# THE LAST BRAHMIN

# THE LAST BRAHMIN

## HENRY CABOT LODGE JR. AND THE
## MAKING OF THE COLD WAR

*Luke A. Nichter*

Yale UNIVERSITY PRESS
*New Haven and London*

Published with assistance from the foundation established
in memory of Amasa Stone Mather of the Class of 1907,
Yale College.

Yale University Press books may be purchased in quantity
for educational, business, or promotional use. For
information, please e-mail sales.press@yale.edu
(U.S. office) or sales@yaleup.co.uk (U.K. office).

Set in Scala type by Westchester Publishing Services.
Printed in the United States of America.

Library of Congress Control Number: 2020935981
ISBN 978-0-300-21780-3 (hardcover: alk. paper)

A catalogue record for this book is available from the
British Library.

This paper meets the requirements of ANSI/NISO
Z39.48-1992 (Permanence of Paper).

10  9  8  7  6  5  4  3  2  1

*For Jennifer and Ava, my partners in everything I do*

# CONTENTS

# Introduction

The overthrow and assassination of South Vietnamese President Ngo Dinh Diem in November 1963 was one of the most important events in Cold War history. It is widely regarded as a turning point that led to formal American military entry in Vietnam.

Our understanding of the coup continues to evolve. There is an active debate about the extent to which the United States supported it; how the decision was made to execute Diem and his brother, chief political adviser Ngo Dinh Nhu; and whether President John F. Kennedy had foreknowledge of these events. The publication of Kennedy's instructions to newly appointed American Ambassador Henry Cabot Lodge Jr. before his departure for Vietnam helps to clarify these issues. One thing is certain. While the coup was intended to increase political stability, it had the opposite result. In March 1965, instability in South Vietnam necessitated the first deployment of U.S. Marines to the beaches of Danang.

The events leading up to the November 1963 coup are some of the most closely studied of the entire Vietnam War. But they have never been explained from the point of view of one of the most significant figures in the entire drama, Henry Cabot Lodge Jr., who has been largely forgotten by history.

The reason is not only that Lodge preferred to remain behind the scenes and that he was brought up to consider it crass to trumpet one's own accomplishments. It is also that Americans disregarded the "Best and the Brightest" generation, which was responsible for the U.S. involvement in Vietnam. For scholars and journalists living through the disillusionment of the post-Vietnam, post-Watergate period, it was unfashionable to treat the Vietnam era, its decisions, and its decision makers as worthy of serious study.

The story of Lodge's life and career illustrates America's coming of age as a superpower. The searing experience of World War II—when he became the first sitting senator since the 1860s to resign his seat for military service—dramatically transformed him from an isolationist into an internationalist. With a convert's zeal, Lodge embraced the United Nations as a force for good and emerged from his grandfather's controversial shadow and long battles with Woodrow Wilson over national sovereignty.

The Cold War tested Lodge's and the country's faith in democracy and our ability to project our system of values abroad. The belief in our superiority and even infallibility led directly to our involvement in Vietnam and other adventures of empire. Lodge occupied a series of key positions of influence throughout, and when the nation began to fear we had overreached our role, the American people reacted by turning decisively against those who caused us to doubt ourselves. The decline of Lodge's reputation reflects a shift away from a generation of leaders who overextended our international presence at the price of domestic unrest and turmoil.

Throughout his life, Lodge was motivated by a deep sense of patriotic duty and his family's history of public service that went back to the Washington administration. "This country and this government must have the support of people who feel a deep sense of devotion, who have a desire to give something," he wrote in his diary, echoing Henry Stimson's call to defend the nation's institutions and traditions. "This country has done a great deal for all of us. I know it has done much for me. We should in turn be willing to do what we can for our country."[1] After Lodge's father died tragically when he was just seven, his grandfather's tutelage molded him into a kind of nineteenth-century figure dropped into the high-level politics of the more visceral twentieth century. Believing in the old-fashioned notion that "the best man" should be chosen as the party's presidential nominee, Lodge never engaged in the endless modern campaigning that is as exhausting for the candidate as it is for voters.[2] His life came to a close in a Cold War twilight after a fifty-year career.

Lodge was the last true Brahmin of the Eastern Establishment to be active in government. Steeped in the views typical of his social class regarding race, gender, and colonialism, he also represented their highest ideals and conducted himself as a "vital centrist" long before Arthur Schlesinger Jr. coined the term.[3] "I don't think a difference of opinion means a difficulty," Lodge told journalist Stanley Karnow late in life. "I mean, if you spent your life in a forum the way I have, the Massachusetts Legislature and the United States Senate and the UN, every day is spent cheek by jowl with people that you disagree with. But for that reason, you don't get all hot and bothered and angry and so forth."[4]

Lodge's views harked back to a time period when compromise was an art and comity a virtue, when those in public life could disagree without being disagreeable. It was these qualities that allowed a Republican Episcopalian from Massachusetts to be trusted by Democrats, Catholics, and five presidents from Dwight Eisenhower through Gerald Ford. A perennial theme of Lodge's political and military service was that he was trusted by those in power and to stand in for those in power.

Thrice Lodge gave up his political career to serve the greater good: first when he resigned from the Senate to serve in World War II, second when he sacrificed his Senate seat to manage Eisenhower's campaign for the presidency, and third when he willingly accepted an appointment from a Democratic president to the most challenging diplomatic post in the world. Yet no one, including those who benefited from Lodge's sacrifices, was there to help him in 1964 when he had a genuine chance for the presidency and his success would have helped those who withheld their support.

As journalist Neil Sheehan once concluded, the self-containment of the aristocrat, the sensitivity of the politician to human factors, and a perspective on the military that reached back to the pre–World War II era made Lodge difficult to stereotype.[5] He left his mark on the nation but failed to create a lasting impact on the Republican Party.[6] He was too much a loner to have left successors. On rare but significant occasions, he could abandon his bipartisanship and engage in shrewd, tough, even vicious political maneuvers. While many politicians have claimed to be uninterested in higher office, Lodge genuinely was. Higher office was irrelevant to the social status he already possessed. However, privilege led not to selfishness and decadence but to a willingness to serve his country.

The events set in motion shortly after Lodge's arrival in Saigon in August 1963 contributed to the greatest misunderstanding of all. But to understand them, we have to understand Lodge—and where he came from.

# PART I
# THE MAKING OF A BRAHMIN

# 1 • Early Life

Henry Cabot Lodge Jr. was born on July 5, 1902, to George Cabot "Bay" Lodge and Mathilda Frelinghuysen Davis Lodge at the family's summer house in Nahant, Massachusetts. He was born into a family of Boston Brahmins and named in honor of his grandfather, Republican Senator Henry Cabot Lodge. Six Lodge forefathers served in the Senate during the eighteenth, nineteenth, and early twentieth centuries. His grandfather was Woodrow Wilson's nemesis, and his great-great-great-grandfather was Washington-Adams-era Senator George Cabot.

The Cabot-Lodge family was among the "first families," which included the Appletons, Lowells, Peabodys, and Saltonstalls. A famous saying about these families sums up their social hierarchy:

> And this is good old Boston,
> The home of the bean and the cod,
> Where the Lowells talk to the Cabots,
> And the Cabots talk only to God.

Many of these families settled in the Beacon Hill area of Boston, where they inherited grazing rights on the Boston Common. Proper Bostonians, as they were called, were fiercely proud—and proud to be distinguished from other upper-class societies in Philadelphia and New York. In Philadelphia, what mattered was *who a person is*. In New York, it was *how much he is worth*. However, in Boston, it was *what he knows*. While Philadelphians cared who your parents were, Bostonians asked about your grandparents. Proper Bostonians did not happen by accident; they were socially engineered to produce leaders and maintain the wealth and influence of their families. Oliver Wendell Holmes, in

1861, referred to them as "the Brahmin caste of New England."[1] Many favorite sons of Boston's first families went to Harvard and became doctors, judges, chemists, politicians, and attorneys—professions that continue to be dominated by these same families today.[2] These families, and their sons, were united in their belief in a single American social character and a Calvinist sense of duty and class authority.[3]

Establishment families intermarried like European royalty—marrying narrowly to preserve wealth, and sometimes more widely to attract new wealth. They were active and autonomous participants in society at a time of rapid social change, yet they were surprisingly insular and tarnished by the racial and ethnic prejudices of the day.[4] Even before the term "establishment" came into common usage in the mid-twentieth century, these families had certain characteristics.[5] They were never too impressed by their own importance; they built and maintained institutions rather than tearing them down. While they were not always brilliant or given to introspection, their self-assurance prompted them to avoid making enemies. They were guided in words and actions by a sense of historical proportion, and their bureaucratic rivals often came away believing they were sympathetic to opposing views whether they were or not.[6] They had a strong belief in the nation's founding documents and referenced history in their decision making. They preferred their upper-crust religion of Episcopalianism.[7] Adoption of children was discouraged and strictly monitored.

In the eighteenth century, the American upper class became less an aristocracy and more a caste.[8] Power and wealth were retained within the family and passed down through a series of trusts that became increasingly time-consuming and complicated to manage. Typically, these families are not descended from *Mayflower* passengers, nor from Boston's founders. Family names came and went before Boston's social structure solidified—and stratified. For many, it was the period between the American Revolution or the War of 1812 and the Civil War when a prominent family member, acting as economic patron, dramatically expanded the family's wealth, usually in a field that emerged during the Industrial Revolution, such as textile mills or maritime shipping.[9] However, these families were more than simple traders between the "golden years" of 1820 and 1860. The epicenter of this activity in Massachusetts was in Lowell, named for Francis Cabot Lowell.

Like most other upper-class families at the time, the Cabot-Lodges did not have an ancestor on the *Mayflower*. By Bay State standards, they were not an old family.[10] Even though they adopted the coat of arms of the French Chabots, there is no definitive link to them. The Cabots instead emigrated from the Isle of Jersey—not England—around 1700. John Cabot and his wife, Anna Orne, arrived on Boston's North Shore and built wealth from trade in tea, copal, rubber, sandalwood, otter skins, linseed oil, peppercorns, molasses, and rum between the West Indies, England, and colonial Boston. There was a rumor that they were involved in the slave trade, but there is no documentation to confirm this.[11] Their sons Joseph and Francis multiplied their wealth during the French and Indian War. Joseph married Elizabeth Higginson, who was a descendant of Francis Higginson, the first minister of the Massachusetts Bay Colony and the earliest American ancestor on either side of the Cabot-Lodge family.

Both sides of the Cabot-Lodge family descended from prominent merchants. On the Lodge side, Giles Lodge was born in London in 1770 but immigrated to the West Indies at the age of twenty-one as an agent for a network of merchants that stretched from London to Liverpool. He fled Santo Domingo during the August 1791 slave rebellion and went to Boston. He decided to stay in the United States and married Mary Langdon, the daughter of Revolutionary War captain John Langdon. By age twenty-eight, Lodge had a dozen shipping vessels under his command, built in places like Mystic, Connecticut, and Medford, Massachusetts, which carried gold prospectors to California and made trips to China, the Spice Islands, Sumatra, and New Zealand.[12]

On the Cabot side, George Cabot built the early family fortune as a privateer during the Revolutionary War, authorized by a letter of marque from the Continental Congress. Cabot, an amiable pirate, was the seventh child of Joseph and Elizabeth Higginson Cabot. He was expelled from Harvard during his second year for disciplinary reasons and took the helm of a cod-fishing boat, joining the family business.[13] He was given command of a merchant ship, and, following the American Revolution, his shipping business grew to the point where he had vessels all over the world. One of them carried the first American flag to St. Petersburg in Russia. Some traded salted cod and rum with East Africa and Zanzibar, while others could be in Hawaii or Brazil or California, helping Salem, Massachusetts, become an important hub for sea trade. Cabot, a dreamer by temperament, was an autodidact, a world traveler, and a Federalist whose friends included George Washington, Alexander Hamilton, and John Adams. At twenty-nine, he was a delegate to the Massachusetts state constitutional convention and became known as the "president of New England."[14] Later appointments included senator, member of the executive council of Massachusetts, and secretary of the navy.[15] Cabot's vocational and avocational pursuits inspired an interest in politics and public service in later generations.

The Cabot-Lodge dynasty was formed through the nineteenth-century marriage of John Ellerton Lodge and Anna Cabot. Their son, the future Senator Henry Cabot Lodge, was born in 1850 at the corner of Winthrop and Otis Places in Boston. Neighbors included George Bancroft, the nation's first great historian, and Senator Rufus Choate. Frequent visitors to the Lodge home included Charles Sumner; Henry Wadsworth Longfellow; Henry Jacob Bigelow; historians William Prescott, John Lothrop Motley, and Francis Parkman; and the naturalist Louis Agassiz.[16] In 1876, Lodge earned one of Harvard's first PhDs in history, following an AB in 1871 and an LLB in 1875.[17] His dissertation was published under the title *Essay in Anglo-Saxon Law* in 1876, and that fall he was appointed to teach colonial American history.[18] It seemed likely that Lodge would become an academic, specializing in the work of Alexander Hamilton and the age of independence.[19]

He spent seven years at Harvard and married Anna Cabot Mills Davis, the daughter of Rear Admiral Charles Henry Davis, who founded the Naval Observatory and the National Academy of Sciences. For their honeymoon, they spent a year in Europe traveling and studying. He became a prolific writer and speaker, focusing on a range of subjects from Anglo-Saxon law to American politics. Lodge wrote a series of biographies dubbed the "American Statesmen Series," including volumes on Alexander Hamilton (1882) and Daniel Webster (1883).[20] By the age of thirty, he was earning $3,000 a year, a not inconsiderable sum in those days. One of the first articles he accepted as editor of the *International Review* was "Cabinet Government of the United States," by Thomas Woodrow Wilson, who was then a senior at Princeton. Wilson later cited Lodge's work in American history as one of the reasons he felt able to pass an entrance examination in colonial history when he applied for graduate work at Johns Hopkins. However, when Lodge received a second Wilson manuscript for consideration, he dismissed it with "R.R.R."—received, read, rejected.[21] No longer content to simply write about politics, Lodge threw his own hat in the ring by running for the Massachusetts House of Representatives in 1880. He later served in the U.S. House of Representatives from 1887 to 1893 before winning a seat in the Senate.

In the Senate, with the government subject to more generous recesses, Lodge spent the winter term in Washington when the Senate was in session but escaped north during the warmer months. He always felt more comfortable at the family home in Nahant, as opposed to Boston. Nahant is a slender tongue of land extending into Massachusetts Bay, "thrust out into the open ocean," he once observed, "with nothing between it and Portugal, all rocks."[22]

It was developed as early as 1640 as a home for fishermen and became one of the first true nineteenth-century vacation spots in the region, even before Martha's Vineyard or Nantucket. Early developers hoped to make it the rival of Newport.[23] It is fourteen miles northeast of central Boston, a single square mile of granite jutting southward from the Essex County shoreline, "as though," wrote Henry Adams, "directing the Bostonian homeward."[24]

The rides up to the North Shore permitted time for reading the poetry of Sir Walter Scott, Thomas Gray, Alexander Pope, and William Shakespeare. The Lodge home, a cavernous, gray clapboard with nine bedrooms, nine bathrooms, and roses climbing up the veranda, was located at East Point, where young men learned to row and sail. It was the easternmost point on the peninsula, a prestigious location with unmatched views of the Atlantic Ocean and the Boston skyline.[25] The nearby cliffs provided privacy for men and boys of all ages to skinny-dip in the natural pool formed by Cupid Rock. "The earliest and most prized memories of my life," young Henry Cabot Lodge Jr. recalled later, "are of Nahant, of its great cliffs and the roar of the surf beating on the headlands, of its streets lined with elms, and its houses in so many of which I have been . . . I remember the red light of Egg Rock and the horse-drawn carriages which used to take us from Lynn to Nahant."[26]

Teddy Roosevelt, Henry Adams, Edith Wharton, and Henry James, among others, gathered in Nahant for political meetings during the summers. Senator Lodge's best friend was Roosevelt, who said, "[Lodge was] my closest friend personally, politically and in every other way and occupied toward me a relationship that no other man has ever occupied or will occupy." "TR" was also a regular fixture at the family's winter home in Washington, DC, at 1765 Massachusetts Avenue NW.[27] Ever since he was a young civil service commissioner, Roosevelt had visited for Christmas dinner. Before dinner, Lodge read while Roosevelt said grace; then Roosevelt carved the goose while Lodge carved the turkey. Roosevelt was just about the only person who could talk candidly with Lodge, and to whom Lodge would listen. When Lodge asked with dismay "why these writers persist[ed] in calling [him] cold, and reserved, and a Brahmin," Roosevelt's response was simple: "I can tell you . . . —it's because you are."[28] Roosevelt made enough of an impression on young Cabot, as Henry Cabot Lodge Jr. was known, that the latter once wrote his grandfather, "When I am a big boy I want to take care of the president's horse. Will you ask the president?"[29]

Cabot grew up in a unique environment, even when compared with other Establishment families. His upbringing was intentionally similar to his father's and his grandfather's. It was an atmosphere of almost constant intellectual stimulation—painting, writing, reading, engaging in multilingual conversations, and receiving distinguished visitors from all over the world. The whole family was a community of scholars of one kind or another.[30]

Cabot's father, Bay, short for "Baby," was a poet who had no interest in business, government, or the pursuit of power.[31] Henry Adams said that Bay was "as elementary and simple as the salt water." He was a "big, handsome man with white teeth, blue eyes, thick light brown hair, and a deep tan," an admiring Cabot reflected later.[32] Bay devoted his time to reflection and literature, writing as much as six hours a day.[33] Roosevelt once wrote about Bay to his father, Senator Lodge, "Of all the men with whom I have been intimately known, he was the only man I have ever met who, I feel, was a genius."[34] At Harvard, Bay displayed talent for French language and literature, Spanish, and Italian. He also displayed signs of what might today be termed depression.

Bay, listed as an assistant clerk in a 1908 congressional directory, was assigned primarily to the Senate's Philippines committee. He worked as his father's secretary in the Senate but, feeling too constrained by his duties, quit to become a poet. While not a great author, he was at the very least a respectable minor one.[35] Bay had a first-rate intellect but never did well in school. The expectations of the family were a heavy demand on him, and he cried out for help in his correspondence. He constantly reminded himself of his insufficiency, and his career was symptomatic of the stresses borne by many other modern American writers. Bay drifted where the wind blew him, enjoying the stimulating company of other writers in places such as Paris. "I ought to go home in order to get into the tide of American life if for nothing else: . . . I oughtn't to be dreaming and shrieking inside and poetizing and laboring on literature here in Paris, supported by my father, and . . . I ought to go home and live very hard making money," he wrote. "I said to myself that I knew I could not be very quick at money-making, but that at any rate in the eyes of men I should lead a self-respecting life."[36]

Bay returned home in 1896 and almost immediately found himself in rebellion. "I hate the philistine-plutocrat atmosphere of this place . . . I sincerely thank God I shall never be a rich man . . . If I haven't it in me to write a poem, what a sordid farce my life will be!"[37] In his suffering, he managed to find motivation to publish his first collection of poems, a volume called *The Song of the Wave*. The final verse of one sonnet is haunting:

> We know how wanton and how little worth
> Are all the passions of our bleeding heart
> That vex the awful patience of the earth.[38]

Perhaps family friend Edith Wharton summed up Bay best: "He grew up in a hot house of intensive culture. [He] was one of the most complete examples I have ever known of the young genius before whom an adoring family united in smoothing the way."[39] Proper public recognition of Bay's work never came during his lifetime. He remained financially dependent on his father during adulthood and lamented his "crying inability to adapt" himself to his time and "become a moneymaker." He poured out his heart in correspondence to his mother. "I am almost crazed with the desire to be independent," he wrote.[40]

Bay married Mathilda Elizabeth Frelinghuysen "Bessie" Davis, the belle of Washington society, on August 8, 1900. Her grandfather, New Jersey's Senator Frederick Theodore Frelinghuysen, was Chester Arthur's secretary of state. Of Cabot's mother, Henry Adams once remarked that she was "another survival of rare American stock: Davis of Plymouth, Frelinghuysen of New Jersey, Griswold of Connecticut, with the usual leash of Senators, Cabinet officers, and other such ornaments in her ancestry."[41] Like Bay, Bessie cared little for the expectations placed on her by her ancestors. They made their home at 1925 F Street NW in Washington in a rented house near Massachusetts Avenue and Sheridan Circle, backing up to Rock Creek Park. The couple had two other children besides Cabot: John Davis (1903) and Helena (1905).

On August 18, 1909, Bay and his father visited Tuckernuck Island for a quiet day at the home of William Sturgis Bigelow, a close family friend. Tuckernuck, a one-mile-by-two-mile-wide rectangle almost completely encircled by white sandy beaches, is a remote island to the west of Nantucket, a good half hour's run in a motorboat away. Algonquin for "picnic," it evokes a sense of the past, pristine and undiscovered. The waves are gentle due to the sand bar about one hundred yards from the south shore. At the time, the island was covered with scrub pine and oak and beach plum, nothing much more than about five feet tall.[42] Grazing cattle freely roamed, and a telephone to Nantucket provided the only communication with the outside world. The island had no year-round residents because of the severe winters and lack of creature comforts such as electricity and running water. It was an elemental place to work and relax, free of the interruptions of civilization, which was why Bay loved it.[43]

They stayed for a dinner of steamed clams with a Professor Brown of Harvard.[44] That evening, Bay developed serious indigestion. Was it a bad clam? No one seemed to know. Another theory was that he had an overstressed heart from working too hard in a role that did not suit him.[45] His stomachache kept him up all night, but he felt better by the morning and was able to get some sleep. "I asked him how he was, and he said that he had had a hard night—a violent indigestion, vomiting, diarrhea, etc.," his father recalled. "He thought he had eaten a bad clam, and the doctor subsequently said that he seemed to have been poisoned acutely enough, he thought, for ptomaine poisoning."[46]

The pains and nausea returned later the next day and were severe enough that Lodge called a doctor in Nantucket. When the doctor arrived, he administered nitroglycerin and digitalis. When that did not help, Lodge called another doctor and wired his wife, Nannie, to come down quickly. At that point, Bay had not slept normally for thirty-six hours. The second doctor, who was trying to comfort him so he could sleep, abruptly called out to Lodge in the next room. "There is a sudden failure," he said. "Is he going?" Lodge asked. The doctor administered another powerful injection and checked Bay's chest with a stethoscope. "He is gone," the doctor said.[47]

"So he died," Lodge wrote to Bigelow. "Perfectly quietly, without a gasp or a struggle, in my arms, sitting in your big chair in the parlor by the dining table. So he died in my arms. You will know the lonely agony of that moment for me. I cannot write of it even without wanting to cry out as I did then."[48] Lodge never set foot on Tuckernuck Island again. Bay's death at the age of thirty-five deeply wounded the family and represented a break in the security and pattern of Cabot's childhood.[49]

Cabot was just seven years old at the time of his father's death, so young that because he and his grandfather shared a name, people mistakenly assumed he was his grandfather's son. His grandfather focused his future hopes for the family on Cabot; his brother, John Davis Lodge; and his sister, Helena. "Mother told us in a gentle and lovely way that father was gone," John recalled later. "I remember a tremendous feeling of desolation and bursting into tears. Mother was very brave. She faced up to all tribulations with complete courage. I never knew her to indulge in self-pity."[50]

Neither of Senator Lodge's sons had shown any interest in politics, so Cabot received all his grandfather's direction on the subject in concentrated form. "Discussion of politics is one of the first things I can remember," he recalled later. "The haze of cigar smoke and the emphatic utterances of such words as 'caucus' or 'campaign' made politics very vivid to me."[51]

Although Cabot learned a lot about politics up close, his grandfather did not pressure him. "You have shown, what I never doubted to be true, that you are able to control your mind and apply it to any subject that you choose. This is the most important thing in education," his grandfather observed.[52] Young Cabot certainly got an education in politics. It seems that in each year of his young life, his grandfather was engaged in a political battle. The year Cabot was born, 1902, Senator Lodge spoke against a proposal for the direct election of senators, which he said would cause the upper chamber to lose its "character and meaning" by requiring that its members be chosen in the same manner, by the same constituency, as the House.[53]

Following their father's death, Cabot and John attended Miss Ward's classes near St. Albans School for Boys in Washington, DC, for two years. In the autumn of 1911, Cabot moved to St. Albans, where he had difficulty adjusting.[54] A year later, his mother moved the family to Paris to get away and enable the children to perfect their French. Cabot had learned German from their nurse, Fraulein Schultz.[55] His multilingual childhood gave him an exposure to cultures and the world that set him apart, even among his upper-class peers. The change of scenery was also a way for Cabot's mother to recapture her memory of happier days, when Bay was alive. Cabot's brother, John, later recalled the influence of their mother. "It's always supposed that the greatest influence on my brother was our grandfather—and that is not true at all!" he reflected. "We did occasionally spend a few days' vacation with him at Nahant, and of course there were family Christmas or Thanksgiving dinners sometimes—but the greatest influence in all our lives was our mother. She brought us up; we always lived with her."[56] Emily Lodge, Cabot's granddaughter, wrote, "Whenever I asked my grandfather about his mother there was that mysterious pause and then a quiet response, 'She had a difficult time.'"[57]

The family set sail in early November on the *Oceanic* to Cherbourg, and from there took the train to Paris. Edith Wharton met them and secured rooms for the family at the small Hotel de Tremoille near the Étoile. They could afford a valet, a cook, a chambermaid, and tutors—the standard luxuries expected of their social class but no more. Wharton's friend Walter Berry paid "the tradesmen."[58] The family read aloud after dinner and gathered around the piano to sing from Gilbert and Sullivan. Cabot's mother giggled at her children's jokes and listened with fascination and admiration. He picked mulberries in Henry James's garden, rode horses with George Patton, and visited Wharton.[59] However, the boys were homesick and did not do well in boarding school in the Paris suburb of St. Cloud.

Cabot's study of French language, culture, and history left a deep impression on him, especially the "hard work and long hours," he recalled later. "I feel to this day such ability to concentrate as I have is due to a significant extent to the training I received."[60] At first he struggled, as the boys' French when they arrived was not as good as their German. Little did he know how much his foreign-language ability, and in particular his fluency in French, would help him during his career. At Christmastime 1912, they moved to 55 Avenue Marceau, and the boys attended a day school run by Monsieur Goy at 18 Rue Matignon.[61]

For Bessie, finding a new routine in a new place served her well. She liked France better than Washington or Nahant. Her children accompanied her to some of the finest salons in Paris. They spent the summer of 1913 at Villa de Guets d'Or at Paris Plage on the sea at Normandy. The Lodges found the swimming that took place in the bathhouses of France, which had moveable enclosures that could be wheeled to the water's edge in order to preserve the modesty of female bathers, to be quite different from the nude swimming in the foaming sea adjacent to Cupid's Rock in Nahant.[62]

During the summer of 1914, the guns of August arrived. The rumors of war made for an exciting time for the Lodge boys. "I can remember the drum beat through the village, summoning men to report for military service," Cabot recalled. "I can remember the horses being brought into the village from all the surrounding farms to have their hooves branded with a number, so that they could be returned to their owners if they ever survived the war."[63] Travel became difficult. Trains were standing-room only and not guaranteed, luggage cars were used for passengers, and it was difficult to cash checks. Young men started disappearing. Bessie was adamant about remaining in France and helping with the war effort.[64] However, Lodge dispatched his son-in-law Congressman Augustus Peabody "Gussie" Gardner to France on August 4 to tell them to leave.[65]

The family fled to London, where Senator Lodge and Nannie had been vacationing. The boat departing Le Havre was so overloaded that the children became separated from their mother, the two servants, and their twelve trunks of belongings. Telegram traffic between France and the United Kingdom had been cut, all roads were blocked to civilian traffic, and the passenger boats were crowded with soldiers and ammunition. The family took up a flat on Half Moon Street near St. James Place and Green Park, but they did not stay long.[66] As the war set in, departing Americans jammed every boat that was sailing for New York. Senator Lodge booked them a return journey as soon as he could, in October 1914.

The outbreak of World War I was enough to move the Lodges home for good. The family sailed on the *Olympic* under complete blackout conditions out of fear of German submarines. Childhood friend James J. "Jerry" Wadsworth recalled later how much the boys had changed since the last time he had seen them. Now when they fought, they used their feet, and "they were pretty well imbued with the European idea of young boys, what they did and how they played."[67] Bessie sent the boys, who were completely bilingual at that point, back to St. Albans. They liked to spend evenings in their grandfather's library, and he took a more direct role in their education after Nannie died in September 1915. She had been a shield against her husband's more unilateral ideas, but now he was freer to overrule the independent Bessie.[68]

Senator Lodge thought the boys should go to school in their home state, so Middlesex School in Concord, Massachusetts, was a good choice. He had been concerned that too much time away might cause them to lose their roots. On at least one occasion, he even threatened to withdraw Bessie's allowance.[69] On April 26, 1915, she wrote the headmaster of Middlesex School. "The boys are grandsons of Sen. Lodge," she said.[70] That was enough to guarantee admission. Enrolling in the autumn of 1915 just twenty miles from Nahant, the boys generally did well—especially in French, German, English, and natural science. They scored better in French than they did in courses in their native English.[71] On Sundays, the boys would swim at Nahant, then dress in coats and ties for Sunday dinner, which might include a course of lobster with mayonnaise, then roast beef. "What gastronomic orgies!" Cabot recalled later.[72]

Both boys incurred disciplinary punishments known as "rounds," in which they were required to run laps around the oval driveway circling the school. On one occasion, Cabot was caught smoking and was nearly expelled. Other infractions included talking after lights-out, roughhousing, failing to call a master "sir," being fresh with seniors, lying, and sneaking out.[73] On another occasion, Cabot and two friends were pulled over for speeding while returning from a dance. The officer asked their names. "I am Henry Cabot Lodge, sir," he said. The other two answered "Alexander Hamilton" and "Paul Revere." "That's enough out of all of you," the officer said, and took them down to the station.[74] In all, Cabot endured 144 rounds in his first year at Middlesex—"too many," his report card said.[75]

Cabot developed an interest in current events and international affairs thanks to his grandfather's insistence that he be imbued with important lessons common among Eastern Establishment families: an emphasis on public service, activism, and the desire to help those less fortunate, rooted in an Americanized notion of noblesse oblige. These are constant themes in their correspondence, especially during the years 1912 to 1918. "Work at your lessons & learn all you can," his grandfather wrote. "It is not so important what you learn as that you should work at your task, whatever it is. Whatever you try to do—do it with all your might & do your best."[76] When Cabot asked about his ancestors, his grandfather responded, "My boy. We do not talk about family in this country. It is enough for you to know that your grandfather is an honest man."[77] Cabot and his siblings learned more than politics from their grandfather. He told them stories of adventure and conquest that stimulated their imaginations, some of which they passed down to their children and grandchildren.

Cabot's maturation coincided with his grandfather's most important years in the U.S. Senate, when he became best known for his opposition to President Woodrow Wilson's League of Nations. Wilson and Lodge presented competing visions of American foreign policy. It was a rivalry that was intense and personal. Lodge believed Wilson was guilty of nothing less than destroying American ideals after his extended hesitation to support military preparedness.[78] The Democrats, on the other hand, were effectively able to run against Lodge's vitriol and "United States first" nativism in successive elections. The epic battle served as Cabot's political education. As he recalled later, "I got tremendously caught up in the excitement of the whole thing."[79] Cabot spent hours in the evenings in front of the fire, talking with his grandfather.[80] "It was interesting to see how he treated Cabot as an equal in age," Harvard classmate John Mason Brown wrote in his diary.[81]

Senator Lodge had liked the idea of an international organization to ensure peace until Wilson claimed it as his own in his 1917 "Peace without Victory" speech.[82] While they both wanted the Allies to win and keep the United States out of World War I, the ways they proposed to reach that goal were fundamentally different. Wilson wanted to prove that his desire for peace was genuine by refusing to arm.[83] Lodge, however, believed that the best way to maintain peace was for the nation to prepare for war so much that no other nations would fight it. He did not believe it was possible to enforce peace without an international military force. Lodge also believed that Wilson's proposal for the League of Nations was an unacceptable loss of American sovereignty and that it would be the eventual duty of the United States to inherit the mantle of the British Empire and preserve civilized order in the world.[84] He was not convinced that the league would preserve that order—or be effective in achieving an end to war. He used his knowledge of Senate rules and procedures to delay league debates, but the use of filibuster was never considered because it was seen as almost too extreme to be even a last resort.[85] Forty Republican senators, including Lodge, submitted a resolution to Congress on March 4, 1919, stating their objections to American participation in the League of Nations "in the form now proposed."[86] What Lodge wanted more than anything was what he considered missing—a clear statement of policy.[87]

As these battles raged in Washington and sometimes even at the Lodge dinner table, Cabot was completing his education at Middlesex School, from which he graduated on June 10, 1920. There was hardly any doubt that he would go to Harvard.[88] There was some concern that he was weak in two subjects, geometry and Greek, which prompted a letter of gentle reprimand from his grandfather. "It would be a terrible disappointment for me if you should fail any of your Harvard examinations," he wrote. Cabot realized that all the pushing from his grandfather prompted him to achieve more than he would have otherwise. "I certainly try and hope that someday through my work I shall be able to give any children which I may have an advantage, such as you have given me," he promised.[89] His grandfather was in Chicago preparing to chair the 1920 Republican National Convention when Cabot's Middlesex headmaster sent his assessment for Harvard: "H.C. Lodge, Jr. is a grandson of the Senator and comes honestly by a real interest in intellectual things and in government and history. He is able, somewhat opinionated, and somewhat stubborn, but he has a winning smile and he intends to do right. I wish there were more fields of intellectual endeavor at Harvard outside the classroom, because he is one of the men who needs such fields to keep him stimulated."[90] University life would force him out of the shadow of his grandfather more than ever.

At Harvard, Cabot enjoyed rowing on the Charles River and acting (in French) with the Cercle Français. Cabot majored in French; one of his classmates commented that his speaking ability was better than the instructor's due to his time living in France.[91] He wrote a political piece in the *Advocate* entitled "Political Sentimentalists" and found a home for his political ideas in both the Republican and the Conservative Clubs. "I inherited my party affiliation from my grandfather, who was the Republican leader of the Senate, and always my beloved counselor and friend," Cabot said. "His Republicanism stemmed from the Civil War, slavery, the Union, and Abraham Lincoln."[92]

In his spare time, he learned to be a good dancer and sought the status offered by Harvard society. Cabot was snubbed by the Porcellian Club, chosen by the Fox Club, and eventually elected to Harvard's most erudite club, the Signet Society. He enjoyed socializing and parties, but he did not drink much. He was arrested once for intoxication, on October 28, 1922, in the Roxbury District of Boston.[93] At a time when raccoon coats were popular, his grandfather gave him a mink coat at twice the cost. Classmate John Mason Brown remembered that, "above all, he liked to talk. Talking was his favorite exercise . . . Bull sessions were his meat, political arguments his delight. In the course of them he hit hard and took hard hits, and had the ingratiating quality of enjoying the hits he received as much as those he gave you."[94]

Cabot graduated cum laude in 1924 with a major in Romance languages. He had finished the degree the year before, after which his grandfather and mother arranged for a summer job with the *Boston Evening Transcript* that started on July 1, 1923, four days before his twenty-first birthday.[95] "He never seemed to study," Brown said. "And he graduated cum laude!"[96] There was also no doubt about what he would do after Harvard. "My grandfather encouraged me to enter journalism instead of studying law," he said. "As one who was himself a member of the bar he felt that journalism was at least the equal of the law as training for political life."[97] "Whatever you choose to do, don't be an amateur!" his grandfather warned.[98]

The *Transcript* was the newspaper of the Establishment. It was published six days a week and arrived at teatime. A popular story illustrates the difference between the reputation of the *Transcript* and other newspapers: A Back Bay butler answers the door and announces the visiting journalists. "Four reporters and a gentleman from the *Transcript* to see you, sir."[99] Requiring transportation in his new job, Cabot drove a secondhand Ford that was a source of jokes from his grandfather due to its state of disrepair.[100]

While writing a front-page story on the Ku Klux Klan, Cabot gained access to KKK secret meetings and interviewed top leadership. There is a suggestion in his personal papers that he even temporarily joined the KKK in order to obtain this access. While there is no hard evidence of this, at a minimum the episode suggests youthful naïveté. After publication of the piece, he received a threatening letter from the Klan. More routine assignments included covering dance, culture, and the arts—as well as a review of the Pavlova tour that required him to don a dinner suit and boiled shirt and attend the ballet every night for two weeks.[101] Sometimes he wrote about fashion, such as in his article on September 15, 1929, about why men should adopt the dress jacket. "Dancing with it on hot nights becomes a different experience from the miserable pirouetting which men must now indulge in with a thin coating of wool enveloping their trunk," he wrote.[102] Cabot prided himself on being an elegant dresser.

"I believe that I am going in an intelligent way and shall try to be animated by an intelligent spirit," he wrote in response to his grandfather's concern that he was not serious enough.[103] Cabot came home from a day's work, sat at the head of the dining room table like the chairman, and held court. He liked to debate late into the night, almost to the predawn hours, then sleep late and do it all over again the next day. His mother wondered whether he was a little too headstrong in his arguments, too sure for his age, and too vehement in his stands. "His mind is a joy . . . He becomes so interested in the idea on the table that he loses sight of personalities—and persons—and talks with a gorgeous detachment," John Mason Brown wrote in his diary.[104]

Cabot would take any assignment given him by the city editor. On one occasion, he covered city hall to fill in for the beat reporter, who had the day off. The assignment was his first interaction with Boston Mayor James Michael Curley, who was "handsome, with a massive head, regular features, and rich baritone voice," he remembered.[105] Curley dominated Boston politics for nearly forty years; even Yankees like Cabot submitted to his power.[106] At Curley's daily press conference, a reporter for the *Globe* asked him whether he had heard anything further about Senator Lodge getting more navy contracts for Boston Navy Yard. The reporter had no idea that Lodge's grandson was in the room, and perhaps Curley did not, either. "Why yes," Curley responded. "I had a letter from the old son of a bitch today, asking me to please lay off him in the public prints and saying he would do the best he could for the Yard."[107] These were surely different political lessons from the type Cabot learned from his grandfather, although they were every bit as valuable.

In early 1924, Cabot took an extended trip to Europe. His grandfather had promised him that if he took his studies seriously at Harvard and graduated a year early, he would pay for the trip.[108] It was time to cash it in. His grandfather took him to see President Calvin Coolidge to obtain letters of invitation. "This young man finished Harvard in three years, but I had to bribe him to do it," he told the president. Coolidge gave Cabot a "To whom it may concern" letter, as did Secretary of State Charles Evans Hughes. The tour of western Europe was a combination of the personal and the professional. In addition to meeting up with friends, Cabot arranged interviews for the *Transcript* with Austrian President Michael Hainisch, French President Raimond Poincaré, and Italian Prime Minister Benito Mussolini. "He really was a disappointment. I had expected to see a rather handsome, distinguished man. But he is swarthy, thickset, striking looking but a thug, through and through," Lodge recalled of Mussolini.[109]

In Venice, he and Harvard classmate John Mason Brown visited a prostitute, according to Brown's diary. "She smiled—we thought it might be fun to see what it was like so we followed—mother drunk upstairs—a bed-room opposite," he wrote. There is no description of what occurred in the bedroom, or anything at all in Lodge's private papers, but Brown wrote, "We thanked her for her courtesy and retreated."[110] In Paris, they visited Dr. and Mrs. Henry Sears, who were old Boston friends of the Lodges. Among the sights to be seen in Paris, the young men showed the most interest in the Searses' attractive blond daughters, Emily and Jean. "Cabot, the dog," Brown recalled later, "he'd see Emily in the morning, then meet me for lunch and never let on where he'd been."[111]

Cabot's most prominent assignment was covering the 1924 Republican National Convention in Cleveland.[112] His grandfather had intervened with *Transcript* Washington bureau chief Theodore G. Joslin to ensure his grandson got the job. "I could of course take him with me, but I would prefer to have him go as a working newspaperman," his grandfather said. No doubt Senator Lodge hoped the experience would help to spark an interest in politics. "My fondest hope is that the time will come when he will see his future as I believe I foresee it," he recalled.[113] Cabot not only dutifully covered the convention for the *Transcript* but rewrote his dispatches in French for front-page publication in *Le Matin*, France's leading political newspaper.[114]

The convention would be the last for his grandfather, who was embarrassed by Coolidge's rejection of his bid to be chairman of the state delegation. The move was payback for Lodge's refusal to endorse the Northampton, Massachusetts, native for the presidency in 1920. Senator Lodge was not used to being embarrassed or reduced to the status of an ordinary delegate. Once in office, Coolidge consolidated power in his home state of Massachusetts. "I have had every possible convention honor that could be given," Lodge wrote later. "They will not hurt my feelings by keeping me out of any place that I may be fitted for at Cleveland, and if it gives them any satisfaction to do it I shall hold no ill-feeling against anybody."[115] Boston Mayor James Michael Curley sent Lodge a telegram of condolences, along with a key to the city. It was a gracious tribute from someone who had, at times, been Lodge's sparring partner.

Not long after the convention, Senator Lodge was admitted to Charles Gate Hospital in Cambridge to have his prostate removed. The operation went as planned and he returned to recover in Nahant. He had outlived Wilson, who died on February 3, and was now an elder statesman. After learning of the former president's death, Lodge took to the Senate floor to say a few words of respect for his old rival, whose funeral he was delegated by the Senate to attend. However, Edith Wilson requested that Lodge not attend.[116] "As the funeral is private, and not an official one, and realizing that your presence then would be embarrassing to you and unwelcome to me I write to request that you not attend," she said. Lodge assured her that he would make nothing of it. "You may rest assured that nothing would be more distasteful to me than to do anything which by any possibility could be unwelcome to you."[117]

One day on their way to swim near Cupid Rock, Cabot, John, and John Mason Brown walked by Lodge. "When he saw us," Brown recalled later, "his face took on the most angelic expression. He rose to his full height, and threw his arm out in our direction, in the pantomime of beginning a speech. He looked like an old Roman Senator standing there, beaming down at us with his smile." In hindsight, "it seemed like a sort of hail and farewell."[118]

Senator Lodge was standing in his library at Nahant on November 9, 1924, when a cerebral hemorrhage struck him and he fell backward onto the floor.[119] He died that evening at the age of seventy-four.[120] He had spent thirty-seven years in Congress and was a mixture of contrasts: bullying, arrogant, and selfish, but also a devoted husband, father, grandfather, scholar, and statesman.[121] He left an estate valued at approximately $1,249,825.[122] After his death, the Nahant house was rarely used. The federal government purchased it, tore it down, and built a big gun emplacement to protect Boston Harbor. Cabot inherited his grandfather's library and paintings.[123]

Cabot had lost his father young, and now his grandfather. "In the last years of his life we had a remarkably close relationship," he recalled. "I was always interested in government. When a boy hears so much of that sort of thing at home, he either revolts against it or else he likes it. I liked it. We had wonderful, long conversations about government."[124] He continued his work in journalism, including a hard-to-get interview with Charles Lindbergh that had been arranged by Coolidge partly to make up for the 1924 convention. He moved to Beacon Hill to be closer to his primary beat of the state house. With a name like Henry Cabot Lodge—after his grandfather's death, he and others stopped appending the "Jr."—it was not long until people started to ask when he might step out on his own into the political realm. After a veteran member of Congress from Gloucester, Massachusetts, died, the Essex County Republican Council unanimously recommended that he run for the seat. The only problem was that at age twenty-two, he was still three years shy of the minimum age.[125]

Lodge was already tall (6 feet 2¾ inches) and handsome, with deep-blue eyes and a baritone voice that held no trace of a Boston accent, and he was a gifted speaker.[126] He had a sharp wit and could be brutally blunt when he was irritated. He was looking for his next adventure, so he stopped in to see Julian Mason, managing editor of the *New York Herald Tribune*. Lodge brought a few samples of his assignments from the *Transcript* with him. Mason knew his work, especially his coverage of President Coolidge's activities at White Court, his summer White House in Swampscott, during his stay at the twenty-eight-room mansion from June to early September 1925.[127] Lodge was offered a position in the Washington bureau for fifty dollars a week, beginning in October 1925. It was the first thing he had done since his grandfather's death, and he had done it on his own. He submitted his resignation to *Transcript* editor James Williams and publisher George Mandell and received very gracious replies. "You made your own way and you did it well," Mandell wrote. "You came into the office with everyone skeptical, you left it with everyone your friend. I am glad you came so quickly into a worthy job."[128]

Lodge's assignment was the White House, with ancillary responsibility for the War and Navy Departments. He moved into an apartment at 1718 H Street and spent evenings at the Metropolitan Club. There, former club president Judge John Davis, his maternal grandfather, watched over him and other diners from his portrait that hung in the main dining room. Lodge liked entertaining and dressed the part. A colleague later remembered that he was "an uncommonly agreeable and good-looking young man . . . he always looked, even in the hot, suspended days of summer, as though he had just left the shop of an expert tailor."[129]

Lodge picked up with his grandfather's social circle on Capitol Hill, including Senators William Borah of Idaho and Hiram Johnson of California and Brigadier General Frank McCoy, who marched up San Juan Hill with Theodore Roosevelt. They strongly encouraged him to run for Congress in 1926, but he refused, saying, "I have always felt and still feel that the holding of public office is a great public trust and that, even if I could get elected, I should not aspire to office until I was certain that I was wise enough and experienced enough to discharge the duties of whatever office I might hold in the best possible way."[130] It would be only a matter of time. The fact that Lodge almost seamlessly inserted himself into his grandfather's former life in Washington would be a significant boost to his professional career.[131]

One of Lodge's more memorable assignments was covering national political conventions. The most colorful characters he ran into were often not would-be elected officials but rather journalists, including H. L. Mencken. "Arriving in Chicago in 1932, a few days before the convention opened, Mencken asked me if I would like to join him in an informal investigation of how well Prohibition was working in Chicago," Lodge remembered. They took a taxi to a local bar. "Standing behind the bar was a young lady who could best be described as 'gorgeous.' At the end of the room was a piano and a species of singer, in vogue at the time known as a 'crooner.' Mencken and I ordered drinks and, as we stood drinking, the crooner's voice became more and more objectionable. Finally, Mencken said to the young lady behind the bar, 'I'd like to shoot that son of a bitch.' The young lady did not bat an eye or change her supercilious expression. She reached under the counter, pulled out a Thompson submachine gun, laid it on the counter and with a condescending fluttering of her eyelids said, indifferently, 'Go ahead.'"[132]

Even without his grandfather to direct him, as Lodge matured, public service became more important to him. Upper-class elites like Henry Stimson, who had served as William Taft's secretary of war, wrote about the importance for Lodge's generation of military preparedness and learning to defend the country's institutions and traditions.[133] When he was twenty-three years old, Lodge was commissioned a second lieutenant in the U.S. Cavalry of the Army Reserve. "My interest in military matters attracted me to the yearly tours of active duty of about two weeks' duration," he said.[134] Lodge learned a lot about the military during long conversations at the Metropolitan Club with Major Willis D. Crittenberger. "I was amazed at the man," Crittenberger recalled. "It was no easy transition from desk to horseback, pounding those trails out west. Yet Lodge never complained. And he was a good officer. If you told him to take a hill, you knew it would be taken." Lodge remembered fondly those early days of night marches and bivouacking in the army: "I'll always miss the maneuvers in Texas and New Mexico, before the cavalry was mechanized. There's no more pleasant experience than waking up at first light and watching your horse's ears take shape against the far horizon."[135]

In the army, Lodge was one of the first cavalry officers to switch from horses to tanks. He was promoted quickly during the 1920s from second lieutenant, to first lieutenant, and then to captain, and he refused compensation for his military service. In 1931, he was reunited with Crittenberger and the First Cavalry Division at Fort Bliss, in West Texas. High in the Sacramento Mountains, they were outfitted with campaign hats, olive-drab shirts, breeches, high-laced boots, and spurs. Lodge spent May and June on active duty, capping the cavalry division maneuvers at a celebratory dinner at the Central Café in Juarez, Mexico. The army got good publicity from Lodge, too, because he wrote about his experiences in the *Herald Tribune*.[136] His efficiency report from 1935 concluded that he was "an unusually high type reserve officer. In spite of the demands made upon his time by the duties of public office he devotes himself enthusiastically to his military training. He is militant, aggressive, quick to make an analysis of a situation, and is a natural leader."[137]

Another officer recalled how that positioned Lodge at the outbreak of World War II. "By the time the war came along, he knew as much about the Army as anyone. Because of his name, he might have asked for special privilege. But he started at the bottom and earned his way to the top," Major General J. K. Herr recalled. The experience in the army also forced Lodge to get to know people from other walks of life and different parts of the country. "It was not until I had my military training, working under difficulty and hardship with men of every background, that I really appreciated the texture and quality of our people," he said.[138]

Lodge ran into Mencken again on another assignment, in Houston, Texas, for the 1928 Democratic Convention. The two were chatting in the lobby of the Rice Hotel when Amon G. Carter, publisher of the *Fort Worth Star Telegram,* adorned in Stetson, boots, and spurs, came in.[139] He introduced Lodge to the sheriff of Fort Worth, Carl Smith, who pointed out his badge made of "real diamonds, pearls, and rubies." Mencken invited Lodge up to his room to sample a keg of German beer that had just arrived from Galveston—unimpeded by Prohibition. They took the stairs since the elevators were malfunctioning. When they got there, Carter, the sheriff, and a reporter for the *Baltimore Sun* were already enjoying the keg. "Mr. Carter had just finished his drink and had walked out into the corridor to press the button for the elevator," Lodge recalled. "No elevator stopped. Finally, after the fourth elevator had flashed by, Mr. Carter took the sheriff's pistol and fired three or four shots through the glass elevator door, turned back into the bedroom and fired two or three more shots through the open window (I had dived under the bed, Mencken had gone into the closet, and the reporter from the *Baltimore Sun* had jumped into the bathroom) and then calmly took to the stairs." Because there were about fifty thousand people in the hotel at the time, "the uproar was tremendous. Nobody was damaged, but the Rangers had swarmed into the lobby."[140]

After being transferred to the New York office, Lodge began to devote more time to editorial writing, but he also covered the 1928 and 1932 Republican conventions, as well as military and naval issues, including Coolidge's commission to restore order in Nicaragua.[141] Then came his first major international assignment.[142] "They wanted me to do a series of articles comparing the colonial system of the French in Indochina with the British system in Malaysia with the Dutch system in the Dutch East Indies and with the American system in the Philippines," Lodge said. "So I was making a tour of those four countries. It was in 1929, by the way, and we came up on the train from Bangkok to Batdambang in Cambodia, then we drove across Cambodia and across South Vietnam to Saigon. The thing that I remember, 'cause it was a long time ago now, was the tremendous peace and quiet. There was no uproar, there were no problems for the police, there was nothing of that kind. The only act of violence that I witnessed was one which my party committed against an enormous black snake. It must have been twelve feet long who started across the road and we ran over it. So as far as he was concerned the presence of Americans in Vietnam was not something welcome."[143]

Lodge kept detailed diaries during this trip, including many photographs, which helped him to churn out numerous articles for the *Herald Tribune* and other publications. His diaries highlight his first impressions of places such as French Indochina. "We reached Saigon for lunch which we had at the Continental Palace Hotel (!) and good it was too, except for the ether-like coffee, which, however, was no worse than lots of similar ink that has been placed before me in France itself . . . I sat at one of the side-walk tables of the hotel, drinking Dubonnet and beer and enjoying the life of the streets, which was killingly funny," reads one entry.[144] "It used to be the fashionable thing to say that the French were not good colonizers and that they did not have the gift of other nations for administering dependencies . . . There is law and order in Indo-China. There is prosperity, health, and education. Your life and property is as safe in Indo-China as in the United States—safer, indeed, than in certain communities at home, for without being harsh, the French officials give the natives to understand that there must be no 'funny business.'"[145]

Among the articles that sprang from these experiences were "The Meaning of the Kellogg Treaty" (*Harper's*, December 1928), and "Our Failure in the Philippines" (*Harper's*, January 1930).[146] Lodge's reporting reveals how his opinions formed and evolved over time. He was sometimes condescending toward "backwards" people, perhaps because he had insufficient exposure to people from Asian cultures. When writing about Vietnam or the Bombay riots in 1929, Lodge was sympathetic to those who maintained order over the "funny business" on the part of the natives. "The oriental mind is so different from ours," he said, reflecting the common prejudices and colonial views of his class.[147] "I remember Manuel Quezon's remark, the great Filipino leader, a remark that he made to a House Committee and I was there as a newspaperman, in which he said 'I would rather live in a government run like hell by the Filipinos than run like heaven by the Americans.' And that is a very human impulse and I think it is still—has a lot of life to it."[148]

He expressed these views in his first book, *The Cult of Weakness*, which was written during a leave of absence from the *Herald Tribune* and published by Houghton Mifflin in 1932. Lodge believed that the book, a kind of political treatise, was "of no importance." It was a slim volume of five chapters with titles such as "The Mirror of War and Peace," and "The Peace Fight," and Lodge saved his strongest critiques of American political leaders for the final chapter. It is clear that his military training shaped his emerging views. Critiquing what he termed the "peace at any price" lobby, he made it clear he was not in the isolationist camp. He argued for the need for stronger political leaders and a complete reexamination of the way government operated. "The activities of the federal government are so extensively intertwined that only volumes of complicated analysis would separate the wheat from the chaff," he wrote. He displayed his Republican roots in his argument that the government had gotten too far from its areas of expertise: "A public temper must develop which is so angry that it will not draw careful lines, but will blast great mounds of government away, carrying some good along with the bad."[149]

Lodge's political views fell somewhere between isolationism and internationalism. "Certainly some of our problems would be nearer solution if the gap between thinkers and doers were narrower," he wrote.[150] At the heart of the book, he made a case for realism and against "political sentimentalists."[151] He argued for a middle way, born out of disenchantment with big-government liberalism. While Lodge advocated for a bigger army and navy, it was not because he thought the United States should play a bigger role in European affairs. He believed increased preparedness was the best way to avoid being entangled in Europe. "The believer in preparedness, on the other hand, after agreeing that nothing fundamental is being done to remove the war danger, seeks for a quarantine for his country against that danger," Lodge argued. The book sold just 350 copies but received mostly favorable reviews.[152] The *New York Times* praised it as "incisive, sometimes audacious and almost always provocative" and stated that first-time author Lodge had "the gift of clear, virile, and interesting expression."[153]

## 2 • First Political Steps

Following publication of *The Cult of Weakness,* Henry Cabot Lodge Jr. advanced quickly at the *New York Herald Tribune.* However, journalism was training for a higher calling, not the end game, and New York was not home. The gap in political succession left by Bay and John Ellerton Lodge would be filled by Henry Cabot Lodge Jr.[1] But not until he found his way back to Massachusetts.

At a debutante party around Christmastime 1924, he became reacquainted with Emily Esther Sears, "a long-suffering young lady who says that, whatever else I may have done, I have never bored her," he recalled later.[2] She was tall (five feet ten), slender (about 135 pounds), blond, and eighteen years old. She attended Miss May's School in Boston and spent three years in Paris at the Convent of the Assumption and Institut Catholique. It took eighteen months to convince her and, most importantly, her family that he was worthy of her.

Emily's father was Dr. Henry F. Sears, a wealthy Boston blue blood. Her grandfather, David Sears, was said to have "owned half the West Coast and all of Alaska."[3] He was an early developer of Newport, Rhode Island, and was the richest man in America until John Jacob Astor overtook him. Considering that their ancestor Richard Sears emigrated from England to Plymouth in 1633, the Searses liked to joke that the Lodges were upstarts.[4]

Lodge and Emily fell in love, and their wedding took place on July 1, 1926, at the small Episcopal church in Beverly, Massachusetts, with the reception at the sixty-acre Sears estate on the oceanfront. The Victorian home is long gone, but one can still envision the original seventeen-acre tract and its graceful slope opening up to Massachusetts Bay.[5] Lodge's brother, John, was the best man, and John Mason Brown served as an usher. It was the North Shore event of the summer, replete with tents, an orchestra, and the Sears cellar of prewar champagne—although, due to Prohibition, they did not openly toast. Many guests arrived by private yacht. Emily would provide partnership and companionship for the rest of Lodge's life, as well as bringing an important balance to him. They would have two sons: George Cabot Lodge, born in 1927, and Henry Sears Lodge, born in 1930.[6]

On land carved from the Sears estate, they moved into an L-shaped brick oceanfront home on Beverly Cove that would be their only permanent refuge for the remainder of their lives. The house was modeled after Edith Wharton's villa at Hyères, where they stayed on their honeymoon tour of Europe. At low tide, the adjacent sea retreated to reveal flats of rocky sand, laced with shallow pools teeming with flounder, eels, and mussels. There, Lodge took up another serious preoccupation of the Establishment—sailing. In 1930, he purchased *Delilah*, an eighteen-foot Swampscott dory. It reminded him of a boat he had sailed as a boy in Nahant. He later left *Delilah* to his son George, who would develop his own love of boats. "I hate to spend money, generally having been without much to spend, but spending it on boats is different; they cannot consume enough; nothing is too good for them," George reflected later.[7]

In 1932, at twenty-nine years of age, Lodge was wooed by a suggestion that he should seek a seat in the state house, officially called the lower chamber of the General Court of Massachusetts. John Trowt, a local car salesman from Beverly Farms, had taken him under his wing, and they had long conversations about Lodge's grandfather, who was Trowt's political hero. Two days after Trowt made the suggestion, moved by the need to correct what he considered the negative attitude of the Republicans, Lodge announced his candidacy. "It was one of my snap decisions," Lodge said.[8] Trowt, "who could sell a refrigerator to an Eskimo," arranged a speaking tour at organizations such as the Beverly Republican Club.[9] The members of the Republican Club included small businessmen, mechanics, and insurance salesmen. It was a crowd that generally frowned upon expanded governmental relief programs.[10] Lodge, who was the vice president of the Beverly Chamber of Commerce, knew how to talk to them.

The district included Beverly, Hamilton, and Wenham. The area was both a manufacturing hub and a trading hub, with thirty products manufactured in Beverly alone. It also served as the headquarters of the United Shoe Machinery Corporation, the largest factory of its kind in the world. Essex County's only airport was located there, as was one of the nation's oldest seaports. Beverly, which at the time had about twenty-five thousand inhabitants, was perhaps the best-known town on the North Shore, the nine-mile stretch of rocky, surf-flecked coast that rivaled the finest scenic oceanfronts on the Eastern Seaboard. The city's train station was served by sixty-one daily passenger trains that could reach Boston's North Station in thirty-two to forty minutes.

Lodge had two opponents in the Republican primary, each of whom labeled him a carpetbagger. They questioned why Lodge did not run from Nahant, his birthplace. He pointed out that he and Emily had lived in Beverly for five years, and Emily had grown up there. "Everything I own and everything that I prize is in Beverly," Lodge said in one of his earliest campaign speeches.[11] The main street in Beverly was even called Cabot Street. Lodge made up for any shortcomings in residential status while he was on the campaign trail. He made 2,300 house calls, created an elaborate card index of supporters, attended house parties, and even strolled by the shops during the day in order to reach women—the nation's newest voters.[12] "My name is Henry Cabot Lodge. I'd like to get your views on the election," he said when he went door to door. Most people had never encountered someone so famous who was so eager to meet them.

There was no doubt that he would run as a Republican. "The Republican Party . . . was founded on human rights and we must not relinquish our great heritage. I believe in plain speaking and in meeting every issue frankly," he said. Lodge explained how his political beliefs served his community at a time of economic depression. "The leading industry of the district is the United Shoe Machinery Company, which seems to be meeting the present Depression satisfactorily. My only thought is that with my interest in public affairs and my knowledge on public questions and my interest in good government I should be useful to the district and the state. I am sure that I would be able to represent all the people of the district. I do not believe in class distinctions in public life. We are all Americans, equal before the law, and I am sure that I could represent the district in the legislature with fairness to all of its people."[13]

Lodge's first campaign reflected the era before business rose to dominance in the Republican Party. At the time, especially in New England, the party looked for aristocrats and thought it was more important to find candidates who reflected a high moral purpose than to choose those with a big payroll. Lodge, despite having no specific policy proposals, squeaked by his primary challengers with a majority of 1,400 votes and was elected to the Massachusetts state house. He was following in his grandfather's footsteps, as the latter had launched his own political career there when first elected in 1878.[14] Teddy Roosevelt's sister Corinne Roosevelt Robinson wrote, "Another Henry Cabot

Lodge is now going to be prominent in the service of his country." Walter Lippmann and Arthur Krock sent notes of congratulations in recognition of the dawn of the next phase of a political dynasty.[15] Lodge had no reason to believe he was anything but another politician—except for his famous last name.[16]

His foray into politics coincided with the first year of Franklin Delano Roosevelt's presidency and its revolutionary economic policies, which would reshape the nation, usher in a generation of political wilderness for Republicans in Washington, and begin an era of big government that would last until Richard Nixon's presidency. It was among the most economically turbulent periods of the entire twentieth century.

Lodge took his seat under the gold-leafed dome of the State House on Beacon Street in Boston. He got some good advice from Speaker Leverett "Salty" Saltonstall, who recalled that Lodge looked so young at thirty that "he hardly looked old enough to be allowed to work." Salty advised him to keep quiet and support bills that would benefit his district. One allowed the Beverly harbormaster to shoot "an occasional seagull" in order to keep the birds away from the fishing boats. Another ordered the health department to investigate sewage in Salem Bay. These types of legislative actions ensured that Lodge was socializing in non-Brahmin circles. Two men in particular helped Lodge avoid the aristocratic label: James P. Meehan, the secretary of state for the building trades council, and Hyman "Honey" Manevitch, a shrewd local politician from Boston's Twelfth Ward.[17]

Lodge was a strong backer of FDR's National Industrial Recovery Act, which established minimum wages and maximum hours for workers. It also provided funding to create public-sector jobs for the unemployed as a kind of employer of last resort. Lodge was in support: "The economic system should be changed to provide a better distribution of wealth, although I'm against any system which [favors] the lazy and spendthrift at the expense of the industrious and the thrifty." These stances were early signals of his pragmatic, accommodating views, and the beginning of his journey as what he would call a "practical progressive."[18]

Lodge also showed an interest in environmental issues.[19] He took a stand against the manufacturers of Salem & Peabody for dumping grease from tanneries into the sewers, which polluted Salem Bay. Lodge introduced nearly a dozen bills to address the issue, including an outright ban on polluting that included a fine of $250,000 to pay for cleaning up the bay, which had been too polluted to swim for forty years. When the company threatened to move out of the district and take its jobs with them, Lodge met with the company leaders at Peabody City Hall. Over the course of several hours, Lodge tried to explain his position. "You gentlemen have me wrong. I don't want to ruin you. And now that I see some of my bills are a little expensive, I'm willing to with-draw all the others if you'll only agree to the two that'll stop the grease dump-ing and provide the sludge basins," he said. "I'm just as anxious to cooperate as you are." The company leaders agreed to the compromise, and the bills passed without opposition.[20] Lodge's support of these environmental issues helped him to be reelected by a large majority.

Lodge obtained a reputation for rebelling against Republicans when he thought it was principled to do so. This was especially the case when it came to labor issues, since Lodge was appointed chairman of the labor commission—an assignment that could mean a Republican's political death. Salty originally suggested he take that committee assignment. "If you want to do a job and put yourself in a position to get some publicity and a reputation for open-mindedness on the labor question, why don't you go on this committee?" he advised. It was a good fit for Lodge. Saltonstall later recalled, "He did so well on it that he had the support of labor thereafter."[21] Lodge watched as the na-tion underwent a significant economic and social upheaval—the collapse of the banking system, the rise of demagogues such as Governor Huey Long and Father Charles Coughlin, rising calls for social protections such as old-age pensions, and the emergence of increasingly radical state-sponsored ideas to get the economy going again and restore Americans' confidence in it.[22]

On the labor committee, Lodge was on the front line during the Depres-sion in Massachusetts. He sponsored more than thirty bills related to workers' compensation, the employment of women and children, and maximum hours for workers, as well as a far-reaching one that required that any totally dis-abled worker be paid for the rest of his or her life.[23] "I have been on this com-mittee for three years," recalled New Bedford Democrat Leo J. Carney. "This is the first time an honest effort has been made in behalf of labor. The chair-man sat up until three in the morning working on these bills."[24] They all passed, which helped create the impression for some that Lodge was a threat. His success permitted him to think about higher office—much higher office. "I am steadily working on the problem of running for the U.S. Senate . . . It's a tremendous leap for me, but I have the temperament for that kind of thing and I can afford to take chances," he wrote his mother.[25] Lodge was critical of some aspects of FDR's New Deal but did not suggest that the whole thing be thrown out. "But I resent taking our money to give to southern farmers for not growing cotton and to southwestern farmers for irrigation projects so that they can grow more cotton," Lodge said.[26] He believed that doing nothing was not an option.

The result of his success on the labor committee was that Massachusetts's big business detested him "for his realistically liberal opinion on labor and relief legislation," Joe Alsop and William Kintner wrote.[27] Lodge and Alsop were friends from the time they both worked at the *Herald Tribune,* where Lodge helped him to begin his journalistic career. "In the legislature, my experience as House Chairman of the Committee on Labor and Industries convinced me that the interests which men have in common and which bind them together are more numerous and important than those which drive them apart," Lodge reflected.[28] He disagreed with fellow Republicans who seemed to think that if they simply waited out the New Deal and said no to everything, FDR's efforts for reform would go away. Lodge felt the opposite, that Republicans were betraying their progressive origin, which he argued "stems from the mind of Alexander Hamilton, the spiritual father of our party." Lodge encouraged Republicans to modernize and review "some of our own inspiring and now forgotten traditions."[29]

In between legislative sessions, Lodge continued his duties with the army reserve. His summers were split between maneuvers with the cavalry and riding lessons. In 1933, Lodge wrote for the *Herald Tribune* about how outdated the horse-drawn cavalry had become in the face of modern trucks and trailers. Within two years, it had become mechanized. From Fort Knox, First Lieutenant Lodge wrote, "The most modern regiment in the U.S. Army clattered out of its station one night last week under orders to repel an imaginary threat to the City of Louisville and in two crowded hours spread itself like a huge claw over central Kentucky, gripping the road so as to make any immediate attack impossible . . . It proved that it could bring its 175 vehicles into action more quickly than man had ever done before. It showed that it could, for example, leave New York City at sundown and launch a full-strength attack on Boston next morning." The executive officer of these maneuvers was Lodge's old friend Willis D. Crittenberger, now a lieutenant colonel. Lodge was known to all the top army commanders, and his book *The Cult of Weakness* was required reading at West Point.[30]

In 1936, just five years after Lodge's entry into public life, he challenged sitting Governor James Michael Curley for a seat in the U.S. Senate. Lodge was then thirty-four, the same age that John F. Kennedy would be when he first ran for the Senate against Lodge in 1952. Again, the impetus to run came from Trowt, who told him, "Cabot, I think you ought to get out and run for that Senate job next year." The incumbent, Democratic Senator Marcus A. Coolidge, had just died, creating a vacancy that it was presumed would be filled by another Democrat. Given FDR's popularity, few Republicans wanted to give it a try. Curley was the legendary longtime mayor of Boston. "You know about him," Lodge wrote his mother. "I think I can give him some exercise, too, and it will be impossible for him to pin the reactionary label on me as he has on other Republicans."[31]

Lodge wondered whether running for the state senate might be a safer option. Nonetheless, he announced his candidacy to the *Beverly Times:* "For some time Republican friends of mine have suggested that I become a candidate for the United States Senate . . . I have given the suggestion deep thought. I have concluded that my work as a member of the legislature would enable me to be of service to the people of Massachusetts. I desire, therefore, to submit my candidacy to the people." The announcement brought a quick endorsement from the *Herald Tribune.* "Mr. Lodge, we believe, is of the kind of stuff to leaven the lump of mediocrity that burdens our national councils," the endorsement read.[32] However, he faced a Republican primary challenger. Sinclair "Sinnie" Weeks was the mayor of Newton, the son of Calvin Coolidge's secretary of war, and the director of several large local and regional institutions, including the United Shoe Machinery Corporation, the First National Bank of Boston, the *Boston Herald,* the National Economy League, and the National Association of Manufacturers.[33] Most newspapers endorsed Weeks.

It would be a tough race. As Lodge was tied up with duties in the state house, he would only be able to engage in delegate hunting over the weekend. One of the first things he did was to get a big map of the state and put a red pushpin anywhere he had visited. Each Saturday that winter, he set out no matter how severe the weather, with sand, a towrope, and a shovel in the back of his car. If there was a spot on the map undisturbed by pushpins, he was likely to be going there soon.[34]

The long hours on the road gave Lodge plenty of time to think about the race. Assuming Lodge could find a way to get past Weeks, Curley would be no average rival, even if he had passed his zenith. Curley's most recent two-year term as governor had not been a success; he had promised "work and wages" to the state's 180,000 unemployed but was not able to deliver. On top of that, FDR did not like him, so the White House offered no help. If he were to win, he would need to do it on his own.[35] Across Curley's political career, his record of defeats was at least as impressive as his record of victories, rising from city councilor, to alderman, to state representative, to two-term congressman, to mayor, and, finally, to governor. He was defeated twice for the governorship and six times for mayor—although he did win four times. His recent victory for the governorship involved defeating incumbent Governor Marcus Coolidge by strong-arming the entire state Democratic convention. Perhaps Curley's most impressive two terms served were those in the Federal Correctional Institution in Danbury, Connecticut, for impersonating a constituent on a civil service exam and mail fraud.[36] Due to the passage of "Curley's law," he was allowed to remain mayor while serving time and drew his full salary.[37]

The first thing Lodge did was to put together an experienced political team. By the standards of Lodge's later political life, it was a little rough around the edges. One exception was "Uncle" Tom White, who played a critical role. White had been Calvin Coolidge's chief political adviser and served as Boston's collector of internal revenue. White was motivated to help because of a feud that he had had with Weeks's father, John, when the latter was secretary of war.[38] White, a genial but hardened New Englander, had retired from politics when Lodge came to see him. Joe Alsop and William Kintner once wrote that White's talent was that he could "think of thousands of things; nice things; clean things; beautiful things; things that cost you nothing and get you everything."[39] White looked Lodge up and down and decided he had promise. The former mentor of a president agreed to become the thirty-four-year-old Lodge's secretary right then and there.

Others on the Lodge team included lifelong bachelor Robert "Bobby" Cutler, who was Lodge's finance chairman and would later serve as President Dwight Eisenhower's national security advisor—the first to hold that position. Cutler was an old friend of the Lodges, having even vacationed with them in the Caribbean, Bermuda, and Antigua.[40] Together, they strategized to come up with a simple message. "Although we are eighth in population and ninth in our contributions to Uncle Sam's treasury, we are [forty-fifth] among the [forty-eight] states in the percentage of our relief load paid for by Washington," Lodge said in what became the theme of his campaign.[41] He was particularly critical of the fact that Massachusetts had received only $1 for every $181 the federal government spent in the South.[42]

"We didn't raise much money," Cutler recalled later about the campaign. "Most of it came from the Sears family. However, you didn't need to spend much in those days—telephones, mostly."[43] The Sears clan, including Lodge's wife, Emily, contributed about three-quarters of what was raised for the campaign—more than they were permitted to contribute according to law, so some had to be returned.[44] Others on the campaign included Malcolm W.

"Mally" Greenough, Chandler Bigelow, Mason Sears, and Charlie Barnes. This core helped Lodge visit some faraway district every weekend, while weekdays were spent speaking in the Boston area. As Lodge spoke in more and more places, White would arrange for invitations to the places he had not visited, and when Lodge visited them, White would write down the names of the people Lodge met. When they returned to the office, Lodge sent thank-you letters to everyone he met, referencing the content of their conversations.[45] It was said that, with White's help, Lodge met with seven hundred delegates personally, many of whom had been hit hard during the Depression.[46]

Lodge and White were outspent and outorganized, but they gradually overcame the Weeks machine. Each side competed for the attention of the delegates. Weeks had a brass band, doled out favors, and had powerful party endorsements such as that of Speaker Joseph "Joe" Martin Jr. Lodge and White bought roses for the delegates' wives and tried to greet every delegate as they arrived at the convention in Springfield, a White suggestion. "Get down to the hall a little early and stand out in the lobby and smile and shake hands. Be sure to smile, because then they'll think you've got it in the bag," he said.[47] That might have been a slight overstatement. The truth was, it was hard work to figure out which delegates at the convention were willing to consider Lodge, especially since, as state senate President Erland Fish warned, "No one here will vote against Weeks."[48]

White worked behind the scenes to sway party members one at a time. Perhaps his biggest conversion to Lodge was Maxwell Rabb, a young attorney from Brookline who had graduated from Harvard the year before. His views were typical of those willing to switch their allegiance from Weeks. "I liked Lodge's looks," he said. "He had a liberal record, and labor liked him. He could win a lot of independents and Democrats. Weeks was too conservative. I didn't think he could beat Curley." Rabb was the first Weeks man to defect, signaling to others—including Horace Cahill, manager of the Saltonstall campaign team, and Dick Saltonstall, the candidate's brother—that it was OK to jump ship. "Weeks' big band was waiting outside," Bobby Cutler recalled later. "It had to go home without even sounding taps. It was 4 p.m. when we won—we had balloted right through the lunch hour. We were starving. We all rushed over to some restaurant, only to find the goddamn thing closed. But a big crowd was cheering the new 'Senator' so the owner came to open it up. We ordered bottles of champagne and chicken salad—Cabot, Emily, Mrs. Sears, Tom White, Chan Bigelow and I—and began drinking toasts. We were a bit delirious, you might say, because we had put the boy over."[49]

Lodge won by thirty-seven votes, and rather than challenging the result, Weeks immediately moved to make the nomination unanimous. "The reason that I won was that I went into farmhouse kitchens and sat and talked with the men who were going to be the delegates," Lodge reflected. Returning to Beverly following his primary victory, he was greeted with a torchlit parade. He took a short vacation to Murray Bay, where he picked up a few French Canadian phrases that he could use in his speeches during the general election to that segment of the Massachusetts population, an important constituency.[50]

Lodge understood the changing demographics in Massachusetts. The state was becoming less English and less Protestant, and more Irish and more Catholic. By 1950, the state was 48.4 percent Catholic. Lodge always believed that once the Irish had a respectable candidate on the ballot, there was nothing he could do to win. Until then, however, he knew what Irish voters wanted, and he went out of his way to make sure they got it. Lodge's grandfather had operated the same way; Arthur Krock once said he was "more Irish than Daniel O'Connell."[51] The Irish were reliable supporters of Republicans in each election until 1952. The challenge for Lodge in 1936 was determining how to reach people who now worked for the government as an employer of last resort through agencies like the Works Progress Administration or who were receiving public assistance and had dropped out of the formal economy.[52] His opponent faced the same challenge.

Curley was not the respectable Irish candidate that Lodge feared. Although most actual physical altercations were the specialty of his brother, Carl, Curley proved that he was still more than able with his fists. Some called him "the Mussolini of Massachusetts." In a political brawl with Curley, someone was bound to get bloodied. Dozens of acts of violence at Curley political rallies have been documented, many involving the candidate himself. "Make a path for the gentleman," he would call out from the stage, challenging a catcaller. Rather than being engaged in a debate over the merit of some policy proposal, the unfortunate soul would receive a vicious uppercut when he reached the podium. No one ever accused Curley of being honest, but the Irish American boss was from a more honest era when politicians did their own fighting, and Curley had been gut fighting in politics since before Lodge was born. Charles W. "Chuck" Colson, who served as Leverett Saltonstall's administrative assistant before working for Richard Nixon, referred to Boston politics as "knee 'em in the groin politics."[53]

By the election, Curley had alienated many in his political base. A third-party candidate, Suffolk County district attorney Thomas O'Brien, whittled away at Curley's support after aligning himself with the National Union for Social Justice.[54] The way Curley defeated the respectable Marcus Coolidge was particularly abhorrent, so much so that the Democrats put up Coolidge's son-in-law, Robert E. Greenwood of Fitchburg, in the primary. But Curley had too big a lead and was not afraid to show it—by waiting to open his campaign headquarters until five days before the primary. Curley won by a twenty-five-to-one margin. "I didn't even send out a postcard. Yet I got 240,000 votes," he boasted. "That showed how much they love me."[55] Curley could quote the Bible, Whittier, or Lincoln. Some said he had a kind of Oxford accent, and when he spoke, if you did not hold on to yourself, you could be carried away. He could remember the names of people he had met once a dozen years before.[56]

Curley had built up enemies along the way. He had stretched executive power to the outer limits of democracy and had an almost dictatorial grip in office. Most voters were entertained rather than shocked by his antics. Democratic state legislators were repulsed by how many high posts had been given to Republicans, and the failure of Curley's "work and wages" program—an attempt at a localized version of the New Deal—was evident by the long lines of unemployed registering for benefits, as many as four thousand in a single day.[57] His strategy for dealing with Lodge was to treat him as something other than a serious candidate. "When my youthful rival was still wearing diapers, I was serving the Commonwealth of Massachusetts in the halls of Congress," Curley would say, sometimes referring to Lodge as "Little Boy Blue" for additional effect.[58] Lodge was "a young man who parts his hair and his name in the middle," he added for emphasis.[59] "You young Republicans," Curley told a rally in Springfield, "have no more chance to join the Somerset Club than I have, if your ancestors didn't get rich in the first two or three generations by selling opium to the Chinese, rum to the Indians or getting it in the slave racket."[60]

Despite all that Lodge had done for labor, which had come at some political cost, the Massachusetts State Federation of Labor endorsed Curley. Lodge refused to attack Curley directly. "My opponent has charged my grandfather with having scorned the working man," Lodge said during a political rally in Brockton, twenty minutes south of Boston. "Well, my grandfather did not fail loyally to represent the people of Massachusetts in the Senate. I suppose my opponent would rather have us involved in a European war than be spared entanglement in the League of Nations. I suppose my opponent prefers that ruinous competition of foreign sweat shops to the policies of my grandfather and protection for the American workman. I am proud of my grandfather's record."[61] Still in his midthirties, Lodge continued to defend isolationism.

Apart from Curley's penchant for personal attacks, there were few differences between them on the issues. "I could think of nothing prophetic of doom to say about Lodge," he said in his memoir.[62] Lodge ran as a cleaner version of Curley. He reminded voters of his liberal record on labor and economic relief issues. Both candidates were pro-labor, pro–Social Security, and for or against various New Deal programs when it served them locally. Lodge needed at least some of his opponent's votes in order to win. He had an ample supply of surrogates willing to do his bidding, such as Michael Hennessey of the *Boston Globe*, who responded to Curley's favorite quip with the retort, "When I was still wearing diapers, Curley was serving a six-month sentence in Charles Street Jail." The *Falmouth Enterprise* also chimed in:

> Little Boy Blue
> Come Blow Your Horn
> Lodge Will Be in the Senate
> When Curley is Gone.[63]

Columnist Raymond Clapper referred to the contest as "the best provincial political drama of the year . . . a drama of flesh and blue blood."[64]

On White's instructions, Lodge never mentioned Curley's name during the campaign. He did defend himself, however. "Since this campaign began attempts have been made to ridicule me because of my age, the color of my eyes and even my complexion. It has been insinuated that I am too young to take a seat as U.S. Senator in spite of the fact that the Constitution says that 30 is the age and I am well over that limit. An attempt has been made to take my name off the ballot because I have a Junior after my name so as to prevent any confusion between me and my grandfather. When this failed I was attacked on the ground that I was masquerading as my grandfather," he said during a speech on October 19, 1936.[65] "I still bear the name with which I was born, a fact which is proved by the official records," Lodge said.[66] "The funny thing was that Curley's birth certificate—we checked that, too—was different," Bobby Cutler recalled. "He didn't have the middle name, Michael, on the certificate. But we didn't attack him on it."[67]

Lodge worked day and night, an average of ten to twelve hours per day. He reviewed years of index cards that he had kept for every supporter and every public speech, and he made 2,300 house calls. From those contacts he formed various "Lodge for Senate" committees. He skipped events that he did not think would help him, instead focusing on Syrian picnics, French Canadian clambakes, and hostile events full of swing voters—such as Congress of Industrial Organizations meetings. Lodge tailored his message to each group. He attacked federal spending, while at the same time promising to get a fair share for Massachusetts. Lodge never attacked FDR, who remained popular, and even declared support for aspects of the New Deal, such as the Townsend Plan.

Curley kept up his fiery rhetoric until Election Day. "I'll beat this little lad by more than 150,000 votes, yes, nearer 200,000 votes," he swore in the closing days of the race.[68] "Mr. Lodge is a charming young man, whom I shall regret exceedingly having to chastise." Curley labeled Lodge "a sweet boy with an illustrious name," "little Henry," "big blue eyes," and "my puny opponent" and warned, "Don't send a boy to run a man's errand." Lodge rarely acknowledged or addressed these attacks or turned negative, and Curley's attacks on Lodge's youth started to backfire with voters who had just come of voting age.[69]

Lodge traveled forty-three thousand miles, gave 680 speeches, and criticized the methods but not the aims of the New Deal. On the campaign trail he was an avid handshaker, but not a backslapper. In one night he made fourteen appearances before different types of voters. Lodge possessed the necessary liberal legislative record and the communication skills to convince even an evolving voting demographic that he was a different kind of Republican— not the kind who could be defined and defeated by old stereotypes.

Lodge's hard-earned victory put him in the national spotlight for the first time. He won by more than 135,000 votes, including in every part of the state except Suffolk County, an impressive win for a thirty-four-year-old running in his first major election—and an auspicious sign of things to come. It also gave him "a slightly exaggerated ego," he admitted later.[70] FDR's coattails were long in 1936, and Lodge was the only Republican in the nation to win a seat held by a Democrat. FDR won every state except Vermont and Maine, contributing to the greatest majority held by any party in Senate history. He won Massachusetts by 174,103 votes.

"I intend to remain silent until I have something worthwhile to say," Lodge said after his victory. "My aim is to work for legislation which will achieve the results intended, not legislation which merely looks good on the surface."[71]

# 3 • U.S. Senate

Henry Cabot Lodge Jr. arrived at the Senate in the midst of the Great Depression, in 1937. Thanks to his grandfather, he was well acquainted with Washington—and its hot, miserable summers. "Summers in Washington are not healthy," Lodge wrote to his brother, John, long before the days of modern air conditioning.[1] The British Foreign Office classified it as a hardship post for diplomats due to the "climate"—which presumably referred to meteorology and not politics.

The Republicans, as a national party, were basically extinct. The Grand Old Party held only seventeen seats, and five of those were La Follette Progressives who were barely hanging on. There were a few old-time, Reconstruction-era members of the upper chamber still around, and such longevity ensured that the institutions of the Senate were not only maintained but designed to be resistant to change. The Senate was a place of courtesy, courtliness, dignity, and refinement. The more genteel older members spoke to each other in private as they did in public, addressing each other not by name but by title, duplicating the excessive formality of the Senate floor.[2]

Senator James E. Watson (R-IN) was legendary for telling stories, and he was not the only one. Watson had served at various times in the Senate since 1916. He told Lodge a story about his reelection campaign of 1932, when he refused to take a stand on Prohibition. "He said he wanted to wait until all the evidence was in," Lodge recalled. One day Watson received a fiery group of women who were fervent supporters of Prohibition, and they demanded that he support their cause. "When he refused and said he would continue to maintain an open mind, one of the ladies shook her finger at him and said, 'Well, Senator, it's going to be tit for tat. If you fight us, we'll fight you.' Senator Watson replied, 'In that case, I start off at a great disadvantage. You have two tits and I have only one tat.'"[3]

"Reminds me of an afternoon in the United States Senate at the time that I was a member," Lodge later reflected. "And one senator was talking, and he said to the presiding officer, 'Mr. President, I've seen a lot of changes and I've been against them all.' That was the kind of colorful, picturesque character we used to have in the United States Senate in those days."[4]

Newcomers like Lodge who were born in the twentieth century presented quite a contrast. Lodge's correspondence later in life illuminates what he thought it meant to be an effective senator: "a man who does not go through life fitting everything into the rigid framework of by-gone prejudices."[5] While he was raised among such formality and traditions, he broke from them when it suited him. The young junior senator from Massachusetts breathed life into an aging Republican caucus that did not have much else going for it. "I have no fixed prejudices or policies," Lodge said. "I would like [to be known] as a practical progressive."[6] His staff included representatives of big voting blocs in Massachusetts, including Yankees, Irish, Jews, French Canadians, and Italians, and he boasted that his secretarial staff was the most efficient on Capitol Hill, enabling him to carry on a massive correspondence—typically two hundred letters a day. Joe Alsop and William Kintner wrote a profile about Lodge during his early days in the Senate for the *New York Herald Tribune*.[7] "The vital statistics of the author of so much Democratic anguish are rather simple," Alsop and Kintner wrote. "He is the grandson of the first Henry Cabot Lodge, and the seventh member of the United States Senate in his family in a direct line of succession. He is tall, personable, athletic looking, and only thirty-four. He belongs to the highest caste of the Boston Brahminate, but he has neither the Brahmins' manner, nor their accent, nor their opinions."[8]

Due to the lopsided number of Democrats in the Senate, Lodge argued that Republicans needed to develop responsible social legislation. They could not afford to simply be against everything proposed by the FDR White House. He voted for the Works Progress Administration, was one of only two Republicans to support the Fair Labor Standards Act, and supported an increase in Social Security payments to the elderly and crippled children, as well as efforts to ensure the payment of union wages to workers on housing projects administered by the Federal Housing Authority. "We must look to government to provide actual relief when unemployment overwhelms the nation," he said to the Republican Club of Massachusetts. "And we have a right to demand of government that it do nothing to prevent conditions from existing in which the day of the good job can return."[9]

Lodge voted with Republicans on other issues, including against the Civilian Conservation Corps, crop insurance, and a 1939 relief bill.[10] He voted against Supreme Court nominee Hugo Black on the grounds that he had once been a member of the Ku Klux Klan. Lodge's criticism of FDR's policies concerned how aid was distributed. "I think he would have obtained greater results in federal relief, for example, with local control," Lodge said.[11] He also became a lead critic of FDR's plan to expand the membership of the Supreme Court. In a nationwide broadcast, Lodge said the plan might "establish a precedent which could be used to destroy this republic."[12]

Since the minority party was so marginalized, Lodge expertly learned how to manipulate the rules in order to have greater influence. His philosophy was that the minority should be "the voice of conscience though not of power," undertaking a "calm and deliberate reappraisal of the facts" while offering "constructive suggestions."[13] Lodge knew when to cast a vote for or against, when to buck the Republicans for the purpose of symbolism at home, and when to curry favor with the White House. He knew how to manipulate the amendments process, in terms of both substance and timing—including attaching poison pills to popular bills. Lodge was one of two Republicans to vote for the Wages and Hours Bill, harking back to his labor support in the state house. He defended the Wagner Act, better known as the National Labor Relations Act. He proposed a bill to have postal employees take a more accurate census of unemployment. Lodge was one of four senators who voted against the nomination of William Douglas to the Supreme Court in 1939, having been convinced by Senator Lynn Frazier (D-ND) that Douglas was a pandering opportunist who had become "the fool of Wall Street."[14]

In 1938, FDR criticized Republicans for being against the elderly and pensions when they voted against the Social Security Act. In response, Lodge introduced an amendment that would have increased spending by one-third.[15] When he told Senator Charles McNary, the Republican leader of Oregon, who had been a protégé of Lodge's grandfather, what he planned to do, "McNary's little blue eyes twinkled; his pink lined cheeks, like the well-ripened cheeks of a winter pippin, wrinkled in a grin," Alsop and Kintner recalled.[16] Democrats would be put in the awkward position of voting against the White House in order to deny a Republican proposal.

George Norris (D-NE) condemned the amendment; James Byrnes (D-SC) had a sharp word to say about Lodge. Majority leader Alben W. Barkley (D-KY) also criticized Lodge, but in doing so he revealed that he did not understand the details of the Social Security Act. The opposition was tongue-tied by the unexpected proposal. Byrnes moved that the Lodge amendment be tabled, to place it in an administrative bog. Barkley tried to prevent a recorded vote. Democrats assumed that Lodge's amendment alone would cost them one or two seats once word reached the country's seniors that the Senate did not do something to help them when it had a chance to do so. Barkley once described the typical pattern of Lodge's tricks: "Put the amendment in the bill, and the bill is sabotaged. Keep it out, and the Senators who keep it out are sabotaged."[17]

While the impulse would have been to vote down Lodge's troublesome amendment, Hiram Johnson (R-CA) insisted on a recorded vote in order to establish a record. "Mr. President, is there no fairness in this body, to give us the yeas and the nays?" he asked. "Instantly a wild pandemonium broke loose," Alsop wrote in the *Saturday Evening Post*.[18] Fearing the recorded vote, some Democrats voted for the amendment. In the end, it was defeated thirty-nine to thirty, but Lodge's manipulation of the rules caused some Democrats to believe the issue cost them some seats in the next election.[19] Reflecting on his strategy, Lodge said, "Such measures, I thought, were socially good; they also helped to change and modernize the Republicans, and they helped to reveal the contradictions within the Democratic party."[20]

Lodge loved the political game. It became a forum for him to display his Harvard debating skills, as well as the skills he acquired during his journalistic training and years of watching politicians up close. He learned how to be a thorn in the side of the Democrats. The lesson for Lodge was that a just majority is better for all when challenged by a responsible minority. On several occasions, the White House put pressure on Senate Democrats in response to a Lodge proposal, including through direct intervention by FDR. When the president pressed for the passage of the Public Housing Act in the hope that the unions could compromise and maintain wage discipline or even decrease wages in return for a large, guaranteed quantity of work, Lodge saw another opportunity. He proposed an amendment that federally financed projects pay "prevailing rates of pay for work of a similar nature." The White House was forced to admit that labor was being undercut in the proposed bill, which vastly increased the cost of the administration's measure. To vote with Lodge, and labor, would have killed public housing. To vote against Lodge would be a vote against the unions. The Senate ended up approving Lodge's amendment, but FDR intervened in conference to strip it out. He violated his personal rule of not singling out a member of Congress for criticism by name, stating that Lodge was "playing unjustifiable politics" in Senate.[21]

During final passage, Alben Barkley made a strong speech against the amended version and Lodge's meddling—yet later tried to remove his condemnation of Lodge from the *Congressional Record*. In the end, the Lodge provision was defeated, but by only two votes. "It is smart politics on the part of the Senator from Massachusetts," said Sherman Minton (D-IN). Another senator commented, "Cabot, I wish to God you'd go back to Massachusetts where you came from. We don't mind having a few Republicans around, but you're a real nuisance."[22]

Lodge learned that if he wanted to stay in the Senate, he had to cultivate and retain Irish support. His grandfather had taught him that even largely symbolic gestures can go a long way. He walked in South Boston's St. Patrick's Day parade, the Bunker Hill Day parade in Charlestown, and the Patriot's Day parade in Lexington and Concord. In South Boston, Lodge wore a top hat, a morning coat, and striped pants, like any other Irish district captain. In Charlestown and Concord, he wore a well-worn suit with a battered felt hat. Lodge did not miss an important funeral. He wore green on St. Patrick's Day and attended so many Irish funerals that Truman secretary David K. Niles once told him, "You oughtn't to go to so many Irish funerals, Cabot, because it looks as if you just like to see dead Irishmen."[23] Over time, the term "Lodge Democrats" came to be used to refer to those voters who voted a straight ticket with the exception of Lodge.[24]

Lodge discovered an old rule that Irish immigrants had to pledge allegiance to the King of England. It had long outlasted its importance; Ireland was an independent nation. Lodge proposed a bill making it unnecessary. It passed easily since no one cared, yet it was popular with the Irish, who treated Lodge as though he had freed them from the last vestige of England's power. It was called "one of the shrewder political moves of the century" at the time, and Lodge's name was added to the Irish pantheon of St. Patrick, Daniel O'Connell, and Charles Stewart Parnell.[25] He also voted in favor of federal aid to parochial schools, supported plans to send an ambassador to the Vatican, and voted for UN membership for Ireland. He continued to prod Republicans to purge themselves of reactionaries if they ever hoped to regain power in Washington. "It must become a party of the people," he said. "It ought to go back to Abraham Lincoln and get some real liberty."[26]

Lodge proved himself astute at fulfilling his campaign promise to get more federal funds for Massachusetts. He voted sometimes liberal, sometimes conservative, and sometimes evasively.[27] Few freshman senators demonstrated an understanding of pork-barrel politics as completely as Lodge. In one case, he asked for $1.2 million to retool the Springfield arsenal, an outdated facility. If some investment occurred, it would probably save those jobs. During a Senate hearing chaired by Democratic Senator Royal Copeland of New York, the proposal was addressed. "Without objection, it is so ordered," Copeland said. Then he asked Lodge whether an appropriation was also needed for the fortification of New York Harbor. Lodge said there was no greater advocate of harbor fortification than he was—and that Boston could use the same. "I see $750,000 down here for Boston," Copeland said. Some Brahmins complained that Lodge used too many federal funds in Massachusetts, but the moves were popular.[28]

Tom White continued to be a font of wisdom and sage political advice.[29] McNary was the Senate Republican leader. They were "rather like a pair of elderly, immensely experienced horse trainers who have spotted a promising yearling."[30] Other mentors who had known Lodge's grandfather included Hiram Johnson, Styles Bridges (R-NH), Lister Hill (D-AL), and C. Wayland Brooks (R-IL). Lodge also befriended Arthur Vandenberg of Michigan. They were both journalists by training, liked storytelling and laughter, and were from the progressive wing of the party. They were chastised by conservatives such as George Moses (R-NH) as "sons of the wild jackass."[31]

For most of his adult life, Lodge lived in the family home in Beverly Cove, tucked away in Boston's North Shore.[32] Great front rooms opened to the Atlantic Ocean and a private beach. A breeze carried a faint smell of lilies, and ivy climbed the brick walls. A large, copper beech tree shaded the square gravel courtyard.[33] The interior was French provincial, including the expansive library with floor-to-ceiling bookcases that held twenty thousand books, many of which had been his grandfather's—whose portrait held court in the small sitting room.

The house was a living museum of Cabot-Lodge family artifacts—gigantic seashells that had served as ballast on John Ellerton Lodge's clipper ships, a cannon used by Admiral Charles Davis at the siege of Vicksburg, Louis XVI tables, and Ming porcelain. Visitors who ascended the grand staircase could view George Cabot's parchment commission from John Adams as the nation's first secretary of the navy, as well as John Trumbull's portrait of Alexander Hamilton—a gift from Hamilton to Cabot.[34] A handsome rendering of the Great Seal of the United States in the front hall hung among portraits of generations of generals, admirals, senators, and governors. "Individually and collectively, they radiated patriotism, love of country, and a sort of unsullied certainty: traits well embodied by my father," Lodge's son George Cabot Lodge said.[35]

Whether on the Senate floor or at his home in Georgetown or Beverly, Lodge put in a twelve-hour workday on average. He attended committee meetings and rarely left the Senate during session. These were the days before air travel was considered routine and safe. The correspondence he maintained with constituents was so vast that he had to use personal funds beyond his congressional allowance to hire extra secretaries. Even though he was happily married with two sons, he received many offers of marriage by mail. When he was asked for a signed photograph, he made sure to send one of him with his beaming family. Lodge did not turn down a duty connected with some public service. Even when Vice President John Nance Garner assigned Lodge the job of trustee to a federal institution for juvenile delinquents in Washington, Lodge took the job seriously. He showed up unannounced to request a tour, talked to everyone, stayed for lunch, and ate with the boys.[36]

Lodge tried to shake off the reputation that he was an isolationist—a label that had also been applied to his grandfather. On balance, before World War II, Lodge tended to follow his grandfather's views on foreign policy. "I was always for strong preparedness, which true isolationists weren't," he would say, even while he held to his belief that a strong America could avoid war. Lodge thought that the United States should not be involved outside the Western Hemisphere, and even with war on the horizon, he avoided becoming unnecessarily entangled in it.[37]

Lodge opposed the Neutrality Act of 1937, which was designed by the Roosevelt administration to keep the United States out of foreign conflicts as well as the Spanish Civil War, because he did not think it went far enough. Specifically, he did not believe in the amended version that allowed "cash and carry" sales of armaments to Britain and France. "I believe we should be absolutely neutral in the European conflict. To enact a 'cash and carry' law would mean that ultimately we would be drawn into the European war and be obliged to send an army there to protect the financial interests of our traders in war goods." Prominent Americans such as Charles Lindbergh and Joseph Kennedy agreed, and public opinion polls showed that a clear majority of Americans were opposed to U.S. involvement in an overseas conflict.[38] Winston Churchill later referred to the passage of the Neutrality Act as the "green light" to Hitler and remembered that Lodge was one of the six senators who voted against it.[39]

Around this time, Lodge had a hand in helping Leverett Saltonstall, his Bay State colleague, get elected to the U.S. Senate in 1938. They had met in the early 1920s, before Lodge first ran for the state house, when Saltonstall asked *Boston Evening Transcript* publisher George S. Mandell for publicity to help his fledgling political career. When Mandell told him that Lodge would be coming to see him soon, Saltonstall was excited, thinking that Woodrow Wilson's nemesis was paying him a visit. Instead, cub reporter Lodge turned up. Lodge asked whether Saltonstall was planning to make any speeches he could cover. "I wasn't going to make any speeches," he recalled. Lodge asked whether he planned to hold any political meetings. "We don't have meetings in Newton," Saltonstall said. "Well, how do you expect me to give you any publicity in the paper if you're not going to attend any meetings or make any speeches?" Lodge asked.[40] In 1938, Lodge not only campaigned for his friend but helped him organize a major political rally at the Boston Garden on election night. It was the beginning of an alliance.

As war came nearer, Lodge became more pro-defense and advocated closer ties to the Allies. He took a similar position in *The Cult of Weakness*. Lodge wanted to stay out of European affairs but believed that a weak nation was open to attack. The purpose of building up defenses was not to go to war but rather to avoid war by dissuading a would-be attacker.[41] The logic sounds surprisingly similar to the neoconservative doctrine of "provocative weakness" that many espoused in the final third of the twentieth century. Lodge argued for more warships in 1938, called for more planes in 1939, and supported the selective service in 1940.[42] He opposed reciprocal trade bills and a repeal of the Neutrality Act. Lodge also spoke against a repeal of the arms embargo on October 10, 1939, following the German invasion of Poland.[43] He wrote Major General J. K. Herr to "request that [he] be ordered to active duty immediately upon the commencement of hostilities," in case the United States were to join the war early.[44]

Due to Lodge's own military experience, he sometimes suggested isolationism or even pacifism. In a secret Senate session after Germany invaded Poland, he said, "The fight in Europe is not our fight. If the British and the French empires can't stand without our help, they deserve to fail." He did not believe Hitler could conquer London or Paris, and he hoped that the Russians would be able to fend off the Nazis.[45] This view was popular in Massachusetts, as Irish Catholics did not really care whether Britain was prepared for war.[46]

Lodge repeated the same refrain in September 1940: "I hate war, now more than ever . . . I have one supreme determination—to do all that I can to keep war away from these shores for all time." In Dayton, Ohio, in October, he said the military was a deterrent because "it is the strongest guarantee for peace."

He reiterated that sentiment in Boston later in the month: "Our objective is to keep any potential attacker as far from our continental shores as we possibly can."[47] Lodge's commentary would make his eventual conversion to internationalism even more dramatic.

Lodge had started to surface on Gallup polls beginning in late 1936 as a possible Republican candidate for president.[48] While he did not express any interest in campaigning for the top of the ticket, he did use his popularity to help Wendell Willkie in 1940. Lodge seconded him at the convention, and he was chosen on the fifth ballot.[49] Willkie was a controversial choice because he had been a lifelong Democrat before switching parties. Longtime Senator James E. Watson (R-IN) was shocked by his eventual nomination. "I don't mind admitting the fallen woman to the church," Lodge recalled Watson saying in the Senate, "but I don't want to make her leader of the choir."[50]

Lodge helped write the platform at the convention in Philadelphia, and he later spent hours on Willkie's campaign train. Believing the best man should win, he was not troubled by Willkie's lack of Republican ties. "The Republican Party strives for Americanism, preparedness and peace; no foreign war; an air force, army and navy so strong that no one unfriendly power can successfully attack America or its essential outposts; . . . [and] no third term for president," Lodge said in a typical speech. He campaigned for three weeks and wrote an article for *Life* chronicling the experience, telling a nationwide audience that Willkie, a World War I veteran, "has looked war in the eye—he hates it!"[51]

He went further in an essay titled "Cutting the Cables," in which he recalled the changed attitude toward war in the wake of World War I. "Soon after the war some of the groups who gave special attention to the question of peace believed that the United States could best remain at peace by joining with foreign nations in punishing any nation which went to war," he argued. "This theory of starting a war to stop a war manifested itself in the desire for American membership in the League of Nations and its Court. Fortunately, I believe, the suicidal character of this method became apparent and, for the time being anyway, it was dropped." In a speech before the World Court, Lodge said, "Let us not substitute an international flag for the American flag," harking back to his grandfather's argument about the loss of sovereignty required by the League of Nations.[52]

Only after the 1940 Battle of France did Lodge's views privately start to shift. He supported the Selective Training and Service Act of 1940, which created the first peacetime draft in American history.[53] Lodge voted to arm merchant ships and advocated universal military training in a September 1940 edition of *American Magazine.* He called for an immediate buildup in the air forces and urged compulsory military service months before FDR spoke out on the issue.[54]

For Lodge, the ideological debate came to a head with FDR's Lend-Lease Bill in 1941, a proposal to lend American allies food, oil, and materiel needed for the war effort. The bill struck a careful, if precarious, balance between engaging in World War II and remaining on the sidelines. Lodge warned that FDR might become an "internal dictator." FDR had never faced such criticism before. He said the attacks against him were "the rottenest thing that has been said in public life in a generation."[55] The episode showed how rough Lodge's bare-knuckled political attacks could be. Later in life, after his conversion to internationalism, he felt differently.

For the first time in his legislative career, Lodge lost sleep over a vote. The outcome hinged on the central issue of choosing war or peace. He drew up the list of arguments in favor of lend-lease on one sheet of paper and the list of arguments against it on another. "The bill is naturally not perfect but far better than no bill at all in the present emergency, where time is of the essence," he said.[56] Years later, Lodge reflected that FDR's "lend-lease agreement with Britain to assist that nation was an act of foresight and courage masterfully timed." It was just a single bill, but it served a greater purpose. "Another great achievement of FDR's was the skill and courage with which he prepared public opinion in the United States for what he, before many, saw as the inevitability of World War II . . . In this, as in so much else, he showed mastery of timing."[57]

What broke the deadlock in Lodge's thinking was the opinion of his friend, army chief of staff George Marshall, who wrote, "The prompt enactment of the bill into law is a matter of great importance to the proper and expeditious development of our measures for national security. The munitions program in prospect presents a colossal task which can only be accomplished under the most favorable circumstances, meaning absence of confusion, and simplicity of procedure. This bill has been drawn with this in mind." With this guidance, Lodge broke from all of his key political allies—Arthur Vandenberg, Hiram Johnson, and Robert Taft—and joined the sixty senators who voted in favor of H.R. 1776. It was a step toward war.[58]

Given world events, Lodge's maneuvers with the artillery reserve in Louisiana in the summer of 1941 started to seem more serious. Many of the reservists remained in disbelief that France had fallen to Hitler. "Why, that's impossible!" said General Hugh Drum. "The French are the best artillerists in the world." Lodge spent part of the summer with Major General George Patton's Second Armored Division in a one-hundred-mile "battle" against the "enemy," led by Lieutenant General Ben Lear—whose chief of staff was Colonel Dwight D. Eisenhower, a relative unknown identified as "Eisenberg" in a local newspaper's write-up of the war game. Eisenhower played the role of the chief of staff of the opposing army in the exercise. Lodge heard Patton say, "I'll give fifty dollars to anyone who captures a son-of-a-bitch named Eisenhower." It was the first time Lodge had heard his name.[59] They met during the army exercises in Leesville, outside the post theater. The maneuvers continued on and off through the fall, concluding on December 2, 1941. Patton's final report noted that his men had "met every test short of war."[60]

On Sunday, December 7, Lodge and Emily were in Groton to visit their son George, then fourteen, who was enrolled at Groton School. After an uneventful lunch, they stopped to get gas on the drive back to Beverly. "Can you believe what the Japs did?" the attendant said. They listened to the radio reports about the attack on Pearl Harbor during their trip home. Emily remembered later how grim Lodge was.[61] When he flashed back to the summer of 1914, which he was spending in France with his family when war broke out, it became real and threatening. They arrived in Beverly with reporters pushing microphones in Lodge's face, seeking comment.[62] Lodge went on the air in Boston the same day and called for all Americans to unite.[63] "The time for united action has come. The time for words has passed."[64] He did the first thing he thought of: get the next train to Washington.

# Part II
## The Making of
## an Internationalist

# 4 · World War II

"The president will see you now."

It was hardly the first time that Henry Cabot Lodge Jr. had heard those words. When entering the White House, he was awash in memories. The building was an integral part of his upbringing. "I like this hotel! I'm going to come here again," his sister, Helena, had said when, as children, they dined with the Roosevelts.[1] The family had known plenty of presidents. Their birthright entailed access to elites and membership in a class in which everyone was exceptional, but also an expectation to use one's talents for the betterment of the nation. Being a Lodge came with obvious privileges, as well as responsibilities that were less visible.

But February 1, 1944, was different. Lodge had requested an emergency meeting with President Franklin D. Roosevelt, and Lodge was about to make the most important decision of his life. The tall, lanky forty-one-year-old had taken a taxi to the White House and used the east entrance, where he was not likely to be spotted by the press. He had asked to see FDR off the record "about a personal matter."[2] "Although I had, of course, seen President Roosevelt when he appeared before Congress and had been invited to some large affairs at the White House, this was the first time I had ever sought an appointment with him alone," Lodge said.[3] He was shown into the Cabinet Room to wait, and as he stared out the window, he spotted a plume of smoke that rose from the president's long cigarette holder. FDR was being wheeled rapidly along the terrace by the Rose Garden, Admiral William Leahy at his side.[4]

"Hello, Cabot!" FDR said with a wry smile. Press Secretary Stephen Early remained in the room as FDR started to tell a dramatic story about the Battle of Kwajalein, which was ongoing. "Mr. President," Lodge interrupted,

"I have decided to resign my seat in the Senate and go into combat duty in the Army."[5]

FDR and Early were caught off guard by the announcement. The only precedent, an ominous one, was Senator Edward Baker (R-OR), who became the only sitting senator to be killed in action at Ball's Bluff in 1861. "The President's eyebrows shot up and so did Early's. I shall always remember those two sets of eyebrows," Lodge wrote later. "Cabot, that's splendid," FDR said. "I congratulate you! I wish I were going with you!"[6]

Lodge must have had some concern that he could be talked out of his decision—whether by FDR or by family and friends. "What I plan to do," Lodge explained, "if you will give me your blessing, is to fly to England . . . before my resignation is announced in the Senate." FDR said, "Certainly you have my blessing." Lodge told no one of his plans other than Emily, his two sons, and his friend army General Willis D. Crittenberger. After meeting with FDR, Lodge informed his administrative assistant, Maxwell Rabb, as well as his friend Senator D. Worth Clark of Idaho, who was acting president of the Senate. "I'll never forget Clark's expression," Rabb recalled. "He was visibly awed. As a Senator he knew what a tremendous job it is to get and keep a seat in the Senate and what a wrench it would be to give all that up voluntarily."[7]

The Pearl Harbor attack on December 7, 1941, had compelled Lodge, the man who had rejected the League of Nations and the World Court, to make a dramatic shift. He still strongly advocated neutrality after Germany's invasion of Poland. He held mostly firm after the London Blitz and the occupation of France. But Pearl Harbor challenged him to rethink his positions.[8] The event also forced him to consider his own future. Upon hearing of the attack, his first instinct was to rejoin his army unit and deploy right away. However, he decided he was better off in Washington.

The army liked the fact that they had a friend in Washington. The veteran officers, including Generals George Marshall, George Patton, and Crittenberger, considered Lodge to be the one senator who understood their needs. Lodge knew that resources were needed; he donated his March and April 1942 salaries of $833.34 "as a gift to the United States of America as a contribution on [his] part towards winning the war."[9] He continued his service in the army reserve and the Second Armored Division, which had moved to Fort Benning, Georgia.[10] "Throughout the Army you are probably more favorably known for actual field service well done than any other Reserve Officer," Crittenberger wrote.[11] Remaining in Washington permitted Lodge the opportunity to inspect army facilities as requested by Senate Military Affairs Committee Chairman

Robert R. Reynolds (D-NC) on February 5, 1942: "It would be most helpful . . . if you were able to make a personal inspection of our military units."[12] Lodge could make sure they had what they needed and report back to Washington.

While the United States was rapidly preparing for war, Lodge was planning for another tough campaign. His Senate term was up in 1942, and he faced challenges from several high-profile Democrats, including Congressman John McCormack and Ambassador Joseph Kennedy's father-in-law, Boston Mayor John "Honey Fitz" Fitzgerald.[13] Fitzgerald, seventy-nine, had not run for Congress for three decades.[14] Kennedy gave an early boost to the Fitzgerald campaign by writing $1,000 checks from himself and his two sons—Joseph Jr. and Jack. He felt threatened by Fitzgerald's primary challenger, Congressman Joseph E. Casey, whom FDR had asked to run against Lodge.[15]

Casey was considered by many to be the Irish New Dealer in the House of Representatives.[16] Joe Kennedy felt differently. If there was to be a young Irishman in the U.S. Senate, it would be a Kennedy, not a Casey.[17] Kennedy denounced Casey, a respected member of Congress, so thoroughly that Tom White used a recording he had made of it in the general election. The bruising primary had drained Casey's finances and badly wounded him by the time he faced Lodge in the general election. Backing Honey Fitz in 1942 was a Kennedy play to end Casey's political career; that way, the seat would be open when a Kennedy was prepared to run.[18]

There was no shortage of people who would have liked to make the Republican gadfly Lodge a one-term senator, not the least of whom was in the White House. Several Massachusetts newspapers chimed in, too. "Mr. Henry Cabot Lodge should make up his mind and be either a soldier or a Senator," the Fitchburg *Sentinel* editorial page opined on March 2. "The same person cannot hold both a military and a civilian commission as U.S. Senator," Charlie McGlue wrote for the Lynn *Telegram-News*. Yet some were supportive. "While some of the experts on Constitutional law assert that a man cannot be in both Congress and the Army, the best proof that it can be done is that Lodge is doing it," Roslindale's *Parkway Transcript* opined.[19]

Lodge maintained his reserve status and reached the rank of captain in 1941. Combining that with the rank of U.S. senator meant that he had access to top political and military leaders, such as Winston Churchill, who visited Washington for the first time as prime minister during the spring of 1942. After his address to Congress, a group of senators was invited to the British embassy for a private gathering. "Mr. Churchill stood up and talked in his inimitable way," Lodge recalled. "Everyone else was seated when I noticed that on the shoulder of Mr. Churchill's jacket, a button had been sewn on." He noticed that the other members of Churchill's entourage also had the extra button. "The purpose of the button was to prevent Prime Minister Churchill's gas mask from sliding off—the button was there to catch it," Lodge remembered being told.[20] For an American, this was a simple but sobering reminder of what was going on in Europe.

Lodge's reserve status in the U.S. Army was activated and his first tour began in 1942. He was ordered to report to Fort Benning, where he would join the Second Armored Division, later known as General Patton's "Hell on Wheels" Division. Unlike most politicians, Lodge wanted to see action. He wrote General Dwight Eisenhower on April 29, 1942, to make himself available for any interesting assignment the general might become aware of. "I am hopeful that soon I will give you definite advice on a likely assignment involving action," Ike responded.[21]

Lodge made an impression at Fort Benning. An officer remembered that Lodge "was worshipped by the men in that tank division. He was a born leader."[22] Lodge liked the egalitarian nature of the army. It was a place where individuals were responsible for their own actions. Lodge was eager for a substantive active-duty assignment. He went to the Munitions Building in Washington to see Eisenhower, then in charge of army operations.[23] "He advised me to wait a month and then get in touch with him again," Lodge reported to Patton. Eisenhower was hesitant to send any of the newly trained armored units across the Atlantic due to the heavy losses inflicted by the German U-boats. Instead, he decided to handpick certain tank crews, fly them to the front, and put them under British command.[24]

Lodge's friend Crittenberger recommended that Lodge be chosen to lead one of these missions. Crittenberger had succeeded Patton as commander of the Second Armored Division, leading to the promotion of Jacob "Jake" Devers as chief of the Armored Force at Fort Knox. Since Lodge was both a trained tank officer and someone with extensive government experience, he seemed like an ideal candidate to lead a team of tanks into the Libyan Desert. It would be an experiment to see what it would be like to fight Germans there, specifically Field Marshal Erwin Rommel's Afrika Korps. Eisenhower agreed. Lodge's orders on May 15, 1942, were to report to Fort Knox, then Miami, from where he would travel by sea via the South Atlantic to the British Gold Coast, Anglo-Egyptian Sudan, and finally Cairo.[25] Devers hoped to get two hundred officers and their men with the tanks "to get them blooded" and teach the British how to service and maintain American tanks.[26]

Lodge again captured the element of surprise. While the press at home was reporting that he was taking part in maneuvers, he turned up in Tripoli. When asked for comment, even Tom White was caught off guard. "As far as I knew Mr. Lodge was at Fort Knox only 10 days ago."[27] Lodge had told no one about his secret mission. After the six-day trip to reach Egypt, Lodge reported for duty on May 28, 1942, to Colonel Lewis H. Ham of the Third Armored Division.[28] He was assigned as an observer with the British Eighth Army. That made Lodge one of the first Americans to go into combat against the Nazis.

Travel weary and consumed by thoughts about the war, Lodge slept little that first night. "A soldier in action, I learned, is much too preoccupied to have sustained periods of fear," he recalled. "Fear requires concentration. Even when he is being fired at, the soldier in the desert has plenty to think about just to supply his bodily wants—finding a cool spot, getting the sand out of his eyes, trying to down biscuits and brackish water."[29] Lodge and his tank crew joined the British Fourth Armored Brigade. There had been little for the British to celebrate in the war. Since late 1940, after Italy joined the Axis powers on June 10, both sides had waged military offensives in the western desert. However, while they were greatly outnumbered by Italian forces stationed in Libya, the British had managed to capture Bardia and Tobruk in January 1941 during Operation Compass.[30]

Rommel had dominated that theater of war. Egypt was considered especially vital. It was a gateway to oil in the Middle East and its route to the British Empire, and it was a major naval base on the Mediterranean and a center of communications to more remote parts of the empire. Lodge's tanks were placed in a safe area at the extreme end of the British line, far from the minefields.[31] Little did Lodge know that Rommel and the German Panzers were about to make a push toward Alexandria that would put him in the line of fire as he trained with the British tank units.[32]

With three tank crews in training behind him, Lodge reconnoitered the front, which consisted of forty miles of mines laid by the British. "The wire," as it was known, extended from the Mediterranean southward to a point after which the desert opened up and armies would run out of gas. While that seemed like a safe buffer, the Germans were sometimes close enough to observe them through field glasses. Rommel ordered the use of minesweepers on a large scale for the first time, presumably in an attempt to construct an accurate map of the wire. The observation of dust clouds through field glasses indicated a lot of movement to the south on the German side.[33]

On the Tobruk-Bardia road on June 11, Lodge and a British colonel saw nine German Stukas peel off and blast an entire truck convoy.[34] Lodge dove into a slit trench dug by the side of the road for that very purpose. It was the first time he had seen the Germans up close. "A man would have to be blind not to see that the German soldiers were superbly equipped for the peculiar rigors of desert fighting," he reflected later. This message was reinforced by a German prisoner of war, who said, "We will win because our equipment and organization are better." The experience served as a wake-up call for Lodge. The United States was obviously not prepared to face this type of enemy.

While still officially training, Lodge was nearly taken prisoner during a visit to a command post west of El Adem. The post was guarded by a half dozen American light tanks. When three German mediums approached, the Americans and British jumped into their vehicles and drove "hell for leather" back to Cairo. The Germans could easily have taken them but chose not to pursue.

On another late afternoon, the Germans engaged at four thousand yards, and fire was exchanged until dark. The Americans moved to higher ground and resumed the battle at three o'clock the next morning. The fighting continued throughout the next day, with the two sides coming as close as seven hundred yards. Two British tanks were destroyed, resulting in a British order to retreat after the Nazis unveiled 88 mm guns.[35] As Lodge fled, he could see the tracer bullets set fire to the mess truck, killing the mess sergeant. Although shell fragments and armor-piercing projectiles struck Lodge's vehicle, he survived. "I understand this was the first time American land soldiers had fought against the Nazis," he said. The Americans held out better than expected. "We were on the receiving end of practically everything they had to throw at us. We took it, but we gave back, too. When the smoke had cleared away, we had knocked out at least eight German tanks."[36] In the press coverage of the Battle of Tobruk, there was no mention of Lodge. British censors had a "stop" on any mention of his name.[37] Within weeks, the British would start new offensives that would stop Rommel's advances in Egypt and culminate in the Second Battle of El Alamein in October 1942.[38]

Lodge's training, which had seemed more like actual combat, came to a close. The tank units were ordered out of action and returned to Fort Knox, where Lodge and his colleagues could share their battle experiences. Upon filing his final report, Crittenberger wrote Lodge, "General [Jacob] Devers, on the phone, was so enthusiastic about your report to him, [and] said you are one of the outstanding observers so far developed in this war."[39] Lodge was interviewed about his combat experience by the Associated Press. "I must lead a charmed life," he said. "Men were killed within a half-dozen yards of me. Once I was nearly taken prisoner . . . Believe me an experience like that makes you think—and it isn't about politics either."[40]

On July 26, Eisenhower wrote, "General Marshall told me that you had gained most valuable experience in North Africa, and had made some very pertinent observations concerning your own and the British troops."[41] While Lodge had faced more combat that most members of Congress, he was careful to downplay any talk than he was a war hero. "I was under fire, but not in a tank. I was never in a tank in a fight. I was bombed and machine-gunned from the air," he clarified. The experience changed Lodge's mind about the need for international cooperation, a shift that would dramatically affect his political views—and later his support of the United Nations and the North Atlantic Treaty Organization. "Serving with soldiers of many nationalities convinces you that we Americans can't repeat the mistakes we made after the last war. We must assume our responsibility in maintaining the peace of the world. As I see it, we shall have to do it by cooperating with like-minded powers, but our cooperation will be meaningless without the strength to back it up," he said, adding, "Although there will be great pressure within our own country to do it, we must never again disarm by ourselves alone in the vain hope that other nations will follow our example."[42]

Back in Washington, enough members of Congress were out contributing to the war effort that the government had ground to a halt. FDR issued an executive order that contained an ultimatum—serve in government or serve in the military. It stated, "All members of the House and Senate who are now serving in an active status will be placed on inactive duty July 1, 1942, or immediately on returning to the U.S., except those who wish to remain on active duty for the duration of the war."[43] The order made it impossible for members of Congress to retain their seats and go on active military service. Lodge received a personal letter from Secretary of War Henry Stimson: "I cannot but feel, there, that you will render more service to the American people by performing the important duties of a United States Senator rather than to devote your energies solely to the purely military phase of the war as a junior officer."[44] Lodge received similar letters from Marshall, Patton, and Crittenberger.

Back in Washington, Lodge looked to his reelection in the fall. Despite Lodge's emphasis on military preparedness, Casey branded him an isolationist—something he never really shook off.[45] Casey had the support of many Brahmins and ran a "support FDR 100 percent" campaign, so much so that Lodge branded him a rubber stamp. They traded barbs throughout the fall. Lodge was called "foxy, unreliable, and ambitious," while he made political hay out of Casey's vote to increase the pay and pensions of members of Congress—always an unpopular position. After Casey belittled Lodge's military service as "Cook's tour of the Libyan desert," Lodge released the letter he had received from Stimson praising his deployment.[46] That did not settle the matter. Congressman John McCormack attacked Stimson for his "pernicious political activity," while Casey and members of the press, including Drew Pearson, questioned the legitimacy of Lodge's military mission.[47]

Lodge struck back, calling such questioning "a slur directed at [him], insofar as that expedition is concerned, [that] also slurs the brave men who carried their country's flag across shell-torn desert sands and into the smoking mouths of enemy guns." "And I resent that, too," he said.[48] "I can assure it wasn't a Cook's tour. I did what was expected of me, obeying orders, as did every man in the outfit."[49] Lodge gave a briefing at Fort Knox on July 10 for two thousand noncommissioned officers that provided a play-by-play account of his mission.[50] According to the *New York Times* reporting of the briefing, Lodge received a standing ovation. Not only was he well known for his military service, but on Capitol Hill he fought for a 15 percent increase in the twenty-eight-dollar monthly allotment to soldiers' wives and forty dollars to their families.

The November 1942 contest was close, but the unbeaten Lodge won again, 721,239 to 641,042. He even carried Lowell, the first Republican to do so. "The Irish saved him, just like they did his old man," was a popular sentiment. Lodge was grateful for the work he had done to cultivate the Irish vote. He returned to Washington no longer a first-term senator but rather a more mature politician, a more constructive critic, and less of a gadfly prone to harassing the opposition through the deft manipulation of Senate rules. Due to his military experience, he spoke out for GIs, against bureaucratic waste, and for the creation of a unified command structure.[51] Lodge did not vote with the farm bloc to raise food prices. He joined with the Roosevelt administration to reinstate the domestic branch of the Office of War Information, an important forerunner to postwar intelligence reorganization. Lodge voted to override the Smith-Connally anti-strike bill and against the National Resources Planning Board and the Rummel plan.[52]

Despite his return to Washington, Lodge gained additional international experience. He wrote Eisenhower what was arguably their first political communication, on January 7, 1943. "I do not presume to comment on your military success which is self-evident," Lodge wrote. "I did, however, want to give you my opinion, for what it is worth, that you have the confidence of the average American in a substantial degree. Your handling of the political factors involved, appeal to the real people of this country as realistic, energetic, and smart . . . I thought you might be interested to get this opinion from one who has recently come through an election campaign and is, therefore, in close touch with public sentiment."[53]

Lodge's background earned him a place on an around-the-world congressional delegation with fellow senators James Mead (D-NY), Richard Russell (D-GA), and Owen Brewster (R-ME) in June 1943. It was another opportunity to see the war up close, which Lodge craved. At the request of General Marshall, the group inspected American activity in the African and Southwest Pacific areas. This was no easy junket. Five senators departed Washington on July 25 on their own four-engine converted B-24 Liberator and traveled forty-one thousand miles over the next nine weeks to London, Casablanca, Marrakech, Sicily, Cairo, Basra, Calcutta, Chungking (where they attended a meeting with Chiang Kai-shek), Australia, Guadalcanal, Fiji, and Honolulu.[54] They came under fire from a Japanese air attack while visiting the Solomon Islands.

At each stop, Lodge put his training as a reporter to work. His priority was to learn the experience of the men at the front—what they had, what they needed, and how they were treated. He kept careful notes of his conversations, just as though he were on the campaign trail, typed them up in the evening on his portable, and submitted them to Marshall's office. "Luckily for me, I was a working newspaperman for many years, which has given me some training in asking questions, and my military service has given me a wide personal, first-name acquaintance with members of the army."[55] The trip gave Lodge the chance to consult with figures such as King George VI, Winston Churchill, Anthony Eden, Lord Mountbatten, Sir Dudley Pound (First Lord of the Admiralty), and Sir Alan Brooke (British chief of staff), as well as old friends such as General Jacob Devers.

Lodge found his visit with Churchill particularly memorable.[56] "We went through his conference room with its long tables and bookcases done in white and gold," he recalled. "In the ante-room are hooks for the hats of the ministers, with the name of each minister over each hook. He took us into the garden and talked very frankly. He wants to bear down hard on Germany. He is not at all disturbed about Russia getting too strong. He looks forward to the day when British and American fleets will use the same bases, that the joint chiefs of staff will keep on working together for 10 years, and there will be joint British and American citizenship." At a private dinner hosted by Churchill's

Minister of Information Brendan Bracken, Bracken conveyed a political message to Lodge that Churchill thought he could work just as well with conservatives as with liberals—in case the Republicans were to win the White House in 1944.[57] Lodge had been shortlisted as a possible running mate on a ticket with General Douglas MacArthur, until the latter decided his higher calling was liberating the Philippines.

On behalf of the Senate Foreign Relations Committee, Lodge flew to Algiers to meet with Eisenhower. The latter's temporary headquarters was at the Hotel Saint George, overlooking the Mediterranean. It was there, in his role as commander in chief of the Allied Expeditionary Forces in North Africa, that Eisenhower planned the D-Day invasion, from November 1942 to December 1943. Lodge hoped to obtain permission to see the front in Sicily. However, Eisenhower was too busy to see him, and his chief of staff, Major General Walter Bedell Smith, told Lodge it was too dangerous.[58]

After Lodge met with Generals Carl "Tooey" Spaatz and Lauris Norstad, Smith called to say Field Marshal Bernard Montgomery would permit Lodge's visit to Sicily the next morning—in a B-25 with two fighters as escorts. At Palermo, Lodge visited with Patton and his staff, including Colonel Paul Harkins, a childhood friend. Patton took Lodge in his car to the front, including to towns that were so full of rubble and wrecked German vehicles that there was only room for a single vehicle to maneuver. "You fellows have worked hard enough," Patton bellowed at an American lieutenant. "Get these local bastards to dig this out."[59]

Upon his return to the United States, Lodge spoke on the Senate floor about the trip—and the public's need for more information. "I cannot describe the impression made upon me by the infantry company," he reflected. "They had no sleep for two days and were eating their first food in 12 hours." During his Senate speech on June 18, 1943, he said, "It has become plain as day, and it is common sense, to recognize that our British and Russian allies are not only dedicated to the broad purpose of crushing Nazism and Fascism, but that they have a number of very definite and very practical national aims which have been frankly revealed to the world. One of them—Britain—frankly intends to maintain the Empire, and the other—Russia—has clear intentions regarding Eastern Europe."[60]

Massive military bases were being constructed around the world at a cost as high as $500 million with, in Lodge's view, little oversight. "Most of these have not been constructed in territory belonging to the United States, and military secrecy forbids my stating just where they are," he said. Such vast growth was indicative of what American leaders thought would be necessary to defeat Japan. MacArthur warned that it would take a million American casualties to defeat Japan unless the United States got access to bases in Siberia. Lodge's concern was not only how the United States was fighting the war but also what this investment in military power meant for postwar American intentions.[61] Preparation was being sacrificed in the name of the waste he saw all around him. While the military faced manpower shortages and newspapers were being told to cut back on newsprint, Lodge saw needless high-profile wartime desk jobs being created around Washington.[62]

As he provided a report of his recent tour, the Senate floor buzzed and the public and press galleries were filled to capacity. He criticized the Roosevelt administration but also defended it. He praised allies but also spoke of their shortcomings. At some points, Lodge sounded like an internationalist, while at others he cautioned against such a stance. There were a few consistent themes: the need for more energy resources and better communications, the increasing importance of air power, and finally, the need for the individual service branches to integrate more closely. As Lodge put it, these were "lessons learned in the white heat of actual combat experience." His inspection tour especially convinced him of the last point. "The fact which is most striking is the close integration of forces in land, sea, and air. None can exist without the other."[63]

Lodge criticized what he felt was a dearth of information among GIs on the front lines. "Our fighting men are mad because of the false optimism of our news . . . When suffering intensely they will hear a bland radio announcement saying, 'The enemy is routed. Our losses are negligible. There is little if any enemy resistance,'" he argued. Lodge saved special criticism for the Russians. He believed many American lives could be saved if the United States had access to the Pacific coast of Russia. "For reasons of security I shall not say how many American lives would be spared if we receive this aid."[64] These issues gradually shifted Lodge's voting record. He became a greater advocate for the military and the role it could have in the postwar period. Lodge and his mentor, Senator Arthur Vandenberg, whom he called Van, were among the thirty-two who were "undecided" on the need for a postwar international force to preserve peace. That was a decisive shift for each of them from their stances during World War I. Senators such as Robert Taft remained among those opposed to the creation of such a force.[65]

Lodge's Senate presentation was widely praised by the press. Arthur Krock of the *New York Times* called it "especially constructive and clear. He spoke as a good reporter writes, in the light of high journalistic standards, having had his pre-Senatorial training in that field." While Lodge delved back into his Senate work, he could not help feeling as though he belonged in the army. He said as much to Crittenberger during a late-night conversation at Lodge's home in Georgetown.[66] Crittenberger said he would like to have Lodge with him as his personal assistant on his next assignment, and they agreed to see if they could work out the details without mentioning it to anyone.[67]

The major obstacle was FDR's 1942 edict curtailing members of Congress from active duty. Lodge was willing to resign, but he had to do so carefully. If he did and was assigned to some remote outpost, he might not even see combat and, to add insult to injury, it could end his political career when he returned home.

"As the first year of my second six year term drew to a close, I reached the definite conclusion that it was my duty to resign from the Senate and serve in combat in the Army overseas," Lodge wrote in his diary. "My age, my military training and my previous military service in Libya in 1942 all impelled me to this view as did the fact that the United States was only just then entering the period of large-scale ground fighting."[68] Lodge's friends and colleagues were helpful—including Colonel Bobby Cutler in Secretary of War Stimson's office, Stimson himself, and General Patton. Their advice was to make all of the preparations necessary and then inform FDR of the decision. "If you have his approval nobody can send you anywhere else, and I am sure he would gladly give it to you," Marshall said.[69]

That was how Lodge became the first senator since the Civil War to resign his seat to go to war on February 3, 1944, when he received his orders reassigning him to the European Theater of Operations, London.[70] When Lodge went to the White House to notify FDR of his decision, he had already received his inoculations at Walter Reed Hospital and was ready to leave. If FDR did not give his assent, he would do so knowing that everyone else involved in the decision had already agreed and made preparations.[71]

Lodge sent a letter to be read to the Senate at 11:00 a.m. on Friday morning, after he had departed, "confident that [his] political career was finished," he recalled.[72] "The fact that the United States is entering the period of large-scale ground fighting has, after grave thought, brought me to the definite conclusion that given my age and military training, I must henceforth serve my country as a combat soldier in the Army overseas," his letter read. "In order to serve in combat I hereby resign from the United States Senate."[73] The announcement stunned his colleagues on both sides of the aisle, who took to the Senate floor as news spread and paid him tributes as though they would never see him again.

Lodge's Democratic colleague from the Bay State, Senator David Walsh, said, "Mr. President, the announcement of the resignation of my colleague as a member of the United States Senate comes to me—and, I feel certain, to the other members of the Senate—with mingled sentiments of regret and admiration for the high patriotic motives that prompted his decision."[74] Michigan's Arthur Vandenberg, Lodge's mentor, friend, and ally, rose and echoed the remarks. "Mr. President, this contemplation moves me very deeply because I think it is the disclosure of a great and patriotic soul at its best," he said. "I think it is a challenge to America. It seems to me this resignation is simply the final and conclusive demonstration of a superb character and an incorrigible courage." Vandenberg's diary reveals even more. "In all my twenty years in the Senate no single episode ever thrilled me so deeply as the quiet drama which saw young Lodge in his usual Senate seat on a late afternoon in February and the next morning heard his resignation read at the desk after his overnight departure to the fighting front," he wrote. "No one, including myself, had any idea Cabot planned to quit the Senate and go to War. It was typical of him. He made no valedictory speech to his colleagues and there was no band to escort him to the station. He just quit the Senate and went."[75]

FDR was no less effusive in his praise, writing Lodge after their meeting on February 1, "I want you to know I am awfully glad that you came to see me this morning. And I am writing you this note to tell you that I would do just what you are doing if I could. I missed being with the guns in 1917–18. It's too late now. I envy you, the opportunity that is yours, and I congratulate you on the decision you have made." The balance of Lodge's Senate term was carried out by former Lodge rival Sinclair Weeks, who was appointed by Governor Leverett Saltonstall.

Lodge was commissioned a major with the American Sixth Army Group and assigned to active duty on the European front. He reached the preinvasion planning headquarters in London's Grosvenor Square at the same time as the news of his resignation began to spread, and he received orders to report to Algiers.[76] He joined Crittenberger's IV Corps just south of Anzoo, and every day they flew over the front in a small reconnaissance plane. Lodge was a good choice for the assignment. He spoke fluent French, had a track record of dealing with difficult problems in the Senate, and had twenty years of service in the army reserve. In late February 1944, they flew to Lake Averno, ten miles north of Naples, to set up the new IV Corps headquarters. While many in the command staff had not yet seen action, Lodge had. "We all looked up to him as a veteran, he had already had his baptism of fire," Lieutenant Colonel Edward A. Stephenson said. Lodge's job as deputy chief of staff IV Corps was to be a troubleshooter.[77] He would go to the front, see what was working well and what was not, and make arrangements to improve it on the spot. Lodge would usually travel in a single-engine aircraft or Jeep, and he regularly had to watch for antiaircraft gunfire and minefields.[78] Crittenberger, in a pep talk to his officers on April 11, 1944, said, "I challenge each and every one of you to get tough. Toughen up mentally, morally, and physically for the stupendous job at hand. That is the surest way to kill Germans. And killing Germans is the only way this war can be won."[79]

Before he could see combat, Lodge suffered an onset of serious stomach problems. At first, he thought it was dysentery or the recurrence of an ulcer from two decades earlier. It was sufficiently severe that he was ordered to Walter Reed Hospital in Washington on April 24.[80] "It is with deep regret that I have just put Cabot Lodge on an outgoing plane for the homeland where an immediate operation for removal of a stomach ulcer appears necessary," Crittenberger wrote to General Wilton B. "Jerry" Persons. "I need not tell you what a strong right arm he has been to me in the past; this you know."[81] Bobby Cutler, Lodge's old friend from his Harvard days, thought he was dying, so he sent for a top specialist from Boston. Lodge's medical history was spotless aside from an appendectomy in 1927, a tonsillectomy in 1916, and the earlier ulcer. His situation was serious enough that he could have requested discharge, and he later stated that his "darkest" day was when he thought his doctors might decide to recommend that he be involuntarily discharged from the army.[82] After his first week in the hospital, he was down to 165 pounds from his normal wartime weight of 190–195 pounds, and he had to be fed intravenously.

"By the time this letter reaches you I hope your operation will have been completed and that your first hurdle on the course back to join us thus will have been successfully negotiated," Crittenberger wrote Lodge on May 2, boosting his spirits with the suggestion he would return to action soon.[83] After intravenous feeding was no longer necessary and his diet was changed, Lodge perked up and insisted on being returned to Italy. His weight was back up to 192 pounds. "I honestly believe that I am in better shape than at any time since I left college," he wrote Persons.[84] "All I ask is a chance to go back to the front (where I am wanted and where I can be useful) and share the dangers of my fellow soldiers," he wrote Cutler.[85]

Lodge was released from Walter Reed on June 28, 1944.[86] He returned to Beverly for a brief leave, took part in the July 4 parade, and was ordered to return to Crittenberger's IV Corps.[87] He was back on July 6, serving as deputy chief of staff to Crittenberger. He caught up on what he had missed in the intervening ten weeks, then flew to inspect a unit that was bogged down by a German Panzer division. He recommended that the commanding officer be relieved, and Crittenberger did as Lodge suggested. "He was always with me when I was in my battle station," Crittenberger recalled. "Most of the time he was operating at the Chief of Staff level. He was frequently under fire, was strafed and bombed by planes, and often had to travel through mines." On July 29, 1944, General Jacob L. Devers informed Crittenberger that he wanted to take a small detachment to establish an advanced headquarters. "This will require me to have a good, reliable officer who speaks French fluently, and I would like to steal Lodge from you for this purpose," he wrote.[88] Lodge's orders were so modified on August 3.[89] He picked up a Bronze Star on August 7 as a result of the IV Corps's pursuit of the enemy from north of Rome to the Arno River. "Major Lodge displayed unusual qualities of leadership and by his poise, calmness, and personality under difficult conditions obtained the maximum in high morale, loyalty, and efficiency among the officers and men working under him," the citation said.[90] Lodge landed on the beaches just north of Toulon with French General Joseph Magnan's Ninth French Colonial Infantry during the D-day of the U.S Army's Third Armored Division on August 15. The Free French forces, the military of the French government in exile led by General Charles de Gaulle, were under the command of General Jean de Lattre de Tassigny.[91]

Under Devers, Lodge was assigned to the Senior Liaison Office.[92] He described his duties as "to liaison with the French Army and Corps commanders; to liaison with the Commanding General and Chief of Staff, 6th Army Group with the French high command; to serve as an interpreter for the Commanding General and Chief of Staff, 6th Army Group; prepare summaries of proceedings or matters when acting as interpreter; translate correspondence to the Commanding General and Chief of Staff from the French command; work directly for Commanding General and the Chief of Staff, 6th Army Group."[93] He handled interallied communications and also visiting dignitaries, including Eisenhower, Churchill, and de Gaulle.[94]

Lodge was a good fit for the job—and with Devers, a former superintendent of West Point who was close to Omar Bradley, Eisenhower, and Patton.

"Devers was deeply interested in other people's motivations . . . He believed in management by walking around; talking with and listening to the troops that served in his command."[95] Lodge had Devers's full confidence in dealing with de Lattre and the French. Devers did not speak or understand French well, and Lodge knew how to finesse delicate problems. He knew Devers would not harass his subordinates; he empowered them so each man felt he was "in business for himself."[96]

On August 21, Lodge accompanied Devers on their first meeting with de Lattre at the latter's new headquarters at an insane asylum in Pierrefeu.[97] The location was a few miles from Edith Wharton's house, where Lodge spent time as a child. "He made an immediate impression upon de Lattre," wrote his biographer, British General Guy Salisbury-Jones, "who summed him up not only as a man of exceptional intelligence but of great uprightness of character. Cabot Lodge understood de Lattre better than most of his American compatriots, and was to render a great service, not only to de Lattre, but to the greater cause of Allied cooperation."[98] Lodge would later refer to de Lattre as one of the great influences in his life. "While he was a man whose superficial appearances had great variety, there was a core of steel inside his soul. He knew what he wanted, when he wanted it and how he wanted it done," Lodge wrote.[99]

Lodge shuttled back and forth, serving as a liaison between Devers and de Lattre. On August 23, 1944, they took Toulon in the face of fierce German resistance.[100] Lodge wrote to update Devers the next day: "At noon today, 24 August 1944, the French Ninth Division held the eastern edges of Toulon, the arsenal de Terre, and the arsenal Maritime. The Mourillon section is still held by the enemy."[101] Lodge was also at the seizure of Marseille, the advance up the Rhône valley, the formation of a French sector on the right of the Allied line, the forcing of the Belfort Gap, and the advance across Alsace and the Colmar pocket.[102] Lodge was the link between the Sixth Army Group and the French First Army, in which he sometimes received the full force of de Lattre's blasts. Lodge socialized with de Lattre and the French, hearing stories of the general's rise from a junior officer in World War I, his capture by the Germans following the fall of Paris, his escape from prison, and then his recovery to lead the French First Army. After being promoted to lieutenant colonel on August 28, Lodge worked even more closely with the French army. Devers considered Lodge his secret weapon. "I am using all my personality and psychology on the French," Devers said. "They are a great people but one must understand them and their problems. Lodge is most helpful for he speaks and writes fluent French and is smart and wise."[103]

Lodge was trusted enough to stand in for generals when there was no time for more conventional methods. On one occasion, Lodge urged de Lattre to go up to the Rhône, where German units were fleeing across the river trying to get out of southern France and Spain. American troops were pouring up the east bank as de Lattre's forces went up the west bank. When they met north of Lyon, there was a major traffic jam. Devers and Lodge flew ahead, and Lodge translated Devers's orders into French. Armies usually moved based on written orders, but there was no time for formality. Without formally clearing every detail with the American chain of command, Lodge directed de Lattre's forces to move between advancing American units. "Whose orders were those we were following?" de Lattre asked Devers later. "They were mine," said Devers, displaying absolute confidence in Lodge at a critical moment, "but they were oral. I couldn't have handled it as well if I had been able to speak French. I had the benefit of another man's mind which was well-equipped to do the job."[104]

The advancing momentum northward required precise and frequent communication between American and French forces. De Lattre complained to Lodge that he would prefer his headquarters to be in Besancon, a site important in French history due to its bombardment by the Germans during the Franco-Prussian War. De Lattre wanted to build up the image of the French army for the French people, who had been through so much during German occupation. Lodge, knowing French history, understood the symbolism.[105] He intervened with Devers, and de Lattre was permitted to move his headquarters from Aix-en-Provence. Not long after, Lodge was summoned by de Lattre for another heated discussion about how the French forces were in such a woeful state that they did not even have warm clothes. "Some of his FFI's [French Forces of the Interior] have already been shot as spies by the Germans because they were in civilian clothes," Lodge wrote in his notes.[106] He intervened once again with Devers to keep the peace between the French and the Americans, managing to acquire fifty thousand clothing sets.

As winter came, so did plans to envelop Strasbourg and reach the Rhine. Devers drew up plans for an offensive scheduled for November 13, 1944. "We were well-prepared for this," he recalled, "but I could never get de Lattre to say he would jump off. All of a sudden, four days before jump-off time, I received word that Churchill and de Gaulle were going to visit de Lattre and would be there the very day of the jump-off. I was certain their visit would slow things up. I couldn't speak French, moreover I had to be with the Seventh in the North. I told Lodge to go down and tell de Lattre to treat him as if I were right by his side, giving the orders—and for Lodge to give them."[107]

It was late in the war. Churchill planned to inspect the First French Army close to the French-Swiss border, a staging area before continuing the slog toward Germany. The prime minister arrived at Besancon Station in the midst of a blizzard. "A truly Scandinavian landscape," Lodge described it. "Snow had been falling ceaselessly for hours and reduced visibility to a few yards." Accompanied by his daughter, Mary, Churchill said to de Lattre, "You're not going on with your attack in this weather, are you?" De Lattre, always mindful of maintaining the secrecy of troop movements, responded ambiguously, "There is no question of it, Mr. Prime Minister." Churchill then spoke of his plans, including taking the night train to Paris and seeing Eisenhower in the morning. Lodge recalled, "I was standing nearby in the snowstorm with General Devers' mission in my mind, which was to get the battle started," despite what de Lattre said. Churchill remembered meeting Lodge in Washington. "I have since noted your decision to resign from the Senate for military service. This is a patriotic and unselfish act which you will never regret," he said.[108]

As Devers recalled later, "[Lodge] managed somehow to get both Churchill and de Gaulle out of there and on the train by midnight before the jump-off day. And he got de Lattre to agree to jump off at Noon the following day, right through the snowstorm. Lodge called me with the pre-arranged code word that signified the jump-off, and when. They killed the German corps commander and captured his aide with all his paper. This clearly showed that nobody was expecting an attack in that weather. De Lattre's forces took Belfort and went right on to Mulhouse and hit the Swiss border. As far as I'm concerned, Lodge was more than my liaison that day. He was acting in my place." The Third Armored Division cleared a path for General Jacques Le Clerc's French Second Armored Division to liberate Strasbourg just as it had liberated Paris.[109]

Due to the high water and fierce fighting, the French army was unable to take Colmar, which had been heavily reinforced by the Germans. Some of the heaviest fighting of the war followed. Devers commanded more French troops than any non-Frenchman in history, including the First French Army, the Army Detachment of the Atlantic, and the Army Detachment of the Alps.[110] Lodge recommended that, in order to advance more quickly, de Lattre be given control of American forces sent in to reinforce the French. While all of the senior American officers were opposed on the basis that Devers could never explain the decision to the War Department in Washington, Lodge argued that foreign command of American forces was acceptable in that instance on account of the fact that de Lattre was universally recognized as competent—and because command of the American forces would give him a strong incentive to push his own troops as hard as possible.[111] Devers sided with Lodge. Approximately 150,000 American troops, the entire XXI Corps, were now under the command of de Lattre. It would not be long until it was clear that Devers had made the correct decision.[112] "Since December 2 the enemy has entirely changed his attitude," Lodge reported.[113]

Lodge liked to be at the front, to get close to where the firing was. General Edward R. Brooks, commander of the VI Corps, said, "I remember having to tell Lodge to get down. We were under German observation and he's such a tall fellow I was afraid he would draw fire. I asked him, 'What are you trying to do, get killed or just wounded?' He laughed and said, 'I don't suppose it makes any difference.'" On another occasion, Devers wondered how Lodge managed to stay alive. "Lodge has tremendous ability, excellent judgment[,] a very high standard of integrity. He risked his life innumerable times, I don't know why he didn't get killed. He was always at the front. He rode thousands of miles through those mountains of the Vosges, ice everywhere, slipping and sliding, I can't say enough about his courage."[114]

When General Eisenhower came to inspect the Sixth Army Group's front in November 1944, Lodge was assigned to accompany him on his two-day tour.[115] Lodge briefed him on the First French Army, showed him maps of the area, explained the working relationship between Devers and de Lattre, and acted as translator. It was the last time Lodge saw Eisenhower during the war. Not long after, the German dominoes began to fall. Lodge was part of not only the liberation of southern France but also that of Germany. First, Stuttgart fell. Then the Third Armored Division plowed all the way to Salzburg, and the 101st Airborne took Hitler's Berchtesgaden. The entire German Army Group G, more than two hundred thousand men, surrendered on May 5 in Haar, southeast of Munich. "It was my privilege to be present at the historic occasion when all the German armies facing the allied troops on the southern end of the western European front gave their unconditional surrender," Lodge wrote in his journal.[116]

Since Lodge spoke German, he was on hand with Devers to accept the surrender at Haar. When German General Hermann Foertsch, commander of the First German Army, tried to insert some conditions in the surrender document, Lodge quietly changed it from "conditions" to "specifications"—*Bedingungen*.[117] That allowed the Americans to maintain a commitment to secure an unconditional surrender while helping the Germans to save face. Devers was insistent that there be no misunderstanding, that this was unconditional surrender. "Do you understand that?" Devers asked. "General Foertsch flushed a little, looked down for a moment and said: 'I understand it. I have no choice. I have no power to do otherwise,'" Lodge recorded as he observed the exchange.[118] He was also present at the liberation of the Dachau concentration camp. The horrors he witnessed, captured in the "restricted" photographs he kept in order to never forget, affected his views of Germans for the remainder of his life.

Meanwhile, Lodge's brother, John, serving in the navy, continued to cross paths with officers who had seen or heard something about his brother. "Everywhere I go there is very much interest in you and your plans about which, of course, I know nothing," John wrote.[119] Lodge stayed with the occupying forces for a few weeks after the war ended, where he received the Legion of Merit. De Lattre, who had awarded him the Croix de Guerre with palm after the capture of Belfort, presented him with a scroll, signed by General de Gaulle, awarding him the National Order of the Legion of Honor. On June 15, de Lattre paid his respects to the American forces in a festival held at Lake Constance, Germany, with Eisenhower attending. Late in the evening, de Lattre rose to pay tribute to Devers, with Lodge serving as translator.[120] After describing the searing experience of the war that brought them together, they had more than a friendship.[121]

Word got around about Lodge's wartime success. General Bradley asked Devers whether Lodge was available for duty in the Office of Strategic Services in the China theater, because of his knowledge of French.[122] However, Devers recommended that Lodge be permitted to take leave before reassignment. In the final days of the European Theater, Crittenberger sent for Lodge a final time. "If you have no other plans, why not return to IV Corps to terminate together our service in the European Theater?" he wrote on July 2, 1945.[123] Lodge had orders to return to Washington, but he and Crittenberger were back in Europe together on new orders only a month later, when they were reassigned to the Mediterranean Theater on August 20.[124]

At the end of the war, Lodge was owed one month and twenty-four days of leave following his twenty-one months and three days of active duty overseas. He returned to Beverly before being honorably discharged from active duty on December 2, 1945.[125] It was a good Christmas for the family. Lodge was home; his youngest son, Henry, was home from Groton; and his eldest son, George, was safe on naval duty.[126]

However, politics was never far from Lodge's mind. He was disenchanted by both political parties. "Party labels mean little now. The Democrats have grown away from Jefferson, and the Republicans have grown away from Lincoln," he said. Lodge returned from war a different man and an unemployed civilian. He was decorated after capturing a German four-man patrol. His American decorations included a Legion of Merit; a Bronze Star; six European–African–Middle Eastern service stars for Egypt-Libya, Rome-Arno, Southern France, Rhineland, Central Europe, and Ardennes-Alsace; and a bronze arrowhead. He came home with more than a service record. While in Europe, he made lifelong friends, and his experiences fundamentally changed the way he viewed conflict and international affairs. "I was 100 percent wrong in believing that we could stay out of the Second World War," he said. "But that was my first incarnation. I'm now an older and wiser man—or at least I hope I am."[127] He was firmly convinced that collective action was essential to peace. An internationalist had been born.

# 5 • Return to the Senate

After he returned from the war, Henry Cabot Lodge Jr. began to speak out more and more against what he believed was a reactionary, isolationist Republican Party. He had challenged Republicans to modernize before World War II—and now the need was greater than ever before. "I do not see our future in terms of a choice between an undynamic preservation of individual rights on the one hand and government by labor racketeers on the other," he wrote his friend Henry "Harry" Luce, the publisher of *Time* magazine. "I certainly think that liberal Republicanism can be equally articulate." In a speech to Republicans in Oregon, he said, "If we are restricted to these alternatives I fear for the Republican Party—for the Democratic Party—and for the U.S."[1]

Lodge was eager to test these ideas in another run for public office; he would not have to wait long. Legendary seventy-three-year-old Democratic Senator David Walsh was up for reelection in 1946, and Lodge announced his candidacy in April. He sensed Walsh was more vulnerable than people realized. According to Robert Bradford, who would be elected governor of Massachusetts that fall, Walsh rode a tide of some kind each time he had been elected. He was first elected as lieutenant governor in 1912 as a result of the Bull Moose split that divided Republicans between Teddy Roosevelt and Robert Taft, putting Woodrow Wilson in the White House.[2]

Despite his advanced age, Walsh was still a fiery, isolationist, anti–New Deal Democrat. That was a difficult platform to have maintained over the nearly thirty years he had served in the Senate. Walsh endorsed James Farley over FDR in the 1940 presidential election, which helped Walsh win some Republican votes. No Republican had dared to challenge the fearsome Democrat during his peak, but in 1946, Lodge believed he had an opportunity.[3] With his military record and international service, he would have been a strong candidate even if he were not an experienced former senator just reaching his midforties.

As soon as Lodge announced his candidacy, rumors began to swirl that he was on the short list for the Republican vice-presidential nomination in 1948. The assumption was that he would easily return to the Senate in 1946 and then begin making a push for national office. "I have heard many reports hereabouts concerning you as a possible vice-presidential Republican nominee," Lodge's brother, John, wrote. "I believe these reports are based on Walter Winchell and Drew Pearson. What's cookin'?"[4] Lodge's friend Mason Sears drew up a list of pros and cons of running for president and presented it to Lodge. "Politically set for life" was one of the key reasons to run.[5] "If Lodge can defeat the most consistently potent vote-getter in the history of Massachusetts then Republican leaders seeking presidential timber for 1948 or later can hardly afford to overlook him," wrote the *Providence Journal*. "Lodge is gambling his immediate political future in challenging the veteran of nearly 50 years in public life. If Lodge wins he gains inestimable prestige as a giant-killing vote puller, and a spot in the national limelight. If he loses he faces at least a temporary political oblivion."[6] Lodge did have national political ambitions at the time, though he would not later in life. He did not deny the rumors, but for now his focus was on 1946.

It would be the campaign without acrimony. Lodge did not once attack his opponent, instead campaigning against the government in Washington. He was particularly critical of the fact that the American standard of living continued to slump following the war. "I did not expect on coming home from Germany to see American women standing in line to buy essentials," he told a Newbury veterans group. "There is no meat available even though there is more cattle on the hoof than ever before." Lodge blamed "a low grade of leadership which is endangering the whole peace for which we fought and for which our government was completely unprepared."[7] Leverett Saltonstall, Lodge's colleague and friend from Massachusetts, was more political: "Bureaucracy has indeed been built up to a fine art. No sugar. No meat. No shoes. No shirts. Is that a Democratic idea of a high standard of living?"[8] The nation's foreign and military policy was in an even greater mess. "By the summer of 1946, we did not have a single division in our army, nor a single group in our air force considered ready for combat," Dean Rusk reflected later. "Joseph Stalin could look out across the West and he saw all the divisions melting away."[9]

What may have hurt Walsh the most in his 1946 bid was his alleged involvement in a sex scandal. His name turned up in the FBI investigation of a brothel, and the *New York Post* reported that he was involved in a sordid sex and spy scandal going back to 1942 at a Brooklyn male brothel apparently infiltrated by Nazis. The investigation into the "swastika swishery," as it was called by the *Daily Mirror,* consistently mentioned the involvement of "Senator X," without disclosing the identity of the unnamed legislator. However, brothel owner and émigré Gustave H. Beckman confirmed that lifetime bachelor Walsh was a regular customer.[10] The combination of sex and swastikas was especially unsavory. Even though the FBI failed to confirm the *Post*'s allegations, the charges lingered and Walsh's relationship with the White House degraded so much that he feared it might support a primary challenger.

Walsh ran unopposed in the Democratic primary, but he did not perform up to his usual standard against Lodge. The two met privately to agree on campaign rules of engagement at the Algonquin Club on Boston's Commonwealth Avenue on April 20, 1946. Lodge wanted Walsh to understand that his decision to run against him was not intended to show any disrespect for the kindnesses that Walsh had shown to his grandfather, who welcomed Walsh to the Senate in 1919. Lodge said he was more interested in running for governor but did not want to face a brutal primary. "Assure you no word of attack either public or private out of me," Lodge scribbled in his record of what he and Walsh discussed. "I thought you'd do this. It's just like the man of honor that you are," Walsh said.[11]

Lodge urged voters to support activist-minded Republicans like himself, and his plea worked. He ended up decisively defeating Walsh by nearly 350,000 votes—982,613 to 653,260, the largest plurality of his legislative career and the biggest majority received in state history. Lodge benefited once again, as he did in 1936, from running against a scandal-ridden, if legendary, opponent. He never mentioned the brothel issue during the campaign, saving Walsh from the embarrassment, but he also did not speak out against the charges.[12] Lodge carried every county and almost half the vote even in big union cities like Lynn, Springfield, and Worcester. Walsh recognized the lopsided result. "In such an overturn, no man may justly harbor a feeling that his own record has been repudiated," he said. Lodge saw the termination of Walsh's long political career as the end of an era. "I recognize and pay tribute to the faithful service which has been rendered by Senator Walsh. The people of Massachusetts will long remember all that he did for our state and nation and the spirit of tolerance and justice in which he acted."[13]

Lodge even won Boston, a Republican's dream. His victory was every bit as impressive as his 1936 victory against James Michael Curley had been. It was sweet for another reason, too. It was the first he shared with his brother, John Davis Lodge, who won his first election to Congress from Connecticut. John entered the House of Representatives in a freshman class with Richard Nixon of California, beginning an association between the Lodges and the Nixons that would endure for the remainder of their lives.

In the span of a decade, Lodge defeated three leading Irish politicians in Massachusetts, where having the Irish vote was what it took to win. In doing so, he also inadvertently cleared a path in the Democratic Party for a fresh face. The Kennedys, in the midst of celebrating their own 1946 election victory, which sent John F. Kennedy to the U.S. House of Representatives, studied Lodge's technique. "The Lodges are different," a Democratic report read. "His brother, John, a former movie star, the same year racked up an impressive win running for Congress in Connecticut. They are blue bloods with all the advantages of blue bloods. But they are also the most thorough practical politicians I have ever seen operate. They use all the tricks we do—and more."[14]

Lodge's system of index cards documented every move he made during a campaign. He cataloged voters, supporters, and interactions with the public. "Cabot Lodge had reduced political appeal to an exact science," a Washington reporter concluded. Four former court stenographers took down the information that would end up on the cards. A typical card might read something like, "Arthur Green, Fall River—three boys in service, one disabled—punch press operator—sore at local union." After a meeting with Lodge, a letter would follow, citing what they discussed. If Lodge met him again, the card would brief him. Voters were amazed that Lodge could recall a casual conversation from three months before. One reporter commented that Lodge's organizational system was worth one hundred thousand votes.[15]

Lodge also had a strong political network. He had a good staff that included Chandler Bigelow, Francis McCarthy, Cammann Newberry, and Maxwell Rabb. Lodge was an active member of the American Legion, the Veterans of Foreign Wars, and the American Veterans' Committee, and he had a bona fide service record himself. He used his fluent French with French American voters, who were an important constituency in Massachusetts. He even won a medal from the Société du Bon Parler Français of Montreal for his frequent—and correct—use of the language. And Lodge continued to woo the Irish vote. One observer commented, "The average Yankee Republican acts as if he were doing the voters a favor by running for public office. Cabot tries to make the voters feel that they're doing him a favor—and that's what the Irish like." In his three Senate campaigns, he soundly beat Irishmen on their home turf.[16]

If not for his wartime service, Lodge, at age forty-four, would have been the most senior Republican in the Senate—more senior than Robert Taft, who succeeded Charles McNary as Republican leader. At the first meeting of the Republican caucus in the Eightieth Congress, Senator Charles Tobey (R-NH) moved to restore Lodge's Senate seniority, which had been lost during World War II. If the motion had carried, Lodge would have outranked Taft and could have moved into the position of Senate majority leader—just like his grandfather—with all of the attendant power to influence the selection of committee chairs. Or, at a minimum, Lodge would have been chairman of a powerful committee, such as the Committee on Finance or the Committee on Foreign Relations. There was absolute silence following Tobey's motion. Lodge broke the silence by standing and downplaying his military service. "I was only doing my duty, like millions of others. I therefore would be grateful if the Senator would withdraw his resolution," he said.[17]

Lodge did receive a key committee appointment to the Committee on Foreign Relations, which would shape his career. His old mentor Arthur Vandenberg, now chairman of the committee, supported Lodge's views that the Republican Party needed to modernize and liberalize. He was able to stack the ideological deck of the committee in his favor due to the Congressional Reorganization Act of 1946, which liberalized how members of the committee were appointed.[18] Lodge also served as president pro tem, since there was no vice president between the end of World War II and the 1948 presidential election after Harry Truman ascended to the White House following Franklin D. Roosevelt's death.

The new generation of political leaders faced a new set of challenges. The onset of the Cold War ensured that the immediate postwar period was a golden era of bipartisan cooperation when it came to foreign-policy-related legislation. Lodge was at the center of the action. "The Senate at that time was at its best," he said. The United States was taking its first step as a superpower, and the Senate was an integral part. Under Vandenberg's chairmanship, the Senate Foreign Relations Committee played a great role in the recovery of Europe and the creation of the United Nations, the European Economic Community, the North Atlantic Treaty Organization (NATO), and the Marshall Plan.[19] The nation was entering a more complex era that included supersonic flight, guided missiles, and thermonuclear power, and it was characterized by dramatic differences in wealth between wealthy nations and newly independent, emerging ones.

The late 1940s were a period of Republican soul searching. Senator Robert Taft's increased power during the Eightieth Congress was disturbing to the sixteen freshmen Republican senators, who were more internationalist and did not share his conservative values.[20] The first signs of the McCarthy era blossomed following Truman's nomination of David E. Lilienthal as chairman of the Atomic Energy Commission. Republicans had been waiting for the opportunity to fire the opening shots at Lilienthal, the former head of the Tennessee Valley Authority—itself a target of "creeping socialism." Taft criticized Lilienthal as "soft on issues connected with Russia and Communism," and "a real threat to national safety." Lodge was not so quick to condemn. After conducting his own study of Lilienthal's background, he wrote a letter to Truman: "Accusations made against his character and patriotism are without proof and without foundation." Lodge believed Lilienthal's experience running the Tennessee Valley Authority made him more qualified to run the Atomic Energy Commission, not less.[21]

Lodge devoted significant attention to foreign aid. He gave a major speech on the eve of St. Patrick's Day 1947 at Boston's Clover Club on the need for a responsible foreign policy to meet the coming challenges. He argued that due to the devastation of World War II, many of the great nations of Europe had ceased to be great powers "and may not be able to stand up to communist doctrines without outside help. That there will be demands on our generosity is almost a foregone conclusion." He proposed a program of loans and economic aid "in the name of religion and humanitarianism," believing that the American people would support such loans because they, as "the descendants of immigrants who sought to escape the curse of Europe, are a generous people." Lodge cautioned against the isolationism in his own party. "One thing we cannot do is to avoid a decision, for refusing to make a decision in an affair of this kind is itself a decision."[22]

When Truman proposed such aid to Greece and Turkey, Lodge strongly supported it. He argued that the aid could prod Europe not only to organize the rebuilding effort but also to create an economic union. "In the large sense we have defeated the enemy, but we have not won the peace," he said. "We were utterly, completely and abysmally unprepared for the end of the war . . . our leaders did not tell us that it was absolutely essential to the national well-being that the U.S. maintain armed forces after the end of the hostilities." Lodge believed that victory in World War II would not truly be achieved unless an organizational structure was put in place in Europe following the rebuilding effort.[23] On June 22, 1947, Truman appointed a three-man commission to determine what the nation could "safely and wisely undertake, on what basis," and "what reciprocal benefits" Europe would offer in return to guarantee success.

That same month, Secretary of State George Marshall delivered a Harvard address in which he outlined the core tenets of what would become the Marshall Plan, explaining that Europe must help itself by organizing; the United States could not dictate the actions it should take. Lodge gave 335 speeches in support of the plan.[24] He understood the potential benefits to the United States, and the role the aid would play as an important component of what became known as the American containment strategy for communism. "The recovery of Western Europe is a twenty-five year proposition . . . the aid which we extend now and in the next three or four years will in the long future result in our having strong friends abroad," Lodge wrote to Vandenberg.[25] The estimated total cost of $3 billion was shocking to many, especially after the human cost of World War II. But for Lodge, not going through with the plan would be even more costly. "The end of the Marshall Plan now would mean the communization of Europe and the price of $3,000,000,000 is not much to pay when you compare it, for example, with the cost of World War II, which Secretary of the Army [Gordon] Gray has estimated at $1,500,000,000,000," he wrote in his confidential journal.[26]

Lodge argued that there was an even more important reason for the plan's passage. "My broad conclusion is that in Western Europe we are losing the battle for men's minds," he told Vandenberg. "The lies that communists are spreading about us are being repeated so often that, like a drop of water wearing away a stone, they are making a real impression." Vandenberg gave Marshall a copy of Lodge's twelve-page memo written after multiple inspections of American army, navy, and air facilities in Europe during 1946–1947. One example cited was based on a conversation Lodge had with a French doctor: "We realize that medical science is way ahead in America of what it is in France, but then we also know that you have all those colored people over there on whom your doctors constantly experiment."[27] Lodge was appalled by the anti-American propaganda that the Soviets were spreading in Europe. It turns out that the doctor was not totally incorrect. Lodge must not have known about the Tuskegee syphilis experiments, which did not become public until 1972.

At the end of 1947, Congress committed to provide $587 million in aid to Europe. Vandenberg and Lodge insisted on strict accountability of how the money was spent. Lodge proposed that a portion of the funds be used to translate American newspapers for European distribution in order to counteract the experience he had talking to the French doctor.[28] Vandenberg and Lodge had conducted a series of hearings under the auspices of the Senate Foreign Relations Committee in which they called some ninety witnesses, and they had determined from their testimonies that the total cost of a larger aid package to Europe would be approximately $17 billion over four and a half years.[29] The committee vote was thirteen to one for the increased aid. "The Senate of that time was at its best," Lodge wrote.[30] The final Senate vote came at five minutes past midnight on March 14, 1948. Kenneth Wherry (R-NE) found sixteen others to vote against it, while Taft actually voted for it. The final vote was sixty-nine to seventeen. The bill had many contributors, but arguably none contributed as much as Lodge.[31]

With the same zeal, Lodge attacked government waste. "I was amazed then, and still am, with the ineffectiveness of government," he said. "Very often, after legislation has been enacted, funds appropriated, and personnel appointed, nothing much happens. It was a little-known fact in 1948 that there had been no effort to organize the government in the interest of economy and efficiency since the founding of the United States in 1789." He repeatedly took to the Senate floor with his criticism, pointing out that twenty-nine agencies were engaged in lending government funds, thirty-four in buying land, twelve in home and community planning, and ten in forestry. Lodge finally had the leadership ability to do something, since Republicans were the majority party in both the House and the Senate.[32] He looked to the House of Representatives to find a collaborator, settling on Clarence Brown (R-OH). They began work on a bill calling for the creation of a bipartisan commission to make recommendations on reducing government waste. The Lodge-Brown bill passed unanimously in July 1947. Speaker Joe Martin got former President Herbert Hoover to chair the commission, which became known as the Commission on Organization of the Executive Branch of the Government or, simply, the Hoover Commission.[33] The Lodge-Brown Act was one of Lodge's proudest achievements during his time in the Senate. Arthur Krock of the *New York Times* wrote, "A federal project of this magnitude, set on an absolutely nonpartisan basis and conducted by citizens chosen in the same spirit, is rare enough to be called unique." Joseph and Stewart Alsop hailed it as "one of the most important enactments of the present Congress."[34] Hoover Commission

I cut approximately $7 billion from the budget, and 72 percent of its recommendations became law. Hoover Commission II identified about $3 billion more in savings, and 64 percent of its recommendations became enshrined in law.[35] In its various phases, the Hoover Commission made 273 recommendations to the White House.[36] However, Hoover later said that much of the savings were eaten up by the Korean War.[37]

Vandenberg's role on the Foreign Relations Committee had given him national prominence that convinced him to run for the Republican presidential nomination in 1948.[38] Lodge supported him over Governor Thomas Dewey, who was from the same wing of the Republican Party. Lodge chaired the Resolutions and Platform Committee at the 1948 Republican convention, with his friend Bobby Cutler serving as his chief of staff—a "mighty tough assignment and both the party and the country should be grateful to you," Dewey wrote Lodge.[39] The convention, which took place in Philadelphia over June 20–25, was uncommitted, meaning there was no party consensus on a nominee. Typically, the Resolutions and Platform Committee produces a short, well-written platform outlining the primary goals of the individual candidates and the party. However, when a convention is uncommitted, all the party members want to have their ideas and beliefs included. Lodge had to pull it all together.[40] He later referred to it as "the most laborious and back-breaking task which [he had] ever had to perform in time of peace."[41]

Lodge inserted many of his own liberal philosophies—and the ideas behind the Marshall Plan—in the foreign affairs plank.[42] He later said that he "had shrewdly thrown in a few more expansive statements of bipartisan cooperation for the purpose of giving the little coterie of isolationists on his committee something to knock out."[43] "I was prepared to fight to the finish," Vandenberg confided in his diary, "to protect the GOP against reversion to 'isolationism' or against desertion of the peace plans, including 'collective security' and the European Recovery Program . . . It wasn't necessary—thanks to the superb job done by Lodge."[44]

While working on the platform, Lodge hoped to block Dewey's nomination on the first ballot, hang the vote on the nomination, and work behind the scenes to throw the nomination to Vandenberg. "Before Lodge (Bless Him!) went to Philadelphia he asked me for a working paper on a foreign policy plank," Vandenberg wrote. "I gave it to him. He put it all the way through his sub-committee and his full committee and the convention practically intact. I think it is of historical importance to nail down this fact."[45] Vandenberg's loss was devastating to Lodge. Still, Lodge wrote to Dewey, "As you may have heard, my support at the Convention went to my old friend and close associate Senator Vandenberg, but I was truly happy at your victory because I felt that you stood for the good things in public life and because I have liked and admired you ever since our first meeting."[46] Lodge campaigned hard for Dewey, becoming close to him during long hours on the campaign train, the "Victory Special." Republicans hoped for a second rejection of Truman after picking up fifty-four House and twelve Senate seats in the 1946 midterm elections. Even Truman's old Senate seat had been lost to a conservative Republican in the mold of Taft.[47] The Buckeye State senator looked more and more like a viable presidential candidate. The last Republican to win the White House had been Herbert Hoover in 1928, and Lodge thought his party would continue to be locked out for as long as Taft maintained control.

Truman thought it was remarkable that Lodge had gotten Republicans to adopt such a progressive foreign policy agenda. He suspected it gave him a political advantage, believing that many Republicans did not actually support the measures. On July 14, Truman shrewdly called a special session of Congress and asked the Republican leadership to endorse Lodge's foreign policy platform. They debated for three weeks but did not have the votes to approve it. It was a risky move that paid off for Truman, and it might have cost Republicans the White House and control of Congress. The year was a Democratic sweep, including the presidency and both houses of Congress. The Republicans would be the minority party once again.

Many Republicans blamed Dewey for his 1948 loss to Truman. However, some of the blame should be apportioned to Lodge, who knowingly crafted a platform that was close to the Democrats' and that, once it failed to be endorsed in the special session of Congress, only served to enlarge the spotlight on Taft. "The freedom of the people of the United States is in serious danger from the foreign policy of the present administration," Taft wrote. "Our international relations have been conducted with so little foresight since 1941 that six years after vast military victories in Europe and Asia we face a more dangerous threat than any that has menaced us before."[48] Lodge and the moderate Republicans blamed the Old Guard. Their time in the majority had been brief, and Lodge's own state of Massachusetts was quickly turning Democratic. "We've been told we had the heavier and more powerful crew," Lodge recalled. "But they didn't win us any races. I'm sick of that. I want to see the Republicans serve the people, not lecture them. When a man comes into a gasoline station for gas, you don't argue with him. You give him the gas."[49]

"The epic set-back of November may well be a blessing in disguise to Republicans," Lodge said. "It is in defeat that the Republican Party will become a modern party and take its proper place in our political system."[50] Vandenberg saw Lodge as the future. "I fully expect him to be a Republican president of the United States," he said. "And I hope I live long enough to have the chance to put him in the White House."[51] However, the warning signs in the Republican Party had been flashing red long before. Early in the Eightieth Congress, a March 1947 Gallup poll showed that Republicans had slipped six points since the 1946 midterm elections. Lodge, along with fellow Republicans George Aiken (Vermont), Irving Ives (New York), and Wayne Morse (Oregon), lobbied against the extent to which Taft politicized legislation such as the Taft-Hartley Act, rent controls, and foreign and economic aid. Each of these hot-button issues deeply divided conservative and liberal Republicans.[52]

Lodge increasingly focused on what he considered another pernicious threat: the electoral college. A generation of Americans who had never lived under a Republican president had been born and grown to adulthood. Lodge questioned a system that could permit a candidate to win the presidency without either a majority or even a plurality of the popular vote.[53] That result had occurred on three occasions: Jackson-Adams in 1824, Hayes-Tilden in 1876, and Cleveland-Harrison in 1888. "This possibility is due to the fact that the electoral vote in each state is counted as a unit," Lodge testified before the Senate Judiciary Committee. "This means that under our present system the minority votes in every state are thrown away and not counted at all. In the final count, the winner received credit for literally millions of votes actually cast against him."[54] For example, in the 1944 presidential election, Dewey would have won 245 electoral votes against FDR's 286 had the electoral votes been apportioned according to the popular votes in each state. Instead, FDR won 432 to 90, a landslide.

Americans have complained about the electoral college since the founding of the republic. Lodge's effort to replace it was the last serious effort to have achieved any measurable success. His goal was simply to produce the electoral result that was what the voters intended, and he modeled his proposal after one that FDR had endorsed in 1934 and introduced to the House Rules Committee.[55] "Under our present system, as amply demonstrated in history, the electoral votes often do not run parallel to the popular vote," Lodge wrote his friend T. Jefferson "Jeff" Coolidge of the United Fruit Company. "If it could be said that the judgment of the elector was a particularly wise judgment, this failure to conform to the popular vote might be tolerated. But the fact is, as you know, that the verdict of the 'electoral college' does not reflect the opinion of a selected group of especially wise citizens. Although this was the original purpose of the founders in establishing the 'electoral college,' the members of the 'college' in modern times are—and are meant to be—rubber stamps for the popular vote. If they are not accurate rubber stamps there really is no excuse for their existence."[56]

Armed with reams of data, Lodge introduced a constitutional amendment that would replace the electoral college with a direct election of both the president and vice president, a winner-take-all system.[57] Some Republicans believed that a proportional division of electoral votes based on the popular vote in each state, an added provision of the Lodge-Gossett amendment, would help Republicans make headway in the South, since many states were effectively one-party states. Taft disagreed, citing the example that, under the Lodge proposal, William Jennings Bryan would have defeated William McKinley in 1900.[58] "There is no doubt that the Republican Party would be far worse under this amendment than under the present system, other things being equal. This is because the Republicans would receive a smaller proportion of the electoral vote in the southern states than the Democrats would receive in the northern states. We would have been somewhat worse off in every state," Taft said, suggesting that Lodge should no longer be a Republican.[59]

Writing Taft directly, Lodge said, "I not only do not think that this proposal will be harmful to the Republican Party; I believe it gives us our greatest opportunity in years."[60] Basil Brewer, publisher of the *Standard-Times* of New Bedford, Massachusetts, was a leader of the resistance movement against Lodge. While he had previously used the pages of his newspaper to endorse his Bay State senator, he and other Republicans were uneasy about Lodge's internationalist backers. "I urge that Judiciary Committee not yield to high pressure tactics of Senators Lodge, [Estes] Kefauver, [Matthew] Neeley [*sic*] and [John] Sparkman to force approval Lodge-Gossett Bill before country wakes up to real consequences," Brewer telegrammed Taft.[61] Brewer even testified at a judiciary subcommittee meeting on March 9, 1949, where he confronted Lodge.

Over the opposition of Taft Republicans, Lodge steamrolled the bill through the Senate, gaining passage by the required two-thirds majority, sixty-four to twenty-three. It was the first time in history that one of the houses of Congress voted by a two-thirds majority to amend the system for electing a president. On March 1, Lodge met with Truman at the White House "and told him that thanks to his help it had passed the Senate and was further along than at any time in American history." Lodge asked for his help to get the measure through the House, but Truman warned "that the alliance of Right Wing Republicans and Northern Democrats in the Rules Committee was hard for him to understand."[62] Some Republicans, like Homer Ferguson (Michigan), were concerned that the bill might strengthen Democratic control in the South, a power bloc that Lodge hoped to break down since there would be an incentive for Republicans to organize better, even in de facto one-party states, if electoral votes were distributed in proportion to the state's popular vote.[63] When the bill went to the House, it did not receive the required supermajority.[64] Only forty minutes of debate was scheduled in the House, and the measure was defeated 134 to 210, killed by the Republican leadership. Others were also opposed, such as the Congress of Industrial Organizations, which did not like the provision for removing the role of Congress in the case of a tie.[65] Lodge later referred to Brewer's attacks on him in the *Standard-Times* as "a mass of incandescent nonsense" from a man "who is unable to take a licking, and who knows no code but that of underhanded attack on men whom he is unable to intimidate."[66] The defeat did not stop Lodge from trying to fix what he thought was a broken electoral system. In 1949, he introduced legislation for public financing of presidential campaigns, "to the exclusion of all other methods of financing." He hoped the effect would be to reduce the corrupting effect of money on politics. Electoral reform was not a typical Republican issue, but Lodge was not the typical Republican.[67]

During the late 1940s, Lodge became the unofficial spokesperson for liberal Republicans after Vandenberg's failed run for the presidency and his subsequent resignation from office due to illness.[68] In the wake of Dewey's loss, it was a lonely job. Lodge voted for a higher minimum wage and expanded Social Security coverage. He partnered with conservative Senator John Bricker (R-OH) to push for more intervention in desegregating federal housing and aid to education.[69] Lodge's support of these policies further alienated him from Old Guard Republicans. "I don't see why we must choose between state socialism and no social progress at all," he argued. "I don't see why we shouldn't use the power of the government to fill in the chinks that private enterprise can't fill for us."[70]

When the Eighty-First Congress met, Lodge was the unrivaled leader of the progressive Senate Republicans, a caucus of sixteen eager to oust the Taft-Wherry leadership. "Our feeling is that the party under Bob Taft is not going forward," said Senator Ives of New York. It was business, not personal. Lodge found Taft to be an "extremely likeable and honorable man, but whose views seemed to be wrong for the times." He recalled a list of Taft's votes that he simply did not understand, including voting against arming American vessels in the lead-up to Pearl Harbor, the Selective Service Act, lend-lease, reciprocal trade, and NATO. "It would be best for the party, and for Taft, if he would voluntarily step aside," Vandenberg confided to his diary. Lodge was encouraged to challenge Taft for the position of head of the Republican Policy Committee. Still, Taft remained popular, and even supporters of Lodge did not believe in bucking the established seniority system. "But in their view the fight is worth making if only to draw public attention to the fact that a Republican *revolt* is under way after five successive defeats for the presidency and the loss of its Congressional majority gained only two years ago," Arthur Krock reported for the *New York Times*.[71]

Like other senior Republicans, Vandenberg acknowledged Taft's long record of public service, as well as the fact that he had unfairly gotten a bad reputation. That made it difficult for Lodge to unseat Taft for the leadership position. "I deeply regretted that I could not vote for Lodge in this instance. He is one of my most precious friends. He has been of great assistance to me," he reflected. Vandenberg's chief concern, expressed to Lodge privately, was "to change the leadership without disturbance," and Lodge would have caused a disturbance.[72] When it came for the Republican caucus to vote, Lodge was supported by senators from the coastal states but lost twenty-eight to fourteen. Lodge feared that if Taft remained unchecked, there would be further Republican disintegration. Assuming Taft won his reelection in 1950 by a solid margin, he would be in a good position to run for president in 1952.[73]

Lodge hardly had time to dwell on the defeat. While the Marshall Plan anchored the foreign policy achievements of the Eightieth Congress, the ideas behind it were picked right back up in the Eighty-First. The impetus was the twenty-three Soviet vetoes in the UN Security Council, which ground progress to a halt in the UN. American allies needed to collaborate but be free of the menace of the Soviet veto. Vandenberg, Lodge, and Robert Lovett, Secretary of State Marshall's undersecretary, started meeting at Vandenberg's Wardman Park apartment in Washington beginning in the spring of 1948. The fifteen-month Berlin blockade showed the Allies that they needed some means of self-defense distinct from the options available at the UN. From those meetings emerged the ideas behind what was initially known as the Vandenberg Resolution, which endorsed Allied efforts to develop "regional and other collective arrangements for individual and collective self-defense" conducted in a way consistent with the American "constitutional process"—the latter clause being all it might have taken for Woodrow Wilson to have avoided a fight with Lodge's grandfather over Article X of the proposed League of Nations.[74]

The Vandenberg Resolution (Senate Resolution 239) of June 11, 1948, created a legal path for NATO to be created in a way that was consistent with American law and tradition. Truman negotiated the treaty, which then came to the Senate for a vigorous debate. "The purpose is to show that we are in sympathy with the broad trend of strengthening the freedom-loving countries, but it does not commit us to anything," Lodge argued. "They must make the showing. If they make a good showing and if it is advantageous to our national security to help them, we shall help them." As with passage of the Marshall Plan, Vandenberg and Lodge did the heavy lifting. John Davis Lodge—then a member of the House Foreign Affairs Committee—also played a key role in making sure Italy was included. Originally, Vandenberg did not include Italy, because he did not consider it to be an Atlantic nation. France insisted on Italian membership, because Italy would serve as a buffer to Yugoslavia and the communist world. Assistant Secretary Ernest Gross and Major General Alfred Gruenther came to Lodge's office on March 3, 1948, to make a strong case for including Italy.[75] "I told Secretary Gross that I was not sufficiently familiar with the argument for the admission of Italy and that I would like to hear a presentation," Lodge recalled.[76]

John Davis Lodge lobbied his brother that evening for two hours over dinner at the former's Wardman Park apartment, preparing him to then lobby Vandenberg. "I remember this so well because it was one incident in which you and I were able to collaborate most successfully," he wrote to Cabot.[77] Lodge found Vandenberg in the Marble Room in the capitol, next to the Senate chamber. "When Vandenberg said to me that Italy was not on the Atlantic, I asked him whether it was not at least as much on the Atlantic as Alaska was, if not more." Alaska was not a state at that time, yet it was included in the North Atlantic Treaty. "With a smile, Vandenberg said: 'you go along now and leave me alone.'"[78]

The Senate Foreign Relations Committee met the next day, March 4, with Vandenberg in the chair's seat. Before he called the meeting to order, Lodge saw him writing something on a piece of paper. "I also remember well your telling about Senator Vandenberg writing on a piece of paper and rolling it up in a ball and tossing it over to you at a Senate Foreign Relations Committee meeting," John Lodge later recalled to his brother. "He had written, 'Italy will be in.'"[79] Lodge showed the piece of paper to Gross, who was sitting behind the dais, against the wall. Gross immediately called a meeting with a visiting French delegation that had refused to discuss the issue further until Italy was accepted. Upon receiving the news, France reversed its position and signed the treaty, and the idea of NATO came into existence.[80]

The opposing voices in the Senate were the usual ones—Taft, Wherry, William Jenner, Joseph McCarthy, George Malone, and so on. Taft called the treaty "a tremendous mistake" that would provoke war, not prevent it. "It seemed to me that he treated both these subjects as political all the time, that they were subjects which he knew very little about and in which he was unable to differentiate between his advisors," Lodge recalled.[81] "In 1914, the United States Army was not in Europe, . . . in 1939 the United States Army was not in Europe, and . . . if the United States Army had been in Europe on those two occasions, we would not have had World War I or World War II," he said later to John Foster Dulles.[82] After a single day of debate in the Senate, it passed overwhelmingly, sixty-four to six. Less than a month after the vote, Robert Lovett began negotiations with the ambassadors of Canada, Britain, France, and the Benelux nations to create the structure of what became known as the North Atlantic Treaty.[83]

Woodrow Wilson's ghost surfaced during Senate debates over the proposed Article 5, which would require member nations to come to one another's defense. No one knew better than Lodge what a difficult issue that was, but rather than cause a standoff, as had occurred between Wilson and Lodge's grandfather, Lodge carefully rewrote that passage with Vandenberg's oversight. Each member nation would take "such action as it deems necessary, including the use of armed force," which provided a way out that the League of Nations did not. Vandenberg, Lodge, and the new chairman of the Foreign Relations Committee, Thomas Connally (D-TX), called ninety-six witnesses during sixteen days of testimony after Secretary of State Dean Acheson signed the treaty on April 4, 1949. The committee endorsed the treaty with a unanimous thirteen-to-zero vote.[84]

When the treaty went to the full Senate, Taft once again led the opposition. Lodge forcefully argued that it was weakness, not strength, that provokes adversaries. Vandenberg, in decline due to cancer, spoke for nearly two hours in what would be the last major speech of his life. He called the treaty "a fraternity for peace . . . it spells out, beyond any shadow of a doubt, the conclusive warning that 300,000,000 people, united in competent self-defense, will never allow an armed aggressor to divide and conquer them." Former Secretary of

State Cordell Hull called Vandenberg's oration "one of the greatest speeches ever made." It took eleven days of debate, but the result was worth it: final passage by a margin of eighty-two to thirteen.[85] It was "a complete revolution in American foreign policy in the attitude of the American people," Acheson later said.[86]

Soon another menace appeared on the horizon. Throughout 1950, newspapers were filled with stories about a communist scare, and this scare would reach its crescendo in the McCarthy era. Lodge and Senator Theodore F. Green made recommendations to improve American diplomatic facilities around the world on the heels of Senator Joseph McCarthy's charges of rampant disloyalty and security risks.[87] The dozens of suggestions that Lodge and Green made were intended to get ahead of the growing hysteria on Capitol Hill.[88] The University of California fired 157 employees for refusing to sign an anticommunist oath. At its annual convention in Boston, the National Association for the Advancement of Colored People agreed to drive all known communists from its membership rolls. In Washington, a federal judge denied pleas for acquittal from three screenwriters, part of the "Hollywood Ten" who had refused to testify before the House Un-American Activities Committee. A photograph of former army Sergeant David Greenglass in handcuffs was featured on the front page of the New York Times after he was charged with being associated with the Klaus Fuchs spy ring in Los Alamos, New Mexico. Even UN Secretary General Trygve Lie faced accusations that he was a communist.

Lodge became more directly involved after McCarthy made the charge that the State Department was "riddled" with communists. Lodge was a member of the Tydings subcommittee tasked with investigating McCarthy's charges.[89] The Tydings report ultimately concluded that the charges McCarthy had made about employee loyalty within the State Department were unsubstantiated.[90] Lodge believed that McCarthy's ability to make such allegations without evidence "tended to besmirch the reputation of innocent persons, hamper the work of the government investigative agencies, impair the position of the U.S. before the world, reflect unjustly on the many excellent persons in the State Department, and discourage other excellent persons from entering the service of the State Department." Lodge's goal was not to silence McCarthy; it was to discredit him through hearings that would demonstrate that there was no evidence to support his charges. Lodge called for the creation of a special commission. "This business will never end at all clearly or otherwise if the practice of having the majority party investigate the majority continues to hold sway. Nor will satisfactory results be obtained if the minority investigates the majority. The investigation must be non-political," he said.[91] Truman was relieved when he received a note from Lodge stating that he had reviewed eighty-one cases of alleged communism by McCarthy and found no evidence to support the claims.[92]

In the face of such rising xenophobia, it took particular courage for Lodge to introduce a bill to expand the enlistment of foreigners in the American armed forces. Known simply as the Lodge Bill, or the Lodge Act, it was passed on June 30, 1950, and provided for the enlistment of 2,500 aliens in the U.S. Army. In return for five years of military service, American citizenship was offered to enlistees who were to be recruited primarily from strategic areas of Eastern and Central Europe. "The bill permits the Secretary of the Army, with the approval of the Secretary of State, to accept qualified enlistments and re-enlistments in the Regular Army from among qualified aliens between the ages of 18 and 35," Lodge testified before the House Armed Services Committee.[93] Privately, Lodge said, "The best arguments for it cannot be stated publicly."[94] These included the need for the United States to build up a coterie of trained personnel who could add to American intelligence capabilities in Eastern and Central Europe, which had something to do with why the bill passed so easily even as the temperature rose during the McCarthy era. The CIA took an immediate interest in screening those selected and even recruiting some for intelligence-related work.[95] One of the earliest groups of fifty alien soldiers recruited under the bill, forty-two of whom were former refugees from behind the Iron Curtain, were sent to Camp Kilmer, New Jersey, under the command of—surely no coincidence—General Willis Crittenberger. Lodge later said the Lodge Bill was the thing he was most proud of from his entire Senate career.

A provision in the bill that enlisted Germans helped to reduce the pressure by some for Germany to rearm, similar to why Germans occupied 60 percent of the French Foreign Legion.[96] Lodge's initiative was introduced during discussions regarding the Pleven Plan, named for French Premier René Pleven, a proposal for a European army. With President Truman and Secretary of State Acheson supporting German rearmament, a compromise was reached that would create an integrated force under Dwight Eisenhower. The compromise allowed the French government to more fully commit to the organization of NATO and forces of the Supreme Headquarters Allied Powers Europe in December 1950.[97] Lodge served as a critical backchannel between the Truman White House, the Senate, and the French government in the effort to convince the French that the United States did not want Germany to dominate Europe. One lobbying session between Lodge and skeptical French parliamentarians was referred to by Ambassador to Paris David Bruce, who was in attendance, as "the most interesting" that he had seen since he had arrived in the city.[98] Due to Lodge's language ability and experience in Europe, he was able to talk to the French in a way most Americans could not.

The Cold War at home and abroad provided Lodge ever-greater opportunities to be involved in military affairs. Korea tested his newfound faith in collective military operations and was arguably the first such known exercise in the history of modern foreign relations.[99] Lodge believed the decision to respond to North Korean aggression was allowed under the UN Charter and supported Truman's decision to deploy troops on June 30, 1950, even though there had been no congressional authorization.[100] He became more critical after the White House did not provide adequate protection for the troops.[101] He called for an air force group of 150 instead of 95 and expanded enlistments in the army, including a 250,000 Volunteer Freedom Corps made up of enlistees from Europe and Asia who would be equipped and maintained by the United States. He even called for the possible use of tactical nuclear weapons.[102]

Lodge excoriated Truman's handling of the Korean War, which he called "inexcusable and terrible negligence." In sworn testimony before the Senate Foreign Relations Committee, General Omar Bradley revealed to Lodge that General Douglas MacArthur had not been consulted in advance before deploying troops.[103] Lodge was summoned to the office of Secretary of Defense Louis Johnson on Tuesday, September 5, 1950. "I have asked Senator Lodge down here because he doesn't think we are doing enough," Johnson said to those assembled, which included all of the military chiefs—General Bradley, General J. Lawton Collins, General Hoyt Vandenberg, Admiral Forrest Sherman, Admiral Arthur Davis, and General James Burns—and Undersecretary Stephen Early. "I then stated my position in brief, which was that the American people would support a major effort, that it ought to be undertaken at top speed so that definite results could be obtained in between three to five years and that, if we regain the initiative, we might organize lasting peace and avert World War III with all its bloodshed," Lodge said.[104]

Meanwhile, Lodge continued his charge to "modernize the G.O.P.," the title of his March 1950 article in the *Atlantic Monthly*. Lodge believed the party should refocus on issues such as taxation, social legislation, veterans, health care, the expansion of Social Security, farm legislation, and job security. His commitment to civil rights prompted him to call for the creation of national civil rights weeks, which brought praise from the American Civil Liberties

Union.[105] "We must press our own program—bold, different, practical, constructive," Lodge said, urging the creation of "a climate in which the strength and self-reliance of the individual human being will grow and flourish." He called this expansive domestic program "a welfare society without a welfare state."[106] Lodge believed the Republican Party needed new ideas. He opposed the all-or-nothing approach to the Taft-Hartley Act. Instead, Lodge believed in providing legislative relief for specific labor grievances when they arose. He believed the Republican Party's biggest problem was that it needed a new face.

Lodge's challenge was that Republican elders and those representing business interests seemed intent on making Taft their nominee in 1952. Lodge was convinced he would lose, and a sixth consecutive Democratic victory in capturing the White House would tear the Republican Party apart. Permanent rule by one party, he believed, put no pressure on that party to lead with its best people. Lodge believed this problem was already on display in some of the lower levels of the Truman administration. The American political scene needed a charismatic figure who could breathe life back into a system that had become stale. Such a figure had to not only unite the Republican Party but also be appealing enough to win independents and crossover votes from the Democrats. Lodge believed that the only person who could lead the Republicans and preserve a viable two-party system in the United States, whose political abilities he first recognized in 1943, in the midst of war, was former Columbia University President Dwight D. Eisenhower.[107]

There were just three problems: First, Eisenhower was in Paris as the newly appointed head of NATO. Second, he had never run for office, and Lodge did not know whether he would consider doing so. And third, Lodge had no idea whether Eisenhower was a Republican.

# 6 · Drafting Ike

The year 1952 was the most consequential in the career of Henry Cabot Lodge Jr. He led the "draft Eisenhower" movement after securing his agreement to run, was the General's first campaign manager, and wrestled control of the Republican Party away from Robert Taft and steered it in an internationalist direction in his own image. Without Lodge, the Republicans would have remained mired in isolationist, anti–New Deal rhetoric, and the Democrats would have extended their twenty-year control of the White House. It was also the year that Lodge lost his Senate seat to rising star John F. Kennedy, never to serve in elected office again.

Eisenhower had been courted by both political parties since the end of World War II. No other politician had the relationship with Eisenhower that Lodge did, formed as it was in the fire of World War II. Lodge first mentioned the idea of running for president during lunch on February 16, 1949. "I told him that a situation might very well occur in which the isolationist elements in the Republican Party got so strong that the Party would be faced with a definite turn in the wrong direction," Lodge recalled.[1] "I stay completely clear of any hint of personal partisanship," Eisenhower responded.[2] Lodge felt that the nomination of Taft would result in either Taft's election, "in which case we would have an administration which would be backward-looking at home and utterly ignorant of the facts of life abroad," or Taft's defeat, "in which case the two-party system in America would be at an end."[3]

Lodge believed the nation needed a figure of renewal who would break with the past. Eisenhower received an estimated twenty thousand letters and telegrams from people all over the country requesting that he run for the presidency.[4] But it was not until their first serious political meeting at Columbia

University in June 1950 that Lodge began in earnest to try to convince Eisenhower to run. He used a variation of the argument that would eventually succeed—that Eisenhower should consider whether it might be his duty to the nation.[5] Eisenhower was resistant. "It would be the bitterest day of my life if it ever became my duty to run. But if it is my duty, I would not flinch from doing it." Lodge began publicly backing Eisenhower for president in October 1950, before anyone else.[6] New York Governor Thomas Dewey and Eisenhower's old army friend, General Lucius Clay, also began publicly proclaiming his virtues as a presidential candidate.

At the end of 1950, President Harry Truman appointed Eisenhower to become Supreme Allied Commander Europe, a position established before that of secretary general when NATO was dominated primarily by military affairs. The position included command of one hundred thousand U.S. troops who were part of the new Atlantic alliance that Lodge helped to form in the Senate. A cynic could assume that Truman's appointment eliminated a popular rival for the White House, but no one in the mainstream took an Eisenhower candidacy seriously at that point.

The appointment was far more controversial than initially imagined, requiring three months of debate. The usual opposition in the Senate, led by Taft, argued that Truman's appointment would make war more likely. It fell to Lodge to marshal support for Eisenhower's confirmation. After Senator George "Molly" Malone (R-NV) proposed withdrawing the appointment, Lodge said, "It is hard to understand how anyone can contend the development of a defensive holding force in Europe could look like aggression to such realistic men as the rulers of the Kremlin. I do not want to stand on the Himalayas nor do I want to fight on Cape Cod. We've got to pick the spots where we can bring our force to bear."[7]

The back-and-forth stalemate was finally broken by Eisenhower himself, who flew to Washington to serve as a witness during the hearings. In a large public session in the Library of Congress auditorium as well as a closed joint session, he argued that the United States had no choice but to play an active role in NATO. "If we Americans seize the lead," he said, "we will preserve and be worthy of our own past." The nationally televised appearance allowed Eisenhower to win over the nation. *Time* magazine summarized his performance: "Eisenhower had done for the president what Harry Truman could not do for himself[:] . . . routed the calamity-howlers and the super-cautious—the Hoovers, the Kennedys, the Wherrys, and the Tafts." Not only was Eisenhower's confirmation approved, but he gained important national exposure in the process.[8] Before he departed for Europe, Eisenhower offered Lodge the opportunity to join him as his chief of staff.[9]

Building on the momentum of Eisenhower's confirmation hearings, Lodge did not wait long before approaching him again about running for the presidency. He did not think that Eisenhower would accept, as he wrote his old army commander Willis Crittenberger: "It looks as though the Ike business was not going to amount to anything and I like to keep my hand in in case of future emergencies." Lodge was so sure that Eisenhower would not run that he asked Crittenberger to let him know if any interesting army assignments popped up.[10] He was tiring of the Senate, especially as the Taft forces came to dominate more and more.

In July 1951, Lodge accompanied the Senate Armed Forces Committee to Paris for an inspection of NATO. Eisenhower worked out of the Hotel Astoria on the corner of the Champs-Elysées and the rue de Presbourg in Paris while the Supreme Headquarters Allied Powers Europe was being built in Rocquencourt, near Versailles, about thirteen miles from Paris. Lodge had another purpose for his frequent trips to Europe, and particularly to France: to consult with various foreign leaders on missions authorized by Truman's special assistant Averell Harriman. Lodge's background uniquely qualified him to serve as a discreet messenger from the highest levels of the U.S. government. In a meeting with Prime Minister René Pleven, Lodge encouraged the French to stop criticizing the integration of Germany into NATO, which was fueling isolationist politicians in the United States against the entire Atlantic pact.[11]

These visits to France allowed Lodge to check in with Eisenhower on July 16. They chatted for two hours in the morning, had lunch, and then talked for another hour in his office. Eisenhower criticized Truman's Korean policy, saying that the United States should have gone all out in mobilizing in order to send a message to the Soviet Union. Eisenhower said that Truman wanted him to return home for consultations, but Lodge said it was a bad idea as long the military assistance bill was being debated in Congress. If he were in the United States, there would be no way to avoid an invitation to testify and be torn to shreds by the Taftites. Eisenhower was grateful to Lodge for making him aware of that. "Today was the best time I have had since I have been over here and Lodge was very witty and interesting," Eisenhower told a colleague. After their conversation, Lodge wrote, "I am left with the feeling that he will think that his duty is to prevent the Taft victory from taking place, and I do not foresee much trouble in the word going out privately in January."[12]

When Lodge returned from Europe, he spoke about Eisenhower during an appearance on *Meet the Press* on August 5. He walked a careful line between being supportive of Eisenhower in his current position and also stating that he thought he should consider a political future. "Nothing would destroy Eisenhower's military effort quicker than for it to get in partisan politics," Lodge said, but he added, "I certainly would be very happy to see him president of the U.S." Lodge got a very positive reaction from just about everyone, except for members of the Taft wing. The *Boston Herald* commented on Lodge's remarks: "He may have flown in the face of the party's reactionaries, but he just as surely put himself on the side of what the Republican Party most needs in 1952—a winner."[13] Senator Richard Nixon said Lodge was Eisenhower's "leading supporter" on Capitol Hill.[14] In John Eisenhower's memoirs, Lodge is at the top of the list of those who convinced Ike to run.[15] Sherman Adams later referred to Lodge's contribution in getting Eisenhower to run as "the most effectual" and stated that it "largely paved the way for the political decision that Eisenhower subsequently made."[16] Lodge's Bay State colleague in the Senate, Leverett Saltonstall, said, "Lodge was the first to sound him out, and he secured Ike's tentative pledge."[17]

Lodge visited Eisenhower again at the Hotel Astoria on September 4, 1951. Eisenhower later said it was a "significant" visit.[18] Lodge told him that his candidacy was critical to the preservation of the two-party system, that the Republicans had lost five straight presidential elections, and that the party's current leadership was unable to cope with the challenges facing the nation. "You will have to make up your mind," Lodge told him, "and not later than January." Eisenhower did not like to be pressured. "Thank God I have until then," he responded.[19]

Lodge pressed harder. "In June of 1950, General, more than a year ago, I saw you at Columbia and said that in my opinion the neutralist and defeatist influences in the Republican party might get so strong that it would be your duty to enter politics to prevent one of our two great parties from adopting a disastrous course," he said. "I come to you today to say that the arguments which were persuasive then are a great deal more persuasive now and I urge that if you come to the conclusion that it is your duty to run for president, you let that fact leak out quietly through your political supporters, without necessarily being quoted, not later than January."[20] What was supposed to be a short meeting ended up lasting two hours. Lodge boldly requested that Eisenhower permit the use of his name in the upcoming Republican presidential primaries.

For the first time, Eisenhower answered in a new way. Up to then, he had rejected the idea. "[Lodge] argued with the tenacity of a bulldog and pounded
away on this theme until, as he left, I said I would 'think the matter over,'"
Eisenhower wrote in his memoirs, adding that the conversation had been a
"turning point."[21]

Lodge was making progress, but time was short. "He, more than any other
individual, was able to convince Eisenhower that the people wanted him,"
Adams recalled.[22] Eisenhower had confided in a friend that he had come to
believe a Taft nomination "would nullify all the things [he had] fought for and
worked for" in Europe.[23] Lodge sensed that Eisenhower could be convinced if
he spoke to him not as a politician but as a fellow soldier—emphasizing that
it was his duty. "I think a man who definitely has a public duty to perform and
doesn't perform it is in the same category with Benedict Arnold," Eisenhower
had told Lodge.[24] While Lodge did not write about the importance of his role,
he later told Rufus Phillips in Saigon that he "convinced him to run and was
thereafter instrumental in ensuring his nomination and managing his campaign."[25] Eisenhower felt the same way. "From that time onward, both alone
and through correspondence, I began to look anew—perhaps subconsciously—
at myself and politics," he wrote.[26]

Lodge thought Eisenhower could win votes from independents and Democrats in a way that someone like Dewey could not. "I am an extrovert and people
think I am honest," Eisenhower said.[27] Only someone with Eisenhower's stature could transform the Republican Party into an internationalist party.[28]
Lodge wrote, "At the end of this meeting I felt moderately sure that he would
consider it his duty to respond to a bona fide draft and I thought we would be
able to get this fact known to politicians around the country sometime in January, but I also realized that he would refuse to come back and campaign for
the nomination. Therefore, getting him nominated by the convention in opposition to so formidable an adversary as Senator Taft would involve Hercu-
lean labors."[29]

Lodge was not the only one actively lobbying Eisenhower, even if he was
the most influential. Eisenhower adviser General Lucius Clay sold him on the
idea of cooperating with Dewey and Lodge.[30] He hesitated to be more open
about his intentions because of the dilemma he found himself in. If he said
he would not run, he could put Taft over the top. If he said he would run, it
meant he must resign a job he had barely started.[31] On October 14, his sixty-
first birthday, he wrote James Duff, "I have been and am an adherent to the
Republican Party and to liberal Republican principles."[32] Eisenhower asked a

military aide in Paris what it would take "to get Mamie and [him] back home."[33] There were still many details to sort out. "The question was, could he be induced to stand for the highest public office as a Republican, and in time for the Republican convention?" Saltonstall reflected later.[34]

Truman had not yet made up his mind about his own reelection chances. On November 5, 1951, he privately told Eisenhower that "his offer of 1948 held good for 1952," meaning that he would be willing to run with Eisenhower as his vice-presidential running mate.[35] Eisenhower's response was that no professional military man should be president.[36] "As I told you in 1948 and at our luncheon in 1951, do what you think best for the country," Truman wrote. "My own position is in the balance. If I do what I want to do I'll go back to Missouri and *maybe* run for the Senate. If you decide to finish the European job (and I don't know who else can), I must keep the isolationists out of the White House. I wish you would let me know what you intend to do. It will be between us and no one else."[37] Eisenhower's response can be seen as a little disingenuous given later events. "You know, far better than I, that the possibility that I will ever be drawn into political activity is so remote as to be negligible," Eisenhower wrote on January 1, 1952.[38] Truman denied he had made the offer after he realized a political marriage with Eisenhower was never going to work.[39] Some of Truman's staff hoped the president would attack him. But instead, Truman said Eisenhower was "a grand man," stating, "I have utmost confidence in him, and I gave him one of the most important jobs that this government had to offer. If he wants to get out and have all the mud and rotten eggs and rotten tomatoes thrown at him, that is his business, and I won't stand in his way."[40]

Taft was moving full speed ahead in his pursuit of the nomination and already had an impressive number of delegates committed. With Truman's public approval rating hovering around 23 percent, the lowest of any sitting president at that time, only Eisenhower could stop the coming Taft surge.[41] While Lodge had been working on Eisenhower, Dewey had been meeting with Republicans in Washington to gauge potential support. What he discovered was positive enough that he thought it merited establishing a more formal organizational system. They needed someone to run their operation day to day. "What we need is someone to head this thing up," said Duff. "We need an office, a staff, people to compile mailing lists, and send things out to leading Republicans."[42] The decision to appoint Lodge as campaign manager was made in Dewey's smoke-filled suite in the Roosevelt Hotel on Sunday, November 11.[43] Besides Lodge, others in attendance among the "Initial Advisory Group" included Herbert Brownell Jr., Clay, J. Russell Sprague, Duff, and Barak Mattingly. Eisenhower considered Kansas his home state, and Lodge thought it would be best if a westerner like Mattingly, who was from St. Louis, ran his campaign.[44] Duff objected. After many other names were suggested and rejected, Lodge was asked to be manager.[45] He represented the new generation of Republican, and he had experience doing a little bit of everything. "Cabot Lodge is the man to be campaign manager and he is the only man with whom you can win," Duff said. Lodge initially protested, saying someone from "the effete East" was "all wrong for that purpose."[46] However, Dewey argued he was the only one who could do it, since he was not affiliated with any particular Republican, not even Dewey.

Lodge knew that the Eisenhower campaign needed to be associated with a fresh face. "We knew, and Governor Dewey knew—Governor Dewey was magnificently realistic about it—that as we got down toward the finish line in July of 1952, that the Taft people would say that the Eisenhower movement was just a rehash of the Dewey campaign of '48, and Dewey had been defeated and this was more defeatism. And we had a campaign in which there were many people who had not been for Governor Dewey. I had not been for Governor Dewey," Lodge reflected. "That's one of the reasons I was chosen to be campaign manager. I'd been a Vandenberg man."[47] Dewey promised Lodge full access to his fund-raising network, a weak spot of Lodge's organization, thereby ensuring Lodge would have Dewey's assets but not his liabilities.[48]

Lodge's immediate problem was that Duff and Dewey did not get along. The latter had never forgiven the former for trying to stop his nomination in 1948. Lodge sought the guidance of Maxwell Rabb.[49] They met in Beverly, Massachusetts, joined by Mason Sears. Lodge told them he had been asked to head the Eisenhower campaign. "Of course, we don't know whether we will have a candidate or not. And I have my own campaign to run against Jack Kennedy. He's going to be a tough man to beat and my own campaign will suffer if I do this," he said, asking, "Should I take it on?"[50] Rabb pointed out that Lodge had felt his hands were tied by being in the minority, and he advised him to take a chance on his Senate career and go for it.[51] Sears agreed. "Good," Lodge said. "We start on Monday." He called Dewey and said he would take the job if Duff also agreed, and he did. Dewey rented Suite 922 at the Commodore Hotel, which Lodge used when he was in New York. Lodge hired Senator Vandenberg's former secretary, Geraldyne Creagan. Rabb joined Lodge as his unpaid assistant. Vandenberg's son Arthur Jr. also pitched in.[52]

On November 16, 1951, a national headquarters was established in Topeka, Kansas, but the bulk of the work was done out of a small office set up in the Shoreham Hotel in Washington. There, with the help of Dewey's friend Thomas Stephens, the secretary of the New York State Republican Committee, Lodge handled public relations. He decided that his "workshop" at the Commodore Hotel in New York should be "kept confidential as long possible," he wrote, in light of its connection to Dewey. "I plan to conduct the following activities: talks with political leaders and delegates who arrive from other parts of the country; strategy meetings where I get in complete privacy the benefit of the uniquely successful convention experience of the Dewey organization; our research organization; current day-to-day estimate of the situation as regards delegates; and contact with the treasurer and the financial side of the campaign."[53]

Eisenhower's formal approval of these arrangements was not sought. Wearing an "I Like Ike" button on his lapel, Lodge called a press conference at the Commodore Hotel on Saturday, November 17, 1951.[54] He was the front man, trusted to stand in for the candidate himself until the General decided to return from duty. Not knowing Eisenhower's positions on matters of public policy, if he even had them, the views of the campaign that were disclosed to the press were Lodge's. "We've got a candidate and we've got the one who is sure to win," he announced. "I know he is a Republican, period. I can assert that flatly. There is no doubt about that."[55] Lodge was in way over his head, and he knew it.

Reporters did not believe it when Lodge said Eisenhower was considering a run for the presidency. "If he confirms what I've said, you'll have a good story. And if he fails to confirm what I've said, you'll still have a good story," Lodge said. "In fact, you'll have me over a barrel." The surprise announcement was praised widely by the press. Lodge's friend Arthur Krock called it "an act of unity" in the New York Times. "Senator Lodge is a skillful politician," he wrote. "He can walk on eggs when he thinks that is indicated by circumstances and not break any."[56] Lodge got to work quickly. Dewey wrote him, "There is an urgent need for a large staff of superior and experienced field men traveling through almost every state to spread the gospel. They certainly do not grow on trees but I hope we can find some more."[57] With the New York office open, Lodge returned to the Washington office to expand operations, upgrading to Suite 600-G at the Shoreham and putting former chairman of the Kansas State Republican Committee Wes Roberts in charge.

"This surprised me," Lodge recalled later about the early days of the Eisenhower campaign, "as I never thought of myself in this role."[58] He networked
for Eisenhower, lining up commitments coast-to-coast and spreading word of
the General's candidacy. Lodge and his top lieutenants methodically and repeatedly reviewed the situation in every state and chose assignments to address
weaknesses in their network. Lodge was totally committed. "For the nine
months following November 16, I accepted every invitation on TV and radio,
never turned down a press conference, and never slept more than three nights
in a row in the same bed." He was convinced Eisenhower had unique qualifications to be president, while Lodge himself had unique qualifications to run
Eisenhower's campaign. "My political background enabled me to bridge the
gaps between factions and thus be the man on whom all could agree." He was
naïve about the historic challenge ahead. "We had not really faced up to the
fact that, in every sense of the word, we would have to organize a draft," Lodge
recalled.[59]

Initially, the major challenges were practical ones. With no candidate in the
flesh and Eisenhower himself denying that he was seeking the presidency from
four thousand miles away, it was very difficult to raise the necessary funds to
keep the operation going. Even with a very meager campaign, they still had to
pay rent, staff members' salaries, office expenses, telephone bills, and travel
expenses. Lodge did not want to simply dip into Dewey's funds or use fund-
raisers associated with him, even though many of them were, since he was
the nominee in 1944 and 1948. If he did, it would have meant taking sides in
a Republican fight right from the start. The goal was for Eisenhower to transcend such divisions. Nothing would have ignited the Taft wing of the party
more quickly than if Lodge had put Dewey men in key positions in the Eisenhower campaign. In an extraordinary move, Lodge's family personally helped
bankroll the initial campaign expenses through his wife Emily's younger
brother, Henry Sears, a New York investment banker.[60]

The other major problem that Lodge had was that U.S. Army Regulation
600–10 forbade Eisenhower from actively seeking political office.[61] "There is
no slightest doubt in my mind as to the impropriety, almost the illegality, of
any preconvention activity as long as I'm on this job," Eisenhower wrote in his
diary. "I've just prepared a letter to Cabot saying that he and his friends must
stop the whole thing, now."[62] Lodge had to be careful; if Eisenhower too forcefully condemned the effort to draft him, it would fail. Some rank-and-file Republicans were less patient about Eisenhower's noncandidacy. When a
devastating late-November Gallup poll showed that support for Eisenhower

was slipping, Dewey wrote, "This ought to be hammered and hammered and hammered by mail and by personal interview on every party official and county chairman."[63] Lodge reached out to William Robinson of the *New York Herald Tribune,* an old card-playing friend of the Eisenhowers. Robinson went to Paris for Christmas to see if he could get any answers out of Eisenhower. When he returned, he met Lodge at the Commodore. "If we enter him in the primary," he said, "the General won't repudiate it. He is willing to return in June, but he can do nothing publicly before that time. And after that time he will not lift a finger to get the nomination himself." Lodge wondered what he had gotten himself into.[64]

On January 4, 1952, Lodge wrote New Hampshire Governor Sherman Adams.[65] "I therefore authorize you to enter the name of Dwight Eisenhower in the primary election for the expression of the preference of the Republicans of the State of New Hampshire for President of the United States," he said.[66] Typically such an announcement would be made by the candidate, but this was an unusual situation. Eisenhower's problem was that by being entered into a prominent primary, he could be accused of seeking the nomination instead of being chosen at the convention. "Time and again, I've told anyone who'd listen I will not seek a nomination," he wrote in his diary. "I don't give a damn how impossible a 'draft' may be. I'm willing to go part way in trying to recognize a 'duty,' but I do not have to seek one, and I will not." It is hard to imagine anyone but Lodge making such a bold move, and he had much to lose if it were to backfire. Lodge gambled that he would get away with it based on his previous conversations with Eisenhower, and he was right.[67]

On January 6, the uncertainty reached a crescendo as Lodge called a press conference at the Shoreham. It was a Sunday morning, which would maximize press coverage since Monday's papers would otherwise be light because of the government's recess. With the unofficial candidate still in Paris, Lodge announced that he had entered Eisenhower's name on the New Hampshire Republican primary ballot. Lodge's advisers said it was an extremely risky move to provoke Eisenhower.[68] He had not spoken to him once since becoming his campaign manager.[69] "I remember very well getting a very fiery telegram from the General," Lucius Clay recalled, "because he was very unhappy about this. He had not gone that far at the time, and he was quite disturbed at what Cabot said."[70]

Eisenhower wrote in his memoirs, "[Lodge] took it upon himself to say, on his own authority, that he could assure the New Hampshire officials that I was a Republican. He made this announcement without consulting me, probably to save me embarrassment."[71] It was a brilliant move by Lodge, but it also exposed a personal flaw. When Lodge became fixated on something, his blind spots to outside advice grew and he could go rogue. In one of the only instances in which Eisenhower criticized Lodge, he said he could become "a victim of his own fixations."[72] The press reached Eisenhower's office in Paris, and the colonel who answered said he knew nothing of the matter.[73] "My hand was forced by Lodge," Eisenhower recalled, "and either I had to repudiate him or I had to admit that I was a Republican."[74] Eisenhower had until February 10 to remove himself from the New Hampshire primary; silence would signal his availability.[75]

Eisenhower's supporters did not even know for certain whether he was a Republican. "It has never occurred to me to wonder whether my convictions can be interpreted as pertaining to the right or to the left. In fact, these terms annoy me," he wrote to Lodge.[76] The town clerk in Abilene, Kansas, said that he was not a registered voter and had never declared an affiliation with a political party.[77] A study of the speeches he made while president of Columbia University suggested he was closer to being a Republican than a Democrat. In one speech to the Saint Andrews Society, Eisenhower chided a liberal as "a man in Washington who wants to play Almighty with your money."[78] Lodge claimed that Eisenhower voted Republican in 1948.

There was also evidence that Eisenhower was not a Republican. The *Chicago Tribune* found the text of a November 9, 1909, speech that Eisenhower gave to the Young Men's Democratic Club of Abilene, Kansas, which was labeled his "first public speech." Truman described Eisenhower as having been a Democratic precinct worker in Kansas while a young man. The *Newark Evening News* reported that Eisenhower voted for Roosevelt in 1944, even though his family was Republican.[79] Some military officers of Eisenhower's generation did not even believe in voting while in uniform, as they wished to remove themselves from politics as much as possible. It was up to Lodge to make the case that Eisenhower was a Republican and to frame the issues that would form his campaign and the policies of the eventual administration. Eisenhower would accept most of the New Deal and be tough on the Soviet Union in an internationalist foreign policy. "I consider it incumbent on me to divulge certain conversations I had with General Eisenhower while he was serving in a civilian capacity at Columbia University," he said, framing the issue in a way to shield Eisenhower from potential accusations that he had made political remarks while wearing the uniform. "During these discussions, he specifically said that his voting record was that of a Republican. He also pointed out that his political convictions concurred with enlightened Republican doctrine."[80]

Lodge was asked for Eisenhower's position on his press conference. "Ask him and see," Lodge said. "That was a pretty grim Monday in Lodge's office just waiting around," Maxwell Rabb recalled of the day spent hoping that Eisenhower's office would confirm. "It looked as if we were out on a limb. Reporters were still flocking around, complaining about his calling them out on a Sunday."[81] On Monday, January 7, Eisenhower confirmed that he would accept if nominated.[82] "Senator Lodge's announcement of yesterday as reported in the press gives an accurate account of the general tenor of my political convictions and of my Republican voting record," he said in a vague statement.[83] Eisenhower addressed the matter in his diary. "On the seventh, due to a series of incidents, I decided to issue a short statement of my convictions concerning any possible connection between me and the current political contest in the United States."[84] Even more importantly for his backers, Eisenhower hinted he would leave his current post at the right time. He said that being the Republican candidate for president would constitute "a duty that would transcend [his] present responsibility."[85] Those were the words that Lodge needed to hear. The announcement dominated the front page for three straight days, pushing coverage of Winston Churchill's visit to Washington inside. Truman could not help but feel misled. "I'm sorry to see these fellows get Ike into this business," he said. "They're showing him gates of gold and silver which will turn out copper and tin."[86]

The campaign got off to a slow start. Lodge had spent too much time simply getting Eisenhower to permit a draft to be run in his name and not enough on getting local leaders to corral delegates. That allowed Taft to get off to a huge lead. Lodge was unable to quote Eisenhower in any campaign correspondence or political advertising, so he scoured past speeches and remarks for anything that might provide even fragments of usable content. Unlike Eisenhower, Taft was free to campaign as he liked, including in New Hampshire. "The New Hampshire primary marked the first big turning point in the Eisenhower campaign," Lodge recalled later.[87] The closest thing to campaigning that Eisenhower could do was grant nonpolitical interviews, as he did to Drew Pearson. "In many respects, Eisenhower reminds me of F.D.R.—the same contagious charm, the same ability to talk, and the same tendency towards pleasant-sounding generalities," Pearson wrote.[88] That kind of endorsement might have been better than any campaign appearance.

By the end of February, the Eisenhower boom was being deflated.[89] With some saying that New Hampshire would be in the bag for him, the campaign became overconfident. Expectations were so high that if Eisenhower achieved anything other than a landslide in New Hampshire, Lodge feared people would call it a disappointment.[90] He saw reports that sentiment for Taft was starting to grow—a potentially ominous sign. "It becomes increasingly apparent that Taft's vote-getting record and his obvious knowledge of government are stimulating a growing confidence and respect," Basil Brewer wrote to Taft's administrative assistant, I. Jack Martin. If the Eisenhower effort flopped, what kind of political career would Lodge and others have?[91]

The campaign was also running out of money. A lot of funds had been spent on a February 8 rally at Madison Square Garden, in addition to hiring new staff in New Hampshire. Herbert Brownell and Paul Hoffman were brought in to run the campaign headquarters.[92] Former Minnesota Governor Harold Stassen's campaign meant a drain on moderate support for Eisenhower, but it also helped him in that Stassen denied Taft outright victories and increased the odds that the nomination would be settled at the convention.[93] Stassen actually hoped that Eisenhower, being unable to campaign, would withdraw, as Stassen wanted to position himself to acquire his delegates.[94]

Despite the obstacles, Eisenhower won the New Hampshire primary on March 11 by more than 10,000 votes against "Mr. Republican" Robert Taft, 46,497 to 35,820. He won without shaking a single voter's hand. As a result, Truman announced he would not seek reelection on March 29.[95] The day of the primary, Eisenhower, in Paris, was playing bridge with his pals, including his personal physician, Howard Snyder. Snyder left the game early to listen to the returns in New Hampshire and said he would call Eisenhower if there was any important news. "Don't call me," Eisenhower said. "I'm not interested. Call Al [General Alfred Gruenther] if you want to speak to anyone. He's got some money on it."[96]

The Friday before the primary, Taft had attacked Eisenhower as an absentee candidate, not realizing that doing so gave Lodge an opportunity. New Hampshire Governor Sherman Adams went on the offensive against Taft, issuing a thirteen-page statement that appeared in the state's major newspapers. Adams went issue by issue—Taft-Hartley, civil rights, Korea, and other domestic and international issues—to rebut Taft's charges that Eisenhower had not made up his mind on the major issues of the day and was therefore unprepared to be president. It was so successful that as soon as Taft announced an appearance, Adams bought a full-page ad. Besides New Hampshire, he also did it in Massachusetts and Nevada.[97] In the Minnesota primary, Eisenhower was not even on the ballot but got 106,946 votes as a write-in against favorite son Stassen's 128,605 votes. "They just wrote in Ike or whatever if they couldn't spell the name," Eisenhower recalled later.[98] Winning New Hampshire and coming in second in Minnesota was respectable and showed that Eisenhower was a serious candidate who could do battle against Taft.

Lodge immediately began a coast-to-coast tour to meet with the heads of the state Eisenhower organizations.[99] He used these performances as leverage to convince the General to return home earlier than planned, embrace his popularity, and actively campaign. However, Eisenhower made it clear he would not be coming home. "As long as I am performing a national duty and doing it as well as I know how, I am possibly providing as much ammunition for your guns as I could in any other way."[100] Even more was on the line when the Radio Corporation of America released its "I Like Ike" advertisement just days after New Hampshire in order to capitalize on the victory.[101] The phrase, which first appeared in the October 1950 premiere of the Irving Berlin musical *Call Me Madam*, quickly became part of the nation's political lexicon. The Taft side shot back with a song entitled "I Like Ike, but What Does Ike Like?" to play up the fact that so little was known about his personal views. Another Taft campaign theme was "We like Ike BUT Bob can do the job," a way of promoting the Ohioan without insulting the five-star general.[102]

Taft was in the lead in terms of committed delegates, so he withdrew from some primaries, such as that of New Jersey, to avoid going head-to-head with Eisenhower in states where Ike was likely to be popular. In mid-March, Taft was estimated to have 509 prospective delegates versus Eisenhower's 262.[103] Lodge believed that the Taft campaign had peaked too soon, and when he was asked whether the Eisenhower campaign was ready to go into high gear, he said, "No, we'll move into second now. We won't move into high gear until after the first of June," as this was when Eisenhower was expected to return, just before the Republican convention to be held in Chicago.[104] On April 4, 1952, Lodge flew to Paris to meet with Eisenhower, which marked the first time they had met since November 1951. Lodge later said it was the first time that he and Eisenhower had overtly talked politics.[105] Lodge was mobbed by press at the airport, around Paris, and at his hotel, the George V.[106] Eisenhower and Lodge escaped some of the crowds by meeting at Rocquencourt, with its ground floor filled with the flags of the NATO countries. In Eisenhower's corner office, Lodge brought the General up to date on everything that had happened, in addition to briefing him on a list of sixty policy issues. Over lunch at the officers' mess, where they were served trout that Eisenhower had caught from a fish pond adjacent to his house, they discussed how to ensure his campaign was not associated too closely with Dewey.[107] The conversation continued over dinner. The General remained firm that he would accept the nomination but would not campaign for it. "There is a vast difference between responding to a duty imposed by a national convention and the seeking of a nomination," Eisenhower said.[108]

Lodge needed help. Sigurd Larmon, head of the advertising agency Young & Rubicam, offered his services. Larmon worked, without pay, to set up billboards, newspaper ads, and radio and television time, marking the 1952 campaign as one of the most modern in terms of the use of advertising and marketing specialists.[109] Madison Avenue would play an unprecedented role in making sure Americans would "like Ike."[110] Young & Rubicam worked directly with the networks to ensure maximum coverage and prepared the first television spot announcement. The agency got CBS and NBC to spend $100,000 to contract with AT&T for the construction of temporary microwave relays that would cover Eisenhower's campaign speeches, including the kickoff in remote Abilene.[111] These efforts prompted the political paradigm shift that made the television audience more important than the event audience and, over time, resulted in the extinction of the whistle-stop campaign, which had been a mainstay of American politics for a century. "With the availability of television, you don't have to take this traditional backbreaking ride around the country for 23 or 24 days," Eisenhower campaign spokesman James Hagerty recalled.[112]

Lodge had to gain some momentum for Eisenhower with respect to the seating of delegates. On April 11, the White House announced that Eisenhower would be relieved of duty and return on June 1.[113] His eventual return was something tangible Lodge could sell to delegates. It did not help that there were issues related to the legitimacy of delegates in five states, including Texas. Because there were two candidates—Taft and Eisenhower—and there were two slates of delegates, no one knew which set should be seated. It came to a head at the Texas state convention in Mineral Wells, where twelve thousand Republicans converged on the town on May 28. Approximately fifty county sheriffs who were providing security took it upon themselves to refuse admission to anyone not wearing a Taft button. Of the 519 delegates contested because the Eisenhower campaign challenged the process by which they were selected, the pro-Taft Republican State Executive Committee in Mineral Wells decided to seat only 30 for Eisenhower. That decision was affirmed by the credentials committee and a 762–222 vote of the whole convention.[114]

The result prompted a walkout of the Eisenhower forces, who set up shop across the street with signs reading "Rob with Bob" and "Graft with Taft." What happened in Mineral Wells became known as the "Texas Steal." Lodge brought to bear all his political abilities to turn the tide to Eisenhower, calling in personal favors to anyone who could help, in arguably the most aggressive moment of Lodge's entire career. He sought to maximize exposure of the process, and he got a boost from an unlikely source: the media. As he did at certain points in his career, he used his background as a journalist to help the press to frame the story he wanted. He was willing to engage in the same corrupt practices that he accused the Taft side of. Lodge asked his old friend Joe Alsop to place a story, and it was devastating to Taft: "With the on-the-spot approval of Sen. Robert A. Taft's personal representatives, the Texas delegation to the Republican National Convention has been stolen for the Ohio Senator. And the steal has been accomplished by a system of rigging as grossly dishonest, as nakedly anti-democratic, as arrogantly careless of majority rule, as can be found in the long and sordid annals of American politics." Lodge was delighted. "You made the Texas vote steal an issue," he said to his old friend, "and now we're going to win on it."[115] Lodge's political propaganda was a success. The big newspapers sent reporters to cover the state convention and the seating of divided delegations. Even Taft noted how much it hurt him. "The making of a moral issue out of the Texas case was only possible because every internationalist paper sent special writers to blow up a contest which ordinarily would have excited a few days' interest," he recalled.[116]

As in his early days in the minority in the Senate, Lodge manipulated the rules to his benefit. He hosted visiting VIPs, such as South Carolina Governor James Byrnes and John Roosevelt, FDR's son, each of whom came to stump for Eisenhower. Allan Shivers showered Eisenhower with as big a welcome as one could get in Democratic Texas. In Houston, twenty-three Republican governors met to decide whether to accept Lodge's argument that the Taft side was being unfair in the way it was seating contested delegations. If the problem was not dealt with, it would only spread to other states with contested delegations. The result of their deliberations, which informally became known as the "Houston Manifesto," would take on even greater importance at the convention in Chicago. Sherman Adams helped draft the agreement, which said that in the case of disputed delegates, they should not be seated until the entire convention had a chance to vote on their status.[117] The governors ultimately sided with Lodge's proposal to permit the Eisenhower delegates, changing the tide and producing momentum for Eisenhower. The ruling was effectively a warning to the Taft camp that if it was going to win the nomination, it needed to do so fair and square—and that senior figures in the Republican Party were watching.[118]

Lodge and former Dewey campaign manager Herbert Brownell arranged a series of coast-to-coast dinners for various state delegations, providing an opportunity for the state representatives to hear how victory was achieved in Texas with regard to the seating of split delegations and helping each state to strategize how to do the same. Lodge also launched a PR offensive in major newspapers across the country. "As fast as improprieties were committed, we pamphleteered and propagandized them," Lodge recalled later. In the July 10, 1952, edition of the *Pittsburgh Post-Gazette,* Lodge surrogate Lamar Cecil, a pro-Eisenhower attorney from Beaumont, Texas, argued that the Chicago convention needed to "wipe out the infamy of Mineral Wells so that we can go before the American people with clean hands."[119] The work that went into these state-by-state Eisenhower rallies ultimately became the core of what would be known as the "Fair Play" amendment, which, if approved, would keep contested delegates from being seated at the national convention. It proposed rules that would forbid many contested delegates from voting in Chicago, where Taft-controlled forces organized the convention schedule.

Lodge made plans for Eisenhower's return. He took a substantial campaign trip as a surrogate for the General right into the heart of Taft country—the West. "He and I went out most everywhere, into every kind of meeting," Maxwell Rabb recalled later. "They were strong for Taft there but they listened" as the team barnstormed all the way to California. In the May 1952 issue of *Harper's,* Lodge wrote of Eisenhower, "His fame as a world statesman rests on his having brought about a greater degree of European unity than had been possible in centuries of stormy history. In these achievements Eisenhower learned the arts and developed the gifts which fit him perfectly for the Presidency."[120] With Lodge acting as the surrogate for the General, he became more than a campaign manager. He internalized Eisenhower and became comfortable writing, talking, and fielding questions as Eisenhower would. It was an extraordinary assignment.

"General and Mrs. Eisenhower will arrive in Washington Sunday morning June 1," Lodge said in a public statement. Expecting that their settling in would take a few days at most, Lodge hoped to get him out on the campaign trail the morning of June 4. Plans for the convention needed to be made. Dewey reserved the entire eleventh floor of the Conrad Hilton in Chicago for the Eisenhower team. National Chairman Guy George Gabrielson, a strong Taft supporter, was eager to meet with Eisenhower to discuss convention plans. During their summit at Eisenhower's Morningside Heights home in New York, Gabrielson tried to determine whether Eisenhower planned to cause any embarrassment over the Texas vote fraud issue.[121] Lodge explained that he planned to introduce the Fair Play amendment at the opening of the convention. "We hope it won't be necessary for the party to wash its dirty linen in public," Gabrielson said. Lodge exploded. "We have no dirty linen to wash!" he said. "Your dirty linen has already been washed in public at Mineral Wells, and the nomination won't be worth having unless you clean up that mess." Gabrielson was taken aback. "That's just your opinion," he said. "There was misbehavior on both sides." He claimed that he had heard rumors of questionable behavior on the Eisenhower side. Lodge dug in. "I challenge you to name one single instance of misbehavior," he said, "and if you can I will publicly repudiate it. And I challenge you to repudiate what was done in Taft's name in Texas."[122]

The Eisenhower campaign was running at an all-time high in terms of popularity, primarily because the candidate had returned from France and was making personal appearances. There were 1,205 delegates in Chicago, so 603 were needed to win the nomination. A March 12 estimate of delegate commitments showed that Taft had 600, Eisenhower had 469, and the rest were split among California's Earl Warren, Harold Stassen, and Theodore McKeldin, the moderate governor of Maryland. By June, Eisenhower's campaign estimated his delegate strength was over 500, slightly ahead of Taft. Neither candidate had enough to win on the first ballot. The Eisenhower forces believed their numbers would enable them to win on a second or third ballot.[123]

Lodge and James Hagerty, who had been Dewey's press secretary, began to set up camp in Chicago ten days before the beginning of the convention. They, along with Brownell, chose Sherman Adams as Eisenhower's convention floor manager.[124] Bobby Cutler was also on hand, convinced there was "dirty work" to clean up regarding delegates.[125] Lodge's brother, John, was also part of the Eisenhower convention-floor team.[126] He was, in effect, the anchor man on the Fair Play amendment.[127] Lodge's primary function was public relations as delegates started to pour into the city. His team went to work, assuming correctly that the Taft side did not want to hold a public "final knockdown dragout fight," as Taft called it. The Eisenhower campaign put out two statements a day, one each for the morning and evening papers. The point was to ensure that the delegates, regardless of when they arrived and which hotel they stayed in, could not pick up a newspaper without reading fresh content directly from the campaign. Lodge rented two rooms at the adjoining Stock Yard Inn where they could loosen up stubborn delegates with refreshments.[128]

Lodge began working on the party regulars, starting with Gabrielson. Meeting him alone in his Hilton suite on July 6, Lodge's strategy was to address the credibility of the nominating process. Gabrielson did not hide his admiration for Taft, so Lodge argued that nominating him under the specter created by the delegate issue would irreparably damage him as the nominee that fall.[129] "If these things happen, the winner of the nomination will have a nomination that is worthless, and those who are responsible for such a miscarriage of the democratic process will lose their reputations for life," Lodge said.[130] Was that really something Gabrielson wanted to have happen on his watch? Lodge also paid a visit to former President Herbert Hoover, who officially endorsed Taft on July 9.[131] Hoover expressed "constantly greater anxiety" about the "pre-convention campaign," the Texas issue, and the "effect on Republican chances in the election."[132] Lodge asked the former president to stay out of any intraparty disputes.[133] Even if Hoover would not help Eisenhower, Lodge wanted to make sure he would not actively hurt him.[134] Meanwhile, Walter Judd met privately with Taft. "Conventions are where we choose the best man *who can win*," he said. "However many votes you'd get, Ike will get more. He'll get pretty near all the regular Republicans. He'll get more youth. He'll get more veterans and their parents. He'll get more of the intellectuals coming as he does out of Columbia and so on. He's a war hero and let's recognize it, that is an asset. He's fundamentally sound on government. He doesn't know government as well as you do, but he'll be a good chief executive."[135]

By the start of the convention, an AP poll showed Taft ahead of Eisenhower in the delegate count, 533–427.[136] Taft proposed a compromise on the Texas delegation whereby he would receive 20, and Eisenhower 16. Eisenhower thought it sounded like a good deal, but Lodge vetoed it and doubled down, seeing it as an opportunity to make an even bigger deal with Richard Nixon for California's delegates.[137] Lodge and Dewey subsequently discovered that thirty-seven delegations were chosen using irregular procedures, just as in Texas. For example, the Taft-controlled National Committee voted sixty-two to thirty-nine to exclude the Georgia delegation, which included fourteen of the seventeen Eisenhower supporters elected at the state convention. Instead, the National Committee voted to seat seventeen Taft delegates. Senator Richard Nixon said it raised the issue of whether the convention would be "conducted with complete integrity and fair play." Eisenhower set out from Denver on a two-day train journey to the Chicago convention, saying, "I'm going to roar out across the country for a clean decent operation. The American people deserve it."[138]

Ten minutes before the start of the convention on July 7, Gabrielson asked to meet Lodge behind the speaker's platform with Senator William "Bill" Knowland of California and three Taft managers—Dave Ingalls, Tom Coleman, and Clarence Brown—to discuss the Fair Play amendment.[139] Brownell had advised Lodge that any rules changes needed to occur at the very opening of the convention in order to have maximum effect. "The purpose of the Fair Play motion is to rehabilitate the Republican party in the eyes of the public and to establish confidence in our procedures," Lodge explained. Knowland said the California delegation, including Nixon, had agreed to support it and they preferred that the convention adopt it without a bitter fight.[140] Under pressure, the Taft side conceded. "If Taft had had one good manager instead of four lousy ones, he might have won," Lodge recalled.[141] Brown said that Taft agreed to have the contested delegations not vote until the right to their seats had been determined, yet Lodge insisted on a public vote to prove the point that the Taft side was trying to steal the nomination. "The delegates are thoroughly familiar with the issue. The way to avoid bitterness is to vote this up or down on the floor of the convention. I have confidence in the delegates," he said. "We were counting so much on the psychological effect of the showdown on the Fair Play amendment," Maxwell Rabb recalled. "The worst thing *would be for Taft to accept it,* to deny us the chance to *win* a vote on it."[142]

The Taft side fought it. Brown proposed an amendment that would exempt seven contested delegates in the Louisiana delegation since they had been chosen by a normal state convention. It was defeated. The longer the issue dragged on, the worse it looked for the Taft side. As Arthur Krock wrote in the *New York Times,* the Taft managers "were from the start outgeneraled by the Eisenhower group led by Senator Lodge." California's Warren announced that all seventy of his delegates would go to Eisenhower. Dewey delivered all but one of New York's votes for the General. Michigan, Pennsylvania, and Maryland all followed.[143] The tide turned. While Taft denied that anything improper had been done in the seating of state delegations, the convention voted 658 to 548 on Monday morning to adopt the amendment. Divided delegations were to be seated—a major boost to Eisenhower, especially in the South, since it reduced the influence of state party bosses who were pro-Taft. The Texas delegation ended up voting thirty-three to five for Eisenhower.[144]

The result did more than clear a path for Eisenhower. It "thereby definitely insured [his] nomination," Lodge wrote.[145] Some of Lodge's deputies floated the idea of trying a first ballot on Monday night to capitalize on the momentum. "The possibility of winning the nomination for president seemed suddenly and vividly to open up before us," he recalled, even though the decision would not take place until Friday. Lodge feared overextending. If Eisenhower lost on the first ballot, in the wake of that loss the Taft forces could regroup. Between the adoption of Fair Play on Monday and the vote on Friday, both sides used television to wage a propaganda battle in a way never seen before in a presidential campaign.[146] Lodge recalled Jim Farley's management of FDR's 1932 campaign, which he covered as a journalist. "If the campaign manager looked so buoyant, all must be in the bag," he remembered. The problem was that the Taft forces looked buoyant in Chicago. Their ninth floor in the Hilton was full of "bustle, noise, banners, and pretty girls." Two floors above, the Eisenhower floor was "too quiet, orderly, and dignified." Lodge changed the tone. "I sent a campaign worker out to remedy the situation, which consisted of more pretty girls, more noise, trumpets, and red curtains with gold tassels," he said.[147]

Thursday of the convention was dedicated to nominations. Lodge hoped to find someone to nominate Eisenhower who was not associated with either the fight with the Taft wing of the party or that between the moderates, Dewey and Duff. It would be even better if it were someone who added to Eisenhower's chances to be nominated on a first ballot. He found him in Maryland Governor Theodore McKeldin, who had been a short-lived presidential candidate. Senator Everett Dirksen (R-IL) nominated Taft and used his speech to attack Dewey and the moderate wing of the party for leading Republicans behind Eisenhower "down the garden path to defeat. We say unto you, we have been down that path before. Do not lead us down that road again!" After the nominations, at nearly midnight, Lodge huddled with Sherman Adams and his sixty convention-floor deputies at the Stock Yard Inn. It looked as if the Michigan and Pennsylvania delegates would swing their support to Eisenhower.[148] By Friday, Lodge predicted 592 delegates in support of Eisenhower. State after state called out its vote, beginning alphabetically with Alabama, and the tally seesawed back and forth. When it came time for Minnesota's vote, Ed Thye announced, "Minnesota casts nineteen votes for Harold Stassen." Stassen had gambled that neither candidate would win on the first ballot and that he might then be able to strike a deal with one side or the other. The actual vote was 595 for Eisenhower and 500 for Taft. The remaining votes were split among Warren (81), Stassen (20), and Douglas MacArthur (10). Neither Eisenhower nor Taft had reached the 603 necessary for nomination on the first ballot.

The chairman of the convention, Joseph W. Martin (R-MA), began preparing for a second ballot.[149] Minnesota called a quick huddle, and then Thye rose again to speak. "Mr. Chairman," he said, "Minnesota wishes to change its vote. Minnesota now casts nineteen votes for Dwight D. Eisenhower, the next President of the United States!"[150]

State after state followed in Minnesota's footsteps. When the revised first ballot had been calculated, Eisenhower won 845 to Taft's 280, with Warren taking 77 and MacArthur receiving 4. Then a representative from the Taft side rose to propose that Eisenhower's nomination be made unanimous. However, one delegate, Basil Brewer, the publisher of the New Bedford *Standard-Times*, was unwilling to support anyone other than Taft. He planned to get even with Lodge later. Eisenhower walked across the street from the Blackstone Hotel to the Hilton to visit with Taft. It was a magnanimous gesture, just as Lodge had made with Curley, Casey, Walsh, and later Kennedy. While Eisenhower and Taft did not know each other very well, they agreed to work together for a Republican victory.[151] Taft wanted a Republican to win in 1952. His concern, expressed privately, was, "I don't believe General Eisenhower really understands the differences which exist between the two branches of the Republican Party."[152] Nonetheless, Taft put his differences aside and campaigned in twenty-one states on behalf of Eisenhower, even riding with him on his train from Cincinnati to Cleveland.[153]

After Eisenhower's nomination, it was time to choose a running mate. Lodge had secretly been preparing Senator Richard Nixon from California to be the vice-presidential nominee since earlier in the year. Nixon offered the best geographical balance as well as youth, and his brass-knuckled approach would complement Eisenhower's softer disposition.[154] "I approached him on the Senate floor, well before the convention, and asked him if he would be interested in the vice presidency," Lodge said. "Who wouldn't?" Nixon responded.[155] Dewey and Lodge introduced Nixon to parts of the country where Eisenhower would not be able to campaign himself. Lodge brought Nixon to a Republican town committee meeting in West Newberry, Massachusetts, where no one had heard of him. "He gave us a wonderful speech," recalled one attendee. "It was exciting; it got us all exercised. I couldn't put it out of my mind. I still remember it as one of the best speeches I ever heard."[156]

At least one journalist was onto Lodge's efforts to get Nixon on the Eisenhower ticket. Two days before balloting at the Chicago convention, John S. Knight of the *Chicago Daily News* published a story predicting that Eisenhower and Nixon would win the election that fall. Lodge "laughed off" the column, while Nixon said, "That's news to me."[157] But Lodge added to the speculation when he was seen with Nixon at the convention on the night of the latter's nomination. To avoid a premature press conference, he quickly herded Nixon past reporters and simply told the press, "He had done as much to rid this country of communists as any man I know," thereby introducing Nixon as a national candidate for the first time.[158]

Republican leaders, including Lodge, met to discuss Nixon as though no one had considered him before then.[159] When Brownell called Eisenhower with their selection, Eisenhower approved, although he later told journalist James Reston that he had very little to do with the selection.[160] "July 11, 1952 was the most exciting day of my life," Nixon wrote about his selection and meeting with Eisenhower at the Blackstone Hotel.[161] Senator Barry Goldwater wrote later that it was his understanding that Earl Warren had agreed to step aside and let Nixon lead the California delegation because he was told that if he did, he would be repaid by being appointed as U.S. Supreme Court chief justice.[162] Brownell let it slip at the 1952 Gridiron Club dinner that Nixon might be chosen as vice president if he could ensure the state's shift in support from Taft to Eisenhower.[163] There was no controversy over Nixon, who had anticommunist credentials that appealed to the Taft wing of the party. Nixon was also a war veteran, he had a photogenic family, and he demonstrated talent and energy.

After the convention ended, Taft wrote an extraordinary nine-page reflection of what had transpired in Chicago, observing, "The whole strategy of the other side was to change the rules and get enough votes to steal all the contested delegates, and it was difficult to see how this could be prevented if the Eisenhower people were supported by the Warren and Stassen forces." Taft identified Lodge's manipulation of the press as a factor. "It was clear, therefore, when the Convention began that if Warren, Stassen and Eisenhower all ganged up on us on preliminary votes, we might not be able to win unless we held on to every vote, or replaced them with additional votes. Neither of these results were we able to achieve."[164] Lodge saw the result in Chicago differently. "I do believe the Party has been saved from itself," he wrote to Dewey, "and that now if we all work hard enough it can save the country and the free world."[165]

Eisenhower told Lodge that he was "lost in admiration" at what he had pulled off—and without incurring a single political obligation to be repaid later.[166] Lodge believed that a clear path to victory had become possible only because manipulation of the delegate issue allowed for the maximum possible publicity to discredit Taft. While Lodge would pay a heavy personal price later for his role, in Chicago he was jubilant.[167] He received messages of congratulations from all over the country, including some that proved to be prophetic. Rear Admiral James E. Arnold wrote, "We who admire you realize that you compromised your political career on this convention." The words of a constituent, George Maroney of Boston, were even more ominous: "We'll be very happy to retire you to private life in favor of Congressman Kennedy this coming November for your actions in this convention."[168]

It was soon clear whom Eisenhower would oppose that fall. "We should assume that this is going to be a hard fight regardless of whom the Democrats nominate," Lodge said in his first act as newly appointed chairman of Eisenhower's Campaign Advisory Committee.[169] Even with the nomination behind him, Lodge was still not free to concentrate on his own Senate race. The Democratic Party nominated a ticket of Adlai Stevenson and John Sparkman. Stevenson was young at fifty-one, able, progressive, and the governor of a major industrial state in which he had won a majority of 570,000 in his first campaign for any office. He was known as a champion of honest government and represented a welcome new face in politics.[170] He privately wondered whether he had a real chance, and whether Americans were tired of Democrats since they had been in power for so long.

Lodge's strategy was simple: "We must not insult the Democrats; we want millions of them to vote for us," he advised his team. "We can attack the mistakes that have been made by those who are in the seats of the mighty in Washington without offending the average Democrat at the crossroads."[171]

# 7 · A Lodge-Kennedy Rematch

Henry Cabot Lodge Jr. was about to suffer the first serious—and surprise—setback of his political career in Massachusetts: the emergence of John F. Kennedy. Lodge may have won the nomination for Dwight Eisenhower in Chicago, but Robert Taft's supporters got their revenge that fall. John F. Kennedy—and his father, Joe Kennedy, who had been close to Lodge foes Taft and Herbert Hoover—saw an opportunity. Lodge's efforts on behalf of Eisenhower had kept him out of the state for much of the year, making his Senate seat vulnerable. What he did to embarrass the Taft campaign created a lifelong break from what he considered the unprincipled right wing of the party. His son George Cabot Lodge said later that it was the only time in his life that he made enemies.[1] In his confidential journal, the elder Lodge wrote, "I did not know it at the time, but it turned out that my refusal to compromise on the issue of the Texas vote fraud and my unwillingness to yield an inch on the matter of the fair play amendment were factors which would lead to my defeat in Massachusetts in the following November."[2]

Kennedy was a freshman at Harvard when Lodge was first elected to the Senate in 1936. "I don't suppose I ever thought in those days that I would someday run against him and defeat him for the Senate," Kennedy reflected. Kennedy was a fellow Beacon Hill Brahmin, but from new money. He and Lodge had a lot in common. They both had graduated from Harvard cum laude; they both had published books advocating for greater military preparedness before World War II; they both had been decorated for their wartime military service; and both were tall, handsome, and privileged.[3] "I first heard of John Fitzgerald Kennedy in 1943 at the time of his heroic conduct in the Solomon Islands," Lodge recalled. "Then I got to know him when he became a Congressman from Boston. I always enjoyed seeing him."[4] Lodge was partly responsible for Kennedy's quick rise, as Lodge had cleared a path by wiping out three of the biggest names in Democratic politics in Massachusetts—James Curley, Joseph Casey, and David Walsh.

Using the Lodge campaign model and improving upon it, Kennedy covered all corners of the state long before the general election, even before he knew which office he was running for, since he had the luxury of having one of the safest House seats in the country.[5] Kennedy determined he could not rise to national prominence quickly as a member of the lower chamber.[6] Whether Kennedy decided to run for governor or the Senate depended on whether Governor Paul Dever challenged Lodge for the Senate or played it safe and ran for reelection. Kennedy leaned toward running for Senate, because he wanted to work on national policy in Washington, where the action was. "I hate to think of myself up in that corner office deciding on sewer contracts," he said, referring to the governor's office.[7] Lodge would be tough to beat, but Joe Kennedy said his son "would murder" Lodge for the Senate if it became necessary.[8] During JFK's fourth meeting with Dever on Palm Sunday 1952, the governor told him he would run for reelection. "Well, that's fine. I'm a candidate for the Senate," Kennedy responded.[9] On April 6, 1952, thirty-four-year-old Kennedy announced his candidacy for the Senate seat that had been held by Lodge and his grandfather for forty-five of the previous sixty years.[10]

Kennedy was weak outside his Eleventh Congressional District in Boston.[11] "At the outset I doubted that Kennedy could do it," longtime aide Lawrence "Larry" O'Brien wrote.[12] Likewise, McGeorge Bundy told Kennedy to stay out of the race. "I thought Cabot Lodge was a hell of a vote-getter," he said.[13] The Massachusetts Democratic Party was not going to be of any help. They considered Kennedy a rich kid who had entered an impossible race. In their view, he wanted a job for which he had not yet paid his dues. After Eisenhower and Adlai Stevenson were nominated, the Kennedy camp was not optimistic, either. Kennedy's views, to the extent that he had deep convictions, were arguably closer to Taft's than to Lodge's or to the orthodoxy of many northern Democrats—and certainly Stevenson's.

However, if there was one thing the Kennedys knew how to do, it was how to get elected. Kennedy took the campaign operation that Lodge had first put in place against more senior rivals in 1936, 1942, and 1946 and turned it against him. "I had in politics to begin with a great advantage of having a well-known name and that served me in good stead," Kennedy reflected.[14] He shifted right just enough to capitalize on the popularity of Eisenhower and figures like Taft and Joseph McCarthy yet distanced himself from Lodge. His charm and good looks canceled out what had been a consistent advantage for Lodge, and his Irish background, two generations removed from immigrants, canceled out yet another advantage that Lodge had traditionally enjoyed: support from the Irish. Kennedy started campaigning early, never actually ending his previous House campaign of 1950. He made an appearance in all 351 state communities, in large cities eight or nine times each, and, like Lodge, he directly targeted women.[15] The Kennedys had accumulated an enormous trove of voter data, more than what Lodge had gathered.[16] The race also showed that, by the third generation, the Catholics and the Irish wanted to elect a Brahmin of their own.[17]

Kennedy worked hard during his Senate campaign and was extraordinarily ambitious, although that might have been more due to his father. Joe Kennedy's focus for his son was always the presidency and not just a mere Senate seat. "I will work out the plans to elect you president," he said. "It will not be more difficult for you to be elected president than it will to win the Lodge fight."[18] "Anybody who wants to know how I beat Lodge can look into it and he'd find I beat Lodge because I hustled," JFK recalled.[19] "In 1952, I worked a year and a half ahead of the November election . . . a year and a half before Senator Lodge did."[20] One of Kennedy's aides recalled, "I'll bet he talked to at least a million people, and shook hands with 750,000."[21] One recent biographer said Kennedy's 1952 campaign was the most methodical, most scientific, most thoroughly detailed, most intricate, and most disciplined campaign in Massachusetts history.[22] In the Democratic primary, Kennedy needed 2,500 signatures to be eligible for nomination. Lodge's son George Cabot Lodge was on-site at the state house as a reporter for the *Boston Herald* when the signatures were delivered.[23] Kennedy garnered 262,324 signatures, scaring away any potential primary challenger.[24]

Running against Kennedy was one problem for Lodge, but the other came from within his own party: the Taft Republicans' effort to defeat him. With Eisenhower at the top of the ticket, Lodge assumed he would benefit from long coattails. He underestimated how divided the Republican vote would be after Eisenhower's nomination. It forced him to look outside the state to fund-raise, an effort that was headed up by Paul Hoffman of the Ford Foundation—who gave $2,000 of his own money.[25] Lodge's inattention to his own campaign in favor of Eisenhower's was another strike against him. Lodge aide Cammann Newberry said that Lodge "neglected his campaign outrageously . . . he just paid no attention to his race up here at all." Mason Sears wondered whether

Lodge wanted to run for reelection at all. "Cabot had been solidly in the Ike business for about a year. He was very tired and it took a great deal of spark out of him," he said.[26]

The newspapers run by Taft supporters, most prominently Basil Brewer's *Standard-Times* in New Bedford, ran front-page editorials denouncing Lodge.[27] "We engaged in a very ardent campaign on behalf of Senator Kennedy," Charles Lewin of the *Standard-Times* said later. "We distributed thousands of copies of texts of the press conference in which Mr. Brewer answered questions . . . And we carried on a considerable consultation campaign with the Kennedy leadership."[28] Brewer went to *Boston Post* publisher John Fox, a reliable supporter of Lodge's, and argued that Lodge had no convictions and was soft on communism. Fox, a McCarthy supporter who had purchased the *Post* on June 18 for $4 million, told Lodge that he could never endorse a Democrat and would endorse him. After a phone call from Joe Kennedy, Fox switched his endorsement to JFK.[29] Since it was worth forty thousand to fifty thousand votes, Joe Kennedy also arranged for a $500,000 loan to Fox, who grew up in the poor, numbered streets of South Boston's Bayview. The endorsement ran on the front page of the *Post* on October 25.[30] Kennedy recalled the loan sixty days after the election, with interest, and the *Post* went bankrupt in 1956; Fox died penniless.[31] Years later, Bobby Kennedy recalled that "there was a connection between the two events—the endorsement and the loan."[32] *Look* magazine writer Fletcher Knebel wrote a fifteen-thousand-word piece on the activities of the Kennedys during the 1952 Senate race. When JFK read it, he let Knebel know he was not pleased. "You know, we had to buy that fucking paper or I would have lost the election."[33]

While five of the six most important newspapers in the state still supported Lodge, Kennedy had seriously chipped away at his base. Even the *Boston Globe,* which by tradition did not make political endorsements, suggested in its coverage of the campaign that it favored Kennedy.[34] Newspapers refused to run ads paid for by the Lodge campaign. Lodge created an ad that highlighted his voting record in the Senate, displaying it side by side with Kennedy's in the House on the important votes of the Eighty-Second Congress. Doing so showed how many votes Kennedy had missed, due to either campaigning or health reasons. Brewer called the ad "undemocratic" and refused to run it. The *New York Times* described Brewer as Lodge's "implacable enemy."[35]

Lodge made a special effort to woo Catholic leaders, who had supported him in previous elections. To the delight of the archbishop of Boston, Richard Cushing, Lodge had supported federal aid to parochial schools and insisted that the 1949 Federal Education Bill include such funding. Cushing had previously reminded Catholic voters, "Lodge has been with us one hundred percent on this particular matter."[36] Lodge even borrowed a passage from a Cushing speech to use as a theme in his reelection campaign: "In this solemn hour of world history, America is the special object of God's providence. America must have some mighty vocation awaiting her, so wonderful are the means which God has given her toward its fulfillment. Her wealth and power inevitably impose the heavy responsibility of leadership."[37]

Kennedy ran increasingly to the right, criticizing Lodge for supporting the Truman White House while it "lost China" to the communists. Kennedy called Lodge a New Dealer and claimed that Lodge had the number one voting record of those who had supported Truman's appeasement foreign policy.[38] The fact that Truman had appointed Lodge to the 1950 UN delegation seemed to indicate how close they were. The Kennedy-Lodge war of words was played out on the billboards. When Kennedy put up a billboard challenging Lodge with "Kennedy will do MORE for Massachusetts," Lodge responded with "Lodge has done—and will do—the MOST for Massachusetts." When Kennedy and Lodge faced off in a debate at Waltham Junior High, ten minutes west of Boston, more than one thousand people crammed into the school auditorium to hear the candidates address issues facing the Democratic and Republican parties in the upcoming election.[39]

Kennedy criticized the Truman administration, but both candidates were polite and even had nice things to say about each other. "It was hard to attack Lodge on his record, because his record reflected Massachusetts in those days," Larry O'Brien recalled. "I always found him an extremely likeable man with whom it was impossible to be angry," Lodge said of Kennedy.[40] "I've always been fond of Cabot," Kennedy told journalist Hugh Sidey.[41] Commentary by attendees, as published in the Waltham News-Tribune, claimed that both performed well and were likeable. While there was no clear winner on the substance of the debate, it elevated Kennedy's status even further—and Lodge declined the invitation for additional debates. He doubted whether debates benefited both candidates equally, especially when one was more senior. "We never saw Henry Cabot Lodge again in the campaign," O'Brien said.[42] One prominent endorsement did come in for Lodge, from James Curley, after Kennedy refused to sign a pardon petition for Curley when he was in jail.[43]

The two big national issues during the fall of 1952 were the Korean War and McCarthyism—on which both candidates were silent. McCarthy was an icon in Massachusetts. He had the perfect ideological combination of Irish

Catholic roots and strong anticommunist views. He had served with Kennedy during World War II in the Solomon Islands, and they shared a "sense of fun and love of women."[44] McCarthy later dated two Kennedy sisters, the brainy Eunice and the beautiful Pat, and served as godfather of one of Robert Kennedy's children—something the Kennedys did not publicize. McCarthy was a guest at Eunice's wedding to Sargent Shriver, and JFK attended McCarthy's wedding at St. Matthew's Cathedral. The families vacationed, played softball, and boated together.[45] Bobby Kennedy worked as assistant counsel to Roy Cohn, McCarthy's infamous attorney on the U.S. Senate Permanent Subcommittee on Investigations.[46] McCarthy's friendship with the Kennedys allowed JFK to portray himself as the ultimate anticommunist to the state's 750,000 Irish Catholics.[47] McCarthy's personal loyalty to Kennedy and his professional loyalty to Lodge put him in a difficult spot. "I told them I'd go up to Boston to speak if Cabot asked me," McCarthy recalled. "And he'll never do that—he'd lose the Harvard vote."[48] Whether that would have been true or not, Lodge needed McCarthy to not only speak for him but also speak against Kennedy. And that did not seem likely. William F. Buckley wrote that McCarthy's friendship with the Kennedys cost Lodge the election. McCarthy campaigned for every Republican seeking a Senate seat that year except Lodge.[49] Lodge and McCarthy were fellow Republicans, but they were from different social classes and ethnic backgrounds, and they had very different temperaments. Lodge had defended McCarthy against some of his critics' charges that his anticommunist investigations were based on partisan politics. But there is evidence that a sizeable contribution by Joe Kennedy to McCarthy's campaign was what truly kept him out of Massachusetts that fall.[50] To save face with Lodge, McCarthy did send him a telegram that he could use in the final days of the campaign, but Lodge chose not to publicize it.[51] The damage was done.

Many voters considered Lodge to be to the left of Kennedy, which did not serve him well.[52] "I always knew if there came a man with an honest, clean record who was also of Irish descent, he'd be almost impossible to beat," he said.[53] While Taft's defeat had brought applause in Boston at the 1952 Congress of Industrial Organizations convention, it did not for many large Republican gatherings that fall. Lodge's mere presence on the ballot was resented by Taft Republicans. This could be seen in the fact that the Democratic primary turnout, even with Kennedy running unopposed, was nearly twice the Republican turnout, 855,339 votes to 458,425.[54] These numbers must have been shocking to Lodge. "I recognized that I had started campaigning too late, but I really felt that with my own attention back on Massachusetts, I could pull it off," he recalled.[55] He did not take Kennedy seriously enough. The only asset that he had that Lodge did not was his father's mammoth fortune, widely believed to be ill gotten, to go with his desultory House record and his father's reputation for anti-Semitism.[56] The coup de grace might have been the thirty-three tea parties Kennedy held to win the Irish vote, which tore the "lace curtain" in half at last. In the final weeks of the campaign, thousands of women—the same women Lodge had wooed in his earlier runs for the Senate—received invitations to receptions "in honor of Mrs. Joseph P. Kennedy and her son, Congressman John F. Kennedy." In a single afternoon at the Commodore Hotel in Cambridge, 8,600 cups of tea were poured during just one of these receptions.[57] These receptions were presented in a way that drew no formal connection between them and Kennedy's campaign, even though they gave him a captive audience for a short talk.[58] "It was those damn tea parties that beat me," Lodge said later. Kennedy catering bills totaled approximately $100,000.[59]

In the August 1952 Pittsfield statewide survey of name recognition, 97 percent recognized Eisenhower as a candidate on the ballot, 68 percent recognized Lodge, and 35 percent recognized Kennedy. By October, the figures for Eisenhower and Lodge had held steady, but Kennedy's had jumped to 52 percent. It did not hurt that he picked up the endorsement of every major labor union in Massachusetts, even though Lodge had a pro-labor record that went back to the 1930s. Lodge's Taft-Hartley vote obviously hurt. While Lodge had criticized how many votes Kennedy had missed in the House of Representatives, almost half of his House votes in total, it did not seem to significantly affect Kennedy's political fortunes.[60]

Eisenhower made a final campaign swing to Massachusetts to stump for Lodge. He was greeted by ten thousand people in Harvard Square, arriving in an open car seated between Lodge and Saltonstall in the back seat. Republican gubernatorial candidate Christian Herter and Bobby Cutler rode in the front seat.[61] "Until the final week of the campaign, I was of the opinion that Cabot would prevail," Saltonstall wrote. "But in the closing days I felt Kennedy had forged ahead. Basil Brewer, who was so strong for Taft, had hurt Lodge."[62] Anti-Lodge Republicans were so well organized in Massachusetts that they had set up a political action committee, Independents for Kennedy.[63] When Eisenhower and Lodge campaigned at Boston Garden on November 4, there was still a lingering, pungent smell in the air from the Wild West show that had taken place there the night before.[64] It was an auspicious sign for Lodge as he introduced Eisenhower, who was predicted to defeat Stevenson. "At the end of the campaign it is fitting that I should be introduced to you here tonight by

Senator Lodge," Eisenhower said in a tribute to his first campaign manager. "He was one of the very first seriously to suggest that I might undertake this great crusade upon which so many of us are now engaged. If on occasion I have singled out Senator Lodge to say how much I will need his leadership in the Senate it is because I consider him a man of courage and conviction . . . and because I have observed him in the field of battle."[65]

In November, Eisenhower won handily. Lodge was simply outmatched. "Cabot was simply overwhelmed by money," Eisenhower recalled. "There was simply just too much money spent." The final tallies were $349,646 spent by the Kennedy campaign against $58,266 spent by Lodge.[66] Seven members of Joe Kennedy's family spent a total of $35,000. He once listed the three things that got someone elected: "The first is money, the second is money, and the third is money." The candidate himself spent somewhere between $15,866 and $70,000 in 1952; the precise figure is unknown.[67] The campaign spent $250,000 on billboard advertisements alone.[68] None of this was a surprise to Lodge. According to his confidential journal, he knew he could not "attack corruption in government and then practice corruption in political campaigning," so he did not even try to compete with the Kennedys when it came to money.[69] There were rumors that if a Sunday collection was $950,000, Joe Kennedy would write a check for $1 million to Boston's Cardinal Cushing. Kennedy would take the tax deduction for $50,000, and in return he would get nearly $1 million in untraceable funds. The Boston Archdiocese said it was familiar with these stories and volunteered information about other Kennedy schemes. For example, the family had pledged a donation to name a new convalescent home and hospital for poor children in Brighton, in Kennedy's congressional district.[70] But after the building was named and the Kennedys had enjoyed the publicity, they never quite fulfilled the pledge.[71]

Lodge did not make money or JFK's private life an issue during the race. Kennedy's philandering, which was influenced, according to one account, by his father's sexual promiscuity and his relationship with his mother, had become a poorly kept secret.[72] As Thomas Dewey once said, "That's the one thing you can't discuss in a campaign. It will boomerang on anyone who tries."[73] The furthest Lodge went was to arrange for the publication of some embarrassing Nazi documents that mentioned Joe Kennedy during his time as U.S. ambassador to Great Britain. In one, the German ambassador reported to the foreign minister that Kennedy said about Hitler, "It was not so much the fact that we wanted to get rid of the Jews that was so harmful to us, but rather the loud clamor with which we accompanied this purpose."[74]

JFK emerged as a viable candidate as Massachusetts began a significant shift. Democrats dominated state politics from 1958 onward, and after Eisenhower, the next Republican president to win the state would be Ronald Reagan in 1984. On election night 1952, Massachusetts television and radio stations called the race for Lodge as late as midnight.[75] Kennedy defeated Lodge by 70,737 votes, 1,211,984 for Kennedy to Lodge's 1,141,247—a margin of 51.5 to 48.5 percent—in a state that Eisenhower won handily by 208,800 votes and that elected Herter as governor. Eisenhower was the first Republican since Calvin Coolidge to win Massachusetts. Voter turnout was an estimated 90.94 percent of those eligible to vote, and the number of ballots they cast was a record in state history.[76] Kennedy became just the third Democrat to win a Senate seat in state history. If the outcome had been reversed, Kennedy aide Patrick J. Mulken said, it would have been Lodge who would become president one day. Instead, Lodge was out of a job and had no clear political future. He never held elected office again, and, after his brother, John Davis Lodge, was defeated for reelection as governor of Connecticut in 1954, the line of public service by the Cabot-Lodges going back to the founding of the country was broken. No Lodge has served in elected office since.[77]

Lodge secured Eisenhower's candidacy and party nomination, but at a high personal cost, ending his Senate career. "It's pretty much of a landslide for Eisenhower," Drew Pearson confided to his diary. He was more concerned about Kennedy's defeat of Lodge. "I don't know whether this latter is a plus or minus. Lodge was a good Senator. Kennedy probably will revert to the thinking of his old man."[78] Governor Dewey was especially upset after seeing how hard Lodge had worked on behalf of Eisenhower. "I am desperately unhappy about the unfair defeat visited upon Cabot," he wrote John Davis Lodge.[79]

Lodge blamed his defeat on his role in the "draft Eisenhower" movement. He pointed to the fact that 34,708 fewer Republican ballots were cast for Lodge than were for Herter.[80] "If you study the election returns, you'll see that in the Democratic cities I ran ahead of Congressman Herter," Lodge recalled, "and he ran way ahead of me in the Republican towns."[81] Lodge did all right with Irish voters, but the Taft Republicans who voted for Kennedy damaged him the most. One of Lodge's deputies even suggested that if Lodge had asked Taft to come to Massachusetts to speak on his behalf, he would have done it out of party loyalty. Lodge had doubts. "I fought Taft with everything I had," he said. "I simply could not ask him to come and speak for me. There are worse things than political defeat." The fact is, of the photographers who captured Lodge after his defeat, none found him looking gloomy. He was elated that Eisenhower had won.[82] Of all the letters that poured in following Election Day 1952, perhaps none was more significant to him than a handwritten letter from George Marshall. "I am terribly sorry that the electorate failed you in your state," he wrote on November 6. "They made a great error for you were among the most conspicuous statesmen in public office." Marshall was optimistic that an Eisenhower victory might provide even greater opportunities for Lodge than another term in the U.S. Senate would have. "Personally, I want to see you Secretary of State preferably . . . if ever the country needed a man it needs you!"[83]

# PART III
## THE EISENHOWER YEARS

# 8 · The UN (1953–1957)

If there was anyone who had earned a position in the new administration, it was Henry Cabot Lodge Jr. Dwight Eisenhower chose him to coordinate his White House transition team, assigning him responsibility for all agencies except the Bureau of the Budget.[1] Lodge now had something to focus on aside from his Senate loss. He went to the Bahamas with his family for their first real vacation that year, but he also began to plan for a transition meeting with President Harry Truman.[2] Beginning on November 14, 1952, Lodge worked closely with officials such as David K. E. Bruce on a sketch of foreign policy issues likely to require decisions early in the new administration, including Eisenhower's trip to Korea, decolonization and the independence of Tunisia and Morocco, and the European Defense Community.[3] Bruce later told Lodge that it "was the first time in our political history that such a transition was successfully implemented."[4]

On November 18, Lodge and Eisenhower rode in an open-top car to the White House. It was just a year earlier that the "draft Eisenhower" group had rented two rooms at the Commodore Hotel in New York. Now, Truman, Eisenhower, and Lodge were meeting at the White House, then the Pentagon, to discuss transition issues. Truman described Eisenhower's demeanor that day as "frozen grimness" and "tense." To lighten the mood, only somewhat successfully, Truman presented him with a gift of a globe that Eisenhower had used during World War II.[5]

Eisenhower had Lodge in mind for White House chief of staff, a newly created position influenced by his military background. He intended it to be a kind of assistant president. "I was particularly interested in Cabot," he reflected later, "because I wanted someone who understood the staff system of operating.

His military experience would give him that. He had both the political savvy, from his long experience in the Senate, and he had the military training to know the staff system. I think he would have been a damn good one. I have always found him a keen observer and a man who had a helluva fund of common sense."[6] However, Lodge took himself out of the running. "You should maintain the homegrown atmosphere as long as possible. Roosevelt maintained it all the time," he wrote. For Lodge, who had spent almost his entire career in the minority, Eisenhower's victory was a chance not just to take back the White House but to remake politics—a chance for Eisenhower to become a kind of Republican FDR. Lodge advised Eisenhower to make amends with conservative Republicans. "I recommend that Senator Robert A. Taft be placed on the Supreme Court at the first opportunity with the assurance that he would be made Chief Justice," Lodge wrote.[7]

John Foster Dulles, who had known Lodge since the late 1940s, when he used to meet with Republican members of the Senate Foreign Relations Committee, thought it would be a waste of Lodge's talents not to use him in a foreign policy role. Dulles suggested to Eisenhower that a change in representation at the UN was needed due to the age of outgoing Ambassador Warren Austin.[8] General Lucius Clay asked Lodge to go to Augusta, Georgia, where Eisenhower was staying, to talk it over. Lodge agreed. "Look," he told Eisenhower, "you don't owe me a thing. Don't feel you have to give me a job." Eisenhower would not hear it.[9] "Oh, no," he said. "I need you." Eisenhower offered Lodge the post of U.S. permanent representative to the UN, more commonly abbreviated as UN ambassador. It was a U.S. "mission," not an embassy, since it was not accredited to a country.[10] "I regard this job," Eisenhower told him, "as next in importance to the Secretary of State. You will rank immediately below him, and have Cabinet status. And I'll want you to sit in on meetings of the National Security Council." The position became a central part of Eisenhower's "New Look" policy.[11] The UN had been the victim of Cold War tension between the United States and the USSR, which had broken its pledges at the June 1945 San Francisco Conference. Eisenhower used a portion of his 1953 inaugural address to mention his intention of transforming the UN from "an eloquent symbol" to "an effective force."[12]

The UN was not a new assignment for Lodge. He had been part of the UN delegation during the 1950–1951 session, along with Dulles, Eleanor Roosevelt, and Senator John Sparkman (D-AL). Still, one can only wonder what Lodge's grandfather would have thought about his grandson's choice of vocation. Lodge was an obvious choice, not only due to his work on the Senate

Foreign Relations Committee but also for his advocacy of the UN, NATO, the Marshall Plan, and what later became known as the European Economic Community.[13] Lodge saw the post as a stepping-stone, and that is how Eisenhower intended it.[14] "[It would] add a lot of experience to my life, for a year or a year and a half or so, fit me for even higher work and put me in the reserve for secretary of state," Lodge said. He stressed the importance of developing American support for the UN. "The American case should be presented at the UN with life, cleverness and effectiveness," he said. The U.S. Mission to the UN had to deal with dozens of governments, in addition to working closely with policymakers in Washington. Eisenhower once said that the UN is "a place where the guilt can be squarely assigned to those who fail to take the necessary steps to keep the peace," as well as "the only real world forum where we have the opportunity for international presentation and rebuttal."[15]

Lodge served at the United Nations for both terms of Eisenhower's presidency, longer than anyone else in that role before or since. Unlike bodies such as the National Security Council, which have a membership defined by statute, the Cabinet does not, allowing a president to designate other members.[16] That gave Eisenhower the discretion to add Lodge. They exchanged as many as three letters a day during their peak correspondence of 1953–1954. Lodge received about 150 letters from Eisenhower during his time at the UN, as well as participating in telephone calls, weekly Cabinet meetings, private meetings, and social events.[17] Typically, he had breakfast with the president twice per month. None of Eisenhower's political advisers spoke more directly with him than Lodge, such as when he advised the president that possibly losing control of the House or Senate in 1954 due to the failures of some "shop-worn Republicans" would be no great setback as long as it did not involve a "sacrifice of the Eisenhower popularity."[18] Due to Eisenhower's lack of political experience, and the lack of political experience of many of the people he had brought into government, he planned to count on newly appointed White House Chief of Staff Sherman Adams, Attorney General Herbert Brownell, Vice President Richard Nixon, and especially Lodge as his top strategists.[19]

The addition of Lodge to the Cabinet was an unprecedented distinction that demonstrated how much he was relied on as a senior member of the Eisenhower foreign policy team, a kitchen cabinet with no shortage of heavyweights: Secretary of State John Foster Dulles, CIA Director Allen Dulles, Nixon, and National Security Advisor Bobby Cutler. Even among this select group, it was Lodge who found the most favor with Eisenhower, in large part because of the trust that had developed between them beginning in wartime. Lodge was given a special status not out of any requirement but because Eisenhower wanted him to remain close.

At the UN, Lodge was a heavyweight debater whose presence gave real legitimacy to the international body that served as a multilateral vehicle for U.S. engagement with the world.[20] He was a skilled propagandist at what he called "the art of popular government."[21] Lodge was Eisenhower's ambassador to the world at a particularly difficult time, facing numerous challenges in what was arguably the most turbulent decade of the Cold War. In those days, a majority at the UN could usually be found to support American initiatives. In January 1953, the UN had fifty-six members. These were drawn from NATO allies, British Commonwealth nations, nineteen Latin American countries, and three strong anticommunist Asian allies—the Philippines, China (Taiwan), and Thailand. It was relatively easy for the United States to obtain a majority.[22] The Eisenhower administration monitored the UN and looked for ways to take advantage of its proceedings to an unprecedented degree, from maintaining a semipermanent State Department contingent in New York during each fall session, to installing direct phone lines from Lodge to John Foster Dulles and the White House, to maintaining the "hot line," a continually open phone line between the UN General Assembly and the assistant secretary of state for international organization affairs. "So they were never caught by surprise—at least not very long," James J. "Jerry" Wadsworth, Lodge's deputy, recalled. "We almost always knew within a matter of minutes exactly how the Department felt about anything."[23]

When receiving briefings from his staff, Lodge liked punchy, succinct, colorful language suited to this approach. He made it a priority to respond immediately to Soviet attacks and, when possible, to issue an official response in the same news cycle as the attack. He came to have a close relationship with the CIA, which regularly briefed him on subjects such as international communism.[24] The CIA provided Lodge with materials that he could use during UN debates, including maps and "ideas and themes."[25] These were provided directly to Lodge without clearance through the State Department.[26]

Lodge and Eisenhower believed that the UN, and, in particular, General Assembly and Security Council debates, had not been used to the full propaganda effect during the Truman administration.[27] The Soviet Union had done a far better job of utilizing the UN for its purposes. The Soviets would level some charge at the United States, and the American response would come far too late—or not at all.[28] That changed during the Eisenhower administration. "My guiding principle is never, never, never let a communist speech take place without having a speech from the U.S. on the same day, so that always the news story that is going out over the world has got something of the U.S. position in it," Lodge recalled later.[29] The result was to "break up their headlines, interfere with their news stories and, actually, take the news play from them."[30] On Lodge's first day on the job, acting on instructions from Eisenhower, he refused to pose for photographs with the Soviet representative.[31] "Don't you know there's been a change of administration in Washington?" he asked.[32]

Lodge's enthusiastic and effective support of the international organization was in direct contrast to his grandfather's efforts to block U.S. participation in the League of Nations. His self-confidence at the UN was based on his strong relationship with Eisenhower, as well as his political and military experience.[33] While at the UN, Lodge did not consider himself to be a mere ambassador of a single diplomatic post. "He [Dulles] told me at the very beginning that he wanted me always to call him direct, and not to go through the lower channels, for the simple reason that things move too fast," Lodge recalled. "And so I was on the telephone to him—often, four or five times a day—and almost every morning about 8:15. We'd talk almost every morning. I was in his office by telephone more than anybody in Washington was physically."[34] The UN was perhaps the only place outside Washington to view almost the entire spectrum of American foreign policy. "I knew President Eisenhower so well that I could pretty well anticipate what he would think about a given subject," Lodge recalled. "Of course, we always had instructions whenever there was time to draft them," but that was not always possible with the quick pace of activity at the UN. "A member will suddenly make a motion in the middle of the voting and the U.S. Representative has to meet the issue then and there. He must either vote 'Yes' or 'No' or abstain. Under those circumstances there is not even time to make a telephone call. But Washington never had to repudiate any decision that I took because I was so familiar with the thinking in Washington."[35] Eisenhower and Dulles seemed happy with the fact that Lodge exercised some independence. "I was told by the president that whenever I thought I should have direct access to him, I should talk to him directly—man to man. I was to be the judge of whether to see him or not," Lodge recalled.[36]

One of the first things Lodge did after taking his new post was to request that J. Edgar Hoover investigate American personnel at the UN.[37] Within two weeks, 1,200 completed dossiers had been sent to the State Department. "Since the last meeting of the General Assembly, there has been a change in the government of the U.S., a change in which the losers have neither been disgraced nor, may I say, liquidated," Lodge said. "The American people wish to establish a lasting peace and regard the UN as a vital means to that end." His statement was a reference to the Korean War, which was still being negotiated. Lodge immediately increased the security of the U.S. Mission, including staff training and additional security sweeps and security personnel. He added U.S. Marine Corps guards, as had been done for other diplomatic missions around the world. These changes were meant to be visible, address the legitimate security concerns, and enhance Lodge's prestige in the process. He explored moving the offices of the U.S. Mission, but due to cost, availability, and the organization's unique spatial requirements, that would not be possible until 1959. Lodge tried to move his personal accommodations out of the Waldorf Astoria, which was too small and lacked security, as it was a major hotel. He instituted small shifts such as more carefully controlling visas issued to communists, limiting their movements to Manhattan, and threatening deportation for violating these rules. Whether these changes made a difference was questionable. Communist diplomats in Washington already enjoyed greater freedom and greater access to secrets, and any tightening of restrictions on communists would almost assuredly result in reciprocal tightening on American diplomats overseas.[38]

To improve security in other ways, Lodge had CIA officers embedded in his staff and used the agency for a wide range of activities, such as preparing for upcoming debates, gathering research materials for speeches, and assembling investigative reports.[39] These staffers were heavily involved in regular mission functions.[40] Lodge regularly requested reports from the CIA, which came to be known as Sponge reports, that he used to document cruel and inhuman treatment beyond the Iron Curtain. They came primarily from Germany and were based on intelligence coverage of sources that was often derived from the interrogations of defectors, including those who worked for the Soviet regime. When the Soviet Union raised the issue of human rights and American misbehavior during the Korean War, Lodge wanted facts at his fingertips about "communist inhumanities." Such inhumanities included forced assignments to labor camps, forced confessions, government manipulation of the food supply, omnipresence of police informers, fines and imprisonment for "crimes" such as giving public speeches, and persecution of minority groups, especially Jews.[41]

Lodge chose as his deputy James "Jerry" Wadsworth, a childhood friend who stayed with Lodge all eight years. "He's here not because I knew him when but because he's the best man I know for the job," Lodge said.[42] Wadsworth had been the acting director of the Federal Civil Defense Administration.[43]

After hours, they sang duets, and Wadsworth was known to bring out his guitar.[44] Lodge also appointed James Barco as minister-counselor, designated Charles Cook as deputy counselor, and persuaded AP correspondent Frank Carpenter to serve as his press officer. With these appointments, Lodge began a lifelong pattern of appointing young, capable, ambitious men who worked hard, questioned the conventional wisdom, and remained loyal. They were all around thirty years of age, were virtually unknown, and had no obvious party affiliations. It was a high-quality, tightly run, efficient staff.[45] When Adlai Stevenson replaced Lodge during the Kennedy administration, he retained Lodge's entire staff except the top political positions.[46]

Lodge's usual routine was to wake up by seven-thirty and have a quick breakfast of orange juice, toast, and coffee in his suite. He preferred to walk the sixteen blocks from his eight-room apartment on the top floor of the Waldorf Astoria to the U.S. Mission at 2 Park Avenue, the only U.S. embassy on American soil. The *New Yorker* once commented that he must have covered more of New York as a pedestrian than any contemporary. On Mondays, Lodge held a senior staff meeting and consulted with key allies Britain and France on the week ahead. Throughout the week, he briefed key congressional representatives and senators, consulted with the Soviets, and attended evening diplomatic receptions and dinners.[47] In the office, he liked to tackle work quickly and not let things back up. "He wouldn't let things rest on a back burner," secretary Rosemary Spencer said. "He knew what he wanted. He would ask for it and if you could provide it, you were 'in.' If you could not do what he wanted, he would go somewhere else. He got things off his chest. He liked people who stood up to him, even if he disagreed with what they had to say. His biggest dislike was indecisiveness," she added. Lodge rarely went to lunch. He might eat a box of Portuguese sardines at his desk or walk home to have lunch with Emily. Lodge also liked to eat baby food, a habit he had nurtured since his wartime stomach illness. At the Waldorf Astoria, he might order cream soups made with baby food chicken or spinach. He liked to go to parties and entertain, but drank little.[48]

Lodge's most important assignment early in his tenure at the UN was to get to know Dag Hammarskjold, who had become secretary general on April 10, 1953. After Trygve Lie's retirement and attempts to nominate various successors, the five great powers met in secret on March 31. That official gathering followed an unofficial gathering at Sir Gladwyn Jebb's house with Lodge and the Soviets, including Valerian Zorin and Andrei Gromyko, on March 25. At that meeting, just as the three sides had agreed to compromise, there was a loud clap of thunder, followed by torrential rain. "It is the voice of God," Lodge said. Gromyko grinned, responding, "But He doesn't say what side He's on."[49] The Soviets agreed "to replace the person currently fulfilling the functions of Secretary General," refusing to mention Lie by name. They decided on Hammarskjold, the slender, blond, Swedish diplomat. "On the basis of my sketchy information about Mr. Hammarskjold I am inclined to think that he would be satisfactory and that he may be as good as we can get," Lodge cabled Dulles.[50]

Lodge and Hammarskjold did not make for an obvious pairing, at least not at first. They did not know each other well, which made them a little uneasy about working together. As soon as work permitted, Lodge invited him to his Beverly estate. They even took a cruise, flying both the UN and U.S. flags.[51] It provided a far more relaxed atmosphere than Hammarskjold's office on the thirty-eighth floor of the UN Secretariat Building. "It's a clan, a tribe," Hammarskjold said of the Lodges, "where everyone is independent but still a part of the whole."[52] The Lodge-Hammarskjold relationship was arguably the most important one during this period, helped by the fact that Lodge enjoyed entertaining Hammarskjold at his official residence at the Waldorf Astoria. Working closely with Hammarskjold elevated Lodge's status and the status of the UN. When the UN responded to Soviet attacks, its response would carry more weight.[53] They grew closer, and Hammarskjold felt increasingly comfortable taking more and more authority to act independently, including by organizing a mission to China in 1955 to release fifteen American pilots who had been held since the end of the Korean War.[54] However, in making overtures to China, Lodge drew the line at UN membership, something that Hammarskjold believed in. "The UN, I said, was not created to be a band of international adventurers not bound together by a common love of peace," Lodge recalled saying. "The San Francisco conference envisaged a moral sanction in the words 'peace-loving' which are in the Charter. Were the conditions prevailing now prevalent then, the U.S. would undoubtedly have opposed Soviet membership." Hammarskjold dropped the issue.[55]

Hammarskjold helped to ensure the UN was free of spies. He announced in his first press conference, on May 12, 1953, that he intended to carry out full security investigations at the start of the new session in 1953.[56] He appointed a committee to oversee all investigations of UN employees for potential subversion.[57] Lodge felt that Hammarskjold understood the effect of McCarthyism on American domestic politics even if he was willing to overlook previous Communist Party membership as long as a UN staff member currently had a clean record of activity.[58] The United States insisted that American citizens applying for positions with the UN be cleared first by Washington. Lodge criticized the director general of UNESCO for not dismissing all Americans on his staff who had received negative loyalty reports.[59] Eisenhower wanted to remove any actually or potentially subversive employees from the U.S. Mission and the UN itself. With the help of the FBI and the civil service, Lodge oversaw a process to review all 1,800 American employees of the UN. Lodge told Eisenhower, "[It is] a scheme which I pushed from the first, which received the cooperation of the Secretary General, favorable consideration by the General Assembly (41 votes in support, 4 abstentions, and 13 against) and which is so well under way now that, with luck, it should result in this problem being cleaned up once and for all by early autumn."[60] Lodge called for an increase in the security of all aspects of UN operations, instead of simply relying on the prior practice of having the State Department screen applicants' police records and political affiliations. Eisenhower was especially concerned about the offices of the U.S. Mission at 2 Park Avenue, which already had their own facility for burning secret papers and were swept three times a year for electronic listening devices.[61]

The Senate Internal Security Subcommittee of the Judiciary Committee, chaired by Patrick McCarran (D-NV), interviewed current American employees of the UN.[62] In the hearings, a total of twenty-three invoked their Fifth Amendment right when asked whether they were a current or past member of the Communist Party. That allowed McCarran to conclude that the U.S. Mission was infiltrated by disloyal Americans, and those who had invoked the Fifth Amendment were fired. Eisenhower himself took a rhetorical middle road, preferring not to use the inflammatory language that the UN was a nest of spies. He simply agreed that Americans not wholly loyal to the government had breached the UN. That tone set the policy that followed.[63]

Lodge reassured Americans that no U.S. classified information was transmitted to the UN. While he did not believe any American should be charged with espionage, he also did not think that the U.S. government should employ known communists. Lodge's goal was to diffuse the hysteria of the various investigating committees, and he told McCarran that the Eisenhower administration would remedy the mistakes of the Truman years. Lodge proposed a twelve-member loyalty review committee that would take the key findings from the congressional hearings and use them to investigate all UN personnel, him included. Lodge did not see the irony that he had opposed similar efforts by McCarthy. In carrying out this proposal, Eisenhower issued some of the most significant executive orders of the Cold War—E.O. 10450, which established loyalty tests for federal workers and banned those with undesirable character traits, such as homosexuality, and E.O. 10459, which pertained directly to the UN. The latter established the International Organizations Employees Loyalty Board within the Civil Service Commission.[64]

The FBI's investigation of Lodge turned up rumors, including that he was a homosexual, that he had had an affair with a Senate page boy, and that he had had an affair with a woman. The accusations were not passed on to the Eisenhower White House since they could not be verified.[65] Despite Lodge's efforts to get the UN security problem out of the way as soon as possible, a lack of appropriated funds and a profusion of congressional bills and executive orders confused more than clarified. With Hammarskjold's help, however, the security review of the UN was completed in December 1954.[66]

Over time, the UN became a forum for worldwide opposition to the rhetoric and the policies of the communist bloc. Eisenhower was fond of saying that psychological warfare was "just about the only way to win World War III without having to fight." This view was consistent with his broader "New Look" approach, articulated in October 1953.[67] The goal was to create the best possible image of the United States abroad and exploit events that reflected poorly on the communist world, "from the singing of a hymn up to the most extraordinary kind of physical sabotage." Eisenhower appointed Charles David "C. D." Jackson to coordinate psychological warfare for the White House, and, with Lodge's help, the UN became a key battleground where these efforts played out, as it was a unique worldwide forum for the dissemination of American propaganda. These efforts at the UN became internally known as the "Lodge Project."[68]

Lodge's long experience as an insurgent in the Senate Republican minority was good training. He amassed a reputation at the UN for his handling of various crises, as well as his sometimes unconventional approach to problems. British colleague Gladwyn Jebb commented, "In no way an intellectual, Cabot was a first-class operator in the Security Council when he sometimes gave the impression of being, as it were, a power in his own right." Lodge was popular with the staff, even the receptionists, guards, and other "little people." He regularly greeted them, smiled, shook hands, and sang at staff parties.[69] "If they have a good time at your parties it's only natural that they may want to please you," he said.[70] However, not everyone was pleased during the workday. One of Lodge's aides said, "You learn three things right off around here. The first is that everything must be disposed of immediately. The second is that Lodge can't stand intrigue. Everything must be completely straightforward. The third is that he can't tolerate yes men. He wants you to tell him exactly what you think."[71]

Lodge's range of duties for Eisenhower went well beyond those of U.S. permanent representative to the UN. Lodge frequently counseled him on the full range of political and domestic matters. Eisenhower called Lodge "one of [his] friendliest and yet most severe critics."[72] He played a key role in helping Eisenhower keep his campaign pledge to end the Korean War. The United Nations General Assembly had passed a resolution relating to the return of prisoners of war, but negotiations had hit a stalemate under Truman. Eisenhower supported the Truman policy on nonforced repatriation of POWs—based on the finding that many communists did not want to return home. On March 28, 1953, China and North Korea offered a transfer of sick and wounded POWs. Their health was so bad that Lodge filed a petition with the UN General Assembly, adopted by a vote of forty-two to five, with nine abstaining, regarding at least 6,113 American servicemen who had suffered illegal, torture-like conditions while in custody.[73] Agreement on repatriation was reached on June 8, and South Korea released 25,000 POWs ten days later. According to the *New York Times,* Lodge had used his status to receive expedited permission from the State Department to place the issue on the UN agenda.[74] The POWs released by South Korea quickly disappeared into South Korea, as opposed to returning home to China or North Korea. Finally, on July 27, after three years of inconclusive fighting, the thirty-eighth parallel was established as the boundary between North and South Korea, meeting the UN goal of returning to prewar borders.[75] Lodge presented the issue of Korean reunification at the UN on August 17, 1953, and a peace conference that included the United States, both Koreas, and China was planned in Geneva. The talks began and ended quickly, with both sides repeating their prewar positions.

Lodge continued to advise Eisenhower on Washington politics. He advocated "modern Republicanism" against would-be reactionaries and urged Eisenhower not to purge Republican mavericks before the 1954 midterm elections, which saw control of both chambers returned to the Democrats after flipping in 1952 thanks to Eisenhower's long coattails.[76] He advised Eisenhower to reject McCarthy's smears against Foreign Service officials such as John Service, John Carter Vincent, and Charles Bohlen. Lodge insisted that those chosen to testify before Congress have expertise in how Congress worked, not just on the issue that was the subject of the presentation.[77] Senator Stuart Symington was one of the few who came to discover how much Eisenhower relied on Lodge for political strategy. At the beginning of 1954, Congress considered hearings related to the Senate decision to censure McCarthy. Lodge surfaced as a possible witness due to his role in initiating a meeting with Brownell and Adams where they set policy to create distance between the White House and McCarthy and between McCarthy and his counsel, Roy Cohn.[78] Given McCarthy's aggressive pursuit of army officers, they decided to intervene on behalf of Eisenhower because they concluded that he was McCarthy's ultimate target.[79] Lodge's chief concern, as expressed to Eisenhower, was that "the Senatorial investigation of the Army, while ostensibly aimed at making sure that the Army is secure against communist penetration, is actually a part of an attempt to destroy you politically and it is wishful thinking, as well as imprudent, not to proceed on this assumption."[80] When Symington learned of the meeting, he wondered why that was within the purview of the U.S. ambassador to the United Nations. Lodge's involvement did not make sense unless he had a broader role in advising Eisenhower.[81]

Lodge believed the UN could serve Eisenhower's political interests, which in turn served Lodge's political interests. He believed Eisenhower's enormous popular appeal could be used to enhance the UN and promote world peace. He also believed the UN could work hand in hand with U.S. foreign policy interests, since a major goal was "having people respect us and have confidence in us. We want a lot of people around the world who feel they are in business for themselves, and we don't want satellites. It should be the worst thing in the world for us to have satellites. We want people who are with us because they agree with us out of mutual respect."[82]

At the end of Lodge's first year as UN ambassador, Eisenhower gave his "Atoms for Peace" speech, calling for the creation of an international atomic agency in order to avoid the "fearful atomic dilemma" in which "two colossi glower at one another across an atomic abyss." The dark rhetoric was intended to match that dark period of the Cold War. The proposal was universally received, even by neutral and communist nations.[83] "The reaction in the free world was immediate and enthusiastic on all sides," Lodge reported to Eisenhower. "Leaders of such neutral countries as India and Indonesia hailed the proposal as an important step toward peace. The Soviet Union, surrounded by this universal attitude of acclaim, agreed after long hesitation to join the agency." These high-profile events at the UN, often televised, as were regular debates, helped Lodge to become a household name for millions of Americans.[84]

Robert Murphy, who took over the State Department's UN desk in 1953 and was the person Lodge officially reported to, realized that managing Lodge would be no easy task. Within a few months at the UN, Lodge had become "one of the best known personalities in American public life," Murphy wrote.[85] He observed, "Cabot had the advantage of having strong pull with Ike because Ike was grateful to him for his work in the 1952 campaign."[86] Due to Lodge's personal relationship with Eisenhower, as well as his political career and heritage, he did not expect to be treated like a mere ambassador. The only explanation for the unusual political autonomy Lodge had was that he was receiving personal protection from Eisenhower. "I would have to practice a form of diplomacy in my new post which I had not anticipated," Murphy recalled. "During the Korean debates, a resolution was proposed on which the vote promised to be closely divided. There were discussions at the Office of UN Affairs in Washington about how the U.S. should vote, and after due consideration we decided that the American vote should be 'Yes.' We submitted our conclusions to Secretary Dulles and he approved it, so instructions were sent to the U.S. Mission in New York. But the next morning I was dismayed to read in the newspapers that Lodge had voted 'No.' As soon as I could talk to him by long distance telephone I said, 'Apparently our instructions failed to reach you.' Lodge repeated, 'Instructions? I am not bound by instructions from the State Department. I am a member of the President's Cabinet and accept instructions only from him.'" When Murphy explained the situation to Dulles, the secretary of state was not much help. "This is one of those awkward situations which require special consideration. If it happens again, just tell me and I'll take care it," Dulles advised.[87]

Francis "Fran" Wilcox, former staff director of the Senate Foreign Relations Committee during Lodge's tenure, said that these examples were exaggerated. "I know it is sometimes said that Ambassador Lodge was a bit of a free-wheeler and voted against the instructions of the Department of State from time to time," he reflected. "I don't think there is any justification for this charge. He had his own notions, and he expressed himself, of course, but so far as I can tell he never voted against the instructions of the United States government."[88] However, enough of these stories exist that they must touch on the emergence at the UN of a more selfish side of Lodge. He dismissed such criticism, emphasizing how much pressure he was under. The second half of 1954 was especially difficult for Lodge. His mother was in and out of the hospital with blood anemia, a broken hip, high fevers, and the lesion of a heart valve. In the middle of it, her doctor had a heart attack and was sidelined. Lodge and Emily alone cared for his aging parent, as his sister, Baroness de Streel, lived in Belgium, and his brother, John, was running for governor in Connecticut.[89]

On occasion, Lodge's wit and sense of humor were put on display. He was disarming in a way that charmed both sides of the aisle, and this remained a lifelong skill that enabled him to have a fulfilling career under Democrats as under Republicans. His work at the UN was good for him for another reason, too. Lodge had proved that he was sufficiently anticommunist to gain the respect of the Taft supporters. He wrote Eisenhower, "The feeling of the strong Taft adherents which was so extremely bitter against me in 1952 has now very much diminished, both because they like what they see of my work at the United Nations on television and in the press and because of the death of Senator Taft."[90] It is difficult to find anyone who disliked Lodge for any extended period of time throughout his life. He was genuinely likeable and worked hard to maintain relationships. Once, when Lodge discovered that Senator John F. Kennedy was recovering in a hospital not far from him, he stopped by to drop off a get-well message handwritten on the back of his business card. "It was the nicest thing I have ever heard of—your sending him your card—and you can't imagine how much something thoughtful like that means to people who are sick," Jackie Kennedy wrote to Lodge.[91]

With the Korean War over, Lodge soon had a series of other crises to deal with. The first of these was Guatemala, which would be one of the most difficult issues Lodge handled at the UN and the first of the U.S.-Soviet proxy wars that would mark one of the most intense periods of the Cold War, leading to the Cuban Missile Crisis. In May 1954, a cache of weapons, identified as "optical goods" in the bill of lading, was shipped from Czechoslovakia to Guatemala. The United States reacted quickly, and the next month, on June 29, Colonel Carlos Castillo Armas successfully led a coup, backed by the CIA, U.S. air support, and a force of 150, and overthrew President Jacobo Arbenz Guzman. Arbenz supporters in the UN called for an investigation, backed by the Soviet Union, and made charges that American aggression toward Honduras and Nicaragua had assisted the rebels in the coup.[92]

For Lodge, the episode represented the "malignant growth" of the "Soviet menace in the western hemisphere."[93] Lodge had obtained a ten-to-one endorsement that the issue belonged under the purview of the Organization of American States, but Hammarskjold disagreed with the American position, which was inconsistent with his effort to transform the UN into a forum with the authority to consider and debate any threat to the independence and territorial integrity of member states regardless of whether any other organization considered it. He warned Lodge that the U.S. position had serious consequences for the UN's future.[94] While normally an advocate for the UN, Lodge showed he was willing to push some ethical boundaries in the U.S. treatment of Guatemala given the American criticism of European colonial practices.

Lodge had argued that because the Organization of American States was looking into the issue, the UN did not need to become involved, too. The investigation discovered warehouses in Guatemala containing propaganda from Moscow, as well as plans to create a "proletarian revolutionary dictatorship." What rattled Lodge was that American allies Britain and France voted in support of the Soviet resolution calling for a UN investigation. Britain liked Arbenz because he had dropped any territorial claim to British Honduras (Belize). Lodge was authorized to use the veto for the first time against Great Britain and France. Lodge threatened the British and French representatives, telling them, "If Great Britain and France felt that they must take an independent line backing the present government in Guatemala, we would feel free to take an equally independent line concerning such matters as Egypt and North Africa."[95] In the final UN Security Council tally, the veto was not necessary because Britain and France abstained. Denmark, Lebanon, and New Zealand voted for it, while Lodge managed to cobble together a "no" bloc of Brazil, China (Taiwan), Colombia, and Turkey, which was sufficient to defeat the resolution.

Tension in Indochina was another serious issue that the United States and the UN had to face early in Eisenhower's presidency. As Indochina moved toward independence from France, Eisenhower's primary concern was that it remain noncommunist. As close as Lodge was to Jean de Lattre de Tassigny, the former commanding general of French forces in Indochina, one wonders what he might have learned from him had he not died in 1952. The United States wanted France to be a strong contributor to the proposed European Defense Community, but Eisenhower did not think France could do that while being bogged down in Southeast Asia—not to mention the fact that there was intense French opposition to German armament at the heart of the community.[96] France wanted to keep Indochina out of the UN, where it assumed it would be condemned for colonialism. Eisenhower, Dulles, and Lodge disagreed. However, the United States did not force the issue.[97]

For France, the matter came to a head during the spring of 1954 after the loss at Dien Bien Phu. On March 25, Eisenhower's National Security Council debated and rejected deploying ground forces to prevent a communist takeover. Eisenhower believed that UN approval was needed for any new action. During his April 7 news conference, he said that the question of deploying forces is "the kind of thing that must not be handled by one nation trying to act alone." Lodge did not completely agree. He had argued as early as 1950 that the United States should become more involved in Indochina, the same position taken by de Lattre, not only to increase the odds of French participation in the European Defense Community but also because Lodge wanted greater French involvement at the UN.[98] The Geneva Conference convened on April 26, 1954, and Indochina was divided at the seventeenth parallel, the Ben Hai River. The northern half, North Vietnam, was backed by the communists, and the southern half, South Vietnam, was backed by the United States. They were separated by a demilitarized zone ranging from two to three miles in width on either side of the Ben Hai River, running from Laos to the sea.[99] Neighbors Cambodia and Laos agreed to be neutral. Critics of the Eisenhower administration believed that after seeing a division in Korea and another in Vietnam, the United States was not doing enough—and certainly not achieving enough.

The first serious disarmament talks between the United States and Soviet Union were initiated in 1954. Eisenhower's proposal in December 1953 for an international atomic energy association did not go anywhere. He did not give up, using a Labor Day 1954 speech to say that he remained committed. On September 22, the USSR responded that it was willing to continue negotiations. Lodge argued that the United States needed to commit to a specific quantity of nuclear material to show the Soviet Union it was a serious offer, so on November 15 he said the United States was willing to commit to 100 kilograms of fissionable material. The last hurdle to conducting serious talks was cleared when the USSR agreed to internationally supervised verification inspections.[100] On February 20, 1955, Lodge flew to London to present a two-pronged American proposal: a "tamper-proof" proposal for disarmament and a "fool-proof" proposal for inspections and monitoring. The meetings went on for three weeks, but the Soviet Union did not seem interested in negotiations, as Lodge reported to the Cabinet on March 18.[101] The exercise provided the Western allies the chance to harmonize their positions, even though they agreed that total disarmament was not attainable.[102] Another attempt at negotiations took place in Geneva in July.[103] Eisenhower's "Open Skies" plan proposed aerial inspections to verify disarmament compliance. "I welcome you . . . to share in a great opportunity to give each other a complete blueprint of our military installations from beginning to end, from one end of our country to the other," Lodge said when presenting the proposal. "Next, to provide within our countries facilities for aerial photography to the other country—reconnaissance . . . you to provide exactly the same facilities for us . . . by this step to convince the world that we are providing as between ourselves against the possibility of great surprise attacks, thus lessening the danger and relaxing tension."[104]

Harold Stassen was appointed assistant to the president for disarmament.[105] Lodge and Stassen knew each other well.[106] He was also named the U.S. deputy representative on the UN Disarmament Commission—a somewhat awkward position in which he had to report to one of three bosses depending on whether he was advising the White House (Eisenhower), talking to foreign nations (Dulles), or taking part in meetings at the UN (Lodge).[107] The press labeled him the "Secretary of Peace."[108] Nothing immediate was achieved during the Eisenhower administration, but Stassen's work became the blueprint for the creation of the Arms Control and Disarmament Agency during the Kennedy administration.[109]

On June 20, 1955, Eisenhower addressed the UN in San Francisco to mark its tenth anniversary. He pledged that the United States would rededicate itself to the ideals of the UN.[110] A public opinion poll showed that "satisfaction for the progress of the UN" rose from 50 percent in 1953 to 74 percent in 1955, a sharp increase during Lodge's first two years as ambassador. Support for the UN among Republicans in particular, those most likely to fear the threat of a "world government," increased from 19 percent in May 1951 to 58 percent in December 1953.[111] Lodge correctly assumed that Americans would see, as he did, that there was a gulf between communist doctrine and Soviet actions and a political advantage to be gained in aggressively exposing that gulf. The percentage of Soviet speeches at the UN that were anti-American declined from 80 percent in 1952 to 40 percent in 1953, then to 16 percent in 1955.[112] Lodge unquestionably helped establish the U.S. Mission to the United Nations as the powerful organization it would become in successive administrations, even though no successor was permitted to have quite the independence that Lodge had.[113] "In its first decade, the UN has developed into the greatest single engine in the world for mobilizing public opinion—a force which no government can withstand forever, no matter how dictatorial it may be," Lodge wrote.[114]

In the span of just seventeen days in the fall of 1956, Lodge faced his biggest challenges. On October 23, students and workers overthrew the Hungarian communist government led by Erno Gero. In response, Russian tanks rolled into Budapest, where they were confronted by Hungarian troops, fellow communists, and citizens united in resistance, and brutal street battles broke out. Leaders around the world condemned the Soviet actions to suppress Hungary, which was landlocked and surrounded by Warsaw Pact countries.

It was inaccessible by land or water without going through neutral Austria or an East European communist state.[115] On October 28, Lodge, along with Britain's Sir Pierson "Bob" Dixon and France's Bernard Cornut-Gentille, asked Hammarskjold to call an emergency session of the UN Security Council. Lodge publicly blasted the Soviet suppression of the Hungarian uprising, which he referred to as "wholesale brutality." The Soviet representative, Arkady Sobolev, protested the meeting, calling it a "gross interference in the domestic affairs of the Hungarian People's Republic." While the UN was powerless from a military standpoint, it could raise the issue as a moral one. "The Hungarian people are demanding the rights and freedoms affirmed in the Charter of the UN and specifically guaranteed to them by the peace treaty to which the governments of Hungry and Allied and Associated Powers are parties," Lodge argued. "We fervently hope that the action taken in bringing this matter to the Council and the Council's decision to consider the grave events in Hungary will move those responsible for the repression of the Hungarian people to discontinue such measures."[116]

During this Security Council meeting, another crisis developed.[117] Israel attacked Egypt, asserting self-defense following Gamal Abdel Nasser's decision to nationalize the Suez Canal. This more complicated problem was an outgrowth of Egyptian and Arab nationalism, Islamic solidarity, Arab-Israeli hostility, and transatlantic tensions.[118] Egyptian forces, backed by the Soviet Union, had assembled near the border with Israel, having pledged to destroy its neighbor. Israel, armed by the French, responded militarily to the provocation. On October 30, the UN Security Council met. "The government of the United States feels that it is imperative that the Council act in the promptest manner to determine that a breach of the peace has occurred, to order that the military action undertaken by Israel armed forces should be immediately withdrawn behind the established lines," Lodge argued.[119] The British and the French issued an ultimatum to Israel to cease hostilities, which was ignored.

American intelligence determined that Paris and Tel Aviv had exchanged an abnormally large number of messages in the twenty-four hours before the Israeli aggression, leading Eisenhower to believe that the British and the French were playing a double game.[120] "I was not a diplomat and did not know what diplomatic customs were but I felt that when one had an urgent situation, when one wanted to stop a war, one had to act quickly," Lodge wrote in his confidential journal.[121] He had to immediately distance himself from the two allies at the UN in order to prevent the issue from causing damage to

American foreign policy. "The UK lost a great part of its influence at the United Nations when it attacked Egypt," Lodge advised Dulles.[122]

The United States did not seem to appreciate the ripple effect the problems had on British and French interests elsewhere in the Middle East and Africa.[123] Both nations were outraged, as they depended heavily on the canal for trade and oil shipments and were the primary investors in the Suez Canal Company. Britain did not want the issue referred to the UN because of the time it would take to get any kind of action.[124] On October 31, Lodge called Eisenhower to inform him that the UN had offered enthusiastic and near-unanimous approval of the American proposal to call for Israel and Egypt to cease hostilities, for Israel to withdraw behind the armistice line, and for all UN members to refrain from the use of force.[125] The problem was that the British and French military forces had already been deployed for the purpose of "temporary occupation" of the Suez Canal area. That created an insoluble problem for Lodge, whose earlier proposals had met with the British veto, the first ever, after he pressed passage of a resolution that called for an immediate cease-fire and withdrawal of forces.

"I, together with my French colleague, registered a negative vote on the United States resolution which failed with 7 votes in favor and 2 abstentions (Australia and Belgium)," Dixon reported.[126] "Our friends among the maritime powers were appalled at the rift which was revealed between us and the United States," British Prime Minister Anthony Eden recalled.[127] Eisenhower and Dulles wanted the UN to consider the issue even less than did Dixon, who threateningly conveyed to Lodge that the British were considering leaving the UN over the matter. "It simply did not make sense that two of the great powers should be publicly put in the dock in the United Nations in this way . . . Was that what Mr. Lodge wanted?" Dixon quizzed him.[128] Lodge saw it as another unpopular issue at the UN for the United States, with a growing number of third-world nations likely to block any Western resolution.

The Soviets were also opposed to the idea of British-French occupation of the Suez, which temporarily meant Lodge was closer to the Soviet position than to the one held by America's strongest allies. He voted with the USSR on a seven-to-two vote to call the General Assembly to "try" Britain and France for aggression. "I *know* President Eisenhower felt—and I think that Secretary Dulles felt, and I know that I felt, that if the United Nations did not oppose the use of force, other than in self-defense, it would cease to be a respectable organization," Lodge reflected.[129]

At a press conference, Secretary of State Dulles said that the United States, Britain, and France were not allied in all parts of the world, further inflaming the matter. He flew up from Washington on November 1 to present the American side of the case. Eisenhower was hesitant to do it himself in the final weeks of the presidential campaign.[130] Privately, Lodge told Bob Dixon that the British "had been guilty of aggression and what we had done was indefensible." Arriving at the UN, Dulles was frail and shaky. Within days his cancer would be discovered. For that reason, his appearance was more than symbolic. "I doubt that any delegate ever spoke from this forum with as heavy a heart as I have brought here tonight," Dulles said. "We speak on a matter of vital importance, where the U.S. finds itself unable to agree with the three nations with whom it has ties, deep friendship, admiration and respect, and two of whom constitute our oldest, most trusted and reliable allies." The debate continued until three o'clock in the morning on November 2, capped by a 4:20 a.m. vote of sixty-four to five, with six abstentions, that demanded a cease-fire and a stop to the movement of arms and military forces into the Suez area.[131] The decision effectively determined that the Suez Canal belonged to Egypt and not to the colonial powers.

At virtually the same time, on November 4, while the UN was distracted by the Suez Crisis, Soviet troops broke through the last resistance in Hungary. Tanks rolled into Budapest even while the Soviets tried to be more involved in the UN on the Suez Crisis, perhaps as a distraction. The struggle that killed an estimated 2,500 Hungarians was condemned by a UN vote of fifty to eight, with fifteen abstentions. Little else was done, because Western nations did not want to risk another war.[132]

In the midst of the colliding crises, Hammarskjold paused to write Lodge, "This is one of the darkest days in postwar times. Thank God you have played the way you have. This will win you many friends."[133] Even with all of Lodge's talents, one cannot but wonder whether the episode was a failure for him and American diplomacy. "It will be said that here are the great moments and when they came, and these fellows [Hungarians] were ready to stand up and die, we were caught napping and doing nothing," Eisenhower wrote.[134] "The United Nations failed on Hungary—so did the United States, incidentally, and so did everybody else," Lodge recalled.[135]

"The truth is that every initiative taken in the United Nations regarding Hungary was taken by me—the initial call for the Security Council meeting, the Security Council resolution, the 3 A.M. meeting last Sunday, the Assembly resolution after the Security Council had been vetoed, and now another resolution," Lodge wrote to U.S. Ambassador to France Douglas Dillon. "The plain fact is that I have opposed the French and British action in the Middle East because it was the United States policy to oppose it—a policy formulated at the very highest level by the President himself."[136] The American attitude during the Suez Crisis gave rise to anti-American feelings among the French, which Charles de Gaulle was able to fully exploit later.[137] Lodge was unable to prevent a public break over Suez, and the crisis took away precious time for the UN to act on Hungary.[138]

The dual crises took a toll on Lodge, as well as the State Department, which considered them the "most intense responsibilities since World War II."[139] Lodge barely made it home at night during the seventeen-day period, worked exceptionally long hours, and endured regular late-night sessions. In a letter to Henry Luce, Lodge compared the experience to that of the intense 1952 convention. "I never worked harder or longer hours at Chicago than I did for the 17 days and nights the Hungarian crisis was at fever heat and during the long weeks and months that elapsed thereafter," he said.[140] In the March 4, 1957, issue of *Life,* Lodge was accused of sitting idly by and not doing anything during these crises. He issued a rebuttal stating that he had introduced nine resolutions and made twenty-five speeches during the crisis period.[141] Resolutions and speeches did not translate into action, however, and any failures that belonged to Lodge also belonged to other American officials. The episode put on full display both the limitations of the UN and how the Eisenhower administration used it as part of its overall foreign policy-making strategy. The United States had misread the actions of key allies, and Eisenhower had been hesitant to act forcefully for fear of playing politics mere days before the election.[142] In neither Hungary nor Suez was the rhetoric backed by the willingness to go to war, and in both cases the real diplomacy occurred bilaterally, outside the UN.[143]

Eisenhower was reelected decisively against Adlai Stevenson, 457 electoral votes to 73. He won the popular vote everywhere except a portion of the South.[144] Lodge did not have time to campaign with him, but, acting as a clearinghouse for his political speeches, he sent plenty of speech material that Eisenhower used. "This is a job which must be done by someone to avoid dangerous and needless errors . . . in order to remove from them anything which could be harmful," Lodge argued, proposing the unusual arrangement on account of the fact that his continued role at the UN meant that he should "preserve the bi-partisan nature of this office which deals with our foreign relations."[145]

In the wake of his reelection, Eisenhower summed up the role that Lodge had played during his term in a letter of December 28, 1956. "Particularly in these last months of international crises and great strain, it has been a source of tremendous satisfaction to me to know that you were so ably representing us in the council of nations," the president wrote. "I truly cannot adequately express the proper measure of my gratitude for your tireless and dedicated efforts."[146]

# 9 · The UN (1957–1960)

By the start of Dwight Eisenhower's second term, Henry Cabot Lodge Jr. had settled into his role at the UN. The General Assembly had grown to seventy-three members, making it more difficult for the United States to achieve an automatic majority. The new idea of universal human rights, recognized in international law, was taking hold, but John Foster Dulles had no expertise in the area and Lodge argued that the UN was better off focusing on its traditional roles of maintaining peace and security.[1] "There is an interesting contrast in the Ambassador's techniques," one Lodge aide recalled. "On the one hand he does a very mature, subtle, diplomatic job of negotiating and has held the support of more than two-thirds of the UN members by a course of moderation; on the other hand, he's a polished, literate, saloon-fighter . . . he knows the tricks when no holds are barred." His deputy, Jerry Wadsworth, went further: "Cabot has developed a far greater warmth and humanness than he had at the beginning, and is sympathetic to other views and suggestions. He is far more of a disciplined diplomat. He can be terrifically charming when he wants to be, and he is far more willing to be than when he started out. He has an appreciation of the job itself, aware that he can do the world a lot of good or harm. He has grown tremendously."[2]

The job at the UN was unpredictable. On July 14, 1958, Lodge was behind the wheel of his thirty-nine-foot fishing boat, *Horse Conch,* off Porpoise Bay, Maine, enjoying an afternoon cruise with Emily and their two nieces when the ship's radio started to crackle. A military coup in Iraq had resulted in the murder of King Faisal II and Premier Nuri al-Said at the hands of Nasser-inspired followers of General Abd al-Karim Qasim, who had become disillusioned with Faisal's pro-Western government.[3] It was a significant setback in the U.S. effort to reorient Iraq on the American side of the Cold War balance sheet. As Lodge made his way to the UN, Wadsworth called an emergency meeting of the Security Council for the next morning, and after he picked Lodge up at the airport, they strategized all night.[4]

Both the United States and the Soviet Union had increased their activity in the Middle East following the Suez Crisis. The Soviet Union encouraged Gamal Abdel Nasser's aggression, which threatened neighboring Lebanon. Nasser's Radio Cairo called for the overthrow of President Camille Chamoun, a pro-West Christian, and Lebanon's border was being flooded with arms and terrorists from Syria. Eisenhower wanted to avoid another coup. The UN had been discussing the issue of Lebanon, and on May 22, Lebanon requested an emergency meeting of the Security Council to address Nasser's interference. A resolution was passed on June 10 authorizing observers to be sent to Lebanon to detect any territorial infiltration of arms or personnel.[5] John Foster Dulles called a meeting of his top staff, Lodge, Allen Dulles, and Francis Wilcox at his house on June 22. "If we used troops that would create widespread enmities, run the risk of bringing in the Russians, put ourselves in a weak position before world opinion, and turn certain countries in the Middle East over to Nasser," John Foster Dulles said, according to Lodge's notes of the meeting. "But if we did not use troops it could be even more serious as the losses would be even greater and the world would have lost confidence in us . . . This may be another Munich in which those of us who believe in freedom and democracy should not hesitate to stand up," he added.[6]

Eisenhower had maintained the Sixth Fleet in the eastern Mediterranean, and when the coup in Iraq occurred, Chamoun asked him for American protection.[7] Within twenty-four hours, the U.S. Marines had secured Beirut's airport—"until the UN can act," Eisenhower said.[8] Lodge was in a tough spot. During the Suez Crisis, the United States had criticized Britain and France for taking unilateral military action to deploy troops to the region, bypassing the UN. Now, the United States had taken unilateral military action to defend Lebanon, once again bypassing the UN. The fact that Chamoun had requested the protection was an important difference, but UN Secretary General Dag Hammarskjold was unhappy, and the American action was called "legally indefensible." Lodge was isolated and received little help from the White House yet was being criticized for not doing anything. The Soviet Union telegrammed Eisenhower four times, on July 19, 23, 28, and August 5, calling for action.[9] It was the only time during Lodge's tenure at the UN that he disagreed vehemently with the American position. "As President Eisenhower explained this morning our forces are not there to engage in hostilities of any kind—much less to fight a war," he told the Security Council. "Their presence is designed for the sole purpose of helping the government of Lebanon at its request in the effort to stabilize the situation . . . until such time as the UN can take the steps necessary to protect the independence and political integrity of Lebanon." Critics of American policy, including the *New York Times,* referred to it as "another Suez" and a scheme to restore a pro-Western regime in Iraq.[10] Arkady Sobolev did not let up, stating that Eisenhower's policy was similar to Adolf Hitler's. "Well, I must defer to Mr. Sobolov in the knowledge of Adolf Hitler," Lodge responded, "because his government was once an ally of Adolf Hitler when Mr. Molotov made a pact with Mr. Ribbentrop of unfragrant memory."[11]

Hammarskjold had been trying to transform the UN from a static conference to a more dynamic instrument with enhanced political powers, and when a nation like the United States went around it, Hammarskjold was undermined.[12] "We face a great, rough brutal fact," Lodge said. "The fact is the fomenting of civil strife by assassins in plain clothes instead of by soldiers in uniform. Make no mistake about it, my colleagues, history will hold us responsible. We cannot avoid an answer to the question: Is the United Nations to condone a subversion in plain clothes, controlled from outside a country? If the United Nations cannot deal with indirect aggression, the United Nations will break up."[13] Eisenhower delivered a speech at the UN on August 13 in which he proposed a broad plan for peace in the Middle East that included a three-part settlement: there would be no second term for Chamoun; General Fuad Chehab, a moderate nationalist, would become president; and the new president would agree to grant Chamoun amnesty. The only remaining issue was when U.S. forces would be withdrawn: "The U.S. troops would be totally withdrawn whenever this is requested by the duly constituted government of Lebanon or whenever, by action of the UN or otherwise, Lebanon is no longer exposed to the original dangers," Eisenhower said.[14] Nasser saw that the United States was prepared to use force, and peace was restored. "We should have no illusions about what kind of men they are," Lodge said about the Soviets after the crisis was over, learning from the experience of Hungary and Suez. "They are not soft. They are not stupid. They are not lazy. While their basic way of looking at the world must be described as malignantly irrational, they are very thorough and often clever in the methods they use to give effect to their fallacies . . . our greatest struggle is with ourselves rather than with the Soviet Union. We face the simple fact that enthusiasm for a bad idea can prevail over lack of enthusiasm for a good idea."[15]

Despite his words, Lodge struggled with Soviet attacks on the floor of the General Assembly. When he proposed nuclear disarmament, calling for an end to the production of nuclear weapons under strict international supervision, followed by a treaty to eliminate "all nuclear test explosions,"[16] the Soviets responded by criticizing Anglo-French "aggression" and then launched into an attack on Eisenhower's Middle East proposals.[17] "Five years here have convinced me that we must proceed on the theory that the Soviets are using disarmament for propaganda purposes without any sincere desire to reach a settlement on the problem itself—except on their terms," Lodge wrote to John Foster Dulles.[18] However, it was not only the Soviets he had to win over, but Britain and France as well. Eisenhower feared that unless the United States proposed greater help in developing those countries' nuclear arsenals, they were unlikely to support the American proposal. Expanding bilateral cooperation would not be easy either, since it would require a congressional amendment to the Atomic Energy Act. The General Assembly rejected the test ban treaty twenty-four to thirty-four, with thirty abstentions. "No matter how many votes we are able to cajole in support of our position, we have a position which fundamentally lacks appeal," Lodge said to Dulles.[19]

To improve Lodge's national visibility, Eisenhower chose him to escort Soviet leader Nikita Khrushchev on a highly public tour of the United States from September 15 to 27, 1959. Lodge had proved his ability to strongly rebuke the Soviet Union in public forums at the UN, while still being amiable in private. That was just the balancing act needed to host Khrushchev, who was America's least likely tourist. Eisenhower counted on Lodge to show the Soviet leader the country and effectively counter Khrushchev's propaganda with a little of his own.[20] When the Soviet leader arrived in Washington, he arrived on a Russian TU-114 turboprop, reputed to be the largest aircraft in the world.[21] "Who would have guessed, twenty years ago, that the powerful capitalist country would invite a communist to visit?" Khrushchev said.[22] When Lodge introduced himself, it was obvious Khrushchev had done his homework. "Before coming over here, I read your speeches. And after I read them, I thought I would be scared of you, but now that I have been with you, talked with you, and seen what a nice man you are, I don't feel scared anymore," the Soviet leader said.[23] "Mr. Lodge, I want you to understand one thing," Khrushchev said. "I have not come to the United States to learn anything about America. We know all we need to know about America and we learn it through our Marxist instructions." Hosting Khrushchev was unlike anything Lodge had done before in his career. "Our Soviet visitor was obviously a diplomat, a politician, and a polite guest, with a marked sense of the ridiculous," he said.[24]

Lodge found ways of charming Khrushchev, who was seemingly uncharmable. "When things went right, he showed pleasure," Eisenhower wrote in his memoirs, and "when he was displeased or heckled, he displayed a scowling, enraged countenance."[25] Khrushchev and Lodge seemed to settle in with each other quickly. In the Soviet Union, ambassadors were often mere messenger boys. The fact that Lodge was also the president's personal representative was a substantive difference for Khrushchev. He described his American host as "radiating strength and good health; he had been an officer during the war and held the rank of major general (the equivalent of that rank in the Soviet Union)."[26] The Soviet leader admired Lodge's wartime service, but was quick to inform his American host that he had outranked him during World War II. "Therefore you're my subordinate and I'll expect you to behave as befits a junior officer," he said. Lodge took it in stride. "General Lodge reporting for duty, sir!" he said. Khrushchev and his entourage, which included Mikhail Menshikov, Foreign Minister Andrei Gromyko, and translator Oleg Troyanovsky, could hardly contain a smile at Lodge's antics. However, Lodge was consistently frustrated with Khrushchev's bodyguards, who kept shoving him out of the way of the Soviet leader.[27]

Their itinerary did not get off to a flying start. Khrushchev revealed that he was afraid of helicopters, despite assurances by Eisenhower that it was safe to fly in them. "Oh, if you're going to be in the same helicopter, of course I will go," Khrushchev said.[28] Traveling was made more difficult by the fact that four hundred reporters trailed them everywhere they went. One of the first stops on the itinerary was a visit to the U.S. Agricultural Research Center, located in Beltsville, Maryland. The visit would give Khrushchev an early opportunity to compare American and Soviet agricultural techniques.[29] Secretary of Agriculture Ezra Benson told his guest that "capitalism has enabled American farmers to develop an agriculture unequaled anywhere in the world in total efficiency, productivity, and prosperity."[30] Khrushchev responded, "If you don't give a turkey a passport you couldn't tell the difference between a communist and a capitalist turkey."[31]

"He was a good listener and gave the impression of being a man with an open mind, but on certain subjects only," Lodge said of Khrushchev. He showed a Western politician's shrewdness with the press, choosing which questions to answer, which to dodge, and which to bull through.[32] During a visit to the

National Press Club, he called the press "comrades" and explained why he thought capitalism was doomed based on the "scientific proof" of Marx, Engels, and Lenin. They loved his unique allegories to illustrate differences between political systems. For example, Khrushchev spoke of the different way that people of different nations drank. "The French are used to drinking wine. When they drink whisky, they say, 'it burns.' When the English drink it, they say, 'we'll have a go at that.' When a Russian drinks it in a highball, he gulps it down and says, 'they've just invented it, and already they are diluting it.'"[33]

Lodge took Khrushchev to an "afternoon tea" with the Senate Foreign Relations Committee, where Chairman William Fulbright of Arkansas had both tea and cocktails ready for members and his visitor. Fulbright did not shy away from needling Khrushchev, asking whether he was willing to accept the peaceful triumph of capitalism over communism. The Soviet leader responded that he would be the first to favor capitalism if it proved more able than communism, but that he would not want to choose between Republicans and Democrats. "I don't think there's much difference," he said.[34] "I feel that I have known practically all of you a long time but, until now, you have been sort of ethereal beings to me." Khrushchev's remarks suggested an awareness of Congress and the specific role of the committee in the making of American foreign policy. And after extolling Abraham Lincoln as one of humanity's great progressive leaders, he said that the progress of communism over capitalism must have "disappointed" the members of the committee. "Who of us has not been disappointed sometimes in life as when a daughter was born instead of a son?" Such crude sexism was shocking. Khrushchev complained about "appropriations by the Congress of funds for subversive activities" against the USSR. Senator Richard Russell, chair of the Senate Committee on Armed Services, responded, "I know of no appropriations anywhere for subversive work in Russia." While the senators each received Khrushchev's customary finger wagging, the session was light and good-natured.[35] Khrushchev's visit to Capitol Hill enabled him to be more than the caricature that American media had made him out to be.

At times, the itinerary was too much for Khrushchev. Commenting to an associate about Lodge, he said, "He is making me suffer through this program that we have. But at the same time, *he* is suffering, too. That certainly makes my sufferings easier." Khrushchev thought he was being tested, too. "I realize that you were prompted in inviting me by the desire to see what sort of man this Khrushchev is—to see what he's like. Well, here I am!" he said, spreading his arms in a sort of "ta da!" Khrushchev had plenty of opportunities to compare the American and Soviet systems, but he did not always think what he was seeing on his visits reflected the reality for most Americans. "To characterize our attitude toward each other's system, I think the most apt saying is the Russian proverb 'each duck praises its own swamp.' Thus, you praise your capitalist swamp," he said. "I wouldn't want to say that we are praising our socialist swamp because I can't call socialism a swamp, but . . . ," he trailed off.[36]

At the Waldorf Astoria in New York, where Khrushchev was given the palatial presidential suite on the thirty-fifth floor, at a cost of $150 per night, billed to the State Department, the elevator got stuck between the thirty-third and thirty-fourth floors. Khrushchev, Lodge, interpreter Alex Akalovsky, the hotel manager, Soviet security officer General Nicolai Zukharov, and the elevator operator ended up having to crawl out. "This is the famous American technology," Khrushchev commented. Lodge, who helped push Khrushchev's large rear end up and out of the elevator, tried to see humor in the situation. "It's history. You can tell it to your grandchildren," he told the elevator operator.[37] The remainder of Khrushchev's visit to New York hardly went better. At a rough reception following a speech he gave for two thousand guests of the New York Economic Club, he said he brought his personal greetings to the "American toilers who create the wealth of society." Lodge used his introductory remarks to try to educate Khrushchev about capitalism. "If robber baron is the definition of capitalist, then we are not capitalists at all. In fact, on July 2, 1890, we declared war on monopoly capitalism when the Sherman Anti-Trust Act became law," he said. "There are, for example, 14 million Americans who own shares in American industry . . . Three out of four families own their own automobile. Three-fifths of all homes in America which are not on farms are owned by the families who occupy them . . . We have this system today because the rank and file approves it and because it has given them the highest standard of living in the world." Khrushchev broke in to contradict Lodge. "Only the grave can correct a hunchback," the Soviet leader snarled. "He who wants to have eggs must put up with the hen's cackle."[38] Lodge was not pleased.

Khrushchev demonstrated that he was a sophisticated politician. While he could be very curmudgeonly in public, he was much warmer in private. He privately referred to Lodge as "my capitalist." On the Boeing 707 heading to Los Angeles, Khrushchev toasted brandy to Lodge, admitting that, despite his protests, he was happy to be on an American jet aircraft that could fly across the country in five hours as opposed to a Soviet plane that would take eight.[39] After such toasts, which were frequent, Khrushchev turned his glass upside down and placed it on his head. Lodge reported later that it was "a symbol of our good relations." He remembered, "And, although it was hardly my usual routine, I survived rather pleasantly."[40] For a brief time, things were going well. "What I remember most about Los Angeles was how many flowers there were, how warm it was, and how high the humidity was," Khrushchev wrote later.[41] He was complimentary of American freeways, noting that the bumpy Soviet roads irritated his kidneys.[42]

Khrushchev had hoped to visit Disneyland, but Los Angeles Police Chief William Parker said he could not be responsible for their safety if they visited the park. The complex was too vast to protect against every possible risk. The crowd gathered there was considered hostile, and a tomato had been thrown at a local police officer checking the route. "A fresh one, I hope," Khrushchev said sarcastically.[43] He was deeply unhappy, not being accustomed to being told no.[44] To add insult to injury, Khrushchev was forced to sit through the musical *Can-Can*. "You and we have different notions of freedom," he complained to Lodge. "The girls who dance have to pull up their skirts and show their backsides, adapting to the taste of depraved people. Soviet people would scorn such a spectacle. Showing that sort of film is called freedom in this country. You seem to like the 'freedom' of looking at backsides. But we prefer the freedom to think, to exercise our mental faculties, the freedom of creative progress."[45]

Khrushchev encountered protesters during his visit to Los Angeles. "Death to Khrushchev, the Butcher of Hungary," one sign read, referring to the 1956 Hungarian crisis. Khrushchev demanded to know why the woman holding the sign was along the route of their itinerary. "Well, Mr. Chairman, this is a woman who does not agree with certain aspects of your foreign policy," Lodge explained. "If Eisenhower wanted to have me insulted, why did he invite me to come to the United States?" Khrushchev asked. "Do I understand that you think that President Eisenhower invited you to come to the United States and then arranged to have this woman stand on this street corner in Los Angeles so as to insult you?" Lodge asked. "In the Soviet Union, she wouldn't be there unless I had given the order," he said.[46] Khrushchev continued to boil until the tension came to a head at that evening's banquet at the Ambassador Hotel. While most public officials had avoided confrontation with Khrushchev, Los Angeles Mayor Norris Poulson pointed out the lack of personal freedom in the USSR.[47] It was the only time that Khrushchev was outwardly critical about his trip. Everything was going south, and in a hurry. "Clearly, the Khrushchev visit to America is becoming a horrible failure," Lodge thought.[48] Khrushchev continued to criticize his itinerary, the protesters, and his hosts. "I am the first head of either Russia or the Soviet Union to visit the United States. I can go. But I don't know when, if ever, another Soviet premier will visit your country," he said. Khrushchev believed that it was the public officials who were critical of him, not the American people. "Now Lodge, I want you to notice one thing. The plain people of America like me. It's just these bastards around Eisenhower that don't," he said.[49] Lodge managed to defuse the situation by apologizing for the mayor's remarks. He guaranteed that nothing like it would happen again. Eisenhower later wrote in his memoirs that at this event Khrushchev began to understand a free press and the fact that even the president could not control a mayor. "Now I begin to understand some of the problems of President Eisenhower," he said.[50]

Khrushchev enjoyed his visit to San Francisco much more. "You slaves of capitalism live well," the Soviet leader commented while touring the city.[51] The mayor and the chief of police showed him the hospitality he had not been shown in Los Angeles. "San Francisco made me happy with a display of solidarity from workers," Khrushchev wrote in his memoir.[52] After a welcome speech, he was greeted with a long ovation. "You see," he turned and said to Lodge, "the ordinary people of America like me!"[53] Lodge believed that what Khrushchev saw of the United States affected his whole outlook and made him realize the inadequacies of the standard Moscow line. He was repeatedly impressed by the standard of American roads, cars, factories, farms, housing projects, and drive-ins, as well as the fact that everywhere he went, members of the American public appeared healthy and well dressed. Lodge recalled, "I had the feeling that he looked at us quite differently on September 27 than he had on September 15." However, Khrushchev insisted that he'd learned nothing new about America.[54]

Khrushchev's visits with Eisenhower at the end of the trip represented the first true summit meeting between the United States and the Soviet Union since Harry Truman met Stalin at Potsdam in 1945.[55] Khrushchev agreed they could issue a joint communiqué stating that negotiations would be reopened on Berlin and that restrictions on Western rights of access to Berlin would be relaxed. Khrushchev's send-off from Andrews Air Force Base included a 125-foot red carpet, a fifty-six-piece army band, and a 75-mm howitzer to fire the twenty-one-gun salute. He thanked Lodge, "my capitalist," shook his hand, and invited him to visit him in Russia. "Thank you all," Khrushchev said, "from the bottom of my heart for your hospitality and, as we say in Russia, for your bread and salt."[56] Lodge reflected, "He has an amazingly quick, clear mind, a capacity for comprehension of human situations. He is a natural debater. He always takes the offensive and tries to put the other man on the defensive. He can carry on a tremendous bluff—like a poker player."[57]

Lodge's prestige continued to rise at the UN and across the country as a result of successfully hosting Khrushchev. "The UN Assembly meeting really seems to be getting somewhere," columnist Drew Pearson wrote. "Henry Cabot Lodge, I understand, deserves some of the credit though perhaps most of it goes to Dag Hammarskjold."[58] Plans for the Khrushchev trip had been made while John Foster Dulles was in the final months of his life. After he died on May 24, Lodge became the de facto secretary of state in everything but the title. According to Joseph Sisco, Dulles had convinced Eisenhower not to appoint Lodge as secretary of state. He did not want a flashy successor who could overshadow him. The title was given to Christian Herter, but Herter never had the authority over the department that Lodge did.[59] More and more, Lodge was consulted as a heavyweight on international affairs. He had traveled to Rome, Tehran, Kabul, Peshawar, Karachi, New Delhi, Paris, and London, and the CIA was eager to be briefed on his experiences.[60] They were particularly interested in India.[61] "India, because of its size and strategic position, is bound to be of increasing importance as time goes on," Lodge wrote.[62] "If we allow her to slip away from us, it will be a blow to our world position quite as serious as the loss of China."[63]

Lodge mainly went with the tide of self-determination, such as in the cases of Algeria, Cyprus, and South Africa. He regularly advised Eisenhower to "go much harder on the anti-colonial side than we are going . . . they can be made to like the United States without its costing us a nickel—merely a different policy position, a somewhat different line of talk."[64] He spoke in favor of human rights in Tibet and urged caution when Fidel Castro came to power in Cuba.[65] He condemned the massacre that killed thirty-four at Sharpeville in South Africa in March 1960, one of the rare times that the United States and the Soviet Union were in accord, even though Britain, France, and Italy expressed concerns about the UN's jurisdiction in the matter. The increasing number of postcolonial states in Africa and Asia demanded action following the massacre, in which white police officers had gunned down unarmed black demonstrators.[66] "The U.S. approaches this question with no false pride at all," Lodge told the Security Council. "We recognize that many countries, and the U.S. must be included in that list, cannot be content with the progress which they have made in the field of human rights . . . but we think there is an important distinction between situations where governments are actively promoting human rights and fundamental freedom for all without distinction as to race, sex, language or religion, and situations where government policy runs counter to this." The council passed a unanimous resolution condemning South Africa's apartheid regime and requested that Hammarskjold use his authority to compel South Africa to change its laws. The action was not as strong as the economic sanctions that some members wanted, which the UN had no authority to enforce, but, in Lodge's words, "it seeks to build a bridge and not a wall."[67]

Lodge's private correspondence with Eisenhower demonstrates that his words and actions at the UN helped racial relations at home, too. Following the events at Little Rock Central High School in 1957, Lodge recommended subtle shifts in U.S. foreign policy, including "that our diplomatic representatives make a sustained effort to extend hospitality to distinguished colored people." He noted, "This should not be confined merely to US diplomats in colored countries or posts like mine here [at the UN], where I entertain nonwhites regularly. In 'white' countries distinguished colored people who may be visiting should be given hospitality. I know from experience here how much it means."[68] Lodge was limited in his ability to have authority on the issue given race relations in the United States, which he thought could only be overcome through personal diplomacy.[69] "Ever since I have been here [at the UN] US policy has been negative. This has hurt us," he argued. Lodge did what he could, helped by like-minded advisers such as Mason Sears and Maxwell Rabb. Lodge successfully lobbied John Foster Dulles to ensure that at any official July Fourth celebrations held by the United States in South Africa, a typical practice for American embassies and consulates abroad, Americans disregard official South African policy "so that we cannot be accused of excluding Negroes from this celebration."[70]

Early in 1960, Lodge visited the new nation of Cameroon in Africa, attended President William Tubman's inauguration in Liberia, and traveled to Dakar in Senegal. In February, he was reunited with Khrushchev, who had invited him and Emily to visit the Soviet Union. It was a personal trip, as they did not travel as official guests of the government. "Lodge asked to be received by me, and we met as old friends," Khrushchev wrote in his memoirs.[71] The fifteen-day trip included stops in Baku, Tashkent, and Samarkand, in addition to Moscow. Lodge had time for extended conversations with Khrushchev, and they reminisced about the latter's trip to the United States. The Soviet leader spoke about his American tour in glowing terms. During the intermission at Tchai-kovsky's *Swan Lake* ballet at the Bolshoi Theater, Khrushchev warmly feted the Lodges with caviar, champagne, and Ukrainian wines.

Lodge submitted a full report to Eisenhower upon his return. He said the Soviets no longer seemed as eager for a summit due to the recent criticism from China that they were "selling out" their revolutionary principles in or-der to make some accommodation with the United States. Lodge's trip was an informal advance mission to see whether Eisenhower might be able to make a trip to the USSR in the way that Khrushchev had visited the United States.[72] "I have just about come to the conclusion that Mr. Khrushchev withdrew his invitation to you because he was terrified at the thought of the welcome which you would have received," Lodge reported. "There are many little things which happened to me on [the] trip with Khrushchev and my trip to Russia in Feb-ruary that make me think this."[73]

Following the failure of Eisenhower's "Open Skies" inspection program, the United States invested more heavily in surreptitious surveillance designed to intercept information related to ballistic missile development. U-2 reconnais-sance planes flew at high altitude (seventy thousand feet) and high speed (five hundred miles per hour) and flirted with a weaving border while they captured their imagery. In May 1960, the Soviets shot down a U-2 plane near Sverd-lovsk and captured the pilot, Francis Gary Powers, who was a CIA employee. The White House fumbled in its explanation of the event, which added to the crisis. First, they said the U-2 was a "weather plane" that strayed off course. Then Eisenhower admitted that he personally ordered the spy mission and took responsibility for it.[74] Soviet Foreign Minister Andrei Gromyko said it was evi-dence of American duplicity and demanded that the UN condemn such flights as a threat to peace. Gromyko canceled a planned Paris summit and cooled further American talk on improving relations.[75] Lodge had no clear way to counterattack since it was hard to deny that the United States had been the aggressor. He needed to do something to regain the offensive.

Lodge sent his security advisor, Richard Petersen, to Washington to pick up a large, wood-carved eagle, a replica of the Great Seal of the United States, which Secretary of State Herter had agreed to loan Lodge.[76] It had been a gift to U.S. Ambassador Averell Harriman years before from Soviet schoolchildren and had adorned the ambassador's office in Moscow.[77] On May 26, 1960, with his secret package next to him, Lodge decided not to deal with the U-2 issue head on. "A very few minutes convinced me that it would not be wise or suc-cessful to attempt a legal argument," he recalled. Lodge rejected Soviet claims of American aggression by emphasizing that the Soviet Union "has repeatedly used force in its relations with other sovereign states" and stated that he had concrete evidence of Soviet espionage. He then unwrapped the eagle and showed how the Great Seal was hollowed out in the middle. Flipping it over, he pointed out a hidden microphone sensitive enough to have captured conversations for Soviet eavesdroppers in the ambassador's office for years. "It is quite a beautiful piece of carving. And you will note how it opens up into two pieces. Here is the clandestine listening device. You see the antenna and the aerial and it was right under the beak of the eagle," Lodge said. "I might add that in recent years the U.S. has found within its embassies, mission and residences in the Soviet Union and the satellite countries well over a hundred technical clandestine listening devices." Lodge's presentation caused a ripple of laughter throughout the Security Council. "The uproar was gratifying," Lodge recalled. "Even the Russians could not help but smile." Sobolev, the Soviet UN ambassador, who was usually stoic, said, "The next time we put one of those Soviet-American friendship plaques in the ambassador's office, we will put the microphone under the eagle's tail."[78] Following the episode, Lodge received 531 favorable letters and telegrams and just 8 unfavorable ones.[79]

The crisis ended with a resolution calling on the United States and the Soviet Union to continue discussions to resolve outstanding issues between the two powers. However, the incident cast doubt on American intelligence capabilities. The White House response had created a difficult situation for Lodge at the UN. Eisenhower was careful not to criticize in public, but Lodge's brother, John, said that the CIA was to blame and that Allen Dulles should be fired. Eisenhower never went that far, but he privately revealed to Lodge that "the administration and training of some of our intelligence units were weak" and suggested that Lodge might want to "hint" at the UN that the United States already had better "methods" than the U-2.

The newly independent states in Africa created a variety of challenges for American policy. Lodge's strong civil rights record influenced his work, and whether taking a stand against white supremacy in South Africa or helping newly independent states like Ghana form a delegation at the UN, Lodge believed the importance of these tasks extended beyond foreign policy. He believed that black American voters were watching.[80] However, when the Congolese army rebelled against Belgian forces on July 6, 1960, it came at a particularly bad time for the United States. Herter was still getting up to speed, and Lodge was about to be nominated as the Republican vice-presidential candidate.[81] The Congo asked for American assistance when

Belgium sent paratroopers to restore order—a violation of the treaty for Congolese independence—while the Soviets pledged assistance to Premier Patrice Lumumba and told the West, "Hands off the Congo!"[82]

Eisenhower had three options. The United States could ignore the request, which presumably would allow the Soviet Union to take advantage of the situation; the United States could take unilateral action, which might provoke a superpower conflict; or the United States could go to the UN and seek to obtain Belgian withdrawal.[83] Lumumba went before the UN Security Council to request UN peacekeepers. "Speed is essential," Lodge said. "The longer the present state of near anarchy continues, the heavier the toll of lives, the greater the prospect of hunger and epidemic, and the greater the difficulties in future economic development."[84] On July 13, Lodge led the charge at the Security Council for an eight-to-zero vote, with three abstentions, for the UN to provide military and technical support officials to the Congo.[85] To the Soviet demand that Belgium withdraw its troops within three days or face military intervention from the Soviets, Lodge responded with clever language stating that the United States "would do whatever may be necessary to prevent the intrusion of any military forces not requested by the United Nations."[86]

Belgium did not withdraw its forces, which led to a rare alliance of the United States, the Soviet Union, and African nations. Then, both Lumumba and Khrushchev demanded that the UN peacekeeping force leave the Congo, feeding growing suspicions about Lumumba's political orientation.[87] The UN force had been carefully drawn from twenty-nine nations, all under the UN flag, which intentionally excluded participation from the Soviet Union and the United States. Lodge doubted that the UN force could stay if the government of the Congo was determined to kick it out.[88] It became clearer later that a war of succession was going on in the Congo, and on September 14, Joseph Mobutu declared himself dictator. Eisenhower was convinced, however, that the Congolese people wanted the UN to remain, and he gave a September 22 speech at the General Assembly calling for increasing aid to Africa. As a result, the UN World Food Program was created on October 27. It was not endorsed by the Soviet Union. "What's the hurry?" the Soviets responded. "People have been hungry for a long time."[89] Lumumba was arrested by Mobutu's forces on December 2 and was assassinated the next month.[90]

While the Democrats were meeting to nominate Senators John F. Kennedy of Massachusetts and Lyndon Johnson of Texas to be the presidential and vice-presidential candidates, Lodge was on television in his final days on the job, addressing the UN regarding the downing of another American reconnaissance plane, an RB-47, which he said had been more than fifty miles from Soviet territory and turning away. Lodge argued that the RB-47 was forced by a Soviet fighter to land in Soviet territory, and when that plan did not succeed, it attacked the RB-47.[91] Unlike the previous U-2 affair, the RB-47 incident would play a role in the 1960 presidential election, a kind of Russian collusion, as, unbeknownst to Lodge or anyone else at the time, a Nixon request to return the captured American crew was denied at the height of the campaign. The Russian refusal was an intentional move to show favoritism toward the Kennedy campaign.

As the final months of Eisenhower's presidency played out, Lodge thought about his future and that of his political party. When Lodge left his post at the end of August, 80 percent of Americans expressed support for the UN, in large part because of Lodge and his effective use of the media to thwart the best efforts by the Soviet Union to discredit him. The frequently televised debates at the UN, especially during the U-2 affair and the crisis in the Congo, brought Lodge into millions of American homes.[92] He played a critical role in returning Republicans to the majority by convincing Eisenhower to run for the presidency in 1952, and Lodge believed the General, an internationalist, had saved the Republican Party from itself. However, despite Eisenhower's enormous popularity, he had no leadership to pass on. Eisenhower was an effective leader, an effective manager, and an effective commander in chief, but he did not embrace the roles of political leader and leader of a political party. He protected the New Deal, but put up with Joseph McCarthy longer than he should have, and he did little to steer the Republican Party for the long term.[93] Lodge was unclear what that meant for him. His time in the Senate, his wartime service, his contributions to the postwar international structure, and his eight years at the UN were a crescendo leading to some unknown destination.

# 10 • The 1960 Campaign

Henry Cabot Lodge Jr.'s work at the UN had earned him widespread appeal across the country, and he polled higher than John F. Kennedy, Lyndon Johnson, or even Richard Nixon. "Something changed, and for the better, when Mr. Lodge took his seat in the UN," the *Seattle Times* reported. "Until that time the sounds from the UN seemed largely anti-American . . . Then Mr. Lodge began to speak up with firmness and clarity, for the U.S. and the free world."[1] His efforts were rewarded with the Sylvanus Thayer Award on March 16, 1960, granted by the United States Military Academy to an outstanding non–West Point graduate whose accomplishments in the national interest exemplify personal devotion to the ideals contained in the West Point motto, "Duty, honor, country."[2]

The names Nixon and Lodge began to appear together more and more as the desired Republican ticket in 1960. Dwight Eisenhower had privately told his friends about his preference for a Nixon-Lodge ticket as early as the summer of 1958.[3] In a confidential memo to Nixon on January 13, 1960, he said Lodge should be at the top of the list of possible running mates.[4] According to Lodge's confidential journal, the first conversation that he and Nixon had about being running mates occurred on January 25. "Some have asked what the role of President Eisenhower had been in my becoming the nominee for Vice President. His role has been great," Lodge wrote.[5] "I stated that I did not wish to be Vice President, and that I wished he would count me out completely in any of his calculations on that score," Lodge said.[6] Nixon wanted to return a favor, given Lodge's role in getting him on Eisenhower's ticket in 1952, and he made another offer, but Lodge again said he was not interested. "I'm not seeking it," he said to Nixon. "I won't campaign for it. But if you need me, I'll take it. Don't commit yourself until you see whom the Democrats nominate."[7] On February 26, Lodge wrote his personal attorney and lifelong friend Charles Barnes, "For me to be the nominee for Vice President is not the best way to help Mr. Nixon or the Republican Party or the nation."[8] An aggressive lobbying campaign that could only have originated with Eisenhower was under way by March 1960 to convince Nixon that Lodge was "the perfect man and would [bring] prestige to the Republican Party."[9] Lodge and Nixon had additional conversations on March 9 and April 7. Lodge offered a continuity with Eisenhower that Nixon desired, and it would have been difficult to find someone to whom both Nixon and Eisenhower owed more. Lodge's unwillingness to campaign for the vice-presidential nomination was not due to a lack of gratitude. He had so little spare time given that he was bouncing from crisis to crisis at the UN, and the United States could not have an absentee ambassador in such a critical post.[10]

Nixon's challenge at the Chicago convention from July 25 to 28 was whether he could unite the Republican Party. He was, by definition, a compromise candidate in a political party that hoped to avoid another bruising, bloody primary like the one in 1952. The experience of national leadership as vice president caused Nixon to begin moving toward the center and away from the anticommunism for which he was famous during the Alger Hiss trial. Nixon learned to straddle the center but could shift right or left depending on the issue. He met with Nelson Rockefeller in New York in July to discuss the party platform. Rockefeller reminded him that he had no interest in being the candidate for vice president, even if Eisenhower asked him.[11] "My own opinion is that Nixon went to New York ... to secure Rockefeller's (and [Thomas] Dewey's) support and the quid pro quo was Lodge," prominent Republican Richard Kleindienst wrote.[12] Writing later, Nixon revealed, "Eisenhower had also urged me to select him."[13]

Nixon maneuvered behind the scenes at the convention to ensure there would be no fissure between the liberal and conservative wings. The 103-member platform committee passed a slightly diluted version of the platform that Nixon and Rockefeller had proposed—and it was even stronger in its support and recognition of the desegregation movement. "I believe it is essential that the Republican convention adopt a strong civil rights platform, an honest one, which just deals specifically and not in generalities with the problems and with the goals that we desire to reach in these fields," Nixon said.[14] The 12,485-word platform passed on a voice vote on July 27. Nixon was nominated on the first ballot, winning 1,321 of 1,331 votes.[15] That evening, Nixon assembled party leaders past and present in the Sheraton Room of the Black-stone Hotel. He announced that there were four candidates he was seriously considering for vice president: Lodge; Senator Thruston Morton of Kentucky, who was also national chairman; Robert Anderson, Eisenhower's treasury secretary and a former Democrat; and Representative Walter Judd of Minne-sota, a former missionary to China.[16]

Nixon maintained the appearance that it was an open contest.[17] "I have not made my choice and I will make it on the basis of the opinion expressed by you, my friends, who represent every section and every viewpoint in the Re-publican Party . . . I'm entirely free to make a decision here tonight," Nixon said. Judd took himself out of the running to support Lodge, as did Morton.[18] The four active Cabinet members lined up behind Lodge, including the De-partment of Commerce's Fred Mueller, the Department of Labor's James Mitchell, Postmaster General Arthur Summerfield, and the Department of the Interior's Fred Seaton. Midwesterners, including Illinois Governor William Stratton, liked Morton.[19] While conservatives preferred the "firepower" of Judd, they were willing to accept Lodge.[20] He was popular and had good name rec-ognition. "Not even the NAACP can be against his superb liberal record," said Eisenhower administration official E. Frederic Morrow, the first African Amer-ican to hold an executive position in the White House.[21] In fact, Lodge gave annually for years to the NAACP.[22] "The final decision was Lodge," Morrow said. "Nixon wanted him, and perhaps it would have been Lodge no matter what the majority voted."[23]

Nixon learned from Lodge's problems in 1952. He was from the moderate wing of the party, like Lodge, although not as liberal, but he also had strong anticommunist credentials that appealed to conservatives. Since he was a com-promise between the two wings of the party, he had greater freedom to choose a running mate who was more liberal. Lodge would secure the eastern intel-lectual wing of the party. "Lodge was more liberal than Dick," Nixon's brother Ed recalled, "but Dick thought he would balance the ticket with his broad na-tional appeal."[24] Judd offered to nominate Lodge. "He's very good in debate," he told Nixon. "I've watched him in action and he's a match for anyone." On top of that, Judd pointed out that Lodge could get votes from internationalists and independents, and the other three contenders could not.[25] Dewey said, "It all simmers down to this. If we want to send the delegates home happy, we ought to agree on Morton. And, let it be said, he would be a good vice presi-dent and one whale of a campaigner. But if we want to make the *people* happy, it should be Lodge. He would make a superb vice president, and he would put the emphasis on foreign policy, where it should be."[26] That was the final word. Nixon called Lodge at three o'clock in the morning to inform him that he would be the vice-presidential nominee. "Everybody in the group wants you," Nixon said. "Thank you very much," Lodge responded. "I'm very touched and I'll do the best I can."[27]

"Never having thought of myself presidentially or vice-presidentially, I tried to figure out why I had been chosen," Lodge recalled.[28] He later said he had been "pitchforked into a national campaign for vice president."[29] Lodge's patrician upbringing had instilled a sense of public duty. He was a good fit for Nixon's campaign theme of "positive, progressive conservativism."[30] Since he was currently the U.S. ambassador to the UN, he had to be relieved immediately of those duties. Lodge called in James Barco, his chief of staff, and gave him instructions. The Lodges left for Chicago, where he was greeted by hundreds of cheering Republicans. In a sign of unity, Robert A. Taft Jr. seconded Lodge's nomination, as did Gerald Ford. After the states cast their ballots, making Lodge's nomination official, the Lodges and the Nixons appeared together on the platform in the International Amphitheater as the band played "Yankee Doodle Dandy." Cheers erupted, strobe lights flashed, and they posed for an official photograph next to the presidential and vice-presidential seals.[31]

In his nominating speech, Judd said that Lodge was "tested and proved in the fires of today's world—and found completely worthy—and trustworthy."[32] Unlike Nixon, Lodge was confirmed unanimously.[33] In his seconding speech, Ford called Lodge "a true disciple" of fellow Michigander Arthur Vandenberg. "The American people can be assured that with Richard M. Nixon and Henry Cabot Lodge—giants of courage and foresight—as their leaders, the economic, military and ideological challenge of world communism will fade in the sun of a progressive, powerful, forward-looking America," he said.[34]

Lodge's acceptance speech, which he wrote himself, sought to unify the party and state the foreign policy strengths of the Republican ticket. "We could lose our country . . . all at once, by all-out nuclear war, or gradually by being isolated and nibbled to death," he said. "Of course, we are not going to lose our country. We are going to keep our country. More than that, we are going to advance, using the strengths and the talents which God gave us to build a world in which freedom will be secure; a world in which the rights of small nations will be respected; a world of open societies which practice tolerance and are truly devoted to the dignity of men . . . ultimately we will win the struggle on a spiritual basis—or victory will elude us . . . we have the most glorious purposes of any nation in history. Purposes which, as Lincoln said, give 'hope for the world and all future time.'"[35]

After the convention, the Lodges took a week's vacation at home in Beverly before he returned to work at the UN. He submitted his letter of resignation to Eisenhower on August 17. "I accept your resignation as the Representative of the United States to the United Nations and to the Security Council, effective, as you wish, September third," Eisenhower replied on August 19. "The deep regret I feel at contemplating your leaving your United Nations post is mitigated by the knowledge that you do so only to offer yourself to the nation in an elective post of high responsibility and opportunity for service. The country could ill afford in these times to lose the service of a man of your abilities."[36] On the evening of August 31, Lodge hosted a reception for 1,500 guests at the Waldorf Astoria, and he said a final round of farewells at the UN on the evening of Friday, September 2.[37]

Nixon and Lodge would face off in the national election against Democratic Massachusetts Senator John F. Kennedy and Texas Senator Lyndon Johnson. It was the first time that two current U.S. senators had run for the nation's two highest offices against two former U.S. senators.[38] People were crazy for Kennedy. "If he had come out for abortion, sodomy, and divorce, the crowd would still have voted for him," journalist Theodore White wrote.[39] Following his nomination, Kennedy characterized Nixon as someone who had "charity toward none and malice toward all."[40] It was the first warning that it would be a rough campaign. Kennedy was critical of the Eisenhower administration, and Nixon by inclusion, for being weak on defense. He falsely cited a "missile gap" with the Soviet Union as a way of arguing that the United States had fallen behind its Cold War foe in terms of military preparedness—resulting, he claimed, in the nation falling behind the USSR more generally as a world power at a time when many new nations were looking for direction.[41] The press had never heard a presidential candidate talk the way he did, such as when he said he would "fucking well take Ohio."[42]

Lodge matched up well against Johnson, a friend since Senate days, who had no strong following outside the South. Lodge was a national political figure who could out-debate any of the other three on the two tickets. Both Nixon and Kennedy made their running-mate selections by choosing someone older who would not be threatening. Clay Blair of the *Saturday Evening Post* wrote that Lodge was the most widely known vice-presidential candidate since Theodore Roosevelt in 1900.[43] The only people who did not praise Nixon's choice of Lodge were conservative Republicans.[44] Many hoped for a midwestern vice-presidential nominee, which they thought would bring better ideological balance to the ticket.[45] Former Brooklyn Dodgers star Jackie Robinson called Lodge a "distinguished statesman and diplomat for the vice-presidential nomination [who] is in sharp and refreshing relief to the shoddy political deal which resulted in the designation of Lyndon Johnson for the Democratic second spot." Robinson was especially upset when Kennedy invited Arkansas Governor Orval Faubus to sit on the dais during his convention acceptance speech, a reminder that Kennedy had voted against sections of the Civil Rights Act of 1957, the same year Faubus had called out to the National Guard to "preserve peace and good order" and keep black students from entering Little Rock Central High School.[46] Johnson had reached Senate leadership with an almost 100 percent voting record against civil rights.[47]

Lodge kicked off his campaign on September 3, when the Lodges met New York Governor Nelson Rockefeller for the first stop in upstate New York. He had not campaigned for himself in eight years. In the Catskills, he ate lox and kosher egg rolls at Grossinger's and shook hands with 400 guests. From there, he went to Monticello and the 2,600 guests who awaited him at the Concord resort. He spoke on a street corner in South Fallsburg, at the Flagler resort, and made an appearance with Rockefeller at the Nevele.[48] Despite later accusations that Lodge was not a strong campaigner, he only missed one campaign appearance. He did not even make his own schedules; the Nixon side of the campaign did. Nixon himself directed that Lodge was to campaign in large metropolitan areas near seaports—Boston, Philadelphia, New York, and so on—where his speeches on international affairs would be popular. "I would be delighted to approve schedules on a weekly basis if I ever obtained one but to date I have had only the haziest notion of what was expected of me, and with no specific times set forth," Lodge wrote Nixon campaign manager Leonard Hall. "I will do all I can for the campaign but I live from one 24-hour period to another and from long political experience I know I can't do my best without a sensible day-by-day schedule."[49]

Lodge did his best to work from the schedules that were given to him. "I come to you tonight after eight years at the UN where I spoke for all the nation—north and south, east and west, regardless of party," Lodge would often start his campaign speeches. It was a unifying technique that usually drew prolonged applause. Tom Wicker of the *New York Times* covered much of Lodge's campaign. "Mr. Lodge brings a ready-made personality—a fully-created image—to the voters," he wrote. "Through the medium of TV, which has brought into the pine-paneled game rooms his frequent rhetorical jousts

with the Soviet representatives to the UN, the handsome Bostonian has become something like the all-American boy defending American virtue and cas-
tigating communist evil." Wicker, who also covered Johnson's vice-presidential
campaign for the Democrats, considered the contrast between Lodge and Johnson. "Mr. Lodge also seemed to possess another Eisenhower-style asset: a
considerable appeal to women . . . He shared the platform in Los Angeles with
movie star Ronald Reagan and a breathless blond was heard to murmur, 'Aren't
they divine?'"[50] Lodge understood that physical health and a good appearance
were more important in politics and diplomacy than intellectual ability.[51] As
another journalist put it, "In Henry Cabot Lodge the American people have
a hero so exactly tailored to their dreams that no script could have improved
on him."[52]

Lodge laid down just two rules for his staff to follow in preparing him for
public appearances. "No. 1) I must make sense in my speeches. No. 2) I must
be good-humored. If I'm irascible, I might as well stay home. I hope I don't
talk claptrap. The idea that the more you talk the more votes you get is fallacious. Being a politician is something like being an actor. You don't stay on
too long. In a campaign you've got to think it's worthwhile, and then you've
got to think it's fun, and then you've got to think it's funny," he said. Campaign Director Cammann Newberry had been Lodge's administrative assistant in the Senate, and Lodge's personal secretary, Francis McCarthy, had been
with him since 1932.[53] They worked hard and had a lot of energy, and Lodge's
staff saw a fun-loving side of him. After long days, they would unwind together.
On one occasion when Lodge was asked whether he would like a drink, he said,
"I could beat around the bush. I could give you an elaborate and circumlocu-
tory answer. But the short answer is 'yes.'" On another occasion, Lodge returned to his campaign plane to find one of his aides, Charles MacCarry,
sound asleep. "Here's a man who was really moved by my oratory," Lodge
cracked. "I'll award him the Order of the Silver Tongue." At one point, moments before the cameras started rolling for an interview, Lodge quipped, "I'm
a private citizen; I'm off the payroll trying to get back on. I'm not exactly private—at least I can't get any privacy—but I'm unemployed; just an angry
taxpayer."[54]

Lodge's most important campaign "aide" was Emily, who made many appearances at his side. "Mrs. Lodge is a woman of gentle manners," Neil Mc-
Neil of Time wrote. The Washington Post did an extensive profile of the four
leading ladies that year—Jacqueline Kennedy, Lady Bird Johnson, Pat Nixon,
and Emily. Mrs. Lodge was "the most fascinating character of the quartet. She

is the oldest, tallest, slimmest, vaguest, and the one with a built-in sense of humor," the profile concluded.[55] "Her face is open and candid, and her behavior on the stump, on the reception line, and in private is one of almost girlish enthusiasm, kept from mere silliness by her grace, her inherent sense of dignity, her quite obviously intellectual sensitivity. This woman has been a politician's wife for a third of a century and her mind and her manners are untouched and unaffected by even the suggestion of cynicism—a remarkable achievement."[56] The *Post* said that in addition to her intelligence and skill in dealing with people from all sorts of backgrounds, she was "the most unobtrusively sophisticated and stimulating of the four."[57] Emily was also Lodge's editor, critic, and sounding board. "She loves to tear Cabot's arguments to shreds, force him to strengthen them," McNeil continued. "She gets up in time, sees that Cabot is properly fed, getting to him a glass of milk and a sandwich when he runs short of food. She sees that he gets some rest, making him take naps when he has a half-hour break during the day."[58]

It was a tight race right from the start, especially in the coveted South. A Gallup poll at the end of September showed the Kennedy and Nixon campaigns tied at 46 percent in the South, with 8 percent undecided.[59] Nixon promised, should they be victorious in November, that he would put Lodge in charge of all nonmilitary aspects of the Cold War.[60] That was a significant assignment for a vice president, a position with few constitutional duties. It would not be too different from Lodge's approach to public relations at the UN. "My job will be getting quick decisions out of all the various agencies involved in foreign relations, so that we can seize the initiative and hold it at all times," he said.[61] He reinforced this message in variations of his stump speech, in which he made it clear that he and Nixon were running not against Kennedy but rather against Nikita Khrushchev. In Sacramento, Lodge was told the crowds were the biggest any Republican had ever received. He told Fred Seaton that many people wearing Kennedy buttons came up to him after his speech and said they were going to switch their vote from Kennedy to Nixon.[62]

Lodge's most critical moment in the campaign came on October 12 during a visit to Harlem. Lodge laid out a progressive vision of race relations in a Nixon-Lodge administration. He called for appointing blacks to the Cabinet and to various positions in the Foreign Service, including that of ambassador. He proposed to end segregation and discrimination in public schools, public eating places, and all public facilities. He pledged to seek new legislation that would guarantee the right to vote everywhere in the country.[63] It was the most expansive position ever taken by a major-party nominee, building on the Eisenhower proposal that had become the Civil Rights Act of 1957—the first civil rights legislation since Reconstruction. "That is our program," Lodge said. "It is offered as a pledge—and as a pledge that will be redeemed in January 1961, if you elect Richard Nixon president." A Republican administration, he said, would "erase the last vestiges of segregation."[64]

Lodge's statement accurately reflected his own views regarding race relations and civil rights. He did not clear the speech with Nixon, who was about to start a campaign swing to the South, where these points, especially regarding Cabinet appointments, would be troublesome. Lodge accused the *New York Times* of manipulating his pledge in its coverage of his speech—in his words, "hornswoggling" him—by making it appear that he was talking out of both sides of his mouth. In campaign appearances later that week in upstate New York, Lodge doubled down on the pledge rather than retreating from it. "There ought to be a Negro in the Cabinet," he said to reporters in Albany. "I'm for it before the election. I'll be for it after the election."[65] Nixon was desperate to make headway against the Democrats in the South, but such progress would be more difficult with Texan Lyndon Johnson as Kennedy's running mate. Nixon refused to endorse Lodge's views, saying that the number two man on the ticket was unable to promise anything.[66] "I will attempt to appoint the best man possible without regard to race, creed, or color," Nixon corrected.[67] That not only did damage with those in favor of what Lodge said but also looked weak to those who were against it.

The episode has been viewed almost universally as proof that Nixon and Lodge were mismatched on an ill-fated ticket. That is incorrect. A deeper look at the record suggests that even if he did not clear the text with Nixon, Lodge discussed the subject with him in advance.[68] It was Nixon who suggested to Lodge that Ralph Bunche replace him at the UN, a Cabinet-level position.[69] Bunche, who had a long-standing relationship with Lodge, was the kind of figure Nixon and Lodge could have used to improve the Republican image on race and civil rights. He was light-skinned, had a PhD from Harvard, and was an expert on French West Africa.[70] Ever since his trip to Ghana, Nixon had had "a very high regard for Bunche." Nixon said he would "certainly be given very serious consideration."[71]

In the heat of the campaign, Nixon overreacted. By focusing so much on the South, he missed opportunities in the six big states that could have elected him. Nixon had a good record on civil rights. As vice president, he had visited fifty-five countries, and 95 percent of them were nonwhite. He had chaired

Eisenhower's committee to ensure nondiscrimination in federal contract jobs, had criticized southern use of the filibuster in the Senate, and was a strong supporter of the Civil Rights Act of 1957.[72] "He was considerably more forthcoming about the civil rights of minorities than Eisenhower ever had been," Wicker wrote.[73] Like Lodge, Nixon understood the relationship between civil rights at home and American foreign policy. "It is awfully hard to preach the dignity of men abroad, and to have to explain the prejudices at home in the United States," he said.[74] While it was possible for individual politicians to maintain liberal records with regard to civil rights, each of the two major political parties consistently made politically expedient decisions that resulted in shallow national commitments to black equality.[75] Lodge encouraged Nixon to campaign more in northern cities with large black populations, such as Chicago and Philadelphia, where Lodge believed Kennedy and especially Johnson were weak.[76]

Lodge continued to feel strongly about the need for a black Cabinet member, even if his belief overstepped the official boundaries of the platform. He appointed Jewel Stratford Rogers as his special consultant on civil rights during his campaign.[77] Political polls at the time showed that Lodge's image and message resonated with voters. He visited the offices of the *Chicago Daily Defender,* something no other candidate would do. In Los Angeles, Lodge made himself available to speak to racial minority groups, but the local Nixon-Lodge headquarters claimed to be unaware of his interest and therefore unable to coordinate such visits. The *Defender* later accused the Nixon campaign of saying different things about race in different parts of the country. Any real momentum that Lodge had established for the campaign, based on credentials that both he and Nixon had on the issue of race relations, was lost in the face of political inconvenience. Nixon embraced Lodge as his running mate, but Nixon's campaign never fully embraced what Lodge stood for.

Not only was Lodge popular, but Gallup polls showed that he was more popular than Nixon or Kennedy—and far more popular than Johnson. Of those with an opinion about Lodge, 96 percent viewed him favorably.[78] Paul Hoffman wrote that Lodge's mere presence on the ticket added at least 6 percent to the combined ticket's potential vote. Lodge was especially popular with the estimated twenty million voters of foreign origin because of his stance against communism.[79] The Nixon campaign made so many demands for Lodge to speak that he felt he could not accept them all without risking that he would be tired and ineffective. He insisted on rest between morning and evening appearances.[80] This rest was often not sleep but simply a period to unwind. "But the two-hour nap in the middle of the afternoon is a myth," recalled Lodge press secretary Vincent O'Brien.[81]

Accusations that Lodge was a lazy candidate do not hold up when one looks at his campaign schedule.[82] "I never took a nap during the 1960 campaign," he wrote his brother, John. "These are all so called 'reasons' given by people who don't wish to state their real reasons. What they also don't tell you is that the vice-presidential candidate is always and inevitably a secondary figure. How could he be anything else?"[83] One loyal Lodge follower, Joseph Delehant, recalled being on hand for a rally at eleven o'clock at night in New Haven. Lodge's plane was late, but when he arrived, he was enthusiastic and shook approximately two hundred hands. Nixon campaign press secretary Herb Klein later downplayed the criticism. "Henry Cabot Lodge was a subject of controversy in internal debates within the Nixon staff—and [Spiro] Agnew was likewise [in 1968]. But then so was Nixon when he ran with Eisenhower," Klein reflected.[84] "I may seem ruthless and mean," Lodge said, "but dammit, I can't give it to these pros who want me to run myself ragged. I gave Eisenhower this advice in '52: 'There are just two things, stay in character and don't get tired.' I'm not going to stagger across the finishing line. I want to stay fresh and stay in character."[85]

At fifty-eight, Lodge was the most experienced of the candidates. He was sixteen years older than Kennedy, eleven years older than Nixon, and six years older than Johnson. "As far as physical energy for a campaign is concerned, I would point out that of the four who were running in 1960, I was the oldest and I was the only one who did not have a single sick day during the whole campaign," Lodge said. "The purpose of the campaign is not an endurance contest, but to try to make sense. People who talk about a campaign as an endurance contest do not realize what television has done to political campaigning."[86] Lodge had more experience with television than the other three. Wicker later reflected, "I think Lodge, in retrospect, looks better and better . . . I think Lodge felt probably under less pressure than any of those three."[87] Lodge was the only one who did not have anything to prove. He represented the generation in between the grandfatherly Eisenhower and the younger Nixon.[88]

Some Republicans criticized Lodge for not doing enough negative campaigning. "I won't attack the Democrats as such; I want and expect to get some of their votes," he responded. "I've never been narrowly partisan. Let them present their case, we ours, and let the voters decide."[89] Remembering how he was treated by James Michael Curley in 1936, Lodge said, "Never,

never during this campaign will I refer to Jack's age. I know just how he feels." Lodge covered more ground than in any of his previous campaigns. Some made an issue of Kennedy's Catholicism. Lodge shrugged it off, defending him. "I do not want anybody to vote for me on religious grounds," he said. "I refuse to accept the proposition that my three Catholic grandchildren are debarred from becoming president because of religion . . . even for a journalist to bring it up violates the spirit of the Constitution."[90] Instead, Lodge gently took aim at Kennedy's inexperience without mentioning him by name. "This is no time for on-the-job training in the presidency," Wicker remembered him saying.[91]

Lodge believed the thing that doomed the Republican campaign was Nixon's willingness to debate Kennedy.[92] Lodge understood this philosophically as well as practically. Debating Kennedy in 1952 had hurt his own Senate campaign. And just as Lodge had done in 1952, Nixon boosted Kennedy's status in 1960 by doing so.[93] By one account, Nixon already had 93 percent of the support of Republicans going into the first of the four debates scheduled. Where he needed to make inroads was with independents and Democrats, who were not likely to be won over with the kind of tough, partisan attacks a debate forum makes possible.[94] Lodge cautioned Nixon that these "debates" tended to be "competitive press conferences" as opposed to "real debate[s] hand to hand."[95] "You don't debate when you think you're ahead," he said. "Curley thought he was behind and wanted to debate. We obfuscated, stalled and diverted the reporters till the idea got lost."[96]

Before the first debate, Kennedy spent the day sunning, napping, and listening to Peggy Lee records. He declined makeup, using only some Max Factor Crème Puff to reduce the sheen on his tanned face.[97] Nixon followed suit, applying some Lazy Shave to minimize the effect of his five o'clock shadow, but it added a sheen to his pale complexion. "As a former actor," Lodge's brother, John, advised, "in my opinion a darker make-up might be helpful; perhaps grease paint rather than pancake make-up."[98] The advice was not followed. Nixon took exactly one telephone call before the debate, and it was from his television expert running mate.[99] "Erase the assassin image," Lodge advised.[100] Nixon decided he would play it low key and be "gentlemanly."[101] "Nixon worked in isolation on his opening statement, and generally he accepted counsel from Henry Cabot Lodge (by telephone) . . . the result was that he was apologetic and defensive from the opening second of the debate and not only disappointed his own followers but lost vast numbers of undecided voters who had expected to see a strong, statesmanlike, tough leader," Klein wrote.[102] Lodge cringed while watching the debate, which had a television audience of eighty million, the biggest since Nixon's 1952 Checkers speech. He thought Nixon agreed with Kennedy too much, which gave the appearance that Kennedy had the initiative.[103] "That son of a bitch has just cost us the election," Lodge said.[104] The first Gallup poll after the debate showed Kennedy up 49 to 46 percent, and on the question of who won the debate, 43 percent said Kennedy, 23 percent said Nixon, and 29 percent said it was a tie.[105] "The time has come for the Vice President to stop stressing his agreement with Kennedy on goals and their disagreement only on methods," John Davis Lodge said. Nixon defended himself. He believed the importance of the debates was blown out of proportion by the Kennedy side. "My recollection was that immediately after the first debate the headlines read 'Rated Even or Slight Edge Kennedy.' By the end of the week, the Kennedy partisans had blown this up into a decisive victory," he recalled.[106] "The newspapers, magazines and T.V. are giving us a thorough brainwashing on Kennedy," Lodge recalled.[107]

The Nixon-Lodge campaign was dealt another piece of bad luck, this time through no fault of their own. Nixon made a public call to Moscow to return Francis Gary Powers, the captured American U-2 pilot, as well as the two survivors of the RB-47 reconnaissance plane that had landed inside the Soviet border. Had Moscow agreed, it would have shown that Nixon could get results from the USSR, just as his campaign rhetoric promised. Khrushchev understood what Nixon was after and wanted none of it. "Father didn't intend to keep Powers in prison for very long," his son Sergei recalled. "'What use is he to us,' Khrushchev said. 'We just have to feed him. Let a little time pass and we'll release him.'" It was an intentional move to influence the election, a move that Khrushchev believed was worth half a million votes. "Father intended to wait for the new administration before resolving the matter of the RB-47 crew members, who were being held for violating Soviet borders. Of course, he didn't know who would win the election. If Kennedy were defeated, the pilots would be returned to Nixon. But after the election, not before."[108] Sergei Khrushchev later said his father made a mistake by not supporting Nixon. "He [Nixon] ended up being a pretty good politician."[109]

The Kennedy-Johnson side was handed another gift late in the campaign, again due to a gaffe by the Nixon side. On October 19, Martin Luther King Jr. was arrested after a sit-in at Rich's department store in Atlanta. He was transferred to a rural Georgia jail to serve a four-month sentence. Kennedy seized the political moment, calling Coretta Scott King to express his sympathy and pressuring local law enforcement officials to release him while Nixon initially

East Point in Nahant (ca. 1880), where Lodge spent much of his childhood.
Collection of the Massachusetts Historical Society

Lodge was his grandfather's namesake. Here, Senator Henry Cabot Lodge (1860–1924)
stands outside the U.S. Capitol in 1922. Library of Congress, Prints & Photographs
Division, photograph by Harris & Ewing, LC-H234-A-4034

The Lodges, ca. 1906. From left to right, sitting are Henry Cabot Lodge Jr., George Cabot Lodge, and John Davis Lodge. Standing are Helena Lodge and Mathilda Elizabeth Frelinghuysen Davis Lodge. Collection of the Massachusetts Historical Society

The Pool at East Point, where Lodge spent summers as a boy, ca. 1910–1915.
Collection of the Massachusetts Historical Society

Newlyweds Cabot and Emily on their six-month around-the-
world honeymoon, December 1928 to June 1929.
Collection of the Massachusetts Historical Society

Cabot and Emily during his first campaign for the Senate in 1936. He carried on a
family tradition of public service that began in the Washington administration.
Courtesy of the Boston Public Library, Leslie Jones Collection

Lodge on the stump during his 1942 campaign for the Senate.
Courtesy of the Boston Public Library, Leslie Jones Collection

Lodge was the first to resign a Senate seat for military service since the
Civil War. Here, he inspects a destroyed "baby" tank in Messina, Sicily, ca. 1943.
Courtesy of the Dwight D. Eisenhower Presidential Library

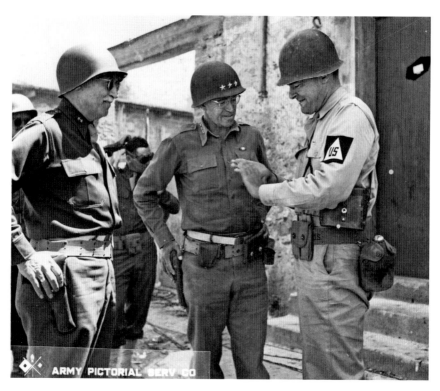

Lodge and General Omar Bradley at Brolo, Sicily, ca. 1943.
Due to his foreign-language ability, Lodge spent most of his war service
at the front as a liaison between American and French generals.
Courtesy of the Dwight D. Eisenhower Presidential Library

Lodge and Congressman John F. Kennedy during their 1952 Senate race.
Courtesy of the John F. Kennedy Presidential Library

Lodge with President-Elect Dwight Eisenhower and Joseph Dodge at the White House on November 18, 1952, following a transition meeting with President Harry Truman. Abbie Rowe, National Park Service. Harry S. Truman Presidential Library

Lodge, as permanent representative to the United Nations, was a full member of President Dwight Eisenhower's Cabinet, May 8, 1953. Courtesy of the Richard Nixon Presidential Library

Lodge served in a variety of roles for Dwight Eisenhower, including as one of his closest political advisers. Here, he conducts a briefing for the press on July 23, 1953. Courtesy of the Dwight D. Eisenhower Presidential Library

Lodge's role as the senior American at the UN—sometimes called the "little State Department"—could be lonely. Here he waits for the General Assembly Steering Committee to begin on September 20, 1957. Courtesy of the United Nations Photo Library

Lodge dramatically reveals a Soviet microphone used to spy on the U.S. ambassador in Moscow, May 26, 1960. Courtesy of the United Nations Photo Library

The Eisenhower-Lodge relationship was forged in the fire of World War II. He was one of the few who could talk to the General like a peer. Lodge was the leader of the Draft Eisenhower movement in 1952 and his campaign manager. Courtesy of the Richard Nixon Presidential Library

Lodge served as Vice President Richard Nixon's running mate in 1960.
Here they are at the Chicago convention on July 25.
Courtesy of the Richard Nixon Presidential Library

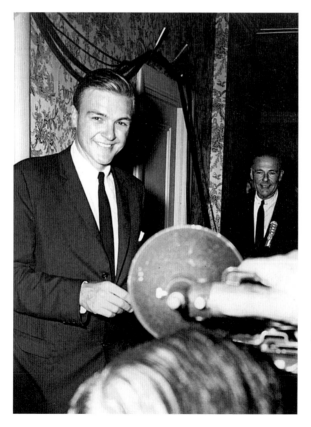

George Cabot Lodge was
a steady—and sometimes
covert—source of support
during numerous phases
of his father's career.
Courtesy of the
Richard Nixon
Presidential Library

Lodge was a leader of the moderate-to-liberal wing that dominated the
Republican Party for most of the twentieth century. Here he is in August 1960 with
fellow moderates Richard Nixon, Gerald and Betty Ford, and Dwight Eisenhower.
Courtesy of the Gerald R. Ford Presidential Library

President John F. Kennedy appointed Lodge to be the next U.S. ambassador in
Saigon at a critical time. Here, in his Oval Office farewell on August 15, 1963,
Lodge receives the instructions that would reshape the American commitment to
Vietnam. Courtesy of the John F. Kennedy Presidential Library

Lodge was en route to Washington when he learned of John F. Kennedy's assassination. Dwight Eisenhower encouraged him to resign and run for president in 1964, but Lodge believed his duty was to help new President Lyndon Johnson. Here, they meet on November 23, 1963, along with Dean Rusk, Robert McNamara, and George Ball. Courtesy of the LBJ Presidential Library, photo by Cecil Stoughton

Lodge served President Lyndon Johnson in a variety of capacities. Here, they have a quick huddle on July 13, 1965, just before Johnson's announcement that Lodge would return to Vietnam for a second tour as ambassador. Courtesy of the LBJ Presidential Library, photo by Yoichi Okamoto

President Lyndon Johnson honored Lodge for his exceptional career with a
VIP White House dinner on May 16, 1966. At the cocktail party preceding the dinner,
familiar faces include George Cabot Lodge, Dean Rusk, Robert McNamara, and
Vice President Hubert Humphrey. Courtesy of the LBJ Presidential Library,
photo by Yoichi Okamoto

Lodge spent more time in more capacities working on Vietnam than anyone else—
at the UN, in Saigon, as ambassador at large, as one of Lyndon Johnson's
Wise Men, and, later, as head of the American delegation to the Paris peace talks.
Courtesy of the LBJ Presidential Library, photo by Yoichi Okamoto

South Vietnam considered Lodge a close friend and staunch anticommunist ally. Here he is in 1966 with Nguyen Cao Ky and Nguyen Van Thieu. Courtesy of the LBJ Presidential Library, photo by Yoichi Okamoto

President Richard Nixon appointed Lodge to lead the American delegation at the Paris peace talks. Here, Nixon greets Lodge in Paris in February 1969. Courtesy of the Richard Nixon Presidential Library

In 1970, Richard Nixon appointed Lodge as personal representative of the president to the Vatican. In this role, Lodge, pictured here at the time of his appointment, paved the way for full diplomatic relations with the Holy See.
Courtesy of the Richard Nixon Presidential Library

Lodge's other duties during the Nixon years included leading a twenty-fifth anniversary commemoration of the UN. In addition, here he meets with Henry Kissinger and Charles Colson in June 1972 to support ratification of the Anti-Ballistic Missile Treaty.
Courtesy of the Richard Nixon Presidential Library

Lodge continued his duties at the Vatican through the Ford administration. Here, he introduces President Gerald Ford to Pope Paul VI on June 3, 1975.
Courtesy of the Gerald R. Ford Presidential Library

remained silent, saying he had "no comment."[110] Lodge sent eight wires to civil rights leaders and NAACP chapters to say, "I utterly deplore the treatment being given Reverend King . . . You can count on me to help in any practical way I can."[111] Each side's reaction was calculated. Kennedy improved his image with black voters, while Nixon appealed to southern whites who were eager to vote against a Catholic. Nixon, who had previously had good relationships with black leaders, saw his support crumble. Brooklyn Dodgers owner Branch Rickey intervened with Jackie Robinson to ensure the star's continuing support of the Nixon ticket following the King affair.[112] Robinson wanted Nixon to be more involved in the black community and campaign in Harlem himself as opposed to Lodge's being sent.[113]

Lodge's most substantial appearance of the campaign took place on October 20 at Vocation High School in Minneapolis. In a major speech broadcast live for thirty minutes on national television, he said, "Two thirds of the world lacks the food, the housing, the industrial sinews, the social and economic foundation, to take full part in the adventure of the 20th century. The people of the new nations demand a better life and they should have it. If they do not achieve it and achieve it quickly there is every prospect that the world will be plunged into further turmoil and instability, and inevitably impelled toward tragic tests of power between East and West, as the communists try to exploit the discontent of the rising peoples." Lodge called for bold initiatives, including proposals for international cooperation and humanitarian programs. More so than the other three candidates, Lodge also had the experience of working with the Soviet Union to back up his foreign policy proposals. "I have been with Chairman Khrushchev in this country and I have met him in the Soviet Union and I assure you that he is no clown. He is a man who must never be taken at face value."[114]

Khrushchev's name was invoked many times by Nixon and Lodge during the campaign. Four days before Election Day, in Rochester, New York, Nixon reminded voters that he and Lodge were the best qualified to protect Americans from international menaces. "I tell you I do know this: I do know that Cabot Lodge and I have been through the fire—the fire of decision. We have sat opposite Khrushchev and we have never been fooled by him and we never will."[115] It was a concerted effort to make the campaign about foreign policy, where they were viewed as strongest, as opposed to domestic policy, where the Democrats had the edge. "If you ever let them [the Democrats] campaign only on domestic issues, they'll beat us—our only hope is to keep it on foreign policy," Nixon said.[116]

Nixon and Lodge had the awkward challenge of running both for and against the Eisenhower record.[117] "I had a great advantage from being Vice President and being able to use the argument of experience," Nixon recalled, "but there was a corresponding disadvantage in being required in effect to stand for the status quo and not being able to advocate for 'bold new programs.'"[118] Nixon, who believed "the best way to keep religion out of the campaign was not to discuss it," later reflected that he probably missed an opportunity to win more Catholic votes. He won just 22 percent, lower than the 26 percent for Republican candidates in 1958. "I probably made a mistake in resisting the strong recommendations of virtually every one of my advisers two and a half weeks before the election that I should take the issue on frontally rather than to continue to ignore it," he wrote in 1961.[119] What also hurt the Nixon campaign was his stubborn promise to campaign in all fifty states, although Kennedy visited nearly as many. Nixon traveled sixty-five thousand miles and delivered 180 major speeches. By the time he visited Alaska late in the campaign, he was exhausted, having worked from dawn to midnight every day.[120] Nixon also micromanaged the campaign too much, a claim made later by his friend and national campaign director Robert Finch. "He went over his own speeches, rewrote them, nit-picked the schedule, scrutinized everything down to the ethnic appeals," Finch said.[121]

In fact, it was only after the election that history started to turn on Lodge. In 1961, supporters of Barry Goldwater levied accusations against him concerning his "weak campaigning."[122] Conservatives did not embrace the Nixon-Lodge campaign.[123] A July 1960 Young Republican National Federation poll showed 37 percent preferred Goldwater as the vice-presidential candidate, as opposed to 11 percent for Lodge, even while Lodge was more popular according to all the national polls.[124] Some of the criticism came from Republicans who never forgave Lodge for what he did to Taft in 1952. Others criticized him for being defeated once before by Kennedy, in the run for the Senate. Unpublished portions of Nixon's memoirs, written in the late 1970s, echo the revisionist perception that the Lodge selection was a mistake. Nixon blamed Lodge for promising a black member in the Cabinet, for not campaigning hard enough, and for canceling a Yonkers event because Lodge was tired. It was convenient to blame Lodge for the loss in 1960; he appeared to have no political future.[125] The charges contained in the drafts of Nixon's memoirs were largely removed before publication.[126] "I shall always be proud that you were my running mate in 1960," Nixon wrote to Lodge in late 1972, "and I shall always be grateful for the services you have rendered not only to the

Eisenhower Administration but to our Administration over the past four years."[127]

In his memoirs, Lodge strongly denied that he had been a weak campaigner in 1960. While "demonstrably untrue, undoubtedly some believed it," he said.[128] He never criticized Nixon or the campaign, leaving his private reflections on the "defects in [the] Nixon campaign" in his papers:

- no centralized study, strategy, planning + execution
- no adequate liaison bet. P. candidate + h.q. and VP candidate
- no stockpile of speech material—affirmative proposals for future
- no [illegible] work with negros + latinos
- no bracing up of weak state orgs: S.F., Pa.
- became trapped by South = see loss of N.J. by 20,000, Mich., N.Y.
- experience—[illegible] intelligence argument hard to tell; became impossible after TV "debates"[129]

Would Nixon have been victorious with a different running mate, as conservative critics later alleged? Few believed that at the time. If Eisenhower had more fully embraced his role as a political leader and a leader of a political party, two obvious weaknesses among many strengths, it might have made a difference.[130] Eisenhower's facetious comment that if he thought for a week, he might be able to think of something Nixon had done as vice president "burned Nixon up," Goldwater recalled. "He said he'd win his election without Ike's help." The Eisenhower quip "was *the* factor in his decision that he'd make it on his own," Goldwater was convinced.[131] Whether Lodge or Eisenhower, almost any target for blame would do to keep Republicans from admitting that Kennedy ran a strong campaign.[132]

The campaign concluded with a ticker-tape parade in New York from Wall Street to Macy's at Herald Square. With President Eisenhower and Governor Nelson Rockefeller in tow, Nixon and Lodge greeted a crowd estimated at a half million people.[133] It was too little, too late. Secret Service Agent Clint Hill was assigned to the Sheraton Park Hotel in Washington, where Eisenhower was expected to visit with Lodge just before giving a speech to supporters in the grand ballroom. Hill's orders were to protect Vice President Elect Lodge if Nixon and Lodge were declared the winners. "At some point after midnight, Mr. Lodge came out of the suite and said, 'agent, you might as well go home. We have lost the election,'" Hill wrote.[134]

Kennedy and Johnson won the election by 112,000 votes, less than 1 percent of the popular vote. Earl Mazo of the *New York Herald Tribune* launched an extensive investigation into allegations of voter fraud in Texas and Illinois, which were decisive states in the result. He discovered "ballot-box stuffing and jamming the Republican column on voting machines to misreading ballots cast for Republicans and double-counting these for Democrats."[135] "Typical was the result in precinct twenty-seven, Angelina County, when 86 individuals cast ballots and the officially reported vote was 148 for Kennedy-Johnson, 24 for Nixon-Lodge . . . a minimum of 100,000 votes officially tallied for the Kennedy-Johnson ticket simply were non-existent."[136] Kennedy and Johnson won Texas by 46,233.[137]

Lodge did not discuss the allegations of fraud until years later, after Johnson reappointed him for a second tour as ambassador to South Vietnam. "You've got a gentleman in the White House right now who has spent most of his life rigging elections," Lodge told Department of Defense consultant Daniel Ellsberg in Saigon. "I've spent most of my life rigging elections. I spent nine whole months rigging a Republican Convention to choose Ike as a candidate rather than Bob Taft . . . Nixon and I would have taken Chicago in 1960 if there had been an honest count. The Republican machine there was simply lazy; they didn't get out the vote, and they didn't have anyone watching the polls. But I don't blame Democrats for that. I blame the Republicans."[138]

After the election, Lodge wired Kennedy, "Sincere congratulations on your election as president of the United States. You have my very earnest and genuine good wishes for an administration filled with useful and valuable accomplishments for the American people. Now that the voters have spoken Americans should close ranks and present a united front before the world."[139] Eisenhower called it "the biggest defeat of my life."[140] He cabled Lodge, "I salute you for a magnificent campaign in the finest tradition of a great American family. I shall be forever grateful for your effective service to my administration and the country during these past eight years."[141] One of the warmest letters that Lodge received after the election was from his ticket mate. "Words, I find, are most inadequate to express my grateful appreciation for your service to the nation over these eight years and your tremendous contribution in the campaign of 1960," Nixon wrote. "As I said over and over again, as distinguished from the President-elect, I was always proud to appear with my running-mate in any state in the nation."[142]

And with that, Lodge was a private citizen for the first time in twenty-eight years and had no immediate plans for his future.

# PART IV
## THE KENNEDY YEARS

# 11 • Saigon

After the 1960 election, Henry Cabot Lodge Jr. was at a loss in terms of what to do next. "I'm too old to run for office, but too young to retire." He thought about returning to journalism as a commentator but worried that after such a long political career, he might be seen as someone with an ax to grind. His son George suggested, "Pa will go on active duty in the Army. We tease him about his 19th century concept of public service, but it's his whole life."[1] Instead, Lodge disappeared to Caneel Bay, St. John, in the U.S. Virgin Islands to think. His "chaotic and disorderly" career would continue one way or another, "resembling the journey of a drunken man on a blind horse," he reflected.[2]

Despite his personal conundrum, Lodge was highly sought after, given his international status. Nelson Rockefeller called Lodge on December 30 to tell him that the Rockefellers planned to recruit him.[3] James W. Barco, who had been Lodge's deputy at the UN, fielded inquiries on behalf of his former boss, including the offer from the Rockefeller Brothers Fund of the position of international chairman of the Institute of International Education.[4] Lodge took the part-time, volunteer position, in which he helped to launch a fund-raising campaign for educational exchanges with third-world nations. "International education puts the idealism of youth to work," Lodge said. "An organization like the Institute fills a need which government cannot fill because many students are wary of all government-sponsored education."[5]

Lodge's friend Henry Luce also invited him to join Time, Inc. as a consultant on international affairs. When Luce offered the position, Lodge did not know what to say. However, when the salary of $40,000 was mentioned, considerably more than he earned as a member of Dwight Eisenhower's Cabinet,

Emily broke the silence to speak for him: "Cabot says yes!"[6] "I had for many years been impressed by what I could see of Time, Inc., i.e. its published product," Lodge wrote, thanking Luce for the offer. "Now I am on the inside I am lost in admiration at its efficiency—and I am grateful."[7] He would be a general consultant to *Life, Time,* and *Fortune* magazines.[8] His duties included "lectures, speeches, and helping that enormously talented man, Henry Luce, with memoranda on public policy," Lodge wrote.[9]

In the same week that he accepted the Time position, Lodge was offered the opportunity to become the Atlantic Institute for International Affairs' first director general. As a result of the 1959 Atlantic Congress, several large American foundations had provided funding to start the organization.[10] Its purpose was to link the United States and Canada with Western Europe and Japan and promote relations between NATO member states as well as between NATO member states and the rest of the world. Its founders, as well as President John F. Kennedy and new Secretary of State Dean Rusk, encouraged Lodge to take the position.[11] Rusk told Lodge on April 8, 1961, that it was "an utterly vital organization" to which Lodge could provide "strong, experienced and imaginative leadership," according to Lodge's notes.[12] His only condition was that he did not want to be involved in fund-raising.[13] Rusk agreed, and Lodge took the job, heading off to Paris to help set up the institute's offices.[14] The chairman was Paul van Zeeland, former premier of Belgium, and the vice chairman was Lord Gladwyn Jebb of Britain, who had also served on the UN Security Council. Other members of the board of governors included Kurt Birrenbach, a member of the German Bundestag; Jacques Reuff, the former French finance minister; Paul-Henri Spaak of NATO; former Canadian Prime Minister Lester Pearson; Norway's Haakon Lie; Britain's Lord Franks; and former U.S. Secretary of State Christian Herter and former U.S. Undersecretary of State Will Clayton. Lodge chose Pierre Uri, who had been a protégé of Jean Monnet's, as staff director, and a research staff was formed under Marc Ullman, who was recruited from the European Coal and Steel Community.[15] The group quickly became a major center of debate regarding the future of European-American partnership. Lodge did not take a salary, and the Ford Foundation and contributions from a dozen European countries, among others on both sides of the Atlantic, helped get the Atlantic Institute off the ground financially.[16]

Lodge ran the organization like a think-tank, an "idea factory," as he called it, composed of some of the brightest thinkers from the Western nations, with the purpose of making recommendations to European nations and the United

States on how to improve transatlantic relations.[17] In a speech on November 14, 1962, Lodge proposed a kind of "super NATO," an organization not limited to discussions of defense issues, in order to enhance transatlantic cooperation. He shuttled back and forth between Beverly and Paris to direct these conferences. Many of the best ideas from them were published in *Partnership for Progress: A Program for Transatlantic Action,* edited by Uri, and to which Lodge contributed the preface.[18] Privately, Lodge said one of the primary purposes of the publication was to fill the gap created by the French veto of British membership in the Common Market.[19] Many of the ideas caught the notice of Kennedy, who planned to make a major summit tour of Europe during the summer of 1963.[20] Both Kennedy and Lodge insisted that an Atlantic community of shared values existed, even if these were never precisely defined.[21]

Ironically, it was a meeting with Kennedy about the book that was to change the course of Lodge's future. Lodge delivered a copy to Kennedy in the Oval Office on June 12, 1963.[22] When Lodge handed it to him and summarized a few of its key points, Kennedy listened with interest. But when he spoke, it was not about the book. "Cabot, I'd like to persuade you to go to Viet Nam," he said.[23] The situation there was serious, and it endangered American policy elsewhere in the region.[24] Kennedy emphasized that Lodge was the only American with the credentials for the job.[25] It was not a totally unexpected request.

During meetings about the Atlantic Institute, Rusk had brought up the problem of Vietnam more and more. In a conversation on October 12, 1961, he had indicated that the United States might need to introduce troops at some point in the near future.[26] Lodge told Rusk, "If events evolved in Vietnam so that young American military men were being fired at, then I would offer my services and would be very glad to do whatever I could."[27] Some of the army officers, noticing Lodge's interest during his U.S. Army Reserve duty in early 1963, asked whether he would be willing to go to Vietnam to study the situation firsthand. He was interested and asked whether he could do an actual tour of Vietnam.[28]

The Battle of Ap Bac, regarded as the first major combat victory of the Viet Cong, occurred on January 2, 1963.[29] There was controversy over the fact that Washington wrote it up as a success while the American reporters wrote it up as a "defeat" and an "extraordinary screw up" and said "it was all the fraud of the war tied up in one battle."[30] Two weeks later, on January 14, Lodge attended a retirement dinner at the Mayflower Hotel for General Lauris Norstad, the retiring commander of NATO. Kennedy, surprised to see Lodge there, asked him what he was doing in town.[31] Lodge explained that he had spent a couple of weeks of his reserve duty at the Pentagon. Kennedy had not been aware of Lodge's military service, and General Chester Clifton, Kennedy's military aide, told the president that "Lodge is as good a General as any of us." Four days later, Lodge was at the Pentagon for a briefing with Clifton.[32] "The president would like to know if you are available for an embassy," Clifton said. "Well," Lodge responded, "I'm not looking for a job. I have a job. But if something challenging and difficult arises where my experience could be useful, I'll be glad to accept."[33] Lodge heard nothing more about it until he saw Kennedy in the Oval Office five months later.

"This is the phrase he used, 'I'd like to persuade you to go to Vietnam,'" Lodge recalled. "'Well,' I said, 'Mr. President, you're not going to have any trouble persuading me because I have already made it clear to Secretary Rusk that I am available.' And that was how that happened."[34] Kennedy was moved by Lodge's energy and the fact that he put service to the nation ahead of his political career or a political party. One could speculate that Lodge was also motivated by personal ambition, but Vietnam was not viewed as a place to make one's career. Lodge wanted to discuss it with Emily first, however, and while it was considered the most difficult post in the entire Foreign Service, she was supportive. Lodge also spoke to Eisenhower, who had been concerned about the future of Indochina since before he ran for president.[35]

If the position Kennedy had offered were simply a political one, Lodge might have thought about it differently. "This is the toughest post in our service," Rusk said, according to Lodge's confidential journal. "We need an Ambassador out there who is tough; who can act as a catalyst; who will take responsibility and make decisions and not refer many detailed questions to Washington. We want to make the political side of things go as well as the military side has been going."[36] Lodge did not view it as a stepping-stone to higher office. "I am 61," Lodge said. "I will never run for elective office again. A Republican administration is too far away for me to hope for a high appointive office. I want you to know that if it will serve the United States, I am expendable. Just don't do it for unimportant reasons."[37] At that point, fewer than fifty American lives had been lost in Vietnam. A total of eleven thousand U.S. troops were in country as advisers to the South Vietnamese army.[38] Part of the reason why there were so few Vietnam experts in the government was that it was an appendage of the American embassy in Paris, and the Vietnam Desk at the State Department was largely staffed by French-speaking Foreign Service officers with experience in Europe.[39] The New York Times called Vietnam "a graveyard for the reputations of American diplomats" on June 28, 1963, long before the war started to look unwinnable. No doubt the Kennedy administration would have focused more closely on the problems if it had not spent so much time on others, such as Cuba. According to Rusk, by May 1963, Vietnam was taking more of Kennedy's time than any other issue.[40]

The White House was determined to avoid another Bay of Pigs disaster. Like his predecessor, Kennedy deemed Vietnam to be the future of Southeast Asia.[41] The Viet Cong had approximately five thousand guerillas who controlled a significant portion of the countryside. After a fact-finding mission in January 1961, General Maxwell Taylor and Deputy National Security Advisor Walt Rostow recommended sending as many as ten thousand American combat troops to Vietnam to prevent infiltration of the Ho Chi Minh Trail. "[Kennedy] was deathly afraid that it would get out that he had said no American troops, and that the opposition would say 'Kennedy's soft on communism,'" State Department Director of the Bureau of Intelligence and Research Roger Hilsman recalled. "He was willing to give them aid and advisors, but no American troops."[42] Policy in Vietnam was further damaged after the Kennedy administration accepted the neutralization of Laos, negotiated by Averell Harriman in 1962, a treaty that was "structurally flawed at several points," resulting "in its breakdown almost from the moment it was signed."[43] Both Thailand and South Vietnam were concerned about the thirty thousand to forty thousand North Vietnamese soldiers in Laos who might infiltrate neighboring nations.[44] "We provided in the declaration on Vietnam which they all signed, that no country could use the territory of Laos to move any troops into any other country," Harriman recalled. "The North Vietnamese never paid any attention to it, but it specifically provided that the Ho Chi Minh Trail, as it was later called, could not be used."[45] While the Viet Cong continued to use Laotian territory to plan attacks on South Vietnam, the United States agreed not to violate the borders.[46] However, American policymakers were aware of the extent to which the treaty was being violated by North Vietnam.[47] "If President Kennedy had insisted, even at the risk of some military action, that the Laos Accords be honored ... If we had been as tough in enforcing the agreement as we were in negotiating it, I think the tragedy in Southeast Asia would have ended then," Rostow said.[48]

Kennedy, like Lyndon Johnson after him, feared right-wing retaliation should things go badly in Vietnam. President Ngo Dinh Diem had considerable American support, especially from the anticommunist American Friends of Vietnam, whose past members included Mike Mansfield, Francis Cardinal

Spellman, and Tom Dooley. Yet when the group fell apart early in his administration, Kennedy was not as fearful of conservative retaliation.[49] He made key personnel changes that amplified the anti-Diem voices around him. Harriman, who had been nicknamed "Crocodile" by National Security Advisor McGeorge Bundy because of his short, snappy answers at presidential meetings, was promoted to undersecretary of state for political affairs on April 4.[50] Hilsman became assistant secretary of state for Far Eastern affairs on May 9. He might have been the first person to bring up the idea of regime change, and he did so repeatedly in conversations with fellow anti-Diemists Harriman and Michael Forrestal.[51] If these personnel shifts were the signal that a policy change with respect to Diem was in the making, Ambassador Frederick Nolting missed it. "No doubt I underestimated Harriman's influence, tenacity, and vindictiveness," Nolting wrote.[52]

In January 1963, Hilsman argued that Nolting needed to be replaced by a "single, strong executive"—a military figure or a civilian public figure who could dominate all aspects of the mission.[53] Lodge did not need the job, but the job found him. As someone with a political background, a military background, and skill in responding to communist rhetoric, Lodge felt it was his duty to help stop the spread of communism in Vietnam.[54] Kennedy saw politics, not the military, as the bigger problem in Saigon.[55] He wanted a strong ambassador who could handle the press, and an ability in French was a plus. "Dear Cabot," Kennedy wrote on June 18, "I am delighted that you are going to South Viet-Nam. This is a most important assignment and I know you will do an outstanding job."[56] Lodge was tough and competent and would help ensure that Kennedy could respond to facts, not the claims of the American journalists in Saigon.[57] "[David] Halberstam, [Neil] Sheehan, and [Malcolm] Browne just didn't report what was going on over there," Lodge's soon-to-be deputy said of the American newsmen in Saigon. "They influenced it in mark and measure. And they influenced Lodge's appointment."[58] Kennedy had sent over umpteen fact-finding delegations, only to have them return with conflicting information. Appointing Lodge was a way of appointing a kind of permanent fact finder. Kennedy trusted Lodge to stand in for him and be his personal ambassador. It was a savvy political move that helped remove mainstream Republican opposition to Kennedy's (and later Johnson's) growing attention to Southeast Asia.

Lodge's appointment drifted over the summer due to Kennedy's trip to Europe. It was also subject to approval by Lodge's former colleagues on the Senate Foreign Relations Committee. He was unanimously confirmed, even though some conservative Republicans were unhappy that he would take an appointment from the "enemy." He shrugged off the criticism. "Service in any situation—foreign or domestic—which acutely involves American security must always be considered from a totally unpartisan viewpoint, without regard to party politics, important though party politics are," he told Congresswoman Frances Bolton (R-OH). Nolting could not believe how quickly he had been re-placed. He returned to Washington in early June for consultations and ob-served, "Clearly, serious opposition had developed to what had been viewed as a successful policy in Vietnam."[59] Kennedy ordered Nolting to return to Sai-gon immediately, as a lame-duck ambassador, and he arrived on July 11.[60]

On August 14, Lodge had a full day of final briefings, including with Rusk, Harriman, and Secretary of Defense Robert McNamara. That evening, he had dinner at the South Vietnamese embassy with Ambassador Tran Van Chuong and his wife, Than Thi Nam Tran. Devout Buddhists, they had lived in Wash-ington since 1957. Lodge knew them well from his days at the UN. Their daughter was Tran Le Xuan, aka "Madame Nhu," who was married to Diem's brother, Ngo Dinh Nhu, and served as de facto first lady of Vietnam. Madame Nhu posed a special problem, not just for Diem or Kennedy but also for her soon-to-be estranged parents. Le Xuan translates to "beautiful spring" in En-glish, and she was known to be beautiful and sensual, but also decadent and dangerous. Some called her a dragon lady, which she dismissed. "I believe that when they call me like this it is just because they see that I looked fearless, and it is true," Madame Nhu said.[61] Her parents called her "power mad" and said they "did not wish to know her" anymore.[62] Lodge was shocked to hear Madame Tran Van Chuong say, "Unless they leave the country, there is no power on earth that can prevent the assassination of [President] Diem, of his brother Nhu, and of my daughter, Madame Nhu."[63]

Before Lodge even arrived in Saigon, the situation was serious. "I never be-lieved that the Vietnam war was basically a war against communism," Lodge said later. "It was not an ideological matter. The North wanted to conquer the South. I recognized the demand and need for revolution in both North and South Vietnam to rid the region of the old structures of colonialism and feu-dalism and to build new structures." While the tension had been building since Kennedy took office, Lodge felt the crisis really took hold beginning on May 8, 1963, with the Buddhist crisis in Hue.

Diem quietly had continued the 1950 French colonial Ordinance No. 10, which permitted Catholics to display religious banners, but the Buddhists were defined as members of an "association" rather than a religion, so on May 6, the government issued a ban on Buddhist flags.[64] However, Buddhist flags were already flying in Hue in preparation for the 2,527th birthday of the Buddha on May 8 at Tu Dam Pagoda, the center of Vietnamese Buddhist activity.[65] A parade of young people kicked off the festivities with banners containing various messages of religious freedom. That evening, a monk took a tape of a speech by Buddhist leader Thich Tri Quang to the government radio station, where it was to be broadcast on air as well as by loudspeaker. The director of the radio station refused to play the tape, claiming he had not had time to review its content.[66] Word of the incident spread, and angry crowds marched to the radio station to listen to monks make speeches critical of the Diem regime, the first time ever that such a gathering had been formed. A local security officer, Major Dang Sy, ordered soldiers to disperse the crowds. When that did not work, fire trucks were brought in and water hoses were turned on the crowd, to no great effect. The local government quickly assembled army detachments as well as members of the civil guard.[67] According to journalist Peter Arnett, there were two hand-grenade explosions. The crowd panicked, tear gas disoriented them, and some were trampled to death. Eleven Buddhists were killed, including several children, and dozens were injured. Buddhist leaders claimed that the troops fired on their peaceful protests, while the Diem government initially said that a Viet Cong terrorist threw a hand grenade into the crowd. Some of the dead were so badly battered that it looked as if they had been run over by an armored car.[68]

While relations between the minority government and the Buddhist majority had been fragile, the incident created unprecedented tension.[69] The Catholic Church in Vietnam, led by Apostolic Delegate Salvatore Asta, published a letter signed by all Vietnamese bishops, save for Diem's brother, the archbishop of Hue, expressing sympathy for the Buddhists. A pastoral letter on the subject of religious tolerance was issued by Paul Nguyen Van Binh, archbishop of Saigon, to all churches and chapels of the diocese to be read at all masses. These were extraordinary acts of official Catholic protest against the Diem government.[70] The Buddhists, led by Tri Quang, understood the power of the printed image, and they conducted a series of public hunger strikes that provided material for the Western press, which was already predisposed against the Diem government. That power was never stronger than on June 11, when seventy-three-year-old monk Thich Quang Duc sat down in the lotus position at the intersection of Le Van Duyet and Phan Dinh Phung streets near Xa Loi Pagoda and another monk doused him with gasoline and lit him on fire. "As he burned he never moved a muscle, never uttered a sound, his outward composure in sharp contrast to the wailing people around him," David Halberstam reflected.[71] Malcolm Browne of the Associated Press had received a tip about what was going to happen, and he took the famous photo of the Buddhist priest calmly burning to death. Monks and nuns gathered around him with banners that contained messages such as "A Buddhist Priest Burns for Buddhist Demands."[72] It was the first of seven suicides that would grip the nation's attention.

Critics later said that this assisted self-immolation occurred because Duc had been drugged, and they pointed out that the "monk" who poured gasoline on him later became a member of the post-1975 Vietnamese Communist Congress. Nevertheless, Duc's charred heart was placed in a jar and became a draw for pilgrims and protesters alike.[73] Diem said in a radio broadcast that he was grief stricken that a number of people "intoxicated by extremist propaganda" had caused an "undeserved death."[74] Madame Nhu went further, saying that the Buddhists had barbequed an intoxicated bonze with imported gasoline.[75] Kennedy was infuriated. "That goddamn bitch," he told his friend Paul "Red" Fay. "She's responsible . . . That bitch stuck her nose in and boiled up the whole situation down there."[76] Kennedy was stunned by the turn of events and felt pressured to act quickly. The Associated Press photo was displayed prominently on his desk during his meeting with Lodge the next day when he offered him the job as ambassador. It was ultimately one of the factors that caused the White House to turn against both the Diem regime and the American press in Saigon.[77]

As a result of the Buddhist crisis, some American reporters in Saigon no longer made even a pretense at objectivity. At the July 4 Independence Day party at Acting Ambassador William Trueheart's residence, Halberstam refused to take part in the traditional toast to Diem and announced in a loud voice, "I'd never drink to that son of a bitch."[78] The CIA's Lucien Conein recalled that during a conversation at the Caravelle bar that evening, General Tran Van Don had told him that there was "a plan afoot" among the generals to remove Nhu and possibly Diem.[79] It was stunning how quickly Americans in Saigon and Washington were eager to dump Diem, their longtime ally, in favor of the Caravellistes—so named because the insurgents often gathered at the hotel bar.

The White House considered three possible scenarios for the Diem regime. One involved the overthrow of the entire Ngo family, while another kept Diem in power while ridding him of the Nhus, and a third assumed that Nhu planned to overthrow Diem. There was a concern that Nhu secretly planned to broker a peace agreement with North Vietnam. Rufus Phillips recalled a meeting with

Secretary of Defense Nguyen Dinh Thuan on July 9, "friend to friend and off the record." Thuan told him that Diem was "completely a prisoner of his own family" and that "the Nhus, particularly Mrs. Nhu, have gone out of their minds." And of Diem, he said, "The president is going to let the family ruin him; nobody can do anything to prevent it."[80] When Phillips met with Diem ten days later, on July 19, Diem tried to reassure his old friend, saying, "I do not believe everything I am told and I have my own private sources of information."[81]

Journalist Joe Alsop warned Lodge that his sources said Diem was exploring the possibility of some kind of North-South rapprochement.[82] Diem had received a gift of a flowering cherry branch from Ho Chi Minh, which he displayed prominently in the Gia Long hall where diplomatic receptions were held.[83] It was "very ugly stuff," and Alsop published a version of his finding in the *Washington Post* on September 18, 1963, the only journalist to do so.[84] Alsop's source was none other than Nhu himself.[85] According to Alsop, Nhu said he had been engaging in secret negotiations with the North Vietnamese through French Ambassador Roger Lalouette, and Nhu expected to reach a settlement. Nhu, who bragged to Alsop that he was the world's greatest living guerilla expert, said he would bring Diem along on any agreement reached. Madame Nhu later confirmed that the talks were taking place, but she claimed it was the North that had first approached Nhu.[86]

"Nhu had gone stark, raving mad," Alsop said.[87] He believed that Kennedy had given Diem plenty of chances. "He increased the American military aid to Vietnam very greatly, as was urgently needed. And he replaced an ambassador who had led scores of breast-beating attacks on the Diem government with a friendly and helpful ambassador, Frederick Nolting, who was bitterly criticized by the breast-beaters in my trade precisely because he tried to be friendly and helpful to Diem and Nhu," he told Lodge. "I base my opinion that Ngo Dinh Nhu was very close to a madman at the end of his life on direct personal observation."[88]

Nhu said he would like to see half of the American military personnel stationed in Vietnam leave the country.[89] In hindsight, that might have been a better outcome for the United States. According to Polish diplomat Mieczyslaw Maneli, Nhu said, "I am not against negotiations and cooperation with the North; you know that suggestions have been presented to me by many western diplomats. Even during the most ferocious battle, the Vietnamese never forget who is a Vietnamese and who is a foreigner. If we could only begin a direct dialogue, a rapprochement could be reached."[90] Lodge found this very alarming. "We should consider a request to withdraw as a growing possibility," he said.[91]

Lodge's Oval Office farewell with Kennedy took place on August 15, 1963. Presidential farewells to new ambassadors are rarely substantive. They involve a handshake, a photograph, and a few words of encouragement. In his memoir, Lodge only very generally recalled the conversation. Kennedy told him that Nhu's practices of arbitrary imprisonment and torture, persecution of Buddhists, and use of other civil and oppressive measures must be stopped. He also said Lodge and Diem should explore the possibility of Nhu leaving the country for a period of time.[92] Lodge needed to get control over the CIA station in Saigon, which had responsibility for training Diem's special forces. Beyond those things, Lodge never spoke of the meeting in any detail—and certainly not in terms of Kennedy issuing any specific instructions to him. In 1991, the State Department stated that "no record of their discussion has been found."[93] However, Kennedy secretly recorded the conversation, and it is being published here for the first time.

"The time may come, though, we've gotta just have to try to do something about Diem, and I think that's going to be an awfully critical period," Kennedy told Lodge, a statement that was close to an authorization for a coup, although not quite an order. While remaining vague, Kennedy was obviously talking about Diem's removal. Becoming more specific, he added, "I don't know how well prepared you are for that out there, or who we would sort of support, or who we would—and—I think that's going to be the key—your key problem this year." Kennedy's concern was much more about Diem's replacement and having the whole thing wrapped up in 1963, before the start of the election year.[94]

Lodge warned Kennedy that should a coup take place, there was a strong likelihood that Diem and members of his family, in particular Nhu and Madame Nhu, would be assassinated. Lodge repeated this warning more than once, emphasizing that it was not possible to control a coup. Kennedy did not seem particularly concerned. "It may be that they ought to go, but it's just a question of how quickly that's done, and if you get the right fellow," he said. Kennedy gave his authorization, leaving Lodge with a caution: "Well, as I say, I think we have to leave it almost completely in your hands and your judgment. I don't know whether we'd be better off—whether the alternative [to Diem] would be better. Maybe it will be. If so, then we have to move in that direction." Lodge replied the only way that he could. "That's very helpful. That's very helpful," he said. "I'll certainly give it my very best."[95]

It was August 1963, six months before the start of the 1964 presidential primaries, less than a year from the Democratic and Republication conventions, and a little more than a year from the 1964 presidential election. The recording suggests that Kennedy was not in favor of making a wider commitment to Vietnam, but he was even more afraid of "losing" Vietnam, as Harry Truman had been blamed for losing China. Kennedy emphasized this point to Lodge. Their conversation gave Lodge a mandate—not an order for a coup, but an instruction to plan for its possibility, a green light to make contact with the Vietnamese generals and, if it seemed the coup plotters were sufficiently organized, to remain in contact with them and ensure their success. While Lodge has been criticized by some for being despotic, Kennedy chose him to take charge in Saigon.

Lodge and Kennedy downplayed the fact that the appointment was a policy change, but it obviously was. The diplomatic corps in Saigon understood, too, and it was a regular topic of conversation among them.[96] Lodge was to take charge of the U.S. mission, exert influence on the American press operating there, and present a tougher line to the Diem government. After reading the transcript of the Kennedy-Lodge conversation of August 15, Rufus Phillips, who is the last American to have known Diem and was opposed to a coup, commented, "I can see how Lodge interpreted it to be an authorization."[97]

Lodge suggested that Ed Lansdale, who had briefed him before he left for Vietnam, be adviser to Diem.[98] Lansdale had warned the Kennedy administration in 1961 that South Vietnam was undergoing an "intense psychological attack," and he was universally praised for his previous work in advising Diem in the 1950s.[99] Lodge recalled that Kennedy approved Lansdale's transfer, but no action was taken.[100] Writing Rusk on September 13, 1963, on a "top secret—eyes only" basis, Lodge said, "What I ask is that General Lansdale be sent over here at once to take charge, under my supervision, of all U.S. relationships with a change of government here . . . I therefore ask that he be put in charge of the CAS station [Central Intelligence Agency Station] in the Embassy, relieving the present incumbent, Mr. John Richardson." Lodge typed the letter himself and sent it by messenger so no one else would see it.[101] McNamara threatened to resign if Lansdale were sent to Vietnam.[102] The CIA was also opposed. "I'm certain that I was considered a maverick by many people in the government, military and civilian," Lansdale said.[103] He also had a "reputation as an independent and sometimes insubordinate operator," and he had made it clear that he would not support a coup against Diem under any circumstances.[104] Lansdale was arguably the last best chance to save the Diem regime.

On August 17, the Lodges departed Boston with stops planned in San Francisco, Hawaii, and Tokyo before landing in Saigon. Lodge insisted on bringing his own people to Saigon. "I will have the last word on personnel, who I want to have and who I do not want to have," he said. "I will have priority on people, money, and everything else, just as though this were a war theatre." He chose John Michael Dunn and Frederick "Freddy" Flott as his personal aides.[105] Dunn, a fellow Bay Stater from Natick, west of Boston, was an academic military officer who knew Lodge from his army reserve days. Dunn would be responsible for overall routine mission management, "as an extension of [Lodge] himself," and he would serve as a liaison to the military. He was closer to Lodge in Saigon than anyone else. They even lived together for several months during the most sensitive period of Lodge's first ambassadorial tour.[106] Flott had been a career Foreign Service officer, was fluent in French, and was a friend of George Lodge's.[107] He was close to the Kennedys and had traveled to the Soviet Union with Robert Kennedy. Lodge liked the idea of having someone to talk to the Kennedy White House when questions arose, and Flott could also handle liaison duties with the Vietnamese and the French. Flott went up to Beverly for an interview with the Lodges before he was offered the job. "Lodge had me take the wheel of his yacht, which I guess is how New Englanders analyze character," Flott recalled. "I didn't drive the boat into any rocks or anything. But, more seriously, we talked about the Mission and his plans, and I think it was largely just a question of being personally acceptable to Mrs. Lodge and to him."[108]

Lodge's first Vietnam crisis hit even before he arrived.[109] Nhu declared martial law in Saigon on August 21, and his CIA-trained special forces conducted a number of raids of Buddhists centered on Xa Loi Pagoda in Saigon that were presumably timed to be finished before Lodge's arrival. Monks and nuns were beaten, their furniture was smashed, and their bedding was ripped with bayonets. The entire pagoda was emptied out, and at least eight were killed, thirty injured, and hundreds arrested.[110] Another tally found that 1,426 monks and laymen had been arrested.[111] The swiftness in the force used against the Buddhists was the result of a kind of "half-coup," whereby Diem remained as the head of the government but Nhu could exercise as much power as he wanted to, yet blamed the military for carrying out the raids.[112]

During a briefing with Nolting and Hilsman in Honolulu, Lodge received word that all telephone lines to the U.S. mission in Saigon had been cut, except for one line to the military.[113] "They thought they'd take the interregnum between those two ambassadors and just eliminate the Buddhist thing and present Lodge with a *fait accompli*," CIA Far East Division Chief William Colby reflected. "Well, Lodge is not one that takes that kind of gesture lightly and this affected his entire attitude towards him [Nhu]."[114] Lodge was supposed to go on to Hong Kong after a stop in Tokyo, but Kennedy sent a telegram to the embassy asking him to go directly to Saigon the next morning. "There wasn't any doubt that that pagoda incident marked the beginning of the end of the Diem regime," Lodge recalled.[115] Nhu's pagoda raids were effectively a declaration of war on the Buddhists that defied Nolting's soft diplomatic efforts and directly resulted in a tougher American policy. Nolting bid farewell to Diem on August 14 with Diem's personal word that there would be no further violence against the Buddhists.[116] He warned Diem that if he did not repudiate Madame Nhu's remarks, "it would be impossible for the U.S. government to continue our present relationship."[117] The British government came to the same conclusion. "It looks as though the time is approaching when we will have to reexamine our long-standing position on the Diem regime," including support for a coup, the Foreign Office wrote following the Buddhist crisis.[118] Even those Vietnamese officers who remained loyal to Diem felt betrayed by his insistence that no bonzes, or monks, be hurt during the August pagoda raids.[119]

Lodge arrived in Saigon on August 22 at 9:30 p.m. in a "hot tropical blackness." His first official act in country was to violate the strict government-imposed curfew, which had started a half hour before.[120] Straw hat in hand, wearing a dark suit, *Đại sứ* (Ambassador) Lodge—known by some as "Cabalodge" (like "camouflage"), "Cabbage Cod," "Hydrochloric Acid" (a reference to his initials, HCL), and even "sabotage"—was alone at the cabin door at the top of the steps. He was tall, lean, and chiseled in the handsome way that New England Yankees were supposed to look, according to legend.[121] "I remember thinking this celebrity was coming into our lives," recalled Charles "Charlie" Trueheart, son of Deputy Chief of Mission William Trueheart.[122] Lodge had been featured in *GQ* for his poplin suits with open patch pockets, a three-roll-two jacket that betrayed a middle-age paunch, just enough sleeve, and trousers hemmed short over white socks and Belgian loafers. "We have had some bad Ambassadors, and we have had some good Ambassadors—but as far as I know you are the only pin-up Ambassador we have had," C. D. Jackson wrote.[123]

Taking in his first sights of Saigon, Lodge uttered a greeting in Vietnamese ("Toi ret ben long den Viet-Nam"), then descended the stairs that had been wheeled up next to his plane. "My wife and I are delighted to be back in Saigon," he said.[124] "Henry Cabot Lodge arrived on the scene with an outstretched hand. We clutched at it eagerly," Peter Arnett recalled.[125] If there were any

cheers, they were drowned out by the sounds of flash bulbs and cameras working furiously to capture the moment. William Trueheart and U.S. Commander General Paul Harkins met Lodge at the airport, along with a small
group of American officials and a protocol officer from the foreign ministry.
Lodge asked, "Where are the gentlemen of the press?"[126] Although he had ra-
dioed ahead that he did not plan to make a statement, once he had arrived and
saw the forty newsmen clamoring for a bite for the next morning's news, he
walked up to them and did just that. U.S. Information Service Chief John
Mecklin recalled that Lodge "talked for five minutes about the vital role of the
press in American democracy and how much he welcomed any opportunity
to help the newsmen do their jobs . . . This was a first glimpse of Lodge's mas-
terful way with newsmen. As far as the U.S. Embassy was concerned, the so-
called press problem ended then and there."[127] Robert Eunson, the Associated
Press's Asia chief, descended from the plane behind Lodge and whispered to
Arnett, "The ambassador's on our side." Dunn overheard and nodded in agreement.[128] "He was not going to fight us," Halberstam thought.[129]

Lodge's arrival gave Kennedy's Vietnam policy a new, bipartisan halo.[130]
Halberstam said that there were impossible expectations for Lodge: "Everyone here, Americans and Vietnamese alike, expects much too much from him,
more than any man could ever produce."[131] Various American agencies under
the U.S. mission pursued their own projects, protected their own budgets, and
did not share information.[132] A strong ambassador was needed to bring order
to it all. "Saigon was seething," Mecklin recalled about Lodge's arrival, "and
at least part of the situation was popular anticipation that Lodge had come to
put things right, meaning to apply American power to destroy the Diem regime. A good many Americans in Saigon, perhaps a sizeable majority, felt the
same way."[133]

The next morning, Lodge began his term as ambassador in his fifth-floor
office at 39 Ham Nghi Boulevard. The U.S. embassy was in a former commercial building on a broad, busy avenue situated between the riverfront and Diem's Gia Long Palace, about three blocks from the Saigon River. In the
ten-minute drive from his villa to the embassy in the big black Checker sedan
that was the official limousine of the embassy, one experienced the sensory
overload that was Saigon—a city of great contrasts. "Imagine a charming
French city in the tropics with, without doubt, the prettiest girls in the most
graceful dresses," Emily Lodge wrote.[134] The breeze from the river only occasionally interrupted the thick heat. City streets were alive with the sights,
sounds, and smells of strong Vietnamese people—including women dressed

in the beautiful yet versatile traditional *áo dài*. "The Vietnamese are a beautiful race of people and the ladies have a national costume which accentuates the positive more than any costume I have ever seen," Lodge wrote his friend John Mason Brown.[135] The city had—and has, although it is fading—an aura of a tropical Paris. Saigon had wide, Hausmann-inspired boulevards, with delicate bougainvillea climbing up the walls surrounding pastel-colored colonial villas. "You will not believe the Mekong Delta," Halberstam reflected. "You know, the beautiful rice paddies, the farmer, the water buffalo, the docks, the fish in the canal, everything . . . You go down there and then suddenly in this biblical setting, you know, be in a fire fight and you'd come back that night and you go out to a wonderful French dinner with some beautiful Vietnamese girl. I mean, it was at once romantic and unreal and very tough."[136]

Lodge's embassy staff was uniquely young and ambitious. It included William A. K. "Tony" Lake, Richard Holbrooke, John Negroponte, Peter Tarnoff, and Frank Wisner II—junior Foreign Service officers on the first or second assignment of their careers.[137] Seven of them, including two on Lodge's personal staff—Lake and Joseph Luman—would receive the State Department's Superior Honor Award within the year.[138] Lodge credited his "open-door policy" for his success in recruiting the most talented staff. Some ambassadors hire those known to be friendly to them. Lodge preferred to hire the best people he could find—more often than not, prep-school-educated young liberals from good New England families. "This was not only so he could secure information himself, but also to prevent people from feeling a sense of injustice," Neil Sheehan said.[139] Foreign service in Vietnam attracted a certain niche, and there was a demand in Saigon for French-speaking bachelors.[140] These were young officers of uncommon intelligence with a willingness to take risks for public purpose and the ability to rise to the occasion as the circumstances demanded. Many joined the Foreign Service because they were inspired by Kennedy to choose careers in public service. Twenty-six thousand took the Foreign Service exam in the first year of Kennedy's presidency.[141]

These young officers were a good fit for Lodge, who was not the ordinary ambassador because of his dislike for administration and mistrust of bureaucracy. "You can fall in love with the girls, but don't fall in love with the country," he told his young staff.[142] The embassy contained not a single Asia specialist. Lodge did not have to break his staff of their ways because they had not yet established any. They learned from him and liked him, and he got a lot of work out of them. "I loved Lodge," Dunn reflected later. "I make no bones about it. I don't think there was ever anybody in my life I liked as much . . .

He was a patrician, but that's all right if a guy handles it well, and he did. His ability to laugh at himself was unparalleled in my experience."[143] It was exciting to be in a place like Saigon and work for someone like Lodge, who not only questioned the conventional wisdom but in some cases was actively opposed to it.[144] "The thing about Lodge that got him in trouble in Vietnam and kept him, in my judgment, from being vice president of the United States was that he just didn't suffer fools gladly—and he reserved the right to define who was a fool," Dunn said.[145]

From the moment of Lodge's arrival, the news coming out of Saigon was grim. CIA Station Chief Richardson cabled to Washington that the "situation here has reached point of no return. Saigon is armed camp. Current indications are that the Ngo family have dug in for last ditch battle."[146] Lodge saw tanks and armored cars guarding intersections against a backdrop of graceful palm trees and lush foliage. Soldiers donned oversize American rifles, and Jeeps on the streets were mounted with .30-caliber machine guns.[147] It was the first sign that Diem was not fully in control of Saigon, let alone the rest of the nation. "[The] U.S. can get along with dictators (See Thailand) but not this kind," Lodge wrote in his confidential journal.[148] At one intersection near Saigon University, two thousand bicycles, scooters, and motorbikes were piled up, waiting patiently for their owners, who had been rounded up and remained in jail.[149] Greeting Lodge upon his arrival were threats against his life, a warning from Madame Nhu that he was on probation, and a pile of urgent cables that required his personal attention.[150]

On that first day, Lodge delicately insulted the Ngo family by conspicuously driving to the U.S. Agency for International Development headquarters next to the Xa Loi Pagoda, where the monks were sheltering, and telling them they were welcome at the embassy. Some Buddhists, including their informal leader, Thich Tri Quang, requested asylum the next day, and Lodge granted it, giving them a conference room as living quarters. He even had fresh food brought into them daily that adhered to their vegetarian diet.[151] The South Vietnamese government strongly resented the fact that the United States refused to turn Tri Quang over to Saigon authorities, who considered him the primary instigator and leader of a revolutionary effort to overthrow the government.[152] Lodge and Tri Quang became friends. "He was a very sharp, clever, determined, energetic man," Lodge reflected. "And he detested what Diem was doing. He was very suspicious by nature."[153] The Saigon government erected barricades around pagodas and other locations deemed sensitive, including the U.S. Operations Mission building. The American civilian officials who were giving more than a million dollars per day to the Diem government were harassed and could not get to work. There had been four more self-immolations, and Nhu had ordered the arrest of Malcolm Browne and Peter Arnett.[154] A security officer at the embassy warned Lodge that they were after him, too. "They have a plot to kill you," he whispered to Lodge. "If these people have a plot to kill me," he responded, "why do we have to whisper and be so careful about keeping their secret for them?"[155]

Frustrated Americans in Saigon who demanded action were told to wait for Lodge's arrival. Until then there would be no response to the actions of the Diem government. The gap between Nolting's departure and Lodge's arrival had been meant to show U.S. displeasure with the Diem regime, but it was time to get to work. The Kennedy administration now had the means to make a policy change with respect to Vietnam, as well as the motive (the 1964 presidential election) and opportunity (the anger of the generals, and the questions raised by Americans following the Buddhist crisis). "I'm running things here, and I intend to run them with a firm hand. If Washington wants a weasel for this job it can find someone else," Lodge was quoted as saying in the New York Times, although he denied these were his exact words. Critics were fair in saying that Lodge ruled more like a colonial proconsul than an ambassador.[156] Just as at the UN, he took instructions from no one except the president, and he had received his instructions from Kennedy on August 15.[157]

Shortly after his arrival came State 243, the most infamous cable of the Vietnam War. The cable, "in effect, directed Lodge and the Mission to start exploring ways to find alternative leadership to Diem," Deputy Assistant Secretary for International Security Affairs William Bundy said.[158] This was to be done through calculated broadcasts on the Voice of America as well as by "salami-slicing" U.S. aid to Diem, which he needed to survive.[159] The cable reinforced the instructions that Kennedy had given Lodge nine days earlier and further conditioned the atmosphere for a coup.[160] Thus, the content of the cable was not a surprise to Lodge. For him, its message was simply, "Go ahead." The shock was that such instructions were committed to writing and sent via regular State channels, especially so early in his tenure. The cable read, "We must . . . tell key military leaders that U.S. would find it impossible to continue to support GVN [Government of Viet Nam] militarily and economically unless . . . steps are taken immediately which we recognize requires removal of the Nhus from the scene. We wish to give Diem reasonable opportunity to remove Nhus but if he remains obdurate, then we are prepared to accept the obvious implication that we can longer support Diem. You may also tell appropriate military commanders we will give them direct support in any interim period of breakdown central government mechanism . . . concurrently with above, ambassador and country teams should urgently examine all possible alternative leadership and make detailed plans as to how we might bring about Diem's replacement if this should become necessary."[161]

Assistant Secretary of State for Far Eastern Affairs Roger Hilsman drafted the cable at Kennedy's suggestion.[162] Thomas Hughes, director of the Bureau of Intelligence and Research at the State Department, made a detailed record of his conversations on August 24 at the White House with Hilsman and National Security Council staff member Michael Forrestal, published for the first time here, that he called his "coup planning week" notes. Forrestal said he "was in direct touch with JFK, could reach him at any time, aware of JFK's communications to and from Lodge, and of JFK's political requirements." Forrestal had sent Kennedy the latest cable traffic on the Buddhist crisis, concluding that Nhu was the mastermind and was calling the shots independently of Diem. He criticized Hilsman's instructions to Lodge in what would become State 243. "They were terrible! Imagine sitting out in Saigon with Buddhists in your garden and refugees and demonstrators outside your house, and you get instructions from us saying 'press Diem for liberal reforms.'"[163]

Much of what Hilsman wrote had to be rewritten. The CIA's input had to be modified, as it argued for at least twelve more months of the Diem administration to allow for the consolidation of military campaigns against the Viet Cong. In the White House, Forrestal said, it was understood that "another 12 months of Diem is absurd."[164] Hilsman told his wife, Eleanor, that "this week would separate the men from the boys."[165] He contacted Under Secretary of State George Ball, who was on the ninth hole of the golf course at the Chevy Chase Club, outside Washington, DC, to request that he approve the cable.[166] "We had really run our course with the Diem regime," Ball recalled. "Unless he got rid of the Nhus and straightened up, it was impossible to go forward."[167] Ball then called Kennedy in Hyannis Port, Massachusetts, and the president concurred, pending approval from Rusk, who was at Yankee Stadium.[168] Rusk agreed, pending Kennedy's and Harriman's approval. Harriman approved. Nolting later reflected, "I think Harriman was determined to get on with this thing at a faster rate, and I think a part of that was his political instinct to get Kennedy re-elected."[169] Richard Helms cleared the text on behalf of the CIA, since he considered it a matter of policy rather than an intelligence matter.[170] He applauded the cable and called it a welcome policy shift.[171]

Lodge interpreted State 243 as a "go ahead" from Ball. If Lodge had had any doubts about what he and Kennedy had discussed on August 15, Ball had offered a critical confirmation. The portions of the cable that Lodge underlined included the directions that Diem be given an opportunity to rid himself of the Nhus and to notify the generals that the United States would find it impossible to support the Saigon government unless these steps were taken. Lodge considered the telegram significant enough that he kept it in an inner safe inside his office safe, out of the embassy filing system. It became the first document in a special folder of cables documenting White House approval of the coup, a folder that remained at the embassy until it was evacuated in 1975, when it was hand-carried by Ambassador Graham Martin to the United States.

"I was thunderstruck," Lodge said in a 1977 BBC interview. While he was well aware of the implications of his August 15 meeting with Kennedy, there had been nothing in his Honolulu briefings to warn him of the imminent arrival of the telegram.[172] "So I get on down to Saigon on Friday and then Sunday comes this telegram for me to do whatever I could to overthrow Diem, and to, in effect, press the button. I thought about asking for clarification of instructions and then I thought no, that I wouldn't do that. I can read English, I could understand perfectly well what the telegram said. I thought it was very ill-advised, but I only had had twenty-four hours in the country and my opinion wasn't worth very much to me or anybody else. So I said I'm going to carry it out."[173] Lodge cabled back only to Rusk and Hilsman, asking for his instructions to be revised. He said that the "chances of Diem's meeting our demands are virtually nil." Lodge suggested that "we go straight to generals with our demands, without informing Diem."[174] It was a bold suggestion, but how else was Lodge to carry out his White House orders? "They were asking me to overthrow a government I hadn't even presented my credentials to."[175] Part of the reason for Lodge's suggestion was that "by the time that cable was received, events were already moving and had a momentum and life of their own," Dunn said.[176] The generals were in motion, even if they did not agree on the direction.

In a meeting of Kennedy's top Vietnam advisers at noon on Monday, August 26, according to records declassified in 2016 in response to a request by the author, there was no regret in sending State 243 to Lodge. Kennedy reemphasized that he did not want Halberstam's reporting from Saigon to create policy in Washington. "When we move to eliminate a government, we want to be sure we're not doing it just because the *New York Times* is excited about it," Kennedy said. Hilsman believed that what was even more dangerous was "to sit still, or to wait, to delay."[177] Most of the rest of the conversation focused on the importance of a coup being successful. Kennedy wanted more information on the relationships between the generals and which ones were loyal or dissident. Rusk argued that the reason a coup was necessary was that Nhu was anti-American. "If the coup was unsuccessful," he said, "the decision for the United States would be, therefore, to get out and let the country go to the Communists or to move U.S. combat forces into South Vietnam and put in a government of our own choosing."[178] No one disagreed with Rusk's analysis.

In Saigon, Lodge presented his credentials to Diem on the same day as the meeting in Washington.[179] He returned to the palace later that day for a private conversation with Diem. "I believe the government suspects us of trying to engineer a coup," Lodge reported.[180]

Kennedy polled his National Security Council. Each member could vote whether to (1) cancel the cable, since Lodge had taken no action, (2) go with the original cable as written, or (3) go with the original cable, but with Lodge's proposed revisions—to not warn Diem that the generals were plotting against him. "All present—including General Taylor—voted to go with the cable as modified by Lodge," said Hilsman.[181] Without a coup, Harriman said, "we cannot win the war" and "must withdraw." Hilsman added that the United States "cannot win the war unless Diem is removed."[182] Hilsman, Harriman, Ball, and Forrestal led the charge against Diem, and even Kennedy was turned against the Saigon government once he came to believe a failed foreign policy could affect his chances for reelection in 1964.[183]

Attorney General Robert Kennedy, so outspoken in his later oral histories in denying the president's assent to a coup, was not present for any of the most significant discussions. Most of those took place when Vice President Lyndon Johnson was out of the room, too. A review of all of the relevant Kennedy tapes indicates that the president was not strongly in favor of a coup or strongly opposed to one. He only wanted to do what would be successful and improve the image of his handling of the war. The others in the room during these meetings, despite their later views regarding Vietnam, were all in agreement— except Nolting, who said that it would be "a bad principle and a bad practice" to support a coup "for the purpose of establishing a government with which we can deal more effectively and which we hope to give us a better basis for winning the war against the Viet Cong."[184]

William Colby defended his stance in support of a coup by saying, "The situation there seems to have reached a point of no return . . . the overwhelming majority of general officers except [Ton That] Dinh and [Huynh Van] Cao are united . . . We believe they will act and have a good chance to win." Ball agreed: "I strongly urge that we now proceed on things. The decision is made that we're going to see this thing through and going to see it successful. Because I think that to pull back or not to be willing to do what's necessary is going to result in the worst of both possible worlds for us." McNamara said they should make it clear to Lodge and Harkins that they should not permit a coup unless they felt it could succeed. "Because I personally believe we're going to be identified with a coup if it starts, whether it succeeds or fails. If a coup starts and fails, it seems to me we've almost lost South Vietnam." Harriman stated, "We've lost South Vietnam if we do not succeed in the coup. I'm utterly convinced that we cannot win with the combination of Diem/Nhu. I've felt that way for—since you asked me to take this job." Hilsman pointed out, "The generals are committed, sir. In my opinion, they are going to either make it or they're going to die. I don't think you can stop it now." The most important decision maker, Kennedy said he was for a coup unless "the Diem forces outnumber the coup forces."[185]

At times during the secretly recorded conversations, Kennedy seems surprisingly uninformed. He had to be reminded who Colby was, even though he was a CIA briefer at some of the meetings. Kennedy could not keep straight the names of the principal coup leaders, such as Big Minh. Part of the problem was that there was not merely one coup effort but rather as many as six distinct groups, Richard Holbrooke wrote later.[186]

Rusk told Lodge that Kennedy "will support a coup which has a good chance of succeeding but plans no direct involvement of U.S. armed forces."[187] It was Lodge's job to make sure any coup effort succeeded. He was later criticized for not communicating with Diem more regularly during this period, but that was how he was being directed by Rusk to operate. Rusk warned Kennedy, "One possibility, for example, we cannot dismiss, is that if Lodge sees him and says you have got to rid of the Nhus or else, that Diem could call the North Vietnamese for assistance in expelling the Americans from Vietnam and we'd have no shred of legality left and a great problem on our hands." Kennedy agreed that "operationally it is a mistake to try this with Diem until the generals are really ready for whatever it is they are going to do."[188] Yet Kennedy's staff blamed Lodge for not seeing Diem.

Even if Lodge were threatened or declared persona non grata by the Diem government, the United States was prepared to "stall on the removal of our officials until the efforts to mount a coup have borne fruit," Hilsman wrote to Rusk on August 30.[189] As far as what was to happen to Diem and Nhu, "our approach to the generals specified that the decision on whether or not Diem should be retained was up to them," Hilsman told Kennedy.[190] "I think the next steps are really one of reassuring the generals that we are indeed with them."[191] Hilsman was among those who denied any advance knowledge of the coup in an Associated Press news story following the release of the Pentagon Papers in June 1971. That denial, along with others, established the basis for the claim that Kennedy did not have any direct knowledge and that it must have been Lodge, exceeding his authority, who set out with the generals in Saigon to overthrow Diem.

Lodge received another cable from Kennedy, affirming State 243 but adding one caveat: "Until the very moment of the go signal for the operation by the generals, I must reserve contingent right to change course and reverse previous instructions. While fully aware of your assessment of the consequences of such a reversal, I know from experience that failure is more destructive than an appearance of indecision." The latter was presumably a reference to the Bay of Pigs.[192] Lodge acknowledged Kennedy's message: "I fully understand that you have the right and responsibility to change course at any time. Of course, I shall always respect that right. To be successful, this operation must be essentially a Vietnamese affair with a momentum of its own. Should this happen, you may not be able to control it, that is, the 'go signal' may be given by the generals."[193]

# 12 · Diem

As ambassador, Henry Cabot Lodge Jr.'s primary job was to oversee a mission called to train, supply, and advise Vietnam's political and military officials, but not engage in actual combat. The U.S. embassy in Saigon was normally a relaxed post where a young, ambitious Foreign Service officer could enjoy the food, the music, and tree-lined boulevards featuring colonial architecture. There was nightlife, history, and opportunities to practice one's French while pursuing the opposite sex. The doors were typically locked in the evening at six o'clock, and the occasional unrest or act of Viet Cong terrorism did not disturb the leisurely pace of life in Saigon.[1] But when Lodge arrived, it was more chaotic. So many new American support offices were being created in Saigon that the embassy telephone book was regularly out of date before the new edition arrived.[2] The Pentagon had to buy a computer to keep track of the explosion of personnel in Vietnam. The American post exchange could not manage all the credit accounts it had. And there was a severe housing crisis for apartments suitable for Americans, with rents rising as high as $1,000 per month.[3]

One of the first things Lodge did was to reestablish relations with the American press in Saigon. He was appalled that they did not trust anything being told to them by the military or the embassy. "I don't think there's any doubt that the press are instinctively—a lot of them are liberal, and some very—and they harry against every authoritarian regime, they rebel," John F. Kennedy said to Lodge on August 15, 1963.[4] "And, in addition, you know, they're a lot of fellows who haven't had that much experience. A lot of them have been out there a year or so . . . so that we do have a problem with them," he said. "I mean, that fellow—*New York Times* fellow [David Halberstam], I guess he's a bright fellow, just wrote a story about how we're losing the war . . . you're going to have a difficult time maintaining a satisfactory relationship with them," Kennedy added.

Lodge, the former reporter, went to work, inviting the three regular correspondents—Halberstam, Neil Sheehan of United Press International, and Malcolm Browne of the Associated Press—to a series of lunches in the embassy residence drawing room. They had never experienced that kind of treatment before.[5] Each warned Lodge that the Ngo family was mad, and "if they were replaced by a military regime there was no guarantee that a junta of generals would do better, but there was hope that they might."[6] "Except for his arrival and departure ten months later," John Mecklin recalled, "Lodge gave no press conferences, no off-the-record briefings. Instead he met frequently but always alone with individual American newsmen, thus at once flattering them and minimizing the risk of broken confidences. He was not an exceptionally good news source, but he knew how to talk to newsmen so they went away happy."[7]

There was serious talk of a coup the week that Lodge arrived, so in addition to reining in the American press, he had to get a better feel for the political situation. It was a city full of gossip, and Lodge had to determine which sources of information were reliable.[8] He had inherited a mission that contained four major divisions. General Paul Harkins, a friend of Lodge's since 1925 when they served at Fort Bliss, commanded Military Assistance Command Vietnam.[9] Harkins's primary duty was advising the Vietnamese military and overseeing all Americans in uniform. John "Jocko" Richardson, the CIA station chief in Saigon, had arrived in Saigon in 1961 and was living in the same villa used by the Japanese Imperial Army's intelligence service during World War II.[10] Richardson's duties included advising the Vietnamese government, helping to create a modern Vietnamese intelligence system, and training paramilitary forces as well as Ngo Dinh Nhu's special forces. Harkins and Richardson were arguably the closest to their Vietnamese contacts and potentially had the most to lose as a result of any political changes in the Diem government.[11] Joseph Brent was in charge of the U.S. Agency for International Development, which included economic assistance to South Vietnam ranging from radio transmitters to fertilizer. Finally, Mecklin ran the U.S. Information Service, which worked with the South Vietnamese government to develop propaganda programs.[12]

Lodge presented his credentials to President Ngo Dinh Diem at Gia Long Palace on the morning of August 26. He and the eight members of the mission who accompanied him were dressed in their *protocolaire* white suits.[13] Lodge was so concerned about his safety that day that he told Harkins not to come.[14] Diem greeted him graciously, even though relations with the United States had deteriorated significantly. Lodge handed him a letter that Kennedy had given him in the Oval Office on August 15, in which Kennedy wrote, "I think it is important that Ambassador Lodge establish with you as quickly as possible a close working relationship based upon mutual confidence." It included the awkward closing, "With cordial wishes for your personal welfare." Lodge was the most dangerous American Diem had ever met.[15]

Lodge first met Diem during the latter's visit to the United States in 1957 at the invitation of President Dwight Eisenhower. The administration's policy toward Vietnam had been one of full support of Diem and no compromise regarding world communism.[16] During his trip to Washington, Diem received the red-carpet treatment—a full diplomatic ceremony at Andrews Air Force Base, a motorcade to Blair House, and a ticker-tape parade down Broadway in New York. Diem had been premier of the new Republic of South Vietnam since June 1954.

When the French persuaded Diem to become premier, they assumed he would fail at the impossible job. South Vietnam had never been a nation in the Westphalian sense. A people whose most important social, political, and economic unit was the village, where even the residents of the next village were "dirty foreigners," had no sense of a distant capital city run by French-trained political and military officials. Diem had to create, implement, and reinforce— for internal as well as external stakeholders—the idea of South Vietnamese identity and statehood using a mix of French and Vietnamese traditions that composed the unique personality cult of his democratic mandate of heaven.[17] People in South Vietnam had survived the French, the Japanese, the French again, and the Viet Cong, and they would soon survive the Americans as well.[18] They were accustomed to turbulence and conflict. Diem's new government faced instability from the start yet managed to suppress each uprising.[19] "The main weakness of Ngo Dinh Diem in the early days of his holding office, the highest office in the land, was that he didn't trust his subordinates to get a job done correctly," Ed Lansdale said. "In other words, he wasn't a good executive."[20]

Born on January 3, 1901, Diem, the son of an adviser to Emperor Thanh Thai in Hue, had set out to be a priest but became disenchanted and quit when he came to believe the church was "too worldly," although he maintained his vow of chastity and spent hours in meditation.[21] Diem graduated from the National College at Hue for the training of mandarin administrators, became a provincial governor in 1929, and then became interior minister four years later under the young Emperor Bao Dai. He supervised roughly three hundred villages in Annam, later known as central Vietnam.[22] His job was to ride around on horseback, wearing a conical hat and a mandarin robe, and settle peasant disputes—serving as part sheriff, part tax collector, and part public works director. He quit government and lived in solitude from 1933 to 1944. Fluent in the classical texts, he demonstrated the expected scholarly elitism.[23] He read, wrote, rode, hunted, tended flowers, and practiced photography. The Japanese occupation asked him to become a puppet prime minister, but he refused. In September 1945, Diem was arrested by Ho Chi Minh's Vietminh near Hue. They held him in the jungle for months, where he nearly died from malaria and dysentery. In February 1946, Ho asked Diem to join him in Hanoi. Despite Ho's apology for arresting him and killing his brother Ngo Dinh Khoi, Diem refused Ho's invitation. He was released and went to live with another brother, Archbishop Ngo Dinh Thuc, near Saigon. In 1949, Emperor Bao Dai invited Diem to be prime minister and again he turned down the offer. Diem left the country in 1950 and lived in monasteries in Japan, New York, and Belgium. In the United States, he spent most of his time at Maryknoll Seminary in Lakewood, New Jersey. In an article titled "Democratic Development in Vietnam," he wrote that in the government, "the magistrate" "must conduct himself as one participating in a religious rite." Diem was a twentieth-century politician, but European political ideology influenced him as much as Vietnamese nationalism and Confucian thought.[24]

Once in power, the Viet Cong increasingly challenged the ability of South Vietnam to function.[25] The conflict that might have started as a civil war became a brutal military conquest by communist North Vietnam. Diem responded by consolidating his power.[26] The Ngos' interests were as autocratic as they were nationalistic, implementing a synthesis of Eastern and Western cultural elements in a modern political philosophy uniquely their own.[27] By 1962, they had virtually total control over the South Vietnamese government, a "one-family dictatorship that is worse than any party," according to future premier Nguyen Cao Ky.[28] Diem was president and minister of national defense. His brothers held other key positions—Ngo Dinh Nhu was his political counselor and alter ego,[29] Can was proconsul in central Vietnam, Thuc was archbishop in Hue and leader of the nation's two million Catholics, and Luyen was ambassador to London. Tran Van Chuong, Nhu's father-in-law, was ambassador to Washington. Due to Diem's status as a lifelong bachelor, Nhu's wife was the de facto first lady of South Vietnam, the leader of the Women's Solidarity Movement, and an outspoken advocate of the Diem government.[30] Madame Nhu fascinated President Kennedy, who wondered whether she was a lesbian and assumed that she and other women he considered masculine "resent[ed] getting their power through men."[31] Journalist Stanley Karnow found her "so coquette always flaunting her sexiness" and a "loose cannon; no one could control her."[32]

There was the facade of a normal government, with the various ministries, the directorates-general, and the civil service, but the only two people who made important decisions were Diem and Nhu. One U.S. embassy official likened working with the Saigon government to "dealing with a government of madmen, whose words were meaningless, where nothing that was supposed to have happened had really happened."[33] There were a series of coup attempts before 1963. What they showed is that the more the regime drew inward upon itself, and the more it seemed interested in survival as opposed to defeating the Viet Cong, the more it cut itself off from the increasingly serious problems confronting South Vietnam.[34]

Lodge was a shrewd, tough operator, which made him a good match for the Ngos.[35] Initially, Diem had favorable things to say about Lodge's appointment. "Vietnam remembers the warm interventions of this High American Representative to the United Nations in the Security Council in favor of the admission of the Republic of Vietnam in the past," Diem told the *Chicago Tribune*. "The appointment of a man of such stature and having such experience of communism is an honor for my country." When he met Lodge on August 26, he had no reason to believe that the new American ambassador would be anything other than a strong anticommunist ally. Diem warned Lodge not to believe the foreign journalists in Saigon and told him he should visit the provinces for himself in order to see the real situation.[36]

Lodge needed to determine as quickly as possible whether Diem was savable. He did not rush into a coup.[37] Instead, he demanded human rights, political freedom, military competence, and accountability.[38] "And I brought up this question that President Kennedy wanted me to bring up, of getting Nhu out of the country and of appointing new people and bettering and improving and strengthening the government," Lodge recalled. "And he absolutely refused to discuss any of the things that I was instructed to discuss. And it gave me a little jolt, frankly. I think that when an ambassador goes to call on a chief of state and he has been instructed by the President to bring up certain things, the chief of state ought to at least talk about them. But he wouldn't talk about

them at all and he looked up at the ceiling and he'd start talking about absolutely irrelevant subjects and I really wasn't accomplishing anything."[39]

Lodge followed a measured, gradualist approach to increase pressure on
Diem to make reforms while simultaneously using his green light from Kennedy to determine how a coup might be carried out.[40] The problem with a coup
was that Diem's family controlled South Vietnam as the Romanovs had controlled Russia before World War I. "They're completely cut off from everything," Lodge told Kennedy on August 15. "It's very hard to get in to the palace.
They don't have the slightest idea what's going on in the country."[41] It would
be difficult to remove just one of them, and that was in addition to Madame
Nhu. He planned to treat her as a private citizen since she had no official
role in the Saigon government—even though the *New York Times* called her
"the most powerful" woman in Asia.[42] She played a very public role during
Vice President Lyndon Johnson's visit to Saigon in 1961.[43] Lodge's appointment
was a shift in policy from "ultra pro-Diem to doubtful on Diem."[44]

It became clear rather quickly that Lodge and Diem would not work well
together. Diem's habit of engaging in long monologues that prevented direct
conversation while puffing on cigarette after cigarette was not Lodge's style.
Once Diem started talking, it was impossible to change the subject or even
get his attention. He had an impressive body of knowledge on a range of subjects. Even the casual remark "It's a nice day" could result in a twenty-minute
discussion about Vietnamese meteorology.[45] Lodge knew that in order to avoid
these traps, he should raise the most important subject right away. Senior diplomats in Saigon had learned to schedule meetings with Diem during the late
morning or early evening so they could escape with an excuse to get to lunch
or dinner. "Diem couldn't possibly run the country; the president couldn't even
speak coherently," Halberstam wrote. While Lodge ticked off American grievances and recommendations, his host stared at the ceiling, and when the ambassador was finished, the president poured out a babble of words about
something totally unrelated.[46]

Lodge said that by the time he arrived in Saigon, Diem's "rule was clearly
entering its terminal phase, regardless of what the United States did."[47] He
hoped a coup would not be necessary. The United States had poured nearly $3
billion into South Vietnam since 1955, and since 1961, the investment had been
backstopped by eighteen thousand civilian and military advisers.[48] Destabiliz-
ing Saigon further would do nothing to provide a return on the American
investment. Also, a coup was not likely to be peaceful. "Prudence demands
that we assume some bloodshed. If the Nhus see defeat staring them in the

face, their Gotter Dammerung complex is such that they would gladly see Saigon in flames before they perished. This means that all Americans would be in hostile territory," Lodge cabled to Averell Harriman.[49]

Lodge was arguably the reason a coup did not occur sooner. In late August, he reported that the White House had misjudged the generals, who were not as ready to act as Washington hoped. The CIA estimated that "the arrest of four or five key figures among the generals might bring this operation to a halt . . . It is puzzling that action of this nature had not already been taken."[50] Lodge argued that they did not have the necessary strength and support and that the United States should stand down.[51] "We have an 'Organization de Confusion' with everyone suspicious of everyone else and none desiring to take any positive action as of right now. You can't hurry the East," Harkins reported.[52] Rather than deserving blame for the coup, as many have assumed, Lodge was a moderating influence. Late in Lodge's life, he revealed to his friend Karnow that he had made up his mind about the need for a coup around mid-September 1963. "This is after I'd been there about three weeks," he said.[53] However, he told Karnow he was not yet convinced that a coup was the only option. Newly declassified CIA records from that month seem to validate Lodge's claim that he arrived in Vietnam without his mind made up. In a surprisingly informal and chatty three-page letter dated September 19 from CIA Director John McCone to Lodge, McCone explained the different back-channel communication options that Lodge had. In addition to the CIA channel, which "would mean that a few people on both ends would have access," there was the special messenger, Deputy Saigon Station Director David Smith, who could hand-carry sensitive communications between Saigon and Washington.[54]

More proof that indicates Lodge had not made up his mind about a coup was his request that Lansdale replace John Richardson as CIA station chief in Saigon. Lansdale, who was vehemently opposed to a coup, could have used his long friendship with Diem to make suggestions for reforms that might have saved his government. Lodge's unpublished notes show that he thought the Saigon station was "badly organized" and that Richardson was "too prominent" and "has not got good sources."[55] However, in his letter of September 19, McCone reminded Lodge why the CIA could not accept Lansdale's return to Vietnam. "Although I do not resist a change of Station Chief," McCone wrote, "to have a Station Chief in as an important a station as Saigon who is unacceptable to this organization would be unmanageable. Unfortunately General Lansdale would not be acceptable to the organization or to me personally. I

will not go into details as to why this is true but some time when we are together I can tell you." McCone argued that Richardson should be kept because
of his "valuable contacts and the confidence of some individuals in the regime, particularly Nhu, as well as certain generals, and these might be lost
with his departure." It was up to Lodge to decide what was ultimately one of
the most important foreign policy decisions of the Cold War. Should the
United States continue to work with the Diem regime, try to separate Diem
and the Nhus, or eliminate the whole family? If one of the first two options,
then Richardson could be useful. "However, if the decision is to abandon all
hope of working with the regime," McCone wrote, "then Richardson probably should be replaced."[56]

The Americans could have ordered Diem out of office, but that would have
smacked of colonialism and outraged the Vietnamese.[57] The preference was
for Diem to separate himself from the Nhus, thus eliminating the need for a
coup. Before his father died, Diem had promised he would take care of his little
brother. Lansdale proposed a plan to separate the two brothers in a way that
he thought was consistent with Diem's commitment. He pitched the idea of
setting up a Vietnam policy group at Harvard and asking Nhu to move there
as a member. "Kick him upstairs," Lansdale told Harriman and fellow Kennedy administration official John Kenneth Galbraith. "Tell him he's an intellectual. Listen to him and give him a job there. He'd come and Diem would
let him go." Galbraith shut the idea down, saying that Harvard does not do
such things.[58] The Americans never seemed to understand how Diem's promise to his father influenced his thinking. They would never succeed by coldly
asking Diem to send his brother away. Yet at the same time, Diem seemed to
understand that the Nhus were poison. He once said that Madame Nhu had a
"bad character" (*mauvaise caractère*).[59]

Lodge wasted no time getting to work. "This is an extremely active and interesting place," he wrote his brother, John, on September 4. "Life is a succession of surprises all day long and sometimes well into the night!"[60] That was
an understatement. "He has inherited a nightmare task," the British embassy
reported to the Foreign Office.[61] The uniqueness of Lodge's personality and
mode of operation would itself play a role in the unfolding events.[62] He later
told Karnow that he immediately recognized that the U.S. government, and
the embassy in particular, did not have good sources in Saigon. Lodge had to
find his own people. These included Patrick J. Honey, a professor from the University of London, who was, in Lodge's words, "the only westerner" he had
"ever heard of who could speak, read and write Vietnamese on very abstruse,

philosophical subjects." Lodge also got to know the apostolic delegate, Archbishop Salvatore Asta. "In everything that I did, I was in the closest possible contact with Archbishop Asta . . . who had a relationship with the million and a half Vietnamese Catholics which was quite remarkable," he recalled.[63] Finally, Lodge needed someone with contacts among the Buddhists to get a better grasp on the movement, whether it was strictly religious or more political—and whether it had been compromised by communists, as some believed. So he added a third member to his kitchen cabinet trifecta, Buddhist priest Quang Lien, who was a graduate of Yale University. Taken together, the trio were Lodge's barometer of Vietnamese public opinion, and he trusted them more than he did any American expert.

On his second full day on the job, Lodge authorized Lucien Conein to meet with General Tran Thien Khiem, chief of staff of the Joint General Staff, and tell him the United States was in agreement that the Nhus had to go and support would be available in the event that an attempted coup might result in an interim period of breakdown of the government.[64] The latter meant that the United States was willing to recognize a replacement government for Diem no matter its composition. Conein met with General Tran Van Don, acting chief of staff of the Vietnamese Armed Forces, and provided intelligence information on things such as the location of armaments and secret bases used by Nhu's special forces.[65] Conein was also authorized to say that the U.S. government would look favorably upon the generals' efforts to depose Diem and Nhu.[66]

Conein, who in the fall of 1963 was nominally an adviser to Diem's Ministry of Labor, did not have a good first impression of Lodge. "At first I didn't talk to the ambassador," he said. "I was scared of him." Conein liked to joke that Lodge's initials, HCL, stood for "hydrochloric acid." "The rumor had it you couldn't smoke in front of him, all kinds of things. Once I got to know him, though, he wasn't all that bad. He was very in love with his position, and he was going to knock that American team together, even if he had to fire everybody." That the Lodges were something to be scared of was a myth both Lodge and Emily worked to debunk. It took time to shake the reputation that had preceded them to Saigon. Shortly after their arrival, Emily ran into an embassy aide who was chatting away in French to a half dozen Vietnamese children. Fluent in French herself, she asked the aide why the children did not play on the wide embassy lawn. The aide assumed that the Lodges had rules that proscribed such behavior. "I have 10 grandchildren, you know," Emily said. "I adore them, especially when they are naughty. These Vietnamese children seem very well behaved. Tell them to come over and play on the grass often. I like to watch them."[67]

Conein preferred to meet with Lodge face-to-face. He gave oral reports and took notes longhand. "I would get his clearance prior to attending any meeting with any senior official of the Vietnamese Army," Conein recalled. "And immediately upon returning from the meeting, I would report to him verbally, then I'd make up my own written report for the files."[68] He quickly learned Lodge's preferred style. "The secret to success with Lodge was to be amusing, in the French sense of the word," John Michael Dunn recalled. "One of the things we did was put on a lot of acts for him, and Conein was one of the stars. He was very entertaining. Besides, you had to talk to Conein in person to have any hope of believing what he was going to tell you. It would have been very hard to understand some of the maneuvering that he has going on without seeing this fellow in the flesh."[69] Lodge had inherited a Gordian knot of intrigue. "Everybody was using back channels," Dunn remembered. "It was getting to the point where I thought that regular machines must have been standing idle. The military had their channels; the Agency had their channels; and even the State Department had their channels."[70]

Conein was perhaps the most knowledgeable American on Vietnamese affairs, serving almost without interruption in country from before U.S. entry into World War II until 1971.[71] The Vietnamese were like his brothers. They drank and womanized together, and on at least one occasion, according to Conein's second ex-wife, Monique Denise Veber, Conein had to check himself into a hospital in Toulouse for treatment of what was politely called a "social disease."[72] Dunn chuckled about how Conein and Lodge were supposed to work together. "You know, you could understand that if you were a graduate of Exeter or Andover and then Harvard, Lou Conein wouldn't be necessarily your chosen role model for your eldest son," he said.[73] Many Americans had Vietnamese girlfriends, mistresses, or wives, and womanizing seemed to form a bond among political officials, the military, and the journalists. Sex was part of the experience of Vietnam for the many single men in Saigon, and Vietnamese women were "a white man's dream," Richard Holbrooke said.[74] CIA officials like Conein racked up some of the most impressive tallies of conquests. "They would fuck everything in sight and tried to," journalist George McArthur recalled after spending a decade in Vietnam. "That's no great secret. Any CIA billet on any given night, the sound of fucking was as loud as the shell fire from outside the town."[75] Conein was just as effective at seducing the military men. He gave out unregistered CIA firearms as gifts. "He had a relationship with these generals that nobody else could match," William Trueheart said. "He had known them since he was a lieutenant and they were corporals and sergeants."[76]

Conein knew he was being watched by Nhu's secret police and was sometimes followed, so he met Don secretly. "The meetings were generally arranged ahead of time and it would be in a dentist's office, which is all right, except that I had to have my teeth repaired in the dentist's office so that in case the— the Secret Police would check up, they could see that I had been legitimately at the dentist's office," Conein recalled.[77] He would always get permission from Lodge for these arrangements, knowing that without his approval, "good old Cabot Lodge would have seen that [Conein] would never work for the United States government again."[78]

During Conein's meeting with Don on Lodge's second day on the job, Don told him that the generals had decided to impose martial law, which was the first step in tightening control.[79] Don also said that the generals had nothing to do with the raids on the pagodas. Those had been carried out by units loyal to Diem. Many of the generals were Buddhists, and at the beginning of the crisis, just four of Diem's seventeen cabinet members were Catholics; most of the others were Buddhists.[80] Nhu had forced the generals to sign predated statements that suggested they had foreknowledge of the raids.[81] Don said Diem made the final decisions about the pagoda raids, even if Nhu was the driving force. That was part of the problem—figuring out who was actually calling the shots in Saigon.[82] According to Halberstam, the raids had been led by Colonel Le Quang Tung's troops. This was particularly sensitive for the United States because, as Halberstam discovered, "highly reliable sources" said the CIA paid Tung $250,000 in cash on the first of each month, a total of $3 million per year.[83] The cash continued to flow even after Lodge's arrival in Saigon, without his input.[84] Halberstam considered that finding so sensitive that he had to smuggle his notes for a story on it out of the country with a false dateline and no byline.[85] It was only after CIA Station Chief John Richardson was finally recalled to Washington that Lodge notified Tung that the cash would flow only if it were used to fight the Viet Cong.[86]

Don, one of the leading advocates for replacing Diem, discussed alternatives to Diem and Nhu but rejected the available political exiles as unfeasible.[87] "The trouble is nobody around here has a lust for power," Lodge told journalist Keyes Beech.[88] The coup plotting during the final week of August seemed too premature and too chatty. There were far too many people who claimed to know the details, whether in the American community or even in leaks to the press that resulted in local press attacks against the CIA station for allegedly being the source of the information. Nhu caught wind of the plot almost immediately and put an end to it.[89]

On August 26, Lodge and Harkins authorized Conein to outline a new American policy to General Khiem and General Nguyen Khanh. The policy stated that Nhu must go, and the question of whether to retain Diem would be up to the generals. Bonzes and others who had been arrested would be released immediately. The United States would not be of any help during any initial action of assuming power; however, it would provide direct support during any interim period. If the Nhus did not go and the Buddhist situation was not addressed as indicated, the United States would no longer continue military or economic support. The policy stated that the United States hoped bloodshed could be avoided or kept to a minimum and, finally, that it hoped to retain and increase the necessary relations between Vietnamese and Americans that would allow for progress and successful prosecution of the war.[90]

Khiem responded almost immediately to say the generals were in agreement but that the policy also should be discussed with General Duong Van "Big" Minh, military adviser to the president. Big Minh was dissatisfied with the government because he had no substantive role and was merely a figurehead for the other disaffected officers.[91] The generals agreed that a coup would occur within one week. Conein provided assurances that all possible steps would be taken to assist the families of the generals if the coup failed. Admiral Harry Felt in Honolulu ordered all Pacific-based air force transport planes in readiness for emergency deployment. Big Minh asked for a token of U.S. determination to support the coup group in the form of a cut in American economic aid to Diem. It would be a public signal that the United States no longer supported Diem and would help to rally additional disaffected military forces to the cause of the coup, as well as sending a strong signal to Buddhists that Diem had lost his mandate of heaven.[92]

Lodge concluded that Big Minh had the greatest capability for sparking a coup, as the other generals were too closely monitored by Nhu's agents.[93] Lodge met with Nhu on August 27, and while there is no record of what Lodge and Nhu discussed, a CIA telegram sent by Richardson to Washington stated, "Situation here has reached a point of no return. Saigon is armed camp. Ngo family has dug in for a last ditch battle. It is our considered opinion that general officers cannot retreat now."[94] But Lodge did not send the signal requested by Big Minh, so the generals sought confirmation of American intentions another way. Major General Le Van Kim and oppositionist Dai Viet politician

Bui Diem sought out U.S. Agency for International Development official Rufus Phillips, who was not in favor of a coup but wanted to separate Diem from the Nhus. Phillips told Kim that they could trust Conein and that he acted with Lodge's blessing. However, the British MI-6 station chief in Saigon informed Conein that the Diem government planned to arrest the plotting generals within twenty-four hours, and the warning was passed on to Big Minh.[95] True or not, no one was willing to call Diem's bluff.

On August 31, Harkins met with Khiem, who also concluded the generals were not ready to act. "Perhaps they're afraid to die, like everyone else," Lodge said.[96] At that point, the instructions in the telegrams from Washington had been canceled. "I welcomed that cancellation and I thought we didn't know enough and we didn't have enough muscle to throw our weight around in Saigon," Lodge reflected.[97] The generals did not have enough forces under their control to guarantee success and preferred to lie low following Diem's threat of arrest. Phillips passed this message on to Kim to be sure that all sides received the same message.[98] Besides not being convinced that the generals could succeed, Lodge cabled George Ball that he did not feel he had a good enough grasp of the situation to recommend replacements for Nhu and Diem. "You've got to remember that I had just arrived," Lodge told Karnow. "I was just off the boat, so to speak . . . I was absorbing knowledge all day long, every day, and all my thoughts were in the process of revision."[99]

French Ambassador Roger Lalouette defended Diem and Nhu as the best available option and claimed that it was the American press that needed calming down.[100] It was a moot point to Lodge as the generals were not ready. Part of the reason they were not ready was the United States. Kim, the right-hand man to Big Minh, reported to Phillips on August 31 that the "U.S. should understand it has given so much equipment to Nhu that counter-action cannot be organized in a few days."[101] In light of that fact, Dean Rusk sent modified instructions to Lodge: "Since generals have indicated they are unwilling or unable to act now, U.S. trying to improve situation by diplomatic means."[102]

The generals revealed that Diem and Nhu were considering some type of political settlement with North Vietnam that would result in "uninviting" the Americans. On August 29, French President Charles de Gaulle offered French assistance for "national" reconciliation and stated his belief that peace between North and South was possible.[103] Nhu conferred with Lalouette in Hanoi through Mieczyslaw Maneli, the head of the Polish delegation to the International Control Commission.[104] Nhu did this under the auspices of a "hunting trip" to Khanh Hoa province, where he made several concrete proposals to the

North Vietnamese, including ones calling for the resumption of the postal service and the reopening of the railroad line between Hanoi and Saigon. As a
result, Ho Chi Minh made a ceasefire offer to Nhu.[105] "The North Vietnamese
only negotiated with one person in the South and that's me," Nhu bragged to
Don.[106]

The Kennedy White House was extremely alarmed by this news. Roger
Hilsman wrote Rusk on August 30 that Lodge should warn Diem of the dangers of such a move and prepare for the possibility that Diem and Nhu could
make a political agreement with the North. Lodge should "encourage the generals to move promptly with a coup," Hilsman wrote.[107] Lodge was critical of
the chaos in Washington. "Jack Kennedy would never approve of doing things
this way. This certainly isn't his way of running a government," he said.[108]

The Diem government held the CIA station responsible for fueling much
of the gossip related to a possible coup. The pro-government *Times of Vietnam*
ran a banner headline on September 2: "CIA Financing Planned Coup d'Etat."
The article reported that a coup had been planned for August 28 but was canceled because Diem got wind of it.[109] That same day, Lodge met with Nhu and
Monsignor Salvatore Asta. Nhu told them that he agreed to resign and move
to Dalat after martial law in Saigon was lifted.[110] The papal delegate said Madame Nhu had agreed to leave the country on September 17, and Asta said
Archbishop Thuc would be responsible for issuing official orders to move Nhu
out of the country. The meeting appeared to be a genuine attempt by Lodge
and the Vatican to save the Diem government. "We are in fortunate position
where (a) we can pursue our demands directly with Nhu and Diem and (b) at
the same time we have the generals' trump in reserve," Lodge reported.[111]

The American journalists in Saigon actively tried to influence policy through
their overtly anti-Diem coverage, which emboldened the coup plotters, who assumed the journalists represented the views of the United States. They said
openly to anyone who would listen that they wanted to see Diem overthrown.[112]
"Neil [Sheehan] and I have been pulling no punches for the last two months,"
Halberstam wrote U.S. Army official John Paul Vann during the summer of
1963. "There is a time and a place for everything, and this was the time to go
for broke and use all of our ammo—while people were really watching," he
added.[113] They knew they were advocating for the overthrow of Diem, yet they
denied they played any role. Richardson, who got along with Sheehan, once
told him that the CIA had determined that there were no viable alternatives to
Diem. "Do you want us to take a flying leap in the dark?" Richardson asked.
"Yes," Sheehan responded.[114] Dunn remembered seeing the American

journalists frequently in the embassy. "I don't care what they say now," he said. "They used to come into my office at the embassy and fill me in with what was going on. They weren't sitting out there as neutral observers. They were players."[115]

Halberstam later reflected that he had been criticized for not writing more about the political problems of Vietnam, but he had no pegs for major stories until the Buddhist crisis.[116] "We did as well as we could have expected ourselves to do under the circumstances," he said to Sheehan.[117] They traveled around the countryside more than any American diplomat in Saigon, and they knew the horror stories. "The job of the reporters in Vietnam was to report the news, whether or not the news was good for America," Halberstam wrote in *Commentary*.[118] The journalists sided with the demands of the Buddhist movement, and the Buddhists took advantage of this and Diem's unpopularity.[119] "We have taken an unmerciful beating from the Kennedy administration for David Halberstam's reporting on Vietnam," Tom Wicker wrote to William F. Buckley.[120] Halberstam and Sheehan were effectively Lodge's cheerleaders. "He's what my Irish mother would call a crafty Yankee," Sheehan said to Halberstam.[121] Lodge's background as a journalist convinced them he was one of them, and instead of seducing their source, the journalists were seduced *by* their source. "The leak is the prerogative of the ambassador," Lodge told Mecklin. "It is one of my weapons for doing this job."[122] Lodge gave the reporters what they wanted—attention, respect, occasionally information, and even Diem, eventually. But he was never to be an attributed source unless he approved explicitly. "When I speak, I speak for the United States Government," he wrote to his friend Clay Blair of the *Saturday Evening Post*. "To date I have not given out one interview—or even made one speech . . . A man in a diplomatic post like this simply cannot be a talker."[123]

Lodge's bona fide military experience and longtime association with Eisenhower meant that "he did not think that the generals were necessarily more competent to judge wars than he was."[124] "The brightest spot is Lodge who's [*sic*] performance for my money has been near perfect," Halberstam said to Vann. "He's tough and intelligent and he has few illusions about this situation; he doesn't intend to see the U.S. kicked around, and he impresses me as the right man in the right place."[125] There was a different sentiment about Harkins. "He's so stupid," Halberstam said.[126] "Most of us still feel that the war won't start to improve in the Delta until Harkins and Diem go," Sheehan wrote to Vann, who resigned as an army colonel, in part, because he thought Harkins was lying about war progress.[127]

Sheehan later wrote that he did not know his reporting was affecting policy in Washington. "We did not realize that our dispatches had been arming Averell Harriman . . . and Roger Hilsman . . . in their attempt to persuade Kennedy to authorize the overthrow of Diem and his family," he said.[128] In a column called "The Crusaders," Joe Alsop wrote, "The reportorial crusade against the [Saigon] government had also helped mightily to transform Diem from a courageous, quite viable national leader, into a man afflicted with a galloping persecution mania, seeing plots around every corner, and therefore misjudging everything."[129] Journalists Marguerite Higgins and Keyes Beech also criticized the Saigon journalists for the reporting excesses.[130] The journalists in Saigon became unexpected heroes to many Vietnamese, especially Buddhists, while Diem's press and radio remained heavily censured. However, to the Kennedy White House, they became an enemy just as the Congress that questioned the continued desire to support Diem became the enemy.[131] Americans and readers around the world continued to see self-immolations by monks on the front page, descriptions of rampant corruption, economic turmoil, and dissent even among those who were close to Diem and Nhu. Because the journalists' reporting was vastly different from what the government was putting out, many were led to believe that what they were saying must be closer to the truth.[132]

In early September at his Hyannis Port, Massachusetts, house, Kennedy gave a significant and unusually long interview to Walter Cronkite. In the interview, which was edited down to twelve minutes for broadcast on CBS, Kennedy suggested that continued American support for South Vietnam might depend on changes in the Diem government. "With changes in policy, and perhaps in personnel," Kennedy said, it might be able to win back the support of its people and win the war. "If it doesn't make these changes, I would think the chances of winning it would not be very good."[133] White House Press Secretary Pierre Salinger later said that the way the interview was edited made Kennedy's statement more dramatic than it was intended to be. CBS admitted that it cut Kennedy's line, "I admire what the president [Diem] had done." If Lodge's appointment was the first signal that the United States was shifting from its ironclad support of Diem, Kennedy's interview was the second.[134] It occurred as Lodge had his second meeting with Diem on September 10. He warned him to send the Nhus away at least until after Congress voted on appropriations for Vietnam.[135] Diem's ambassador to Washington, Tran Van Cuong, had provided a similar warning on August 16 and offered his resignation. Diem's response was not only to ignore the warning but to terminate his ambassador.[136] Diem appeared not to be even superficially aware of the profound dissatisfaction among the articulate and the opinion makers in Saigon, let alone in the rebellious countryside. "I thought the removal of Nhu was one of those things that is frightfully desirable and as a practical matter there's absolutely no chance of its taking place, because the brother Diem would never do it," Lodge reflected.[137]

Diem unwilling, Lodge then made another proposal: appoint a prime minister under Diem to reduce the influence of the Nhus. Lodge suggested that if that proposal were rejected, Lansdale could return and counsel his friend Diem. "If American opinion is in the state you describe," Diem said to Lodge, "then it is up to you, Ambassador Lodge, to disintoxicate American opinion."[138] Lodge later reflected on the experience of visiting Diem. "He had this office where he received foreign visitors and he had a big armchair and a table with a tea set on it and you had a big armchair and a table and the differences between the two tables though, were rather important because the tea that was in front of me contained a diuretic which created an irresistible urge to do that thing which nobody else can do for you," he said. "And I gather his tea was not the same kind of tea that I had. So he sat there chain-smoking cigarettes, one right after the other, and I sat there with this urge growing on me and it grew so strong that finally I had to leave and I never took another cup of tea in his palace again."[139]

For Washington, the noise level coming out of Saigon was too high, in particular due to the consistently negative stories about the Nhus. Lodge was expected to turn the volume down. During a public hearing of the Senate Foreign Relations Committee's Far East Subcommittee, Democratic Senator Frank Church of Idaho questioned what to do with "this mandarin," adding, "There has been nothing like him since the Borgias." Church threatened to introduce a resolution to end American foreign aid to South Vietnam, which Lodge passed along to the Saigon government.[140] Lodge suggested more closely scrutinizing the sources of American foreign aid going to Diem. "If there are effective sanctions which we can apply, we should apply them in order to force a drastic change in government," Lodge wrote in an eyes-only cable to Rusk on September 11.[141] When Kennedy was asked on September 12 whether he supported the Diem government, he responded, "What helps to win the war, we support; what interferes with the war effort, we oppose."[142] It was not the first time that Lodge had heard the line. He had said it himself to Kennedy during their August 15 conversation almost verbatim.

Kennedy sent Joe Mendenhall and Major General Victor "Brute" Krulak to Saigon for a firsthand look at what was going on. Mendenhall once had been the number two man at the embassy, while Krulak was close to Harkins.[143] Upon returning to Washington, Mendenhall repeated Lodge's concerns that the Diem government was disintegrating, while Krulak reported Harkins's view that things were fundamentally sound. "On the one hand we get the military saying the war is going better. On the other hand, we get the political thing—the deterioration that's affecting the military," Kennedy said.[144] They presented such vastly different views that Kennedy asked, "Are you sure you two gentlemen visited the same country?"[145]

Rufus Phillips, who had been in Vietnam off and on since 1954 and knew the Vietnamese people intimately, offered an explanation for the different estimates. Rather than advocating for Mendenhall's or Krulak's position, Phillips suggested that a middle option would be to take "a series of steps to show where we stand."[146] Those steps would include "a calculated psychological warfare and political warfare campaign" to "isolate the Nhus to discredit them and to build up confidence in the loyal opposition." He believed Lansdale was the right man to carry out this effort. "I have discussed this with the ambassador. He agrees with me. He believes he should come out," Phillips said. When Kennedy pressed him for more specifics, Phillips said he would cut off aid to Colonel Tung, which would hurt the Nhus without endangering the war effort, and reduce assistance to special programs that the Nhus liked, and he "would not assist in any repression of the Buddhists or any other religion—would not materially assist the buildup of the Nhus," as "what you get is the possibility—the increasing possibility of splitting Nhu off from the president."[147]

Kennedy liked the idea. He adopted a policy of undermining the Nhus while sending signals to Diem regarding needed reforms and different signals to the generals that the American government supported them. "It seems to me, after listening to General Krulak and the fellow from State [Mendenhall] that they were probably both right. There hasn't been a real deterioration yet, but . . . unless there's some change there, they're probably going to be worse off in three to four months," Kennedy said.[148] The president decided to send Robert McNamara and Maxwell Taylor to Vietnam to move forward with a plan that was basically the one proposed by Phillips.[149] "For the first two weeks it seems to me we did follow a policy of doing our best to encourage a coup," Kennedy said. "Now we were not successful. Whether we should or shouldn't have I don't know. I think it was worth making the effort."[150]

"Life continues to be so exciting that we don't notice the heat and the other discomforts," Lodge wrote his brother, John, on September 24. "We are particularly busy here now getting ready for the arrival of the Secretary of Defense and General Taylor."[151] Kennedy's orders were for them to "see Lodge and get his whole feeling about this thing," and to "leave it up to Cabot" whether he should talk further with Diem. Washington was prepared to "rock along on either basis."[152] "If, in our judgment, our prospects on the war are not hopeful then we should determine what actions must be taken to improve that prospect by the Vietnamese government and what steps the United States can take to compel that action," Kennedy said, reaffirming his confidence in Lodge. "He has enough experience to know."[153]

Taylor said that part of the purpose of their visit was to see whether the CIA was out of control in Saigon, as had been rumored.[154] Joe Alsop said that some of the tensions that purportedly existed between Harkins and Lodge were invented by Halberstam. "Harkins carefully specified that he could not judge the political problem, said that he was not convinced that the Buddhist problem affected the progress of the war. Whereas Lodge, carefully specifying that he knew nothing about the details of the military problem, said he considered the Diem regime no longer politically viable and predicted that this lack of political viability would probably affect the military problem later on," Alsop wrote to Beech.[155] Lodge addressed the issue himself with Harriman, stating that any differences between Harkins and himself had more to do with how they saw political events. "For example, I think the Buddhists, and a good many Christians, too have a very real grievance and that there certainly was persecution of Buddhists (and even of some Roman Catholic clergy!) by Archbishop Thuc and that all of this created a genuine state of indignation which had nothing whatever to do with the Communists," Lodge wrote.[156] Halberstam also made a story out of tensions between Lodge and Saigon Station Chief Richardson. Lodge had asked that Rusk recall Richardson after he praised Diem, which in Lodge's view undermined the strategy of increasing pressure on Diem.[157] For Lodge, the decision was never personal. Privately, he praised Richardson and said he was a good man, but he suspected that Richardson might have been the reason a coup did not come off in August as originally planned. Lodge decided that Richardson had to go before talk about another coup became serious.[158] Halberstam wrote that Richardson, who was one of the first people he befriended after arriving in 1962, was very slow to take the turmoil in Saigon seriously.[159]

McNamara and Taylor had a three-hour meeting with Nhu and Diem on September 29, followed by dinner.[160] Taylor later called it "a depressing evening" and noted "the refusal of this stalwart, stubborn patriot to recognize the realities which threatened to overwhelm him, his family, and his country."[161] They visited all the corps and had substantive conversations with eighty-seven members of the advisory system, from low-ranking enlisted men to senior officers, to gauge the effect of "recent events," presumably the pagoda raids and the arrival of Lodge, "upon the attitudes of the Vietnamese in general, and upon the war effort against the Viet Cong."[162] After hearing him complain about being deceived by briefings, Vann told McNamara that he brought it on himself by sticking to the official itineraries. "They've been rehearsing for you for weeks," he said, suggesting that a better option would have been to pick up a security officer and make unannounced visits.[163] While Harkins was in charge of scheduling McNamara's and Taylor's activities, McNamara stayed with Lodge in his villa. That way, no matter what McNamara heard during the day, Lodge had a monopoly on his time in the evening.[164]

The big issue was whether the war could be won with Diem. McNamara and Taylor concluded that it could be if appropriate political reforms were undertaken by Diem, but he was unlikely to undertake those reforms.[165] "President Diem must decide whether he is fighting for his family or his country," the *New York Times* editorial page headlined.[166] The McNamara-Taylor official report of their trip to Kennedy on October 2 is public, but we do not know the full extent of what they reported privately.[167] Following their visit, Lodge stayed away from Diem.[168] While he was later criticized as arrogant for refusing to see Diem, the McNamara-Taylor report defended him. "Your policy of cool correctness in order to make Diem come to you is correct. You should continue it," McNamara and Taylor wrote.[169] The Vietnamese coup plotters also approved of Lodge's shrewd strategy of leaving his door open but insisting that Diem be the one to walk through it.[170]

Lodge moved to get more of the U.S. mission under his control, specifically the CIA station, which had strongly cautioned against removing Diem. On October 2, 1963, Richard Starnes reported in the *Washington Daily News* that Richardson had refused to obey Lodge's orders. Lodge's old friend Arthur Krock piled on in the *New York Times*, portraying CIA operatives in Saigon as being insubordinate to Lodge and refusing to carrying out his orders on two occasions.[171] The fact that an undercover official was named meant that the CIA was obliged to remove him since his identity had been made public. The next day, Max Frankel wrote in the *New York Times* that "President Kennedy was reliably reported today to have recalled 'for consultations' the head of the Central Intelligence Agency operations in South Vietnam, presumably to end his policy dispute with Ambassador Henry Cabot Lodge."[172] Before he departed

Saigon, Richardson gathered Conein and Alfonso C. "Al" Spera and gave them a message for the generals. "Washington is now open to a coup," he said. "Tell them everyone agrees that Nhu has to go. It's up to them whether or not to keep Diem. And please avoid bloodshed—or keep it to an absolute minimum."[173] The CIA again rejected Lodge's idea to appoint Lansdale as Richardson's replacement. They compromised by leaving the position vacant, as Deputy Station Chief David Smith had spent just as much time in Vietnam as Richardson had.[174] The position was not filled until December, with the arrival of Peer de Silva.[175]

These shifts in the wake of the McNamara-Taylor visit suggest that American policy in Saigon was not the product of a rogue ambassador but rather came from Washington. Lodge's influence went up; he emerged the unchallenged commander of American policy in Saigon. The CIA's and the military's—especially Harkins's—went down. Smith let Conein have complete access without interference from the CIA station in Saigon or headquarters in Washington, where Chester Cooper chaired the CIA's Vietnam Working Group.[176] Kennedy authorized Harkins to approach appropriate generals to gauge their coup plans, and he authorized Lodge to announce a suspension in foreign aid and take control of "all operations in Saigon overt and covert."[177] Diem's brother, Archbishop Thuc, was recalled to the Vatican and ordered to cease his controversial anti-Buddhist statements.[178] Asta planned to keep Thuc in Rome "as long as possible."[179] Lodge and Asta's regular conversations helped to ensure that the failings of the Diem regime would never be blamed on his Catholicism and that it would never be alleged that he and other Catholics supported the persecution of Buddhists.

In his unpublished Vietnam memoir, Lodge stated that he first learned of an assassination plan around October 9.[180] In Washington, the Kennedy White House proposed various potential makeups for the postcoup government.[181] General Don told Conein on October 2 that the generals had a "specific plan" and a coup was planned for late October or early November. Conein asked whether Don needed any help, and Don said the generals needed a signal of American moral support.[182] On October 5, Big Minh presented Conein with three specific possible actions: the assassination of Nhu and Ngo Dinh Cam and the retention of Diem; encirclement of Saigon by military units; and direct confrontation between military units in Saigon.[183] Big Minh said the use of assassinations to accomplish a change of government "was the easiest plan to accomplish."[184]

Lodge started using CIA channels to communicate with Rusk and the White House in a way that suggests he was aware of the type of public record he was creating. He sent all communications related to coup planning through CIA channels, while he continued to conduct normal business using State channels. Communicating through CIA channels ensured that the U.S. government could officially say it had no involvement in coup planning, while discussions in the lead-up to the coup could continue covertly. Lodge clarified that the discussion of possible assassinations would not have occurred had Big Minh not raised the issue. Conein was authorized "to review his plans, other than assassination plans."[185] McNamara and Taylor saw that Lodge shared less and less with Harkins and that he reported directly to the White House. "Circulation of cable traffic to and from Washington was cut so drastically that even General Harkins, with responsibility for 16,000 American military personnel, was left in the dark on Lodge's activities and policies," Mecklin wrote.[186]

It was obvious something was in the works as the generals started to stir again. General Khiem told Conein that they had a plan and they were growing more and more concerned about the possibility of a reconciliation between North and South Vietnam sponsored by Nhu. Allen Whiting, a China scholar and State Department intelligence officer, said, "All thought that this Nhu-Diem tie with the North was a very live possibility . . . You don't want Diem and Nhu to cut a deal with the North and tell us to get the hell out." No concrete evidence has ever emerged regarding whether Nhu made any progress in these talks or whether they were meant as more of a threat against the United States. "Without the Americans we could win the war in two or three years. With the Americans . . . perhaps never," he was fond of saying.[187]

Regardless of whether Nhu believed it, his generals did not. Diem was aware of their dissatisfaction, so they made a proposal that the cabinet posts of the Departments of Defense, Interior, Psychological Warfare, and Education be assigned to military men.[188] Diem deliberated on these demands, but no action came. "They have not done anything I asked," Mecklin recalled Lodge as saying. "They know what I want. Why should I keep asking? Let them come to me for something." Lodge did not keep begging, and instead gave Diem the silent treatment.[189] "I believe that for me to press Diem on things which are *not* in the cards and to repeat what we have said several times already would be a little shrill and would make us look weak," he said.[190] Some have criticized his treatment of Diem as arrogant, but McNamara defended him, saying, "Lodge was not given instructions to meet with Diem."[191]

Big Minh continued to line up support for the coup. He met with his military-school classmate and drinking buddy, Major General Ton That Dinh, at the Caravelle bar. The principal coup plotters were all from Diem's former inner circle. It was from these forces that Diem desperately had called reinforcements during the 1960 coup, and they saved him. This time was different. Dinh told Big Minh that he agreed to the use of his troops to overthrow Diem.[192]

Kennedy was about a year out from reelection. He did not want to deepen the American commitment, but also he did not want to turn his biggest foreign policy weakness into an election-year disaster. "We don't have a prayer of staying in Vietnam," Kennedy told his friend and Pulitzer-winning journalist Charles Bartlett. "Those people hate us. They are going to throw our tails out of there at almost any point. But I can't give up a piece of territory like that to the communists and then get the American people to reelect me."[193] Kennedy believed he had a limited time to act. "Somehow we've got to hold that territory through the 1964 election. We've already given up Laos to the communists and if I give up Vietnam, I won't really be able to go to the people."[194]

A few days later, the *Times of Vietnam* announced the signal the generals had been waiting for—a reduction in American aid to Vietnam. While there would be no immediate cuts, the psychological effect was felt right away. The reporting included new rumors of plans to assassinate Lodge. His life had been threatened more and more over time. According to Mecklin, Lodge addressed the threats with an unknown Vietnamese official. "You surely do not intend any harm to Americans in Viet Nam. If you do, of course, we will bring in the Marines. The Japanese tried to fight the Marines. On a lot of those islands in the Pacific there were not enough Japanese left to bury their own dead after the battle. You wouldn't like that, would you?" Lodge operated on the assumption that even his closest associates were adversaries.[195] Mike Dunn, Lodge's deputy, recalled that he kept a .38 on his desk and a Smith & Wesson .44 Magnum in the embassy safe. He was attacked on more than one occasion in public, and twice a young U.S. Marine named Howard Evers helped him.[196] Dunn and Frederick Flott sometimes slept on a rug outside Lodge's bedroom, armed with a Schmeisser submachine gun.[197]

The generals were feeling more confident about moving forward. Big Minh and Conein met on October 10 to review the coup plans in greater detail. Big Minh came away with the feeling that the generals had the support of Conein and Lodge, but not Harkins. Big Minh informed Conein that Don would be the liaison to the generals.[198] According to Department of State official Paul

Kattenberg, the generals fell into one of two categories. The first were those who were opportunistic and corrupt, both afraid to fight and cognizant that there could be no tomorrow so they should grab all they could today. This group was outraged by Diem's attacks on their fellow Buddhists even though their lifestyle of risk taking, hard drinking, and womanizing was anathema to most Buddhists. The second group was smaller, but more enlightened. They were those, such as Big Minh, who might have tried to seek some type of accommodation with North Vietnam if they had had the chance.[199] Every quality of the coup plotters that made them easy to work with for the Americans—they spoke French, thought like Westerners, and were womanizers—made them contemptible to Vietnamese, whether Buddhist or Catholic, because their lifestyles rejected traditional Confucian values such as humility, fidelity, and filial piety.[200] This was a point that few Americans understood. The ragtag group of generals was never going to produce a national leader, whatever "national" meant to a people like the Vietnamese.

Nguyen Van Thieu, the future president, was commander of the Fifth Division, which was stationed at Bien Hoa, fifteen miles from Saigon. "The Americans had created the conditions for the army to revolt," Thieu said. "There were shortages of fuel, ammunition, and medical supplies. Our feeling was that the Americans had turned against Diem, but they would support the military with a new civilian government once Diem was ousted. The American military was a constant Sword of Damocles over our head. Every time the Americans wanted something, they would exert pressure on us by withholding or offering military aid."[201] Kattenberg saw it a similar way. American actions conditioned the coup, while the Buddhists provided the yeast for the brew.[202] "The United States had in fact encouraged the coup, or 'climatized' it, as an accurate designation of the time put it, by a series of more or less calculated broadcasts on the Voice of America as well as by a campaign of what was called 'salami-slicing' U.S. aid to Diem," Kattenberg wrote. "This consisted of slowly drying up Diem's sources of U.S. support while simultaneously Ambassador Lodge kept his distance from Diem, a practice of calculated ambiguity, waiting for Diem to approach him, which Diem finally did only a few days before the coup, far too late for any understanding to be reached."[203] The CIA had made its regular support payment for September, but future payments were held up.[204]

The coup plotters were emboldened by Madame Nhu's absence. She had a sixth sense about coup rumors. Madame Nhu continued to cause problems from afar, and CIA wiretaps in Rome picked up that she had been making contact with visiting North Vietnamese cabinet members. "Madame Nhu presented written proposals that the DRV [Democratic Republic of Vietnam] and the Republic of Vietnam consolidate their positions and work together to liquidate American influence," the Saigon station reported on October 15, making American officials even more anxious about when the coup would take place.[205]

On October 16, Don and Big Minh wanted confirmation that Conein spoke on behalf of Lodge. Don had become upset by Harkins's insistence that the generals stop talking about a coup. Harkins had never really developed anything but a formal relationship with the Vietnamese during his time in their country.[206] Don demanded to know what the American position really was. Conein, according to his instructions, stated that the "U.S. would not thwart a change of government or deny support to a new regime if it appeared capable of increasing effectiveness of military effort, assuring popular support to win the war, and improving working relationships with U.S." He then asked for something in return—proof that the coup plans were well advanced, as well as a postcoup political organizational plan.[207] Just to be sure, even though he had his authorization of August 15, Lodge wanted confirmation from the White House. According to Leslie Gelb, when he was serving as general editor of the Pentagon Papers, he read a CIA transcript of a telephone conversation between Kennedy and Lodge in which Kennedy urged Lodge to get the coup in motion. But the transcript "disappeared" and he never saw it again. It was not used in the Pentagon Papers.[208]

When Conein still had not received a satisfactory plan, he met twice with Don on October 23. Don had asked him to stay home so he could receive an update as soon as it was available.[209] Conein apologized on behalf of Harkins for his lack of support. Harkins had told Don the night before at a party hosted by the British embassy military attaché that he was opposed to their plans, but if the coup happened, he agreed to provide shelter for Don and his family in the Harkins villa. Don had not submitted a written coup plan to Conein, but he said, "Perhaps I could provide something for Ambassador Lodge's eyes a couple of days before the start of the coup."[210] A plan for the coup as well as the postcoup period was what had been missing all along. There was not a lot of disagreement about overthrowing the Diem government. But who would replace it?

# 13 · A Coup

For most people in Saigon, Friday, November 1, 1963, began like any other. The sun rose on All Saints' Day at 5:42 a.m.[1] Henry Cabot Lodge Jr. had long-standing plans to return to the United States, but he canceled them at the last minute.[2] In his memoir, Lodge wrote that John F. Kennedy had instructed him to tell no one of their communications in the weeks leading up to the coup.[3] That morning, Army of the Republic of Vietnam coup leaders met at the Joint General Staff headquarters (JGS) and began moving equipment into Saigon. The coup plotters had shrewdly chosen a Roman Catholic holiday for the big day.[4]

"The air was electric with rumors and tension," Peter Arnett recalled.[5] "I have hope that [the] political [situation] will die down soon and I can get out again," Halberstam wrote to John Paul Vann on October 29, "if I don't get thrown out."[6] Arnett later wrote that Lodge had told him, "Diem said I know there is going to be a coup but I don't know who's going to do it or where he's going to do it, and the coup planners are much cleverer this time than they've ever been before because there are a number of them and I can't find out which is the real one."[7] Early in the morning on October 31, Halberstam received the following message from "a Vietnamese colonel who was a friend of ours": "PLEASE BUY ME ONE BOTTLE OF WHISKY AT THE P.X."[8] It was a code that had been agreed on earlier to signal that a coup was impending.[9] Rufus Phillips later recalled, "Early in the morning on the day of the coup, before it started, I got a call from Lou [Conein]. He said, 'Would you mind staying with Elyette and the kids? I think the balloon is going up today.'"[10]

Even though Lodge knew the Diem government was poised for destruction, he went about his normal routine. He held out hope for Ngo Dinh Diem, who had refused to see him again until the end of October.[11] On Sunday, October 27, Diem invited Lodge to go up to Dalat for the opening of an atomic research center.[12] While preparing for his departure at the airport, Lodge ran into Tran Van Don.[13] Conein had arranged the meeting through Don's dentist.[14] "Mr. Ambassador, what is Conein's relation to you?" Don later recalled having asked. "He is my representative. And I said, 'fine.' And I didn't avoid talking about the coup. I said, 'Well, I'm very happy to know he's your representative.' So then I jumped into the subject. I said, 'Mr. Ambassador, we need a change soon.' I didn't speak of a regime change, merely of a 'change.' He knew I was talking about a coup. He said, 'Well, I'm ready to give you support, and so are the Americans in all that you do.'"[15] According to one account, Lodge told Don that the United States was considering a withdrawal of forces by 1965, after the 1964 presidential election. That comment caused a reaction of "near panic" for the generals. "We took it as a sign that unless we get rid of Diem, the United States would wash its hands of the war no later than 1965," Tran Thien Khiem recalled.[16] "Lodge's declaration that Conein was authorized to speak for him was the unequivocal endorsement the generals had been looking for," Phillips wrote. The interaction caused CIA Director John McCone to warn the White House that Conein had become a little too "overt."[17] Conein said Lodge wanted the coup to take place before he returned to the United States for consultations on October 31.[18]

Lodge headed out of the city with Diem under these conditions. Colonel John Michael Dunn and Emily joined them on the overnight trip to Dalat.[19] The highland city was at an altitude of two thousand feet with welcome milder temperatures. The Lodges and Diem stayed at a palace built by the French, and they dined with the mayor of Dalat and his wife. According to Lodge's record of the meeting, they discussed the recent U.S. aid cuts, repression of the Buddhists, and complaints of CIA intrigues.[20] "I began to see a chance we might begin to get a different kind of behavior out of him," he recalled. "We were up in Dalat sitting in front of an open fire incidentally, that's when he said, 'oh by the way,' he said, 'I've changed my mind about the commercial import programs and we will talk about it,'" Lodge remembered. "We were like two boys on bicycles playing chicken and he gave way first."[21] Diem got what he wanted from their visit. "At last, Mr. Lodge understands what I am trying to do," he said.[22] Diem offered a partial capitulation, but it was too late to halt the coup plotters.[23] "He was rather a nice-looking man and he was very polite and correct," Lodge recalled. "I sensed that he was a man of great courage and great convictions and if necessary he would go down fighting for his country, which of course is what he did."[24] Dunn said the visit was a turning point in their relationship. "I think he sincerely believed at that late date that the Diem regime could be made to work. And he certainly didn't have a great opinion of the triumvirate waiting in the wings."[25]

Despite the exchange of views in Dalat, Diem did not announce any further reforms or offer to send Ngo Dinh Nhu away even temporarily. Lodge referred to his inaction as "frustrating." Diem's assistant, Do Tho, recalled hearing Diem yell in French at Lodge. "Each time he bade farewell to President Diem and left, Ambassador Lodge's face was bright red and angry-looking as he rushed hurriedly out to his car. I can say that this same thing happened repeatedly from the very first day that Lodge arrived to take over the post of U.S. Ambassador in Vietnam."[26] However, nothing seemed to bother Diem in the final days. "There was none of the agitation I had seen in him during the height of the Buddhist crisis," Phillips said after meeting Diem on October 30. "He seemed philosophical about whatever fate brings." During the meeting, Diem puffed on his ever-present cigarette and asked Phillips, "Do you think there will be a coup?" Phillips had no doubt. "I am afraid so, Mr. President," he answered.[27] There is no doubt that the Kennedy White House supported a coup. The concern was that the United States could be blamed for what was now seen as inevitable. "We are particularly concerned about hazard that an unsuccessful coup, however carefully we avoid direct engagement, will be laid at our door by public opinion almost everywhere," McGeorge Bundy cabled Lodge on behalf of Kennedy on October 25.[28]

As Lodge and Diem met that weekend, the Joint Chiefs of Staff quietly deployed a task force to the areas previously identified as possible evacuation zones. Operation Candy Machine was activated, which involved sending three F-102s to Tan Son Nhut. These activities took place even as Paul Harkins stated that he did not know anything about plans for a coup.[29] The generals were also busy that weekend. Don went to Nha Trang to review the latest coup plan with General Ton That Dinh. Both returned to Saigon the next day to meet Duong Van Minh and Khiem at a private club in Cholon. "Dinh insisted on saving the lives of Diem and Nhu," Don wrote, "which Khiem and I fully supported."[30]

On the morning of November 1, Admiral Harry Felt concluded a daylong visit to Saigon from his headquarters at Honolulu. There is no evidence to suggest that the meeting had to do with coup planning, but rather was a routine visit. Felt and Don met at nine fifteen in the morning at the Military Assistance Command office. Big Minh had started to have doubts about the coup plan. "About midway in our planning," Don wrote, "he proposed the idea of assassination to me in lieu of our planned overthrow of the regime."[31] Felt then joined Lodge, who escorted him to Gia Long Palace for a meeting with Diem at ten o'clock in the morning. Since the meeting was scheduled to go until eleven fifteen, Felt got an abbreviated version of Diem's legendary monologues. Then Diem became suddenly direct. He said he knew junior CIA officers were spreading rumors about him. Diem complained that the United States had cut foreign aid and that Americans had misunderstood the role of the special forces used to carry out the August pagoda raids.[32]

Don and Lodge escorted Felt to the airport at eleven thirty that morning for a press conference. Returning to the JGS, Don said, "I gave orders to have combat-ready companies available to set up a defense perimeter around the JGS headquarters beginning at 12:00 Noon."[33] Don was not eager to organize a coup. He had served Diem loyally and urged him on numerous occasions to make reforms. "It was only after we presented a petition many times to Diem to ask him to re-open the pagodas, to free Buddhist monks and nuns, and once he refused two or three times, at that moment, there were many arrests of the students," Don recalled. "The domestic situation was intolerable, and it was then that we decided to make our coup d'état."[34] He called a meeting of top military leaders for one o'clock that afternoon at the JGS. Brigadier General Van Thanh Cao called Nhu to tip him off about the sudden gathering. Cao, who had been trained by the French in Hanoi and the Americans at Fort Leavenworth, said it seemed suspicious. Nhu told him not to worry. The situation was under control.[35] Nhu was confident that his efforts to divide the army's leadership had been sufficient to reduce the chance of a coup.[36]

Harkins and Felt left Gia Long shortly before noon, leaving Lodge and Diem alone. Diem said he was ready to talk about what the United States really wanted.[37] He was concerned about Lodge's return to Washington. "There's an old saying here that every time the American ambassador leaves there is a coup against the government," Diem told him. "And he said there's one being organized now," Lodge recalled in a 1979 interview with Stanley Karnow. "Diem was already getting rumors of plots, but there were so many different rumors he hardly knew what to believe," Lodge said.[38] Diem repeated some of the complaints against the CIA that he had raised with Lodge over the weekend. "Please tell President Kennedy that I am a good and a frank ally, that I would rather be frank and settle questions now than talk about them after we have lost everything," he said. "Tell President Kennedy that I take all his suggestions very seriously and wish to carry them out but it is a question of timing."[39] Lodge sent a summary of their conversation to Washington marked "priority," but it would not arrive until after the "flash" communications related to the coup.[40]

A short drive away, Conein was putting on his colonel's uniform and special forces beret. Don's dentist, who hosted many of Conein's secret meetings, had told Conein that he was to go to the JGS right away.[41] "I had a voice radio," he said. "'Nine-nine' was the prearranged code word to say the coup was on." The generals who cut the phone lines were supposed to leave open certain lines, including one to Conein. "But like everything the Vietnamese do, they screw things up," he recalled.[42] Conein had planned to stay home that day. He had stockpiled firearms, ammunition, and communications equipment, and there was even a police checkpoint on the road outside to control traffic and watch for anything suspicious. But since he was summoned to the JGS, Conein took three million piastres ($42,000) from his villa safe and stuffed it in a briefcase. He had another five million piastres available to him at the CIA station. The money was for the generals to buy food for those taking part in the coup and to pay death claims for those who were killed. He put the briefcase in his Jeep, loaded up some grenades and a submachine gun, and drove to the JGS headquarters adjacent to the airport, arriving shortly after noon.[43] His level of preparation suggests that the United States did more than simply "condition" the atmosphere for a coup. The transfers of cash suggest that the coup plotters were, at times, hired hands. Once he got to the JGS, he provided updates to the CIA station office in the U.S. embassy approximately every five minutes, giving Lodge street-by-street intelligence regarding coup progress.

The streets in Saigon were empty due to the lunchtime siesta.[44] The Gia Long presidential palace was quiet. With Madame Nhu out of the country and the Nhu children up in Dalat, Diem did not have the usual worry of balancing the nation's affairs and family matters.[45] Colonel Le Trung Hien, the air force commander, was flying and had no idea that a coup was in progress. When he landed at Tan Son Nhut Airport late that morning, he learned of the meeting at the JGS. More interested in going to lunch than taking part in a coup, he sent his deputy, Lieutenant Colonel Do Khac Mai. When Hien was overruled on the decision to authorize some T-28s to fly that afternoon, Big Minh sent armed guards to take Hien to the JGS, where he was locked up.

At one-thirty sharp, the Armed Forces Radio Station began playing "White Christmas," the signal to go into action.[46] The coup itself began moments after.[47] The British embassy was onto the fact that something unusual was going on, because while the Saigon Radio Station was surrounded by fully armed marines, there was barely any additional security at Gia Long Palace—meaning that the coup plotters had pulled off a "near-miracle of achieving tactical surprise for their attack."[48] "I was getting ready to return to work after lunch at home when I heard the sound of gunfire," deputy political counselor Robert Miller recalled. "I immediately drove to the embassy, ten minutes away, noting along the way that concertina barbed wire had been strung across the streets leading to the palace and that several armored vehicles had been placed in defensive positions in the area."[49] Truckloads of marines surrounded police headquarters and arrested pro-Diem officials. They seized the two main radio stations, the post office, and the airport.[50] Air force planes equipped with rockets attacked the navy headquarters, bombing naval vessels that resisted by firing antiaircraft shells from the Saigon River.[51]

Don kept phone lines out to the JGS, the U.S. embassy, and Gia Long. "We were just starting to eat around 1:30 when I heard cannon fire, and recognized it as 20 mm. fire and bombing," Lodge recalled. Emily, the Dunns, and their two boys were with them.[52] "It is not yet clear what exactly is happening," the British embassy reported to the Foreign Office in London in an "emergency" cable.[53] But Lodge knew. "A coup had begun," he said.[54] The coup forces attacked the Presidential Guard barracks and the Gia Long Palace. The rebel generals repeatedly called Gia Long and ordered Diem and Nhu to surrender. The British embassy reported hearing reports that Diem and Nhu agreed to resign shortly after the start of the coup, "but we do not, of course, know that this is true."[55]

Big Minh had put off an assault on the palace for as long as possible in order to avoid potential bloodshed. Conein urged him to strike quickly and maintain the element of surprise. "If you hesitate, you will be lost," he said. Deputy Chief of Mission William Trueheart arrived at Lodge's villa and told him Don had announced to the embassy that a coup had begun. Don also called General Joseph Stilwell, Harkins's deputy, to inform him that it was under way.[56] "I decided to stay at the house," Lodge said. "I got one rumor that an attempt would be made to kidnap and hold me as a hostage. I could reach the embassy by telephone, as well as voice radio. There was no telling how long the fighting would last. With Trueheart at the Chancery, the U.S. would have two strings to its bow. Twelve American MPs dressed in civilian clothes arrived to protect me—the biggest men I've ever seen, armed with riot guns and tear gas. They were stationed in the yard and at the upstairs window."[57] Phillips went to the safest place he could think of: Conein's villa.[58]

Diem informed his personal staff by one forty-five that afternoon that a coup had begun.[59] He, Nhu, and key palace staff quickly moved to a bunker under Gia Long Palace shortly after the first shots were fired.[60] That afternoon, he desperately worked the telephone, hoping to receive assurance that reinforcements were on the way to rescue him, just as they had rescued him during the attempted coup in 1960. Members of the Presidential Guard deployed themselves around Gia Long, but there was little firing around the palace. One hundred three truckloads of rebel troops entered Saigon over the bridge from Bien Hoa.[61] "Mortar shells began to fall into the Presidential Guard (Cong Hoa) barracks across the road and less than 100 yards distant from the Chancery," the British embassy reported to the Foreign Office in London. "At this time we had no idea exactly who was involved in the fighting or who was winning, but it was increasingly evident that we were being given a grandstand view of a full-scale coup d'état."[62] Around three o'clock in the afternoon, Diem and Nhu began broadcasting from a Gia Long transmitter asking for confirmation of reinforcements.[63]

Two single-engine aircraft rocketed the Presidential Guard barracks and naval ships on the Saigon River. The navy, which remained loyal to the Diem regime, surrendered, and according to a classified American government history of the coup, Captain Ho Tan Quyen, the naval commander, refused to take part in the coup and was murdered by his escort.[64] Diem held out hope that if everything else failed, he could expect reinforcements from the south from Generals Bui Dzinh and Huynh Van Cao. Diem called Don around three thirty. When Don reminded him of their conversation the day before about the importance of making reforms, Diem said he was ready to do so. "Why didn't you tell me that yesterday? Now it's too late." One by one, Don put the other generals on the phone, to prove to Diem that the coup was real.[65] "He was very alarmed," Don recalled. "Suddenly he seemed to realize that we had been serious. I reminded him of four futile attempts to persuade him of the necessity of reforms. He was frightened enough to listen and make any kind of public proclamation we suggested, but by then it was too late. The troops already had their marching orders. His only course now, I pointed out to him, was to surrender unconditionally and safe conduct would be provided for him and his family to leave the country."[66]

Diem refused to surrender and instead continued trying to reach Dinh on the telephone.[67] Nhu invited the generals to come to the palace to negotiate. Don considered the idea but, after consulting with the others, refused, advising that both resign. They refused. At four o'clock that afternoon, in response to Diem's stubbornness, Don ordered two fighter planes to attack the Presidential Guards' barracks.[68] "Very heavy firing in Embassy area, believed from Presidential Guard. Tanks reported moving eastwards towards Bien Hoa highway," the British embassy reported nearby.[69] Dinh was supposed to arrest the rebel generals who moved against Diem and Nhu, a plan code-named Bravo I, but instead he betrayed them.[70] "Had the revolution been delayed by one day, all the military leaders would have been arrested," Dinh recalled, noting how close Diem had been to uncovering their plot.[71] Diem frantically telephoned all of the divisional and provincial headquarters he could reach, asking for help, but none was forthcoming. "Although tightly besieged, he still called for help," Dinh said. "He also yelled: 'All you officers must come here if you want to negotiate.' That proved he wanted to stall for time."[72]

With rumors swirling around Saigon, Diem penned extraordinary handwritten orders to palace staff and loyalists. These notes, previously unpublished, suggested that Diem had not yet panicked and still held out hope that he might defeat the coup. First, he issued a brief, specific order to Bui Dzinh "to bring four battalions up to liberate the Capital." Dzinh, one of the few who remained loyal to Diem, was commander of the Ninth Infantry Division in Ben Tre, about seventy miles south of Saigon. However, Dzinh's forces were roadblocked on the Trung Luong bridge to keep them from reaching the capital city just twenty-five miles farther. Young American Foreign Service officer Richard Holbrooke was also on his way north into Saigon from the Mekong area and noted that the road into the city at Can Tho was blocked by troops.[73]

Second, Diem wrote a more philosophical order that defended his rule, his presidency, and the South Vietnamese constitution. "Together with citizens and officials in the military, with my position as president and the leader of the military of the republic," Diem wrote as shelling continued outside the palace, "I order every soldier: you cannot listen to anyone's orders except my orders."[74] Read today, the notes show the truly sad ending of the Diem regime and how out of touch he remained until the very end. He remained stubborn, fixated on protocol, unresponsive, aloof, rigid, and, perhaps mostly importantly, utterly Confucian—and he expected that others would understand his circumstances. He lived in a bubble that remained unburst even as shells exploded outside the palace. Diem expected his order to be read when reinforcements arrived. "Because there are some officials who plan to deceive our military in order to deceive our citizens' rights, every department in the military and every related department must stand up and follow me to destroy the rebellion."[75]

The order and his other handwritten notes represent the only evidence of Diem's state of mind that day. It was a stalling technique, just like those he was able to use to delay the 1960 coup attempt long enough to regain power.[76] He counted on support from a formerly loyal division of General Huynh Van Cao's Fourth Corps, but it had been commandeered by the coup leaders. The notes were written at a critical moment when the rebel generals had begun broadcasting on Saigon Radio in the name of the armed forces, explaining why they had taken action against the government, calling on Diem and Nhu to resign, and offering safe passage out of the country. The generals announced that if they refused, they would be killed. "It is important to remember that this offer was made, not once, but repeatedly," the British embassy reported to the Foreign Office.[77] Nhu made frenzied calls to his paramilitary units, including the Republican Youth Corps, but they were futile.[78] "Because of the urgent situation at this moment, I request all of the departments to stand up and use the fastest means to liberate the capital," Diem urged.[79] He wrote the order in his own hand so that recipients would know that their president was alive and demanded their immediate help.

At about four thirty that afternoon, Diem called Lodge. "A group of rebels have started a coup," he said. "What will the attitude of the U.S. government be in this matter?" Diem had a habit of shouting over the phone, so Lodge held it away from his ear. Frederick Flott, seated next to him, could hear almost everything that was said.[80] Lodge demurred. "It's half past four in the morning in Washington," he said. "It's impossible for me to get any opinion from our government at this hour." He told Diem that he was concerned for his safety, although the generals had promised Lodge that Diem and Nhu would be able to leave the country. "Mr. Ambassador, do you realize who you are talking to? I would like you to know that you are talking to the president of an independent and sovereign nation. I will only leave this country if it is the will of my people," Diem said, according to his bodyguard's recollections.[81] Lodge offered him protection on his own authority, without consulting Washington.[82] "I will provide you asylum in my residence. I can provide air passage outside the country. The generals running the coup have promised me their cooperation." Flott said if Diem had accepted Lodge's offer, he would have been the one sent to escort him to safety. "There was a plan and a well thought-out effort by Lodge to save Diem's life," he said.[83] However, Diem held out. According to his assistant, Diem felt insulted. "With an angry look on his face, he refused the offer. Diem slammed the telephone receiver down hard," Do Tho recalled.[84] Lodge later remembered Diem's final words before hanging up as

"'Je vais ramener loi,' or something like that."[85] British Ambassador Gordon Etherington-Smith, in a detailed twelve-page eyewitness report on the coup, wrote that Lodge had confirmed the offer of safe passage.[86]

"The shooting went on and on," Lodge recalled. At around four forty-five in the afternoon, the generals called Diem and Nhu. Colonel Le Quang Tung was on the phone just long enough to tell them that their special forces had surrendered—and then the generals took Tung outside and shot him. Big Minh called Diem again around five fifteen to urge him to surrender. Diem hung up on him.[87] Around six o'clock, the rebels began a heavy bombardment of the Presidential Guard barracks. "It got closer and closer. I didn't know how long it would go on. I decided the sensible thing for me to do was to try to get a little sleep. I had a very dependable man in Mike Dunn who would wake me if necessary," Lodge recalled.[88] Around eight o'clock that evening, there was a lull in the fighting while Big Minh spoke to Diem and Nhu. He urged them again to surrender, and they countered by proposing that a general be sent to Gia Long Palace to negotiate. Big Minh refused, being well aware of Diem's ability to thwart coup attempts. Diem's voice came over the loudspeaker at the palace, stating that he remained in control and had captured the generals. The British ambassador suspected that the announcement was a cover-up for his escape.[89] Diem and Nhu managed to get out of Gia Long Palace in disguise with a briefcase full of U.S. dollars—and depending on which version of the story is accurate, the amount was somewhere between $6,000 and $1 million. Diem and Nhu walked to Le Thanh Street, where they were met by a loyal officer in a small black Citroen and driven to the home of a friend, Ma Tuyen, a Chinese merchant who lived in Cholon.[90] After the attempted coup in 1960, Diem had made several security enhancements, including the installation of a telephone line in Ma's villa so Diem could be reached directly through the palace switchboard as though he were still within its walls. "When the President arrived around 8 o'clock he was very tired and nervous," Ma recalled. "He kept pacing the floor and chain-smoking cigarettes."[91] Nhu suggested splitting up, proposing that Diem head to the Mekong Delta while Nhu went to the Central Highlands. Remembering his promise to watch over his brother, Diem wanted to stay together.[92]

At nine fifteen that night, the mortaring of the Cong Hoa barracks resumed. "Twenty tanks, accompanied by the greater part of a battalion of infantry moved eastwards past the back of the Chancery," the British embassy reported. "At 9:40, they assailed the barracks with all weapons firing, both light and heavy, backed by increased mortar shelling from the radio station."[93] At around ten o'clock, the remaining pro-Nhu forces pledged loyalty to what was being called the Military Revolutionary Council. Diem continued to make offers to save his government. "The President stayed in his room all night, making many telephone calls and not sleeping," Ma recalled.[94] Dinh spoke with Diem around midnight. "I've saved you motherfuckers many times, but not now, you bastards," Dinh told him. "You shits are finished."[95]

"Around 4, I was standing on my second-floor portico when I saw a couple of my neighbors firing tracer bullets at each other from their houses up the street," Lodge said. "Apparently, they were using the coup to work off some private grudge."[96] Phillips, still hunkered down in Conein's villa, remembered, "A tremendous racket of firing, including heavy weapons and what sounded like tank cannons, broke out from the direction of the presidential palace and lasted for over an hour."[97] The CIA station in Saigon reported that Big Minh gave the order to take Gia Long at any cost.[98] Etherington-Smith called it "an impressive spectacle." He reported, "The troops taking part were supported by tanks, artillery and mortars and large fires quickly broke out around the Palace. Observers in the town reported the enormous intensity of fire combined with sniping from roof tops which made observation dangerous. This was the last phase of the battle."[99]

U.S. embassy deputy political counselor Robert Miller, who remained at the embassy monitoring reports of what was happening as it unfolded, recalled that "in the early morning hours came a final tank-led assault on the palace, and by daylight it was all over."[100] Shortly after six o'clock that morning, a white flag went up at the palace. "After heavy fighting lasting over two hours the Presidential Guard surrendered the Gia Long Palace. According to the rebel radio, both Diem and Nhu were captured but the Reuters correspondent who has visited the badly battered Palace denies this and says the troops are still looking for them and questioning Palace guards about hidden tunnels, etc.," the British embassy reported.[101] Colonel Pham Ngoc Thao was one of the first of the rebels who went into the palace, where he was told that Diem and Nhu had fled.[102] Invading forces scratched their heads when they were unable to locate Diem or Nhu. Don ordered a search.[103] The coup forces raided the Gia Long antiques, Nhu's Scotch whisky, and Madame Nhu's lingerie. Flott passed David Halberstam as he was leaving the palace with a ten-foot-long elephant tusk and a Laotian sword in his arms.[104] Flott stooped to pick up some loose .223 ammunition, hard to come by in Saigon, which had spilled on the palace floor.[105] Khiem was told at the JGS that Diem and Nhu could not be found, and that information was presumably passed on to Conein and Lodge.

According to Don's memoirs, "Conein seemed to be irritated by this news, saying that Diem and Nhu must be found at any cost."[106]

Ma sent Diem and Nhu in his car to a nearby Chinese Catholic church. "When we parted the President merely said, 'Thank you.' That was all, there was no emotion," Ma recalled.[107] According to a British embassy source who knew Father Fernand Billaud, the priest at St. Francis Xavier's, Diem and Nhu arrived at the church dressed in religious garments and asked to "wait there for their assassins . . . The decision to capture and execute them had already been taken." Diem and Nhu planned to reckon with their lost mandate of heaven—death to the mandatories.[108] Billaud, a stocky man with white crew-cut hair, steel-blue eyes, and a goatee, at first did not believe it was Diem but realized who he was when a congregant ran up to Diem and cried, "I want to live or die with you." Diem comforted the man. "Have courage, we face difficult times," he said.[109] Another account, however, reported that after a breakfast of steamed rice buns with pork filling, small meat dumplings, and coffee, Diem called Don at six o'clock that morning with an offer to surrender "with honor." Don refused until Diem ordered the Gia Long Palace guard to surrender.[110] Diem called back at six fifty and asked to speak to Big Minh, who was furious that the surrender was offered to Don and not to him.[111] Diem told him it was all over. He was willing to surrender. Big Minh stated that he would accept Diem's surrender as long as he gave the order for his remaining loyal forces at the palace to stop firing.[112] Diem agreed, and the cease-fire occurred just before seven o'clock that morning. The generals still assumed that Diem and Nhu were somewhere in the Gia Long Palace complex. "Generals will soon proceed to Gia Long to get the president and Nhu and escort them to JGS. At that time they will request their preference as to destination and will then seek approval of the government of the country to which they desire to be transported," the CIA station in Saigon reported.[113] Diem put on a business suit and called Khiem to request transportation to negotiate, revealing his location at St. Francis Xavier Catholic Church in Cholon.[114]

The rebels asked Conein to find an aircraft to fly the brothers out of the country, and Conein passed the request to Acting Station Chief David Smith. Khiem wanted to personally retrieve them, but Big Minh refused. Major Duong Hieu Nghia said that Big Minh sent him, General Mai Huu Xuan, Colonel Nguyen Van Quan, Colonel Duong Ngoc Lam, and Captain Nguyen Van Nhung to pick them up and bring them to the JGS, disputing other accounts in which Big Minh said that Diem and Nhu were to be arrested.[115] The convoy included four Jeeps and five M-113 armored personnel carriers (APCs). Nghia felt it was unusual that Nhung was riding atop one of the APCs, since he was an infantry captain. "I thought that General Minh must have given Captain Nhung some kind of special mission to carry out so I did not ask him any more questions because whatever it is has nothing to do with our security escort assignment." Ma arranged for a car to take the brothers to the agreed-on meeting spot.[116] Conein and others were preparing for Diem's arrival at the JGS. "They had a table with green cloth on it, they had the Vice President there to take his dismissal and they were going to bring in the cameras," Conein said.[117] Nguyen Van Thieu was supposed to receive Diem's surrender, so they started sweeping up the cigarette butts and empty Bireley's orange soda bottles. Conein told Don that he had better get out of there before any cameras recorded that he had been there, and Don agreed.[118]

According to one account, Nhung entered the Cholon church alone and spoke to Diem and Nhu. "I invite you two to get in this vehicle," Nghia remembered Nhung as saying. They agreed to leave, but Diem asked Xuan to drop by Gia Long to pick up some personal effects. Xuan and Lam said that was impossible. Nhu complained that an M-113 APC had been sent for them. It was not appropriate for a president, he said, and was a deliberate insult by Big Minh. Diem and Nhu were handcuffed and loaded into the APC, another insult, where they rode alone with their driver.[119] Xuan, Lam, and the others were in one of the four Jeeps behind them.[120] "I clearly saw that there were only three people inside the hull of the vehicle—the President, the Advisor, and Captain Nhung. Later I found out that Captain Nhung had ordered the vehicle commander and the vehicle gunner to get out and ride back in another vehicle . . . I got into my jeep and gave the order to start engines and prepare to move out," Nghia recalled. The vehicles left in the same sequence as they had arrived, with Diem and Nhu riding in the second from the final APC. It was constantly in radio communication with Nghia.[121]

The CIA station notified the generals that no aircraft to take Diem and Nhu out of the country would be available for twenty-four hours. If they needed to get as far as France, in case that was the first place that agreed to take them, it would require a KC-135. The closest option was an American air base in Okinawa. When this information became known and why better contingency plans had not been made is a mystery. Both Lodge's C-135 and Harkins's C-54 sat idly at the airport, as did two helicopters at the Saigon golf course, all on standby to exile the generals in case the coup failed. Washington had sent a special plane for Lodge, Conein's family, and other American officials in case they needed to evacuate. Lodge recalled that no attempt was made to get Diem and Nhu to one of the available planes.[122] Conein said the plan was to take Diem and Nhu to a safe house in Pleiku before evacuating them using a Vietnamese aircraft. However, at the last minute, Big Minh asked to use an American aircraft. "Now this was not in the books," Conein said. "This shows direct support." When Conein said it would be twenty-four hours until an aircraft arrived, Big Minh's response was, "Twenty-four hours? Fine."[123]

The convoy reached the crossing at Hong Thap Tu Street, just past the Tu Du Maternity Hospital, when it was forced to stop at the train tracks and sit there for around ten minutes while waiting for a train to pass. Nhung, known as Big Minh's hit man, got into the APC and began to argue with Nhu.[124] The details remain a little sketchy, but most accounts agree that Big Minh had authorized Nhung to kill them, or at least Nhu.

General Nguyen Khanh described the murders as "savage." Nhung leapt at Nhu and stabbed him with a bayonet fifteen to twenty times, then drew his personal knife and cut out their gallbladders while they were still alive: "Nhu was alive when they put the knife in to take out some of the organs, what they refer to in Chinese medicine [as] . . . the gallbladder.[125] And in the Orient when you are a big soldier, big man—this thing is very important . . . they do it against Nhu when Nhu was alive . . . And Diem had this happen to him and later on they kill him by pistol and rifle. This is murder. A real murder in the fashion that you . . . it's very savage."[126]

Nhung shot Diem in the head. Nhu was still twitching, so he shot him as well, referring to the final unnecessary shots as the "coup de grace."[127] Diem and Nhu could not defend themselves since their hands were tied.[128] When Nghia heard the gunshots, he turned around and drove back to see what had happened. "When I reached the APC carrying the President and the Advisor, I saw Captain Nhung sitting on top of the vehicle in the vehicle commander's position. Looking toward me, he held up one finger as a signal, meaning that everything was all right. I asked him, 'Where did the gunshots come from?' Captain Nhung pointed down into the vehicle but said nothing." The convoy continued forward once the train had passed. "I asked the armored platoon commander what had caused the gunfire in the third APC in the column. The answer I got back was, 'The assistant driver of that vehicle told me that the gunshots we heard were the infantry captain riding in that vehicle shooting the President and his Advisor, killing them both.'"[129] Nghia pressed Nhung about what had happened in the APC: "Major Nhung laughed as he gave me a short, concise answer, acting as if nothing of any importance had happened. He said, 'One man or two, it's all the same. Two was not particularly difficult, but it made our success more certain.' I tried to prod him for more information by saying, 'But there was not an order for two people, was there?' [Meaning, "There was not an order to kill both of them, was there?"] 'Diem resisted [fought back] after I stabbed Nhu to death, so I had to kill him too. I would have done the same thing whether or not there were orders to kill him. Just to make sure. After all, I did not have time to wait for orders, now did I?'" From what he said, it is possible that Nhung's orders had been to kill Nhu but not Diem. "I never dared say a word about this," Nghia reflected.[130] He promised journalist Robert Shaplen in 1972 to tell "the full story some day."[131] As of this writing, based on his health, it is doubtful he will ever be able to do that.

The first report said that Diem and Nhu committed suicide, but that did not hold up once photographs emerged showing their hands tied behind their backs.[132] The fact that they were devout Catholics was another reason why that seemed doubtful. Khanh later told Lodge that when they were shot, Diem was holding a briefcase containing $1 million "in the largest denominations," as well as forty kilograms of gold bars.[133] When Halberstam snickered to Lodge that it was a real shame that they had been killed, Lodge shot back: "What would we have done with them if they'd lived? Every Colonel Blimp in the world would have made use of them."[134]

"Next day I got word that Diem and Nhu had tried to escape, and had been captured and then killed," Lodge remembered. "I was terribly shocked, and terribly sorry that Diem had not accepted American protection."[135] While there is nothing inaccurate about Lodge's recollections, they are incomplete. Lodge rarely answered questions about the coup and assassination, and when he did, he stuck to the version in the Pentagon Papers. He left out a key detail: he had had a second conversation with Diem around seven o'clock on the morning of November 2. This phone call was confirmed by Dunn only after Lodge's death in 1985. "Lodge talked to Diem twice. Once in the afternoon and once the next morning," he said.[136] Diem asked if there was something the embassy could do, according to Dunn, who was with Lodge when he took the call.[137] "Lodge put the phone down and went to check on something. I held the line open," Dunn recalled.[138] When he returned, Lodge told Diem that he would offer him and his brother asylum and do what he could for them. Out of fear of what the generals might do, Dunn asked Lodge whether he could personally pick them up, "because they are going to kill them." Lodge replied, "We can't. We just can't get that involved."[139]

Conein, who had been at the JGS, said that when he returned to his villa that morning, he received an urgent telegram to report to the American embassy. He remembered, "I get there and I'm shown a cable—obviously it was highest authority—wanted to know where Diem was." He thought, "Oh, God." He went back to the JGS to find Big Minh.[140] "The goddamn bastards," Conein said to Phillips upon his return home around eleven o'clock that morning. Conein had been told that an American plane could have taken Diem and Nhu into exile. "His face was ashen. He looked sick," Phillips wrote. "They killed Diem; they murdered him and Nhu," he recalled Conein as saying.[141]

At the appointed hour when Diem was supposed to have reached the JGS to surrender, Don arrived, asking about the news that Diem and Nhu had just been killed. "Why are they dead?" Don asked. "And what does it matter that they are dead?" Big Minh shot back. Don wrote that Big Minh's assistant was lying on the table with a pale face and drawn features, apparently sick over what had happened, and the fact that it had been Big Minh's order to kill them.[142] Xuan interrupted them, saluting and saying, "Mission accomplice."[143]

"I've never ascertained whether it was a private revenge of some sort or whether it was a decision by the new government," Lodge recalled.[144] "Although I had only known him for a few weeks, I was deeply grieved by his death and horrified at the form it took."[145] There is no evidence to suggest that Lodge knew they were going to be killed. However, he must have suspected it, given his warnings to Kennedy as far back as August 15. According to Maxwell Taylor, Kennedy was in the White House Cabinet Room when Mike Forrestal brought in a cable saying that Diem and Nhu had been killed.[146] The CIA Station in Saigon was given photographs of Diem and Nhu dead in the back of an armored personnel carrier, covered with blood and with their hands tied behind their backs. "Photos appear authentic," the CIA station reported to the National Security Agency.[147] Robert McNamara, who was with Kennedy, told *Fog of War* director Errol Morris, "I've never seen him more upset. He totally blanched." Arthur Schlesinger Jr. said he "had not seen him so depressed since the Bay of Pigs. No doubt he realized that Vietnam was his great failure in foreign policy, and that he had never really given it his full attention."[148]

The idea that Kennedy was completely surprised by either the coup or the assassinations should be credited to his formidable acting skills. Many of the telegrams and memoranda cited here leading up to the coup have the words "The President has read" handwritten on them. Kennedy was warned it could happen, beginning with that conversation with Lodge on August 15.[149] According to one source, Kennedy told Francis Cardinal Spellman that he knew in advance that the Vietnamese leaders would probably be killed, but in the end he could not control the situation.[150] The Kennedy White House scrambled to come up with a public position on the murders. "In other words, get a story and stick to it—the true story, if possible," Kennedy said on November 2, agreeing with his top aides.[151] Three days after the coup, he said in a Dictabelt recording that he "encouraged Lodge along a course to which he was in any case inclined." Lodge was the ambassador and the top American official on the scene with day-to-day responsibility for being knowledgeable about the coup planning. The CIA tends to get a greater share of the blame, not just for Conein's involvement but because of the agency's broader legacy during the Cold War of involvement against unfriendly regimes. The Church Committee later found "extensive evidence of CIA participation over a period of months right up to and during the day of the coup, but none of agency complicity in or even advance awareness of the murder itself."[152] The real question is how the Church Committee, with its statutory responsibility to investigate Diem's murder, never knew of the August 15 Kennedy-Lodge conversation or the mid-October Kennedy-Lodge telephone conversation.

Robert F. Kennedy, in his thousand pages of oral history for the Kennedy Library, blamed everyone else for the coup—especially Lodge—and for not defending the president.[153] "He never gave any direction to Henry Cabot Lodge and the result was Lodge was running away with it," Kennedy said.[154] For President Kennedy to have blamed Lodge for the deaths of Diem and Nhu would have meant disowning him. Lodge warned Kennedy numerous times that assassinations are "the kind of thing which will happen in a coup d'état when order cannot be guaranteed everywhere."[155] The coup forces had been strengthening for years and had been set in motion after the May Buddhist crisis— long before Lodge's arrival. They would have attempted a coup (or coups) even if Lodge had never been ambassador. If the Diem coup had occurred in Kennedy's first year, he might have gotten a pass for newcomer naïveté, as he did during the Bay of Pigs. But by the fall of 1963, Kennedy had had his baptism of fire and been through the Cuban Missile Crisis. "We must bear a good deal of responsibility for it," Kennedy recorded in his diary regarding the coup on November 4, 1963, which is surely closer to how he thought at the time than anything he expressed publicly.[156]

"The coup of November 1 was essentially a Vietnamese affair," Lodge wrote in his memoir. "Because of our lack of involvement in the intricacies of Vietnamese political life, we could not have started the coup if we had wanted to. Nor could we have stopped one once it had started."[157] Perhaps if Kennedy had laid out a clearer policy up front and attached strong conditions to American support for the coup plotters, it would not have happened. Kennedy's closest advisers seemed as divided as anyone. "Being tolerably well informed is not the same as 'authorizing, sanctioning, and encouraging' the coup," Lodge recalled, defending his role.[158] "I had nothing to do with the origination of the policy, but I thought it was correct," he said.[159] He was careful to work through an intermediary, usually Conein. There is no record that Lodge ever met with the coup planners or engaged in anything other than a passing conversation in a public place, such as the airport. Lodge preferred not to be involved in the sordid details, and if it had ever leaked out that he was involved, and it surely would have, it would have undermined the entire effort. Lodge's involvement would have smacked of colonialism and would have built more support for Diem from outraged Vietnamese.[160]

According to Ton That Dinh, Lodge had no involvement in the coup. "Although the Americans made no effort to restrain us in either our coup planning or its execution, they were never really part of the plan," Don wrote.[161] The fact that the coup was a relatively bloodless affair and involved no prolonged fighting suggests how isolated the Gia Long Palace had become.[162] The coup leaders burned the offices of the pro-Diem *Times of Vietnam* to the ground. It had added innumerably to the strain in U.S.-Vietnamese relations. "The United States can get along with corrupt dictators who manage to stay out of the newspapers," Lodge said.[163]

Lodge's role will remain controversial. Shortly after the coup, he spoke about the deaths of Diem and Nhu to his close friend John Mason Brown. "I did everything I could to prevent it . . . if my advice had been followed, both would be alive today," he wrote.[164] Diem might have been the only politician that Lodge was unable to charm. The failure to save Diem was a failure for Lodge. However, Diem's former assistant Do Tho defended Lodge. "Lodge respected the President, so he always maintained the correct protocol for members of the diplomatic corps. President Diem frequently refused to see him, giving as his excuse that he was about to leave on an official trip, or, when he learned that the Ambassador was about to come over to Gia Long Palace, President Diem would hastily leave Saigon to visit some place on the city's outskirts. President Ngo Dinh Diem really drove Lodge crazy."[165]

Years later, Lodge composed a "Vietnam memoir," dated March 20, 1978, and classified top secret. Its cover page included the stipulation that it could be published "only after submission to a representative of President Kennedy."[166] He never published any portion of it, instead stuffing it into his personal papers that were donated to the Massachusetts Historical Society. It was opened to researchers after his death. In it, Lodge offered no defense at all. He believed he was simply carrying out the orders given to him. There is no mention in his Vietnam memoir of his August 15 conversation with Kennedy.

The most likely explanation for the murders of Diem and Nhu is either that there was a breakdown in communication between the Americans and the Vietnamese or that the Vietnamese generals betrayed the Americans. Conein testified before the Church Committee in 1975 that Big Minh had asked him to supply a plane for Diem and Nhu, but that the CIA station said the closest plane was in Guam.[167] Lodge would never have ordered the deaths of Diem and Nhu, and there is no evidence that any Kennedy administration official did either. While Conein and CIA officials were involved, the decisions were being made in the White House.[168] The closest Lodge ever came to direct involvement was assuring the generals that the United States would recognize the new government as legitimate.[169]

Don and General Le Van Kim visited Lodge at around four o'clock on the afternoon of November 2.[170] "We went to the American Embassy and Lodge came out personally to greet us," Don wrote. "He was extremely enthusiastic and congratulatory about our achievement, telling us that a full report had been made to President Kennedy."[171] During their one-hour meeting, Lodge said he was very moved by the news of the deaths of Diem and Nhu. "I stressed the importance of getting on with the war, and of no more persecutions," Lodge recalled. "I insisted that there be no reprisals against Christians for the recent opposition of Buddhists." Lodge also stayed out of the new government's push to try Diem government officials for corruption.[172] Lodge agreed to resume all economic aid, which officially became possible once the United States recognized the Minh government on November 7 in Washington.[173] Lodge specifically requested that the British government be the first to recognize the new Vietnamese government so it would not look as though the junta was officially endorsed by the United States.[174] Lodge arranged for a government plane to take Nhu's children out of the country, from Dalat to Saigon to Bangkok and, finally, to Rome.

After the coup leaders came to power, led by Big Minh, they issued two declarations. The first dissolved the government, established the Military Revolutionary Council with Minh as chairman, and abolished the presidential system of the "destitute" Diem. The second suspended the constitution of October 26, 1956, thereby sidestepping the succession process that ordinarily would have elevated the vice president as leader of South Vietnam. Big Minh also dissolved the National Assembly that had been elected on September 27.[175] People were not quite sure what to expect from Big Minh. He had never been referred to as a great soldier until the coup.[176]

Following the coup, congratulations to Lodge poured in from all over.[177] "We send our warm thanks for a day of brilliantly quick reporting," Dean Rusk said.[178] Lodge looked like a "riverboat gambler who has just raked in the post," according to a visitor to the embassy.[179] "He had been sent out by Kennedy to resolve the crisis. He had resolved it with a clean sweep," Phillips recalled.[180] The immediate result of Diem's downfall was positive.[181] There was no greater excitement anywhere than that found in Saigon.[182] "The very great popularity of this coup . . . every Vietnamese has a grin on his face today," Lodge wrote to Kennedy. "Am told that the jubilation in the streets exceeds that which comes every New Year."[183] Lodge also thanked two key people. "I wish warmly to commend the splendid work which has been done here by Acting Station Chief David Smith, who has been accurate, energetic, farsighted, and in every way most resourceful during this vitally important episode," Lodge wrote to McCone. "I wish particularly also to set down the valuable services rendered by Lt. Col. Conein whose contacts with the general's group were of priceless value to us and whose tireless and accurate reporting and transmission of messages have been of the greatest benefit. Both of these gentlemen have rendered outstanding services."[184]

The November 3 editorial page of the New York Times stated that "the overthrow of the Ngo regime by its non-communist opponents in South Vietnam presents the opportunity—and it may be the last opportunity—to establish there a forward-looking democratically oriented government with a broad base of popular support, a government that could in fact carry the anti-communist war to an ultimately successful conclusion." A week after the coup, Le Figaro reported that Saigon had resumed its normal aspect: "traffic jams and swarming masses of pedestrians."[185] Dancing was no longer banned, and soon bars, nightclubs, and cabarets flourished.

Lodge was viewed differently after the coup. Keyes Beech of the Chicago Daily News, who had traveled with Lodge from Tokyo on his initial arrival in Saigon, called him a "switch-blade fighter" and quoted one "longtime U.S. official" in Saigon: "My picture of Lodge before he came out here was of a great handsome zero. I soon changed my mind. That guy can be as tough and mean as they come." "Praise of his performance before, during, and after the coup is well-nigh unanimous among our sources here," a Time correspondent in Saigon cabled to the home office. "Contrary to normal practice, he has apparently been writing many of the cables from the embassy himself, in a succinct, lucid, clear-minded style that officials have learned to recognize as the ambassador's own ... From this poor perspective, it looks as if he has completely absorbed Saigon press corps criticism of the embassy. 'He looks very big and tall right now,' one Department of State source states. His welcome at the White House is certain to be a warm one."[186] Even those who had formerly been critics of Vietnam seemed pleased. "The initial promise displayed by the new Vietnamese government will permit a rapid victory over the Viet Cong and a withdrawal of American soldiers from that country," Frank Church wrote to fellow senator George McGovern.[187]

Of all the congratulations that Lodge received following the coup, a November 7 letter from Kennedy was the most meaningful. "Your own leadership in pulling together and directing the whole American operation in South Vietnam in recent months has been of the greatest importance and you should know that this achievement is recognized here throughout the government," Kennedy said.[188] While that letter was the most meaningful, one from Richard Nixon was the most probing. "I am enclosing a letter I dictated to Cabot and decided not to send," Nixon wrote to John Davis Lodge, who did pass it on.[189] Though it was written on November 12, John waited to send the detailed, three-page memorandum to Lodge until the latter was back in the United States on November 22. A benefit of that was that he could be assured that no one else would see it. Nixon was the only prominent figure to argue that the Diem coup was a terrible mistake. "I could tell from news reports how frustrated you must have been by the obstinacy of Diem, his brother, Madame Nhu and their associates," Nixon said. "But the heavy-handed participation of the United States in the coup which led inevitably to the charge that we were either partially responsible for, or at the very least condoned the murder of Diem and his brother, has left a bad taste in the mouths of many Americans ... This may not seem important now, but I don't need to tell you that the villains of today may become the martyrs of tomorrow."[190] It was a prophetic warning.

Within days of receiving Nixon's letter, Lodge drafted a response to accusations about his role in the coup and the murders of Diem and Nhu. In it, he said that not one single employee of the U.S. government was involved—in planning, in advising, or in execution. He clarified that Conein was never considered part of the U.S. mission or a regular government employee, and in regard to Diem, Lodge said, "I offered to do everything in my power to insure his physical safety and, if possible, to fly him out of the country. But he did not accept my offer." He also said that he advised Nhu to leave the country because he was aware of the widespread hatred for him. "He did not choose to follow my advice."[191]

Lodge's communications to Kennedy suggest that he might have thought that his major purpose had been fulfilled. "Now that the revolution had occurred, I assume you will not want my weekly reports to continue, although I will, of course, gladly continue them if you desire," he wrote. Perhaps Lodge naïvely assumed that with the coup in the past, things would settle down in Saigon, or that he would not stay in position much longer. While Lodge had sent thousands of cables leading up to the coup and in the week following November 1, he sent fewer than two hundred in the same length of time once Big Minh came to power. It seemed as though Lodge was preparing to gracefully disengage and assume a lower profile.[192] He originally planned to return to Washington to brief Kennedy that the situation in Vietnam was worse than anyone realized.[193] The new plan, however, was to stay put, meet with top Kennedy advisers in Honolulu in November, and then continue on to Washington from there. McNamara and Taylor flew out, accompanied by Rusk, McGeorge Bundy, William Bundy, and foreign aid director David Bell. Lodge and Admiral Felt discussed the postcoup political and military situation. While McNamara was still talking about withdrawing a nominal number of U.S. forces at the end of 1965, Lodge was more pessimistic. McNamara told Flott he was eager to find a way to announce that the number of American military advisers was being reduced from sixteen thousand to fifteen thousand. "You know," Flott recalled, "I have the highest respect for his integrity, intelligence, ability, everything else, except that if there was ever a fish out of water, it's the decent, forthright, hard-working personality of McNamara dealing with the opportunistic, self-serving leaders of successive Vietnamese coups."[194]

Lodge learned that some of the events described in optimistic reports by Diem and Nhu, such as securing 219 strategic hamlets, existed only on paper. Reports from the CIA were even more pessimistic, and Bill Colby referred to measurable increases in North Vietnamese infiltration of the South. While there were seven thousand National Liberation Front members in South Vietnam in 1960, the number had ballooned to nearly one hundred thousand in 1963.[195] Hanoi had worked to defeat Diem, and now the Americans had done it for them. The Diem coup was the greatest victory for the North since Dien Bien Phu in 1954. Moreover, the North Vietnamese had shown at least a degree of willingness to negotiate with Diem and Nhu, but not with the "puppets" who came after them.[196] Morale among the Vietnamese was bad, particularly in the countryside, and the situation was worse than the Americans realized, Lodge said.[197] "We should continue to keep before us the goal of setting dates for phasing out U.S. activities and turning them over to the Vietnamese," Lodge said.[198]

Lodge was in San Francisco, on a stopover on his way to see Kennedy, when he learned of the president's assassination. "My thoughts were shock and horror," he wrote.[199] He continued to Washington, but rather than have lunch with Kennedy on Sunday, he would pay his last respects.[200] On November 24, he briefed President Lyndon Johnson at the Executive Office Building. Lodge was the first American diplomat whom Johnson saw as president. He summarized the changes made to the South Vietnamese government as a result of the coup.[201] Lodge said the coup improved the prospects for victory over the Viet Cong. According to Johnson White House aide Jack Valenti, it was not a subject that Johnson seemed particularly concerned about.[202] "But compared with later periods," Johnson wrote in his memoirs, "even the situation in Vietnam at that point appeared to be relatively free from the pressure of immediate decisions."[203] Johnson's primary concern seemed to be not whether the chances for American victory were in doubt but rather to reduce the level of bickering among the leaders of the U.S. mission in Saigon.

Lodge and Johnson had been colleagues in the Senate.[204] Lodge had invited him to visit the UN during the 1950s and coached him on some of his earliest foreign policy speeches, which Johnson referred to as "one of the most thrilling and unusual experiences of [his] life."[205] Johnson told Lodge how thankful he was to have him in Saigon.[206] Lodge said he felt like a catfish that had "grabbed a big juicy worm with a right sharp hook in the middle of it," suggesting that he had no plans to leave his post.[207] Johnson instructed Lodge to return to Vietnam and assure the government that the United States would continue Kennedy's policy of helping Saigon to fight the communists. "I am not going to lose Vietnam," Johnson said. "I am not going to be the president who saw Southeast Asia go the way China went."[208] However, Johnson privately questioned Kennedy's policies. "It is clear to me that South Vietnam is our most critical military area right now," Johnson told Taylor.[209] Johnson was very critical of Kennedy's blessing of the coup. He told Senator Eugene McCarthy, "We killed him [Diem]. We all got together a goddamn bunch of thugs and we went in and assassinated him. Now, we've really had no political stability since then."[210] The coup had created a political vacuum that reduced the choices available to the brand-new Johnson administration, which had inherited 16,732 Americans engaged unofficially in a war.[211] Johnson had developed a rapport with Diem during his visit in May 1961 and believed the United States was not prepared to fill the void left by his death.

While Lodge was in Washington, he called Eisenhower, but there is no record that Lodge told him the truth about the coup or his role in it. Eisenhower did raise the matter of Lodge's future political options. "The General had also spoken to me about my duty to come home and make myself available for the Republican nomination for President," Lodge wrote in his journal.[212] In a follow-up letter, Lodge wrote, "You have a very sure sense of duty and whenever you speak to me about my duty it will always command my most earnest and sympathetic attention. All of this is for your private information and I write it simply because you were kind enough to talk to me about the whole subject when I called you on the telephone."[213] Eisenhower later wrote to Nixon, "I rather suspect the Diem affair will be shrouded in mystery for a long time to come."[214] Johnson made clear that he wanted "our effort in Vietnam [to] be stepped up to the highest pitch and that each day we ask ourselves what more we can do to further the struggle."[215]

# PART V
## THE JOHNSON YEARS

## 14 · Lodge for President

In a December 8, 1963, story, *New York Times* Washington bureau reporter Felix Belair interviewed former President Dwight Eisenhower, who said he hoped Henry Cabot Lodge Jr. would leave his post in Vietnam and come back to run as the "common sense" candidate.[1] The best chance for Republicans to beat Lyndon Johnson in 1964 was with a "moderate, common-sense candidate with an impressive background in international relations." Eisenhower had spoken to Lodge about running for the nation's top office. He believed that Lodge's duty to remain in Vietnam had ended when John F. Kennedy was assassinated. Lodge was the only person who could compete with Johnson on the central issues of war and peace, and he was a "hard-hitting and persuasive speaker."[2]

The *New York Herald Tribune* went even further than the *Times,* predicting that Lodge would run and defeat Johnson. The *Christian Science Monitor* predicted that Lodge would get the Republican nomination.[3] "Maybe the Republicans have to lose in '64. But I'd rather lose with Lodge than anybody else . . . at least he'll fight the campaign on the right issues and he will know how to campaign in the big cities," former Eisenhower aide John Reagan "Tex" McCrary said. "The only one who *might win* is Lodge, because he's the only one with experience in areas of Kennedy failure."[4]

Journalist Roscoe Drummond mentioned that Lodge was being spoken of as a possible candidate in light of "the sensational turn of affairs in South Vietnam since he took over the embassy there some weeks ago," combined with the fact that Republicans wanted "some alternatives to both [Barry] Goldwater and [Nelson] Rockefeller."[5] Richard Nixon had tried his best, losing in his bids for the presidency in 1960 and for the California governorship in 1962.

The Belair *New York Times* story upset Nixon enough that two days later he went to see Eisenhower, who claimed he had been misquoted. "Now both of us agreed that we'd like to see him back here because he is a vivacious man, a leader type," Nixon said, wondering how Lodge might affect the Republican chances in 1964.[6] After saying he had been misquoted, Eisenhower wrote an apology to his friend Belair for implying he had been misquoted. "It isn't true that I have asked Cabot to come home," he wrote to a concerned Harold Stassen. "The most I have said in support of any candidate is that I would be delighted to see all Republican leaders discuss basic issues of the day and the objectives that the Republican Party should be setting for itself."[7]

Eisenhower's comments were worse for Lodge than if he had said nothing at all. Their appearance coincided with Lodge's return to Washington for consultations. "I am receiving increasing pressure from various sources in connection with the forthcoming national campaign," Lodge's brother, John, wrote. "In the light of the splendid publicity which you have been receiving in the United States and the increased mention of you as a Republican dark horse (I refer particularly to Roscoe Drummond's article which you must have seen), it occurred to me that political activity on my part might be of some interest to you."[8] Lodge must have enjoyed the attention, but he denied any interest. "I really and honestly have no political ambition whatever," Lodge said once he returned to Saigon. "I admit that I used to when I was younger. Also I cannot possibly leave here at any *proximate* future without neglect of my duty here and this I will not do."[9]

Lodge could not campaign from Saigon—and if he returned home to do so, he would be campaigning against the president he was serving in his capacity as ambassador. So Lodge did the only thing he could. He maintained an active personal correspondence on nongovernmental stationery with his son George, authorizing him to act for him. Lodge reminded George that he had no intention of running for the presidency. "Of course, this does not prevent anyone . . . from kicking my name around," he wrote. "The next question is: Could anything happen which would cause me to take another look at my attitude? The answer is: Yes." Referring to his own effort to convince Eisenhower to run, Lodge added, "I well remember there were two things which changed his attitude. One was the organization of a really high-powered group with high-ranking professional politicians (with me as 'campaign manager'), and the second the enormous rally which we put on in Madison Square Garden in February which has never been equaled before or since, and of which we made a motion picture film which was flown over to him and which he sat one whole night looking at."[10] Publicly, Lodge said he had no intention of running, and he stated, "The most useful contribution I can make is the work I am doing here in Saigon."[11] It had been little more than a month since the overthrow of the Diem government, and Lodge was helping the new government get established. Progress in the war against the Viet Cong was not going as well as hoped. The job he had been sent to Vietnam to do by Kennedy just four months earlier was not done.

Conservatives in the Republican Party called an emergency meeting on December 8, the day the *Times* article ran, in Goldwater's apartment in Washington. Goldwater wrote later that the GOP activists told him, "This is the conservative hour—it's now or never. The party needs you. Rockefeller, Nixon, [George] Romney, [William] Scranton, and Lodge are not the answer . . . think of the hundreds of thousands of young Republicans out there—the YAF [Young Americans for Freedom], the college crowd, all those young people who came to hear you speak over the last nine years or so . . . you gotta do it, Barry."[12] What was said at the meeting leaked to journalists Rowland Evans and Robert Novak, who published in the *Washington Post* that Lodge was "poison" and guilty of "political treason" for working for Kennedy.[13] "I really am controversial, and it is quite inconceivable that I should be nominated," Lodge wrote to his son George.[14]

Johnson wanted to know whether Eisenhower's published comments had affected Lodge's ability to do his job. "Cabot has indeed begun to think in terms of political responsibilities," McGeorge Bundy reported. Lodge "would very much like to be honorably free of his responsibilities in Saigon," and in two months he hoped to be able to say that "the situation is now so much better that he can now fairly ask for relief" and return home.[15] Johnson decided to publicly express support for Lodge so he would have no reason to resign in protest, return home, or criticize the White House. Johnson told Dean Rusk to "build a record" of support for Lodge to make him think that he is "Mr. God" and has the "maximum attention" of the government. He gave similar instructions to Robert McNamara. "Now I'm thinking politically," he said. "I'm not a military strategist, but I think as long as we got him [Lodge] there and he makes recommendations, we act on them." The point was to keep Lodge happy. However, he also had a warning for Lodge: "While he is on the job he will not engage in politics."[16]

Despite all of this, several people had been working to establish a Lodge campaign for president as early as October 1963, including Victor LeMieux of Manchester, New Hampshire, and Robert Mullen, who discussed the matter with Lodge in Saigon. Mullen, who had known Lodge for twenty-five years, told Fred Seaton, an old Eisenhower adviser and troubleshooter, that he had "been asked" to coordinate the Lodge campaign.[17] George Lodge asked his father about forming a draft effort before and after the Kennedy assassination. Lodge acquiesced but clarified that he would not publicly support or criticize such an effort.[18] On December 21, the group officially began its effort to pursue the nomination of Lodge as the Republican candidate for president. Ten thousand miles away in Saigon, Lodge was elated by the chance of a replay of the success of 1952—except this time with him as the candidate.

On the afternoon of December 23, an anonymous group distributed thirty-three thousand postcards on the outbound commuter trains departing New Haven, Connecticut. Lodge later discovered that the group was led by William Miller of *Life* magazine.[19] They asked respondents to indicate their preference for the 1964 Republican candidate. A surprising 12 percent of the cards were returned, and Lodge earned not only a majority of all votes but more votes than Goldwater, Rockefeller, Nixon, Romney, and Scranton combined. With that, the "draft Lodge" movement had life.[20] But the group had no candidate. "We have not asked him [Lodge] to come back because he is doing a job in the most critical situation in the world as far as the U.S. is concerned," Mullen said. "We want him to do a good job there in Vietnam."[21]

In Saigon, Lodge was dealing with the aftereffects of the coup. Duong Van Minh had been in power for only two months, but there was already wide dissatisfaction. Little had been accomplished by the new government while Lodge was briefing officials in Washington. "The only progress made in Long An Province during the month of November 1963 had been by the communist Viet Cong," Lodge said.[22] He wrote Johnson on January 1 that he was "now just beginning to see the full extent of the dry rot and lassitude in the government of Vietnam and the extent to which we were given inaccurate information."[23] The Viet Cong "believe in something," Lodge wrote. "The communists have conveyed to these men [a] clear picture of a program which they think will make life better. We have not. They are also well organized politically; we are not." He believed that part of the blame was due to Viet Cong propaganda designed to undermine the people's confidence in the Saigon government. "The VC have simply shifted from military to political tactics and are defeating us politically," following "the old Mao Tse-tung maxim," Lodge reported to Johnson.[24]

The second coup to occur on Lodge's watch was even more dangerous to the long-term survival of the South Vietnamese state, for it established a semipermanent instability. Lodge received word on January 29, 1964, that a coup would take place the next day.[25] Thirty-eight-year-old General Nguyen Khanh, commander of Hue, arrived in Saigon and put Big Minh, Tran Van Don, Le Van Kim, and other members of the Military Revolutionary Council under arrest.[26] Less than two weeks earlier, Lodge had forwarded to Johnson a report by Giovanni d'Orlandi, the Italian ambassador to South Vietnam, that alleged that Don and Ton That Dinh were among those who might accept a neutralization proposal from French President Charles de Gaulle.[27] Unlike in 1963, this time, the coup forces struck early and quickly.[28] The generals decided that the diminutive, gung-ho, goateed Khanh would be their new leader, and Big Minh was released to become a figurehead chief of state. Lodge hit it off right away with Khanh, who barely came up to Lodge's neck. "It is safe to say that Khanh's group will be essentially pro-American, anti-communist, and anti-neutralist in general orientation," a CIA report said right after the coup.[29]

"This Khanh is the toughest one they got and the ablest one they got," Lodge told Walker Stone, editor in chief of Scripps-Howard Newspapers. "And he said, 'Screw this neutrality, we ain't going to do business with the communists and get the goddamned hell out of here. I'm pro-American and I'm taking over.'"[30] Khanh was Lodge's type and planned to "rely heavily for political assistance on Lodge" due to his own lack of experience.[31] "Strange as the combination looked from afar, Lodge's French was a help—they seldom if ever spoke English together, and Khanh was always much more at home in French," John Michael Dunn recalled. "Lodge's principal advantage with Khanh was his impressive credentials as a politician. Khanh was eager for practical advice in politics."[32] In Lodge's first conversation with Khanh after the latter became the new head of state, he encouraged him to avoid the mistakes of Ngo Dinh Diem and Ngo Dinh Nhu. Lodge believed that Saigon was most hampered by political, not military, problems, although political problems could spill over into the military sphere. "Any second-class general could win in Indo-China if the political atmosphere were right," Lodge wrote to Eisenhower.[33] He suggested that Khanh get out of Saigon, go to the people, and build grassroots support.[34] He also concurred with the new government's extradition request for Madame Nhu, which was met with a scornful letter in which Madame Nhu referred to Kennedy and Lodge as "the oppressor of [her] country and of [her] people."[35] However, the French refused to give her up.

Lodge recognized the problem of appearing to be a viceroy of the Saigon government. He told Khanh that he "was well aware that he must not appear at any time to be under undue American influence" and that he "would always be sympathetic to any gestures he might feel like making to show that this was not the case."[36] It was a hard image for Lodge to shake off. Lodge trained Khanh on how to take advantage of the power of the media and encouraged him to make "fireside chats" on the radio. Khanh's hold on power was so fragile, Lodge cabled to Johnson, that he slept in a different location each night.[37] Khanh started visiting the countryside and put his newly acquired American campaigning techniques to work shaking hands in a way that would have been expected in any congressional race. "From the way he buttonholed passers-by on Saigon sidewalks, the pint-sized Vietnamese officer in green fatigues could have been Nelson Rockefeller campaigning in the New Hampshire primary," *Time* magazine reported in its February 1964 issue. "He shook hands, introduced himself, asked, 'Have you any suggestions about how we can do a better job for Vietnam?'"[38] It was clearly Lodge's doing, but it was not enough. The coup that toppled Diem and Nhu produced a revolving door of leadership and a vacuum of power that would continue until 1965 when Nguyen Van Thieu established a more stable government. Lodge revealed late in life to his friend Stanley Karnow that the real mastermind behind the January 1964 coup was, in fact, Thieu. "General Thieu did all the thinking," Lodge said.[39]

Johnson was disturbed to read news of another coup in Vietnam.[40] He believed Lodge was too powerful and acted too independently. He thought the answer was to appoint a strong deputy chief of mission to work with Lodge, but Lodge never quite allowed the man he appointed, David Nes, to operate that way. U.S. embassy spokesperson Barry Zorthian called Nes "but a laborer in the vineyard."[41] Johnson feared that if Lodge returned to the United States triumphant, it would pose a threat to his reelection chances. "Lodge is a long ways from here and he's thinking of New Hampshire and he's thinking of his defeats in the Republican party and he's feeling sorry for himself and he's naturally a martyr," Johnson told Rusk.[42] News reports stated that Lodge had privately written friends in Massachusetts that his recommendations to launch bombing attacks against North Vietnam had gone unanswered. "Ambassador Henry Cabot Lodge, the hottest dark horse in the Republican presidential race, has written a number of the same types of letters that got Gen. Douglas MacArthur recalled during the Korean war," one report read.[43] If Johnson escalated, building the war into a bigger campaign issue, it could be good for Lodge. If something went terribly wrong, Lodge could accuse the White House of mismanaging Vietnam. Johnson's best option was to hold the war right where it was through the election. He seemed to limit his range of options due to his domestic political situation, just as Kennedy had in 1963.

As long as Johnson pursued a strategy of appearing to give Lodge every-thing he wanted, Lodge would have no incentive to return home and criticize the White House for not supporting him in Saigon. "Any request for assistance or other Washington action from Ambassador Lodge should be given prompt and sympathetic response," Michael Forrestal reminded John McCone.[44] "He'd be home campaigning against us on this issue every day," Johnson said.[45] He told McNamara that he did not want to escalate, fearing "a third world war or another Korea action" during his presidency. Johnson did not want to appear soft on Vietnam, otherwise he would be handing the Republicans a campaign issue.[46] He assured Lodge that the United States would contribute additional economic aid and military assistance to South Vietnam if Lodge determined it were necessary. Johnson emphasized this expanded commitment in a Feb-ruary 21 speech at the University of California, Los Angeles, his first major Vietnam speech since becoming president.[47] He reiterated it at the March 7 meeting of the National Security Council, where he announced that "all rec-ommendations made by Ambassador Lodge had been dealt with without exception—promptly and generally favorably."[48]

Back in Saigon, Lodge spent time working on the issue of Buddhist-Catholic relations in order to stabilize the Saigon government and fend off protests from one side or the other.[49] He also seemed to take the regular threats of violence against him in stride. "If physical danger had any effect on him, the effect was exhilaration," Dunn recalled. "There were constant assassination threats. I can see him sitting at his desk with a pistol in the drawer, and a heavy Magnum in the open safe. He used to talk about defending the Chancery as enthusias-tically as a Knight of St. John." Visiting American officials were accustomed to wearing bulletproof vests, but Lodge did not wear them. On the streets of Saigon, he had several near misses from Viet Cong terrorist attacks. Trips to the countryside, whether by car or in the old two-engine DC-3 assigned to the embassy, took careful planning to avoid areas under siege by Viet Cong. Some-times it was safe for Lodge to travel without escorts since having an escort drew more attention than desired.[50]

Momentum for the Draft Lodge campaign started to take shape. The goal was to make Lodge a write-in candidate during the 1964 Republican primary. A Boston headquarters was opened on January 3, and a New Hampshire op-erations center was opened in a converted grocery store in Concord on Janu-ary 10.[51] The cochairs were Paul Grindle and David Goldberg, who operated with the blessing of Lodge's son George. Lodge asked them to send him mate-rial on various policy issues so he could remain up to date.[52] He reminded those who asked that Grindle and Goldberg did not act with his authorization. "George passed along to me through George Hinman your message that you will authorize no activity in your behalf in New Hampshire . . . I am frank to say I welcome this decision," Rockefeller wrote to Lodge.[53]

Grindle was a forty-three-year-old scientific instrument dealer from Cambridge, Massachusetts, and was rumored to be a former CIA operative. He had been George Lodge's campaign manager in his Senate bid against Edward Kennedy in 1962.[54] Goldberg was a thirty-four-year-old attorney from Boston who had no previous experience in politics.[55] Grindle and Goldberg met regularly to discuss the political futures of both Lodges and retained publicist Robert Mullen to help with their effort. Mullen had been a founder of Citizens for Eisenhower in 1952 and worked with Paul Hoffman on the Marshall Plan.[56] Officially, the Lodge for President movement had no major source of income and no major political names associated with it. Their entire budget was $25,000, compared with the $150,000 that Goldwater dumped into New Hampshire.[57]

George Gallup found no support for Lodge while Kennedy was president because they were too similar. "I can't imagine anyone could possibly be interested in Lodge," Gallup said, explaining why he left Lodge off his regular public opinion polls.[58] But with a Draft Lodge effort in the works, Gallup added him to his polls, and the results were surprising. Lodge matched up well against Johnson and other Republicans. In the first poll in the Johnson presidency, Lodge garnered 16 percent of voters favoring him in 1964. Lodge, a "Republican Kennedy," was popular in New England, where Johnson was weak.[59] He had long experience in foreign policy, which dominated the news, an area where Johnson was a relative newcomer. Lodge had a high standard of morality and was scandal-free, whereas Johnson had Bobby Baker and Walter Jenkins. And though Lodge was tied to Kennedy's greatest failure, Vietnam, he was poised to potentially capitalize on it in 1964.[60] Whether Lodge's surge in popularity was more sentiment for Kennedy or genuine enthusiasm for Lodge was what his foot soldiers needed to determine. At least of the potential Republican candidates, it looked as if the support for Lodge was strong. Few Republicans or independents were enthusiastic about Rockefeller or Goldwater, and each man's supporters had despised the other side.

Grindle and Goldberg secured a short-term lease on four rooms across from the state capitol for $400 from January 10 to March 10 in Concord, New Hampshire. They brought in telephones and started recruiting locals to assist with their effort. They borrowed furniture from the Republican state headquarters and paid $162 for a huge "Lodge for President" sign.[61] They did not have the tens of thousands of dollars to spend on local television that Goldwater and Rockefeller did, but they made up for these deficits with a surplus of spunk.[62] Their most important recruit was M. Richard Jackman, sixty-seven, who was the head of a $10 million printing business, Rumford Press of Concord, which printed *Reader's Digest*. He helped run the finances and managed the campaign storefront. A Republican delegate, Jackman filed papers favorable to Lodge on January 9, and on January 13 he became the state chairman of the New Hampshire Draft Lodge Campaign.[63] The group also recruited Senator Leverett Saltonstall's niece, Sally, twenty-three, who quit her Peace Corps assignment to join the movement. She brought along Caroline Williams, a former schoolmate, and together they were "two of Boston's finest young ladies."[64] The women ran the phones, Grindle ran the back room, and Goldberg was out in the field.[65] Their collective presence made a party. They were an attractive, young, vivacious, fun-loving bunch that was not immune to getting involved in some pranks and campaign hijinks.

The strategy was to concentrate on relatively inexpensive primary campaigns in small states. The greatest single effort of the movement, innovative for the time, was its concentrated direct mail initiative. Grindle and Goldberg sent out ninety-four thousand unsolicited pledge cards to registered Republicans in New Hampshire. "Don't be satisfied with the available. Select the best," the mailing said, contrasting Lodge with Rockefeller and Goldwater. There was room for all pledges in the household to sign and indicate their support. The return card's address was the Draft Lodge Committee in Concord, with a note that it would be sent to Lodge in Saigon.[66] "We didn't ask them for money," Goldberg recalled. "We didn't ask them to volunteer for anything or to do anything but sign a card and return it. But still we didn't know what to expect by way of returns."[67] The returned cards provided not only key intelligence on voter preferences but also an accurate mailing list from which to recruit district workers and volunteers. They received 8,600 pledges of support, and a second mailing brought the total number of pledges to 26,000. "Whatever happens, this proves politics can be fun," Grindle said.[68] He decided that in order to avoid embarrassment, they needed to win at least five thousand votes. Less than that and they would agree to close up shop. More than twelve thousand and they agreed to move on to the Oregon primary.[69]

There had been some hope that Lodge would lend his supporters the use of his name, as Lodge had compelled Eisenhower to do, but Lodge wrote his brother John, "I am certainly not going into the New Hampshire primaries and have made a public statement to that effect." He even added a handwritten postscript: "In fact I do not intend to go into *any* primaries!"[70] At the same time, Lodge asked both John and his son George to keep him informed.[71]

The media focused almost exclusively on Rockefeller and Goldwater.[72] But then, surprisingly, the two candidates began to publicly criticize Lodge. On February 18, in Newport, New Hampshire, Goldwater said that Lodge had "gotten things all balled up" in Vietnam. Rockefeller piled on, criticizing Lodge later that same week. Goldwater had led the polls up to then, but the criticism provided a burst of publicity for the Draft Lodge effort. "If Rockefeller had defended Cabot, we could have packed our tents, I swear it, and stolen back to Massachusetts," Grindle reflected. Likewise, "had Rocky said Cabot and I are together in this—we have to stop Goldwater—it would have pulled the pins out from under us. Instead, Rocky criticized Lodge later in the week. We feel nothing but gratitude to Rocky."[73] The criticism served to enlarge the spotlight on Lodge.

The more Goldwater, especially, opened his mouth, the more New Hampshire voters had second thoughts. Voters believed it was reckless to criticize someone who was not present to defend himself but had a difficult job in Vietnam—in the bipartisan service of a Democratic president, no less. For Rockefeller, the criticism of Lodge was simply an attempt to score political points. They had similar political positions and were from the same liberal wing of the Republican Party. Rockefeller allegedly called Lodge three times in Saigon to ask him to pull out of the race. When the news of one of those calls leaked, it further boosted Lodge's prospects in New Hampshire.[74] David Palmer, General William Westmoreland's military assistant in Saigon, overheard Lodge's end of what was clearly a political conversation. "There is no doubt this was someone running for office," he said. "I remember Lodge asking 'whose finger do you want on the nuclear button?'"[75]

Lodge was a natural fit for New Hampshire voters. A majority of the state's population lived within fifty miles of Boston, and many regarded Lodge as one of their own.[76] His progressive views concerning foreign policy and aid were popular in New England, as were his views on civil rights. "If we are to win the struggle for the minds of men, particularly in Africa and Asia, we must show at home that we practice what we preach about equal rights for all," Lodge said.[77] He was a suitable surrogate for Eisenhower and Kennedy, representing the best of both presidencies, and gave voters a way out of holding their noses and voting for either Goldwater or Rockefeller.[78] There were two other candidates for the Republican nomination on the ballot: Norman Lepage and Margaret Chase Smith. Lepage was an accountant who received a single, ten-dollar contribution. He campaigned on the need for a balanced budget and better relations with Cuba. Smith, the first woman ever to appear on the New Hampshire Republican primary ballot, was a U.S. senator from Maine and had never lost an election.[79]

Mullen received encouraging letters about Lodge from all over the country. A New Jersey man said, "He is remembered for brilliant and courageous handling of the nation's destiny in the UN." A Kansas man wrote, "I have been impressed by his record in World War II, his devotion to the first Eisenhower campaign, and his acceptance of the ambassadorship to South Vietnam." A California man reported, "The trend has swung to Mr. Lodge . . . He is the only Republican candidate with world-wide appeal." An airline stewardess wrote that she overheard passengers remark that "Lodge is cut out of the same piece of cloth as Kennedy."[80]

In Saigon, speculation swirled that Lodge would throw his hat in the ring. Privately, Lodge had extensive written briefings prepared on a variety of issues, including a fully drafted nomination acceptance speech for the 1964 Republican convention with instructions to his son George that he "hold it very closely."[81] Lodge also made a short list of possible vice-presidential candidates. "I have asked him to stay here until he is elected president," Vietnam's premier Khanh said, joining in the speculation. Grindle and George Cabot Lodge lobbied Leverett Saltonstall to publicly refer to Lodge as a "candidate" and were disappointed when he refused to—not from lack of support but rather because Saltonstall thought doing so could hurt Lodge's relationship with the White House.[82] Bill Treat, the New Hampshire Republican national committeeman, traveled twenty-four hours to Saigon to ask Lodge if what they were doing was going to "piss [him] off." Upon Treat's return, he reported to the Lodge troops, "The ambassador sees no reason to get pissed off."[83]

Grindle bought thirty-nine five-minute spots on WMUR-TV in Manchester, New Hampshire, to show film clips from Lodge's career that reached roughly three-quarters of the state's inhabitants. These were carefully chosen, culminating in a highly edited, clever Eisenhower "endorsement" of Lodge for president. Four of the five minutes were of Eisenhower narrating Lodge's career.[84] The film, including Eisenhower's statement, "I am for this man," was from Lodge's 1960 effort to win the vice presidency.[85] Trumpet blasts were inserted when Eisenhower spoke the word "vice," thereby repurposing the film for a Lodge presidential run and leading the viewer to conclude that Eisenhower endorsed Lodge for the nation's highest office.[86] It was brilliant propaganda, since Grindle used it knowing that neither Lodge nor Eisenhower would refute it. Leftovers from the 1960 campaign were just about the only campaign materials the Draft Lodge effort had, since they were unable—and could not afford—to create new ones. The campaign spent $3,000 on video advertising in New Hampshire, its single biggest expenditure of the primary. That included $500 to edit the five-minute film, with the rest for the television spots, which were spread over twelve days.[87] To those who had returned pledge cards, they sent an additional mailing that showed a mockup of the ballot and instructions on how to write Lodge's name in. Lodge had coverage in New Hampshire that was every bit as good as that of Goldwater or Rockefeller, who spent tens of thousands more.[88]

The group waited out polling day at the New Hampshire Highway Hotel, which was set up as a temporary election headquarters for the campaign as well as the press. Pollster Lou Harris predicted that Lodge would place a respectable third due to the difficulty of pulling off a write-in effort. To further complicate things, a blizzard dropped fourteen inches of snow that morning.[89] Lodge's popularity with voters was the only asset his campaign had, and his surge in the polls demonstrated that there was a lot of last-minute decision making. In the final Gallup poll before the primary, Nixon led Goldwater by a margin of 34 to 17 percent. Lodge held at 16 percent, with Rockefeller at 13 percent. Harris had a similar spread.[90]

Lodge won the primary with a total of 33,007 write-in votes, or 35.7 percent of the votes cast. Goldwater was second with 20,692, Rockefeller came in third with 19,504, and Nixon was fourth with 15,587.[91] In the suburbs, Lodge won by a 45 percent margin. His support from farmers and rural voters was 20 to 36 percent over Goldwater's. Lodge won three Portsmouth districts by a margin of 33 percent. The first poll following the primary found that Lodge had jumped to 42 percent, Nixon was at 26 percent, Goldwater was at 14 percent, and Rockefeller was at 6 percent. When paired against the likely Democratic opponent, Johnson, Lodge did even better at 52 percent, by far the best of any Republican candidate.[92]

When the returns came in, it was Wednesday morning in Vietnam. Secretary of Defense Robert McNamara and Chairman of the Joint Chiefs of Staff Maxwell Taylor were in Hue with Lodge on a fact-finding mission for Johnson, accompanied by Khanh. As they were getting ready to board their return flight to Saigon, Lodge learned that he had won. When the group landed in Saigon, reporters and photographers shifted their attention away from Khanh, McNamara, and Taylor. They wanted to hear from Lodge. "It was a great honor and a great compliment, but Foreign Service regulations preclude my com-menting on political matters," he said. "I have no thoughts of resigning my post." Lodge could not hold back a smile while making his perfunctory state-ment. "Are you happy?" he was asked, according to the *New York Times*. "I am happy by nature," Lodge said.[93] To his son George, Lodge remarked, "It was an unbelievable showing," and "a great honor and a great compliment."[94]

"A somber and wiser group of Arizonans returned to Washington," Gold-water reflected. "We had lost but were not defeated."[95] It was as embarrassing a result for Rockefeller as it was a surprise for Lodge.[96] The excitement was electric. *Time* magazine featured Lodge on the cover of its March 20, 1964, issue with the headline "The Lodge Phenomenon."[97] The Draft Lodge team realized how much trouble they were in. "From a gay and lighthearted group of pranksters who had merrily disturbed the politics of the spring in New Hampshire, they had slowly, in the spring months, come to realize that they had danced into the most serious business of the world—the presidency of the United States."[98]

After Lodge won the New Hampshire primary, he took his potential candi-dacy more seriously. John Davis Lodge appeared on Johnny Carson's *Tonight Show* and began to discuss organizing a campaign, including the need for a spokesman. "I quite agree with you that it should not be either George or me," John told his brother. "Until the matter has been settled, I think Bob Mullen can handle it well . . . while you say that you have authorized no organization I have considered it better for me to check out everything with Bob Mullen who is in constant touch with George."[99] Maxwell Rabb was brought into the campaign to run the overall operation. Milton Katz, who had been director of International Legal Studies at Harvard Law School, would run the campaign's research effort. Major General (Ret.) Charles T. "Buck" Lanham, an Eisen-hower aide at NATO, joined the campaign to write speeches should Lodge return home to make use of them. In the meantime, so many volunteers showed up at the New Hampshire headquarters that the campaign was un-able to harness their energy and enthusiasm. Draft Lodge committees were established in forty-five states, and Republican leaders started to pay attention, providing their home telephone numbers to Mullen so they could respond quickly to requests for help.[100]

In the middle of this, Nixon made his first visit to Vietnam under the spon-sorship of a legal client, Pepsi-Cola.[101] It would be the first of seven visits to Vietnam in the course of his long political comeback; five were hosted by Lodge in his role as ambassador.[102] The former vice president left New York on

March 22 for an extensive tour of South and Southeast Asian capitals. Lodge told Dunn to "keep an eye" on Nixon. "Get on the helicopter with him," he said. "I don't want him ever alone with anybody unless you are there to hear what he is told and what he says."[103] The press were eager to obtain a statement from the 1960 ticket mates. "We had a very interesting discussion and actually we made a deal," Nixon indulged them, according to Palmer. "He is going to put a Pepsi-Cola cooler in the embassy in Saigon," Nixon said about Lodge.[104]

Nixon's stop in Saigon from April 1 to 3 was coincidentally just days after Lodge's New Hampshire win. "You know, Dick, all those stories about how I took a nap every afternoon in the 1960 campaign? They weren't true," Lodge ribbed Nixon.[105] During a two-hour conversation at the Saigon embassy on April 2, Nixon said Rockefeller was through, "not simply because of his re-marriage, but because of deep-seated feelings against him among the delegates." Nixon believed Goldwater had a real chance at the nomination. "If Goldwater should get the nomination, it would be another disaster for the party," Nixon said. "We would lose 30 or 40 Congressmen at least . . . We could all go straight to hell as far as he is concerned." Nixon praised the job Lodge was doing in Saigon and encouraged him to stay on the job.[106] He was surprised to learn that Lodge did not think there was a military solution that could win the war and that U.S. troops were frustrated that they were not permitted to attack the Ho Chi Minh Trail or North Vietnam.[107] "Up to this time there has been doubt and inconsistency about the goal and there obviously has been an inadequate plan as well as considerable inadequacy with regard to the personnel to carry out the plan," Nixon said.[108]

Politics continued to be on Lodge's mind—his own politics. Nixon told him he thought he had a chance to win the nomination. "Of course," Nixon said, "you would under no circumstances leave your post in Saigon, but you should not prevent your friends in the convention from working for you because, even though Johnson is tremendously strong, there is a duty to make a good campaign and make the two-party system work. Also, a good campaign puts pressure of the proper kind on the man who wins." Lodge agreed.[109] But no matter how seriously Lodge took his own campaign, he was constrained by three factors. First, he did not have the national campaign organization necessary to take advantage of the New Hampshire result. Second, he was in Saigon and under the close watch of the Johnson administration. Finally, and perhaps most importantly, he was waiting for key Republican leaders to publicly declare that he should come home and campaign. Lodge was direct with his son George. "There is one way *honorably* to quit this post, and that is in response to a call from the convention," he wrote on April 14.[110] Like Eisenhower in 1952, Lodge needed the offer of a higher duty.

Goldwater supporters and members of the press, trying to account for his surprise victory, perpetuated the myth that Lodge had been a lazy campaigner in 1960. "If a man were thinking of his health and comfort, he would prefer campaigning in New Hampshire to serving in Saigon, a thousand times over," Lodge wrote his son George. "This place is infinitely more uncomfortable, more dangerous, more injurious to health, with more pressure and more hard work than a campaign in New Hampshire would be."[111] Eisenhower, too, rejected the charges. "It certainly wasn't true when he was campaigning for me. Nobody worked any harder," he said. "He's been a damned good Republican all the time I've known him." Eisenhower recalled something Robert Taft had said about the press: "It's the newspapermen who pin the labels on you." They were now sticking labels on Lodge and trying to make sense of his surprise victory.[112]

There were two fundamental differences between Eisenhower's and Lodge's respective draft efforts in 1952 and 1964. First, Lodge did not have his own Lodge in 1964 as Eisenhower did in 1952. Because Eisenhower could not campaign and was four thousand miles away in France, Lodge took the reins. In 1964, Lodge did have his brother, his son, and others rallying the faithful, but they lacked Eisenhower's name recognition and money, and conservative Republicans had never forgotten what Lodge did to Taft in 1952. Second, Lodge needed Eisenhower to be a political leader. Eisenhower said nice things about Lodge, but he was unable to inspire others to act. He could have used his popularity to help other moderate leaders seek office and in so doing marginalize the extreme elements of the Republican Party. His inability to help hurt Nixon and Lodge in 1960, and Lodge again in 1964. "Of course, a call by the Party to anyone who has spent most of his life in national government would be a solemn duty (and privilege), but this has never happened," Lodge wrote to his brother, John.[113] In an unusually critical moment, Lodge said, "Ike hasn't shown the slightest desire to have me come home and bring the Republican Party forward in his image."[114] Lanham, who was close to both Eisenhower and Lodge, said he was "furious" that Eisenhower had done so little to be a leader in the Republican Party for Lodge, who had sacrificed so much. "Your remark about 'if the leader doesn't lead [who the hell will]'[115] is really to the point," Lodge told Lanham.[116] There was really only one condition that Lodge would need to return from Saigon when there was still time to be nominated: Eisenhower's leadership.

Lodge grew frustrated as time slipped away. "There is no doubt that the situation here is fragile and unstable," Lodge cabled to Rusk. "The religious crisis, the grumblings among senior officials, and the delays in administrative action continue," including friction between Khanh and Big Minh.[117] Johnson's strategy through the political season seemed to be the status quo. Lodge proposed making diplomatic overtures to North Vietnam, which Rusk supported, but Johnson showed no interest. Lodge also reported Khanh's frustration that the military was held back by the White House from pursuing the Viet Cong. "This man obviously wants to get on with the job and not sit here indefinitely taking casualties," Lodge said. "Who can blame him? He is clearly facing up to the hard questions and wants us to do it, too."[118] It was as though Johnson were unwilling to try anything new for fear that if something failed, Lodge could return home and capitalize on it.

Lodge dealt with continued rumors about his political future. "My position is so simple I can't get anyone to believe it," he said to *Time*'s Frank McCullough. "I am not a candidate. I say within qualification that I have no intention of returning home to become a candidate. I can say with equal certitude that I have a big job to do here, and I intend to stay here and do it, period."[119] Even as he denied he was running, pollsters detected a growing groundswell for Lodge as the next primary, in Oregon, approached. The fact that Lodge's popularity translated about as far from New England as one could go was considered significant. The Oregon primary was scheduled for May 15, with another big primary looming in California on June 2. There was a brief window in which Lodge could have left Saigon with his honor intact, citing popular demand for him to return, similar to Eisenhower in 1952.[120] "Several years later, in fact," Nixon recalled, "he told me that if he had won the Oregon primary in May he had planned to resign and return home to campaign for the nomination."[121]

At the 1964 World's Fair in New York, the *New York Daily News* set up six mock voting booths inviting visitors to "vote" for the Republican they would most prefer as their nominee. From the first day, Lodge not only led the field but garnered more votes than the rest of the Republican candidates combined. He was both the preferred Republican and the one most likely to defeat Johnson. One comment was heard over and over again: "Lodge really *looks* like a president." John Mecklin described the appeal of the aloof and elite Lodge as "resentment . . . mixed with reluctant admiration . . . some of the same officials whom he had outraged incredulously found themselves tempted to vote for this enigmatic man if he became a candidate." Lodge appealed to both sexes, especially women. Like Kennedy, people saw in Lodge a cultured background, wealth, and charm. He was the most popular Republican nationwide, not only among Republican voters but also independents and Democrats as well.[122]

Those running the Draft Lodge movement believed their biggest obstacle, apart from having no candidate, was the need to convince people, and perhaps even Lodge himself, that they had a real chance. They also had no money, even though privately Lodge agreed to cover the expenses incurred.[123] The best way to avoid going into debt was to establish momentum. To do that, they needed to show that New Hampshire was not a fluke and win a big primary—like California, Florida, or Texas. Winning a big state would help to line up delegates, which would be needed at the convention in San Francisco.[124] Lodge told a visiting Roscoe Drummond, "My overriding responsibility is to stay here on the job to represent the United States as effectively as I can and to help this vital struggle to secure this gateway to Southeast Asia which communists are desperately trying to unhinge. Naturally, I would consider it my duty to run for the presidency if nominated." Drummond came away from this conversation convinced that Lodge was ready to run. "As I see it, Mr. Lodge is willing, even eager, to be nominated. He values what his supporters are doing and wishes them to succeed. But he feels he could not in good faith leave Saigon except as the 1964 Republican presidential nominee."[125]

Throughout April, Lodge led the pack in the polls with 40 percent, plus or minus. On April 26, the field included Rockefeller at 21 percent, Nixon at 15 percent, Goldwater at 12 percent, Scranton at 4 percent, and Smith around 1 percent. Lodge got another boost when the *Portland Oregonian* endorsed him a full month before the primary. Some money started to come into the campaign, and Lodge outspent Nixon $54,000 to $49,000. Still, these figures were dwarfed by Goldwater, who spent $109,000 despite having written off Oregon and already returned to Washington. Rockefeller spent more than anyone else at $460,000 and made a personal tour, unlike every other candidate, reminding voters that he "cared enough to come"—a dig at Lodge. Rockefeller started to surge in the final days, but Lodge still held a lead, 40 to 36 percent, a week before. The Harris poll showed Lodge up 46 to 32 percent two days before, even though Rockefeller was much better organized.[126] If Lodge were to win, he authorized his son George to say that he was willing to return from Saigon if it looked as if the convention would nominate him. It was the first time he had been so direct about the conditions required for his return.[127] Lodge's plan would be to "fly straight to San Francisco, acceptance speech in hand."[128]

The result of the Nebraska primary on May 12 was perplexing. Nixon received 35 percent of the votes, while Lodge came in second with 16 percent. Together, they kept Goldwater under a majority, but the result was not decisive enough to either create a real Nixon candidacy or cause Goldwater supporters to consider switching. Samuel Lubell of Scripps-Howard predicted Lodge would run stronger in Oregon. Lodge had allowed his name to stay on the ballot, which was a boost to his followers. The movement seemed to be rolling, and national sentiment for Lodge was growing. A Draft Lodge headquarters was opened in Portland, television time was purchased to run the five-minute campaign video, the direct mail effort went into action, and celebrity athletes and local politicians lined up to help.[129]

The movement was soon deflated when Rockefeller defeated Lodge, who came in second in the Oregon primary. Rockefeller carried three of the state's four congressional districts; Lodge won in one. The *New York Times* referred to Lodge's "flash and fade experience," while the *Washington Post* said that Lodge "appears to have shot down his political balloon just as quickly as it was inflated."[130] Eisenhower had hurt Lodge in another gaffe. He was asked whether the five-minute campaign video that had been airing on television and was so successful in New Hampshire amounted to an endorsement. Rather than saying something that would help Lodge, he said it was not necessarily an endorsement. After the defeat, George Cabot Lodge asked Lodge supporters to swing their support to Rockefeller.[131] The strategy was that Lodge and Rockefeller were close in ideology, and if Rockefeller were to drop out, Lodge could step back in.[132] "The result in Oregon was, of course, disappointing," Lodge's brother, John, wrote. "On the other hand, it was quite remarkable, considering the enormous effort and money expended by Rockefeller."[133] The Oregon primary showed that the Draft Lodge movement could go no further without the active involvement of its candidate. There was only so much an absentee movement could do, especially in states where Lodge was not even on the ballot.[134]

And while Oregon and Nebraska were not major primaries, California was. The joint Field Poll/California Poll found that Lodge was the most popular candidate in California and, given the necessary resources, he could win both there and in Illinois.[135] "My judgment, Mac, is that Lodge is coming back," Johnson told McGeorge Bundy in a recorded telephone call. "He'll probably be back in June. He's gonna find some trouble. He's gonna fall out with us about something. And I'm not gonna let him have any differences . . . Johnson is not going to have any difference with Lodge. He's gonna have to run and catch me before he does. I'm gonna agree with every damn thing he does. That's my strategy."[136]

In California, Lodge supporters hoped that their candidate might return in time, campaign, and embrace his popularity, but it was not to be. "A few easterners mentioned Henry Cabot Lodge as a possibility," Goldwater recalled, "but his acceptance of the ambassadorship to South Vietnam was a big handicap. He had his hands full in a faraway post."[137] Once again, there was no Eisenhower or other senior party leaders to rally support for Lodge. Due to Lodge's absence, the rules of the primary prevented him from being entered on the ballot. The leaders of the Draft Lodge movement met in Los Angeles on May 18, and they decided that they would encourage all supporters to vote for Rockefeller. "The surest way to endorse Ambassador Lodge in California is to elect Rockefeller delegates on Tuesday," George Cabot Lodge said during a stop in the state the following week.[138] "We did everything we could, but only about a third of our people could work for Rockefeller," one Lodge leader said. Many simply did not vote, and it was enough for Goldwater to win and begin to build some momentum. Even while moderate Republicans continued to deny the possibility that Goldwater could be nominated, the fact that they never organized around an alternative all but guaranteed that he would.[139]

Lodge continued to do well in primaries even as his supporters had less hope and fewer resources were committed to each primary.[140] His friend Charlie Bartlett said Lodge could still "perpetuate a coup of the first magnitude this November . . . it needs to be done."[141] In Illinois, he won 8 percent as a write-in against Goldwater and Smith. He won the New Jersey primary with 40 percent of the vote. In Pennsylvania, against favorite son Governor Scranton, he won 21 percent. He won the Massachusetts primary with an overwhelming 79 percent of the vote. In Texas, he won 8 percent on a write-in with all other candidates appearing on the ballot. While some of these numbers were not large, no other candidate won so much with so few resources. "There is a growing conviction becoming manifest in the American mind that you are the only Republican with the qualities of character and integrity to break President Johnson's hold upon the nation," his old friend and associate Max Rabb wrote.[142] The real question was why party leaders did not embrace a popular, positive candidate. Even with Goldwater racking up delegates, pragmatic Republicans were unwilling to commit to Lodge.[143]

Lodge had his first real opportunity to be relieved of duty after the Honolulu Conference on June 1, 1964. It was not ideal, as Lodge admitted in his top-secret report that the "situation in Viet-Nam can only be described as unsatisfactory. Khanh, contrary to what he has said, has in fact not extended government control over 2,000,000 people."[144] On June 14, Lodge cabled Rusk and requested that he be relieved.[145] According to one source, he asked to be relieved within thirty days for health reasons, not politics.[146] The official explanation was that he needed to care for his wife, Emily, whose health had been affected by the extreme heat and humidity of the Saigon climate. However, Lodge suggested to Rusk on June 18 that he wanted to leave Saigon in order to influence the Republican convention in July. "My presence in the U.S. as a private citizen can make a great difference in deciding whether or not the leadership of one of our two major political parties falls into hands which in foreign affairs would be imprudent and impulsive and unsatisfactory for other reasons in domestic affairs," Lodge wrote.[147] Pollster Lou Harris said that Republicans were so unsure about supporting Goldwater that Lodge could definitely be nominated if he announced that he would attend the convention.[148]

The list of people to replace Lodge in Saigon was long and included Rusk, McNamara, McGeorge Bundy, and Robert Kennedy. Despite Johnson's occasional private complaining about Lodge, he recognized that Lodge would be difficult to replace. Johnson liked Taylor, but Rusk and McNamara thought Taylor would be a mistake, according to telephone calls secretly recorded by the LBJ taping system. Bundy's concern was not Taylor's bad heart, but "the four stars Taylor had on his uniform always shined through his civilian clothing," Barry Zorthian said.[149] Johnson needed someone who could simply hold the situation in Saigon. In an Oval Office press conference on June 23, Johnson announced that Taylor would take over for Lodge in what Max Frankel called "the most difficult, delicate and potentially dangerous output of diplomacy." Johnson made an unprecedented step in naming a deputy ambassador, U. Alexis Johnson. Perhaps it was an honor that two people were needed to replace Lodge.[150] Premier Khanh told Malcolm Browne, "When Lodge quit, I asked Washington to send me another Lodge. Instead, they sent me this 'uncertain trumpet,'" a reference to the title of Taylor's earlier book that criticized Eisenhower's massive retaliation strategy.[151]

Khanh gave a formal reception in Lodge's honor, where he presented him with the nation's highest civilian and military decorations—the Grand Cross of the National Order of Vietnam and the Cross of Gallantry.[152] Khanh pinned these decorations on Lodge, who wore a traditional Vietnamese costume for the occasion, a sign of respect that did not go unnoticed. "You were like my older brother. You always gave me such good advice about politics," Khanh later said to

Lodge.[153] Khanh presented an array of carved gifts, including wooden dragons with elephant tusks. Lodge gave his final press conference, and then he, Emily, and two puppies drove to Tan Son Nhut Airport to board the C-119 jet that had brought Taylor, Johnson, and their team to Saigon.[154] A South Vietnamese honor guard and band awaited them, as well as a receiving line of prominent political, Buddhist, and Catholic officials. Khanh paid him yet another tribute by draping a blue silk tunic around his shoulders. He unveiled a scroll appointing Lodge an honorary citizen of South Vietnam while the band played "The Star Spangled Banner" and the South Vietnamese national anthem.[155]

Lodge had so ingratiated himself with the American press before he left that they also recognized his efforts in Vietnam. "I saw a poll of Republican voters listed your name as the overwhelming favorite," Browne wrote. "Realizing that politics is a forbidden subject of discussion, I'd like to say that while I have generally voted Democratic I would welcome the chance to switch tickets if things develop as I hope they will this July."[156] Even Thich Tri Quang thanked Lodge, giving him a gift of a small Vietnamese Buddhist statue. "It is thanks particularly to you that in a short time my people were able to end a regime that caused us more hardship than all the communists," he wrote.[157] The adulation continued at home. On June 29, Johnson held a White House ceremony to honor Lodge. "He has served without regard to partisanship, keeping the interest of his country foremost at all times," Johnson said. The president asked him to say a few words to the assembled press. "I did not come prepared to make a speech under these circumstances; to tell you the truth I am quite surprised," Lodge said.[158] "My resignation has now taken effect and I am a private citizen."[159]

While Lodge was transitioning from Saigon, moderate Republicans started a desperate effort to support Scranton in a bid to block Goldwater's nomination. In Lodge's view, people all over the country "were worried about having someone rash and impulsive in the White House," and he denied any personal ambition in seeking the nomination despite having a fully drafted nomination acceptance speech in his possession.[160] Even if Scranton could not block Goldwater's nomination, Lodge believed moderates would be better served by supporting the reelection of Johnson than the election of Goldwater.[161] "Regardless of how you feel about civil rights, Social Security, VN [Vietnam], you must oppose a man who has a responsibility for the atomic bomb and who is *impulsive*—which Barry [Goldwater], unfortunately, is," Lodge wrote to his son George.[162] His primary concern was that Goldwater would not insist on the "supremacy of the civil power over the military."[163]

Rockefeller joined the Scranton bandwagon. He thought the symbolism of Lodge's return might prompt others to help, too. "His return, I trust, will encourage others to join in the effort to assure that the Republican party stays in the mainstream of American political thought and action through the adoption of a forward-looking program based on traditional Republican principles and through the nomination of Governor Scranton," Rockefeller said.[164] Moderate Republicans put pressure on Eisenhower to endorse Scranton, but he was hesitant to do so.[165] Eisenhower's former cabinet member George Humphrey, an ally of Goldwater's, convinced him to withhold his support from the Scranton effort even though it was much more in line with Eisenhower's politics.[166]

Johnson believed that Lodge's return ultimately served his own political purposes. "Lodge is going to get in this Scranton thing and I don't mind," he told Chicago Mayor Richard Daley on June 29. "I don't believe they can stop Goldwater."[167] Fanning the flames of discontent in the Republican Party, Johnson said in a speech in Harrisburg, Pennsylvania, that his opponents were not Republicans but extremists who were "contemptuous toward the will of the majorities, callous toward the plight of minorities, arrogant toward allies, belligerent toward adversaries, careless about peace." Johnson praised Republicans like Eisenhower, Arthur Vandenberg, and Lodge, "fine men who had supported a bipartisan foreign policy."[168]

Lodge went home to Beverly for a few days of rest. On July 5, his sixty-second birthday, he flew to Harrisburg to join in the Scranton effort to block the nomination of Goldwater. Lodge felt somewhat obligated to return the support that Scranton had given to George Lodge's ill-fated Senate run in 1962.[169] Reporters called Scranton the "Republican JFK." He was handsome, wealthy, committed to public service, and, somehow, still friendly with the Goldwater forces. He was also the last remaining moderate in the race.[170] Scranton had sent a letter to Goldwater accusing him of treating delegates as "little more than a flock of chickens whose necks will be rung."[171] From Harrisburg, Lodge hit the campaign trail—Chicago, Wichita, and St. Louis—in the hope of finding some uncommitted delegates. However, Lodge's involvement in Scranton's effort backfired. Republicans remembered Lodge's treatment of the Taft delegates, some of the same ones that Lodge was again trying to reach.[172]

As national Republican Chairman William E. Miller and Platform Committee Chairman Melvin Laird prepared for the convention in San Francisco, they had two primary goals: prevent a "runaway" civil rights plank of the kind that had been adopted in 1960 and maintain some kind of balance between moderates and conservatives.[173] Lodge tried to do his part. He appeared before the Platform Committee on July 8 with Milton Eisenhower and George Romney to make a plea for a "Republican-sponsored Marshall Plan for our cities and schools." "Having renounced all personal ambition for future political office, I talk to you here with complete frankness," Lodge began. He argued that there had been "a fundamental failure to do enough in the field of education . . . disgraceful inadequacy at elementary and high school levels, and there is an unpardonable denial of opportunity to youth."[174] Lodge then took direct aim at the lack of positive positions in the Goldwater campaign. He did not mention Goldwater by name, but it was obvious who the target of his remarks was. "No one in his right mind would today argue that there is no place for the federal government in the reawakening of America . . . Republicans must be true conservatives who distinguish between conserving and hoarding and who know that it is possible to conserve when we are willing to innovate and to give every American citizen a chance by his own efforts to have something which he too will want to conserve." Lodge's speech was his farewell to the 1964 presidential campaign—and Republican politics. It fell on deaf ears. "What in God's name has happened to the Republican Party!" Lodge exclaimed. "I hardly know any of these people!"[175]

Lodge continued to the Republican convention at the Cow Palace in San Francisco. The more Lodge tried to win over uncommitted delegates for an anti-Goldwater cause, the more he was shocked to see the changes that had occurred in his party since 1960—and certainly since 1952. "This convention was run by people who have no understanding of the world we live in," Lodge said.[176] He did not even wait until the end of the convention to leave town. "I live on the shores of Massachusetts Bay, and I have a boat. And I think I'll go out on my boat and think," he told Richard Harkness of NBC News. He decided to use his time to advocate for the policies of the Johnson White House that he agreed with—especially on Vietnam. Unlike Eisenhower, whose first act after receiving the nomination in 1952 was to visit privately with Taft, Goldwater did no such thing. The moderate and progressive Republicans were not welcome.[177]

While Goldwater was denied an outright victory on the first ballot at the convention by sixty-two votes, his nomination was inevitable. The moderate to liberal wing of the Republican Party had dominated conventions since 1936, but in 1964 conservatives demanded a change.[178] In 1960, Goldwater had given a rousing speech that unified Republicans behind Nixon, and now it was Nixon's turn to nominate Goldwater. "Before the convention we were Goldwater Republicans, Rockefeller Republicans, Scranton Republicans, Lodge

Republicans, but now that this convention has met and made its decision, we are Republicans, period, working for Barry Goldwater," Nixon said to roaring acclaim.[179] There was a limit, however, to Nixon's happiness with the convention result. Bill Safire later noted how Nixon sat on his hands during Goldwater's famous "extremism is no vice" line during his acceptance speech.[180]

Johnson did not let Lodge rest for long. He sent him on a goodwill trip to American allied nations in Europe from August 16 to September 2.[181] Given the title of special representative of the president of the United States, Lodge was instructed to explain the American actions following the Gulf of Tonkin incident and "to whip up enthusiasm and support for the war in Vietnam."[182] Lodge briefed the NATO Atlantic Council on August 18.[183] "Our presence here today in this Council is the outward manifestation of our common realization that to frustrate the communist design to conquer Europe we had to band together in NATO," he said. "The war in Viet Nam is not only the struggle of a small nation to exist, but it is also an open encounter between the doctrine that 'Wars and Revolution,' as the communists call them, are the wave of the future, and our belief that in the future, nations should be allowed to develop their own destinies free from outside interference."[184] He got a mixed response. While West Germany showed support, primarily because the Berlin issue always caused the Germans to be warier of communist advances than other Europeans, the rest of Europe did not agree that Vietnam was a vital issue.[185] The timing of the trip was not a coincidence, as it took him away from the campaign trail.[186] "Here you are still the most popular of all the Republicans, even after the Convention," Johnson said. "If you had come back a little earlier, you could have had the nomination and it would have been a hell of a contest."[187]

On Lodge's return, he campaigned for candidates he had more in common with, such as his brother, John, in his ultimately unsuccessful run for Senate in Connecticut; John Volpe, who was looking for a political comeback in Massachusetts; and Edward Brooke in his campaign for state attorney general. Volpe and Brooke were among the only non-Goldwater Republicans to win that year despite a backdrop of crushing national defeat for the GOP.[188] It was a complete wipeout, from Johnson's landslide victory over Goldwater on down ballot. "While I don't think any Republican could have beaten Johnson, I do think the election would have been much closer had several Governors, Senators and Congressmen in our Party worked *for* the Party," Goldwater wrote to John Davis Lodge.[189]

Johnson's victory ended two of the longest political streaks in American history. His reelection showed that someone who was viewed as a southerner could not only win but also be pragmatic and accommodating. Vermont, which had voted Republican in every presidential election since 1856, went for Johnson in 1964. On the other hand, Georgia, which had voted Democrat in every presidential election since 1868, went for Goldwater.[190] Lodge returned far too late to save his own candidacy or to have much influence on the 1964 election.[191] But he would not be out of action for long. "You can do anything in this government, I think, and you can do it well," Johnson told Lodge in a secretly recorded conversation. "And I'm not going to let you, the next four years, sit on your tail up there in Boston and play with your grandchildren," he said, getting a chuckle out of Lodge.[192]

# 15 • LBJ and Vietnam

Even though Henry Cabot Lodge Jr. had returned from Vietnam, he continued serving President Lyndon B. Johnson and working on the issue of Vietnam. He undertook special missions to NATO, a tour of a dozen European capitals, and a debate at the University of Oxford.[1] At a state dinner for UN Secretary General U Thant, Johnson singled out Lodge as being one of the four great Americans who represented "all that is best in our country," along with Adlai Stevenson, J. William Fulbright, and Everett Dirksen.[2] The *New York Times* reported that of the four, Lodge received the longest applause from the mostly Democratic audience.

Lodge was part of Johnson's inner circle when the decisions were made to launch Rolling Thunder, the air war on North Vietnam, as well as the first deployments of marines in March and the official beginning of the ground war. Lodge praised both moves and, in fact, had urged them earlier. He felt they were necessary in order to have any chance of saving South Vietnam. General Nguyen Khanh's government was deteriorating both from within in its war effort and in its relations with the United States. Its relations with the Buddhists had gotten so bad that Thich Tri Quang denounced Maxwell Taylor and called for the overthrow of the Khanh government.[3]

In a secretly recorded telephone call on March 24, 1965, Lodge and Johnson discussed the need for politically minded diplomats in Vietnam. "Maybe the thing to do is to send me back," Lodge suggested. "Might be," Johnson said. "I'd hate like hell to murder you by sending you there, but it's something you ought to—we ought to give some thought to," he added. He asked Lodge to think about it and to call him the next day.[4] When he did, Lodge got right to the point. "I think things have gone too far to send a new person out there who is going to have to learn," he said. "You need a man who is right up on the whole thing and thoroughly saturated with it . . . I would be glad to go back if you'd like to have me to do it. I'd be very glad to do it, because, as you know, I believe this thing can work out, difficult though it is." Johnson thought Dean Rusk "would look with some favor on this," and "McNamara was just almost ecstatic last night. He said, 'well, I don't know where in the hell this idea came from, but this is the best thing.'" Lodge also was considered the only one who had been able to tame the American press in Saigon. "Hell, the Halberstams and the rest of them, out there in the early days, they were just almost a member of his family," Johnson recalled Robert McNamara saying, joking that Lodge had done so well with the press that he "must have been sleeping with them."[5]

Johnson sent Lodge on an around-the-world tour from April 19 to May 1 to shore up support for the war.[6] He traveled on a presidential jet with a staff of seventeen to countries that included Australia, New Zealand, India, South Korea, and Japan. The White House arranged meetings with prime ministers, foreign ministers, and even entire cabinets.[7] At each stop, Lodge thanked the nation for its contribution to the war but also discussed whether anything else could be committed while being sensitive to each country's limitations. Lodge made it clear that the United States was not asking Taiwan, Japan, or India for troops, only economic aid. The most Lodge expected to get from India was some ambulances because of their problems with Pakistan. The Australians promised one battalion in return for "complete secrecy" until the government could announce it. New Zealand agreed to an additional combat unit. The Philippines offered a task force. South Korea offered a "few" more combat divisions.[8] Most leaders seemed approving of the expanded American air war over North Vietnam. They also held out hope that increased hostilities would not decrease the opportunities for peace.

Lodge's offer to return to Vietnam had been kept secret from the public for months until Johnson's public announcement appointing him ambassador on July 9.[9] Taylor had suddenly asked to be relieved of his duties. Nguyen Cao Ky's memoirs reveal that he and Khanh were about to call a press conference and declare Taylor persona non grata when the U.S. embassy called to beg that Saigon not expel Taylor.[10] Khanh complained to Lodge that he felt that Taylor wanted him overthrown and that Taylor had not seen him alone a single time.[11] The White House was quick to respond. "The search for the best man . . . was neither very long nor very difficult for the search led first to Ambassador Lodge," Johnson said. "I thought he was the best equipped by training and by experience and by knowledge of conditions there. And when he was first asked, his first and immediate answer was, 'Yes, Mr. President.'" Despite his occasional criticism of Lodge, Johnson liked him. "My people tell me that he is less likely to get us in an Asian war than Taylor . . . He'd like to talk it out, rather than fight it out. And that's pretty appealing these days," Johnson had told Senate Majority Leader Mike Mansfield (D-MN) on June 8.[12]

Lodge was unanimously confirmed by the Senate Foreign Relations Committee, although some Republicans criticized him for serving another Democrat. Even Lodge's brother, John Davis Lodge, questioned his decision to serve in critical roles in two Democratic administrations.[13] Johnson's decision to reappoint Lodge was made to mute increasing Republican criticism of the war. Barry Goldwater urged Johnson to take a tough line on Vietnam, especially when it came to bombing North Vietnam. "I can take my bombs, and I can take my nuclear weapons, as Barry [Goldwater] says," Johnson said to Drew Pearson. "I can defoliate, and I can clear out that brush when I can see anybody coming down that line, and I can wipe out Hanoi, and I can wipe out Peiping . . . But I think that would start World War III."[14]

Lodge was on his way to Vietnam not as ambassador but on a fact-finding mission that had been previously arranged. He was accompanied by McNamara and Chairman of the Joint Chiefs of Staff Earle Wheeler to meet with Taylor and Deputy Ambassador U. Alexis Johnson.[15] LBJ had increased the number of American forces in Vietnam by twenty-one thousand to seventy-one thousand combat troops. The introduction of the first marines in March indicated that the American role would no longer be solely "advisory." Johnson paired that hawkish move with a peace effort: the first bombing halt from May 13 to 18. It provided a chance to see whether North Vietnam was willing to reciprocate with a gesture of its own. Johnson and top advisers Rusk, McGeorge Bundy, Lodge, and many military commanders were skeptical.[16] Lodge welcomed the change in strategy, but he was generally opposed to bombing halts because he thought they would demoralize South Vietnam and drive a wedge between Saigon and Washington.[17] "The bombing must not be stopped without a quid pro quo," Lodge said.[18] He was more in favor of attacking North Vietnam and putting them on the defensive.[19] A huge port had been constructed at Cam Ranh Bay, a little less than two hundred miles northeast of Saigon. When Lodge arrived, he was amazed to see American bulldozers and construction crews working around the clock to handle the substantial influx of soldiers and equipment. At the time, he believed the sight of American power could mean the beginning of the end of communist hostility toward South Vietnam, now that the United States was more fully committed.[20]

Lodge was going back to Saigon because Johnson planned to bring an end to the war, whether through force or diplomacy. Lodge, as the top civilian official in country, was intimately involved in both. His assignment would be very different from that in 1963.[21] The military had far more influence than the politicians and diplomats; thus, with his wings clipped, Lodge's role would be much closer to that of a normal ambassador.[22] He did not believe the military struggle could be effective until the political struggle was fixed, and that was where he hoped to have influence. Lodge also hoped to use the substantial aid that was flowing into Vietnam to improve the lives of people in the countryside. Villagers had "a sense of peoplehood but not the same sense of nationhood that we have," Lodge said. Americans could not force "instant democracy" on villages, but through economic aid, they could provide equipment, materials, and technology to improve and modernize their lives. American aid could build thousands of schools to create a more informed electorate.[23]

While he believed in those policies, however, Johnson was going in a different direction. He met with the Joint Chiefs of Staff on July 21, along with ambassador-designate Lodge, and agreed to an open-ended commitment of military forces.[24] Lodge, McNamara, and Wheeler had just returned from their five-day trip to Vietnam, where General William Westmoreland and other military leaders requested more troops.[25] According to Clark Clifford, who later replaced McNamara as secretary of defense, those present were deeply influenced by the Cuban Missile Crisis and placed emphasis on "flexible response" and "controlled escalation."[26] "What we have done from 1954 to 1961 has not been good enough," Rusk said in self-criticism. "We should have probably committed ourselves more fully in 1961."[27] McNamara proposed an increase in troop strength from 75,000 to 175,000, in addition to a call-up of 235,000 from the U.S. Army Reserve and the National Guard. He argued that 75,000 had been just enough to protect the bases, but not to stabilize the situation and even improve it.[28]

Lodge, McNamara, and Wheeler advised Johnson against a rapid escalation, which had had almost no public debate and not even wide debate within the administration.[29] "Any further initiative by us now would simply harden the communist resolve not to stop fighting," Lodge argued.[30] He said there was an increased risk in deepening the American commitment, but an even greater risk if they did nothing at all. "What makes you think if we put in 100,000 men, Ho Chi Minh won't put in another 100,000?" Johnson asked. "This means greater bodies of men, which will allow us to cream them," Wheeler answered.[31] As Taylor said, it would be "psychologically unsound to get too far ahead in the air campaign while the ground campaign is lagging." The hope was that the gradually escalating air campaign might accomplish a major goal in the north, such as destroying an important railway bridge north of Hanoi, prompting North Vietnam to consider a negotiated end to the conflict in a bombing halt that could follow.[32] Lodge's army background told him it was not wise to negotiate, since "North Vietnam wages war without cost to itself."[33] George Ball argued that the United States would never win the war and therefore should cut its losses.[34] Lodge did not agree. "There is a greater threat of World War III if we don't go in than if we go in," he said.[35] A week after the meeting, the president announced he was increasing American deployments to Vietnam to 125,000, raising draft calls from 17,000 to 35,000 a month, and committing another billion dollars or more to the war.

Privately, Lodge felt he was arriving too late in Vietnam to do anything to improve the situation.[36] Though he had good relations with Khanh, he had no capacity to end the Buddhist-led domestic turmoil or rally the political or military leadership behind him.[37] "There is not a tradition of national government in Saigon," Lodge said. "There are no roots in the country. Not until there is tranquility can you have any stability. I don't think we ought to take this government seriously. There is simply no one who can do anything. We have to do what we think we ought to do regardless of what the Saigon government does."[38]

When Lodge arrived in Saigon on August 20, 1965, conditions looked familiar. "I think I am quite lucky because I have come back after having had one year of duty here already, plus another year in which to think over all the things I observed and learned," Lodge wrote his personal attorney, Porter Chandler. "This place is so complicated and so different from anything that we Americans know about that it really takes that much time to make a man sure-footed."[39] Gone were the white linen suits, and he returned a little more settled down.[40] Lodge landed at the same airport, took the same way into Saigon, and arrived at the same villa he had lived in the year before. His former cook, Canh, awaited him, as did a large supply of baby food that Canh made into the bland soups that Lodge liked. This time Lodge came alone, as dependents had been evacuated for security reasons. Many spouses who wished to stay close remained in Bangkok, while others maintained residences in Hong Kong, Manila, or Honolulu. Emily had a suite in the Oriental Hotel in Bangkok and served in a leadership position in the Saigon United States Operations Mission wives' group.[41] The separation was difficult.

Lodge took the same route to the same embassy. His police escort was larger, and one of the windows in his office had been covered for fear of Viet Cong sharpshooters. In March, the embassy had been shaken by a car bomb that killed two Americans, nineteen Vietnamese, and one Filipino.[42] One hundred ninety were injured. The explosion destroyed Lodge's previous embassy car, and Taylor had been under constant threat of assassination. The embassy was on a busy intersection at Ham Nghi Boulevard, so the site, by design, was not secure. Plans for a more secure embassy between what became Independence Palace and the Saigon Zoo, the site of the American consulate in Ho Chi Minh City today, were started in direct response to the bombing. These kinds of attacks convinced Lodge that the Viet Cong could never achieve any mass political acceptance in South Vietnam. "I have been looking hard for three years for some sign that the Viet Cong have any genuine support or popularity," Lodge wrote his friend Henry Luce. "I have never been able to find such a sign. They have a powerful guerilla organization which is based exclusively on terror, that is, assassination, kidnapping and torture—techniques which we consider 'criminal.'"[43] On the whole, Lodge found upon his return to Saigon a "government in state of grave instability and turmoil." He had no illusions of establishing a democracy in a place with no Western democratic traditions.[44]

While uneven, there had been some progress toward achieving American ends in the Vietnam War. Bringing in William Porter as deputy ambassador in charge of the pacification program was a good move. He had seen his share of conflict, serving in places such as Jerusalem during the partition of Palestine and the creation of Israel, Cyprus during Greek-Turkish fighting, and Algiers during the Franco-Algerian war. He replaced Deputy Ambassador U. Alexis Johnson, who returned to the State Department in Washington. Taylor returned as well, becoming ambassador at large. Westmoreland, with whom Lodge was well acquainted both personally and professionally, had arrived during Lodge's first tour in January 1964, commanding American military activities in Vietnam.[45] Lodge's purview would be the politicians in Vietnam, while encouraging the military to be more aggressive in attacking the Viet Cong, even if it meant bombing in North Vietnam or Laos.[46] Some criticized him for being too hawkish, but Vice President Hubert Humphrey defended him when asked whether Lodge was the driving force behind increased bombing: "Yes, but Cabot is a good professional, and he'll go along. The military aren't so easy to handle."[47]

Lodge had met Premier Ky during his first tour, but they did not know each other well. Ky's political rise had occurred after a series of turbulent events and was a source of both stability and instability in the Vietnamese government. A month after Lodge had departed after his first tour, Khanh promulgated a new constitution in order to make himself president. When there were riots protesting the authoritarianism, he rescinded the constitution and resigned but immediately came back as premier, in a triumvirate that included the popular Duong Van Minh. The generals were under pressure to transition to a civilian government and named a High National Council of seventeen elders charged with drafting another constitution. When Ky played a central role in thwarting a coup against Khanh, he was rewarded with a position in the government. In late January 1965, the generals formed a ten-member National Leadership Committee that appointed Nguyen Van Thieu, a Catholic, as head of state, and Ky, a Buddhist, was chosen as premier.

The American government worried that Ky would challenge the sitting president and further divide the Saigon government.[48] The mustached former air force pilot wore flamboyant scarves and conspicuous pearl-handled pistols; had a young, pretty, Western-looking Vietnamese wife; and once said that his greatest hero was Adolf Hitler. When asked to clarify, he said he admired the methods that Hitler had used to unify the German state.[49] The United States needed someone to fight communism, and Lodge, Rusk, and Johnson convinced themselves that Ky was a real leader.[50] "By any yardstick, he is an exceptional man for 35 years old," Lodge said. Ky was "surprisingly reflective and a very careful listener who will recall conversations going back two weeks, with evidence of having considered what was said. He stands up straight, speaks without notes, and without a hat (something Big Minh could never do)."[51] Some of Lodge's remarks seem like a stretch for someone who saw numerous American presidents up close. Paul Kattenberg said "it is almost incomprehensible that a U.S. statesman of Lodge's stature could have taken a clown like Ky seriously and sold him to Lyndon Johnson as a great war leader."[52]

Lodge and Taylor understood over time that the heterogeneous South Vietnamese were never going to answer the American call to "get together to fight this thing."[53] As one coup followed another in rapid succession, the generals were unable to subordinate their personal ambitions to the war effort, according to Rusk.[54] The immediate beneficiary was North Vietnam. "The Saigon regime, the main instrument used by the American imperialists to carry out their neo-colonialist policies of aggression, collapsed into a state of continual crisis from which it could not recover," the official North Vietnamese history of the war states. "Taking advantage of the convulsions and contradictions within the puppet army and the puppet regime, all our battlefields increased their operations."[55]

It was now the military's war.[56] Lodge was more optimistic once Westmoreland was running the military side of the conflict, which showed how much confidence he had in the general.[57] Johnson had sent Westmoreland to Vietnam during Lodge's first term as ambassador, and they immediately established a rapport. Westmoreland was a South Carolina Brahmin. He had no living quarters when he first arrived, so he and his family lived in a guesthouse on the grounds of the ambassador's residence until a villa was ready. Westmoreland's son, Rip, remembers playing cards with Emily Lodge.[58] It was the "beginning of a rewarding friendship," Westmoreland wrote later.[59]

Lodge got what—or rather *whom*—he had been asking for when General Edward Lansdale came out to help him implement some of his counterinsurgency ideas in the countryside. The CIA once again objected to Lansdale's return, but this time Lodge won.[60] Lansdale arrived in Saigon on November 13, along with about a dozen experts with whom he had worked for many years.[61] "You will be executive agent, responsible for getting an effective political-social program moving in Viet-Nam," in addition to helping Ky become a "true political leader," Lodge said.[62] One expert who arrived with Lansdale was Chester Cooper, who was asked by Lodge to serve as his special assistant. "I spent hours discussing the problems he [Lodge] was likely to encounter," Cooper wrote later, "preparing lists of Americans and Vietnamese he thought would be useful and reading reports and telegrams."[63] Another member of the Lansdale group—officially known as the Interagency Group on Vietnam— was Lodge's personal assistant, Foreign Service officer James Bullington.[64]

The Lansdale team contained an eclectic mix of talents. They were "a motley crew of guerilla fighters, psychological and economic warriors, and unfriendly looking adventurers," Cooper recalled. A few notable members who gathered at Lansdale's Cong Ly villa included Lucien Conein, Belgian-born Mike Deutsch, and Daniel Ellsberg. Lodge's staff assistant Peter Tarnoff later said that Lansdale's parties were a "relaxed" environment where "alcohol flowed freely although people were not dead drunk." For fun, the group liked to record native Vietnamese folk songs for visiting Americans.[65] Embassy political officer Robert Miller characterized the group as ultimately "another gimmick overloading the U.S. mission structure."[66] Lansdale said that he did not have any direct orders from Washington about what he would do. "I didn't have funds from Congress to expend. I didn't have a clear rule of . . . line of authority to do certain things."[67] The Vietnamese regarded Lansdale with "awe" and "mystique," Ellsberg wrote.[68] "Lansdale is without doubt a man of extraordinary gifts," Henry Kissinger said. "He is an artist in dealing with Asians. He is patient, inspirational, imaginative. He has assembled an extraordinary group of individualists—each a remarkable personality in his own right. Anybody who could first collect such a group and then retain its loyalty over two decades is not an ordinary person."[69]

Recognizing that the U.S. mission was not like others around the world, Lodge established a U.S. Mission Council, which included embassy, military, and civilian officials. With Lodge presiding, the two senior members were Porter and Westmoreland. Other members included Charles Mann, the director of the U.S. Agency for International Development; Barry Zorthian, the head of the American psychological war effort; and Leroy Wehrle, the embassy's economic counselor. Lodge also brought in two new faces during his second tour, Philip Habib as political counselor and Samuel Wilson, a loaner from the army who served in the newly created role of mission coordinator. Habib remembered, "[Lodge] was very good to me, and I became in many ways his right hand on political matters, and many other matters, too. We became very close to each other."[70] The group made an ambitious plan to spend hundreds of millions of dollars on securing nearly one thousand hamlets, building 2,500 classrooms, resettling forty-one thousand families who had fled their unsafe villages, and building 150 bridges and six hundred miles of road.[71]

The U.S. mission in Saigon was a small Washington. While the military had its own orders, Lodge was charged with coordinating those orders with the need to fight terrorist activity, as well as with the economic and social programs of the embassy. He was expected to regularly advise the Saigon government, and he took Ky under his wing and sometimes visited him several times per day. Lodge treated him "like [his] own son," and they became good friends.[72] On the surface, these efforts seemed to be working. Commenting on the November 1 National Day parade, Australian counterinsurgency expert Ted Serong wrote in his diary, "Many more aircraft evident. Lots of sophisticated equipment looking well-cleaned, with well-dressed personnel. Pity they can't fight like they look."[73]

Lodge was expected to address all aspects of American activity in Vietnam in his weekly updates to Johnson. When Washington increasingly began to emphasize the importance of a negotiated end to the war, Lodge examined the issue. "I am concerned about the current U.S. stress on a 'settlement' and on 'negotiations' to the neglect of the concept of a satisfactory 'outcome' or 'result,'" Lodge wrote to Johnson as he began his second tour. "We *can* succeed in warding off the communist aggression, but we will not get them to admit it."[74] Lodge was expected to regularly brief a long list of officials, from other Vietnamese government officials to visiting delegations from the United States. In less than a year since the start of his second tour, he hosted Vice President Hubert Humphrey, former Vice President Richard Nixon, four Cabinet members, seventeen senators, four congressmen, thirteen governors, fourteen sub-Cabinet members, and twenty-six four-star generals, in addition to some fifty other visitors.[75]

Lodge gave Henry Kissinger his first serious job in foreign policy.[76] "I ceased being a spectator in early August 1965 when Henry Cabot Lodge, an old friend then serving as ambassador to Saigon, asked me to visit Vietnam as his consultant," Kissinger wrote.[77] He spent a month in Vietnam as Lodge's adviser in October. It was his introduction to Vietnam, a place he was eager to understand better.[78] "This was an area about which I knew very little," Kissinger said.[79] He remarked on how difficult it was in Washington to get straight answers about Vietnam policy. "I have been struck by the fact that in Washington there does not seem to exist any long-range integration of the many diverse operations now taking place. What goes under the name of inter-agency planning is really a device for coordinating essentially autonomous efforts which may be based on different concepts and assumptions."[80] Lodge called Kissinger's prearrival reports "a remarkable contribution from someone who has never been here."[81]

"In 1965, I went to Vietnam as a consultant to Ambassador Lodge and had an opportunity to travel around the country. And I concluded then that there was no way of winning the war in the manner in which it was being conducted and I said so to McNamara, Bundy, and others," Kissinger reflected.[82] Shortly after arriving, Kissinger walked into Habib's office at the embassy to help plan his itinerary. "Professor, you don't know a god-damn thing about this place. I'm a very busy fellow," Habib said. "If you want to learn something about it, I'll give you a couple of my guys who know the language, know the country. You go around the country, spend a couple of weeks looking the situation over, then you come back and I'll have time to talk to you. In the meantime, get the hell out of my office."[83] That is exactly what he did. Kissinger visited Thieu and other leaders, spoke with students, and roamed the countryside. At his first military briefing, he asked what the five- and ten-year goals were. "No one could really explain to me how even on the most favorable assumptions . . . the war was going to end," he wrote in his diary.[84]

Lodge and Kissinger met with Ky at the Nha Trung villa, a kind of Vietnamese Camp David about an hour north of Saigon that had been built for Emperor Bao Dai. Lodge introduced Kissinger, and they had lunch with Ky and his family. "Kissinger handled his chopsticks as easily as any problem he deals with," Ky wrote later. "He put himself out to be charming to Mai, he played with the kids, and later we relaxed in deep, comfortable western-style armchairs while he asked hundreds of questions, storing each answer in the remarkable brain of his, never taking a note."[85] Kissinger came away disenchanted. "Since there were no front lines within South Vietnam and since the Johnson administration refused to pursue the guerillas into the sanctuaries just across the border in Laos and Cambodia, I advocated a negotiated outcome."[86]

On November 1, 1965, his second to last day in Saigon, Kissinger met with eight American journalists. He naïvely revealed his pessimism that South Vietnam could ever defeat the communists. The *Los Angeles Times* published a portion of Kissinger's remarks on the front page the following day.[87] "Recent emissaries from the White House are reporting that there is an almost total lack of political maturity or unselfish political motivation among the current leaders of the South Vietnamese government," the *Washington Post* reported.[88] While Kissinger was not named as a source, Johnson figured it out and went "off the wall."[89] Kissinger became persona non grata at the Johnson White House.[90] "I am depressed and shaken that my effort to be helpful to the Administration and to Ambassador Lodge has ended so ignominiously," he wrote to Clark Clifford.[91] Kissinger apologized, not because his views had been misrepresented, but because he did not realize he had made the remarks on the record. "It was my first real exposure to the press, and I was totally unprepared for it," he said.[92]

Despite his schedule, Lodge was able to visit Emily in Bangkok every fifth weekend, and they enjoyed going to Pattaya Beach. At times when security concerns were lessened, she was able to join him in Saigon for short periods and special events. Lodge had an honorary membership at the private club Cercle Sportif Saigonnais, which had a pool, tennis courts, racquetball, table tennis, badminton, volleyball, and soccer.[93] His noontime dips in the pool helped with his mild arthritis. He could enjoy the horse races every weekend at the Phu Tho Hippodrome. The 2,100-meter track was large enough that the Japanese had used it as an airbase during World War II, and the faint runways could still be made out from the air. Visitors to Saigon, such as journalist James "Scotty" Reston, loved to take advantage of all that the city had to offer, despite its proximity to a war zone. Reston visited Lodge toward the end of 1965 and reported on the unusual aspects of Lodge's job in Saigon. "What Ambassador

Lodge is trying to do is to anticipate the problems that will arise if we ever get to the point of talking to the communists," he wrote. "He spent a number of years . . . at the UN where he had to deal with the negotiating techniques of the communists. He learned from that experience that it is important to be prepared before talking to the communists, so he is being forehanded about the problem of urging his associates in Washington to do the same." While it would be some time until formal negotiations would begin between North Vietnam and the United States, Lodge was learning as much as he could to help with that process.[94]

At Christmastime 1965, Johnson announced the second bombing halt, which, paired with diplomatic pressure on Hanoi, was designed to force the North Vietnamese to reciprocate with some gesture of peace of their own, but none was forthcoming.[95] American casualties were rising, and Lodge even suggested to Rusk and McNamara over lunch that the United States should "get out of I Corps and even Vietnam" or choose to fight communism elsewhere, such as in Thailand. While the situation was the worst in I Corps, the northernmost region in South Vietnam, Lodge wondered whether it would soon spread farther south. When he had agreed to return to Vietnam, his primary duty was to improve political stability. While that had been achieved with the arrival of the Thieu-Ky government, the increasingly poor results of the war were yet another threat of instability against the Saigon government—and one that Lodge had little control over.[96]

In February 1966, Lodge escorted President Thieu and Premier Ky to Honolulu via a presidential jet for a major conference to discuss war progress. Johnson had decided to resume the bombing of North Vietnam on January 31.[97] He paired his decision with an effort by UN Ambassador Arthur Goldberg to seek an international conference to end the war through the UN. However, Ho Chi Minh and the North Vietnamese refused any peace talks. These and other pressing subjects were on the agenda in Hawaii. Johnson's transoceanic trip from Washington to Honolulu with Vietnamese Ambassador Vu Van Thai was the first he had made since becoming president. A White House entourage, including half of Johnson's Cabinet and 125 Americans and Vietnamese from Saigon, took over the Royal Hawaiian Hotel on Waikiki Beach from February 6 to 8.[98] Thieu and Ky had extensive discussions with Johnson, who pledged to give the growing rural construction program the highest priority in the American commitment to South Vietnam. He also promised more experts to help with those efforts, including a czar position over pacification to be filled by Porter.[99]

Some of Johnson's proposals sounded like plans for a Great Society for South Vietnam, with an emphasis on defeating poverty in addition to finding their feet as a nation and defeating communism. Ky was prepared to give the kinds of assurances that he thought Johnson wanted to hear. "We must create a society where each individual can feel that he has a future, that he has respect and dignity, and that he has some chance for himself and for his children to live in an atmosphere where all is not disappointment, despair, and dejection," he said. "Boy, you speak just like an American," Johnson said.[100] Johnson's warm embrace of the diminutive Vietnamese leader in front of the cameras reinforced the image for some that Ky had been summoned and his nation was an American dependency.[101]

During a three-hour meeting in Honolulu, Johnson pressed Westmoreland on how long the war would last. "There comes a time in every battle—in every war—when both sides become discouraged by the seemingly endless requirements for more effort, more resources, and more faith," Westmoreland reflected. "At this point the side which presses on with renewed vigor is the one to win."[102] Lodge's cables to Washington suggest that he had more and more doubts about the American presence in Vietnam. Writing the State Department on May 23, 1966, Lodge said, "The idea that we are here simply because the Vietnamese want us to be here . . . that we have no national interest in being here ourselves, and that if some of them don't want us to stay, we ought to get out is, to me, fallacious . . . Some day we may have to decide how much it is worth to us to deny Vietnam to Hanoi and Peking—regardless of what the Vietnamese may think."[103]

By the spring of 1966, Saigon barely had control of the provinces of central Vietnam. They were exposed to northern infiltration and distant from the government in the South. They were also the hotbed of Buddhist protest activity. After marines tore down Buddhist banners with their bayonets, a local Buddhist leader threatened to burn down the U.S. consulate unless an apology was received. The situation became so tense that the young consul, John Negroponte, called Lodge and Habib. Lodge did not understand how people could get so worked up over some banners. "When I campaigned [in Massachusetts] they wrote 'Fuck you!' all over them!" he said.[104]

Ky made a move to regain control of central Vietnam, but it backfired. He ordered Lieutenant General Nguyen Chanh Thi, an ally of Buddhist leader Tri Quang, removed as commander of I Corps in the northern Hue-Danang area on the front lines of the war. What started as some minor protests fed into what became known as the Struggle Movement, which quickly aligned with Tri

Quang.[105] In late March, the turmoil continued under the guise of protests against the Saigon government's incompetence and spread to other cities, including Hue, Danang, Dalat, and Nha Trang. American officials had evidence that the movement was infiltrated by the Viet Cong, according to James Bullington, a Foreign Service officer who served in Hue.[106] Joe Luman remembered seeing protesters standing up, revealing that they were wearing blue jeans under their saffron robes. "Buddhist monks do not wear blue jeans," he recalled.[107] The Struggle Movement called for various political reforms, including the removal of Thieu and Ky, as well as new elections. They took over Danang, Vietnam's second-largest city, and burned down the two-story French colonial U.S. consulate in Hue. The Danang chief of police was told that unless he surrendered, his wife and children would be kidnapped, his house would be burned down, and he would be assassinated by six o'clock that evening. "The U.S. forces had a big net to catch whales, but neither the Americans nor the government of South Vietnam had the fine-meshed net which was necessary to catch the small but deadly fish of terrorism," Lodge recalled.[108] He advised Ky to eliminate the violence and then turn the situation into an opportunity.[109] Ky promised elections in 1967, at which time experts who had been working on a new constitution would put it to the people by national referendum. In response to pressure from Tri Quang, Ky modified his plans so elections could be held earlier, in September 1966, in order to choose delegates to the constitutional convention that would draft the document. It seemed as though this satisfied Tri Quang, for he made a rare public speech appealing for an end to the demonstrations. However, it resulted in only the briefest of breaks between protests.[110]

The increase in civil disturbances meant that the South Vietnamese government functioned less and less in Hue and Danang. It became clear that the United States was unable or unwilling to match the political, diplomatic, and military will to win of North Vietnam, which many Americans suspected was really behind Tri Quang's Buddhist front. By mid-May 1966, Ky had two options. Either he could let things take their course and watch Tri Quang become even more powerful, or he could take decisive action against the demonstrations. Lodge knew the tension was building and had even met with Tri Quang to hear his grievances firsthand. He told Lodge that he wanted to overthrow Ky. "But just suppose you do overthrow Marshal Ky. Who would you choose to replace him as prime minister?" Lodge asked. Tri Quang thought for a moment before answering. "We will be willing to put Marshal Ky back," he responded.[111]

On May 15, two battalions of South Vietnamese troops—1,500 men—were airlifted to Danang, where they secured the air base and fanned out to clear the city of dissident soldiers.[112] Tri Quang claimed hundreds were killed, but the actual fighting was sporadic. With Lodge's blessing, Ky threw the former mayor of Danang, Nguyen Van Man, in prison. Ky had ended the violence and dispersed the protesters, many of whom came streaming out of Tinh Hoi Pagoda and surrendered voluntarily. Lodge was in Washington at the State Department when he got the news that order had been restored in Danang. On Lodge's return to Vietnam on May 21, Hue was the only remaining dissident stronghold. Ky then moved riot police from Saigon into Hue and the city was brought back under control of the government. A minimum of force had to be used, and no casualties were reported. Ky avoided Ngo Dinh Diem's mistake of eliminating the Buddhist protests with brute force and mass arrests. At the end of the crisis, "Ambassador Lodge aptly likened Vietnam to a man critically ill, yet so irascible that he throws pitchers of water at his doctor," Westmoreland wrote. "That at least shows, Lodge continued, that he is getting better."[113]

Lodge felt Ky handled the crisis extremely well, considering all that could have gone wrong. However, 228 Americans in I Corps had died fighting for South Vietnam during the three weeks of protests.[114] Some thought the United States should have been more involved, but it was an impossible situation. If the United States sided with the Buddhists, then it would have been accused of interfering in a domestic political issue. If it ignored the Buddhists, then the Saigon government must be a puppet government. "It is ironic that many Vietnamese are saying the U.S. should 'fix things up' without ever saying how, it being absolutely certain that if we tried to impose anything there would be first an 'anticolonialist' howl from those with whom we differed and ultimately a howl from everybody," Lodge reported to Johnson. But he also saw how government control of the northern part of South Vietnam was slipping away. "I do not, therefore, think that what is happening now will mean the end of the world, or anything like it, but I wish to heaven that it wasn't happening."[115]

In 1966, Kissinger paid Lodge two more visits as his consultant. He wrote to Lodge that he could "imagine no more vital assignment in today's world," observing, "If we fail there, I foresee decades of mounting crisis. If we succeed, it will mark a historic turning point in the postwar era. Just as the Cuba-Berlin confrontation may have convinced the Soviets of the futility of seeking political breakdowns by military means, so Vietnam can put an end to Chinese expansionism by the use of threat of force." Kissinger privately doubted the chances for victory. He came away even more pessimistic than he had the year before and encouraged American policymakers to seek a negotiated end. "I'm going to give it one more try," Johnson said to Kissinger, referring to negotiations with North Vietnam. "And if it doesn't work, I'm going to come up to Cambridge and cut your balls off."[116]

In 1965 and 1966, Lodge hosted Richard Nixon on two additional visits to Saigon. Lodge played a key role in helping Nixon to better understand American involvement in Vietnam, arranging meetings with political and military leaders, and they had time to discuss American politics, too. The first of these visits occurred on September 2–5, 1965. Nixon was a guest of the Lodges and stayed at the U.S. embassy. Pat Hillings, a friend and California political ally who once occupied Nixon's former seat in the House of Representatives, accompanied him. Hillings recalled, "Each morning we got up before dawn and clambered aboard a helicopter and were flown to the various battle zones."[117] Lodge told Nixon that conditions in Vietnam were better than they had been the year before. Nixon was briefed on the encouraging signs that a negotiated end to the war might be possible, but negotiations posed risks. "If a U.S. settlement interpreted as defeat—greatest effect on 1) Japan, 2) Thailand, 3) Philippines, 4) Malaysia," he wrote in his notes. About Japan, he added, "Growing neutralist sentiment will be drawn into Chinese orbit."[118]

Nixon also spent an evening with the Lansdale group, as he and Lansdale were old friends. "There were about a dozen of us at the house in Saigon," Daniel Ellsberg recalled later. "Lansdale introduced us all to Nixon . . . He seemed intelligent. When we were about to sit down, he said, 'Ed, what are you up to?' Lansdale said, 'We are trying to help make the coming elections the most honest they have ever had in Vietnam.' We then sat down, and Nixon, who was sitting next to Lansdale, said, 'Well, yes. Honest, yes, as long as you win!'"[119] Nixon's notes described Lansdale as "thoughtful," "quiet," and "deliberate in speech." He emphasized to Nixon that the Vietnamese were a people, but not a nation.[120]

Nixon paid another visit to Vietnam on August 5–7, 1966.[121] Nixon arrived in Vietnam just as Lodge and the embassy were preparing for the South Vietnamese Constitutional Assembly elections that would determine the 117 members who would write the new constitution.[122] The September 1966 elections saw an 80 percent turnout rate despite the constant threat of Viet Cong violence against those who chose to vote. It was a substantial milestone considering the "kaleidoscopic" turnover in political power in Saigon. In a report to Johnson, Lodge wrote, "The Viet Cong did its utmost, using hand grenades, ambushes, strikes, broadcasts, printed matter, and every known form of intimidation. Terrorism reached a high tide. And it didn't work . . . For the Vietnamese people to have voted in such large numbers, in the face of terrorism, shows their willingness to defy the Viet Cong in order to take a step which they believe is a step forward for their country. I have asked many Vietnamese in different walks of life why the Vietnamese want to move towards a democratic constitution, and the following answers always emerge: a) A constitutional democracy is a protection against despotism, to which they have been subjected in the past. b) For a Vietnamese to move towards a constitutional democracy is a step towards progress and a step away from coups. They have looked around them and have seen Korea and Japan and believe this is the way to go."[123]

The elections were sufficiently positive for Lodge to recommend to Johnson that another conference be held on the war. Lodge envisioned that it would include not only those who participated in the Honolulu Conference but also representatives of allied governments in the region. The Manila Conference took place in October 1966, and Lodge worked for two months to prepare Thieu and Ky for it. The Americans were particularly concerned that Ky might repeat his demand for an invasion of North Vietnam, which Johnson feared could be an unnecessary provocation of China and the Soviet Union and result in a third world war. In the end, the Manila Conference reaffirmed the American commitment to South Vietnam and pledged an American withdrawal six months after North Vietnam ended intervention. It also pledged a commitment to postwar economic development for all of Southeast Asia, which was supported by the regional allied governments.[124]

Lodge encouraged Johnson to pay a visit to American soldiers in Vietnam after the conference to boost morale. He argued that the security situation at some American military installations in Vietnam was just as strong as in Manila itself. The White House demurred on the decision until the last minute, but finally agreed to visit American forces at Cam Ranh Bay. Westmoreland and Lodge departed first in order to coordinate the details. When Air Force One arrived, Lodge stood at the foot of the ramp to present Thieu and Ky to Johnson. The president awarded decorations to the troops, visited the hospital, and talked with the generals. He was surprisingly informal in his remarks, encouraging the senior officers to "go out there and nail that coonskin to the wall."[125] Lodge praised Johnson for the way he handled the visit. "Your speech to the troops was unique in my experience in the way in which it struck home to your listeners. There is no doubt that your assessment of their importance will lighten the weight of their hardships and inspire them in the hour of danger," Lodge wrote.[126] Johnson thanked Lodge for his work, writing, "I want you to know how much I appreciate your help at the Conference—I shall always cherish the memory. Your good judgment was again confirmed at the Cam Ranh affair yesterday."[127]

Following the Manila Conference, some among the more hawkish urged a million-man military force to move in and crush the communists. The United States had three options: a humiliating withdrawal, a hold on current levels, or an escalation of U.S. military forces. The final option was the only one acceptable to the Johnson White House. At a minimum, forecasters were saying that between 75,000 and 175,000 additional troops would be deployed, with the chance for another 100,000 in early 1967. Another 235,000 could also be pulled from reserve and National Guard forces, in addition to an increased monthly draft.[128] Lodge did not think victory could be achieved through one massive assault. He was more and more opposed to the attrition strategy being followed, endorsed by Westmoreland, which resulted in Lodge's "long and gloomy" cable on November 11, 1966. He reported that the Viet Cong had stepped up the fighting in the central provinces and the Central Highlands. They continued to recruit new units from within South Vietnam, and the equivalent of two or more divisions had been infiltrated from North Vietnam.[129] With superior numbers on the North Vietnamese side, Lodge did not think the United States could ever win by adhering to search and destroy.[130] "I believe that the Vietnamese war will certainly never be won in this way," he wrote to Johnson.[131] At one point, he was so upset that he contemplated resigning and making a public statement of opposition.[132] He told Thieu that South Vietnam would need to absorb the National Liberation Front. "We are a sick man," Thieu responded. "Please don't give us another spoon of microbes. It will kill us. We must get better first."[133]

In Lodge's view, the end of the Vietnam War would be more like Korea, when the enemy had decided it was tired of fighting and would rather negotiate. Lodge continued to believe that whatever mistakes had been in made in Vietnam, the United States was committed to seeing it through in order to prevent Asia from being engulfed in communism. During the summer of 1966, before the elections, he had been authorized to conduct his own secret negotiations. Those "Marigold" negotiations might have been the best chance to reach a peace agreement with North Vietnam. Lodge said later that the talks "so nearly started steps towards a diplomatic settlement some seven years before the 1973 accord was reached."[134] On June 6, Polish diplomat Janusz

Lewandowski reported to Lodge that there was a definite desire in Hanoi for talks. The recent bombings in North Vietnam had badly damaged them. Lodge reported to the White House that it was the best chance for talks that he had ever seen. According to Lewandowski, the Americans had "extended their elasticity further than at any point in the past and perhaps as far as they could do so."[135] Lodge held months of clandestine meetings with Lewandowski, chief of the Polish delegation to the International Commission for Supervision and Control in Vietnam. Lewandowski, in turn, met with the North Vietnamese, with Giovanni d'Orlandi, Italian ambassador to Vietnam, as intermediary.[136] When North Vietnam had a message, they sent it to Lewandowski, who passed it to d'Orlandi, who passed it to Lodge.[137] When Lodge needed to meet with d'Orlandi, he crouched down in the back seat of the car on the drive to d'Orlandi's office or apartment in Saigon.[138] Everyone was happy with the terms of the Marigold talks, even newly appointed Soviet leader Leonid Brezhnev.[139] The talks continued for several months before d'Orlandi warned Lodge that Hanoi was being tightly controlled by China.[140] On December 14, 1966, the North Vietnamese informed Marigold's Polish contacts that the negotiations would be terminated. "We began to have serious hopes that the Marigold exchanges might lead to private meetings with the North Vietnamese, but this prospect soon evaporated," Johnson wrote in his memoirs.[141] There has been no definitive explanation for the sudden change of heart, although some North Vietnamese did not like the American air attacks on heavily populated areas.[142]

Lodge reflected later that Johnson had made two key mistakes that never permitted the Marigold talks the opportunity to produce peace. In December, Johnson moved the location of the Marigold talks from Saigon—where the principals were, including Lodge, d'Orlandi, and Lewandowski—to Warsaw. And later, in March 1968, Johnson decided to move away from private talks in favor of the highly public talks in Paris that began in May.[143] "I realized this channel was a dry creek when the North Vietnamese failed to show up for the critical meeting the Poles had promised to arrange in Warsaw on December 6, 1966," Johnson wrote.[144]

A third presidential conference between American and South Vietnamese leaders took place in Guam in March 1967. After each conference—Honolulu, Manila, and Guam—renewed emphasis on pacification became an even higher priority and could be seen in the declarations and communiqués issued. Lodge continued to argue that the correct American political strategy was based on the necessity of controlling the villages.[145] Only later did it emerge that Lodge had become more disenchanted in Vietnam than he let on. The roller-coaster ride of failed peace attempts had transformed him from someone who believed strongly in the need for a negotiated settlement into someone who was skeptical that peace was possible. "We were forced repeatedly to the conclusion that the hatreds and passions were so deep and the issues so complicated that a negotiated settlement seemed out of the question," he wrote in early 1973.[146]

Lodge indicated to Johnson his desire to retire. "What are you going to do when you leave? Do you want to go back home and sit around with your grandchildren?" Johnson asked. After Lodge responded that he wanted to do something useful, Johnson suggested that he should take a vacation and then come back as ambassador at large and work on projects such as American public opinion regarding Vietnam and take over more of Averell Harriman's portfolio having to do with peace and negotiations.[147] Lodge agreed. He was now nearly sixty-five, past the retirement age of most men of his generation. "As I finish three and a half years of complete involvement in United States policy towards Vietnam, both as Ambassador and as Consultant, I wish to thank you for your unfailing support and for the honor conferred on me by your trust," he wrote to Johnson in his letter of resignation dated February 19, 1967.[148]

Lodge was tired of things he was unable to change and grew eager to escape Vietnam a second time before the situation deteriorated.[149] "It was obviously impossible for someone who was in Saigon to find out exactly who was to blame in Washington. The Viet Nam problem did not fit our bureaucratic system. It did not belong under the State Department. It did not belong under the Defense Department," he wrote in his journal.[150] After two tours in Vietnam, in addition to numerous other visits as Johnson's consultant on Vietnam, Lodge had served longer in Vietnam than any American diplomat and had worked on the subject of Vietnam in more capacities than anyone else. The call of home was getting stronger. His sons, George and Harry, lived next door to him in Beverly. "He'd rather be out in the bay there, in a rowboat, with the youngest grandchild wetting all over the seat or falling all over his legs," his youngest son, Harry, recalled. "I've never seen anybody who can read on as imperturbably as he does with half a dozen yelling kids roller-skating through his hall. There are at least 16 of us when we all get together for supper in the yard, and his laugh is so loud that Ralph Mitchell [the gardener] tells me he can hear it all the way down at his house by the highway."[151]

Before leaving Vietnam, Lodge played host to Nixon one more time. Accompanied by just one staff member, Raymond Price, former chief editorial writer for the *New York Herald Tribune*, Nixon was on a three-week listening tour from April 2 to 23, 1967, starting in Los Angeles, working its way across Asia, and ending in London before returning to the United States. The Lodges invited Nixon to stay at their house as their guest during the Saigon portion of the trip, from April 14 to 17, the longest single stop on the whole Asian trip.[152] The visit included briefings by Lodge and Westmoreland and a meeting with Ky.[153] No doubt they talked about politics, as they had during Nixon's previous visits, but no record of their conversations has surfaced. The "visit was highly useful, Nixon stated, and will provide him with valuable background for public statements he will be making in coming months," Lodge reported.[154]

Johnson had accepted Lodge's resignation on April 12 and appointed Ellsworth Bunker as his replacement.[155] Eugene Locke was appointed as deputy, with Robert Komer as head of pacification activities. Bunker, a Democrat who had been serving as Johnson's ambassador at large, effectively traded jobs with Lodge.[156] As ambassador at large, Lodge had few formal duties other than to advise Johnson on U.S. policy toward Southeast Asia. His value to Johnson was the fact that he had an almost unique bipartisan stature in foreign policy. Johnson also wanted Lodge to be Eisenhower's briefer.[157] As journalist Robert Kintner wrote to Johnson, "Reaction to his statements can have a real effect on informed public opinion and on rank and file public reaction, because he has been on the scene so long; he is prone to make definite statements and he has a camaraderie with Congressmen that may tend to make him speak quite freely to them . . . In addition, as you know, Lodge knows quite a few of the top columnists and newspapermen here."[158] Lodge was appointed as an observer of the South Vietnamese elections on September 3, 1967.[159] The elections were particularly important in order for the new government to have a strong mandate.[160] "Former Ambassador Henry Cabot Lodge accompanied the delegation members at my request to help them in every way possible and to insure that they could travel where they wanted and see what they wanted to see," Johnson wrote in his memoirs.[161] It must have been an emotional experience for Lodge to return to the place that had played such a critical role in his own life.[162]

On November 2, 1967, Johnson convened a gathering of his "Wise Men," a foreign policy kitchen cabinet of sorts to advise him on Vietnam.[163] While the origin of the group is not exactly clear, Lodge had suggested the need to form a "bipartisan citizens' committee in support of your Viet Nam Policy."[164] "I have a peculiar confidence in you as patriots and that is why I have picked you," Johnson told the group. Clark Clifford liked to use another name for it: the "Cold War Knighthood."[165] Johnson preferred the less grandiose "group of outside advisors."[166] Many of the members were Republicans who had supported Johnson over Barry Goldwater in 1964. Johnson consulted them from time to time, especially on the subject of Vietnam. However, the Wise Men as a formal group were short-lived. Some, including Paul Hoffman, George Kistiakowsky, and Arthur Larson, had already fallen out of favor due to vocal disagreement over Vietnam.[167] Such divisions had also become more common among Johnson's staff and Cabinet. When the Wise Men convened for their three-and-a-half-hour session in November, Johnson did not tell them that Secretary of Defense Robert McNamara was the latest to have abandoned the administration's Vietnam policy.[168] Lodge remained loyal to Johnson. However, the coming breakup of the Wise Men, and Lodge's service as ambassador at large, would present him with another public service opportunity in another Cold War hotspot.

# 16 • West Germany and 1968

As the New Hampshire primary approached, Lyndon B. Johnson began to think more and more about his political viability. The Tet Offensive, which began on January 30, 1968, played a role in his thinking, but there were also other important factors. While arguably a military defeat for the Viet Cong, it proved to be a tremendous public relations victory that cast serious doubt on the government's optimistic projections of war progress. "American public opinion cannot stand a *long drawn out war* with *high* casualties," Henry Cabot Lodge Jr. wrote Johnson in February 1968. Unlike World War II, this war could not be won "by killing the enemy by *military means on the ground* in South Vietnam."[1] From the army's point of view, it succeeded at everything it set out to do in terms of logistics and tactics. Over time, it became popular to refer to the fact that the United States had won every battle, yet it lost the war. On the battlefield, the Viet Cong and North Vietnamese army faced terrible losses, but in the end, North Vietnam—not the United States—emerged victorious.[2]

Johnson sent Lodge to Europe on March 10 to brief American officials and NATO allies on America's Vietnam policy following the Tet Offensive. His itinerary included Paris, Bonn, London, Rome, and Belgium. "His long experience in dealing with the Vietnam problem on a high level both in Saigon and in Washington lent special credibility to what he said," the American embassy in Bonn reported.[3] On March 18, Lodge met in Brussels with the three American ambassadors to the European Economic Community, NATO, and Belgium and their deputy chiefs of mission. "His comments on the Tet Offensive and aftermath, and on the ability of the Viet Cong to refill its ranks, were totally candid and indeed gave little comfort to those of us who hoped for significant progress toward bringing the war to a successful conclusion in the near term," the American embassy in Brussels cabled afterward. "At the same time Ambassador Lodge was most convincing in putting the Vietnam issue in perspective of the future of Southeast Asia with its hundreds of millions of people."[4]

Following Lodge's return from Europe, Johnson convened his Wise Men on March 25 in the White House Cabinet Room and again the following day in the Mansion.[5] The membership of the group was almost identical to that when it was last convened in November 1967. At that time, only George Ball was in strong opposition to the war. Now, however, many of even the most loyal and hawkish had turned on the war.[6] "A great many people—even very determined and loyal people—have begun to think that Vietnam really is a bottomless pit," McGeorge Bundy said.[7] Lodge had switched his support to a defensive strategy geared toward protecting the South Vietnamese population.[8]

When General Earle Wheeler remarked that it was "the worst time to negotiate" a way out of the Vietnam War, Lodge turned to Dean Acheson and whispered, "Yes, because we are in worse shape militarily than we have ever been."[9] One of the key problems seemed to have been the lack of a unified command in Vietnam. It had always been a challenge to coordinate the various military and civilian components of the U.S. mission, and it got worse after the arrival of American combat forces in 1965.[10] After each of the Wise Men spoke, Johnson concluded, "Then all of you, except Wheeler, Taylor, [Omar] Bradley, [Robert] Murphy, want to disengage." Lodge wanted to make sure his position was not misunderstood. "No, I don't want to disengage. I want to use our power differently than we have," he clarified.[11] Averell Harriman and Lodge agreed that Johnson had used a poor word choice. "I commented to Lodge that 'disengagement' is not the right word," Harriman said. "Many of us want to start negotiations for a peaceful settlement." Johnson claimed he was not well informed. "You have been hearing things that I haven't," he said.[12]

In a national televised address on March 31, 1968, Johnson announced he would not run for reelection. It was a shock to the nation. Some referred to it as Johnson's "abdication speech." He did not intend for it to be interpreted that way, but it did to some degree mark an abdication in Vietnam, as it signaled the beginning of the end in terms of the deep American involvement in Indochina.[13] Johnson reflected that the problems in Vietnam had escalated after the overthrow of Ngo Dinh Diem. "We found it difficult to put Humpty Dumpty together again. With all Diem's weaknesses, it was not easy to tear that government apart, and put it together again," Johnson said. Some called Johnson a lame duck. However, he believed he would avoid the term simply because of how much he still planned to accomplish that year—engaging in Vietnam peace talks, obtaining release of the Pueblo crew, entering into talks with the Soviets about nuclear weapons, securing peace in the Middle East, and facilitating NASA's planned trip to the moon. Still, he was pressed by many, including congressional leaders, to discuss the political implications of his speech. Johnson said he was tired of "bugging anyone for anything," stating, "I've listened to all the people both for and against our foreign policy and have considered their suggestions carefully . . . Last week we called fifteen men together including Matthew Ridgway, General Bradley, Maxwell Taylor, Arthur Dean, and Henry Cabot Lodge to hear their views, and as a result I made this speech proposal Sunday night."[14]

Johnson's announcement created a wide-open race to the White House. Vietnam would be a major subject of the campaign. Harvard University formed the Study Group on Presidential Transition, 1968–1969. Henry Kissinger was one of the faculty members in charge, along with Phillip E. Areeda, Frank Lindsay, and Ernest May. Among the speakers invited was Lodge, who argued that letting the Viet Cong into the Saigon government would be like "putting the fox into the chicken coup." That is where the Nixon policy with respect to Vietnam differed from what Vice President Hubert Humphrey proposed to do.[15] However, each did say the war should come to an end, which diminished Vietnam as a major issue in the campaign.

Johnson officially disbanded the Wise Men after his announcement. With the administration moving toward a negotiated settlement, they were no longer needed. Lodge, nearly sixty-six, was again called to serve in a Cold War hotspot. On April 19, Johnson appointed him as ambassador to one of the premier European posts in Bonn to relieve George McGhee, who had served for five years. "This new office will prove yet one more illustrious milestone in a record of public service already as impressive as that of any man I know," Ed Brooke wrote in congratulations.[16] Lodge had his farewell meeting in the Oval Office with Johnson on May 17 before heading to Europe.[17]

The Germans, who had been delighted by Lodge during his recent trip following the Tet Offensive, considered the appointment to be high profile. *Die Welt* referred to Lodge as "a well-preserved former Olympiad winner."[18] Chancellor Kurt Georg Kiesinger and Foreign Minister Willy Brandt thought of Lodge as being in the same category as Harriman or John J. McCloy. In Lodge's presentation of credentials, he used part of his official letter to thank Germany: "In Saigon evidence abounded of the willingness and ability of the Federal Government to bring humanitarian assistance to persons far from Germany's shores." Lodge recalled his friends at the German embassy in Saigon, "with whom [he] had such friendly relations."[19] With the Soviet Union presumably behind the latest East German moves to cut off access to Berlin, including proposing a requirement to force West Germans to carry passports and apply for visas, Lodge was the kind of American ambassador needed to stand up to them, just as he had faced them down for years at the UN.[20]

In May, Harriman and Cyrus Vance arrived in Paris to head the delegation to the peace talks to end the Vietnam War. They set up camp at the Hotel Majestic, which had been the site of the former Nazi headquarters during World War II and where negotiations had taken place at the end of World War I. Johnson had originally selected Llewellyn Thompson, the American ambassador in Moscow, to accompany Harriman to Paris, indicating how much Johnson wanted a team that was close to the Soviets to lead the talks and send discouraging signals to South Vietnam. However, since Johnson hoped to make progress on various arms control proposals with the Soviet Union by the end of the year, he decided to keep Thompson in Moscow and instead chose Vance.[21] Harriman and Vance were supported by a team that represented different constituencies in the U.S. government, as well as a handful of junior Foreign Service officers.[22] A number of the delegation staffers had worked for Lodge in Saigon, including Phil Habib, John Negroponte, David Engel, and Richard Holbrooke.

Lodge met with Kiesinger on June 21. The conversation was a warm-up for Dean Rusk's arrival a few days later, when he was supposed to see Kiesinger and Brandt.[23] Lodge emphasized the closeness of German-American relations, and they discussed the seriousness of tensions in Germany and the region. Berlin was again being threatened by the Soviets, which brought back memories of the 1948 blockade, and Czechoslovakia was being destabilized. It was not clear whether these tremors originated from East German leader Walter Ulbricht or directly from Moscow. "If this step were not met firmly it would be followed by a more serious communist escalation," Kiesinger told Lodge. The German people wanted to be reassured that the Americans were tough, and Kiesinger suggested that perhaps the United States should engage more energetically with the Soviet Union.[24] He also suggested that Rusk's visit to Germany would be a very good sign, and that the German and American governments remain in close consultation.[25]

The Germans, who considered the Soviets to be behind many of the region's problems, saw their fears vindicated in August. At about midnight on August 20, some fifteen or sixteen divisions of Warsaw Pact forces rumbled over the Czechoslovakian border. They arrived in Prague virtually unopposed and arrested Alexander Dubcek, the national leader, who had become too independent for Moscow's liking, as well as his liberal allies in the National Assembly. The Soviets reported that they were in Prague "on invitation."[26] Lodge met with Kiesinger on August 21 to assess the situation. He had spoken to Rusk in Washington as well as to Soviet Ambassador Anatoly Dobrynin, and one of the major questions was whether the Soviets planned to continue beyond Czechoslovakia to Romania to bring Nicolae Ceausescu back into line, or whether the invasion was simply a Russian flexing of muscles through power politics.

Lodge and Kiesinger did not meet again until September 17, but by then the initial shock of the invasion had passed, although the situation remained unresolved. Both expressed disappointment at NATO's lack of a firm response to the Soviet invasion of Czechoslovakia. They still did not understand what motivated the Soviet Union. Lodge, borrowing a phrase from Winston Churchill, said their intentions were like "a riddle wrapped inside a mystery inside an enigma."[27] Kiesinger suggested that perhaps a NATO summit would help boost the morale of the allies. "The Germans are nervous," Walt Rostow, special assistant for National Security Affairs, wrote to Johnson.[28] Lodge lobbied in support of the idea of a summit, but it was turned down by the White House, which instead sent a flurry of high-profile visitors and messages of support to calm tensions in Germany.[29] Lodge pressed Washington for action. "The voice of the United States had not been heard in connection with the invasion of Czechoslovakia nor had it been heard for a long time before that," he said. "The leader of an alliance could not remain so silent."[30] It was not just Berlin or Czechoslovakia; Germany was also having severe monetary problems due to massive capital inflows despite low interest rates.[31]

Throughout September, groups of senior State Department staffers met separately with West German party leaders and other influential figures, including Kurt Birrenbach, a senior Christian Democratic Union leader and Kiesinger's newly appointed representative to the United States, and Helmut Schmidt. Lodge sat in on only some of the conversations with visiting Americans. On October 11, Secretary of Defense Clark Clifford and Lodge met with Kiesinger.[32] The chancellor reminded Clifford that the reason the Germans were so concerned about recent Soviet actions, in regard to both Berlin and Czechoslovakia, was that "Germany's best protection are the U.S. troops on Germany's own soil." Kiesinger delicately stated that the United States was not doing enough, either with the troops or through NATO. There was little from a military standpoint that Germany could do, but the Germans could advance bilateral conversations with neighbors in the Eastern bloc that did not want to become the next target of invasion.[33] Brandt began to engage the Soviet Union directly in order to reduce tensions.[34]

There was a hint of movement at the peace talks on October 10.[35] Johnson hoped to trade an unconditional bombing halt against North Vietnam in exchange for South Vietnam's admission to the talks. After months of stalling, North Vietnam agreed. But South Vietnam had already decided that Richard Nixon was going to win the presidential election in November, so there was no point in negotiating with the Johnson White House. The Harriman-led talks from May through the end of the year produced little other than a willingness on both sides to keep talking.[36] The talks established Paris as a site, the delegations involved, and the pattern of both plenary and private meetings, but beyond that they were hardly substantive. Any flexibility that North Vietnam showed was only procedural. Johnson ordered a bombing halt on October 31, partially in response to McGeorge Bundy's and Clifford's urging. In Saigon, the announcement of the bombing halt shattered South Vietnamese confidence in the United States. President Nguyen Van Thieu announced that his country would not attend the Paris peace talks until North Vietnam agreed to negotiate without the participation of the National Liberation Front, the Viet Cong, which Saigon refused to recognize as a separate entity from the North. Washington believed that Thieu had expressed assurances no fewer than four times that the South was in favor of the bombing halt and the Paris negotiations, but Thieu clarified that even while he did express support, he never said his objections had been removed.[37] Johnson spent the final months of his administration and the remainder of his diplomatic capital in an effort to bring the South Vietnamese government into the negotiations, only to find the American ally did not actually want to participate.[38]

Vice President Humphrey lost to former Vice President Nixon in one of the closest popular votes in U.S. history, less so according to the Electoral College result. Vietnam contributed to his defeat, as did the fact that Johnson did little to help him—and, in fact, seemed to enjoy ridiculing him.[39] However, domestic issues such as "law and order" were at least as important in the result, especially as Humphrey and Nixon were in agreement that the Vietnam War should be ended. Humphrey's political advisers pressured him to move beyond the limited Vietnam policy of the Johnson era into a more active advocacy of rapid withdrawal, which is what the left wing of the Democratic Party demanded and was closer to Humphrey's own personal beliefs. The shift came at an inevitable political cost, and a split with Johnson.[40] While rumors circulated that Nixon had encouraged South Vietnam to stay away from the Paris peace talks and claimed that it would get a better deal under a Nixon presidency, there is no evidence that Nixon directly interfered or that there was a chance for real peace.

Lodge saw how far apart the different sides were at Paris. Thieu was rigid, obdurate, and repressive, a kind of Diem without the knowledge of Vietnamese and European history, philosophy, and political theory that Diem had.[41] Thieu had no special love for Nixon. The idea that Thieu was going to bend easily to Johnson's will in 1968 or Nixon's four years later was fantasy. "It flies in the face of the facts to suggest that we could have achieved any kind of substantial or durable peace four years ago," Lodge wrote in early 1973. Lodge desperately worked for a negotiated settlement. "And we were forced repeatedly to the conclusion that the hatreds and passions were so deep and the issues so complicated that a negotiated settlement seemed out of the question," he said.[42] Thieu made his decision based on what was in the interest of his nation.

In Bonn, Lodge and Kiesinger met on November 12, 1968, to discuss American politics and German-American relations during a Nixon presidency. They also talked about the political situation in Spain, the ongoing monetary crisis related to the dollar and gold, and security in Berlin. Kiesinger said he was looking forward to the presidency of Nixon, who was someone who thought clearly, worked hard, and did a lot of reading.[43] However, Lodge came away from his experience in Bonn somewhat disenchanted. "The Chancellor has a hard time thinking his way through his relationship with France on the one hand and with the United States on the other," Lodge commented to David Bruce. "This adds up to a somewhat defeatist state of mind in Germany," Lodge added. "Bruce said that unquestionably my assessment was correct."[44]

In Washington, the transition from Johnson to Nixon had already begun. Secretary of State Rusk asked Nixon to designate someone in whom he had "absolute confidence" to occupy an office next to his at the State Department to run the transition between the two administrations and serve as a liaison to each. Nixon said he was not ready to appoint his secretary of state yet, so whoever he appointed would serve on a temporary basis. Nixon considered appointing Lodge as the head of the White House transition, but the available records suggest that there was no way to recall him from Bonn without upsetting the Germans, who were an important American ally. On the morning of November 14, three days after Nixon's visit to the White House, he called Johnson from New York. They decided that it would be better for Lodge to remain in Bonn. Robert D. Murphy, the veteran diplomat and former undersecretary, would serve as foreign policy liaison between the outgoing White House and the incoming administration.[45]

Lodge met with Nixon on November 9 in Key Biscayne to provide input on a range of possible appointees to the new administration.[46] Nixon told Lodge that he envisioned a kind of "special assignments" role for him, presumably in connection with Vietnam.[47] However, Lodge was focused on the role that Kissinger might play.[48] Lodge envisioned Kissinger in a new position of a Cabinet-level Vietnam coordinator in the White House, a czar for Vietnam issues.[49] Kissinger did not figure prominently in Nixon's thinking before Lodge made the recommendation. Richard Allen was the campaign's lone spokesperson for foreign policy, and while he would go on to join the White House staff, he left by the end of 1969. Lodge and Kissinger had grown close since 1965. "You started the sequence that led to this appointment by inviting me to Saigon. I shall not forget this," Kissinger said to Lodge.[50] They liked each other personally, and they benefited each other professionally. Kissinger acted as Lodge's eyes and ears in Washington, privately reporting on the very candid conversations he heard from figures such as Rostow, William Bundy, and McGeorge Bundy. He also regularly saw George Cabot Lodge, who, in turn, passed along additional information to his father. In return, Lodge continued to elevate Kissinger's status through his trips to Vietnam and the entrée he was given to the country and its political leaders.[51] He liked Kissinger's energy, his cogent ideas, and his ability to work with different constituencies.[52]

Kissinger had his first meeting with Nixon on November 25, 1968. John Mitchell arranged the meeting, and Nixon wrote later that it was in response to Lodge's suggestion. Vietnam was a major topic of discussion. Kissinger argued that Nixon should threaten a veto of any peace agreement that compromised South Vietnam's independence; otherwise the United States would be abandoning its ally. Nixon agreed, believing that Harriman had gone too far to betray Saigon. Nixon offered Kissinger the job of assistant to the president for national security affairs, or national security advisor for short, and the latter obviously did not need to take long to think it over. He accepted on November 27, and Nixon made the news public in an announcement on December 2.[53]

Despite the hesitation about pulling Lodge out of Bonn, Nixon announced on January 5 that Lodge would replace Harriman as the head of the U.S. delegation to the Paris peace talks.[54] The *Washington Post* immediately criticized the choice, referring to Lodge as "a man with a load of ideological baggage" and preferring the promotion of Vance instead.[55] "Mrs. Harriman and I have known him and Mrs. Lodge for many years," Harriman said when asked about the choice of Lodge. "Mr. Lodge is a man in whom Mr. Nixon has great confidence. Mr. Lodge has had long experience in Viet-Nam and in international negotiations as Ambassador to the United Nations."[56]

Lodge quickly put together a statement for the press in Bonn, but it was released by Nixon's headquarters in New York. "My thanks go first to President-Elect Nixon for this mark of confidence," he said. "The meetings underway in Paris offer a hopeful forum for the definition of the interests of all parties involved and for the design of agreements to meet those interests." Lodge thanked Harriman for his efforts to "open the way" and Vance for agreeing to remain in position during the transition. "I am sad at leaving Germany where I have received such a warm and hospitable welcome and I thank President Johnson for having appointed me. It has been a unique experience to live and travel among a people which, in the years since the war, has demonstrated much organizing ability, technical competence, dynamism, vitality and devotion to democracy."[57] Saigon cheered the news of the appointment.[58]

The final meeting in Paris led by Harriman and Vance took place on January 14, 1969, the same day that Lodge left Germany. Harriman was bitterly disappointed by the experience and lashed out at others. Rusk, he said, "had done more damage to America than anyone in our time." Taylor was "a fool." Bunker "regards the preservation in power of . . . Thieu and Ky as the central object of American policy."[59] However, there is no record that Lodge criticized anyone from the Johnson administration. Even while Johnson had criticized him at times, Lodge defended Johnson. "During the whole period from the end of 1963 to 1968 that I worked for President Johnson, I never had the slightest difficulty in getting his attention and therefore had no reason to 'complain' . . . [Johnson] was always courteous and considerate of me. Far from being inaccessible, he gave of himself unstintingly," Lodge told the *New York Times* in 1972.[60]

Johnson was committed to achieving some type of peace agreement in Vietnam before he left the White House, or at least making measurable progress in that direction. Johnson's pattern of activity around the time of the October 31 bombing halt seems to have been motivated much more by self-interest—that is, desire for a legacy as a peacemaker—than by a desire to affect the outcome of the presidential election. Johnson continued these efforts in his final two months with only limited success. Once Harriman and Vance left Paris, Foreign Service officers John Negroponte and David Engel, who also served as translators, were in charge of the American delegation until Lodge arrived.[61]

Before departing Germany, Lodge received a tip from Pyotr Abrasimov, the Russian ambassador to East Germany. The Soviet diplomat said that the USSR was eager for a settlement in Vietnam in order to stabilize the situation in Southeast Asia. They even discussed a possible Russian role in a police force to be created to enforce the eventual peace treaty following formal American military withdrawal.[62] Lodge hoped that this information might help him in his new role in Paris, but based on his experience dueling with the Soviets at the UN, he had no illusions about Soviet offers of assistance to the United States.

Johnson left the White House on January 20, 1969. Much of his legacy— in terms of both domestic and foreign policy—was in the hands of his succes- sor. Johnson left behind a half million men in Vietnam, in addition to thousands more spread across Southeast Asia who were working in support roles for the air and naval units.[63] Before he left the White House, Johnson sent one final thank-you letter to Lodge. "No words could ever thank you prop- erly for all you have given to your country," he wrote. "You have devoted your life to public service, and in so doing, you have given us the inestimable ben- efit of your extraordinary wisdom and skill."[64]

# PART VI
## THE NIXON AND FORD YEARS

## 17 • The Paris Peace Talks

Henry Cabot Lodge Jr. began his duties in Paris on January 18, 1969. Richard Nixon's appointment of Lodge was a statement of policy, given the latter's long-standing ties to Vietnam. Critics charged that the change in administration frustrated the peace process, but Nixon moved quickly to get his Paris team in place.[1] Lodge's expectations for an immediate breakthrough were low. Averell Harriman explained to Lodge why the North Vietnamese would likely not engage in serious negotiations anytime soon, because joining the peace talks would have been an admission that they had failed to conquer the South.[2] Cyrus Vance decided to stay on an extra month in order to help with the transition, and for continuity, Lodge's early negotiating statements were edited by William Bundy and Harriman.[3]

Lawrence E. "Ed" Walsh, a New York attorney and deputy attorney general in the Eisenhower administration, was Lodge's deputy. His staff included Phil Habib, Marshall Green, General George Seignious, William "Bill" Jordan, and Robert Miller.[4] John Negroponte stayed on for a little while and then went to work for Henry Kissinger on his National Security Council staff. Lodge's team was mostly composed of young, ambitious types. They worked under a spell of admiration, fear, and respect for Habib, who loved Paris, French food, wines, and the attention of the press.[5] Habib was effectively Lodge's chief of staff; he would have been a deputy chief of mission or an ambassador at another post, but neither Lyndon Johnson nor Nixon wanted to release him from his work on Vietnam. He believed that the North had no plans to seriously negotiate but that after a time they would come around.[6] It was an exciting place to be for a junior Foreign Service officer, especially those who had started their careers in Saigon. "If there is a better place to be young, single, and gainfully employed, I've not found it," recalled James Dobbins. "One observant boss noted that nightlife was impinging on my professional performance and recommended marriage as a corrective."[7]

Saigon cheered the news of Lodge's appointment. They had even given Lodge a rare mark of respect for a foreigner, a Vietnamese name: Cao Bao Lac (pronounced "Cabah Lod").[8] They had gone from having no good friends in Paris to having one of their best leading the U.S. delegation.[9] "Although I came to admire Harriman, I could never quite trust him," Nguyen Cao Ky wrote. "I had no such problem with Lodge."[10] Harriman had been the North Vietnamese and Soviets' closest collaborator, and they expected Lodge to be more hawkish. For example, the North assumed they would have a much harder time getting Nixon or Lodge to accept the National Liberation Front as a separate entity at the talks.[11]

The first plenary session took place at the Hotel Majestic on avenue Kléber on January 25, 1969. The U.S. delegation was led by Lodge, the North Vietnamese delegation was led by Xuan Thuy, and the newly admitted South Vietnamese delegation was led by Pham Dang Lam, with Premier Ky "supervising."[12] It was the first time that the full delegations had met since having a series of procedural disagreements over the shape of the negotiating table, whether flags or nameplates would be used, and the speaking order to be followed. Vance had resolved these details just before Lodge's arrival.[13] At the session, Lodge was under strict orders to focus on the future.[14] He stressed the need to restore the demilitarized zone, respect Laos and Cambodia, secure an early release of prisoners of war, emphasize mutual withdrawal, and reimplement the basic elements of the 1954 Geneva Accords. Hanoi "flatly refused to negotiate on any basis but its own," Robert Miller wrote.[15] Lodge saw that the United States, South Vietnam, and North Vietnam were nowhere near the point at which a peace agreement would be possible. "We were as close to peace as a man on the moon!" Negroponte said later.[16]

Lodge enjoyed being back in Paris. While he had returned to the city many times during his career, it was the first time he had been able to stay for an extended time since he was a boy. He reunited with friends from the Ecole Gory, including Rodolphe Hottinger, Remy Lebel, Phillipe Mallet, and their wives.[17] Lodge easily settled into a routine. Every Thursday morning at ten fifteen, a procession of black Plymouth Furies carried Lodge and the members of the delegation to the Majestic. During the talks, the group was sequestered behind closed doors and the hotel was carefully guarded by gendarmes, who also closed the sidewalk and blocked traffic. The sessions usually lasted until around three o'clock in the afternoon.[18]

Initially, the Nixon administration followed a path in Paris that resembled the one followed by the Johnson administration, based on a belief that the best way to end American military involvement in Southeast Asia was through a negotiated outcome. During his visit to Paris only a month into his presidency, Nixon gave Lodge and the senior staff of the Vietnam delegation extensive briefings in the eavesdrop-proof "tank."[19] From Washington, Nixon publicly pursued a policy of "Vietnamization," which meant de-Americanizing the conflict and turning the fighting over to the South Vietnamese as quickly as possible. In practical terms, it meant that no matter what the North Vietnamese did on the battlefield, the Americans would progressively withdraw.[20] Lodge's job in Paris, as someone who had seen the military conditions in Vietnam and was an experienced negotiator, was to keep things moving in that direction.

Privately, Nixon and Kissinger authorized Lodge to take a different approach. They launched the first of what would become known as the Nixon backchannels. Nixon preferred private meetings over contact through official channels. "This process started on the day after the inauguration," Kissinger wrote. "The new president wanted to change the negotiating instructions drafted at State that reflected the approach of the previous administration. But he wished also to avoid a controversy. He therefore asked me to phone Ambassador Henry Cabot Lodge, our negotiator in Paris, to suggest that Lodge send in through regular channels as his own recommendation, the course of action that the president preferred. Lodge readily agreed."[21] Lodge was authorized to present a two-pronged approach to the North Vietnamese, separating the political and military aspects of the negotiations. This strategy was born out of a conclusion that the sides were more likely to find agreement on the military aspects than the political ones. Lodge called for a mutual withdrawal from South Vietnam, a shift from the Johnson administration's policy. The United States would withdraw six months after the North Vietnamese (a timetable previously offered at the Manila Conference in 1966), provided the level of violence remained low. He briefed Valerian Zorin, Soviet ambassador to Paris, on these proposals, along with a promise that Nixon was sincere about improved U.S.-Soviet relations.[22]

Lodge had a difficult time separating political and military issues, as the North Vietnamese insisted they were one and the same. The North was adamant that the United States should topple the Thieu government and establish a coalition government that included the National Liberation Front.[23] Madame Nguyen Thi Binh said that Lodge's proposal to raise concrete issues without ending U.S. aggression could not lead to "correct" solutions, and Thuy reminded Lodge that the North had many times rejected American proposals related to restoring the demilitarized zone. The lack of progress in Paris prompted Nixon and Kissinger to try a bolder option to show North Vietnam that the new administration was not bound by limitations set by Johnson. "No substantive negotiating sessions had been held in Paris with our new delegation, headed by Henry Cabot Lodge," Kissinger wrote. "The new administration could hardly have formed its policy. Whether by accident or design, the offensive began the day before a scheduled presidential trip overseas, thus both paralyzing our response and humiliating the new president." While Nixon was on a tour of western European capitals in late February, he called an emergency huddle. The only venue with secure communications was Air Force One, so Nixon and his advisers met on the aircraft while it was parked at Brussels airport. Nixon decided to bomb Cambodian sanctuaries and the Ho Chi Minh Trail, something Johnson had wanted to do but feared would widen the war.[24]

While Nixon and Kissinger studied longer-term alternatives with respect to Vietnam, they authorized Lodge to propose private talks with Thuy, the lead North Vietnamese negotiator in Paris. North Vietnam accepted Lodge's proposal within seventy-two hours, and the first secret meeting took place on March 8, 1969. In all, there would be a total of seven private meetings, five led by Lodge and two by Habib.[25] The first accomplished little other than providing North Vietnam the chance to repeat its demand for an unconditional surrender of U.S. forces and dismantling of the Thieu-Ky government.[26] Lodge did pick up a point from the session that he quickly conveyed to Kissinger. Thuy told Lodge that the United States "should not count on the Sino-Soviet split to help us settle," Kissinger wrote.[27] Downplaying the growing divide between the communist allies had the opposite effect of giving it more attention in the eyes of American policymakers.[28] When Lodge was back in Washington for the somber occasion of General Dwight Eisenhower's funeral, he had a private conversation with South Vietnamese Premier Ky. Lodge mentioned the impact that U.S. casualties were having on overall American support for the war. Ky conceded that Vietnam might be able to speed up the process of Vietnamization. Lodge quickly passed that piece of intelligence to the White House.[29]

Kissinger became convinced that direct, private channels had to be opened with both the Soviet Union and North Vietnam rather than relying on casual contact in Paris, and he needed to be more involved since he was the closest to Nixon.[30] Lodge had begun the talks in the private channel so that they could be taken over by Kissinger.[31] The public talks could then be used to reinforce the private talks, such as when Lodge mentioned a B-52 cutback in a public meeting as a sign of American willingness to deescalate.[32] However, the more that substance was discussed in the secret meetings, the more the public talks were made redundant, since less and less would occur in those sessions—even though the secret talks included only North Vietnam and the United States.

Lodge explained the reasoning to Nguyen Phu Duc of the South Vietnamese delegation. He believed the negotiations had to move beyond the public exchange of diatribes, or else there could be no expectation of results. Lodge also believed that Laos and Cambodia should be included in the conference, because peace in the region depended on their participation. He asked Duc what the South Vietnamese position was on a cease-fire, and the Saigon diplomat said his government was in no hurry for it. However, "if the Viet Cong laid down their arms, repudiated violence and respected the Constitution of the Republic of Viet-Nam, they could enjoy all the civic and political rights, including the right to vote and be candidates in the election," Duc said. That last point surprised Lodge. "To be candidates, too?" he clarified. "I replied yes," Nguyen later wrote.[33] When North Vietnamese leader Le Duc Tho, a politburo member, arrived on May 3 to lead his delegation to the peace talks, it seemed to suggest that the North was taking the talks seriously—and by sending a high-ranking official, they could match the status of Lodge on the American side.[34]

While in Paris, Lodge became an advocate for American prisoners of war as the Nixon administration attempted to correct previous oversight of this issue. Lodge endorsed the efforts of Sybil Stockdale to organize the wives of prisoners of war and to bombard Thuy and the newly opened North Vietnamese embassy in Paris. The wives demanded to know who was dead and who was alive, information they were unable to get during the Johnson administration.[35] "It is difficult to understand how you can claim to be treating our prisoners humanely when you refuse to identify the prisoners you hold so that their families can know the fate of their relatives," Lodge told Thuy on May 22. It was a powerful bipartisan issue for the White House. Lodge's repeated demand for North Vietnam to provide a list of prisoners "so that the wives would know whether they were wives or widows" gave the media and world opinion, which had been critical of the war and the lack of progress in Paris, something else to talk about.[36] Lodge insisted on regular mail exchanges, impartial observation of conditions, and the release of sick and wounded prisoners, which he considered the basic elements of humanitarian treatment under international law.

That summer was Nixon's first chance to meet as president with Thieu and review the war. They met at the World War II fulcrum of Midway Island on June 7. The briefing included Nixon, Secretary of Defense Melvin Laird, Secretary of State William Rogers, National Security Advisor Kissinger, Chairman of the Joint Chiefs of Staff Earle Wheeler, U.S. Ambassador to Saigon Ellsworth Bunker, and Lodge.[37] The main point that Nixon wanted to get across was continued American support for South Vietnam. "Our refusal to overthrow an allied government remained the single and crucial issue that deadlocked all negotiation until October 8, 1972, when Hanoi withdrew the demand."[38] The Nixon position, which Lodge emphasized to Thuy in Paris, was that the United States believed that an enduring settlement was not feasible without the withdrawal of all non–South Vietnamese forces.[39] Nixon briefed Thieu on proposed American troop withdrawals, which began the pattern of unilateral withdrawals that would continue until early 1972, when virtually all combat troops had left Vietnam.[40] Thieu agreed to a sensitive American proposal for the United States and North Vietnam to meet bilaterally, without the South Vietnamese. "We would raise only military issues in these talks but would be willing to listen to proposals on political issues concerning South Vietnam," Kissinger clarified. "Ambassador Lodge believes we should begin an active round of private meetings now with the North Vietnamese."[41]

In July, North Vietnam seemed to be sending signals that they were eager to talk in Paris. "The tone of the session in Paris was the best we have ever seen," Lodge reported. He pressed Thuy to loosen restrictions regarding the sending of gifts to American prisoners in North Vietnam. "It is an unusually positive North Vietnamese gesture, probably intended to underscore Communist interest in getting on with the negotiations and into serious substantive bargaining," the CIA concluded.[42] It bothered Lodge that the North Vietnamese—and the Soviets—preferred to talk in private with Americans but did not want to include the South Vietnamese. Kissinger referred to it as "a substantial shift in tactics for Hanoi."[43] He broke away from the presidential entourage for a detour to Paris and Brussels, ostensibly for the purpose of briefing French officials on Nixon's trip. The real purpose, however, was to meet secretly with the North Vietnamese, and Lodge facilitated the meeting. Although reporters in Paris were keeping a close eye on Kissinger as he went back and forth between Lodge at the U.S. embassy, Prime Minister Jacques

Chaban-Delmas at the Hotel Matignon, and President Georges Pompidou at the Élysée Palace, Kissinger managed to slip away, tucked down in the back of a car as Lodge used to do during the Marigold talks.

Kissinger had his first secret meeting with the North Vietnamese on August 4, 1969, at the apartment of Jean Sainteny, a French banker and former official in Indochina who had been on excellent personal terms with Ho Chi Minh since 1945. The conversation was in French. Thuy was fluent but used an interpreter. Kissinger read better than he spoke, so he used Vernon Walters as an interpreter.[44] Kissinger said that Nixon was determined to "settle this thing," or else he would consider using "violent action." The deadline for results was November 1.[45] While the increased use of private talks would eventually put Lodge out of a job, he believed that there was a much greater chance for the war to be settled in that forum than in highly publicized meetings. "Passage of time convinces me that we had a better dialogue in the Marigold talks than we have ever had during the last twelve months in Paris—where, indeed, it cannot be truthfully said that we have ever had anything deserving of the name," Lodge advised Kissinger.[46]

The former Harvard professor pursued a different path from those of his patrician predecessors, Harriman and Lodge. Kissinger did not trust the Foreign Service, not even Habib, whom he had known since Harvard. He cut out most of those in Paris who had been there since the start of the peace talks in May 1968. Rather than meeting at the grand Hotel Majestic, Kissinger and Walters met at a CIA safe house on rue Darthe in the Paris suburb of Choisy-le-Roi, as well as other locations. Walters was Kissinger's official backchannel.[47] They met with both Tho and Thuy, using rented cars so that the diplomatic plates would not give away their mission.[48] The North Vietnamese were hospitable and friendly. The two sides talked about family, their experiences, life in Vietnam, and sports over the course of four meetings.[49] Since that was the channel more likely to produce results, Nixon struggled to find a reason to keep Lodge at the avenue Kléber.[50]

Lodge's boldest statement yet to the North Vietnamese took place on August 7. Nixon recalled later, "The diplomats and reporters who had become accustomed to Cabot Lodge's usually complacent demeanor were surprised when he rose from his chair, looked directly at the communist delegates, and said, 'We have done all that we can do by ourselves to bring a negotiated peace in Vietnam. Now it is time for you to respond.'"[51] According to proposals that Lodge sent to Kissinger via CIA channels, he wanted to go even further during the meeting, proposing "an immediate ceasefire so that at least the killing may stop while we here in Paris are talking."[52] If the North Vietnamese accepted, that would be a constructive step. If they refused, the United States would be on record as having tried everything.[53] "We have come as far as we are going to until the other side has made some concessions of their own," Kissinger said.[54]

The American people were frustrated that there seemed to be no answers by the fall of 1969, as some had believed that Nixon had a "secret plan" to end the war. This "secret plan" was a creation of the press who covered his 1968 campaign and reflected the fact that he was not willing to reveal his Vietnam policy.[55] In September, members of Congress, led by Senators Edmund Muskie (D-ME), Stephen Young (D-OH), and Charles Goodell (R-NY), introduced resolutions that called for an end to American military involvement in the war. Others, such as Senators Harold Hughes (D-IA) and Thomas Eagleton (D-MO), called for an end to foreign aid to Saigon. Responding to building criticism, Senator Hugh Scott (R-PA) called for a sixty-day moratorium on criticism of Nixon in order to give him "some elbow room" to negotiate a settlement. Lodge, Bunker, and Wheeler continued to meet regularly to strategize on possible solutions.[56]

On October 12, 1969, Nixon called Lodge in Paris to inform him that what became known as the "Support the President" resolution had passed both houses of Congress by wider than expected margins, considering the Democrats had majorities in both chambers. It carried with three hundred votes in the House and fifty-eight in the Senate.[57] Lodge noted that political polls consistently showed that between two-thirds and three-quarters of Americans were in favor of military action against the North.[58] The day after Nixon's call, White House spokesman Ronald Ziegler announced that Nixon would give a major address on Vietnam on November 3. While Nixon had six full-time speechwriters, he did not use any of them. He asked Kissinger to seek input from Lodge, Bunker, Rogers, and Laird. He then retreated to Camp David to write his speech.[59] Lodge asked Kissinger for an advance copy but the latter said, "There is no copy. He [Nixon] is writing it himself."[60]

The result was what later became known as Nixon's "Silent Majority" speech, arguably the most significant of his presidency. Nixon revealed that Lodge had privately met with Thuy four times, but the president said nothing of Kissinger's private talks. "It was great, simply great," British counterinsurgency expert Robert Thompson told John Paul Vann while touring the Mekong Delta.[61] The speech rallied American public opinion behind Nixon, hitting notes intended for both domestic and foreign audiences. The phrase "silent majority" became a watchword for populist pushback against those who criticized the White House. It was one of Nixon's greatest gambles. In Paris, Walters was called in by Mai Van Bo, the North Vietnamese delegate-general, to complain about Nixon's "warlike" speech.[62] Nixon announced his third troop withdrawal from Vietnam on December 15, promising that fifty thousand more troops would leave by April 15.[63]

As Lodge became increasingly frustrated by the lack of progress in Paris, he considered whether he could still be effective in his position. He brainstormed ways "to call attention to the completely negative attitude of the other side," in response to Nixon's instructions "to take a substantially tougher tone" in the plenary sessions.[64] On October 23, midsession at the Majestic, he called for adjournment, canceling the remaining week's talks. The Associated Press reported that Lodge's move was unprecedented in any of the formal meetings since the preliminary negotiations had begun in May 1968.[65] He explained his actions to the press: "The obstacle to progress here in Paris is not the President of the United States. The obstacle to progress here in Paris is the flatly intransigent attitude of Hanoi and the Front who refuse meaningful negotiations with us and who refuse even to have any significant talks of any kind with the South Vietnamese, who have offered to talk about everything."[66]

In November 1969, Lodge asked to resign "for personal reasons" when,[67] Kissinger wrote later, "our position seemed the strongest since the beginning of the Nixon administration."[68] Habib claimed that "Lodge left because he didn't want to hang around any longer."[69] The resignation was timed to punctuate the tenor of Nixon's November 3 speech, providing Lodge an opportunity to slip out quietly. The United States had survived Hanoi's offensives and rising domestic protests.[70] The fundamental problem was that the United States was in a hurry to reach peace, but North and South Vietnam were not.[71]

Accepting Lodge's resignation on November 20, the White House said in a statement, "The President continues to hope that peace can be achieved in Vietnam through successful negotiations. The lack of progress in Paris is a direct result of the refusal of the other side to enter into serious negotiations."[72] Lodge would be unofficially replaced by Habib, but Nixon never appointed a successor with a comparable status, as a way of showing his dissatisfaction with the obstinacy of the North Vietnamese. "Nixon had never liked the plenary sessions at Avenue Kléber," Kissinger wrote. "He considered that they gave the North Vietnamese a weekly forum on television to undermine our domestic support. And he constantly sought ways to diminish their importance. In 1969, he had refused to name a replacement for Lodge for seven months."[73] Kissinger convinced Nixon that a new round of secret talks would be of greater value. By doing so, they excluded not only Saigon but also the State Department. Occurring months after Lodge left his position, Kissinger's next secret meeting in Paris with Tho did not take place until February 21, 1970, a delay that seems to be accounted for at least in part by the death of Ho Chi Minh in September 1969 and the reshuffling of North Vietnamese leadership that followed.[74] "We have no real quarrel with North Vietnam," Kissinger said. "We don't think they are bad, immoral and have to be punished. It's a question of finding a realistic basis for settlement."[75]

Before leaving his post, Lodge affected Nixon-Kissinger foreign policy in a way that would prove profound: he told Kissinger that his contact in Paris had said the Chinese were interested in direct talks with the Americans. Kissinger's assistant Winston Lord remembered talking to him about it.[76] Kissinger's memoirs note only that Lodge had introduced him to a friend, the chargé d'affaires of a West European country in Beijing.[77] Kissinger clarified that he was not sure whether Lodge deserved sole credit for setting up the contact; while he was among the earliest catalysts, the White House was simultaneously pursuing multiple communication channels.[78]

According to Lodge's personal papers, he had picked up the tip from Jacobus Johannes "Koos" Derksen, the Dutch chargé d'affaires in Beijing.[79] Derksen cabled Lodge through a CIA channel with the Dutch Secret Service in China: "More than ever, I feel the necessity to speak with you." Lodge had known Derksen since 1965, when Lodge arrived in Saigon for his second tour as U.S. ambassador and Derksen was serving as the chargé d'affaires in the Dutch embassy. Lodge had also hosted him during a visit to Bonn.[80] Derksen was probably the only senior Western diplomat in Beijing who could speak, read, and write Chinese. That helped him to be on a good personal footing with Chinese officials, including Zhou Enlai. When Lodge learned from Derksen that a breakthrough with the Chinese might be possible, he quickly wrote an extensive memorandum for Kissinger. Derksen said that Tang Hai Kouang, the acting director of the Office of Western European Affairs, had told him on January 13, 1970, that "if the United States really wants better relations then everything becomes easy." Tang said the status of Taiwan would be the major issue to be settled, and relations had become strained between the People's Republic of China and the USSR. "There can be no question," Lodge recorded Derksen as saying, "that all of the above was said on the authority of Zhou Enlai and is the official Chinese line."[81] Lodge hosted Derksen at his home in Beverly on January 30–31 to get his full report.[82] Lodge reported the conversation to Kissinger during a telephone call on February 2 and flew to Washington the next day to brief him on what became known as Operation Valentine.[83] Lodge appeared to be on the shortlist of possible envoys to the People's Republic of China in the spring of 1971. Nixon ultimately decided against him because he had been so closely associated with Vietnam.[84] After Kissinger made his first secret trip to Beijing in July that year, Lodge congratulated him. "My warmest congratulations on your trip to Peking. You obviously conducted yourself with your usual clear-headedness, brilliance and presence of mind. I am proud of you."[85]

While breakthroughs were being made with the People's Republic of China, Nixon struggled to get the facts as they pertained to Vietnam. The complete record of Paris negotiations during the Johnson administration was never shared with him. Nixon's unmet demands for information prompted desperate maneuvers, such as bringing former White House staff member Tom Charles Huston back to the White House to work on special research projects, to compel government agencies to share information with the White House. These efforts were stepped up in the month following the leak of the Pentagon Papers, the top-secret, classified study of how the United States had become involved in the war going back to the Truman administration, and their subsequent publication in a variety of newspapers beginning in June 1971. The Pentagon Papers, presumably created to affect future policy, had been kept from both the Johnson and Nixon White Houses—from the very policymakers shaping future policy.

Lodge was eager to see how the Pentagon Papers characterized a critical period in his career. Ed Brooke was quick to send Lodge copies as soon as they were published in the *Congressional Record* and as additional segments were declassified by the State Department.[86] White House Chief of Staff H. R. "Bob" Haldeman's diary reveals that two days after the *New York Times* began publication of excerpts of the report, Nixon ordered Kissinger to get Lodge's files on the Ngo Dinh Diem coup, information from which he believed was contained both in the Pentagon Papers and in personal files still in his possession.[87] Chief Domestic Policy Advisor John Ehrlichman met with William Colby on November 16 to press for the release of Diem-related documents, but Colby refused and Richard Helms backed him up.[88] Howard Hunt, a former CIA spy, was tasked with using White House and State Department typewriters to re-create a set of cables that would show John F. Kennedy was involved in the planning of the Diem coup, a subject of consistent and intense interest for Nixon—and Johnson before him.[89]

Hunt created an alleged cable from Kennedy to Lodge that read, "At highest level meeting today decision reluctantly made that neither you nor General Harkins should intervene on behalf of Diem or Nhu in event they seek asylum," which put Diem's blood directly on Kennedy's hands.[90] Hunt claimed he was re-creating what he recalled having read contemporaneously.[91] Chuck Colson, Nixon's special counsel, shopped the story to various media outlets and sold it to *Life* shortly before the magazine ceased publication at the end of 1972. What Hunt concocted turned out to be rather mild compared with the now-disclosed truth about Kennedy's role in and knowledge of the Diem coup. Hunt's actions were fraudulent, and possibly illegal, but they were also shocking because they questioned the conventional wisdom that it was inaccurate to question the slain Kennedy for having a role in the Diem coup.

While Johnson started with private talks in Saigon and Warsaw and then moved to public talks in Paris, Nixon started with public talks and moved to private talks. Lodge defended Johnson's efforts in Vietnam in their final exchange of correspondence months before Johnson's death in January 1973.[92] Lodge had been an advocate for a negotiated settlement during the mid-1960s, but he became disenchanted after each attempt faltered. "Nor did I gain any new optimism for a negotiated settlement during my years as President Nixon's representative to the Paris talks in 1969," he wrote in early 1973. "Hanoi had no incentive to negotiate seriously, because they were confident that President Nixon's diplomatic hand was weakened both by war-weariness at home and by the insecure allied military position in the South."[93] Kissinger's secret talks ultimately produced a peace agreement, but one that neither South nor North Vietnam proved willing to implement.[94] Lodge congratulated Kissinger, who would later that year share the Nobel Peace Prize with Le Duc Tho. Recognizing "the miracles which [Kissinger had] wrought," Lodge later called on Republicans to draft him as a presidential candidate on account of his "super human" energy and "brilliant intellect."[95]

# 18 • Envoy to the Vatican

Henry Cabot Lodge Jr., a lifelong Episcopalian, served as special envoy to the Vatican from 1970 to 1977 under Richard Nixon, and later Gerald Ford. Throughout his political career, he had worked with Catholics and cultivated their support, especially in Boston. He had been close to Archbishop Richard Cushing during his time in the Senate in the 1940s, Francis Cardinal Spellman in the 1950s, and Vatican officials while in Saigon—and the last had served as some of his closest confidants. Lodge's relationship with Catholics was based on shared goals and values, as well as political expediency, and his appointment as special envoy to the Holy See was consistent with American tradition going back to the Adams administration and its 1797 decision to appoint Giovanni Battista Sartori as consul to the Holy See.

The position had largely been vacant since the Franklin D. Roosevelt administration, primarily because some Americans, especially southern congressional chairmen, saw a presidential representative to the Roman Catholic Church as a potential violation of the separation between church and state. As the president has no diplomatic representative to any other church, some also felt the Catholic Church did not deserve special status. President Lyndon Johnson became the first U.S. leader to meet with a pope when he met with Pope Paul VI on October 4, 1965.[1] There had been a rumor that Johnson would appoint an envoy, and Lodge was at the top of the list of those being considered.[2] On April 15, 1970, White House spokesman Ron Ziegler announced that Nixon had asked Lodge "to visit the Vatican from time to time. He is glad to say that Mr. Lodge has agreed to make these visits, which, the president believes, are in our national interest."[3]

Lodge presented his credentials as special envoy for Nixon to Pope Paul VI at the Vatican on July 4, 1970, the day before his sixty-eighth birthday. While Lodge would not remain permanently in Rome during his post, this was the first of what would be twenty-two visits to the Vatican. It was the beginning of a fruitful relationship that would ultimately lead to the establishment of full diplomatic relations between the United States and the Holy See in 1984. Not only did closer ties help with Nixon's domestic policy proposals, such as those concerning federal aid to parochial schools and efforts to woo Catholic voters, but Vatican representatives were eager to help on issues such as resolving the Vietnam War and improving the conditions of prisoners of war and securing their eventual return.

While Lodge had ambassadorial status, to avoid potential controversy he was not credentialed to the Vatican, did not run an embassy or diplomatic facility in Italy, and had no permanent staff. "This was a new, and for all practical purposes, unprecedented assignment since the last time the U.S. had been represented at the Vatican was by Myron Taylor in World War II under conditions that were hardly comparable," Lodge wrote. He planned to visit the Vatican a few times per year on a personal basis, although the visits were cleared with the White House in advance. The Vatican was eager to upgrade him, but the advantage of remaining an envoy was a higher Vatican diplomatic status that put Lodge above a regular ambassador.[4] To make it all work, Italian affairs expert Robert Beaudry in the State Department's Bureau of European Affairs was, confidentially, Lodge's liaison to agencies such as State's Bureau of Near Eastern Affairs and Bureau of Latin American Affairs, the Arms Control and Disarmament Agency, and other offices charged with issues concerning prisoners of war.[5] Lodge credited much of his success to Beaudry, who made Lodge's trips work from a diplomatic and practical standpoint. "He has shown himself to be imaginative and broad of view," Lodge wrote later in his journal. "I regard him as a wise counsellor and an officer of extensive knowledge and penetrating intellect."[6] When in Washington, which was, on average, twice per month, Lodge was based out of 365 Executive Office Building.[7]

Nixon agreed that Lodge should use his influence with the Vatican to improve relations with Latin America, including arranging contributions from the United States to Catholic charities in Latin America. "The basic purpose would be to open up a dialogue between the American Ambassador and the Archbishop in the country concerned," Lodge reported to Henry Kissinger. "The President seemed keenly interested," he added.[8] One policy proposal of the Nixon administration in particular piqued the Vatican's interest: what would later become labeled by the media as the "War on Drugs." During Lodge's first visit with the pope, they discussed this subject more than any other. Following their meeting, the Vatican issued a formal statement warning the youth of the world of the dangers of drug use and condemned narcotics trafficking. This was not just to support the White House, as the Vatican was a financial contributor to the UN's Fund for Drug Abuse Control and the UN Commission on Narcotics and Drugs. Lodge gave the Vatican credit for working with the French government to reduce heroin smuggling through the key port city of Marseilles, where it traveled onward to North America.[9]

Despite U.S.-Vatican agreement on the issue of drugs, the dominant issue that arose time and time again during Lodge's early visits was Vietnam. His role was to be sincere, take the advice offered, and then make sure the Vatican did not publicly criticize the United States. Tension rose between Lodge and the White House when he was unable to contain the Vatican's criticism. Nixon vented to Kissinger in April 1971, "I'm really tired of Lodge, anyway. Goddamn it, I sent him over there, fartin' around there with the pope, and he comes in here on this thing [prisoners of war] and now, he wants to take a trip to Vietnam. Goddamn it, leave me alone!"[10] However, for the most part, the relationship between the Vatican and the Nixon White House was a congenial one. The pope seemed to like being the first to have an American ambassador in Rome, especially one of Lodge's caliber. Lodge also seemed to like the assignment. He could come and go as needed, spending as much time in Rome and at home in Beverly as he wished. Lodge, who had several Catholic grandchildren, did not mind attending Mass and other Catholic events, and the Vatican was especially pleased when he attended Easter Mass. It was an ideal job for someone who was semiretired but still wanted to make a public service contribution.

The job was not always easy. Nixon's visit to the Vatican in September 1970 was not particularly warm, again due to differences over Vietnam, but Lodge reassured the White House that the Vatican was a useful Cold War partner that would be in agreement with the United States on many other issues. Writing Nixon on April 13, 1971, amid the beginning of "ping-pong diplomacy" between the United States and the People's Republic of China, Lodge said that the Vatican supported contact with the communist world as well as American efforts toward arms limitation talks with the Soviet Union. The Vatican was also willing to be a vocal advocate for prisoners of war, emphasizing "the humanitarian aspect of their plight, as opposed to its tactical value."[11] Lodge had facilitated delivery of the first letter from an American prisoner in South

Vietnam, Sergeant Leonard Budd.[12] "I believe the prisoner of war issue can probably be exploited to greater advantage and would like to have your thoughts on how we can follow-up on your efforts in Paris," Kissinger wrote to Lodge.[13]

Lodge was also consulted by the Nixon White House on a range of other issues. He had a backchannel set up through Hanscom Air Force Base in Beverly so that he could receive classified messages.[14] In the spring of 1970, after only a few weeks on the job, Charles Colson was assigned to assist with the White House lobbying effort to maintain the anti-ballistic missile (ABM) system and increase public support for the proposed ABM Treaty.[15] Lodge and Colson had been acquainted since the 1950s when the latter was administrative assistant to fellow Bay State Senator Leverett Saltonstall. Under Colson's direction, a bipartisan citizens committee, the Committee to Safeguard America, was formed with Dean Acheson and Lodge as cochairs. A typical message of the committee was "Stop the Arms Race—Support Strategic Arms Limitation by Supporting ABM." When Nixon saw the ad in the *New York Times,* he tore it out and sent it to H. R. "Bob" Haldeman with the annotation, "Powerful! This is the kind of stuff we should be doing." The treaty, combined with the Strategic Arms Limitation Treaty I and the Basic Principles of U.S.-Soviet Relations, were cornerstones of the Nixon détente architecture signed in Moscow on May 26, 1972. Lodge issued statements and gave speeches in support of the ABM Treaty, assignments that were both substantive and an opportunity to reconnect with an old colleague at the end of his life.[16] "I am delighted that we could serve together on the 'Safeguard' Committee and that it turned out so successfully," Acheson wrote to Lodge.[17] The ABM Treaty was easily ratified by the Senate with a vote of eighty-eight to two on August 3, 1972.

Since Lodge's appointment to the Vatican, he was increasingly less willing to make partisan attacks or public political appearances.[18] However, he gave his full support when Kissinger and a group of other notables asked him to contribute to a White House public relations campaign to stop an amendment by Senator Michael Mansfield (D-MT) calling for a withdrawal of U.S. troops from Germany. Mansfield's effort in the spring of 1971 had considerable traction, so Kissinger quickly assembled a bipartisan group with transatlantic ties to speak out against him. In addition to Lodge, those involved included Cyrus Vance, Acheson, Lyman Lemnitzer, and Nicholas Katzenbach.[19] The group met in the Cabinet Room on May 13, 1971. "Nixon was at his best," Kissinger recalled. "He made an eloquent speech. He had never asked those present for their support on Vietnam. But they had never disagreed on NATO."[20]

Lodge was called on to return to the United Nations so it would remain viable for future generations. On July 10, 1970, Lodge was appointed Nixon's representative to the President's Commission for the Observance of the Twenty-Fifth Anniversary of the UN.[21] He was an obvious choice given his long service at the UN under Dwight Eisenhower in addition to his closeness to Nixon and Kissinger. "Added to your job at the Vatican, you certainly have your hands full," his brother, John Davis Lodge, wrote in a letter of congratulations.[22] The work produced a volume of recommendations published in May 1971.[23] "As I had hoped, your report cuts through the haze of preconceptions that have grown around the UN during these past twenty-five years," Nixon wrote, acknowledging Lodge's submission. "You have not only looked at the record of accomplishments, but you have provided a cogent analysis of the shortcomings which must be corrected for humanity to benefit fully from participation in international institutions in the coming years."[24]

A few of the report's more significant conclusions included the following: some states should renounce their right to vote and become associate members; if any state pays less than 0.1 percent of the UN budget, it should become an associate member; and the United States should emphasize electing members to the Security Council based on the contribution they can make; in addition, half of the ten seats should rotate among the larger states.[25] Lodge did not believe the United States should be a hegemon at the UN, but its political influence should be commensurate with its budgetary contribution and the United States and the General Assembly should be used to bring nations together rather than focusing on issues that divide them. The UN was a very different organization in the early 1970s from the one it had been in the late 1940s when Lodge first encountered it, when its membership was primarily the great powers that had emerged following World War II.

Following his return to UN affairs, Lodge was soon back at the Vatican. On August 16, 1971, the day following Nixon's decision to temporarily end the convertibility of the U.S. dollar into gold, striking a fatal blow to the Bretton Woods system, Lodge had another audience with the pope. "The audience was unusual for three reasons," he wrote Nixon on August 17. "I had not asked for it and it was held entirely on his initiative; it was held at Castel Gandolfo his vacation retreat where he rarely has private audiences; and it lasted for one full hour. All this must be attributed to the Pope's tremendous interest in your decision to visit China," referring to Nixon's nationally televised address of July 15. "The Catholic Church, he said, is very much interested in China."[26] "So much time in international affairs is spent in reacting to crisis. A true politician in the best sense of the word must be a prophet who sees far and aims far. This is what President Nixon is doing," the pope told Lodge.[27]

Lodge remained on Colson's radar for yet another reason: rallying Catholic voters for Nixon's reelection. By mid-1972, Lodge's reports of his visits to the Vatican were being directed to Colson in order for him to keep track of the officials Lodge met with and the issues they discussed.[28] Colson sent Lodge lists of prominent Catholic clerical and lay leaders, asking him to remind them in a "totally non-political effort" of the administration's commitment to maintaining close relations with the Vatican.[29] Lodge reported that Nixon had become so popular with Catholics that he thought he had a chance to carry Massachusetts that fall—or at least win more of the popular vote than he ever had before.

Nixon eagerly sought the Catholic vote, but on at least one occasion it backfired. A rumor leaked that Nixon planned to meet with Pope Paul VI in October, only days before the election, to "deliver American Catholics in the hands of the Republican Party." Plans were quickly scrapped.[30] Instead, Lodge embarked on a speaking tour around the country to outline what had been achieved in U.S.-Vatican relations and American foreign policy. "President Nixon has achieved much in many ways, particularly in making this dangerous world a more peaceful place," Lodge said on Boston radio on August 1. "His leadership is directly responsible for bringing about new and more stable relationships with Peking and Moscow and for the shrinkage of American involvement in Viet Nam. He has helped mightily to achieve improved access to Berlin, the cease-fire in the Middle East, the settlement of the Okinawa problem with Japan, and treaties with the Soviet Union to bring the arms race under control. Taken together, these things constitute a notable turn away from war."[31]

In October 1972, Lodge made his eighth visit to the Vatican since becoming Nixon's envoy. If Nixon lost the election, it probably would have been Lodge's final visit. Two years into Lodge's mission, both he and the Vatican had fallen into a routine. There was no talk of upgrading the diplomatic status of Lodge's role, because both sides emphasized the importance of simply "working things out at a practical level."[32] "The informality of the present arrangement—and it is informal when contrasted with the rigid and carefully calibrated niceties of diplomatic protocol and seniority—has practical advantages for both sides," the National Catholic News Service reported on October 7.[33] It was somewhat ironic that one of the nation's greatest WASPs had managed to establish such a good personal relationship with the leaders of the Roman Catholic Church. However, working across the aisle was something

Lodge had done throughout his entire career. He was unique in his ability to be likeable and achieve the results he set out to accomplish.

Lodge attached no special importance to the June 17, 1972, break-in at the Watergate offices of the Democratic National Committee. He knew better than most that it was unlikely anything truly sensitive was stored there, in the party office, as opposed to a candidate's office. The brief embarrassment for the Nixon White House made no apparent difference in the election results, as Nixon won one of the largest landslide victories in American history over George McGovern. However, his victory would soon have the specter of the investigation into the botched break-in hanging over it. Lodge observed how deteriorating White House relations with Congress had spilled over into other areas, such as the president's ability to propose a budget. In April 1973, Lodge wrote a letter to the editor of the *New York Times* advocating a presidential line-item veto in order to overcome congressional riders.[34] The proposal went nowhere.

Following the Nixon White House announcement of a Vietnam peace agreement in January 1973, Lodge reflected on his experiences in and working on the subject of Vietnam. When negotiations stalled in 1971, he had offered to become more involved, just as he had throughout the Kennedy and Johnson administrations. "Over my dead body," Kissinger scratched on a memo conveying Lodge's interest.[35] Once Kissinger began conducting secret talks, he did not want to take any chance that Lodge or anyone else could throw things off pace. "For my part, let me say how wrong were some of my pessimistic views about the prospects for a negotiated settlement of the Vietnam War," Lodge wrote. He had made a full transformation from hawk to peace advocate to pessimist about the chance for peace. "While on duty in Vietnam during the years ranging from 1963 to 1967, I used to discuss with my colleagues in the U.S. Embassy how to achieve a negotiated settlement. Hardly a day went by that we did not speak of it," he wrote, believing that a change in position by the North during the fall of 1972 was what finally allowed peace. "Last October, Hanoi finally dropped its demand for dismantling the Government of South Vietnam and entered serious talks—and now the settlement that eluded us for so long has been negotiated, with solid expectations for peace in Laos and Cambodia as well."[36]

Nixon's resignation and departure from the White House on August 9, 1974, had no apparent effect on his former running mate. Kissinger was happy to continue using veteran diplomats such as Lodge and David Bruce. He offered continuity in Washington at a time when there was not much to speak

of. "Not enough can be said for the dedication and ability with which they ac-
quitted themselves," Kissinger reflected later.[37] President Gerald Ford retained Lodge in his role as special envoy to the Vatican. They had a chance to
talk early in Ford's presidency, on August 29, 1974, while Lodge was on his
way to attend the World Synod of Bishops at the Vatican.[38] Lodge and Ford were
longtime friends. They had served in Congress together, and Ford had seconded Lodge at the 1960 convention. Ford had been a member of the Chowder and Marching Society with Lodge's brother, John, and Nixon, among
others, and was a protégé of Lodge's friend and Ford's fellow Michigan Senator Arthur Vandenberg.[39] Ford and Lodge enjoyed talking about shared memories, especially Vandenberg and the early days of support for General
Eisenhower in 1951 and 1952. Lodge gave him a piece of unsolicited advice:
that Ford needed someone to advise him on the political ramifications of everything he did, just as Lodge had done for Eisenhower. Lodge offered to talk
on the telephone periodically and serve in this role, but Ford did not take him
up on it.[40]

Ford wanted all political activity to be located outside the White House, especially after additional scrutiny was placed on him following the pardon of
former President Nixon. He preferred to keep Lodge around not for political
advice but rather because he got along so well with Pope Paul VI and other
Catholic leaders. Both the United States and the Vatican had an interest in continuing the relationship, and Lodge had encouraged Ford to embrace the opportunity to become closer to the Vatican even when he was Nixon's vice
president.[41] While Saigon was falling to the North Vietnamese on the other
side of the world during the spring of 1975, Lodge reminded the Ford White
House that it was good domestic politics to retain close ties to the Vatican. In
a meeting with Ford and Brent Scowcroft, on April 21, 1975, Lodge pointed
out that Nixon had received a higher percentage of the Catholic vote in 1968
and 1972 than any other Republican, including Eisenhower. "Can you have
an audience with the Pope? This would be a good time because it's not close
to any elections," Lodge suggested. "We will look into it," Ford said.[42] He ultimately did take Lodge's advice and met the pope in the Vatican on June 3,
1975.[43] He later referred to the meeting in the Papal Library as one of the high
points of his life.[44] "He [Pope Paul VI] said how much he had enjoyed meeting you and how deeply impressed he was by your approach to your role in
foreign affairs," Lodge wrote to Ford following the audience.[45]

As of 1975, there were 48.8 million Catholics in the United States, and
many were not thrilled with Jimmy Carter—who had emerged as a chal-

lenger even before the convention in 1976.[46] The decision to appoint a special envoy provided a direct two-way channel between the White House and the Vatican that did not exist before. Lodge encouraged Ford to hold other high-level meetings with Catholic officials and send officials other than Lodge on visits to the Vatican, too.[47] More Catholics were invited to White House functions and took part in Oval Office meetings, and beginning in the early 1970s, Republican presidents increasingly recognized the role that the church played on issues that helped the United States abroad (Vietnamese refugees, Italy, Portugal, and the Middle East) and at home (abortion, voter mobilization). The Nixon and Ford administrations lobbied for things such as the canonization of the first American-born saint of the Catholic Church (Elizabeth Bayley Seton) and proposals for constitutional amendments to ban abortion.[48] The Roman Catholic Church had become more active in American politics following the January 1973 *Roe v. Wade* Supreme Court decision and the rise of abortion as a political issue.[49] Following a three-day conference, a gathering of 250 American bishops called on churchgoers to become involved in the 1976 presidential campaign "according to their consciences."[50]

Lodge, after visiting the Vatican seventeen times between 1970 and 1975, recommended to the Ford White House that his post be elevated in diplomatic status to a full embassy. He took no salary for his work and had no official title other than the "president's special envoy." Lodge normally resided at his home in Beverly and was assisted on visits to Rome by one Foreign Service officer and one Foreign Service secretary attached full time to the American embassy.[51] While the position was not elevated during Lodge's tenure, he gave it a status it had never had before, which ultimately contributed to its being elevated to a full embassy during the Reagan administration.

In perhaps Lodge's last significant meeting with Vatican officials, he hosted visiting Secretary of State Kissinger for an audience with Pope Paul VI in July 1976.[52] The views exchanged during the meeting built up to Ford's major speech the next month at the Forty-First International Eucharistic Congress in Philadelphia on August 8. Pope Paul VI did not attend due to his health, but the total number of attendees was approximately one million, including three hundred thousand in John F. Kennedy Stadium.[53] In the speech, Ford thanked the Roman Catholic Church for its long-standing efforts to address hunger and world peace. "On this occasion of celebrating the church's contribution to building a more peaceful world, we salute you for giving depth and direction to the world community in every age," Ford said. The American government was closer than ever to the Vatican, thanks in no small part to Lodge's efforts.[54]

Vietnam had been on Lodge's mind throughout this period in more ways than one. He continued to reflect during the mid-1970s on his many experiences, including writing numerous memoranda for his personal files as a substitute for writing a comprehensive memoir. Not only had he spent years of his life there, he and Emily had taken in a refugee family at their house in Beverly. Nguyen Ba Thinh did not know the Lodges in Saigon, but he was happy to work as their groundskeeper in Beverly while his wife cooked, their son worked in a local restaurant, and their two daughters attended a local high school.[55] Lodge said little of substance about Vietnam in public. However, given his deep ties to the nation, he did occasionally make comments in statements and correspondence. "We didn't win. We didn't get beaten exactly, we didn't get thrown out, but we didn't win," he once said.[56]

Lodge enthusiastically backed the reelection of Ford. When asked for a suggestion for Ford's running mate, Lodge's first choice was Senator Ed Brooke (R-MA).[57] Lodge saw Brooke as a prototype for the first African American president, and behind the scenes, he strategized with Brooke on ways to prepare him for that.[58] However, Ford lost to Jimmy Carter in November 1976, and following his victory, Lodge wrote a lengthy memorandum to the president-elect outlining his activities since being appointed special envoy. He paid a farewell call on Ford on January 4, 1977, carrying a message from the pope. "He will always think of President Ford not only as a man who is warm and sincere, but as a man with a great reservoir of common sense," Lodge read. "That means a great deal to me," Ford responded.[59]

In his final months in the position, Lodge renewed his call to elevate the position to full diplomatic recognition of the Holy See, pointing out that even countries with a small percentage of Catholics—including Japan, Sweden, and Turkey—had already done so. Lodge argued that it was not a violation of the separation of church and state.[60] He submitted his letter of resignation to Ford on January 21, 1977, although it was not accepted by President Carter until July 6.[61] Carter did not follow Lodge's advice and instead continued the practice of appointing a personal representative. This pattern continued until 1984, when President Ronald Reagan appointed Ambassador William Wilson as the first U.S. ambassador to the Holy See, a matter of months before Lodge's death. He lived long enough to see his wish come true.

# Retirement and Epilogue

Henry Cabot Lodge Jr. never attempted to write anything approaching a comprehensive history of his career. "I have a horror of now-it-can-be-told books," he said. "And I'm not going to do that. Now, I may write something to be published after my demise, as a matter of duty. But I'm not going to write stuff of 'look behind the curtain and see the bearded woman.'"[1] Lodge wrote two short, episodic memoirs but left the most interesting parts of his career unexplored and wrote nothing that could potentially violate or even appear to violate any confidences. "I do not see myself doing a book because if it is interesting, it means I have revealed things which I should not reveal and if I don't reveal them, then the book will be dull," he wrote to his editor, Evan Thomas II.[2] "Never," he once told Barry Zorthian while wagging his finger, "never tell them how you did it."[3] Lodge even failed to defend himself against the charges—by Robert Kennedy, former Kennedy aides, and many historians—of being to blame for Vietnam and the Ngo Dinh Diem coup. "I think he felt that his two books were enough," his son George said. "He naturally shunned self-promotion."[4]

In retirement, Lodge contemplated the world as he had seen it evolve during his life. He was born with a famous name and bred for public service. "It is not often given to a man to play a part, however modest, in such a great adventure and I am deeply grateful," he once wrote Dwight Eisenhower.[5] Lodge reflected on a bygone era that, while being no less civil, represented the world he once knew—a world that was no more. Having been widely read throughout his life, he meditated on his values and philosophy. "Four phrases have particularly impressed me," he wrote in his diary. The first was *homo antiqua virtute ac fide*, which translates to "a man of old-fashioned virtue and trustworthiness."

"That, I think, is a great thing to be," he said. The second was a 1621 letter home to England by the Pilgrims at Plymouth after their first terrible winter in the New World: "It is not with us as other men, whom small things can discourage or small discontentments cause them to wish themselves home again." Lodge was inspired by the statement. "Half of them died that first winter. They had a right to boast. I think it's a wonderful statement," he wrote. Third, there was the line from Tennyson, "to strive, to seek, to find, and not to yield." And lastly, the motto of the U.S. Military Academy at West Point: "Duty, honor, country." These four simple phrases summed up Lodge.[6]

The Lodge family made a permanent break from politics in the middle of the twentieth century after an almost unbroken lineage of service going back to the founding of the republic. No Lodge has held elected political office since the 1950s. In retirement, Lodge spoke out in bipartisan—or nonpartisan, really—fashion on issues of the day. He taught at North Shore Community College, near his home in Beverly, as well as at Gordon College in Wenham. He spoke out in favor of the Carter administration's proposal to return the Panama Canal to the Panamanians on January 17, 1978, even over the private objections of his brother, John. "Let me say that when a President makes a proposal in the complicated field of foreign affairs he is entitled to have the benefit of the doubt—at least at the outset," he wrote to John. "After all, he knows things that we do not know. Later, as we gain in knowledge and experience, we may conclude that the President is wrong, but, at the beginning, he is entitled to the benefit of the doubt."[7] He also praised the Carter administration's environmental protection policies, in particular the increased federal protection of lands in Alaska.[8] Lodge personally lobbied members of the House and Senate to pass pieces of legislation such as the Udall-Anderson bill (H.R. 39), which was also prominently backed by Laurance Rockefeller and Lady Bird Johnson.

At age seventy-seven, on May 25, 1980, Lodge received an honorary degree from Georgetown University. "In all of his activities and assignments, his voice has been one of firmness, of compassion, of wise and prudent counsel. Tenacious in his defense of his country's welfare, he has been no less tenacious in his pursuit of peace and justice in the world," the citation read.[9] What was notable about the May 25 event was that it was his thirtieth honorary degree and the commencement speaker was the nation's youngest governor, William J. Clinton of Arkansas, one generation passing the torch to the next. As Clinton rose to give the commencement address to the 1,877 assembled graduates, Lodge reached over to adjust Clinton's tassel and offered advice about graduation speeches: "You can't be too long, too heavy or too light."[10]

A few years earlier, Lodge had had a chance to do something he had not had much time for during his career—travel for the sake of leisure, as well as to search for clues about his family history. One of his most meaningful trips was when he and Emily took a cruise on the steamer *Delta Queen* up the Mississippi River from New Orleans to Memphis in March 1972. It was partly for leisure but also in search of evidence of his great-grandfather, Rear Admiral Charles Henry Davis, to whom they hoped to pay their respects at a stopover at Vicksburg. Davis had commanded the Civil War First Battle of Memphis and in the fight at Fort Pillow. His successful performance there cleared the Mississippi of Confederate forces from Cairo, Illinois, down to Vicksburg, where Davis's troops met Admiral David Farragut, who had cleared it from New Orleans northward up to Vicksburg. The act earned Davis the thanks of Congress. "At the end of a long spring day we came upon a high bluff rising out of the giant Mississippi," Lodge wrote his brother, John. "On top of this bluff stood a granite obelisk, about 200 feet high. On each one of its four sides, standing at its base, were full-length bronze statues of heroic size of the four Civil War admirals—Farragut, [Andrew] Foote, [David Dixon] Porter and Davis. The effect was stupendous." Lodge had always heard about the memorial, but it was the first time he had seen it in person. "I remembered that my grandfather had once written to me when I was a boy: 'I had rather have you like your great grandfather Davis than anyone else.' Seeing all that, so unexpectedly and in my seventieth year, sent rather youthful shivers down my spine."[11]

At Lodge's seventieth birthday party, held on July 6, 1972, his son George wrote a poem to commemorate the occasion, which he read as a toast to his father:

> Here's to dear old Pa
> Friend to near and far
> Whether driving his boat
> Or seeking a vote
> It's a joy to be with our old Pa.
>
> Diplomat, soldier and seer
> With offspring up to his ear
> He's got three score and ten
> And we all wonder when
> His age will begin to appear.

There is much he is doing right now
The book he's composing's a wow.
He visits the Vatican
But when he comes back again
No rest or relaxing he'll allow.

What will be his next spot
Heaven knows.
But when you look at where he has got
The chances are good
That he'll stand where he stood
And still tell us all what is what.[12]

In 1980, the City of Boston named a park bench after Lodge's old rival, James Michael Curley. Apparently, it was the most that the city could do for its four-time mayor who was also a two-time convict. Yet Lodge, who had made his peace with Curley and struck up a friendship with him before his death in 1958, turned out for the event.[13] "When you had been through a campaign with Governor Curley, you never worried about any other campaign," Lodge said in prepared remarks.[14] Later that year, after Lodge supported George H. W. Bush for the presidency, he learned that David Halberstam's older brother, Michael Halberstam, had died after being shot during a home invasion and robbery. "Emily and I are horrified by the dreadful tragedy which has stricken your brother. We do not find words to express even a small part of what we feel."[15] Halberstam himself would die in a tragic accident in 2007.

Lodge continued to speak on behalf of and advocate for the United Nations. In a speech at the UN on June 16, 1982, he reflected on Franklin D. Roosevelt and what he would have thought about the international organization. "His health prevented him from going to the San Francisco meeting later that year where the UN charter was adopted. He told reporters: 'I wish I could be there if only just to say howdy do,'" Lodge said. "As we advance ever deeper into the nuclear age, will we not prize more than ever our membership in the only organization operating, however imperfectly, on a completely global basis?" With the intensification of the Cold War in its final years, the UN served its purpose. "I am certain that Roosevelt would have been proud of the United Nations—with all its troubles."[16] Lodge was awarded the Christian A. Herter Memorial Award by the World Affairs Council of Boston for his contributions to international affairs.

Lodge suffered a long decline—in terms of both health and finances. Establishment families no longer had the resources they once did. In Lodge's last years of life, decisions were made to sell or donate artwork and family heir-looms in order to provide income and defray taxes. Lodge reasoned that more people could enjoy looking at a portrait of Rear Admiral Davis in the National Portrait Gallery than at the Lodge estate in Beverly.[17] And there were medical expenses. Following prostate problems that started in 1973, he wrote to his brother, John, that he was concerned about "money—and . . . time," declining the opportunity to visit him in Buenos Aires, where John was serving as U.S. ambassador.[18]

"I understand your poor Father's condition is deteriorating," John wrote his nephew George, suggesting that the family might consider a new type of ge-nome therapy to help him.[19] However, the doctors were unwilling to try it. "He is enjoying life, is in excellent physical shape, and although his mind has prob-lems with the here and now it is quite lucid about days gone by," George re-sponded. "He sings, just as always."[20] Just months later, the situation worsened quickly. "Mummy and Pa are coming along but it is becoming increasingly difficult for her to cope . . . Pa is well and happy but pretty much completely gone mentally."[21] Lodge's granddaughter Emily retains a memory of her grand-father shortly before his death. "He had not had any water for days, as he had wanted it. I knelt and took his hand and put my cheek close to his. 'It's Emmy, Grandpa. The sun is shining through the bedroom windows and glistening on the sea. Grandma has gone to Harry's for lunch.' His eyelids fluttered and gathering together all the strength of his courageous spirit, he rasped, 'I love you.'"[22]

Henry Cabot Lodge Jr. died of congestive heart failure at his home in Bev-erly, Massachusetts, on February 27, 1985. He was eighty-two years of age. "Nancy and I were saddened, as well as all Americans, by the recent death of Henry Cabot Lodge," President Ronald Reagan said in a statement. "Few men have played a more prominent role in the events of the last 50 years; Senator, soldier, diplomat, and political figure, Ambassador Lodge served his country long and selflessly . . . Henry Cabot Lodge's sense of personal honor and his devotion to country remain an inspiration to those of us who knew him and will remain so for many generations of Americans to come."[23]

Sympathy poured in from all over the globe. "Ambassador Lodge's entire adult life is one long and distinguished record of personal sacrifice to public service," Henry Kissinger once wrote to President Gerald Ford when nominat-ing Lodge for a Presidential Medal of Freedom. "His military service in World War II, when he was the first Senator since the Civil War to resign his seat to serve in the Army, and his careers in politics, the Senate, the Cabinet, and in diplomacy are, taken together, almost unparalleled in recent history. In particular, the numerous and difficult assignments which he has undertaken in the conduct of our foreign relations under both Republican and Democratic administrations place him in the first rank among American statesmen."[24]

The family was offered the use of Washington's National Cathedral for the ceremony, but they preferred a private ceremony at their Beverly parish, St. Peter's Episcopal Church, on March 2, 1985. Governor Michael Dukakis ordered state flags flown at half staff, saying, "Massachusetts had lost one of her favorite sons." Perhaps the greatest praise came from the Kennedy family, as Senator Edward Kennedy said Lodge "will be honored and remembered most for his extraordinary achievements as a senator and diplomat, but he is also remembered by all of us in the Kennedy family for the warmth and friendship that endured despite our political rivalry."[25] It was an extraordinary statement, not exceeded by anything said by members of Lodge's own political party.

Lodge's body was placed in a simple pine box and slid into the family's brownstone tomb at Lot 3613 Oxalis Path in Mount Auburn Cemetery in Cambridge, Massachusetts. Among the others interred in the tomb are George Cabot and Henry Cabot Lodge. "We shall not look upon his like again," his brother, John, wrote to the grieving Emily.[26] She observed the traditional mourning period of three years, then married Forrester "Tim" Clark, a retired investment banker, in Bermuda. When asked why she wanted to marry again at the age of eighty-two, she said it was "for sex" and to "pay him back" for financing George's Senate race in 1962.[27] Clark had been a longtime friend of the Lodge family and had helped to raise funds for many political and professional initiatives over a period of decades.[28]

When Richard Nixon saw Lodge's obituary on the front page of the *New York Times*, he wrote John a handwritten letter. Nixon had been closer to John, since they had entered Congress together in January 1947, serving as core members of the Chowder and Marching Society. Writing John had always been Nixon's way of saying something about Lodge that he did not want to—or, in this case, could not—communicate directly. "The great 1952 convention where Cabot and you played a decisive part in Eisenhower's and my nomination is still vivid in my mind. His service at the UN, in Vietnam, and as my running mate in 1960, combined with your service in Congress, governor, and ambassador adds up to a record no family in our time has surpassed," he wrote.[29]

Brahmins have never been particularly concerned about being understood by the masses. They have been misunderstood in large part because they have been unknowable. After all, they were privileged. The Brahmins not only were resistant to change and social progress but in fact represented the preservation of an antiquated way of living. Henry Cabot Lodge Jr. was a reincarnation of the noblesse oblige and understood that to whom much was given, much was expected. He had supreme self-confidence, which sometimes came off as arrogance to those who were not cut from the same cloth. Lodge believed in public service because he believed politics was an honorable profession. The federal government was still considered a solution and not the enemy. If asked to do something for his country, he had an overpowering sense of duty and patriotism, a consistent theme throughout his career. He was the embodiment of an American Cold War diplomat. He was handsome, rugged, tanned, scholarly, and all-American, he had *cojones,* and, with the look of a playboy who has to go to work, he was well suited for television.[30] He was conscious of reputation and image, and he could alternate between being extremely charming and being rude.[31] He was a Cold Warrior, the person you wanted on your side opposite a temperamental dictator. He would get what you wanted and make friends with the dictator in the process. Lodge is also a study in contrasts. He had a more consistent civil rights record than any president of his era and also more national security credentials than most.[32]

Lodge was the culmination of his grandfather's ambitions, a softer, gentler kind of Republicanism designed to appeal to the masses. Through his dramatic conversion from isolationism to internationalism, Lodge emerged from his grandfather's long shadow. Yet he remained a Brahmin with a duty to preserve American institutions and traditions. Only now, after a sufficient passage of time since the end of the Vietnam War, can we see that the country lost more than it gained through the exit of these families from politics and public service. With Washington gridlocked, bipartisanship at a nadir, and government the enemy, people long for an era when politicians could disagree without being disagreeable. Lodge went to his grave misunderstood, leaving clues in his archives for future historians rather than telling his side of the story. It was a Brahmin's duty.

# Appendix

President Ngo Dinh Diem's Handwritten Notes,
November 1, 1963

Cùng quốc dân đồng bào và các cán bộ
quân dân chánh

Với tư cách Tổng Thống và Tổng tư lệnh
quân đội cộng hòa

Tôi ra lệnh cho tất cả quân đội
không được nghe lệnh của ai ngoại trừ
lệnh của tôi mà thôi.

Vì có một số sĩ quan đã âm mưu
lừa gạt quân đội ta, để phản bội
quyền lợi dân tộc.

Tất cả các cấp chỉ huy của quân đội
và các đơn vị bảo quân sự phải đứng
lên theo tôi đánh lại bọn phản loạn.

Và những anh em nào đã bị lừa
gạt thì phải lập tức bỏ hàng ngũ
bọn phản loạn đi về với tôi.

## II

21818

Lệnh của Tổng thống VNCH, Tổng Tư lệnh tối cao quân đội

Các đại đơn vị và các đơn vị quân đội – các lực lượng địa phương

Vì tình thế Khẩn trương hiện tại, tôi kêu gọi tất cả các lực lượng thứ bị hãy lên đường bằng các phương tiện nhanh nhất về giải phóng Thủ đô. Muốn tránh ngộ nhận thì Khi về đến Thủ Đô hãy cho người đến liên lạc với Lữ Đoàn Liên Binh Phòng vệ Tổng thống để lãnh chỉ thị của tôi.

BẢN SAO

Tuy nhiên vấn đề chống cộng cũng rất quan trọng nên cũng phải để dành quân số mà bảo vệ lãnh thổ.

Vậy các cấp chỉ huy hãy sáng suốt nhận định thời lễ mà thi hành.

# Translation

## I

To Citizens and Military and Civilian Governmental Cadres

As the President and the Commander-in-Chief of the Army of the Republic

I order the entire army to refuse any orders issued by anyone other than me.

This is because a number of officers have plotted to deceive our army in an effort to betray the interests of our nation.

Commanders at all levels of our armed forces and of our paramilitary units must rise up to join me in fighting off the traitors.

Anyone who has already been deceived must immediately desert the ranks of the traitors and come over to my side.

## II

Order of the President of the Republic of Vietnam and Commander-in-Chief of the Armed Forces

To all large units and armed forces units—to all local forces

Because of the current critical situation, I appeal to all reserve forces to move out using the fastest means available to return here to liberate the Capital. To avoid any chance of mistaken identity, when you arrive in the Capital send someone in to make contact with the Joint Services Presidential Guard Brigade in order to receive my instructions.

However, fighting the communists is still important, so you must also leave sufficient troops behind to defend our territory.

Commanders at all levels should take action based on an intelligent assessment of the situation.

Translated by Merle Pribbenow

# NOTES

## Introduction

1. Henry Cabot Lodge Jr., "Words I Live By," undated, Reel 3, Microfilm Edition, Henry Cabot Lodge, Jr. Papers II, Massachusetts Historical Society.

2. Elsie Lee, *Henry Cabot Lodge*, 14.

3. See Schlesinger, *Vital Center*.

4. Interview with Henry Cabot Lodge Jr., pt. 3 of 5, January 1, 1979, *Vietnam: A Television History*, WGBH Media Library and Archives.

5. Notes, undated, Box 71, Neil Sheehan Papers, Manuscript Division, Library of Congress.

6. Stephen Hess, *America's Political Dynasties*, 491.

## 1. Early Life

1. Holmes, *Elsie Venner*, chap. 1.

2. Amory, *Proper Bostonians*, 12.

3. Baltzell, *Puritan Boston*, 12.

4. Betty G. Farrell, *Elite Families*, 163–164.

5. British journalist Henry Fairlie is commonly credited as the first to use the term "establishment" regularly, beginning in 1955, in his column for the *Spectator*. The historian A. J. P. Taylor also used the word to describe small groups of men who shared personal connections and political beliefs.

6. Bird, *Chairman*, 16.

7. Kabaservice, *Rule and Ruin*, 9.

8. E. Digby Baltzell, *The Protestant Establishment Revisited* (New Brunswick, NJ: Transaction, 1991), ix.

9. Amory, *Proper Bostonians*, 40.

10. Stephen Hess, *America's Political Dynasties,* 367. Following publication of the first edition of this work in 1966, Henry Cabot Lodge Jr. wrote the following appraisal to John Davis Lodge: "I thought it an entertaining compendium with the usual number of inaccuracies and the usual numbers of opinions with which I do not agree. But, after all, they spelled our names correctly!" Henry Cabot Lodge Jr. to John Davis Lodge, November 4, 1966, Box 144, John Davis Lodge Papers, Hoover Institution.

11. John W. Crowley, *George Cabot Lodge,* 15.

12. William J. Miller, *Henry Cabot Lodge,* 417.

13. John W. Crowley, *George Cabot Lodge,* 16.

14. John W. Crowley, *George Cabot Lodge,* 16.

15. Zeiger, *Remarkable Henry Cabot Lodge,* 17.

16. Garraty, *Henry Cabot Lodge,* 4.

17. "Henry Cabot Lodge Loses Fight for Life," *Harvard Crimson,* November 10, 1924.

18. John W. Crowley, *George Cabot Lodge,* 18.

19. William J. Miller, *Henry Cabot Lodge,* 419.

20. Hernon, *Profiles in Character,* 120.

21. William J. Miller, *Henry Cabot Lodge,* 419.

22. Elsie Lee, *Henry Cabot Lodge,* 7.

23. Emily Lodge, *Lodge Women,* 58.

24. William J. Miller, *Henry Cabot Lodge,* 6.

25. The home at East Point was later torn down when the U.S. government acquired the strategic area of East Point as a defensive fortification during World War II. Today, the former location of the home is known as Henry Cabot Lodge Park.

26. William J. Miller, *Henry Cabot Lodge,* 6–7.

27. The home at 1765 Massachusetts Avenue NW was later torn down to make way for the construction of the Brookings Institution.

28. William J. Miller, *Henry Cabot Lodge,* 419.

29. Hatch, *Lodges of Massachusetts,* 156–157.

30. William J. Miller, *Henry Cabot Lodge,* 7.

31. Elsie Lee, *Henry Cabot Lodge,* 24.

32. Henry Cabot Lodge Jr., *Storm Has Many Eyes,* 17.

33. Emily Lodge, *Lodge Women,* 144.

34. Beatty, *Rascal King,* 390.

35. John W. Crowley, *George Cabot Lodge,* 9.

36. William J. Miller, *Henry Cabot Lodge,* 14.

37. William J. Miller, *Henry Cabot Lodge,* 16.

38. William J. Miller, *Henry Cabot Lodge,* 16.

39. Zeiger, *Remarkable Henry Cabot Lodge,* 17.

40. Zeiger, *Remarkable Henry Cabot Lodge,* 18.

41. Zeiger, *Remarkable Henry Cabot Lodge,* 16.

42. Henry Cabot Lodge Jr. to John Davis Lodge, September 3, 1973, Box 200, John Davis Lodge Papers, Hoover Institution.

43. John W. Crowley to Henry Cabot Lodge Jr., July 22, 1969, Box 200, John Davis Lodge Papers, Hoover Institution.

44. Emily Lodge, *Lodge Women*, 245.

45. Blair, *Lodge in Vietnam*, 6.

46. Emily Lodge, *Lodge Women*, 249.

47. William J. Miller, *Henry Cabot Lodge*, 21–22.

48. Garraty, *Henry Cabot Lodge*, 271.

49. Hatch, *Lodges of Massachusetts*, 157.

50. William J. Miller, *Henry Cabot Lodge*, 24.

51. William J. Miller, *Henry Cabot Lodge*, 1.

52. Zeiger, *Remarkable Henry Cabot Lodge*, 20.

53. Hernon, *Profiles in Character*, 124.

54. Hatch, *Lodges of Massachusetts*, 159.

55. Hatch, *Lodges of Massachusetts*, 156.

56. Elsie Lee, *Henry Cabot Lodge*, 8.

57. Emily Lodge, *Lodge Women*, 24.

58. Emily Lodge, *Lodge Women*, 294.

59. Carlson, *K Blows Top*, 76.

60. William J. Miller, *Henry Cabot Lodge*, 30.

61. Hatch, *Lodges of Massachusetts*, 160–161.

62. Hatch, *Lodges of Massachusetts*, 161.

63. Hatch, *Lodges of Massachusetts*, 162.

64. Emily Lodge, *Lodge Women*, 306.

65. Hatch, *Lodges of Massachusetts*, 162.

66. Emily Lodge, *Lodge Women*, 304.

67. Hatch, *Lodges of Massachusetts*, 163.

68. Emily Lodge, *Lodge Women*, 324.

69. Emily Lodge, *Lodge Women*, 295.

70. William J. Miller, *Henry Cabot Lodge*, 36–37.

71. Hatch, *Lodges of Massachusetts*, 164.

72. Henry Cabot Lodge Jr., *Storm Has Many Eyes*, 25–26.

73. George Cabot Lodge, "The Education of George Lodge" (undated, unpublished memoir), Box 68, Folder 21, George C. Lodge Papers, Baker Library, Harvard Business School.

74. Stephen Hess, *America's Political Dynasties*, 472.

75. William J. Miller, *Henry Cabot Lodge*, 39.

76. William J. Miller, *Henry Cabot Lodge*, 24.

77. Amory, *Proper Bostonians*, 18.

78. Widenor, *Henry Cabot Lodge*, 245.

79. William J. Miller, *Henry Cabot Lodge*, 49.

80. Henry Cabot Lodge Jr., *Storm Has Many Eyes*, 26.

81. Excerpt from diary of John Mason Brown, August 31–September 1 and 2, 1923, Reel 2, Microfilm Edition, Henry Cabot Lodge, Jr. Papers II, Massachusetts Historical Society.

82. Emily Lodge, *Lodge Women*, 327.

83. William J. Miller, *Henry Cabot Lodge*, 45.

84. Notes, undated, Box 71, Neil Sheehan Papers, Manuscript Division, Library of Congress.

85. Garraty, *Henry Cabot Lodge*, 352.

86. Hernon, *Profiles in Character*, 130.

87. Garraty, *Henry Cabot Lodge*, 402.

88. Emily Lodge, *Lodge Women*, 14.

89. Whalen, *Kennedy versus Lodge*, 35.

90. William J. Miller, *Henry Cabot Lodge*, 54.

91. William J. Miller, *Henry Cabot Lodge*, 55.

92. Henry Cabot Lodge Jr., *Storm Has Many Eyes*, 27.

93. Theoharis, *Secret Files of J. Edgar Hoover*, 79.

94. Zeiger, *Remarkable Henry Cabot Lodge*, 23–24.

95. Employee Record, *Boston Evening Transcript*, Reel 2, Microfilm Edition, Henry Cabot Lodge, Jr. Papers II, Massachusetts Historical Society.

96. Elsie Lee, *Henry Cabot Lodge*, 34.

97. William J. Miller, *Henry Cabot Lodge*, 60.

98. Elsie Lee, *Henry Cabot Lodge*, 35.

99. Zeiger, *Remarkable Henry Cabot Lodge*, 24.

100. Excerpt from diary of John Mason Brown, August 31–September 1 and 2, 1923, Reel 2, Microfilm Edition, Henry Cabot Lodge, Jr. Papers II, Massachusetts Historical Society.

101. Elsie Lee, *Henry Cabot Lodge*, 36.

102. Zeiger, *Remarkable Henry Cabot Lodge*, 33.

103. Henry Cabot Lodge Jr. to Henry Cabot Lodge, December 15, 1923, Box 39, Henry Cabot Lodge, Jr. Papers I, Massachusetts Historical Society.

104. Excerpt from diary of John Mason Brown, August 31–September 1 and 2, 1923, Reel 2, Microfilm Edition, Henry Cabot Lodge, Jr. Papers II, Massachusetts Historical Society.

105. Henry Cabot Lodge Jr., *Storm Has Many Eyes*, 29.

106. O'Connor, *Boston Irish*, 206.

107. William J. Miller, *Henry Cabot Lodge*, 60.

108. Henry Cabot Lodge to Henry Cabot Lodge Jr., December 8, 1923, Box 39, Henry Cabot Lodge, Jr. Papers I, Massachusetts Historical Society.

109. Henry Cabot Lodge Jr. to Frank Bowker, January 31, 1924, Reel 11, Microfilm Edition, Henry Cabot Lodge, Jr. Papers II, Massachusetts Historical Society.

110. JMB's European diary, Venice, February 10, 1924, Reel 2, Microfilm Edition, Henry Cabot Lodge, Jr. Papers II, Massachusetts Historical Society. When William Miller was preparing his biography of Lodge in the mid-1960s, Brown was asked to comment on a galley. "Too bad, of course, that the shaming facts of the episode in Venice were not revealed, but I'm sure you kept them back to protect me—and thank God you did," he wrote to Lodge. John Mason Brown to Henry Cabot Lodge Jr., September 21, 1966, Reel 2, Microfilm Edition, Henry Cabot Lodge, Jr. Papers II, Massachusetts Historical Society.

111. William J. Miller, *Henry Cabot Lodge,* 63.

112. Emily Lodge, *Lodge Women,* 336.

113. Zeiger, *Remarkable Henry Cabot Lodge,* 26.

114. William J. Miller, *Henry Cabot Lodge,* 64.

115. William J. Miller, *Henry Cabot Lodge,* 65.

116. Edith Bolling Wilson to Henry Cabot Lodge, February 4, 1924, Box 39, Henry Cabot Lodge, Jr. Papers I, Massachusetts Historical Society.

117. Garraty, *Henry Cabot Lodge,* 423.

118. William J. Miller, *Henry Cabot Lodge,* 65.

119. Emily Lodge, *Lodge Women,* 337.

120. Zeiger, *Remarkable Henry Cabot Lodge,* 26.

121. Emily Lodge, *Lodge Women,* 337.

122. Stephen Hess, *America's Political Dynasties,* 472.

123. Emily Lodge, *Lodge Women,* 338.

124. Hatch, *Lodges of Massachusetts,* 155.

125. William J. Miller, *Henry Cabot Lodge,* 66.

126. Elsie Lee, *Henry Cabot Lodge,* 10.

127. Radio interview, Mr. Lodge, Friday, 2:45 [1936], Box 1, Henry Cabot Lodge, Jr. Papers I, Massachusetts Historical Society.

128. William J. Miller, *Henry Cabot Lodge,* 67.

129. Zeiger, *Remarkable Henry Cabot Lodge,* 33.

130. Henry Cabot Lodge Jr. to George H. Norton, August 4, 1926, Box 1, Henry Cabot Lodge, Jr. Papers I, Massachusetts Historical Society.

131. William J. Miller, *Henry Cabot Lodge,* 71.

132. "Some Random Memories by Henry Cabot Lodge," undated, Box 263, John Davis Lodge Papers, Hoover Institution.

133. Stimson and Bundy, *On Active Service,* xxii.

134. Henry Cabot Lodge Jr., *Storm Has Many Eyes,* 43.

135. Zeiger, *Remarkable Henry Cabot Lodge,* 68.

136. William Nalle to Henry Cabot Lodge Jr., June 17, 1931, Reel 17, Microfilm Edition, Henry Cabot Lodge, Jr. Papers II, Massachusetts Historical Society.

137. Efficiency Report—Lodge, Jr., Henry Cabot (0-188725), September 3, 1935, Reel 17, Microfilm Edition, Henry Cabot Lodge, Jr. Papers II, Massachusetts Historical Society.

138. Zeiger, *Remarkable Henry Cabot Lodge*, 69.

139. H. L. Mencken, *Thirty-Five Years of Newspaper Work* (Baltimore: Johns Hopkins University Press, 1994), 171.

140. "Some Random Memories by Henry Cabot Lodge," undated, Box 263, John Davis Lodge Papers, Hoover Institution.

141. Zeiger, *Remarkable Henry Cabot Lodge*, 27.

142. Itinerary for Mr. and Mrs. Henry Cabot Lodge, Jr., Box 40, Henry Cabot Lodge, Jr. Papers I, Massachusetts Historical Society.

143. Interview with Henry Cabot Lodge Jr., pt. 1 of 5, January 1, 1979, *Vietnam: A Television History*, WGBH Media Library and Archives.

144. Around the World Trip, 1928–1929, Diary, p. 95, Box 40, Henry Cabot Lodge, Jr. Papers I, Massachusetts Historical Society.

145. Henry Cabot Lodge, "Saigon," Box 40, Henry Cabot Lodge, Jr. Papers I, Massachusetts Historical Society.

146. Elsie Lee, *Henry Cabot Lodge*, 40–41.

147. Zeiger, *Remarkable Henry Cabot Lodge*, 28.

148. Interview with Henry Cabot Lodge Jr., pt. 1 of 5, January 1, 1979, *Vietnam: A Television History*, WGBH Media Library and Archives.

149. Henry Cabot Lodge Jr., *Cult of Weakness*, 137–138.

150. Henry Cabot Lodge Jr., *Cult of Weakness*, ix.

151. William J. Miller, *Henry Cabot Lodge*, 117.

152. Whalen, *Kennedy versus Lodge*, 38.

153. Zeiger, *Remarkable Henry Cabot Lodge*, 34–35.

## 2. First Political Steps

1. Hatch, *Lodges of Massachusetts*, 155.

2. Henry Cabot Lodge Jr., *Storm Has Many Eyes*, 30.

3. Beatty, *Rascal King*, 390.

4. Emily Lodge, *Lodge Women*, 350.

5. Elsie Lee, *Henry Cabot Lodge*, 38.

6. Zeiger, *Remarkable Henry Cabot Lodge*, 27.

7. George Cabot Lodge, "The Education of George Lodge" (undated, unpublished memoir), Box 68, Folder 21, George Cabot Lodge Papers, Baker Library, Harvard Business School.

8. Elsie Lee, *Henry Cabot Lodge*, 43.

9. Zeiger, *Remarkable Henry Cabot Lodge*, 42.

10. Whalen, *Kennedy versus Lodge*, 39.

11. Reel 1, Speeches, Writings, Etc., Microfilm Edition, Henry Cabot Lodge, Jr. Papers I, Massachusetts Historical Society.

12. Zeiger, *Remarkable Henry Cabot Lodge*, 43.

13. Zeiger, *Remarkable Henry Cabot Lodge*, 44.

14. Zeiger, *Remarkable Henry Cabot Lodge*, 44.

15. William J. Miller, *Henry Cabot Lodge*, 120.

16. William J. Miller, *Henry Cabot Lodge*, 119.

17. Zeiger, *Remarkable Henry Cabot Lodge*, 44.

18. Whalen, *Kennedy versus Lodge*, 38–39.

19. Henry Cabot Lodge Jr. to James Curley, February 3, 1935, Reel 3, Microfilm Edition, Henry Cabot Lodge, Jr. Papers II, Massachusetts Historical Society.

20. Zeiger, *Remarkable Henry Cabot Lodge*, 47.

21. Saltonstall, *Salty*, 45.

22. William J. Miller, *Henry Cabot Lodge*, 121.

23. Robert J. Watt to Henry Cabot Lodge Jr., March 6, 1935, Box 22, Henry Cabot Lodge, Jr. Papers I, Massachusetts Historical Society.

24. Zeiger, *Remarkable Henry Cabot Lodge*, 47–48.

25. Henry Cabot Lodge Jr. to Mathilda Frelinghuysen Davis Lodge, Tuesday [late 1935], Box 1, Henry Cabot Lodge, Jr. Papers I, Massachusetts Historical Society.

26. Reel 1, Speeches, Writings, Etc., Microfilm Edition, Henry Cabot Lodge, Jr. Papers I, Massachusetts Historical Society.

27. Joseph Alsop and William Kintner, "Player of Politics," undated, Box 93, Joseph Alsop and Stewart Alsop Papers, Manuscript Division, Library of Congress.

28. William J. Miller, *Henry Cabot Lodge*, 205.

29. William J. Miller, *Henry Cabot Lodge*, 121.

30. William J. Miller, *Henry Cabot Lodge*, 124–125.

31. Henry Cabot Lodge Jr. to Mathilda Frelinghuysen Davis Lodge, December 20, 1935, Box 1, Henry Cabot Lodge, Jr. Papers I, Massachusetts Historical Society.

32. Zeiger, *Remarkable Henry Cabot Lodge*, 49.

33. Zeiger, *Remarkable Henry Cabot Lodge*, 48–49.

34. William J. Miller, *Henry Cabot Lodge*, 126–127.

35. Whalen, *Kennedy versus Lodge*, 40.

36. Barbrook, *God Save the Commonwealth*, 24.

37. Garrison Nelson, *John William McCormack*, 337.

38. Saltonstall, *Autobiography*, 95.

39. Joseph Alsop and William Kintner, "Player of Politics," undated, Box 93, Joseph Alsop and Stewart Alsop Papers, Manuscript Division, Library of Congress.

40. Cutler, *No Time for Rest*, 134.

41. Whalen, *Kennedy versus Lodge*, 41.

42. Reel 1, Speeches, Writings, Etc., Microfilm Edition, Henry Cabot Lodge, Jr. Papers I, Massachusetts Historical Society.

43. William J. Miller, *Henry Cabot Lodge*, 126.

44. Lodge for Senator Committee, July 9, 1936, Box 1, Henry Cabot Lodge, Jr. Papers I, Massachusetts Historical Society.

45. Zeiger, *Remarkable Henry Cabot Lodge*, 50.

46. Whalen, *Kennedy versus Lodge*, 40.

47. Zeiger, *Remarkable Henry Cabot Lodge*, 51.

48. William J. Miller, *Henry Cabot Lodge*, 128.

49. William J. Miller, *Henry Cabot Lodge*, 128.

50. Zeiger, *Remarkable Henry Cabot Lodge*, 51.

51. William J. Miller, *Henry Cabot Lodge*, 134.

52. Beatty, *Rascal King*, 389–390.

53. Author interview with Charles W. Colson, December 13, 2007, telephone and email.

54. Whalen, *Kennedy versus Lodge*, 40.

55. Zeiger, *Remarkable Henry Cabot Lodge*, 52.

56. William J. Miller, *Henry Cabot Lodge*, 129.

57. Beatty, *Rascal King*, 374.

58. Beatty, *Rascal King*, 393.

59. Whalen, *Kennedy versus Lodge*, 41.

60. Curley, *I'd Do It Again*, 297–298.

61. Whalen, *Kennedy versus Lodge*, 42.

62. Curley, *I'd Do It Again*, 298.

63. Beatty, *Rascal King*, 393.

64. Zeiger, *Remarkable Henry Cabot Lodge*, 52.

65. William J. Miller, *Henry Cabot Lodge*, 131.

66. Statement of Representative Henry Cabot Lodge Jr., September 24, 1936, Box 1, Henry Cabot Lodge, Jr. Papers I, Massachusetts Historical Society.

67. Whalen, *Kennedy versus Lodge*, 42.

68. Beatty, *Rascal King*, 397.

69. Zeiger, *Remarkable Henry Cabot Lodge*, 54.

70. Henry Cabot Lodge Jr., *Storm Has Many Eyes*, 47.

71. William J. Miller, *Henry Cabot Lodge*, 134.

## 3. U.S. Senate

1. Henry Cabot Lodge Jr. to John Davis Lodge, March 18, [1941?], Box 9, John Davis Lodge Papers, Hoover Institution.

2. Caro, *Master of the Senate*, 89.

3. "Some Random Memories by Henry Cabot Lodge," undated, Box 263, John Davis Lodge Papers, Hoover Institution.

4. Interview with Henry Cabot Lodge Jr., pt. 1 of 5, January 1, 1979, *Vietnam: A Television History*, WGBH Media Library and Archives.

5. Henry Cabot Lodge Jr. to Edward Brooke, March 29, 1967, Reel 2, Microfilm Edition, Henry Cabot Lodge, Jr. Papers II, Massachusetts Historical Society.

6. Whalen, *Kennedy versus Lodge*, 43.

7. Henry Cabot Lodge Jr. to Joe Alsop, February 17, 1932, Reel 1, Microfilm Edition, Henry Cabot Lodge, Jr. Papers II, Massachusetts Historical Society.

8. Joseph Alsop and William Kintner, "Player of Politics," undated, Box 93, Joseph Alsop and Stewart Alsop Papers, Manuscript Division, Library of Congress.

9. Speech of Honorable H. C. Lodge Jr., at Republican Club Dinner in Boston on Saturday evening, January 22, 1938, Box 9, John Davis Lodge Papers, Hoover Institution.

10. Zeiger, *Remarkable Henry Cabot Lodge*, 55.

11. Whalen, *Kennedy versus Lodge*, 44.

12. William J. Miller, *Henry Cabot Lodge*, 135.

13. Johns, *Vietnam's Second Front*, 12.

14. Bruce Allen Murphy, *Wild Bill*, 174–175.

15. Zeiger, *Remarkable Henry Cabot Lodge*, 57.

16. Joseph Alsop and William Kintner, "Player of Politics," undated, Box 93, Joseph Alsop and Stewart Alsop Papers, Manuscript Division, Library of Congress.

17. Zeiger, *Remarkable Henry Cabot Lodge*, 56.

18. William J. Miller, *Henry Cabot Lodge*, 136.

19. Zeiger, *Remarkable Henry Cabot Lodge*, 57.

20. Henry Cabot Lodge Jr., *Storm Has Many Eyes*, 56.

21. Zeiger, *Remarkable Henry Cabot Lodge*, 58.

22. Zeiger, *Remarkable Henry Cabot Lodge*, 59.

23. Stephen Hess, *America's Political Dynasties*, 477.

24. Zeiger, *Remarkable Henry Cabot Lodge*, 59.

25. Zeiger, *Remarkable Henry Cabot Lodge*, 60.

26. William J. Miller, *Henry Cabot Lodge*, 138.

27. Stephen Hess, *America's Political Dynasties*, 477.

28. Zeiger, *Remarkable Henry Cabot Lodge*, 61.

29. Saltonstall, *Salty*, 62.

30. Zeiger, *Remarkable Henry Cabot Lodge*, 62.

31. Zeiger, *Remarkable Henry Cabot Lodge*, 63.

32. Elsie Lee, *Henry Cabot Lodge*, 38.

33. Emily Lodge, *Lodge Women*, 341.

34. Beatty, *Rascal King*, 392.

35. George Cabot Lodge, "The Education of George Lodge" (undated, unpublished memoir), Box 89, Folder 1, George Cabot Lodge Papers, Baker Library, Harvard Business School.

36. Zeiger, *Remarkable Henry Cabot Lodge*, 63.

37. Whalen, *Kennedy versus Lodge*, 45.

38. Whalen, *Kennedy versus Lodge,* 45–46.

39. Notes of conversation with Senator Bridges, March 16, 1948, Reel 17, Microfilm Edition, Henry Cabot Lodge, Jr. Papers II, Massachusetts Historical Society.

40. Saltonstall, *Autobiography,* 27.

41. Henry Cabot Lodge Jr., *Storm Has Many Eyes,* 56.

42. Zeiger, *Remarkable Henry Cabot Lodge,* 64.

43. Zeiger, *Remarkable Henry Cabot Lodge,* 65–66.

44. Henry Cabot Lodge Jr. to J. K. Herr, October 10, 1939, Reel 17, Microfilm Edition, Henry Cabot Lodge, Jr. Papers II, Massachusetts Historical Society.

45. Reel 2, Speeches, Writings, Etc., Microfilm Edition, Henry Cabot Lodge, Jr. Papers I, Massachusetts Historical Society.

46. Whalen, *Kennedy versus Lodge,* 45.

47. Zeiger, *Remarkable Henry Cabot Lodge,* 64.

48. Gallup, *Gallup Poll,* 1:46.

49. Saltonstall, *Salty,* 75.

50. "Some Random Memories by Henry Cabot Lodge," undated, Box 263, John Davis Lodge Papers, Hoover Institution.

51. William J. Miller, *Henry Cabot Lodge,* 140.

52. Zeiger, *Remarkable Henry Cabot Lodge,* 64–65.

53. Whalen, *Kennedy versus Lodge,* 47.

54. William J. Miller, *Henry Cabot Lodge,* 141.

55. William J. Miller, *Henry Cabot Lodge,* 141.

56. Whalen, *Kennedy versus Lodge,* 46.

57. "Personal Assessment of the Roosevelt Years, United Nations, New York, Wednesday, June 16, 1982," Francis O. Wilcox Papers, University of Iowa.

58. William J. Miller, *Henry Cabot Lodge,* 141.

59. "The Campaign to Win the Republican Nomination for Dwight D. Eisenhower," undated, Box 23, Administration Series, Ann Whitman File, Papers as President, Dwight D. Eisenhower Presidential Library.

60. William J. Miller, *Henry Cabot Lodge,* 141–142.

61. William J. Miller, *Henry Cabot Lodge,* 142.

62. Whalen, *Kennedy versus Lodge,* 46.

63. Zeiger, *Remarkable Henry Cabot Lodge,* 66.

64. Reel 2, Speeches, Writings, Etc., Microfilm Edition, Henry Cabot Lodge, Jr. Papers I, Massachusetts Historical Society.

## 4. World War II

1. William J. Miller, *Henry Cabot Lodge,* 12.

2. Memorandum for Roberta Burrows, January 27, 1944, President's Personal File 6207–6254, Franklin D. Roosevelt Presidential Library.

3. Memorandum—H. C. Lodge, January 18, 1971, Reel 17b, Microfilm Edition, Henry Cabot Lodge, Jr. Papers II, Massachusetts Historical Society.

4. Memorandum—H. C. Lodge, January 18, 1971, Reel 17b, Microfilm Edition, Henry Cabot Lodge, Jr. Papers II, Massachusetts Historical Society.

5. Memorandum—H. C. Lodge, January 18, 1971, Reel 17b, Microfilm Edition, Henry Cabot Lodge, Jr. Papers II, Massachusetts Historical Society.

6. Memorandum—H. C. Lodge, January 18, 1971, Reel 17b, Microfilm Edition, Henry Cabot Lodge, Jr. Papers II, Massachusetts Historical Society.

7. William J. Miller, *Henry Cabot Lodge*, 2–3.

8. Pruden, *Conditional Partners*, 33.

9. Henry Cabot Lodge Jr. to Division of Bookkeeping and Warrants, Treasury Department, April 18, 1942, Reel 17, Microfilm Edition, Henry Cabot Lodge, Jr. Papers II, Massachusetts Historical Society.

10. Hatch, *Lodges of Massachusetts*, 216.

11. Willis Crittenberger to Henry Cabot Lodge Jr., January 14, 1942, Reel 17, Microfilm Edition, Henry Cabot Lodge, Jr. Papers II, Massachusetts Historical Society.

12. William J. Miller, *Henry Cabot Lodge*, 142.

13. Nasaw, *Patriarch*, 545.

14. Garrison Nelson, *John William McCormack*, 288.

15. Thomas L. Hughes, *Anecdotage*, 50.

16. Stephen Hess, *America's Political Dynasties*, 478.

17. Hersh, *Dark Side of Camelot*, 39.

18. William J. Miller, *Henry Cabot Lodge*, 143.

19. William J. Miller, *Henry Cabot Lodge*, 143.

20. "Some Random Memories by Henry Cabot Lodge," undated, Box 263, John Davis Lodge Papers, Hoover Institution.

21. Henry Cabot Lodge Jr. to Dwight Eisenhower, April 29, 1942, and Dwight Eisenhower to Henry Cabot Lodge Jr., May 5, 1942, Box 72, Office of Dwight Eisenhower, Principal Files, Pre-presidential Papers, Dwight D. Eisenhower Presidential Library.

22. Zeiger, *Remarkable Henry Cabot Lodge*, 70.

23. "The Campaign to Win the Republican Nomination for Dwight D. Eisenhower," undated, Box 23, Administration Series, Ann Whitman File, Papers as President, Dwight D. Eisenhower Presidential Library.

24. William J. Miller, *Henry Cabot Lodge*, 145.

25. Memorandum from War Department to Officers Involved, May 15, 1942, Reel 17, Microfilm Edition, Henry Cabot Lodge, Jr. Papers II, Massachusetts Historical Society.

26. Hatch, *Lodges of Massachusetts*, 216.

27. William J. Miller, *Henry Cabot Lodge*, 144.

28. Zeiger, *Remarkable Henry Cabot Lodge*, 71.

29. Zeiger, *Remarkable Henry Cabot Lodge*, 71.

30. Harper, *Battle for North Africa*, 8–9.

31. Hatch, *Lodges of Massachusetts*, 217.

32. Zeiger, *Remarkable Henry Cabot Lodge*, 71.

33. William J. Miller, *Henry Cabot Lodge*, 146.

34. Legation of the United States of America, Office of the Military Attaché, Cairo, Egypt, undated, Reel 17, Microfilm Edition, Henry Cabot Lodge, Jr. Papers II, Massachusetts Historical Society.

35. Whalen, *Kennedy versus Lodge*, 47.

36. Zeiger, *Remarkable Henry Cabot Lodge*, 73.

37. William J. Miller, *Henry Cabot Lodge*, 148.

38. Harper, *Battle for North Africa*, 4.

39. Wheeler, *Jacob I. Devers*, 317.

40. William J. Miller, *Henry Cabot Lodge*, 148.

41. Dwight Eisenhower to Henry Cabot Lodge Jr., July 26, 1942, Box 72, Office of Dwight Eisenhower, Principal Files, Pre-presidential Papers, Dwight D. Eisenhower Presidential Library.

42. Zeiger, *Remarkable Henry Cabot Lodge*, 74.

43. William J. Miller, *Henry Cabot Lodge*, 144.

44. Henry Stimson to Henry Cabot Lodge Jr., July 7, 1942, Reel 17, Microfilm Edition, Henry Cabot Lodge, Jr. Papers II, Massachusetts Historical Society.

45. Whalen, *Kennedy versus Lodge*, 47.

46. Zeiger, *Remarkable Henry Cabot Lodge*, 75–76.

47. Whalen, *Kennedy versus Lodge*, 48.

48. William J. Miller, *Henry Cabot Lodge*, 149.

49. Whalen, *Kennedy versus Lodge*, 47.

50. S. G. Henry to Henry Cabot Lodge Jr., July 10, 1942, Reel 17, Microfilm Edition, Henry Cabot Lodge, Jr. Papers II, Massachusetts Historical Society.

51. Whalen, *Kennedy versus Lodge*, 49.

52. Zeiger, *Remarkable Henry Cabot Lodge*, 77–78.

53. Henry Cabot Lodge Jr. to Dwight Eisenhower, January 7, 1943, Box 72, Office of Dwight Eisenhower, Principal Files, Pre-presidential Papers, Dwight D. Eisenhower Presidential Library.

54. Dwight Eisenhower to Henry Stimson, August 14, 1943, in Dwight D. Eisenhower, *Papers*, 2:1182.

55. William J. Miller, *Henry Cabot Lodge*, 155.

56. Henry Cabot Lodge Jr. to Winston Churchill, October 8, 1956, CHUR2/527A-B, Winston Churchill Papers, University of Cambridge.

57. William J. Miller, *Henry Cabot Lodge*, 158.

58. "The Campaign to Win the Republican Nomination for Dwight D. Eisenhower," undated, Box 23, Administration Series, Ann Whitman File, Papers as President, Dwight D. Eisenhower Presidential Library.

59. William J. Miller, *Henry Cabot Lodge*, 159–160.

60. Zeiger, *Remarkable Henry Cabot Lodge*, 79.

61. Zeiger, *Remarkable Henry Cabot Lodge*, 80.

62. William J. Miller, *Henry Cabot Lodge*, 152.

63. William J. Miller, *Henry Cabot Lodge*, 169.

64. Zeiger, *Remarkable Henry Cabot Lodge*, 81.

65. William J. Miller, *Henry Cabot Lodge*, 154.

66. Elsie Lee, *Henry Cabot Lodge*, 58.

67. William J. Miller, *Henry Cabot Lodge*, 171.

68. Memorandum—H. C. Lodge, January 18, 1971, Reel 17b, Microfilm Edition, Henry Cabot Lodge, Jr. Papers II, Massachusetts Historical Society.

69. William J. Miller, *Henry Cabot Lodge*, 172.

70. Memorandum from War Department, Adjutant General's Office, to Henry Cabot Lodge Jr., February 3, 1944, Reel 17, Microfilm Edition, Henry Cabot Lodge, Jr. Papers II, Massachusetts Historical Society.

71. Henry Cabot Lodge Jr., *Storm Has Many Eyes*, 57.

72. Henry Cabot Lodge Jr., *Storm Has Many Eyes*, 59.

73. Zeiger, *Remarkable Henry Cabot Lodge*, 82.

74. Zeiger, *Remarkable Henry Cabot Lodge*, 82.

75. William J. Miller, *Henry Cabot Lodge*, 4–5.

76. Memorandum from War Department, Adjutant General's Office, to Officers, February 9, 1944, Reel 17, Microfilm Edition, Henry Cabot Lodge, Jr. Papers II, Massachusetts Historical Society.

77. General Orders, March 19, 1944, Reel 17, Microfilm Edition, Henry Cabot Lodge, Jr. Papers II, Massachusetts Historical Society.

78. Whalen, *Kennedy versus Lodge*, 49.

79. Staff Conference by the Corps Commander, Major General Willis D. Crittenberger, IV Corps in the Field, Lake Averno, Italy, April 11, 1944, Reel 17, Microfilm Edition, Henry Cabot Lodge, Jr. Papers II, Massachusetts Historical Society.

80. Special Orders, Headquarters, 23rd General Hospital, United States Army, April 24, 1944, Reel 17, Microfilm Edition, Henry Cabot Lodge, Jr. Papers II, Massachusetts Historical Society.

81. Willis Crittenberger to Wilton Persons, April 25, 1944, Reel 17b, Microfilm Edition, Henry Cabot Lodge, Jr. Papers II, Massachusetts Historical Society.

82. William J. Miller, *Henry Cabot Lodge*, 5.

83. Willis Crittenberger to Henry Cabot Lodge Jr., May 2, 1944, Reel 17, Microfilm Edition, Henry Cabot Lodge, Jr. Papers II, Massachusetts Historical Society.

84. Henry Cabot Lodge Jr. to Wilton Persons, June 6, 1944, Reel 17b, Microfilm Edition, Henry Cabot Lodge, Jr. Papers II, Massachusetts Historical Society.

85. Henry Cabot Lodge Jr. to Robert Cutler, June 12, 1944, Reel 17b, Microfilm Edition, Henry Cabot Lodge, Jr. Papers II, Massachusetts Historical Society.

86. Letter Orders for Major Henry C. Lodge, Jr. 0188725, GSC, June 28, 1944, Reel 17, Microfilm Edition, Henry Cabot Lodge, Jr. Papers II, Massachusetts Historical Society.

87. Special Orders, Headquarters, North African Theater of Operations, United States Army, July 4, 1944, Reel 17, Microfilm Edition, Henry Cabot Lodge, Jr. Papers II, Massachusetts Historical Society.

88. Jacob Devers to Willis Crittenberger, July 29, 1944, Reel 17, Microfilm Edition, Henry Cabot Lodge, Jr. Papers II, Massachusetts Historical Society.

89. Special Orders, Headquarters Fifty Army, August 3, 1944, Reel 17, Microfilm Edition, Henry Cabot Lodge, Jr. Papers II, Massachusetts Historical Society.

90. Memorandum from Headquarters IV Corps to Henry Cabot Lodge Jr., August 7, 1944, Reel 17, Microfilm Edition, Henry Cabot Lodge, Jr. Papers II, Massachusetts Historical Society.

91. William J. Miller, *Henry Cabot Lodge,* 174–175.

92. Headquarters Final, Senior Liaison Office, August 14, 1944, Reel 17, Microfilm Edition, Henry Cabot Lodge, Jr. Papers II, Massachusetts Historical Society.

93. Wheeler, *Jacob I. Devers,* 317.

94. Zeiger, *Remarkable Henry Cabot Lodge,* 84.

95. Thomas Griess, interview with Henry Cabot Lodge, 1968, tape 5, p. 17, General Thomas E. Griess Research Collection, York County History Center.

96. Wheeler, *Jacob I. Devers,* 465.

97. Notes on Conversation with General de Lattre, August 21, 1944, Reel 17, Microfilm Edition, Henry Cabot Lodge, Jr. Papers II, Massachusetts Historical Society.

98. Salisbury-Jones, *So Full a Glory,* 143.

99. Undated Notes, Reel 3, Microfilm Edition, Henry Cabot Lodge, Jr. Papers II, Massachusetts Historical Society.

100. William J. Miller, *Henry Cabot Lodge,* 174–175.

101. Memorandum from Henry Cabot Lodge Jr. to Jacob Devers, August 24, 1944, Reel 17, Microfilm Edition, Henry Cabot Lodge, Jr. Papers II, Massachusetts Historical Society.

102. Undated Notes, Reel 3, Microfilm Edition, Henry Cabot Lodge, Jr. Papers II, Massachusetts Historical Society.

103. Wheeler, *Jacob I. Devers,* 348.

104. William J. Miller, *Henry Cabot Lodge,* 176.

105. Conversation with General de Lattre at Luncheon Being Given in His Honor, September 8, 1944, Reel 17, Microfilm Edition, Henry Cabot Lodge, Jr. Papers II, Massachusetts Historical Society.

106. Notes of Conversation with General de Lattre, October 6, 1944, Reel 17, Microfilm Edition, Henry Cabot Lodge, Jr. Papers II, Massachusetts Historical Society.

107. William J. Miller, *Henry Cabot Lodge,* 176–177.

108. "Some Random Memories by Henry Cabot Lodge," undated, Box 263, John Davis Lodge Papers, Hoover Institution.

109. William J. Miller, *Henry Cabot Lodge*, 177.

110. Notes on American Command of Foreign Armies and Army Detachments, August 18, 1945, Reel 17, Microfilm Edition, Henry Cabot Lodge, Jr. Papers II, Massachusetts Historical Society.

111. Salisbury-Jones, *So Full a Glory*, 182.

112. William J. Miller, *Henry Cabot Lodge*, 178.

113. Note on the Situation of the II Army Corps on December 15, 1944, Reel 17, Microfilm Edition, Henry Cabot Lodge, Jr. Papers II, Massachusetts Historical Society.

114. William J. Miller, *Henry Cabot Lodge*, 179–180.

115. "The Campaign to Win the Republican Nomination for Dwight D. Eisenhower," undated, Box 23, Administration Series, Ann Whitman File, Papers as President of the United States, Dwight D. Eisenhower Presidential Library.

116. Narrative of Lt. Col. Henry Cabot Lodge, Jr., Former U.S. Senator from Massachusetts, Chief of Liaison Section 6th Army Group, on the German Capitulation on May 5, Reel 17, Microfilm Edition, Henry Cabot Lodge, Jr. Papers II, Massachusetts Historical Society.

117. William J. Miller, *Henry Cabot Lodge*, 180–181.

118. Narrative of Lt. Col. Henry Cabot Lodge, Jr., Former U.S. Senator from Massachusetts, Chief of Liaison Section 6th Army Group, on the German Capitulation on May 5, Reel 17, Microfilm Edition, Henry Cabot Lodge, Jr. Papers II, Massachusetts Historical Society.

119. John Davis Lodge to Henry Cabot Lodge Jr., November 20, 1945, Box 12, John Davis Lodge Papers, Hoover Institution.

120. William J. Miller, *Henry Cabot Lodge*, 183.

121. Salisbury-Jones, *So Full a Glory*, 169.

122. Cable from Bradley to 6th Army Group, June 25, 1945, Reel 17, Microfilm Edition, Henry Cabot Lodge, Jr. Papers II, Massachusetts Historical Society.

123. Cable from IV Corps Crittenberg to 6th Army Group to Lt. Col. H. C. Lodge, July 2, 1945, Reel 17, Microfilm Edition, Henry Cabot Lodge, Jr. Papers II, Massachusetts Historical Society.

124. Memorandum from the Adjutant General's Office, War Department, to Henry Cabot Lodge Jr., August 20, 1945, Reel 17, Microfilm Edition, Henry Cabot Lodge, Jr. Papers II, Massachusetts Historical Society.

125. Special Orders, Army Service Forces, First Service Command, War Department Separation Center, October 8, 1945, Reel 17, Microfilm Edition, Henry Cabot Lodge, Jr. Papers II, Massachusetts Historical Society.

126. Elsie Lee, *Henry Cabot Lodge*, 62.

127. Zeiger, *Remarkable Henry Cabot Lodge*, 86.

## 5. Return to the Senate

1. William J. Miller, *Henry Cabot Lodge,* 184–185.

2. Robert Bradford to Henry Cabot Lodge Jr., February 19, 1946, Reel 2, Microfilm Edition, Henry Cabot Lodge, Jr. Papers II, Massachusetts Historical Society.

3. William J. Miller, *Henry Cabot Lodge,* 185.

4. John Davis Lodge to Henry Cabot Lodge Jr., June 13, 1946, Box 21, John Davis Lodge Papers, Hoover Institution.

5. Mason Sears, "Advantages If You Do Run," 1946, Box 1, Henry Cabot Lodge, Jr. Papers I, Massachusetts Historical Society.

6. William J. Miller, *Henry Cabot Lodge,* 185–186.

7. Whalen, *Kennedy versus Lodge,* 52.

8. William J. Miller, *Henry Cabot Lodge,* 185.

9. Interview with Dean Rusk, June 8, 1982, *Vietnam: A Television History,* WGBH Media Library and Archives.

10. Whalen, *Kennedy versus Lodge,* 51.

11. Conversation with Walsh, Algonquin Club, April 20, 1946, Box 1, Henry Cabot Lodge, Jr. Papers I, Massachusetts Historical Society.

12. Whalen, *Kennedy versus Lodge,* 52.

13. William J. Miller, *Henry Cabot Lodge,* 186.

14. Zeiger, *Remarkable Henry Cabot Lodge,* 87.

15. Zeiger, *Remarkable Henry Cabot Lodge,* 88.

16. Zeiger, *Remarkable Henry Cabot Lodge,* 88.

17. William J. Miller, *Henry Cabot Lodge,* 188.

18. Vandenberg, *Private Papers of Senator Vandenberg,* 333.

19. Zeiger, *Remarkable Henry Cabot Lodge,* 91.

20. Patterson, *Mr. Republican,* 339.

21. William J. Miller, *Henry Cabot Lodge,* 189.

22. William J. Miller, *Henry Cabot Lodge,* 190.

23. William J. Miller, *Henry Cabot Lodge,* 191–192.

24. Whalen, *Kennedy versus Lodge,* 53.

25. Steil, *Marshall Plan,* 373.

26. Confidential Folder, February 7, 1950, Reel 17, Microfilm Edition, Henry Cabot Lodge, Jr. Papers II, Massachusetts Historical Society.

27. Henry Cabot Lodge Jr. to Arthur H. Vandenberg, Confidential, October 10, 1947, Correspondence, Microfilm, Reel 4, Arthur H. Vandenberg Papers, Bentley Historical Library, University of Michigan.

28. Steil, *Marshall Plan,* 228.

29. William J. Miller, *Henry Cabot Lodge,* 192.

30. Henry Cabot Lodge Jr., *Storm Has Many Eyes,* 61.

31. William J. Miller, *Henry Cabot Lodge,* 198.

32. Henry Cabot Lodge Jr., *Storm Has Many Eyes*, 62.

33. William J. Miller, *Henry Cabot Lodge*, 188.

34. "Commission on Organization of the Executive Branch of the Government," Series 5, Box III, Folder 17, Thomas E. Dewey Papers, Rare Books and Special Collections, University of Rochester.

35. Henry Cabot Lodge Jr., *Storm Has Many Eyes*, 64.

36. For more information on these various proposals, see Box 13, Hoover Commission I, Herbert Hoover Presidential Library.

37. Herbert Hoover to Henry Cabot Lodge Jr., December 21, 1962, Reel 7, Microfilm Edition, Henry Cabot Lodge, Jr. Papers II, Massachusetts Historical Society.

38. Vandenberg, *Private Papers of Senator Vandenberg*, 427.

39. Thomas Dewey to Henry Cabot Lodge Jr., July 7, 1948, Series 5, Box III, Folder 17, Thomas E. Dewey Papers, Rare Books and Special Collections, University of Rochester.

40. Henry Cabot Lodge Jr. to Dwight Eisenhower, March 27, 1956, Box 24, Administration Series, Ann Whitman File, Papers as President, Dwight D. Eisenhower Presidential Library.

41. Henry Cabot Lodge Jr. to John Mason Brown, July 8, 1948, Reel 2, Microfilm Edition, Henry Cabot Lodge, Jr. Papers II, Massachusetts Historical Society.

42. Whalen, *Kennedy versus Lodge*, 56.

43. Meijer, *Arthur Vandenberg*, 323.

44. William J. Miller, *Henry Cabot Lodge*, 198–199.

45. Vandenberg, *Private Papers of Senator Vandenberg*, 428.

46. Henry Cabot Lodge Jr. to Thomas Dewey, July 7, 1948, Series 5, Box III, Folder 17, Thomas E. Dewey Papers, Rare Books and Special Collections, University of Rochester.

47. Richard Norton Smith, *Thomas E. Dewey*, 468.

48. Taft, *Foreign Policy for Americans*, 5–6.

49. Whalen, *Kennedy versus Lodge*, 71.

50. William J. Miller, *Henry Cabot Lodge*, 200.

51. Zeiger, *Remarkable Henry Cabot Lodge*, 92–93.

52. William J. Miller, *Henry Cabot Lodge*, 190.

53. Henry Cabot Lodge Jr. to Bert Miller, March 21, 1949, Box 15, Henry Cabot Lodge, Jr. Papers I, Massachusetts Historical Society.

54. Henry Cabot Lodge Jr. to William Bullitt, April 5, 1948, Box 50, William C. Bullitt Papers, Yale University.

55. "Roosevelt for Plan to Change Vote Law," *New York Times*, March 28, 1934.

56. Henry Cabot Lodge Jr. to T. Jefferson Coolidge, July 21, 1948, Box 1, Coolidge T. Jefferson Papers, Franklin D. Roosevelt Presidential Library.

57. Whalen, *Kennedy versus Lodge*, 54.

58. *Congressional Record*, January 30, 1950, p. 1298.

59. Taft, *Papers*, 4:51.

60. Henry Cabot Lodge Jr. to Robert A. Taft, February 25, 1949, Box 711, Robert A. Taft Papers, Manuscript Division, Library of Congress.

61. Telegram from Basil Brewer to Robert A. Taft, May 30, 1949, Box 711, Robert A. Taft Papers, Manuscript Division, Library of Congress.

62. Confidential Journal, May 5, 1950, Reel 17, Microfilm Edition, Henry Cabot Lodge, Jr. Papers II, Massachusetts Historical Society.

63. Homer Ferguson to Robert A. Taft, January 25, 1950, Box 711, Robert A. Taft Papers, Manuscript Division, Library of Congress.

64. William J. Miller, *Henry Cabot Lodge*, 191.

65. Nathan E. Cowan to members of Congress, March 3, 1950, Box 13, Franklin D. Roosevelt, Jr. Papers, Franklin D. Roosevelt Presidential Library.

66. Henry Cabot Lodge Jr. to William F. Carney, August 16, 1954, Box 30, Maxwell Rabb Papers, Dwight D. Eisenhower Presidential Library.

67. Henry Cabot Lodge Jr., *Storm Has Many Eyes*, 67.

68. Meijer, *Arthur Vandenberg*, 320.

69. Finley, *Delaying the Dream*, 122.

70. Whalen, *Kennedy versus Lodge*, 55.

71. William J. Miller, *Henry Cabot Lodge*, 201.

72. Memorandum of Conversation with Vandenberg, November 7, 1948, Reel 17, Microfilm Edition, Henry Cabot Lodge, Jr. Papers II, Massachusetts Historical Society.

73. Henry Cabot Lodge Jr., *Storm Has Many Eyes*, 72.

74. William J. Miller, *Henry Cabot Lodge*, 202–203.

75. Memorandum for Confidential Journal, 1949, Reel 17, Microfilm Edition, Henry Cabot Lodge, Jr. Papers II, Massachusetts Historical Society.

76. "Some Random Memories by Henry Cabot Lodge," undated, Box 263, John Davis Lodge Papers, Hoover Institution.

77. John Davis Lodge to Henry Cabot Lodge Jr., December 5, 1985, Box 271, John Davis Lodge Papers, Hoover Institution.

78. "Some Random Memories by Henry Cabot Lodge," undated, Box 263, John Davis Lodge Papers, Hoover Institution.

79. John Davis Lodge to Henry Cabot Lodge Jr., December 5, 1985, Box 271, John Davis Lodge Papers, Hoover Institution.

80. "Some Random Memories by Henry Cabot Lodge," undated, Box 263, John Davis Lodge Papers, Hoover Institution.

81. Confidential Journal, May 1, 1951, Reel 17, Microfilm Edition, Henry Cabot Lodge, Jr. Papers II, Massachusetts Historical Society.

82. Memorandum from Henry Cabot Lodge Jr. to John Foster Dulles, June 20, 1955, Reel 4, Microfilm Edition, Henry Cabot Lodge, Jr. Papers II, Massachusetts Historical Society.

83. William J. Miller, *Henry Cabot Lodge*, 203.

84. William J. Miller, *Henry Cabot Lodge,* 204.

85. William J. Miller, *Henry Cabot Lodge,* 205.

86. Gaddis, *Strategies of Containment,* 112.

87. United States Department of State, *History of the Bureau,* 132.

88. Theodore Francis Green and Henry Cabot Lodge Jr. to Carlisle H. Humelsine, April 2, 1951, Box 18, Henry Cabot Lodge, Jr. Papers I, Massachusetts Historical Society.

89. McLellan, *Dean Acheson,* 228.

90. Taft, *Papers,* 4:265.

91. William J. Miller, *Henry Cabot Lodge,* 207.

92. McCullough, *Truman,* 773–774.

93. Henry Cabot Lodge Jr. to William Bullitt, February 27, 1950, Box 50, William C. Bullitt Papers, Yale University.

94. Willis Crittenberger to Henry Cabot Lodge Jr., March 7, 1952, Box 13, Henry Cabot Lodge, Jr. Papers I, Massachusetts Historical Society.

95. Deputies' Meeting, Wednesday, October 1, 1952, CIA-RDP80B01676R0023 00110057-5, CREST (CIA Records Search Tool), National Archives and Records Administration.

96. Memorandum of Conversation with Mr. Moch, November 25, 1950, Reel 17, Microfilm Edition, Henry Cabot Lodge, Jr. Papers II, Massachusetts Historical Society.

97. Large, *Germans to the Front,* 105–106.

98. Meeting with French Assemblymen, undated, Reel 17, Microfilm Edition, Henry Cabot Lodge, Jr. Papers II, Massachusetts Historical Society.

99. Wadsworth, *Glass House,* 126.

100. McLellan, *Dean Acheson,* 281.

101. Memorandum for Confidential Journal, September 5, 1950, Reel 17, Microfilm Edition, Henry Cabot Lodge, Jr. Papers II, Massachusetts Historical Society.

102. Zeiger, *Remarkable Henry Cabot Lodge,* 96.

103. Henry Cabot Lodge Jr. to Richard Storey, May 23, 1951, Reel 2, Microfilm Edition, Henry Cabot Lodge, Jr. Papers II, Massachusetts Historical Society.

104. Memorandum for Confidential Journal, September 5, 1950, Reel 17, Microfilm Edition, Henry Cabot Lodge, Jr. Papers II, Massachusetts Historical Society.

105. Patrick Murphy Malin to Henry Cabot Lodge Jr., June 13, 1950, Box 15, Henry Cabot Lodge, Jr. Papers I, Massachusetts Historical Society.

106. Zeiger, *Remarkable Henry Cabot Lodge,* 98–99.

107. William J. Miller, *Henry Cabot Lodge,* 208.

## 6. Drafting Ike

1. Telephone Conversation Regarding Eisenhower Visit on June 9, 1950, Lodge-Eisenhower Correspondence, Dwight D. Eisenhower Presidential Library.

2. Dwight Eisenhower to Henry Cabot Lodge Jr., February 23, 1949, Lodge-Eisenhower Correspondence, Dwight D. Eisenhower Presidential Library.

3. "The Campaign to Win the Republican Nomination for Dwight D. Eisenhower," undated, p. 1, Box 23, Administration Series, Ann Whitman File, Papers as President, Dwight D. Eisenhower Presidential Library.

4. Interview with Milton Eisenhower, June 19, 1969, NXCP87-A941, Columbia Center for Oral History, Columbia University.

5. Dwight D. Eisenhower, *Eisenhower Diaries*, 199.

6. Zeiger, *Remarkable Henry Cabot Lodge*, 101.

7. William J. Miller, *Henry Cabot Lodge*, 211–212.

8. William J. Miller, *Henry Cabot Lodge*, 212–213.

9. Notes from November 30, 1950, Lodge-Eisenhower Correspondence, Dwight D. Eisenhower Presidential Library.

10. Henry Cabot Lodge Jr. to Willis Crittenberger, April 7, 1951, Reel 3, Microfilm Edition, Henry Cabot Lodge, Jr. Papers II, Massachusetts Historical Society.

11. Memorandum of Conversation with Prime Minister [René] Pleven, November 24, 1950, Reel 17, Microfilm Edition, Henry Cabot Lodge, Jr. Papers II, Massachusetts Historical Society.

12. Personal Interview with General Eisenhower, July 16, 1951, 9:00 a.m., Lodge-Eisenhower Correspondence, Dwight D. Eisenhower Presidential Library.

13. William J. Miller, *Henry Cabot Lodge*, 214.

14. Richard Nixon, *RN*, 80.

15. John S. D. Eisenhower, *Strictly Personal*, 306.

16. Interview with Sherman Adams, April 10, 1967, NXCP86-A4, Columbia Center for Oral History, Columbia University.

17. Saltonstall, *Salty*, 152.

18. Dwight D. Eisenhower, *Mandate for Change*, 16.

19. William J. Miller, *Henry Cabot Lodge*, 214.

20. Henry Cabot Lodge Jr., *Storm Has Many Eyes*, 79.

21. Dwight D. Eisenhower, *Mandate for Change*, 18; Dwight D. Eisenhower, *Papers*, 12:608.

22. Interview with Sherman Adams, April 10, 1967, NXCP86-A4, Columbia Center for Oral History, Columbia University.

23. Whalen, *Kennedy versus Lodge*, 73–74.

24. Henry Cabot Lodge Jr., *Storm Has Many Eyes*, 77.

25. Phillips, *Why Vietnam Matters*, 168–169.

26. Dwight D. Eisenhower, *Mandate for Change*, 18.

27. Henry Cabot Lodge Jr., *As It Was*, 11–12.

28. Brownell, *Advising Ike*, 91.

29. Henry Cabot Lodge Jr., *Storm Has Many Eyes*, 79.

30. Pearson, *Diaries, 1949–1959*, 203.

31. Eisenhower's Dilemma, undated, Reel 14, Microfilm Edition, Henry Cabot Lodge, Jr. Papers II, Massachusetts Historical Society.

32. Hitchcock, *Age of Eisenhower*, 57.

33. Richard Norton Smith, *Thomas E. Dewey*, 579.

34. Saltonstall, *Salty*, 152.

35. Barton J. Bernstein, "Election of 1952," in Schlesinger, *History of American Presidential Elections*, 3224.

36. Eisenhower Candidacy, September 18, 1951, Box 963, Robert A. Taft Papers, Manuscript Division, Library of Congress.

37. McCullough, *Truman*, 888.

38. McCullough, *Truman*, 889.

39. Arthur Krock, memo, January 12, 1951, p. 262, Box 1, Arthur Krock Papers, Seeley G. Mudd Manuscript Library, Princeton University.

40. Gibbs and Duffy, *President's Club*, 75.

41. Immerman, *John Foster Dulles*, 38.

42. William J. Miller, *Henry Cabot Lodge*, 219.

43. Report of Progress on "Eisenhower for President" Headquarters, undated, Box 72, Office of Dwight Eisenhower, Principal Files, Pre-presidential Papers, Dwight D. Eisenhower Presidential Library.

44. Henry Cabot Lodge Jr., *Storm Has Many Eyes*, 80.

45. "The Campaign to Win the Republican Nomination for Dwight D. Eisenhower," undated, Box 23, Administration Series, Ann Whitman File, Papers as President, Dwight D. Eisenhower Presidential Library.

46. Parmet, *Richard Nixon and His America*, 236.

47. Oral History Interview of Henry Cabot Lodge, Jr. with Richard D. Challener, February 16, 1965, John Foster Dulles Oral History Collection, Seeley G. Mudd Manuscript Library, Princeton University.

48. Frank, *Ike and Dick*, 25.

49. William J. Miller, *Henry Cabot Lodge*, 221.

50. William J. Miller, *Henry Cabot Lodge*, 222.

51. Interview with Maxwell Rabb, October 6, 1970, NXCP87-A1511, Columbia Center for Oral History, Columbia University.

52. William J. Miller, *Henry Cabot Lodge*, 222.

53. Report of Progress on "Eisenhower for President" Headquarters, undated, Box 72, Office of Dwight Eisenhower, Principal Files, Pre-presidential Papers, Dwight D. Eisenhower Presidential Library.

54. Henry Cabot Lodge Jr. to Dwight Eisenhower, December 3, 1951, Lodge-Eisenhower Correspondence, Dwight D. Eisenhower Presidential Library.

55. Hitchcock, *Age of Eisenhower*, 58.

56. William J. Miller, *Henry Cabot Lodge,* 222–223.

57. Thomas Dewey to Henry Cabot Lodge Jr., December 15, 1951, Reel 4, Microfilm Edition, Henry Cabot Lodge, Jr. Papers II, Massachusetts Historical Society.

58. Henry Cabot Lodge Jr., *Storm Has Many Eyes,* 83.

59. Henry Cabot Lodge Jr., *Storm Has Many Eyes,* 84.

60. William J. Miller, *Henry Cabot Lodge,* 227.

61. Dwight Eisenhower to Henry Cabot Lodge Jr., December 12, 1951, Box 72, Office of Dwight Eisenhower, Principal Files, Pre-presidential Papers, Dwight D. Eisenhower Presidential Library.

62. Dwight D. Eisenhower, *Eisenhower Diaries,* 206.

63. Thomas Dewey to Henry Cabot Lodge Jr., November 23, 1951, Series 10, Box 26, Folder 6, Thomas E. Dewey Papers, Rare Books and Special Collections, University of Rochester.

64. William J. Miller, *Henry Cabot Lodge,* 227.

65. Henry Cabot Lodge Jr. to Sherman Adams, January 4, 1952, Box 23, Administration Series, Ann Whitman File, Papers as President, Dwight D. Eisenhower Presidential Library.

66. Henry Cabot Lodge Jr., *Storm Has Many Eyes,* 96.

67. Blake, *Liking Ike,* 54.

68. Sherman Adams to Henry Cabot Lodge Jr., November 26, 1951, Reel 1, Microfilm Edition, Henry Cabot Lodge, Jr. Papers II, Massachusetts Historical Society.

69. "The Campaign to Win the Republican Nomination for Dwight D. Eisenhower," undated, Box 23, Administration Series, Ann Whitman File, Papers as President, Dwight D. Eisenhower Presidential Library.

70. Interview with Lucius Clay, February 20, 1967, NXCP87-A308, Columbia Center for Oral History, Columbia University.

71. Dwight D. Eisenhower, *Mandate for Change,* 20.

72. Memorandum of Conference, 0930, September 1963, between Eisenhower, McCone, and John Eisenhower, CIA C05579024, CREST (CIA Records Search Tool), National Archives and Records Administration.

73. "The Campaign to Win the Republican Nomination for Dwight D. Eisenhower," undated, Box 23, Administration Series, Ann Whitman File, Papers as President, Dwight D. Eisenhower Presidential Library.

74. Interview with Dwight D. Eisenhower, July 20, 1967, NXCP87-A519, Columbia Center for Oral History, Columbia University.

75. Donaldson, *When America Liked Ike,* 38.

76. Dwight Eisenhower to Henry Cabot Lodge Jr., May 20, 1952, Reel 28, Microfilm Edition, Henry Cabot Lodge, Jr. Papers II, Massachusetts Historical Society.

77. Interview with Sherman Adams, April 10, 1967, NXCP86-A4, Columbia Center for Oral History, Columbia University.

78. Frankel, *Times of My Life,* 104.

79. William J. Miller, *Henry Cabot Lodge*, 223.

80. Kirby, Dalin, and Rothmann, *Harold E. Stassen*, 132–133.

81. Dwight D. Eisenhower, *Eisenhower Diaries*, 209.

82. Text of Eisenhower Statement, January 8, 1952, *New York Times*.

83. McCullough, *Truman*, 889.

84. Dwight D. Eisenhower, *Eisenhower Diaries*, 209.

85. Hitchcock, *Age of Eisenhower*, 59.

86. McCullough, *Truman*, 889.

87. Henry Cabot Lodge Jr., *Storm Has Many Eyes*, 99.

88. Pearson, *Diaries, 1949–1959*, 209.

89. Pearson, *Diaries, 1949–1959*, 189.

90. "The Campaign to Win the Republican Nomination for Dwight D. Eisenhower," undated, Box 23, Administration Series, Ann Whitman File, Papers as President, Dwight D. Eisenhower Presidential Library.

91. Basil Brewer to I. Jack Martin, January 22, 1952, Box 430, Robert A. Taft Papers, Manuscript Division, Library of Congress.

92. Henry Cabot Lodge Jr., *Storm Has Many Eyes*, 102.

93. Stassen and Houts, *Eisenhower*, 24.

94. Interview with Sherman Adams, April 10, 1967, NXCP86-A4, Columbia Center for Oral History, Columbia University.

95. Gibbs and Duffy, *President's Club*, 75.

96. Halberstam, *The Fifties*, 210.

97. I. Jack Martin to G. Harold Alexander, April 24, 1952, Box 424, Robert A. Taft Papers, Manuscript Division, Library of Congress.

98. William J. Miller, *Henry Cabot Lodge*, 235.

99. "The Campaign to Win the Republican Nomination for Dwight D. Eisenhower," undated, Box 23, Administration Series, Ann Whitman File, Papers as President, Dwight D. Eisenhower Presidential Library.

100. Dwight Eisenhower to Henry Cabot Lodge Jr., March 18, 1952, Box 72, Office of Dwight Eisenhower, Principal Files, Pre-presidential Papers, Dwight D. Eisenhower Presidential Library.

101. Blake, *Liking Ike*, 59.

102. Draft Campaign Literature, Dwight D. Eisenhower, 1952, Box 1285, Robert A. Taft Papers, Manuscript Division, Library of Congress.

103. Basil Brewer to I. Jack Martin, March 18, 1952, Box 430, Robert A. Taft Papers, Manuscript Division, Library of Congress.

104. Zeiger, *Remarkable Henry Cabot Lodge*, 106.

105. "The Campaign to Win the Republican Nomination for Dwight D. Eisenhower," undated, Box 23, Administration Series, Ann Whitman File, Papers as President, Dwight D. Eisenhower Presidential Library.

106. Henry Cabot Lodge Jr., *Storm Has Many Eyes*, 103.

107. William J. Miller, *Henry Cabot Lodge*, 236.

108. John Robert Greene, *I Like Ike*, xvi.

109. "The Campaign to Win the Republican Nomination for Dwight D. Eisenhower," undated, Box 23, Administration Series, Ann Whitman File, Papers as President, Dwight D. Eisenhower Presidential Library.

110. Blake, *Liking Ike*, xii.

111. Mickelson, *Electric Mirror*, v–vi.

112. Mickelson, *Electric Mirror*, 102–103.

113. Milton S. Eisenhower, *President Is Calling*, 247.

114. Henry Cabot Lodge Jr., *Storm Has Many Eyes*, 106.

115. Merry, *Taking on the World*, 230–232.

116. Henry Cabot Lodge Jr., *Storm Has Many Eyes*, 106.

117. John Robert Greene, *I Like Ike*, 96.

118. Zeiger, *Remarkable Henry Cabot Lodge*, 109.

119. Henry Cabot Lodge Jr., *Storm Has Many Eyes*, 107.

120. William J. Miller, *Henry Cabot Lodge*, 238.

121. William J. Miller, *Henry Cabot Lodge*, 239–240.

122. William J. Miller, *Henry Cabot Lodge*, 242.

123. Henry Cabot Lodge Jr., *Storm Has Many Eyes*, 109.

124. Richard Norton Smith, *Thomas E. Dewey*, 589.

125. Cutler, *No Time for Rest*, 268.

126. Brownell, *Advising Ike*, 118.

127. John Davis Lodge to Henry Cabot Lodge Jr., March 19, 1973, Box 200, John Davis Lodge Papers, Hoover Institution.

128. William J. Miller, *Henry Cabot Lodge*, 243.

129. Henry Cabot Lodge Jr., *Storm Has Many Eyes*, 115.

130. Memorandum for the File, undated, Reel 23, Microfilm Edition, Henry Cabot Lodge, Jr. Papers II, Massachusetts Historical Society.

131. For Immediate Release, July 9, 1952, Box 432, Robert A. Taft Papers, Manuscript Division, Library of Congress.

132. William J. Miller, *Henry Cabot Lodge*, 243.

133. For background on the Lodge-Hoover relationship following Hoover's presidency, see Box 126, Herbert Hoover Papers, Post-presidential Papers, Herbert Hoover Presidential Library.

134. "The Campaign to Win the Republican Nomination for Dwight D. Eisenhower," undated, Box 23, Administration Series, Ann Whitman File, Papers as President, Dwight D. Eisenhower Presidential Library.

135. Judd, *Chronicles of a Statesman*, 23.

136. Richard Norton Smith, *Thomas E. Dewey*, 589.

137. Taft, *Papers*, 4:395.

138. William J. Miller, *Henry Cabot Lodge*, 244–245.

139. "The Campaign to Win the Republican Nomination for Dwight D. Eisenhower," undated, Box 23, Administration Series, Ann Whitman File, Papers as President, Dwight D. Eisenhower Presidential Library.

140. William J. Miller, *Henry Cabot Lodge*, 247–248.

141. Richard Norton Smith, *Thomas E. Dewey*, 589.

142. William J. Miller, *Henry Cabot Lodge*, 247, emphasis in the original.

143. William J. Miller, *Henry Cabot Lodge*, 250.

144. Henry Cabot Lodge Jr., *Storm Has Many Eyes*, 119.

145. Henry Cabot Lodge Jr. to Dwight Eisenhower, July 7, 1953, Box 24, Administration Series, Ann Whitman File, Papers as President, Dwight D. Eisenhower Presidential Library.

146. Henry Cabot Lodge Jr., *As It Was*, 121.

147. Henry Cabot Lodge Jr., *Storm Has Many Eyes*, 123.

148. William J. Miller, *Henry Cabot Lodge*, 250.

149. Brownell, *Advising Ike*, 118.

150. William J. Miller, *Henry Cabot Lodge*, 251.

151. William J. Miller, *Henry Cabot Lodge*, 251.

152. Memorandum on General Eisenhower, undated, Box 1107, Robert A. Taft Papers, Manuscript Division, Library of Congress.

153. Telegram from Robert A. Taft to Dwight D. Eisenhower, October 31, 1952, Box 1106, Robert A. Taft Papers, Manuscript Division, Library of Congress.

154. William J. Miller, *Henry Cabot Lodge*, 319.

155. John A. Farrell, *Richard Nixon*, 167.

156. Kornitzer, *Real Nixon*, 209.

157. Mazo, *Richard Nixon*, 94.

158. Halberstam, *The Fifties*, 213.

159. Hitchcock, *Age of Eisenhower*, 72.

160. Frank, *Ike and Dick*, 33.

161. Hitchcock, *Age of Eisenhower*, 72–73.

162. Goldwater, *With No Apologies*, 71.

163. Wicker, *One of Us*, 82.

164. Robert A. Taft, "Analysis of the Results of the Chicago Convention," undated, pp. 4–5, Box 431, Robert A. Taft Papers, Manuscript Division, Library of Congress.

165. Henry Cabot Lodge Jr. to Thomas Dewey, July 25, 1952, Series 5, Box 111, Folder 17, Thomas E. Dewey Papers, Rare Books and Special Collections, University of Rochester.

166. Henry Cabot Lodge Jr. to Alfred Gruenther, July 23, 1952, Reel 6, Microfilm Edition, Henry Cabot Lodge, Jr. Papers II, Massachusetts Historical Society.

167. Henry Cabot Lodge Jr., *Storm Has Many Eyes*, 112.

168. William J. Miller, *Henry Cabot Lodge*, 252.

169. Memorandum from Henry Cabot Lodge Jr. to Dwight Eisenhower, July 22, 1952, Lodge-Eisenhower Correspondence, Dwight D. Eisenhower Presidential Library.

170. McCullough, *Truman*, 889.

171. Memorandum from Henry Cabot Lodge Jr. to Dwight Eisenhower, July 22, 1952, Lodge-Eisenhower Correspondence, Dwight D. Eisenhower Presidential Library.

## 7. A Lodge-Kennedy Rematch

1. Author interview with George Cabot Lodge, January 24, 2017, Beverly, Massachusetts.

2. Memorandum for the File, undated, Reel 28, Microfilm Edition, Henry Cabot Lodge, Jr. Papers II, Massachusetts Historical Society.

3. Whalen, *Kennedy versus Lodge*, 7.

4. Oral History Interview with Henry Cabot Lodge, August 4, 1965, John F. Kennedy Presidential Library.

5. Nasaw, *Patriarch*, 652.

6. Donald Ritchie, "Kennedy in Congress," in Selverstone, *Companion to John F. Kennedy*, 37.

7. Schlesinger, *Thousand Days*, 91.

8. Whalen, *Kennedy versus Lodge*, 67.

9. Michael O'Brien, *John F. Kennedy*, 239.

10. Dallek, *Camelot's Court*, 42.

11. Dallck, *Camelot's Court*, 42.

12. Lawrence F. O'Brien, *No Final Victories*, 28.

13. Bird, *Color of Truth*, 150.

14. Belt 39, undated, Presidential Recordings, President's Office Files, Presidential Papers, John F. Kennedy Presidential Library.

15. Whalen, *Kennedy versus Lodge*, 77.

16. Neff, *Vendetta*, 170.

17. Whalen, *Kennedy versus Lodge*, 91.

18. Pietrusza, *1960*, 10.

19. Stephen Hess, *America's Political Dynasties*, 482.

20. Belt 40, undated, Presidential Recordings, President's Office Files, Presidential Papers, John F. Kennedy Presidential Library.

21. Zeiger, *Remarkable Henry Cabot Lodge*, 111.

22. Michael O'Brien, *John F. Kennedy*, 240.

23. O'Donnell and Powers, *"Johnny, We Hardly Knew Ye,"* 90.

24. Barbrook, *God Save the Commonwealth*, 111–112.

25. Henry Cabot Lodge Jr. to Paul Hoffman, July 24, 1952, Box 32, Paul G. Hoffman Papers, Harry S. Truman Presidential Library.

26. Whalen, *Kennedy versus Lodge*, 69.

27. Nasaw, *Patriarch*, 666.

28. Michael O'Brien, *John F. Kennedy*, 247.

29. Henry Cabot Lodge Jr. to John Fox, September 20, 1952, Reel 5, Microfilm Edition, Henry Cabot Lodge, Jr. Papers II, Massachusetts Historical Society.

30. Whalen, *Kennedy versus Lodge*, 129.

31. Beschloss, *Jacqueline Kennedy*, 75.

32. Garrison Nelson, *John William McCormack*, 465.

33. Talbot, *Brothers*, 147.

34. Whalen, *Kennedy versus Lodge*, 132.

35. William J. Miller, *Henry Cabot Lodge*, 254.

36. Richard James Cushing to James Hughes, May 31, 1949, Reel 3, Microfilm Edition, Henry Cabot Lodge, Jr. Papers II, Massachusetts Historical Society.

37. Henry Cabot Lodge Jr. to Richard James Cushing, December 20, 1950, Reel 1, Microfilm Edition, Henry Cabot Lodge, Jr. Papers II, Massachusetts Historical Society.

38. Whalen, *Kennedy versus Lodge*, 111.

39. Whalen, *Kennedy versus Lodge*, 99.

40. Oral History Interview with Henry Cabot Lodge, August 4, 1965, John F. Kennedy Presidential Library.

41. William J. Miller, *Henry Cabot Lodge*, 253.

42. Oral History Interview with Lawrence O'Brien, February 11, 1986, Lyndon B. Johnson Presidential Library.

43. Beatty, *Rascal King*, 511.

44. Whalen, *Kennedy versus Lodge*, 140.

45. Pietrusza, *1960*, 11.

46. Beschloss, *Jacqueline Kennedy*, 75.

47. Whalen, *Kennedy versus Lodge*, 113.

48. Felzenberg, *A Man and His Presidents*, 92.

49. Blake, *Liking Ike*, 59.

50. Donaldson, *When America Liked Ike*, 91–92.

51. Whalen, *Kennedy versus Lodge*, 145.

52. Memorandum from Mr. Landis to Mr. Fayne and Miss Walsh, August 29, 1952, Box 112, Congressional Campaign Files, '52 Campaign, Campaign Effort, John F. Kennedy Presidential Library.

53. Whalen, *Kennedy versus Lodge*, 98.

54. Barbrook, *God Save the Commonwealth*, 121.

55. Whalen, *Kennedy versus Lodge*, 99.

56. Garrison Nelson, *John William McCormack*, 465.

57. William J. Miller, *Henry Cabot Lodge*, 254.

58. Zeiger, *Remarkable Henry Cabot Lodge*, 113.

59. Rose Fitzgerald Kennedy, *Times to Remember*, 326.

60. Barbrook, *God Save the Commonwealth*, 113–114.

61. Cutler, *No Time for Rest*, 281.

62. Saltonstall, *Salty*, 154.

63. Zeiger, *Remarkable Henry Cabot Lodge*, 112.

64. George Murphy, "*Say . . . ,*" 333.

65. William J. Miller, *Henry Cabot Lodge*, 255.

66. William J. Miller, *Henry Cabot Lodge*, 253.

67. Whalen, *Kennedy versus Lodge*, 163.

68. Hersh, *Dark Side of Camelot*, 17.

69. Tactics—1952, Reel 18, Microfilm Edition, Henry Cabot Lodge, Jr. Papers II, Massachusetts Historical Society.

70. Author conversation with Thomas Lester, archivist and records manager, Pastoral Center of the Archdiocese of Boston, October 13, 2016, Braintree, Massachusetts.

71. Nasaw, *Patriarch*, 604.

72. Giglio, *Presidency of John F. Kennedy*, 10.

73. Richard Norton Smith, *Thomas E. Dewey*, 625.

74. Garrison Nelson, *John William McCormack*, 460.

75. O'Donnell and Powers, *"Johnny, We Hardly Knew Ye,"* 92.

76. Whalen, *Kennedy versus Lodge*, 159.

77. Whalen, *Kennedy versus Lodge*, 3.

78. Pearson, *Diaries, 1949–1959*, 230.

79. Thomas Dewey to John Davis Lodge, November 11, 1952, Series 6, Box 83, Folder 16, Thomas E. Dewey Papers, Rare Books and Special Collections, University of Rochester.

80. Whalen, *Kennedy versus Lodge*, 160.

81. Oral History Interview with Henry Cabot Lodge, August 4, 1965, John F. Kennedy Presidential Library.

82. William J. Miller, *Henry Cabot Lodge*, 255.

83. Author interview with Emily Sears Lodge, June 9, 2017, Paris, France. The letter is from the Lodge family private collection.

# 8. The UN (1953–1957)

1. Dwight D. Eisenhower, *Mandate for Change*, 84.

2. Henry Cabot Lodge Jr., *Storm Has Many Eyes*, 128.

3. Lankford, *Last American Aristocrat*, 254.

4. Henry Cabot Lodge Jr., *As It Was*, 21.

5. Chace, *Acheson*, 358.

6. Henry Cabot Lodge Jr., *As It Was*, 46.

7. Henry Cabot Lodge Jr., *At It Was*, 49–50.

8. Henry Cabot Lodge Jr. to Warren Austin, December 4, 1952, Reel 1, Microfilm Edition, Henry Cabot Lodge, Jr. Papers II, Massachusetts Historical Society.

9. Friday, November 21, 1952—Meeting with Eisenhower at the Commodore Hotel, New York, Box 23, Henry Cabot Lodge, Jr. Papers I, Massachusetts Historical Society.

10. Wadsworth, *Glass House*, 174.

11. Gaddis, *Strategies of Containment*, 111.

12. Pruden, *Conditional Partners*, 22.

13. William J. Miller, *Henry Cabot Lodge*, 208.

14. Dwight D. Eisenhower, *Mandate for Change*, 89.

15. Finger, *American Ambassadors*, 72.

16. Maxwell Rabb to Henry Cabot Lodge Jr., April 29, 1957, Box 30, Maxwell M. Rabb Papers, Dwight D. Eisenhower Presidential Library.

17. Pruden, *Conditional Partners*, 6.

18. Memorandum from Henry Cabot Lodge Jr. to Dwight Eisenhower, October 15, 1953, Box 3, DDE Diary Series, Ann Whitman File, Dwight D. Eisenhower Presidential Library.

19. Greenstein, *Hidden-Hand Presidency*, 183.

20. Finger, *American Ambassadors*, 21.

21. Henry Cabot Lodge Jr. to Dwight Eisenhower, October 9, 1956, Box 24, Administration Series, Ann Whitman File, Papers as President, Dwight D. Eisenhower Presidential Library.

22. Henry Cabot Lodge Jr., *Storm Has Many Eyes*, 135.

23. Oral History Interview of James J. Wadsworth with Philip A. Crowl, June 21, 1965, John Foster Dulles Oral History Collection, Seeley G. Mudd Manuscript Library, Princeton University.

24. Deputies' Meeting, Wednesday, August 11, 1954, DM-325, CIA-RDP80B01676 R002300160016, CREST (CIA Records Search Tool), National Archives and Records Administration.

25. Henry Cabot Lodge Jr. to Allen Dulles, undated (date redacted), CIA-RDP-80B01676R003200180018, CREST, National Archives and Records Administration.

26. Deputies' Meeting, Thursday, May 21, 1953, DM-153, CIA-RDP80B01676 R002300130061-8, CREST, National Archives and Records Administration.

27. Henry Cabot Lodge Jr. to Dwight Eisenhower, April 23, 1953, Box 24, Administration Series, Ann Whitman File, Papers as President, Dwight D. Eisenhower Presidential Library.

28. Spaak, *Continuing Battle*, 111.

29. Finger, *American Ambassadors*, 80.

30. Henry Cabot Lodge Jr. to Dwight Eisenhower, April 23, 1953, Box 24, Administration Series, Ann Whitman File, Papers as President, Dwight D. Eisenhower Presidential Library.

31. Telephone Conversation with Ambassador Lodge, February 27, 1953, Box 1, Telephone Conversations Subseries, John Foster Dulles Papers, Dwight D. Eisenhower Presidential Library.

32. UPI Release, February 28, 1985, Research Office, Office of Speechwriting, Ronald Reagan Presidential Library.

33. Finger, *American Ambassadors*, 72.

34. Oral History Interview of Henry Cabot Lodge Jr. with Richard D. Challener, February 16, 1965, John Foster Dulles Oral History Collection, Seeley G. Mudd Manuscript Library, Princeton University.

35. Finger, *American Ambassadors*, 73.

36. Finger, *American Ambassadors*, 74.

37. Confidential Journal, January 26, 1953, Reel 17, Microfilm Edition, Henry Cabot Lodge, Jr. Papers II, Massachusetts Historical Society.

38. Pruden, *Conditional Partners*, 59–60.

39. More than sixty years later, much of this material remains classified for national security reasons. For example, key records of the Psychological Strategy Board were closed during a research visit to the Dwight D. Eisenhower Presidential Library during December 2015. A Mandatory Declassification Review request was submitted, but it was denied. Upon appeal to the National Archives and Records Administration, the records were finally opened in September 2017.

40. Finger, *American Ambassadors*, 78.

41. Memorandum from C. D. Jackson to Henry Cabot Lodge, April 21, 1953, Box 4, C. D. Jackson Records, 1953–1954, Dwight D. Eisenhower Presidential Library.

42. William J. Miller, *Henry Cabot Lodge*, 263.

43. Oral History Interview of James J. Wadsworth with Philip A. Crowl, June 21, 1965, John Foster Dulles Oral History Collection, Seeley G. Mudd Manuscript Library, Princeton University.

44. Gerard C. Smith, *Disarming Diplomat*, 40.

45. Pruden, *Conditional Partners*, 9.

46. Finger, *American Ambassadors*, 77.

47. Wadsworth, *Glass House*, 197.

48. William J. Miller, *Henry Cabot Lodge*, 262.

49. Eyes Only Memorandum for the President and the Secretary of State, March 25, 1953, Box 24, Administration Series, Ann Whitman File, Papers as President, Dwight D. Eisenhower Presidential Library.

50. Telegram 508 from Henry Cabot Lodge Jr. to John Foster Dulles, March 30, 1953, Box 1, Telephone Conversations Subseries, John Foster Dulles Papers, Dwight D. Eisenhower Presidential Library.

51. Dag Hammarskjold to Henry Cabot Lodge Jr., August 13, 1954, Reel 6, Microfilm Edition, Henry Cabot Lodge, Jr. Papers II, Massachusetts Historical Society.

52. Stephen Hess, *America's Political Dynasties*, 488.

53. Pruden, *Conditional Partners*, 61.

54. Dag Hammarskjold to Henry Cabot Lodge Jr., March 28, 1955, Reel 4, Microfilm Edition, Henry Cabot Lodge, Jr. Papers II, Massachusetts Historical Society.

55. Memorandum from Henry Cabot Lodge Jr. to John Foster Dulles, March 25, 1954, Reel 4, Microfilm Edition, Henry Cabot Lodge, Jr. Papers II, Massachusetts Historical Society.

56. Arch Parsons Jr., "U.N. Head Indicates Staff Policy," *New York Herald Tribune*, May 13, 1953.

57. Statement by the Secretary-General Addressed to the Staff of the Secretariat of the United Nations, undated, S-0844-0001-14-00001, Dag Hammarskjöld, Secretariat and Personnel Files, Files of the Secretary-General, Archives and Records Management Section, United Nations.

58. Urquhart, *Hammarskjold*, 67.

59. Stoessinger, *United Nations*, 64.

60. Henry Cabot Lodge Jr. to Dwight Eisenhower, April 23, 1953, Box 24, Administration Series, Ann Whitman File, Papers as President, Dwight D. Eisenhower Presidential Library.

61. Pruden, *Conditional Partners*, 38–39.

62. Activities of United States Citizens Employed by the United States, January 2, 1953, S-0844-0002-02-00001, Dag Hammarskjöld, Secretariat and Personnel Files, Files of the Secretary-General, Archives and Records Management Section, United Nations.

63. Pruden, *Conditional Partners*, 41.

64. Pruden, *Conditional Partners*, 42–43.

65. Theoharis, *From the Secret Files*, 77.

66. Pruden, *Conditional Partners*, 51–52.

67. Bowie and Immerman, *Waging Peace*, 3.

68. Pruden, *Conditional Partners*, 67–68.

69. Finger, *American Ambassadors*, 76.

70. William J. Miller, *Henry Cabot Lodge*, 263.

71. William J. Miller, *Henry Cabot Lodge*, 264.

72. Pruden, *Conditional Partners*, 5.

73. Riggs, *US/UN*, 59.

74. Riggs, *Politics in the United Nations*, 92.

75. Pruden, *Conditional Partners*, 92–93.

76. Henry Cabot Lodge Jr., *As It Was*, 150.

77. Finger, *American Ambassadors*, 73.

78. Bird, *Chairman*, 419.

79. Merry, *Taking on the World*, 272.

80. Henry Cabot Lodge Jr. to Dwight Eisenhower, February 23, 1954, Box 24, Administration Series, Ann Whitman File, Papers as President, Dwight D. Eisenhower Presidential Library.

81. Greenstein, *Hidden-Hand Presidency*, 203–204.

82. Riggs, *Politics in the United Nations*, 178.

83. Henry Cabot Lodge Jr. to Dwight Eisenhower, December 10, 1953, Box 23, Administration Series, Ann Whitman File, Papers as President, Dwight D. Eisenhower Presidential Library.

84. William J. Miller, *Henry Cabot Lodge*, 267.

85. Robert Murphy, *Diplomat among Warriors*, 446.

86. Beichman, *The "Other" State Department*, 109.

87. William J. Miller, *Henry Cabot Lodge*, 267–268.

88. Oral History Interview of Dean Francis O. Wilcox with Philip A. Crowl, June 7, 1965, John Foster Dulles Oral History Collection, Seeley G. Mudd Manuscript Library, Princeton University.

89. Henry Cabot Lodge Jr. to Baroness de Streel, September 3, 1954, Reel 3, Microfilm Edition, Henry Cabot Lodge, Jr. Papers II, Massachusetts Historical Society.

90. Henry Cabot Lodge Jr. to Dwight Eisenhower, September 15, 1954, Box 24, Administration Series, Ann Whitman File, Papers as President, Dwight D. Eisenhower Presidential Library.

91. William J. Miller, *Henry Cabot Lodge*, 270.

92. William J. Miller, *Henry Cabot Lodge*, 271.

93. Immerman, *CIA in Guatemala*, 117.

94. Zacher, *Dag Hammarskjold's United Nations*, 29.

95. Memorandum of Telephone Conversation between the Secretary and Ambassador Lodge, June 24, 1954, Reel 4, Microfilm Edition, Henry Cabot Lodge, Jr. Papers II, Massachusetts Historical Society.

96. Large, *Germans to the Front*, 144.

97. Pruden, *Conditional Partners*, 100–101.

98. Pruden, *Conditional Partners*, 103–104.

99. Bullington, *Global Adventures*, 71.

100. Pruden, *Conditional Partners*, 153–154.

101. Report on the Disarmament Conference, Cabinet Agenda, March 18, 1955, Box 5, Cabinet Series, Ann Whitman File, Papers as President, Dwight D. Eisenhower Presidential Library.

102. "Partial Disarmament of Conventional Forces," October 17, 1955, FO 371/117400, National Archives, United Kingdom.

103. Dwight D. Eisenhower, *Waging Peace*, 469–470.

104. William J. Miller, *Henry Cabot Lodge*, 272–273.

105. Kaplan, *Harold Stassen*, 122.

106. Henry Cabot Lodge Jr. to Harold Stassen, December 9, 1953, 142-A-15-2-F, Harold E. Stassen Papers, Minnesota Historical Society.

107. Werle, *Stassen Again*, 199.

108. Pruden, *Conditional Partners*, 157.

109. Henry Cabot Lodge Jr., *At It Was,* 71.

110. Henry Cabot Lodge Jr., *As It Was,* 79.

111. Scott and Withey, *United States,* 136.

112. Pruden, *Conditional Partners,* 74–75.

113. Beichman, *The "Other" State Department,* 106.

114. William J. Miller, *Henry Cabot Lodge,* 273.

115. Wadsworth, *Glass House,* 127.

116. William J. Miller, *Henry Cabot Lodge,* 273–274.

117. William J. Miller, *Henry Cabot Lodge,* 274.

118. Pruden, *Conditional Partners,* 224.

119. William J. Miller, *Henry Cabot Lodge,* 275.

120. From Washington to Foreign Office, No. 2200, October 29, 1956, FO 371/121746, National Archives, United Kingdom.

121. Confidential Journal, October 29, 1956, Reel 17, Microfilm Edition, Henry Cabot Lodge, Jr. Papers II, Massachusetts Historical Society.

122. Henry Cabot Lodge Jr. to John Foster Dulles, March 25, 1957, Box 1, General Correspondence and Memoranda Series, John Foster Dulles Papers, Dwight D. Eisenhower Presidential Library.

123. Record of a Conversation between the Secretary of State, Mr. Dulles, and Monsieur Pineau in Mr. Dulles' Apartment on October 5, 1956, at 10:15 a.m., FO 371/119182, National Archives, United Kingdom.

124. Pruden, *Conditional Partners,* 225.

125. Dwight D. Eisenhower, *Waging Peace,* 79.

126. From New York to Foreign Office, No. 989, October 30, 1956, FO 371/121746, National Archives, United Kingdom.

127. Eden, *Full Circle,* 591–592.

128. From New York to Foreign Office, No. 993, October 31, 1956, FO 371/121746, National Archives, United Kingdom.

129. Oral History Interview of Henry Cabot Lodge Jr. with Richard D. Challener, February 16, 1965, John Foster Dulles Oral History Collection, Seeley G. Mudd Manuscript Library, Princeton University.

130. William J. Miller, *Henry Cabot Lodge,* 275.

131. William J. Miller, *Henry Cabot Lodge,* 276.

132. Pruden, *Conditional Partners,* 245–246.

133. Pruden, *Conditional Partners,* 244.

134. Hitchcock, *Age of Eisenhower,* 316.

135. Oral History Interview of Henry Cabot Lodge Jr. with Richard D. Challener, February 16, 1965, John Foster Dulles Oral History Collection, Seeley G. Mudd Manuscript Library, Princeton University.

136. Henry Cabot Lodge Jr. to Douglas Dillon, November 9, 1956, Reel 4, Microfilm Edition, Henry Cabot Lodge, Jr. Papers II, Massachusetts Historical Society.

137. Spaak, *Continuing Battle*, 135.

138. William J. Miller, *Henry Cabot Lodge*, 276–277.

139. Robert Murphy, *Diplomat among Warriors*, 524.

140. Henry Cabot Lodge Jr. to Henry Luce, March 4, 1957, Box 13, Henry Cabot Lodge, Jr. Papers II, Massachusetts Historical Society.

141. Pruden, *Conditional Partners*, 260.

142. Hitchcock, *Age of Eisenhower*, 316.

143. Pruden, *Conditional Partners*, 265–266.

144. William J. Miller, *Henry Cabot Lodge*, 279.

145. Henry Cabot Lodge Jr. to Dwight Eisenhower, March 19, 1956, Box 24, Administration Series, Ann Whitman File, Papers as President, Dwight D. Eisenhower Presidential Library.

146. Author interview with Emily Lodge, June 9, 2017, Paris, France. The letter is from the Lodge family private collection.

## 9. The UN (1957–1960)

1. Pruden, *Conditional Partners*, 201.

2. William J. Miller, *Henry Cabot Lodge*, 282.

3. William J. Miller, *Henry Cabot Lodge*, 283.

4. William J. Miller, *Henry Cabot Lodge*, 283.

5. Pruden, *Conditional Partners*, 274.

6. Meeting at Dulles's Home in Washington—5 p.m., June 22, 1958, Reel 5, Microfilm Edition, Henry Cabot Lodge, Jr. Papers II, Massachusetts Historical Society.

7. Dwight D. Eisenhower, *Waging Peace*, 274.

8. Pruden, *Conditional Partners*, 269.

9. Pruden, *Conditional Partners*, 277.

10. William J. Miller, *Henry Cabot Lodge*, 284.

11. William J. Miller, *Henry Cabot Lodge*, 285.

12. Benjamin Rivlin, "The Changing International Political Climate and the Secretary-General," in Rivlin and Gordenker, *Challenging Role*, 11.

13. William J. Miller, *Henry Cabot Lodge*, 287.

14. Pruden, *Conditional Partners*, 283.

15. William J. Miller, *Henry Cabot Lodge*, 287.

16. Kaplan, *Harold Stassen*, 158.

17. Telegram from the United Kingdom Delegation to the United Nations to the Foreign Office, No. 136, January 14, 1957, FO 371/129795, National Archives, United Kingdom.

18. Henry Cabot Lodge Jr. to John Foster Dulles, March 31, 1958, Reel 5, Microfilm Edition, Henry Cabot Lodge, Jr. Papers II, Massachusetts Historical Society.

19. Benjamin P. Greene, *Eisenhower*, 138.

20. William J. Miller, *Henry Cabot Lodge*, 288.

21. John S. D. Eisenhower, *Strictly Personal*, 256.

22. USSR Mission to the United Nations, Press Release No. 18, April 11, 1964, S-0882-0003, Correspondence Files of the Secretary-General U Thant: With Heads of State, Governments, Permanent Representatives and Observers to the United Nations, Archives and Records Management Section, United Nations.

23. Carlson, *K Blows Top*, 77.

24. Henry Cabot Lodge Jr., *Storm Has Many Eyes*, 159.

25. Dwight D. Eisenhower, *Waging Peace*, 441.

26. Nikita Sergeyevich Khrushchev, *Memoirs*, 107.

27. Henry Cabot Lodge Jr., *Storm Has Many Eyes*, 170.

28. Carlson, *K Blows Top*, 77.

29. Nikita Sergeyevich Khrushchev, *Memoirs*, 158.

30. Carlson, *K Blows Top*, 87–88.

31. William J. Miller, *Henry Cabot Lodge*, 289.

32. Barrett, *CIA and Congress*, 339.

33. William J. Miller, *Henry Cabot Lodge*, 292.

34. William J. Miller, *Henry Cabot Lodge*, 290–291.

35. Barrett, *CIA and Congress*, 340.

36. Carlson, *K Blows Top*, 118.

37. Carlson, *K Blows Top*, 118.

38. William J. Miller, *Henry Cabot Lodge*, 293–294.

39. Memorandum of Conversation, September 18, 1959, Box 27, Henry Cabot Lodge, Jr. Papers I, Massachusetts Historical Society.

40. Henry Cabot Lodge Jr., *Storm Has Many Eyes*, 162.

41. Nikita Sergeyevich Khrushchev, *Memoirs*, 108.

42. Memorandum of Conversation, September 19, 1959, Box 27, Henry Cabot Lodge, Jr. Papers I, Massachusetts Historical Society.

43. Sergei N. Khrushchev, *Nikita Khrushchev*, 333.

44. Emmet John Hughes, *Ordeal of Power*, 291.

45. Buckley, *Flying High*, 43–44.

46. Carlson, *K Blows Top*, 165.

47. Sergei N. Khrushchev, *Khrushchev on Khrushchev*, 357.

48. Carlson, *K Blows Top*, 170–171.

49. Carlson, *K Blows Top*, 181.

50. Dwight D. Eisenhower, *Waging Peace*, 445.

51. Henry Cabot Lodge Jr., *Storm Has Many Eyes*, 177.

52. Nikita Sergeyevich Khrushchev, *Memoirs*, 118.

53. William J. Miller, *Henry Cabot Lodge*, 296–297.

54. Henry Cabot Lodge Jr., *Storm Has Many Eyes*, 178.

55. William J. Miller, *Henry Cabot Lodge*, 301–302.

56. William J. Miller, *Henry Cabot Lodge*, 303.

57. Brands, *Cold Warriors*, 163.

58. Pearson, *Diaries, 1949–1959*, 472.

59. Memorandum of Conversation with Joseph Sisco, Confidential Journal, February 19, 1963, Reel 17, Microfilm Edition, Henry Cabot Lodge, Jr. Papers II, Massachusetts Historical Society.

60. Allen Dulles to Henry Cabot Lodge Jr., March 12, 1958, CIA-RDP80B01676 R001000180013-0, CREST (CIA Records Search Tool), National Archives and Records Administration.

61. Deputies' Meeting, Friday, March 7, 1958, DM-621, CIA-RDP80B01676 R002300230063-5, CREST, National Archives and Records Administration.

62. Lodge Statement Concerning India and His General Observations, undated, Reel 2, Microfilm Edition, Henry Cabot Lodge, Jr. Papers II, Massachusetts Historical Society.

63. Henry Cabot Lodge Jr. to John Foster Dulles, May 31, 1957, Reel 5, Microfilm Edition, Henry Cabot Lodge, Jr. Papers II, Massachusetts Historical Society.

64. Henry Cabot Lodge Jr. to Dwight Eisenhower, June 26, 1956, Box 1, General Correspondence and Memoranda Series, John Foster Dulles Papers, Dwight D. Eisenhower Presidential Library.

65. Text of Mr. Lodge Speech on Tibet, U.S. Information Service Wireless Bulletin, October 22, 1959, Box 104, John Davis Lodge Papers, Hoover Institution.

66. William J. Miller, *Henry Cabot Lodge*, 314.

67. William J. Miller, *Henry Cabot Lodge*, 315.

68. Henry Cabot Lodge Jr. to Dwight Eisenhower, October 15, 1957, Box 24, Administration Series, Ann Whitman File, Papers as President, Dwight D. Eisenhower Presidential Library.

69. Pruden, *Conditional Partners*, 219.

70. Henry Cabot Lodge Jr. to John Foster Dulles, March 23, 1956, Box 4, General Correspondence and Memoranda Series, John Foster Dulles Papers, Dwight D. Eisenhower Presidential Library.

71. Nikita Sergeyevich Khrushchev, *Memoirs*, 295.

72. Brands, *Cold Warriors*, 181.

73. Henry Cabot Lodge Jr. to Dwight Eisenhower, May 28, 1960, Box 24, Administration Series, Ann Whitman File, Papers as President, Dwight D. Eisenhower Presidential Library.

74. William J. Miller, *Henry Cabot Lodge*, 315.

75. Pruden, *Conditional Partners*, 83.

76. Oral History Interview of Henry Cabot Lodge Jr. with Richard D. Challener, February 16, 1965, John Foster Dulles Oral History Collection, Seeley G. Mudd Manuscript Library, Princeton University.

77. William J. Miller, *Henry Cabot Lodge*, 316.

78. Henry Cabot Lodge Jr., *Storm Has Many Eyes*, 144.

79. Henry Cabot Lodge Jr. to Richard Nixon, June 6, 1960, Reel 12, Microfilm Edition, Henry Cabot Lodge, Jr. Papers II, Massachusetts Historical Society.

80. Gellman, *President*, 465.

81. Pruden, *Conditional Partners*, 286.

82. Stoessinger, *United Nations*, 110.

83. Pruden, *Conditional Partners*, 287–288.

84. William J. Miller, *Henry Cabot Lodge*, 318.

85. Pruden, *Conditional Partners*, 291.

86. Stoessinger, *United Nations*, 110.

87. Robert Hopkins Miller, *Vietnam and Beyond*, 40.

88. Pruden, *Conditional Partners*, 292.

89. Pruden, *Conditional Partners*, 217.

90. Pruden, *Conditional Partners*, 300.

91. William J. Miller, *Henry Cabot Lodge*, 319.

92. Pruden, *Conditional Partners*, 312.

93. William J. Miller, *Henry Cabot Lodge*, 308–309.

## 10. The 1960 Campaign

1. "Able Man, Headed for Great Things," *Seattle Times*, June 26, 1955.

2. Address by Henry Cabot Lodge, United States Representative to the United Nations, at West Point, on Receiving the Sylvanus Thayer Award, March 16, 1960, Special Collections and Archives Division, U.S. Military Academy Library.

3. Slater, *The Ike I Knew*, 185–186.

4. Dwight D. Eisenhower, *Waging Peace*, 590.

5. Memorandum for the File, undated, Reel 28, Microfilm Edition, Henry Cabot Lodge, Jr. Papers II, Massachusetts Historical Society.

6. Memo for Confidential Journal, January 25, 1960, Reel 17, Microfilm Edition, Henry Cabot Lodge, Jr. Papers II, Massachusetts Historical Society.

7. William J. Miller, *Henry Cabot Lodge*, 319.

8. Henry Cabot Lodge Jr. to Charles Barnes, February 26, 1960, Reel 1, Microfilm Edition, Henry Cabot Lodge, Jr. Papers II, Massachusetts Historical Society.

9. Memorandum from Rose Mary Woods to Robert Finch, March 24, 1960, Box 23, Sub-series A: Alphabetical, Series I: Correspondence, Series 238, Wilderness Years Collection, Richard M. Nixon Presidential Library.

10. William J. Miller, *Henry Cabot Lodge*, 318.

11. Kallina, *Kennedy v. Nixon*, 94.

12. Kleindienst, *Justice*, 27.

13. Richard Nixon, *RN*, 216.

14. Parmet, *Richard Nixon*, 389.

15. Southwick, *Presidential Also-Rans*, 651.

16. William J. Miller, *Henry Cabot Lodge*, 319–320.

17. Graham, *Just As I Am*, 445.

18. Kallina, *Kennedy v. Nixon*, 94.

19. William J. Miller, *Henry Cabot Lodge*, 320.

20. Buckley, *Flying High*, 14–15.

21. Morrow, *Black Man*, 294.

22. Irwin Dorch to Henry Cabot Lodge Jr., March 14, 1941, Box 20, Henry Cabot Lodge, Jr. Papers I, Massachusetts Historical Society.

23. Morrow, *Black Man*, 294.

24. Ed Nixon and Karen Olson, *The Nixons*, 202.

25. William J. Miller, *Henry Cabot Lodge*, 320.

26. Kleindienst, *Justice*, 27.

27. William J. Miller, *Henry Cabot Lodge*, 320–321.

28. Henry Cabot Lodge Jr., *Storm Has Many Eyes*, 183.

29. Gifford, *Center Cannot Hold*, 78.

30. Parmet, *Richard Nixon*, 385.

31. William J. Miller, *Henry Cabot Lodge*, 321.

32. Edwards, *Missionary for Freedom*, 256.

33. Garrison Nelson, *John William McCormack*, 561.

34. Gerald Ford, Seconding Speech for Henry Cabot Lodge, Chicago, July 28, 1960, Box D15, Press Secretary and Speech File, 1947–1973, Congressional Papers, Gerald R. Ford Files, Gerald R. Ford Presidential Library.

35. William J. Miller, *Henry Cabot Lodge*, 321–322.

36. Dwight D. Eisenhower, *Papers*, 21:1620.

37. William J. Miller, *Henry Cabot Lodge*, 322–323.

38. Safire, *Safire's Political Dictionary*, 705.

39. White, *In Search of History*, 478.

40. John Davis Lodge to Robert Finch, October 21, 1960, Box 106, John Davis Lodge Papers, Hoover Institution.

41. Gaddis, *Strategies of Containment*, 174.

42. Bradlee, *Good Life*, 208–216.

43. Gifford, *Center Cannot Hold*, 78.

44. Felzenberg, *A Man and His Presidents*, 91.

45. David R. Derge, "Hoosier Republicans in Chicago," in Tillett, *Inside Politics*, 133.

46. Henry Cabot Lodge Jr., *As It Was*, 99.

47. Gifford, *Center Cannot Hold*, 78.

48. William J. Miller, *Henry Cabot Lodge*, 323.

49. Wire from Henry Cabot Lodge Jr. to Leonard Hall, September 21, 1960, Box 8, Henry Cabot Lodge, Jr. Papers I, Massachusetts Historical Society.

50. William J. Miller, *Henry Cabot Lodge*, 323–324.

51. Blair, *Lodge in Vietnam*, 5.

52. Stephen Hess, *America's Political Dynasties*, 483.

53. "Lodge Staff," *Congressional Quarterly Weekly Report*, No. 39, Pt. 1 (week ending September 23, 1960): 11.

54. William J. Miller, *Henry Cabot Lodge*, 329–330.

55. Mary Von Rensselaer Thayer, "Emily Lodge Is Fascinating One of 'Big Four,'" *Washington Post*, July 29, 1960.

56. William J. Miller, *Henry Cabot Lodge*, 327.

57. Richard Pearson, "Emily Clark, Widow of Sen. Lodge, Dies," *Washington Post*, June 8, 1992.

58. William J. Miller, *Henry Cabot Lodge*, 327.

59. Caro, *Passage of Power*, 144.

60. Henry Cabot Lodge Jr. to Richard Nixon, October 12, 1960, Box 457, General Correspondence, Vice President, Pre-presidential Papers, Richard M. Nixon Presidential Library.

61. Zeiger, *Remarkable Henry Cabot Lodge*, 129.

62. Memorandum from Fred Seaton to Richard Nixon, October 9, 1960, Box 457, General Correspondence, Vice President, Pre-presidential Papers, Richard M. Nixon Presidential Library.

63. Thurber, *Republican and Race*, 125–126.

64. "The Lodge Program to End Segregation," *U.S. News and World Report*, October 24, 1960.

65. Edward C. Burks, "Lodge Foresees Negro in Cabinet," *New York Times*, October 19, 1960.

66. Gifford, *Center Cannot Hold*, 85.

67. W. J. Rorabaugh, "The Election of 1960," in Small, *Companion to Richard M. Nixon*, 126.

68. According to Fred Seaton's notes from a March 12, 1964, telephone conversation with Nixon, Nixon admitted that he "probably would appoint a negro of the stature of Ralph Bunche as delegate to the United Nations and theoretically that delegate has cabinet rank, and that's what he [Lodge] really meant." See Memorandum of Conversation between Fred Seaton and Richard Nixon, March 12, 1964, Box 9, Fred A. Seaton Papers, Dwight D. Eisenhower Presidential Library.

69. Memorandum from Rose Mary Woods to Henry Cabot Lodge Jr., August 1, 1960, Box 23, Sub-series A: Alphabetical, Series I: Correspondence, Series 238, Wilderness Years Collection, Richard M. Nixon Presidential Library.

70. Pedersen, *Guardians*, 321–322.

71. Memorandum from Richard Nixon to Herbert Klein, September 5, 1960, Box 9, Folder 62, Working Files, 1957–1962, Richard Nixon's Early Political Career, 1940–1962, Papers of Herbert G. Klein, Special Collections, University Archives, University of Southern California. In Klein's memoir, he falsely claimed that Lodge made his

speech in Harlem "with no prior consultation with the candidate for president on the eve of appearances in the South." Klein, *Making It Perfectly Clear*, 159.

72. Executive Branch Cooperation with the Commission on Civil Rights, February 27, 1959, Box 17, Henry Cabot Lodge, Jr. Papers I, Massachusetts Historical Society.

73. Wicker, *One of Us*, 238–239.

74. Gifford, *Center Cannot Hold*, 84.

75. Carol Anderson, *Eyes off the Prize*, 5.

76. William J. Miller, *Henry Cabot Lodge*, 325.

77. Gifford, *Center Cannot Hold*, 85.

78. Robert David Johnson, *All the Way with LBJ*, 38.

79. Gifford, *Center Cannot Hold*, 179.

80. William J. Miller, *Henry Cabot Lodge*, 325–326.

81. Stephen Hess, *America's Political Dynasties*, 485.

82. Henry Cabot Lodge Jr. to William J. Miller, undated [April 1967], Reel 11, Microfilm Edition, Henry Cabot Lodge, Jr. Papers II, Massachusetts Historical Society.

83. Henry Cabot Lodge Jr. to John Davis Lodge, March 24, 1964, Box 12, Henry Cabot Lodge, Jr. Papers I, Massachusetts Historical Society.

84. Klein, *Making It Perfectly Clear*, 162.

85. William J. Miller, *Henry Cabot Lodge*, 327–328.

86. Henry Cabot Lodge Jr. to John Davis Lodge, February 20, 1964, Box 144, John Davis Lodge Papers, Hoover Institution.

87. Oral History Interview with Tom Wicker, June 16, 1970, Lyndon B. Johnson Presidential Library.

88. Lodge sometimes reminded Nixon of their age difference. After Nixon's brutal loss in his 1962 gubernatorial bid, Lodge wrote to comfort him. "One thing that I have noticed—and I am older than you are—is that the apparent reverse of today turns out to be the springboard for even better things tomorrow." Henry Cabot Lodge Jr. to Richard Nixon, November 8, 1962, Box 457, General Correspondence, Vice President, Pre-presidential Papers, Richard M. Nixon Presidential Library.

89. William J. Miller, *Henry Cabot Lodge*, 327–328.

90. Stephen Hess, *America's Political Dynasties*, 484.

91. Oral History Interview with Tom Wicker, January 27, 1966, John F. Kennedy Presidential Library.

92. Kallina, *Kennedy v. Nixon*, 123.

93. Beschloss, *Jacqueline Kennedy*, 92.

94. Kallina, *Kennedy v. Nixon*, 125.

95. John Davis Lodge to Richard Nixon, November 2, 1960, Box 106, John Davis Lodge Papers, Hoover Institution.

96. William J. Miller, *Henry Cabot Lodge*, 329.

97. Evan Thomas, *Being Nixon*, 113–114.

98. John Davis Lodge to Robert Finch, October 10, 1960, Box 106, John Davis Lodge Papers, Hoover Institution.

99. Perlstein, *Nixonland,* 53.

100. Matthews, *Kennedy and Nixon,* 18.

101. Kallina, *Kennedy v. Nixon,* 125.

102. Klein, *Making It Perfectly Clear,* 105.

103. Kallina, *Kennedy v. Nixon,* 125.

104. Anthony Summers, *Arrogance of Power,* 208.

105. Matthews, *Kennedy and Nixon,* 155.

106. Memorandum from Richard Nixon to Chuck Lichenstein and Agnes Waldron, September 12, 1961, Box 5, Series VIII: Book Files—Six Crises, Khrushchev and the 1960 Campaign—Drafts, Series 257, Wilderness Years, Richard M. Nixon Presidential Library.

107. 1960 Campaign Notes, Reel 6, Microfilm Edition, Henry Cabot Lodge, Jr. Papers II, Massachusetts Historical Society.

108. Sergei Khrushchev, *Nikita Khrushchev,* 426.

109. Author interview with Sergei Khrushchev, December 22, 2017, telephone.

110. Wicker, *One of Us,* 239.

111. Telegram from Henry Cabot Lodge Jr. to A. R. Traylor, Tarea Hall Pittman, George A. Jones, Sedrick J. Rawlins, L. C. Bates, Raphael Dubard, L. M. Jackson, and James R. Mapp, October 28, 1960, Box 8, Henry Cabot Lodge, Jr. Papers I, Massachusetts Historical Society.

112. Gifford, *Center Cannot Hold,* 86–87.

113. Kotlowski, *Nixon's Civil Rights,* 165.

114. William J. Miller, *Henry Cabot Lodge,* 330–331.

115. Brodie, *Richard Nixon,* 429.

116. White, *Making of the President, 1960,* 206.

117. Hitchcock, *Age of Eisenhower,* 478.

118. Memorandum from Richard Nixon to Chuck Lichenstein and Agnes Waldron, September 12, 1961, Box 5, Series VIII: Book Files—Six Crises, Khrushchev and the 1960 Campaign—Drafts, Series 257, Wilderness Years, Richard M. Nixon Presidential Library.

119. Memorandum from Richard Nixon to Chuck Lichenstein and Agnes Waldron, September 12, 1961, Box 5, Series VIII: Book Files—Six Crises, Khrushchev and the 1960 Campaign—Drafts, Series 257, Wilderness Years, Richard M. Nixon Presidential Library.

120. Witcover, *Very Strange Bedfellows,* 21.

121. White, *Breach of Faith,* 83.

122. Stephen Hess, *America's Political Dynasties,* 484.

123. Felzenberg, *A Man and His Presidents,* 92–93.

124. Gifford, *Center Cannot Hold,* 134.

125. Henry Cabot Lodge Jr. to John Davis Lodge, March 24, 1964, Box 12, Henry Cabot Lodge, Jr. Papers I, Massachusetts Historical Society.

126. Unpublished Memoirs, March 31, 1976, pp. 13–14, Richard M. Nixon Presidential Library.

127. Richard Nixon to Henry Cabot Lodge Jr., November 24, 1972, Box 68, Alphabetical Name Files, White House Central Files, Richard M. Nixon Presidential Library.

128. Henry Cabot Lodge Jr., *Storm Has Many Eyes,* 191.

129. Defects in Nixon Campaign, undated, Box 8, Henry Cabot Lodge, Jr. Papers I, Massachusetts Historical Society.

130. Hillings, *Irrepressible Irishman,* 89.

131. Interview with Barry Goldwater, June 15, 1967, NXCP89-Ao, Columbia Center for Oral History, Columbia University.

132. Kessel, *Goldwater Coalition,* 52.

133. Swift, *Pat and Dick,* 163.

134. Hill, *Five Presidents,* 83.

135. Perlstein, *Before the Storm,* 137.

136. Price, *With Nixon,* 38.

137. O'Donnell and Powers, *"Johnny, We Hardly Knew Ye,"* 4.

138. Ellsberg, *Secrets,* 107.

139. William J. Miller, *Henry Cabot Lodge,* 331.

140. Slater, *The Ike I Knew,* 230.

141. William J. Miller, *Henry Cabot Lodge,* 332.

142. Richard Nixon to Henry Cabot Lodge Jr., January 16, 1961, Box 457, General Correspondence, Vice President, Pre-presidential Papers, Richard M. Nixon Presidential Library.

## 11. Saigon

1. Zeiger, *Remarkable Henry Cabot Lodge,* 133.

2. Henry Cabot Lodge Jr., *Storm Has Many Eyes,* 11.

3. Memorandum for the Record, December 30, 1960, Reel 13, Microfilm Edition, Henry Cabot Lodge, Jr. Papers II, Massachusetts Historical Society.

4. Nelson Rockefeller to Henry Cabot Lodge Jr., March 8, 1961, Box 92, Personal Papers, Projects, Nelson A. Rockefeller Papers, Rockefeller Archive Center.

5. Institute of International Education News Release, February 7, 1961, Box 104, John Davis Lodge Papers, Hoover Institution.

6. Author interview with Frank Wisner II, June 4, 2018, telephone and email.

7. Henry Cabot Lodge Jr. to Henry Luce, April 19, 1961, Box 2, Henry Robinson Luce Papers, Manuscript Division, Library of Congress.

8. "Lodge Plans," undated, Box 34, Personal Papers, Politics—George L. Hinman, Rockefeller Archive Center.

9. Henry Cabot Lodge Jr., *As It Was*, 167.

10. Valerie Aubourg, "The Atlantic Congress of 1959: An Ambiguous Celebration of the Atlantic Community," in Schmidt, *History of NATO*, 354.

11. Oral History Interview with Henry Cabot Lodge, August 4, 1965, John F. Kennedy Presidential Library.

12. Memorandum of Conversation with Secretary of State Dean Rusk, Saturday, April 8, 1961, Reel 1, Atlantic Institute, Henry Cabot Lodge, Jr. Papers I, Massachusetts Historical Society.

13. Henry Cabot Lodge Jr. to Charles Bohlen, May 31, 1962, Reel 2, Microfilm Edition, Henry Cabot Lodge, Jr. Papers II, Massachusetts Historical Society.

14. William J. Miller, *Henry Cabot Lodge*, 333.

15. William J. Miller, *Henry Cabot Lodge*, 333–334.

16. Memorandum of Conversation with John J. McCloy, March 1, 1962, Reel 1, Atlantic Institute, Henry Cabot Lodge, Jr. Papers I, Massachusetts Historical Society.

17. Henry Cabot Lodge Jr., *As It Was*, 167–168.

18. See Uri, *Partnership for Progress*.

19. Henry Cabot Lodge Jr. to Jacob Devers, April 8, 1963, Reel 1, Atlantic Institute, Henry Cabot Lodge, Jr. Papers I, Massachusetts Historical Society.

20. William J. Miller, *Henry Cabot Lodge*, 334.

21. Hatcher, *Suicide of an Elite*, 38.

22. Lodge Calendar, Wednesday, June 12, 1963, Box 42, Henry Cabot Lodge, Jr. Papers I, Massachusetts Historical Society.

23. William J. Miller, *Henry Cabot Lodge*, 334.

24. Confidential Journal, June 12, 1963, Reel 17, Microfilm Edition, Henry Cabot Lodge, Jr. Papers II, Massachusetts Historical Society.

25. This reflects Lodge's recollection, as told to Eisenhower, of what Kennedy said in the Oval Office that day. Eisenhower told John McCone that he was furious that the White House maintained that Lodge had asked for the appointment. Eisenhower advised Lodge to publicize the fact that Kennedy had asked him to go, but Lodge did not do so. See Memorandum of Conference, 0930, September 1963, between Eisenhower, McCone, and John Eisenhower, CIA C05579024, CREST (CIA Records Search Tool), National Archives and Records Administration.

26. Memorandum of Conversation with Dean Rusk, Thursday, October 12, 1961, Reel 1, Atlantic Institute, Henry Cabot Lodge, Jr. Papers I, Massachusetts Historical Society.

27. Oral History Interview with Henry Cabot Lodge, August 4, 1965, John F. Kennedy Presidential Library.

28. Hilsman, *To Move a Nation*, 478.

29. Asselin, *Vietnam's American War*, 106.

30. Interview with David Halberstam, pt. 2 of 5, January 16, 1979, *Vietnam: A Television History*, WGBH Media Library and Archives.

31. Oral History Interview with Henry Cabot Lodge, August 4, 1965, John F. Kennedy Presidential Library.

32. Memorandum for Confidential Journal, undated, Reel 17, Microfilm Edition, Henry Cabot Lodge, Jr. Papers II, Massachusetts Historical Society.

33. William J. Miller, *Henry Cabot Lodge*, 334–335.

34. Interview with Henry Cabot Lodge Jr., pt. 1 of 5, January 1, 1979, *Vietnam: A Television History*, WGBH Media Library and Archives.

35. Logevall, *Choosing War*, 339–340.

36. Conversation with Dean Rusk, Monday, June 17, 1963, Confidential Journal, Reel 17, Microfilm Edition, Henry Cabot Lodge, Jr. Papers II, Massachusetts Historical Society.

37. Hilsman, *To Move a Nation*, 478.

38. Blair, *Lodge in Vietnam*, 8.

39. Thompson, "How Could Vietnam Happen?," 48.

40. Blair, *Lodge in Vietnam*, 11.

41. Gary R. Hess, "Commitment in the Age of Counterinsurgency: Kennedy's Vietnam Options and Decisions, 1961–1963," in David L. Anderson, *Shadow on the White House*, 70.

42. Interview with Roger Hilsman, May 11, 1981, *Vietnam: A Television History*, WGBH Media Library and Archives.

43. Dommen, *Indochinese Experience*, 454–455.

44. Interview with Frederick Nolting, April 30, 1981, *Vietnam: A Television History*, WGBH Media Library and Archives.

45. Interview with W. Averell Harriman, pt. 2 of 4, January 29, 1979, *Vietnam: A Television History*, WGBH Media Library and Archives.

46. Mecklin, *Mission in Torment*, 99.

47. Memorandum from Joseph W. Neubert to Roger Hilsman, June 25, 1963, Box 3, Roger Hilsman Papers, John F. Kennedy Presidential Library.

48. Interview with W. W. Rostow, April 20, 1981, *Vietnam: A Television History*, WGBH Media Library and Archives.

49. Jacobs, *America's Miracle Man*, 229.

50. Interview with W. Averell Harriman, pt. 1 of 4, January 29, 1979, *Vietnam: A Television History*, WGBH Media Library and Archives.

51. Edward Miller, *Misalliance*, 290.

52. Nolting, *From Trust to Tragedy*, 105.

53. Robert Hopkins Miller, *Vietnam and Beyond*, 67.

54. Blair, *Lodge in Vietnam*, xii.

55. Schlesinger, *Thousand Days*, 988.

56. William J. Miller, *Henry Cabot Lodge*, 335–336.

57. Dallek, *Camelot's Court*, 396.

58. Grant, *Facing the Phoenix*, 191.

59. Nolting, *From Trust to Tragedy*, 112.

60. Interview with Henry Cabot Lodge Jr., pt. 1 of 5, January 1, 1979, *Vietnam: A Television History*, WGBH Media Library and Archives.

61. Interview with Madame Ngo Dinh Nhu, February 11, 1982, *Vietnam: A Television History*, WGBH Media Library and Archives.

62. Demery, *Finding the Dragon Lady*, 10.

63. Interview with Henry Cabot Lodge Jr., pt. 1 of 5, January 1, 1979, *Vietnam: A Television History*, WGBH Media Library and Archives.

64. Kiernan, *Viet Nam*, 420.

65. Telegram from British Embassy, Saigon, to Foreign Office, 1783/63, June 12, 1963, FO 371/170142, National Archives, United Kingdom.

66. Telegram from British Embassy, Saigon, to Foreign Office, 1783/63, June 12, 1963, FO 371/170142, National Archives, United Kingdom.

67. Telegram from British Embassy, Saigon, to Foreign Office, 1783/63, June 12, 1963, FO 371/170142, National Archives, United Kingdom.

68. Arnett, *Live from the Battlefield*, 101.

69. Telegram from British Embassy, Saigon, to Foreign Office, 1783/63, June 12, 1963, FO 371/170143, National Archives, United Kingdom.

70. Telegram from British Embassy, Saigon, to Foreign Office, 1783/63, June 12, 1963, FO 371/170142, National Archives, United Kingdom.

71. Halberstam, *Making of a Quagmire*, 113.

72. Dommen, *Indochinese Experience*, 516.

73. Arnett, *Live from the Battlefield*, 103.

74. Telegram from British Embassy, Saigon, to Foreign Office, 1783/63, June 12, 1963, FO 371/170142, National Archives, United Kingdom.

75. Immerman, *Hidden Hand*, 82.

76. Demery, *Finding the Dragon Lady*, 2.

77. Browne, *New Face of War*, 263.

78. Dommen, *Indochinese Experience*, 521.

79. Oral History Interview with Lucien Conein, June 2, 1983, Lyndon B. Johnson Presidential Library.

80. Phillips, *Why Vietnam Matters*, 157.

81. Phillips, *Why Vietnam Matters*, 159.

82. Herken, *Georgetown Set*, 286–287.

83. Dommen, *Indochinese Experience*, 531.

84. Hersh, *Dark Side of Camelot*, 423.

85. Joseph Alsop to Keyes Beech, November 2, 1963, Box 19, Joseph Alsop and Stewart Alsop Papers, Manuscript Division, Library of Congress.

86. Interview with Madame Ngo Dinh Nhu, February 11, 1982, *Vietnam: A Television History*, WGBH Media Library and Archives.

87. Merry, *Taking on the World*, 405.

88. Joseph Alsop to H. E. Gumbel, November 7, 1963, Box 19, Joseph Alsop and Stewart Alsop Papers, Manuscript Division, Library of Congress.

89. Dommen, *Indochinese Experience,* 532.

90. Maneli, *War of the Vanquished,* 146.

91. Chomsky, *Rethinking Camelot,* 80.

92. Henry Cabot Lodge Jr., *Storm Has Many Eyes,* 11.

93. Editorial Note 254, in *Foreign Relations of the United States, 1961–1963,* vol. 3, *Vietnam, January–August 1963,* ed. Edward C. Keefer and Louis J. Smith (Washington, DC: U.S. Government Printing Office, 1991).

94. Tape 104/A40, Oval Office, August 15, 1963, 11:00 a.m., Presidential Papers, President's Office Files, Presidential Recordings, John F. Kennedy Presidential Library.

95. Tape 104/A40, Oval Office, August 15, 1963, 11:00 a.m., Presidential Papers, President's Office Files, Presidential Recordings, John F. Kennedy Presidential Library.

96. Maneli, *War of the Vanquished,* 140–141.

97. Author interview with Rufus Phillips, March 18, 2017, Arlington, Virginia.

98. Oral History Interview with John Michael Dunn, July 25, 1984, Lyndon B. Johnson Presidential Library.

99. Edward G. Lansdale, "Lessons Learned, The Philippines: 1946–1953," September 26, 1962, Interdepartmental Course on Counterinsurgency, Foreign Service Institute, Box 72, Individuals, 1957–1991, Vann-Sheehan Vietnam War Collection, Neil Sheehan Papers, Manuscript Division, Library of Congress.

100. Comment on *To Move a Nation* by Roger Hilsman, Doubleday & Co., undated, Reel 20, Microfilm Edition, Henry Cabot Lodge, Jr. Papers II, Massachusetts Historical Society.

101. Henry Cabot Lodge Jr. to Dean Rusk, September 13, 1963, Box 10, Intelligence File, National Security File, Lyndon B. Johnson Presidential Library.

102. Prados, *Presidents' Secret Wars,* 240–241.

103. Interview with Edward Geary Lansdale, pt. 4 of 5, January 31, 1979, *Vietnam: A Television History,* WGBH Media Library and Archives.

104. Boot, *Road Not Taken,* 505.

105. Grant, *Facing the Phoenix,* 191.

106. Oral History Interview with John Michael Dunn, July 25, 1984, Lyndon B. Johnson Presidential Library.

107. Phillips, *Why Vietnam Matters,* 165.

108. Oral History Interview with Frederick W. Flott, July 22, 1984, Lyndon B. Johnson Presidential Library.

109. William J. Miller, *Henry Cabot Lodge,* 338.

110. Arnett, *Live from the Battlefield,* 105–106.

111. Phillips, *Why Vietnam Matters,* 166.

112. Shaplen, *Lost Revolution*, 195.

113. Oral History Interview with Frederick Nolting, November 11, 1982, Lyndon B. Johnson Presidential Library.

114. Oral History Interview with William Colby, June 2, 1981, Lyndon B. Johnson Presidential Library.

115. Oral History Interview with Henry Cabot Lodge, August 4, 1965, John F. Kennedy Presidential Library.

116. Abramson, *Spanning the Century*, 618.

117. Rust, *Kennedy in Vietnam*, 104.

118. The Buddhist Challenge to President Diem, July 22, 1963, FO 371/170144, National Archives, United Kingdom.

119. CIA Telegram 5978, August 24, 1963, Box 3, Roger Hilsman Papers, John F. Kennedy Presidential Library.

120. Prochnau, *Once upon a Distant War*, 381.

121. Sheehan, *Bright Shining Lie*, 358.

122. Author interview with Charles Trueheart, June 9, 2017, Paris, France.

123. C. D. Jackson to Henry Cabot Lodge Jr., February 12, 1959, Box 68, C. D. Jackson Records, Dwight D. Eisenhower Presidential Library.

124. Statement to Make on Arrival in Saigon, undated, Box 36, Henry Cabot Lodge, Jr. Papers I, Massachusetts Historical Society.

125. Arnett, *Live from the Battlefield*, 107.

126. Hammer, *Death in November*, 168.

127. William J. Miller, *Henry Cabot Lodge*, 340.

128. Arnett, *Live from the Battlefield*, 107.

129. Oral History Interview with David Halberstam, November 1, 1982, Lyndon B. Johnson Presidential Library.

130. Prochnau, *Once upon a Distant War*, 347.

131. Dommen, *Indochinese Experience*, 536.

132. Blair, *Lodge in Vietnam*, 25.

133. Mecklin, *Mission in Torment*, 189–190.

134. Emily Lodge Vietnam Notes, Monday, August 26, [1963], 8 A.M., Reel 25, Microfilm Edition, Henry Cabot Lodge, Jr. Papers II, Massachusetts Historical Society.

135. Henry Cabot Lodge Jr. to John Mason Brown, December 12, 1963, Reel 2, Microfilm Edition, Henry Cabot Lodge, Jr. Papers II, Massachusetts Historical Society.

136. Interview with David Halberstam, pt. 1 of 5, January 16, 1979, *Vietnam: A Television History*, WGBH Media Library and Archives.

137. William J. Miller, *Vietnam and Beyond*, 57–58.

138. Peter Grose, "Young U.S. Aides Score in Vietnam," *New York Times*, July 1, 1964.

139. Lodge #1, undated, Box 28, Correspondence, circa 1950–1984, John Paul Vann, circa 1920–1984, Vann-Sheehan Vietnam War Collection, Neil Sheehan Papers, Manuscript Division, Library of Congress.

140. Interview with Frank G. Wisner, March 22, 1992, Foreign Affairs Oral History Collection, Association for Diplomatic Studies and Training.

141. Packer, *Our Man*, 43.

142. Interview with David Halberstam, pt. 5 of 5, January 16, 1979, *Vietnam: A Television History*, WGBH Media Library and Archives.

143. Grant, *Facing the Phoenix*, 197.

144. Author interview with William A. K. "Tony" Lake, May 25, 2017, telephone.

145. Grant, *Facing the Phoenix*, 197.

146. Telegram 03636 from Saigon to Washington, undated, Box 3, Roger Hilsman Papers, John F. Kennedy Presidential Library.

147. Prochnau, *Once upon a Distant War*, 377.

148. Memorandum, "My Recollection of What Happened in Viet Nam up to Coup of November 1," undated, Reel 19, Microfilm Edition, Henry Cabot Lodge, Jr. Papers II, Massachusetts Historical Society.

149. Arnett, *Live from the Battlefield*, 108.

150. Abramson, *Spanning the Century*, 618.

151. Notes, undated, Box 71, Individuals, 1957–1991, Vann-Sheehan Vietnam War Collection, Neil Sheehan Papers, Manuscript Division, Library of Congress.

152. Government of Vietnam Acting Foreign Minister Cuu's Comments to Ambassador Lodge on the Buddhist Issue and Alleged American Involvement, October 18, 1963, CIA DOC_0000625946, CREST (CIA Records Search Tool), National Archives and Records Administration.

153. Interview with Henry Cabot Lodge Jr., pt. 4 of 5, January 1, 1979, *Vietnam: A Television History*, WGBH Media Library and Archives.

154. Mecklin, *Mission in Torment*, 179.

155. Notes, undated, Box 71, Individuals, 1957–1991, Vann-Sheehan Vietnam War Collection, Neil Sheehan Papers, Manuscript Division, Library of Congress.

156. Rust, *Eisenhower and Cambodia*, 276.

157. Blair, *Lodge in Vietnam*, 1.

158. Memorandum from William Bundy to Bill Moyers, July 30, 1966, Box 263, Vietnam, Country File, National Security File, Lyndon B. Johnson Presidential Library.

159. Kattenberg, *Vietnam Trauma*, 117.

160. For example, see Edward Miller, *Misalliance*, 260–318; Rust, *Kennedy in Vietnam*, 94–178; Kahin, *Intervention*, 146–181; Hammer, *Death in November*, 103–311; Winters, *Year of the Hare*, 29–113; Kaiser, *American Tragedy*, 213–283; Jacobs, *Cold War Mandarin*, 142–181; and Logevall, *Choosing War*, 1–74.

161. Cable from George Ball to Henry Cabot Lodge Jr., State 243, August 25, 1963, Box 8, Saigon Embassy Files Taken by Ambassador Graham Martin, 1963–1975, Na-

tional Security Adviser, Gerald R. Ford Presidential Library. In a follow-up telegram de-classified in 2016, Paul Harkins was even more direct: "In context of State 243 to Saigon 'direct support' interpreted here as indicating that U.S. diplomatic recognition will be forthcoming promptly and that U.S. economic and military assistance to RVN [Republic of Viet Nam] will continue as at present. Even under most extreme contingency of military coup in which not only Nhus but also Diem is removed from scene." Telegram from Paul Harkins to Maxwell Taylor, August 28, 1963, Box 198, Vietnam, Country File, National Security Files, Presidential Papers, John F. Kennedy Presidential Library.

162. Halberstam, *Best and the Brightest*, 263.

163. Thomas L. Hughes, Notes of Conversations with Mike Forrestal and Roger Hilsman during August 24–28, 1963, Coup Planning Week, 1–2. The author was granted access to these notes by Hughes.

164. Thomas L. Hughes, Notes of Conversations with Mike Forrestal and Roger Hilsman during August 24–28, 1963, Coup Planning Week, 1–2.

165. Thomas L. Hughes, Notes of Conversations with Mike Forrestal and Roger Hilsman during August 24–28, 1963, Coup Planning Week, 1–2.

166. Edward Miller, *Misalliance*, 291.

167. Abramson, *Spanning the Century*, 621.

168. Herring, *America's Longest War*, 98.

169. Interview with Frederick Nolting, April 30, 1981, *Vietnam: A Television History*, WGBH Media Library and Archives.

170. Colby, *Honorable Men*, 210.

171. Halberstam, *Best and the Brightest*, 263.

172. Comment on *To Move a Nation* by Roger Hilsman, Doubleday & Co., undated, Reel 20, Microfilm Edition, Henry Cabot Lodge, Jr. Papers II, Massachusetts Historical Society.

173. Shaw, *Lost Mandate of Heaven*, 254.

174. Telegram 292 from Saigon to Department, August 25, 1963, Box 8, National Security Adviser, Saigon Embassy Files Taken by Amb. Graham Martin, Gerald R. Ford Presidential Library.

175. Newman, *JFK and Vietnam*, 350.

176. Oral History Interview with John Michael Dunn, July 25, 1984, Lyndon B. Johnson Presidential Library.

177. Tape 107/A42, Oval Office, August 26, 1963, 12:00 p.m., Presidential Papers, President's Office Files, Presidential Recordings, John F. Kennedy Presidential Library.

178. Memorandum of Conversation, August 26, 1963, 12:00 p.m., Box 4, Roger Hilsman Papers, John F. Kennedy Presidential Library.

179. Hilsman, *To Move a Nation*, 489.

180. Telegram 391 from Saigon to Washington, August 31, 1963, Box 3, Roger Hilsman Papers, John F. Kennedy Presidential Library.

181. Hilsman, "Commentary and Reply," 105.

182. Chomsky, *Rethinking Camelot,* 73.

183. Catton, *Diem's Final Failure,* 200.

184. Tape 107/A42, August 28, 1963, unknown time, and Tape 108/A43, August 28, 1963, unknown time, Presidential Papers, President's Office Files, Presidential Recordings, John F. Kennedy Presidential Library.

185. Tape 107/A42, August 28, 1963, unknown time, and Tape 108/A43, August 28, 1963, unknown time, Presidential Papers, President's Office Files, Presidential Recordings, John F. Kennedy Presidential Library.

186. Holbrooke, "Carpe Diem."

187. Berman, *Planning a Tragedy,* 26.

188. Tape 108/A43, August 29, 1963, 12:00 p.m., Presidential Papers, President's Office Files, Presidential Recordings, John F. Kennedy Presidential Library.

189. Memorandum from Roger Hilsman to Dean Rusk, August 30, 1963, Box 263, Vietnam, Country File, National Security File, Lyndon B. Johnson Presidential Library.

190. Memorandum of Conversation, August 29, 1963, Box 4, Roger Hilsman Papers, John F. Kennedy Presidential Library.

191. Tape 108/A43, August 29, 1963, 12:00 p.m., Presidential Papers, President's Office Files, Presidential Recordings, John F. Kennedy Presidential Library.

192. Cline, *Secrets, Spies, and Scholars,* 198.

193. Blair, *Lodge in Vietnam,* 46.

## 12. Diem

1. Blair, *Lodge in Vietnam,* 8.

2. Mecklin, *Mission in Torment,* 14.

3. Mecklin, *Mission in Torment,* 15.

4. Tape 104/A40, August 15, 1963, 11:00 a.m., Presidential Papers, President's Office Files, Presidential Recordings, John F. Kennedy Presidential Library.

5. William J. Miller, *Henry Cabot Lodge,* 341.

6. Notes, undated, Box 71, Individuals, 1957–1991, Vann-Sheehan Vietnam War Collection, Neil Sheehan Papers, Manuscript Division, Library of Congress.

7. Mecklin, *Mission in Torment,* 15.

8. William J. Miller, *Henry Cabot Lodge,* 341–342.

9. Oral History Interview with Paul Harkins, November 10, 1981, Lyndon B. Johnson Presidential Library.

10. Browne, *New Face of War,* 270.

11. Oral History Interview with Frederick W. Flott, July 22, 1984, Lyndon B. Johnson Presidential Library.

12. Mecklin, *Mission in Torment,* 17.

13. Oral History Interview with Frederick W. Flott, July 22, 1984, Lyndon B. Johnson Presidential Library.

14. Mecklin, *Mission in Torment*, 195.

15. Dommen, *Indochinese Experience*, 537.

16. David L. Anderson, "Dwight D. Eisenhower and Wholehearted Support of Ngo Dinh Diem," in David L. Anderson, *Shadow on the White House*, 43.

17. Robert Shaplen, "Nine Years after a Fateful Assassination—The Cult of Diem," *New York Times*, May 14, 1972.

18. Sorley, *Vietnam War*, ix.

19. Shaplen, "Nine Years."

20. Interview with Edward Geary Lansdale, pt. 2 of 5, January 31, 1979, *Vietnam: A Television History*, WGBH Media Library and Archives.

21. Mecklin, *Mission in Torment*, 28–29.

22. Shaplen, "Nine Years." Shaplen's account is the best of the early accounts. Working for the *New Yorker*, he had time to do research and cultivate sources that a journalist with daily deadlines did not.

23. Kiernan, *Viet Nam*, 407.

24. Shaplen, "Nine Years."

25. Browne, *New Face of War*, 86.

26. Interview with Edward Geary Lansdale, pt. 2 of 5, January 31, 1979, *Vietnam: A Television History*, WGBH Media Library and Archives.

27. Kiernan, *Viet Nam*, 407.

28. Ky, *Buddha's Child*, 91.

29. Hammer, *Death in November*, 591.

30. Mecklin, *Mission in Torment*, 32–33.

31. Beschloss, *Jacqueline Kennedy*, 305–306.

32. Demery, *Finding the Dragon Lady*, 140.

33. Immerman, *The Hidden Hand*, 82.

34. Mecklin, *Mission in Torment*, 33–34.

35. Halberstam, *The Making of a Quagmire*, 136.

36. Notes of Meeting between Diem and Staff, August 27, 1963, 9:00 a.m., Office of the President, 1954–1963 (Phông Phủ Tổng thống Đệ Nhất Cộng Hoà) 60, National Archives Center II (Trung Tâm Lưu Trữ Quốc Gia II), Ho Chi Minh City.

37. Moyar, *Triumph Forsaken*, 249.

38. Arnett, *Live from the Battlefield*, 107.

39. Interview with Henry Cabot Lodge Jr., pt. 3 of 5, January 1, 1979, *Vietnam: A Television History*, WGBH Media Library and Archives.

40. Catton, *Diem's Final Failure*, 200.

41. Tape 104/A40, August 15, 1963, 11:00 a.m., Presidential Papers, President's Office Files, Presidential Recordings, John F. Kennedy Presidential Library.

42. Demery, *Finding the Dragon Lady*, 1.

43. Ngo-Dinh, Ngo-Dinh, and Willemetz, *La République du Vietnam*, 174.

44. Kattenberg, *Vietnam Trauma*, 117.

45. Mecklin, *Mission in Torment*, 39.

46. William J. Miller, *Henry Cabot Lodge*, 342.

47. Henry Cabot Lodge Jr., *Storm Has Many Eyes*, 207.

48. Telegram from British Embassy, Saigon, to South East Asia Department, Foreign Office, 1783/III, August 29, 1963, FO 371/170146, National Archives, United Kingdom.

49. Telegram from Henry Cabot Lodge Jr. to Averell Harriman, August 28, 1963, Box 198, Vietnam, Country File, National Security Files, Presidential Papers, John F. Kennedy Presidential Library.

50. Telegram from CIA to Secretary of State, August 30, 1963, Box 198, Vietnam, Countries, National Security Files, Presidential Papers, John F. Kennedy Presidential Library.

51. Hammer, *Death in November*, 196.

52. Note of Conversation from Paul Harkins, August 31, 1963, Box 198, Vietnam, Countries, National Security Files, Presidential Papers, John F. Kennedy Presidential Library.

53. Interview with Henry Cabot Lodge Jr., pt. 2 of 5, January 1, 1979, *Vietnam: A Television History*, WGBH Media Library and Archives.

54. John McCone to Henry Cabot Lodge Jr., September 19, 1963, C06246225, CREST (CIA Records Search Tool), National Archives and Records Administration.

55. "CAS" Undated Notes, Box 13, Henry Cabot Lodge, Jr. Papers II, Massachusetts Historical Society.

56. John McCone to Henry Cabot Lodge Jr., September 19, 1963, C06246225, CREST, National Archives and Records Administration.

57. Ky, *Twenty Years and Twenty Days*, 36.

58. Grant, *Facing the Phoenix*, 203.

59. Mecklin, *Mission in Torment*, 43.

60. Henry Cabot Lodge Jr. to John Davis Lodge, September 4, 1963, Box 144, John Davis Lodge Papers, Hoover Institution.

61. From Saigon to Foreign Office, Despatch No. 50, September 18, 1963, FO 371/170146, National Archives, United Kingdom.

62. Blair, "Special Consideration," 2.

63. Oral History Interview with Henry Cabot Lodge, August 4, 1965, John F. Kennedy Presidential Library.

64. Dommen, *Indochinese Experience*, 537.

65. Ky, *How We Lost*, 36.

66. Edward Miller, *Misalliance*, 291.

67. Richard Pearson, "Emily Clark, Widow of Sen. Lodge, Dies," *Washington Post*, June 8, 1992.

68. Interview with Lucien Conein, May 7, 1981, *Vietnam: A Television History*, WGBH Media Library and Archives.

69. Grant, *Facing the Phoenix,* 201–202.

70. Oral History Interview with John Michael Dunn, July 25, 1984, Lyndon B. Johnson Presidential Library.

71. E. Howard Hunt, *Undercover,* 42.

72. Interview with Edward Geary Lansdale, pt. 1 of 5, January 31, 1979, *Vietnam: A Television History*, WGBH Media Library and Archives.

73. Oral History Interview with John Michael Dunn, July 25, 1984, Lyndon B. Johnson Presidential Library.

74. Packer, *Our Man,* 85.

75. "George McArthur's Vietnam," interview with George McArthur, *Pushing On* (blog), December 11, 2012, http://lde421.blogspot.com/2012/12/george-mcarthurs-vietnam.html.

76. Rust, *Kennedy in Vietnam,* 110.

77. Interview with Lucien Conein, May 7, 1981, *Vietnam: A Television History*, WGBH Media Library and Archives.

78. Oral History Interview with Lucien Conein, June 2, 1983, Lyndon B. Johnson Presidential Library.

79. Newman, *JFK and Vietnam,* 346.

80. Nolting, *From Trust to Tragedy,* 107.

81. Shaplen, *Lost Revolution,* 195.

82. Richardson, *My Father the Spy,* 175.

83. Undated Notes, Box 1, Folder 2, Papers of David Halberstam, Howard Gotlieb Archival Research Center, Boston University.

84. William Colby to Roger Hilsman, Victor Krulak, and McGeorge Bundy, September 12, 1963, Box 199, Vietnam, Countries, National Security Files, Presidential Papers, John F. Kennedy Presidential Library.

85. Undated Notes, Box 1, Folder 2, Papers of David Halberstam, Howard Gotlieb Archival Research Center, Boston University.

86. William J. Miller, *Henry Cabot Lodge,* 349.

87. "Sequence of CAS Contacts with Vietnamese Generals, 23 August through 23 October 1963," JFK Assassination Records—2017 Additional Documents Release, https://www.archives.gov/files/research/jfk/releases/docid-32283369.pdf.

88. Prochnau, *Once upon a Distant War,* 441.

89. Edward Miller, *Misalliance,* 286.

90. "Sequence of CAS Contacts with Vietnamese Generals, 23 August through 23 October 1963," JFK Assassination Records—2017 Additional Documents Release, https://www.archives.gov/files/research/jfk/releases/docid-32283369.pdf.

91. Oral History Interview with Lucien Conein, June 2, 1983, Lyndon B. Johnson Presidential Library.

92. "Sequence of CAS Contacts with Vietnamese Generals, 23 August through 23 October 1963," JFK Assassination Records—2017 Additional Documents Release, https://www.archives.gov/files/research/jfk/releases/docid-32283369.pdf.

93. Telegram 343 from Saigon to Washington, August 27, 1963, Box 3, Roger Hilsman Papers, John F. Kennedy Presidential Library.

94. Phillips, *Why Vietnam Matters*, 169.

95. "Sequence of CAS Contacts with Vietnamese Generals, 23 August through 23 October 1963," JFK Assassination Records—2017 Additional Documents Release, https://www.archives.gov/files/research/jfk/releases/docid-32283369.pdf.

96. Hilsman, *To Move a Nation*, 493.

97. Interview with Henry Cabot Lodge Jr., pt. 3 of 5, January 1, 1979, *Vietnam: A Television History*, WGBH Media Library and Archives.

98. "Sequence of CAS Contacts with Vietnamese Generals, 23 August through 23 October 1963," JFK Assassination Records—2017 Additional Documents Release, https://www.archives.gov/files/research/jfk/releases/docid-32283369.pdf.

99. Interview with Henry Cabot Lodge Jr., pt. 3 of 5, January 1, 1979, *Vietnam: A Television History*, WGBH Media Library and Archives.

100. Shaw, *Lost Mandate of Heaven*, 258.

101. Talking Paper for Mr. Hilsman for September 3 Meeting, undated, Box 4, Roger Hilsman Papers, John F. Kennedy Presidential Library.

102. Telegram from Washington to Saigon, September 3, 1963, Box 4, John F. Roger Hilsman Papers, Kennedy Presidential Library.

103. From Saigon to Foreign Office, Despatch No. 50, September 18, 1963, FO 371/170146, National Archives, United Kingdom.

104. Tien Hung Nguyen and Schecter, *Palace File*, 75.

105. CIA Memorandum 2352/63, September 14, 1963, Box 4, Roger Hilsman Papers, John F. Kennedy Presidential Library.

106. Tien Hung Nguyen and Schecter, *Palace File*, 75.

107. Memorandum from Roger Hilsman to Dean Rusk, August 30, 1963, Box 263, Vietnam, Country File, National Security File, Lyndon B. Johnson Presidential Library.

108. Parmet, *JFK*, 332.

109. Mecklin, *Mission in Torment*, 201.

110. Dean Rusk wrote Lodge on September 3 to say that he did not like the Dalat plan, because it might enable Nhu to remain the "power behind [the] throne." Telegram 317 from Washington to Saigon, September 3, 1963, Box 4, Roger Hilsman Papers, John F. Kennedy Presidential Library.

111. Talking Paper for Mr. Hilsman for September 3 Meeting, undated, Box 4, Roger Hilsman Papers, John F. Kennedy Presidential Library.

112. Dallek, *Camelot's Court*, 392.

113. David Halberstam to John Paul Vann, July 27, 1963, Box 28, Correspondence, circa 1950–1984, John Paul Vann, circa 1920–1984, Vann-Sheehan Vietnam War Collection, Neil Sheehan Papers, Manuscript Division, Library of Congress.

114. Richardson, *My Father the Spy*, 159–160.

115. Grant, *Facing the Phoenix*, 205.

116. Halberstam, *Making of a Quagmire*, 101.

117. Interview with David Halberstam by Neil Sheehan, May 14, 1976, Box 67, Neil Sheehan Papers, Manuscript Division, Library of Congress.

118. David Halberstam, "Getting the Story in Vietnam," *Commentary*, January 1965, 30–34.

119. Maneli, *War of the Vanquished*, 132–133.

120. Kabaservice, *Guardians*, 209.

121. Prochnau, *Once upon a Distant War*, 382.

122. Prochnau, *Once upon a Distant War*, 382.

123. Henry Cabot Lodge Jr. to Clay Blair, December 16, 1963, Reel 2, Microfilm Edition, Henry Cabot Lodge, Jr. Papers II, Massachusetts Historical Society.

124. Sheehan, *Bright Shining Lie*, 360.

125. David Halberstam to John Paul Vann, October 29, 1963, Box 28, Correspondence, circa 1950–1984, John Paul Vann, circa 1920–1984, Vann-Sheehan Vietnam War Collection, Neil Sheehan Papers, Manuscript Division, Library of Congress.

126. Interview with David Halberstam, pt. 1 of 5, January 16, 1979, *Vietnam: A Television History*, WGBH Media Library and Archives.

127. Neil Sheehan to John Paul Vann, September 16, 1963, Box 28, Correspondence, circa 1950–1984, John Paul Vann, circa 1920–1984, Vann-Sheehan Vietnam War Collection, Neil Sheehan Papers, Manuscript Division, Library of Congress.

128. Sheehan, *Bright Shining Lie*, 359.

129. Herken, *Georgetown Set*, 287–288.

130. Moyar, *Triumph Forsaken*, 239.

131. Chomsky, *Rethinking Camelot*, 76.

132. Mecklin, *Mission in Torment*, 163–164.

133. Douglas Brinkley, *Cronkite*, 261–262.

134. Hammer, *Death in November*, 199.

135. Phillips, *Why Vietnam Matters*, 181–182.

136. Interview with the President of the Republic of Vietnam, Press Office, August 24, 1963, Office of the President, 1954–1963 (Phông Phủ Tổng thống Đệ Nhất Cộng Hoà) 19419, National Archives Center II (Trung Tâm Lưu Trữ Quốc Gia II), Ho Chi Minh City.

137. Interview with Henry Cabot Lodge Jr., pt. 2 of 5, January 1, 1979, *Vietnam: A Television History*, WGBH Media Library and Archives.

138. Hammer, *Death in November*, 205.

139. Interview with Henry Cabot Lodge Jr., pt. 4 of 5, January 1, 1979, *Vietnam: A Television History,* WGBH Media Library and Archives.

140. Ashby and Gramer, *Fighting the Odds,* 168–169.

141. Hammer, *Death in November,* 209.

142. Hammer, *Death in November,* 211.

143. Philip Franchine, "Ariz. Couple Had Adventures, Role in History," *Green Valley (AZ) News,* June 27, 2012.

144. Tape 109/A4, September 10, 1963, unknown time, Presidential Papers, President's Office Files, Presidential Recordings, John F. Kennedy Presidential Library.

145. William J. Miller, *Henry Cabot Lodge,* 344–345.

146. Tape 109/A4, September 10, 1963, unknown time, Presidential Papers, President's Office Files, Presidential Recordings, John F. Kennedy Presidential Library.

147. Tape 109/A4, September 10, 1963, unknown time, Presidential Papers, President's Office Files, Presidential Recordings, John F. Kennedy Presidential Library.

148. Tape 110/A2, September 11, 1963, unknown time, Presidential Papers, President's Office Files, Presidential Recordings, John F. Kennedy Presidential Library.

149. Memorandum of Conference with the President, September 6, 1963, 10:20 a.m., Rufus Phillips Collection, Virtual Vietnam Archive, Texas Tech University.

150. Tape 111/A3, September 17, 1963, unknown time, Presidential Papers, President's Office Files, Presidential Recordings, John F. Kennedy Presidential Library.

151. Henry Cabot Lodge Jr. to John Davis Lodge, September 24, 1963, Box 144, John Davis Lodge Papers, Hoover Institution.

152. Tape 111/A3, September 17, 1963, unknown time, Presidential Papers, President's Office Files, Presidential Recordings, John F. Kennedy Presidential Library.

153. Tape 111/A5, September 19, 1963, unknown time, Presidential Papers, President's Office Files, Presidential Recordings, John F. Kennedy Presidential Library.

154. Maxwell Taylor, *Sword and Plowshares,* 296.

155. Joseph Alsop to Keyes Beech, November 21, 1963, Box 19, Joseph Alsop and Stewart Alsop Papers, Manuscript Division, Library of Congress.

156. Henry Cabot Lodge Jr. to Averell Harriman, September 20, 1963, Box 484, W. Averell Harriman Papers, Manuscript Division, Library of Congress.

157. Moyar, *Triumph Forsaken,* 251.

158. Colby, *Honorable Men,* 206.

159. Halberstam, *Making of a Quagmire,* 123.

160. McNamara, *In Retrospect,* 75.

161. Hammer, *Death in November,* 218.

162. Visit to Vietnam, 7–10 September 1963, JFK Assassination Record 202-10002-10054, David Lifton Collection, Virtual Vietnam Archive, Texas Tech University.

163. Interview with John Paul Vann by David Halberstam, December 15, 1969, Box 67, Neil Sheehan Papers, Manuscript Division, Library of Congress.

164. William J. Miller, *Henry Cabot Lodge,* 345–346.

165. Bird, *Color of Truth,* 258.

166. Hammer, *Death in November,* 217.

167. For a copy of the thirty-two-page report, see "Report of the McNamara-Taylor Mission to South Vietnam," October 2, 1963, Box 263, Vietnam, Country File, National Security File, Lyndon B. Johnson Presidential Library.

168. Herring, *America's Longest War,* 103.

169. Hammer, *Death in November,* 241.

170. Hilsman, *To Move a Nation,* 515.

171. Dallek, *Camelot's Court,* 413.

172. Richardson, *My Father the Spy,* 198.

173. Richardson, *My Father the Spy,* 180.

174. Recall of CIA Station Chief at Saigon, undated, Box 4, Roger Hilsman Papers, John F. Kennedy Presidential Library.

175. Telegram from Lyndon Johnson to Henry Cabot Lodge Jr., December 7, 1963, RAC NLJ-002-001-1-8-2, Lyndon B. Johnson Presidential Library.

176. Dommen, *Indochinese Experience,* 542.

177. Memorandum of South Vietnam Action Items, undated, Box 199, Vietnam, Countries, National Security Files, Presidential Papers, John F. Kennedy Presidential Library.

178. William J. Miller, *Henry Cabot Lodge,* 344.

179. Telegram 933 from Saigon to Washington, November 5, 1963, Box 200, Vietnam, Countries, National Security Files, Presidential Papers, John F. Kennedy Presidential Library.

180. Vietnam Memoir, undated, II-9, Reel 26, Microfilm Edition, Henry Cabot Lodge, Jr. Papers II, Massachusetts Historical Society.

181. Telegram 496 from Washington to Saigon, September 28, 1963, Box 200, Vietnam, Countries, National Security Files, Presidential Papers, John F. Kennedy Presidential Library.

182. Don, *Our Endless War,* 97.

183. "Sequence of CAS Contacts with Vietnamese Generals, 23 August through 23 October 1963," JFK Assassination Records—2017 Additional Documents Release, https://www.archives.gov/files/research/jfk/releases/docid-32283369.pdf.

184. Telegram from Henry Cabot Lodge Jr. to State Department, October 5, 1963, Box 202, Vietnam, Countries, National Security Files, Presidential Papers, John F. Kennedy Presidential Library.

185. Telegram from Henry Cabot Lodge Jr. to Dean Rusk, October 5, 1963, Box 202, Vietnam, Countries, National Security Files, Presidential Papers, John F. Kennedy Presidential Library.

186. William J. Miller, *Henry Cabot Lodge,* 347.

187. William J. Miller, *Henry Cabot Lodge,* 349.

188. "Sequence of CAS Contacts with Vietnamese Generals, 23 August through 23 October 1963," JFK Assassination Records—2017 Additional Documents Release, https://www.archives.gov/files/research/jfk/releases/docid-32283369.pdf.

189. William J. Miller, *Henry Cabot Lodge,* 348.

190. Rust, *Kennedy in Vietnam,* 139.

191. McNamara, *In Retrospect,* 56.

192. William J. Miller, *Henry Cabot Lodge,* 351.

193. Michael O'Brien, *John F. Kennedy,* 865.

194. Shaw, *Lost Mandate of Heaven,* 247.

195. Mecklin, *Mission in Torment,* 227.

196. Henry Cabot Lodge Jr. to Howard Evers, February 16, 1973, Reel 5, Microfilm Edition, Henry Cabot Lodge, Jr. Papers II, Massachusetts Historical Society.

197. Oral History Interview with Frederick W. Flott, July 22, 1984, Lyndon B. Johnson Presidential Library.

198. Don, *Our Endless War,* 97.

199. Kattenberg, *Vietnam Trauma,* 118.

200. Dommen, *Indochinese Experience,* 566.

201. Tien Hung Nguyen and Schecter, *Palace File,* 76.

202. Warner, *Last Confucian,* 220.

203. Kattenberg, *Vietnam Trauma,* 117.

204. Colby, *Honorable Men,* 212.

205. Telegram from CIA Station Saigon to CIA, October 15, 1963, Box 201, Vietnam, Countries, National Security Files, Presidential Papers, John F. Kennedy Presidential Library.

206. Phillips, *Why Vietnam Matters,* 181.

207. "Sequence of CAS Contacts with Vietnamese Generals, 23 August through 23 October 1963," JFK Assassination Records—2017 Additional Documents Release, https://www.archives.gov/files/research/jfk/releases/docid-32283369.pdf.

208. Author interview with Leslie Gelb, October 16, 2018, New York, New York.

209. Oral History Interview with Lucien Conein, June 2, 1983, Lyndon B. Johnson Presidential Library.

210. Don, *Our Endless War,* 98.

## 13. A Coup

1. Boot, *Road Not Taken,* xxiv.

2. Shaplen, *Lost Revolution,* 208.

3. Henry Cabot Lodge Jr., *Storm Has Many Eyes,* 212.

4. Diem, *In the Jaws of History,* 103.

5. Arnett, *Live from the Battlefield,* 121.

6. David Halberstam to John Paul Vann, October 29, 1963, Box 28, Correspondence, circa 1950–1984, John Paul Vann, circa 1920–1984, Vann-Sheehan Vietnam War Collection, Neil Sheehan Papers, Manuscript Division, Library of Congress.

7. Arnett, *Live from the Battlefield*, 121.

8. Undated Notes, Box 1, Folder 2, Papers of David Halberstam, Howard Gotlieb Archival Research Center, Boston University.

9. Halberstam, *Making of a Quagmire*, 164.

10. Grant, *Facing the Phoenix*, 208.

11. Memorandum from William Bundy to Bill Moyers, July 30, 1966, Box 263, Vietnam, Country File, National Security File, Lyndon B. Johnson Presidential Library.

12. Edward Miller, *Misalliance*, 316.

13. Don, *Our Endless War*, 98.

14. Phillips, *Why Vietnam Matters*, 202.

15. Interview with Tran Van Don, May 7, 1981, *Vietnam: A Television History*, WGBH Media Library and Archives.

16. Dommen, *Indochinese Experience*, 538.

17. Phillips, *Why Vietnam Matters*, 202.

18. Don, *Our Endless War*, 98.

19. Emily Lodge Notes, Monday, October 28, 9 A.M., Reel 25, Microfilm Edition, Henry Cabot Lodge, Jr. Papers II, Massachusetts Historical Society.

20. Edward Miller, *Misalliance*, 317.

21. Interview with Henry Cabot Lodge Jr., pt. 4 of 5, January 1, 1979, *Vietnam: A Television History*, WGBH Media Library and Archives.

22. Catton, *Diem's Final Failure*, 1.

23. Bird, *Color of Truth*, 262.

24. Interview with Henry Cabot Lodge Jr., pt. 3 of 5, January 1, 1979, *Vietnam: A Television History*, WGBH Media Library and Archives.

25. Grant, *Facing the Phoenix*, 205.

26. Do Tho, *Nhat Ky Do Tho*, 184.

27. Phillips, *Why Vietnam Matters*, 201.

28. Kahin, *Intervention*, 177.

29. William J. Miller, *Henry Cabot Lodge*, 349–350.

30. Don, *Our Endless War*, 98–99.

31. Don, *Our Endless War*, 101–102.

32. Telegram 854 from Saigon to Secretary of State, November 1, 1963, Box 201, Vietnam, Countries, National Security Files, Presidential Papers, John F. Kennedy Presidential Library.

33. Don, *Our Endless War*, 103.

34. Interview with Tran Van Don, May 7, 1981, *Vietnam: A Television History*, WGBH Media Library and Archives.

35. Edward Miller, *Misalliance,* 318.

36. Warner, *Last Confucian,* 220.

37. Hilsman, *To Move a Nation,* 518.

38. William J. Miller, *Henry Cabot Lodge,* 350.

39. Edward Miller, *Misalliance,* 317.

40. Phillips, *Why Vietnam Matters,* 202.

41. Interview with Lucien Conein, May 7, 1981, *Vietnam: A Television History,* WGBH Media Library and Archives.

42. Oral History Interview with Lucien Conein, June 2, 1983, Lyndon B. Johnson Presidential Library.

43. Grant, *Facing the Phoenix,* 209.

44. Halberstam, *Making of a Quagmire,* 165.

45. Do Tho, *Nhat Ky Do Tho,* 183.

46. Mecklin, *Mission in Torment,* 252.

47. Telegram 842 from Saigon to Secretary of State, November 1, 1963, Box 201, Vietnam, Countries, National Security Files, Presidential Papers, John F. Kennedy Presidential Library.

48. "Military Coup D'état in Viet Nam Summary," November 6, 1963, FO 371/ 170094, National Archives, United Kingdom.

49. Robert Hopkins Miller, *Vietnam and Beyond,* 72.

50. Don, *Our Endless War,* 104.

51. William J. Miller, *Henry Cabot Lodge,* 351.

52. Interview with Henry Cabot Lodge Jr., pt. 5 of 5, January 1, 1979, *Vietnam: A Television History,* WGBH Media Library and Archives.

53. "Military Coup D'état in Viet Nam Summary," November 6, 1963, FO 371/ 170094, National Archives, United Kingdom.

54. William J. Miller, *Henry Cabot Lodge,* 350.

55. "Military Coup D'état in Viet Nam Summary," November 6, 1963, FO 371/ 170094, National Archives, United Kingdom.

56. United States Senate, Committee on Foreign Relations, *U.S. Involvement,* 22.

57. William J. Miller, *Henry Cabot Lodge,* 351.

58. Phillips, *Why Vietnam Matters,* 203.

59. Do Tho, *Nhat Ky Do Tho,* 183.

60. Do Tho, *Nhat Ky Do Tho,* 185.

61. Telegram 842 from Saigon to the Secretary of State, November 1, 1963, Box 201, Vietnam, Countries, National Security Files, Presidential Papers, John F. Kennedy Presidential Library.

62. "Military Coup D'état in Viet Nam Summary," November 6, 1963, FO 371/ 170094, National Archives, United Kingdom.

63. Halberstam, *Making of a Quagmire,* 166.

64. CREST manuscript, blue p. 391, Central Intelligence Agency.

65. Robert Shaplen, "Nine Years After a Fateful Assassination—The Cult of Diem," *New York Times*, May 14, 1972.

66. Don, *Our Endless War*, 105.

67. Jones, *Death of a Generation*, 412.

68. Don, *Our Endless War*, 106.

69. "Military Coup D'état in Viet Nam Summary," November 6, 1963, FO 371/ 170094, National Archives, United Kingdom.

70. Tien Hung Nguyen and Schecter, *Palace File*, 76.

71. Hoi-dong Quan-nhan Cach-mang, *Policy of the Military Revolutionary Council*, 32.

72. Hoi-dong Quan-nhan Cach-mang, *Policy of the Military Revolutionary Council*, 32.

73. Holbrooke, "Carpe Diem."

74. Diem Handwritten Notes, November 1, 1963, Folder 21817, Activities of the President, Office of the President, 1954–1963 (Phông Phủ Tổng thống Đệ Nhất Cộng Hoà), National Archives Center II (Trung Tâm Lưu Trữ Quốc Gia II), Ho Chi Minh City.

75. Diem Handwritten Notes, November 1, 1963, Folder 21817, Activities of the President, Office of the President, 1954–1963 (Phông Phủ Tổng thống Đệ Nhất Cộng Hoà), National Archives Center II (Trung Tâm Lưu Trữ Quốc Gia II), Ho Chi Minh City.

76. United States Senate, Committee on Foreign Relations, *U.S. Involvement*, 22.

77. "Military Coup D'état in Viet Nam Summary," November 6, 1963, FO 371/ 170094, National Archives, United Kingdom.

78. Shaplen, *Lost Revolution*, 209.

79. Diem Handwritten Notes, November 1, 1963, Folder 21817, Activities of the President, Office of the President, 1954–1963 (Phông Phủ Tổng thống Đệ Nhất Cộng Hoà), National Archives Center II (Trung Tâm Lưu Trữ Quốc Gia II), Ho Chi Minh City.

80. Oral History Interview with Frederick W. Flott, July 22, 1984, Lyndon B. Johnson Presidential Library.

81. Jacobs, *Cold War Mandarin*, 2.

82. Henry Cabot Lodge Jr. to William Randolph Hearst, September 6, 1966, Reel 20, Microfilm Edition, Henry Cabot Lodge, Jr. Papers II, Massachusetts Historical Society.

83. Oral History Interview with Frederick W. Flott, July 22, 1984, Lyndon B. Johnson Presidential Library.

84. Do Tho, *Nhat Ky Do Tho*, 186.

85. "I am going to reestablish order." Interview with Henry Cabot Lodge Jr., pt. 5 of 5, January 1, 1979, *Vietnam: A Television History*, WGBH Media Library and Archives.

86. "Military Coup D'état in Viet Nam Summary," November 6, 1963, FO 371/ 170094, National Archives, United Kingdom.

87. United States Senate, Committee on Foreign Relations, *U.S. Involvement*, 23.

88. William J. Miller, *Henry Cabot Lodge*, 352.

89. "Military Coup D'état in Viet Nam Summary," November 6, 1963, FO 371/ 170094, National Archives, United Kingdom.

90. Jacobs, *Cold War Mandarin*, 5.

91. Fox Butterfield, "Man Who Sheltered Diem Recounts '63 Episode," *New York Times*, November 4, 1971.

92. Dommen, *Indochinese Experience*, 555.

93. "Military Coup D'état in Viet Nam Summary," November 6, 1963, FO 371/ 170094, National Archives, United Kingdom.

94. Butterfield, "Man Who Sheltered Diem."

95. Jacobs, *Cold War Mandarin*, 5.

96. William J. Miller, *Henry Cabot Lodge*, 352.

97. Phillips, *Why Vietnam Matters*, 203.

98. Telegram 17 from CIA Station Saigon to National Security Agency, November 2, 1963, Box 201, Vietnam, Countries, National Security Files, Presidential Papers, John F. Kennedy Presidential Library.

99. "Military Coup D'état in Viet Nam Summary," November 6, 1963, FO 371/ 170094, National Archives, United Kingdom.

100. Robert Hopkins Miller, *Vietnam and Beyond*, 72.

101. "Military Coup D'état in Viet Nam Summary," November 6, 1963, FO 371/ 170094, National Archives, United Kingdom.

102. United States Senate, Committee on Foreign Relations, *U.S. Involvement*, 23.

103. Don, *Our Endless War*, 107.

104. Demery, *Finding the Dragon Lady*, 205.

105. Oral History Interview with Frederick W. Flott, July 22, 1984, Lyndon B. Johnson Presidential Library.

106. Grant, *Facing the Phoenix*, 214.

107. Butterfield, "Man Who Sheltered Diem."

108. "Military Coup D'état in Viet Nam Summary," November 6, 1963, FO 371/ 170094, National Archives, United Kingdom.

109. Butterfield, "Man Who Sheltered Diem."

110. Don, *Our Endless War*, 107.

111. Shaplen, "Nine Years."

112. Oral History Interview with Lucien Conein, June 2, 1983, Lyndon B. Johnson Presidential Library.

113. Telegram 19 from CIA Station Saigon to National Security Agency, November 2, 1963, Box 201, Vietnam, Countries, National Security Files, Presidential Papers, John F. Kennedy Presidential Library.

114. Don, *Our Endless War*, 108.

115. Dương Hiếu Nghĩa, "Tường thuật về cái chết của Tổng Thống Ngô Đình Diệm" [Report on the death of President Diem], 1963, https://www.scribd.com/doc /24305345/Tường-thuật-về-cai-chết-của-TT-Diệm-ĐT-Dương-Hiếu-Nghĩa.

116. Tien Hung Nguyen and Schecter, *Palace File*, 77.

117. Interview with Lucien Conein, May 7, 1981, *Vietnam: A Television History*, WGBH Media Library and Archives.

118. Oral History Interview with Lucien Conein, June 2, 1983, Johnson Presidential Library.

119. Dommen, *Indochinese Experience*, 556.

120. Rust, *Kennedy in Vietnam*, 172.

121. Nghĩa, "Tổng Thống Ngô Đình Diệm."

122. Interview with Henry Cabot Lodge Jr., pt. 5 of 5, January 1, 1979, *Vietnam: A Television History*, WGBH Media Library and Archives.

123. Interview with Lucien Conein, May 7, 1981, *Vietnam: A Television History*, WGBH Media Library and Archives.

124. Dommen, *Indochinese Experience*, 556.

125. There is no known connection between Chinese medicine and gallbladder removal. Chinese medicine advises against organ removal as it upsets the balance between "clean" and "dirty" organs. Organ removal, and the grisly way in which it was carried out against Diem and Nhu, is more consistent with Khmer behavior. That could explain why Nhung was the only coup leader to be killed following the coup.

126. Geoffrey Shaw Interview with General Nguyen Khanh, June 16, 1994, Vietnam Center and Archive, Texas Tech University.

127. Nghĩa, "Tổng Thống Ngô Đình Diệm."

128. Jacobs, *Cold War Mandarin*, 6.

129. Nghĩa, "Tổng Thống Ngô Đình Diệm."

130. Nghĩa, "Tổng Thống Ngô Đình Diệm."

131. Shaplen, "Nine Years."

132. Prochnau, *Once upon a Distant War*, 480–481.

133. Henry Cabot Lodge Jr. to Dean Rusk, May 26, 1964, Box 8, Saigon Embassy Files Taken by Amb. Graham Martin, National Security Adviser, Gerald R. Ford Presidential Library.

134. Conversation with David Halberstam, January 6, 1976, Box 71, Individuals, 1957–1991, Vann-Sheehan Vietnam War Collection, Neil Sheehan Papers, Manuscript Division, Library of Congress.

135. William J. Miller, *Henry Cabot Lodge*, 352.

136. Grant, *Facing the Phoenix*, 211.

137. Dommen, *Indochinese Experience*, 555.

138. Grant, *Facing the Phoenix*, 211.

139. Dommen, *Indochinese Experience*, 555.

140. Oral History Interview with Lucien Conein, June 2, 1983, Lyndon B. Johnson Presidential Library.

141. Phillips, *Why Vietnam Matters*, 205.

142. Don, *Our Endless War*, 111.

143. Tien Hung Nguyen and Schecter, *Palace File*, 78.

144. Interview with Henry Cabot Lodge Jr., pt. 5 of 5, January 1, 1979, *Vietnam: A Television History*, WGBH Media Library and Archives.

145. Henry Cabot Lodge Jr., *Storm Has Many Eyes*, 207.

146. Dallek, *Camelot's Court*, 417.

147. Telegram 24 from CIA Station Saigon to National Security Agency, November 2, 1963, Box 201, Vietnam, Countries, National Security Files, Presidential Papers, John F. Kennedy Presidential Library.

148. Johns, *Vietnam's Second Front*, 38.

149. Richardson, *My Father the Spy*, 171.

150. Parmet, *JFK*, 335.

151. Tape 119/A55, November 2, 1963, 9:15 a.m., Presidential Papers, President's Office Files, Presidential Recordings, John F. Kennedy Presidential Library.

152. Prados, *Family Jewels*, 170.

153. Hersh, *Dark Side of Camelot*, 434.

154. Robert F. Kennedy Oral History, March 1, 1964, Tape II, Reel 2, p. 82, John F. Kennedy Presidential Library.

155. Dommen, *Indochinese Experience*, 557.

156. Weiner, *One Man against the World*, 140.

157. Henry Cabot Lodge Jr., *Storm Has Many Eyes*, 209.

158. Henry Cabot Lodge Jr., *Storm Has Many Eyes*, 210.

159. Hersh, *Dark Side of Camelot*, 419.

160. Ky, *How We Lost*, 36.

161. Don, *Our Endless War*, 110.

162. Catton, *Diem's Final Failure*, 202.

163. Demery, *Finding the Dragon Lady*, 161.

164. Henry Cabot Lodge Jr. to John Mason Brown, December 12, 1963, Reel 2, Microfilm Edition, Henry Cabot Lodge, Jr. Papers II, Massachusetts Historical Society.

165. Do Tho, *Nhat Ky Do Tho*, 184.

166. Hersh, *Dark Side of Camelot*, 419.

167. Hersh, *Dark Side of Camelot*, 429.

168. Colby, *Honorable Men*, 215.

169. Arnett, *Live from the Battlefield*, 121.

170. Blair, *Lodge in Vietnam*, 75.

171. Don, *Our Endless War*, 109.

172. Stewart, *Vietnam's Lost Revolution*, 231.

173. William J. Miller, *Henry Cabot Lodge*, 352.

174. "Military Coup D'état in Viet Nam Summary," November 6, 1963, FO 371/170094, National Archives, United Kingdom.

175. Hoi-dong Quan-nhan Cach-mang, *Policy of the Military Revolutionary Council*, 5–6.

176. Warner, *Last Confucian*, 238.

177. David Halberstam, "Diem and Nhu Are Reported Slain; Army Ruling Saigon after Coup; Kennedy Reviews Vietnam Policy," *New York Times*, November 3, 1963.

178. Telegram 683 from Secretary of State to Henry Cabot Lodge Jr., November 1, 1963, Box 201, Vietnam, Countries, National Security Files, Presidential Papers, John F. Kennedy Presidential Library.

179. Dommen, *Indochinese Experience*, 549.

180. Phillips, *Why Vietnam Matters*, 207.

181. Rusk, *As I Saw It*, 440.

182. David Halberstam, "Saigon Coup Gives Americans Hope," *New York Times*, November 6, 1963.

183. Dallek, *Camelot's Court*, 417.

184. Telegram 876 from Saigon to Secretary of State, November 2, 1963, Box 201, Vietnam, Countries, National Security Files, Presidential Papers, John F. Kennedy Presidential Library.

185. Hoi-dong Quan-nhan Cach-mang, *Policy of the Military Revolutionary Council*, 38–39.

186. William J. Miller, *Henry Cabot Lodge*, 353.

187. Ashby and Gramer, *Fighting the Odds*, 174.

188. Henry Cabot Lodge Jr., *Storm Has Many Eyes*, 213.

189. Richard Nixon to John Davis Lodge, November 12, 1963, Box 147, John Davis Lodge Papers, Hoover Institution.

190. Richard Nixon to Henry Cabot Lodge Jr., November 12, 1963, Box 147, John Davis Lodge Papers, Hoover Institution.

191. Statement by H. C. Lodge, U.S. Ambassador to Viet-Nam, undated [attached to a letter dated December 16, 1963], Box 144, John Davis Lodge Papers, Hoover Institution.

192. Blair, *Lodge in Vietnam*, 72.

193. Halberstam, *Best and the Brightest*, 298.

194. Oral History Interview with Frederick W. Flott, July 24, 1984, Lyndon B. Johnson Presidential Library.

195. Gary R. Hess, *Vietnam and the United States*, 74.

196. Dommen, *Indochinese Experience*, 572.

197. William J. Miller, *Henry Cabot Lodge*, 353.

198. Edwin E. Moise, "JFK and the Myth of Withdrawal," in Young and Buzzanco, *Companion to the Vietnam War*, 167.

199. Henry Cabot Lodge Jr. to Jim Bishop, April 13, 1973, Reel 2, Microfilm Edition, Henry Cabot Lodge, Jr. Papers II, Massachusetts Historical Society.

200. O'Donnell and Powers, *"Johnny, We Hardly Knew Ye,"* 389.

201. Memorandum for the Record, South Vietnam Situation, November 25, 1963, Box 1, Meeting Notes File, Lyndon B. Johnson Presidential Library.

202. Caro, *Passage of Power,* 401.

203. Lyndon Baines Johnson, *Vantage Point,* 22.

204. Oral History Interview with Tom Wicker, June 16, 1970, Lyndon B. Johnson Presidential Library.

205. Henry Cabot Lodge Jr. to Lyndon Johnson, June 18, 1957, and Lyndon Johnson to Henry Cabot Lodge Jr., November 20, 1958, Reel 8, Microfilm Edition, Henry Cabot Lodge, Jr. Papers II, Massachusetts Historical Society.

206. William J. Miller, *Henry Cabot Lodge,* 354.

207. Logevall, *Choosing War,* 75.

208. Caro, *Passage of Power,* 402.

209. Logevall, *Choosing War,* 75.

210. Demery, *Finding the Dragon Lady,* 209–210.

211. White, *In Search of History,* 530.

212. Talks with D.D.E. about Running for President, November 1963, Reel 29, Microfilm Edition, Henry Cabot Lodge, Jr. Papers II, Massachusetts Historical Society.

213. Henry Cabot Lodge Jr. to Dwight Eisenhower, December 13, 1963, Box 53, Principal Files, 1963, Post-presidential Papers, 1961–1969, Papers of Dwight D. Eisenhower, Dwight D. Eisenhower Presidential Library.

214. Frank, *Ike and Dick,* 249–250.

215. Logevall, *Choosing War,* 78.

# 14. Lodge for President

1. White, *Making of the President, 1964,* 107.

2. Zeiger, *Remarkable Henry Cabot Lodge,* 7–8.

3. Robert David Johnson, *All the Way with LBJ,* 40.

4. John Reagan "Tex" McCrary to Henry Cabot Lodge Jr., December 9, 1963, Box 11, Henry Cabot Lodge, Jr. Papers I, Massachusetts Historical Society.

5. Roscoe Drummond, "On Viet Horizon—Lodge Looming as a Dark Horse," *New York Herald Tribune,* November 8, 1963.

6. Frank, *Ike and Dick,* 256.

7. Dwight Eisenhower to Harold Stassen, December 13, 1963, Box 64, Principal Files, 1963, Post-presidential Papers, 1961–1969, Papers of Dwight D. Eisenhower, Dwight D. Eisenhower Presidential Library.

8. John Davis Lodge to Henry Cabot Lodge Jr., November 22, 1963, Box 144, John Davis Lodge Papers, Hoover Institution.

9. Henry Cabot Lodge Jr. to John Davis Lodge, December 16, 1963, Box 144, John Davis Lodge Papers, Hoover Institution.

10. Henry Cabot Lodge Jr. to George Cabot Lodge, December 5, 1963, Box 11, Henry Cabot Lodge, Jr. Papers I, Massachusetts Historical Society.

11. Zeiger, *Remarkable Henry Cabot Lodge,* 8.

12. Goldwater, *Goldwater,* 151.

13. Robert David Johnson and Shreve, *Presidential Recordings,* 318.

14. Henry Cabot Lodge Jr. to George Cabot Lodge, January 25, 1964, Box 11, Henry Cabot Lodge, Jr. Papers I, Massachusetts Historical Society.

15. Memorandum from McGeorge Bundy to Lyndon Johnson, "Memorandum for the President," December 9, 1963, Box 1, Memos to the President, National Security File, Lyndon B. Johnson Presidential Library.

16. Robert David Johnson and Shreve, 375.

17. Robert Mullen to Fred Seaton, December 17, 1963, Box 9, Fred Seaton Papers, Dwight D. Eisenhower Presidential Library.

18. Vasilew, "New Style in Political Campaigns," 131.

19. Henry Cabot Lodge Jr. to George Cabot Lodge, January 17, 1964, Box 11, Henry Cabot Lodge, Jr. Papers I, Massachusetts Historical Society.

20. William J. Miller, *Henry Cabot Lodge,* 356.

21. Vasilew, "New Style in Political Campaigns," 135.

22. Logevall, *Choosing War,* 80.

23. Chomsky, *Rethinking Camelot,* 93.

24. Chomsky, *Rethinking Camelot,* 97.

25. Memorandum from Mike Dunn to Henry Cabot Lodge Jr., March 7, 1964, Reel 19, Microfilm Edition, Henry Cabot Lodge, Jr. Papers II, Massachusetts Historical Society.

26. Sorley, *Vietnam War,* 133.

27. Kahin, *Intervention,* 198.

28. Dommen, *Indochinese Experience,* 621.

29. Kahin, *Intervention,* 202.

30. Logevall, *Choosing War,* 106.

31. Dommen, *Indochinese Experience,* 621.

32. William J. Miller, *Henry Cabot Lodge,* 356.

33. Henry Cabot Lodge Jr. to Dwight Eisenhower, April 28, 1964, Box 43, Principal Files, 1964, Post-presidential Papers, 1961–1969, Papers of Dwight D. Eisenhower, Dwight D. Eisenhower Presidential Library.

34. Westmoreland, *Soldier Reports,* 60.

35. Madame Nhu to Henry Cabot Lodge Jr., March 2, 1964, Office of the President, 1954–1963 (Phông Phủ Tổng thống Đệ Nhất Cộng Hoà) 3086, National Archives Center II (Trung Tâm Lưu Trữ Quốc Gia II).

36. Hatcher, *Suicide of an Elite,* 260–261.

37. Hatcher, *Suicide of an Elite,* 22.

38. Moyar, *Triumph Forsaken,* 295.

39. Interview with Henry Cabot Lodge Jr., pt. 5 of 5, January 1, 1979, *Vietnam: A Television History*, WGBH Media Library and Archives.

40. Lyndon Baines Johnson, *Vantage Point*, 63–64.

41. Blair, *Lodge in Vietnam*, 119–120.

42. Beschloss, *Taking Charge*, 261.

43. Robert S. Allen and Paul Scott, "Allen-Scott Report, Lodge Tells Future Plans," *Northern Virginia Sun*, March 19, 1964.

44. Memorandum for the Record by Michael V. Forrestal, February 20, 1964, CIA-RDP80B01676R000100130036-0, CREST (CIA Records Search Tool), National Archives and Records Administration.

45. Moyar, *Triumph Forsaken*, 293.

46. Nguyen Phu Duc, *Viet-Nam Peace Negotiations*, 36.

47. Logevall, *Choosing War*, 115.

48. Robert David Johnson, *All the Way with LBJ*, 79.

49. William J. Miller, *Henry Cabot Lodge*, 356.

50. William J. Miller, *Henry Cabot Lodge*, 357.

51. Robert Mullen to Fred Seaton, January 4, 1964, Box 9, Fred A. Seaton Papers, Dwight D. Eisenhower Presidential Library.

52. Henry Cabot Lodge Jr. to George Cabot Lodge, January 27, 1964, Box 11, Henry Cabot Lodge, Jr. Papers I, Massachusetts Historical Society.

53. Nelson Rockefeller to Henry Cabot Lodge Jr., January 7, 1964, Box 34, Politics—George L. Hinman, Personal Papers, Nelson A. Rockefeller Papers, Rockefeller Archive Center.

54. Parmet, *JFK*, 298.

55. Vasilew, "New Style in Political Campaigns," 133.

56. Zeiger, *Remarkable Henry Cabot Lodge*, 9.

57. William J. Miller, *Henry Cabot Lodge*, 358.

58. William J. Miller, *Henry Cabot Lodge*, 358.

59. Frank, *Ike and Dick*, 250.

60. Kessel, *Goldwater Coalition*, 51–52.

61. White, *Making of the President, 1964*, 136.

62. William J. Miller, *Henry Cabot Lodge*, 358.

63. Vasilew, "New Style in Political Campaigns," 137.

64. White, *Making of the President, 1964*, 135.

65. Zeiger, *Remarkable Henry Cabot Lodge*, 10.

66. Vasilew, "New Style in Political Campaigns," 140.

67. Vasilew, "New Style in Political Campaigns," 140.

68. White, *Making of the President, 1964*, 137.

69. Vasilew, "New Style in Political Campaigns," 138.

70. Henry Cabot Lodge Jr. to John Davis Lodge, January 16, 1964, Box 144, John Davis Lodge Papers, Hoover Institution.

71. Henry Cabot Lodge Jr. to John Davis Lodge, January 25, 1964, Box 144, John Davis Lodge Papers, Hoover Institution.

72. Kessel, *Goldwater Coalition*, 63.

73. Zeiger, *Remarkable Henry Cabot Lodge*, 10.

74. Vasilew, "New Style in Political Campaigns," 142.

75. Author interview with David Palmer, March 2, 2017, Belton, Texas, and email.

76. Richard Norton Smith, *On His Own Terms*, 424.

77. Kessel, *Goldwater Coalition*, 51.

78. Zeiger, *Remarkable Henry Cabot Lodge*, 11–12.

79. Zeiger, *Remarkable Henry Cabot Lodge*, 6.

80. Zeiger, *Remarkable Henry Cabot Lodge*, 12.

81. Draft, May 1, 1964, Reel 14, Speeches, Writings, Etc., Microfilm Edition, Henry Cabot Lodge, Jr. Papers I, Massachusetts Historical Society.

82. Memorandum for the Files, "Political Situation," March 11, 1964, Box 116, Leverett Saltonstall Papers I, Massachusetts Historical Society.

83. Richard Norton Smith, *On His Own Terms*, 425.

84. Vasilew, "New Style in Political Campaigns," 145.

85. Zeiger, *Remarkable Henry Cabot Lodge*, 13.

86. Richard Norton Smith, *On His Own Terms*, 425.

87. Henry Cabot Lodge Jr., *Storm Has Many Eyes*, 194.

88. Vasilew, "New Style in Political Campaigns," 145.

89. White, *Making of the President, 1964*, 137.

90. Kessel, *Goldwater Coalition*, 72.

91. Zeiger, *Remarkable Henry Cabot Lodge*, 6–7.

92. Kessel, *Goldwater Coalition*, 72.

93. William J. Miller, *Henry Cabot Lodge*, 359.

94. Zeiger, *Remarkable Henry Cabot Lodge*, 5–6.

95. Goldwater, *Goldwater*, 161.

96. Zeiger, *Remarkable Henry Cabot Lodge*, 7.

97. Perlstein, *Before the Storm*, 329.

98. White, *Making of the President, 1964*, 170–171.

99. John Davis Lodge to Henry Cabot Lodge Jr., March 13, 1964, Box 144, John Davis Lodge Papers, Hoover Institution.

100. Kessel, *Goldwater Coalition*, 72.

101. Westmoreland, *Soldier Reports*, 67.

102. Douglas Brinkley and Nichter, *Nixon Tapes: 1971–1972*, 459.

103. Anthony Summers, *Arrogance of Power*, 290.

104. Palmer, *Summons of the Trumpet*, 54.

105. Witcover, *Very Strange Bedfellows*, 21.

106. Richard Nixon to Henry Cabot Lodge Jr., May 12, 1964, Box 5, Trip Files, Series II, Wilderness Years, Series 347, Richard M. Nixon Presidential Library.

107. Coppolani, *Richard Nixon*, 323.

108. Charles R. Smith, "Lodge's Job Is Praised by Nixon," *Washington Post*, April 4, 1964.

109. Henry Cabot Lodge Jr. to George Cabot Lodge, April 2, 1964, Box 11, Henry Cabot Lodge, Jr. Papers I, Massachusetts Historical Society.

110. Henry Cabot Lodge Jr. to George Cabot Lodge, April 14, 1964, Box 11, Henry Cabot Lodge, Jr. Papers I, Massachusetts Historical Society.

111. Henry Cabot Lodge Jr. to George Cabot Lodge, January 3, 1964, Box 11, Henry Cabot Lodge, Jr. Papers I, Massachusetts Historical Society.

112. William J. Miller, *Henry Cabot Lodge*, 360.

113. Henry Cabot Lodge Jr. to John Davis Lodge, March 7, 1964, Box 144, John Davis Lodge Papers, Hoover Institution.

114. Henry Cabot Lodge Jr. to Paul Grindle, May 14, 1964, Box 12, Henry Cabot Lodge, Jr. Papers I, Massachusetts Historical Society.

115. Lodge omitted the portion in brackets when quoting Lanham in his response.

116. Henry Cabot Lodge Jr. to Charles Lanham, June 13 1964, Box 12, Henry Cabot Lodge, Jr. Papers I, Massachusetts Historical Society.

117. Telegram 2284 from Saigon to Washington, May 22, 1964, Box 198, Vietnam, Country File, National Security File, Lyndon B. Johnson Presidential Library.

118. McMaster, *Dereliction of Duty*, 94–95.

119. William J. Miller, *Henry Cabot Lodge*, 361.

120. Kessel, *Goldwater Coalition*, 75.

121. Richard Nixon, *RN*, 258.

122. William J. Miller, *Henry Cabot Lodge*, 361–362.

123. David Goldberg to Henry Cabot Lodge Jr., October 19, 1964, Reel 5, Microfilm Edition, Henry Cabot Lodge, Jr. Papers II, Massachusetts Historical Society.

124. Kessel, *Goldwater Coalition*, 73.

125. Zeiger, *Remarkable Henry Cabot Lodge*, 14.

126. Kessel, *Goldwater Coalition*, 76.

127. Henry Cabot Lodge Jr. to George Cabot Lodge, April 14, 1964, Box 11, Henry Cabot Lodge, Jr. Papers I, Massachusetts Historical Society.

128. Henry Cabot Lodge Jr. to George Cabot Lodge, March 27, 1964, Box 11, Henry Cabot Lodge, Jr. Papers I, Massachusetts Historical Society.

129. Kessel, *Goldwater Coalition*, 76.

130. Robert David Johnson, *All the Way with LBJ*, 111.

131. William J. Miller, *Henry Cabot Lodge*, 363.

132. Memorandum from Paul Grindle to Henry Cabot Lodge Jr., May 6, 1964, Box 12, Henry Cabot Lodge, Jr. Papers I, Massachusetts Historical Society.

133. John Davis Lodge to Henry Cabot Lodge Jr., May 16, 1964, Box 144, John Davis Lodge Papers, Hoover Institution.

134. Kessel, *Goldwater Coalition*, 79.

135. Kessel, *Goldwater Coalition*, 73.

136. Beschloss, *Taking Charge*, 320.

137. Goldwater, *Goldwater*, 149.

138. Kessel, *Goldwater Coalition*, 83.

139. David Eisenhower and Julie Nixon Eisenhower, *Going Home to Glory*, 127.

140. Gifford, *Center Cannot Hold*, 144.

141. Henry Cabot Lodge Jr. to George Cabot Lodge, April 29, 1964, Box 11, Henry Cabot Lodge, Jr. Papers I, Massachusetts Historical Society.

142. Maxwell Rabb to Henry Cabot Lodge Jr., April 1, 1964, Box 11, Henry Cabot Lodge, Jr. Papers I, Massachusetts Historical Society.

143. Kessel, *Goldwater Coalition*, 74.

144. Remarks of H. C. Lodge at Honolulu Conference, June 1, 1964, Box 8, National Security Adviser, Saigon Embassy Files Taken by Amb. Graham Martin, Gerald R. Ford Presidential Library.

145. Lady Bird Johnson, *White House Diary*, 166.

146. Frankel, *Times of My Life*, 225.

147. Telegram 207 from Saigon to Washington, June 18, 1964, Box 195, Vietnam, Country File, National Security File, Lyndon B. Johnson Presidential Library.

148. Memorandum from Paul Grindle to Henry Cabot Lodge Jr., May 6, 1964, Box 12, Henry Cabot Lodge, Jr. Papers I, Massachusetts Historical Society.

149. Oral History Interview with Barry Zorthian, January 17, 2005, Vietnam Center and Archive, Texas Tech University.

150. William J. Miller, *Henry Cabot Lodge*, 364.

151. Browne, *New Face of War*, 87.

152. Decree by Nguyen Khanh, June 27, 1964, Office of the Prime Minister, 1954–1975 (Phòng Phủ Thủ Tướng Việt Nam Cộng Hòa) 13360, National Archives Center II (Trung Tâm Lưu Trữ Quốc Gia II), Ho Chi Minh City.

153. Memorandum of Conversation with General Khanh, New York, March 16, 1965, Reel 20, Microfilm Edition, Henry Cabot Lodge, Jr. Papers II, Massachusetts Historical Society.

154. Memorandum from William A. K. Lake to Henry Cabot Lodge Jr., June 27, 1964, Reel 20, Microfilm Edition, Henry Cabot Lodge, Jr. Papers II, Massachusetts Historical Society.

155. William J. Miller, *Henry Cabot Lodge*, 364–365.

156. Malcolm Browne to Henry Cabot Lodge Jr., April 7, 1964, Reel 19, Microfilm Edition, Henry Cabot Lodge, Jr. Papers II, Massachusetts Historical Society.

157. Venerable Tri Quang to Henry Cabot Lodge Jr., June 24, 1964, Reel 19, Microfilm Edition, Henry Cabot Lodge, Jr. Papers II, Massachusetts Historical Society.

158. Press Conference of Ambassador Henry Cabot Lodge, June 29, 1964, Box 80, Background Briefings, White House Press Office Files, Lyndon B. Johnson Presidential Library.

159. "Remarks of the President and Ambassador Henry Cabot Lodge upon the Latter's Return from South Viet Nam in the Cabinet Room," June 29, 1964, Box 112, Statements of Lyndon B. Johnson, Lyndon B. Johnson Presidential Library.

160. Draft, June 12, [1964], HCL Speech, Box 11, Henry Cabot Lodge, Jr. Papers I, Massachusetts Historical Society.

161. McNamara, *In Retrospect*, 264.

162. Henry Cabot Lodge Jr. to George Cabot Lodge, May 16, 1964, Box 11, Henry Cabot Lodge, Jr. Papers I, Massachusetts Historical Society.

163. Confidential Journal, European Visit, August 1964, Box 36, Henry Cabot Lodge, Jr. Papers I, Massachusetts Historical Society.

164. Statement by Governor Nelson A. Rockefeller, June 23, 1964, Box 57, Gubernatorial Press Office, Series 3, Nelson A. Rockefeller Papers, Rockefeller Archive Center.

165. Dwight D. Eisenhower to William Scranton, June 26, 1964, Box 33, William Warren Scranton Papers, Eberly Family Special Collections Library, Pennsylvania State University.

166. William J. Miller, *Henry Cabot Lodge*, 363–364.

167. Beschloss, *Taking Charge*, 444.

168. Kessel, *Goldwater Coalition*, 236–237.

169. Henry Cabot Lodge Jr. to William W. Scranton, December 17, 1962, General Records, Subject File, Folder 37/12, William Warren Scranton Papers, Eberly Family Special Collections Library, Pennsylvania State University.

170. Goldberg, *Barry Goldwater*, 198.

171. Buckley, *Flying High*, 143.

172. Stephen Hess, *America's Political Dynasties*, 487.

173. Kessel, *Goldwater Coalition*, 106.

174. William J. Miller, *Henry Cabot Lodge*, 365–366.

175. Gifford, *Center Cannot Hold*, 145.

176. David Halberstam to John Paul Vann, August 8, 1964, Box 28, Correspondence, circa 1950–1984, John Paul Vann, circa 1920–1984, Vann-Sheehan Vietnam War Collection, Neil Sheehan Papers, Manuscript Division, Library of Congress.

177. Memorandum for the File, January 12, 1965, Reel 7, Microfilm Edition, Henry Cabot Lodge, Jr. Papers II, Massachusetts Historical Society.

178. Kirby, Dalin, and Rothmann, *Harold E. Stassen*, 210.

179. Buchanan, *Greatest Comeback*, 16.

180. Safire, *Safire's Political Dictionary*, 130.

181. Memorandum from Henry Cabot Lodge Jr. to President Lyndon Johnson, September 9, 1964, Box 484, Subject File, Kennedy-Johnson Administrations, 1958–1971, W. Averell Harriman Papers, Manuscript Division, Library of Congress.

182. Notes for DDCI, September 16, 1964, CIA-RDP80B01676R001300100008-1, CREST, National Archives and Records Administration.

183. Report by the Secretary General of Progress during the Period 1st July to 31st December, 1964, C-M(65)33, April 26, 1965, Records of the Secretary General, Archives Division, North Atlantic Treaty Organization.

184. Summary Record of a Meeting of the Council, Held at the Permanent Headquarters, Paris, XVIe., on Tuesday, 18th August, 1964, at 11 a.m., C-R(64)39, Records of the North Atlantic Council, Archives Division, North Atlantic Treaty Organization.

185. Logevall, *Choosing War*, 225.

186. Memorandum from David Klein to McGeorge Bundy, August 11, 1964, Box 197, Vietnam, Country File, National Security File, Lyndon B. Johnson Presidential Library. Johnson dangled another overseas junket before Lodge in early October, to Africa. However, Lodge declined. McGeorge Bundy to Averell Harriman, October 1, 1964, Box 484, Subject File, Kennedy-Johnson Administrations, 1958–1971, W. Averell Harriman Papers, Manuscript Division, Library of Congress.

187. Undated Notes, Reel 8, Microfilm Edition, Henry Cabot Lodge, Jr. Papers II, Massachusetts Historical Society.

188. William J. Miller, *Henry Cabot Lodge*, 369.

189. Barry Goldwater to John Davis Lodge, December 11, 1964, Box 141, John Davis Lodge Papers, Hoover Institution.

190. G. Scott Thomas, *Counting the Votes*, 217–218.

191. Blair, *Lodge in Vietnam*, 138.

192. Conversation between Lyndon Johnson and Henry Cabot Lodge Jr., March 24, 1965, Tape WH6503.12, Lyndon B. Johnson Presidential Library.

## 15. LBJ and Vietnam

1. William J. Miller, *Henry Cabot Lodge*, 376–377.

2. Undated Notes, Reel 8, Microfilm Edition, Henry Cabot Lodge, Jr. Papers II, Massachusetts Historical Society.

3. William J. Miller, *Henry Cabot Lodge*, 377.

4. Conversation between Lyndon Johnson and Henry Cabot Lodge Jr., March 24, 1965, Tapes WH6503.12.7145 and WH6503.12.7146, Lyndon B. Johnson Presidential Library.

5. Conversation between Lyndon Johnson and Henry Cabot Lodge Jr., March 25, 1965, Tape WH6503.12.7147, Lyndon B. Johnson Presidential Library.

6. Visit to Pacific and Asian Countries, April 19–May 1, 1965, Reel 19, Microfilm Edition, Henry Cabot Lodge, Jr. Papers II, Massachusetts Historical Society.

7. William J. Miller, *Henry Cabot Lodge*, 379.

8. Visit to Pacific and Asian Countries, April 19–May 1, 1965, Reel 19, Microfilm Edition, Henry Cabot Lodge, Jr. Papers II, Massachusetts Historical Society.

9. Blair, *Lodge in Vietnam*, 149.

10. Ky, *Buddha's Child*, 113.

11. Memorandum for the Record, March 17, 1965, RAC NLJ-020R-16-2-7-4, Lyndon B. Johnson Presidential Library.

12. Beschloss, *Reaching for Glory*, 348.

13. Blair, *Lodge in Vietnam*, 142.

14. Beschloss, *Reaching for Glory*, 238–239.

15. William J. Miller, *Henry Cabot Lodge*, 374.

16. Schandler, *Unmaking of a President*, 37.

17. McNamara, *In Retrospect*, 220.

18. Schulzinger, *Time for War*, 208.

19. Ellsberg, *Secrets*, 18.

20. William J. Miller, *Henry Cabot Lodge*, 374–375.

21. William J. Miller, *Henry Cabot Lodge*, 378–379.

22. Hershberg, *Marigold*, 109.

23. Lansdale, *In the Midst of Wars*, 369.

24. Blair, *Lodge in Vietnam*, 149.

25. Westmoreland, *Soldier Reports*, 141.

26. Clifford, *Counsel to the President*, 411.

27. Valenti, *My Life*, 226.

28. Barrett, *Uncertain Warriors*, 51–52.

29. Nitze, *From Hiroshima to Glasnost*, 281–282.

30. Berman, *Planning a Tragedy*, 102.

31. Barrett, *Uncertain Warriors*, 52.

32. Drea, *McNamara*, 62.

33. Memorandum of Conversation with General Eisenhower, March 1, 1965, Reel 29, Microfilm Edition, Henry Cabot Lodge, Jr. Papers II, Massachusetts Historical Society.

34. Berman, *Planning a Tragedy*, 150.

35. Clifford, *Counsel to the President*, 413.

36. Undated Notes, Box 14, Henry Cabot Lodge, Jr. Papers II, Massachusetts Historical Society.

37. Kattenberg, *Vietnam Trauma*, 119.

38. Berman, *Planning a Tragedy*, 108.

39. Henry Cabot Lodge Jr. to Porter Chandler, October 4, 1965, Reel 3, Microfilm Edition, Henry Cabot Lodge, Jr. Papers II, Massachusetts Historical Society.

40. Interview with Frank G. Wisner, March 22, 1992, Foreign Affairs Oral History Collection, Association for Diplomatic Studies and Training.

41. Henry Cabot Lodge Jr. to John Davis Lodge, October 27, 1965, Box 144, John Davis Lodge Papers, Hoover Institution.

42. William J. Miller, *Henry Cabot Lodge*, 380–381.

43. Henry Cabot Lodge Jr. to Henry Luce, September 20, 1966, Box 2, Henry Robinson Luce Papers, Manuscript Division, Library of Congress.

44. Herring, *America's Longest War,* 159.

45. William J. Miller, *Henry Cabot Lodge,* 381.

46. Westmoreland, *Soldier Reports,* 148.

47. Pearson, *Washington Merry-Go-Round,* 372.

48. Shaplen, *Road from War,* 155–156.

49. Browne, *New Face of War,* 306.

50. Sheehan, *Bright Shining Lie,* 559.

51. Memorandum from Henry Cabot Lodge Jr. to Lyndon Johnson, December 21, 1965, Box 147, Name File, Confidential File, White House Central File, Lyndon B. Johnson Presidential Library.

52. Kattenberg, *Vietnam Trauma,* 177.

53. Kattenberg, *Vietnam Trauma,* 51.

54. Rusk, *As I Saw It,* 440.

55. *Victory in Vietnam,* 121.

56. Hershberg, *Marigold,* 109.

57. McNamara, *In Retrospect,* 261.

58. Author interview with Katherine "Kitsy" Westmoreland and Rip Westmoreland, December 30, 2017, Charleston, South Carolina.

59. Westmoreland, *Soldier Reports,* 43.

60. Ellsberg, *Secrets,* 99.

61. Memorandum, undated, Confidential Journal, Reel 17, Microfilm Edition, Henry Cabot Lodge, Jr. Papers II, Massachusetts Historical Society.

62. Memorandums from Henry Cabot Lodge Jr. to Edward Lansdale, August 9 and September 14, 1965, Reel 20, Microfilm Edition, Henry Cabot Lodge, Jr. Papers II, Massachusetts Historical Society.

63. Cooper, *In the Shadows of History,* 225.

64. Bullington, *Global Adventures,* 66.

65. Memorandum from Raymond K. Price to Richard Nixon, April 25, 1967, Box 11, Trip Files: 1963–1967, Series II, Wilderness Years, Series 347, Richard M. Nixon Presidential Library.

66. Robert Hopkins Miller, *Vietnam and Beyond,* 92.

67. Interview with Edward Geary Lansdale, pt. 5 of 5, January 31, 1979, *Vietnam: A Television History,* WGBH Media Library and Archives.

68. Ellsberg, *Secrets,* 105.

69. Henry Kissinger to Henry Cabot Lodge Jr., December 3, 1965, Box 99, Folder 23, Series I, Early Career and Harvard University, Henry A. Kissinger Papers, Part II, Manuscripts and Archives, Yale University.

70. Interview with Phil Habib, May 24, 1984, Foreign Affairs Oral History Collection, Association for Diplomatic Studies and Training.

71. William J. Miller, *Henry Cabot Lodge,* 387.

72. Browne, *New Face of War,* 306–307.

73. Blair, *There to the Bitter End*, 118.

74. Memorandum from Henry Cabot Lodge Jr. to Lyndon Johnson, August 31, 1965, Box 212, Vietnam, Country File, National Security File, Lyndon B. Johnson Presidential Library.

75. William J. Miller, *Henry Cabot Lodge*, 390–391.

76. I asked Kissinger what he thought about this statement during a meeting on June 27, 2018. He paused and then said, "Well, you do know that Kennedy sent me to see Adenauer? So that would have been a higher-level assignment." I do not dispute that fact, but the trajectory of U.S. foreign policy in the 1960s was such that it was his assignment to Vietnam that made him a recognized expert, made him useful to the Johnson administration, and got the attention of Richard Nixon.

77. Kissinger, *White House Years*, 231.

78. Ferguson, *Kissinger*, 624–625.

79. Interview with Henry Kissinger, April 17, 1982, *Vietnam: A Television History*, WGBH Media Library and Archives.

80. Henry Kissinger to Henry Cabot Lodge Jr., September 24, 1965, Box 99, Folder 23, Series I, Early Career and Harvard University, Henry A. Kissinger Papers, Part II, Manuscripts and Archives, Yale University.

81. Ferguson, *Kissinger*, 637.

82. Interview with Henry Kissinger, April 17, 1982, *Vietnam: A Television History*, WGBH Media Library and Archives.

83. Interview with Phil Habib, May 24, 1984, Foreign Affairs Oral History Collection, Association for Diplomatic Studies and Training.

84. Isaacson, *Kissinger*, 118.

85. Ky, *How We Lost*, 85.

86. Kissinger, *Years of Renewal*, 467.

87. Clark Clifford to Henry Cabot Lodge Jr., November 8, 1965, Reel 3, Microfilm Edition, Henry Cabot Lodge, Jr. Papers II, Massachusetts Historical Society.

88. Jack Foisie, "LBJ Envoys Find Almost Total Lack of Political Maturity in Saigon," *Washington Post*, November 2, 1965.

89. Clifford, *Counsel to the President*, 429.

90. Dallek, *Nixon and Kissinger*, 58.

91. Henry Kissinger to Clark Clifford, November 10, 1965, Box 99, Folder 23, Series I, Early Career and Harvard University, Henry A. Kissinger Papers, Part II, Manuscripts and Archives, Yale University.

92. Clifford, *Counsel to the President*, 432.

93. Cercle Sportif Saigonnais, Membre d'Honneur, 1965, Box 13, Henry Cabot Lodge, Jr. Papers II, Massachusetts Historical Society.

94. William J. Miller, *Henry Cabot Lodge*, 392.

95. Schandler, *Unmaking of a President*, 38.

96. Blair, *There to the Bitter End*, 123.

97. Lyndon Baines Johnson, *Vantage Point,* 243.

98. Boot, *Road Not Taken,* 486.

99. William J. Miller, *Henry Cabot Lodge,* 394.

100. Ky, *How We Lost,* 81.

101. Kahin, *Intervention,* 417.

102. Westmoreland, *Soldier Reports,* 160.

103. Gaddis, *Strategies of Containment,* 262.

104. Liebmann, *Last American Diplomat,* 20.

105. J. Bullington and H. C. Lodge, "Crisis of Spring, 1966," August 26, 1966, Reel 19, Microfilm Edition, Henry Cabot Lodge, Jr. Papers II, Massachusetts Historical Society.

106. Bullington, *Global Adventures,* 52.

107. Author interview with Joseph C. "Joe" Luman, July 10, 2017, Alexandria, Virginia.

108. William J. Miller, *Henry Cabot Lodge,* 394.

109. Telegram 4887 from Saigon to Washington, May 23, 1966, Box 147, Name File, Confidential File, White House Central File, Lyndon B. Johnson Presidential Library.

110. William J. Miller, *Henry Cabot Lodge,* 395.

111. Ky, *How We Lost,* 89.

112. Bullington, *Global Adventures,* 57.

113. Westmoreland, *Soldier Reports,* 176.

114. Westmoreland, *Soldier Reports,* 170.

115. William J. Miller, *Henry Cabot Lodge,* 396.

116. Dallek, *Nixon and Kissinger,* 58–59.

117. Hillings, *Irrepressible Irishman,* 103.

118. "VNam," Undated Notes, Box 7, Trip Files: 1963–1967, Series II, Wilderness Years, Series 347, Richard M. Nixon Presidential Library.

119. Strober and Strober, *Nixon Presidency,* 52.

120. "VNam," Undated Notes, Box 7, Trip Files: 1963–1967, Series II, Wilderness Years, Series 347, Richard M. Nixon Presidential Library.

121. Schedule for Vice President Nixon's Visit to Vietnam, August 5–7, 1966, Box 8, Trip Files: 1963–1967, Series II, Wilderness Years, Series 347, Richard M. Nixon Presidential Library.

122. Lyndon Baines Johnson, *Vantage Point,* 247.

123. William J. Miller, *Henry Cabot Lodge,* 399–400.

124. William J. Miller, *Henry Cabot Lodge,* 401.

125. Clifford, *Counsel to the President,* 443.

126. Henry Cabot Lodge Jr. to Lyndon Johnson, October 27, 1966, Henry Cabot Lodge, Name File, White House Central File, Lyndon B. Johnson Presidential Library.

127. William J. Miller, *Henry Cabot Lodge,* 402–403.

128. Drea, *McNamara,* 43.

129. Drea, *McNamara*, 118.

130. Henry Cabot Lodge Jr. to Clark Clifford, March 27, 1968, Reel 3, Microfilm Edition, Henry Cabot Lodge, Jr. Papers II, Massachusetts Historical Society.

131. Henry Cabot Lodge Jr. to Lyndon Johnson, November 7, 1966, Box 5, Files of Robert Komer, National Security File, Lyndon B. Johnson Presidential Library.

132. Sorley, *Better War*, 6.

133. Haig, *Inner Circles*, 295.

134. Henry Cabot Lodge Jr., *As It Was*, 170.

135. Ferguson, *Kissinger*, 743.

136. Oral History Interview with William Jorden, March 22, 1969, Lyndon B. Johnson Presidential Library.

137. Cooper, *In the Shadows of History*, 246.

138. McNamara, *In Retrospect*, 248.

139. Ferguson, *Kissinger*, 743.

140. Henry Cabot Lodge Jr., *As It Was*, 171–172.

141. Lyndon Baines Johnson, *Vantage Point*, 251.

142. Drea, *McNamara*, 80–81.

143. Hershberg, *Marigold*, 698.

144. Lyndon Baines Johnson, *Vantage Point*, 251.

145. Elliott, *Vietnamese War*, 252.

146. Henry Cabot Lodge, "A Diplomat's Hail to His Chief," *New York Times*, February 3, 1973, p. 29.

147. Confidential Journal, March 20, 1967, Reel 17, Microfilm Edition, Henry Cabot Lodge, Jr. Papers II, Massachusetts Historical Society.

148. Henry Cabot Lodge Jr. to Lyndon Johnson, February 19, 1967, Henry Cabot Lodge, Name Files, White House Central Files, Lyndon B. Johnson Presidential Library.

149. Sheehan, *Bright Shining Lie*, 668.

150. Memorandum for the File, undated, Reel 25, Microfilm Edition, Henry Cabot Lodge, Jr. Papers II, Massachusetts Historical Society.

151. William J. Miller, *Henry Cabot Lodge*, 407–408.

152. Telegram 21133 from Saigon to Washington, March 25, 1967, Box 2633, POL 7 US/Nixon, Central Foreign Policy Files, 1967–1969, RG 59, General Records of the Department of State, National Archives and Records Administration.

153. Schedule for Visit of Former Vice President Richard M. Nixon, April 14–17, 1967, Box 11, Trip Files: 1963–1967, Series II, Wilderness Years, Series 347, Richard M. Nixon Presidential Library.

154. Telegram 23486 from Saigon to Washington, April 19, 1967, Box 2633, POL 7 US/Nixon, Central Foreign Policy Files, 1967–1969, RG 59, General Records of the Department of State, National Archives and Records Administration.

155. Lyndon Johnson to Henry Cabot Lodge Jr., April 12, 1967, Box 5, Files of Walt W. Rostow, National Security File, Lyndon B. Johnson Presidential Library.

156. Henry Cabot Lodge Jr. to Ellsworth Bunker, March 22, 1967, Reel 2, Microfilm Edition, Henry Cabot Lodge, Jr. Papers II, Massachusetts Historical Society.

157. Memorandum for the Files, May 2, 1967, Reel 17, Microfilm Edition, Henry Cabot Lodge, Jr. Papers II, Massachusetts Historical Society.

158. Memorandum from Robert Kintner to Lyndon Johnson, May 5, 1966, Box 147, Name File, Confidential File, White House Central File, Lyndon B. Johnson Presidential Library.

159. Burke, *Ambassador at Large,* 108–109.

160. Memorandum from William Jorden to Lyndon Johnson, August 26, 1967, Box 13, Vietnam, Country File, Confidential File, White House Central File, Lyndon B. Johnson Presidential Library.

161. Lyndon Baines Johnson, *Vantage Point,* 264.

162. Henry Cabot Lodge Jr. to Ellsworth Bunker, September 14, 1967, Reel 2, Microfilm Edition, Henry Cabot Lodge, Jr. Papers II, Massachusetts Historical Society.

163. Meeting with Foreign Policy Advisors on Vietnam, November 2, 1967, Box 2, Meeting Notes File, Papers of Lyndon Baines Johnson, Lyndon B. Johnson Presidential Library.

164. Memorandum from Walt Rostow to Lyndon Johnson, Box 251, Vietnam, Country File, National Security File, Lyndon B. Johnson Presidential Library.

165. Longley, *LBJ's 1968,* 81.

166. Lyndon Baines Johnson, *Vantage Point,* 416.

167. McNamara, *In Retrospect,* 306.

168. Clifford, *Counsel to the President,* 454–455.

## 16. West Germany and 1968

1. Schulzinger, *Time for War,* 264.

2. Harry G. Summers Jr., *On Strategy,* 1.

3. Telegram 9552 from Bonn to Washington, March 14, 1968, Box 2633, POL 7 US/Lodge, Central Foreign Policy Files, 1967–1969, RG 59, General Records of the Department of State, National Archives and Records Administration.

4. Telegram 5310 from Brussels to Washington, March 20, 1968, Box 2633, POL 7 US/Lodge, Central Foreign Policy Files, 1967–1969, RG 59, General Records of the Department of State, National Archives and Records Administration.

5. Meeting with Special Advisory Group, March 25, 1968, Box 2, Meeting Notes File, Lyndon B. Johnson Presidential Library.

6. Foreign Policy Advisors Luncheon, March 26, 1968, Box 2, Meeting Notes, Personal Papers of Tom Johnson, Lyndon B. Johnson Presidential Library.

7. Leuchtenberg, *American President,* 464.

8. Barrett, *Uncertain Warriors,* 149.

9. Chace, *Acheson,* 358.

10. Rusk, *As I Saw It*, 453.

11. Meeting of So-Called "Wisemen" on Viet-Nam, March 25–26, 1968, Reel 14, Microfilm Edition, Henry Cabot Lodge, Jr. Papers II, Massachusetts Historical Society.

12. Memorandum for Personal Files—No One to See, March 27, 1968, Box 484, Subject File, Kennedy-Johnson Administrations, 1958–1971, W. Averell Harriman Papers, Manuscript Division, Library of Congress.

13. Kattenberg, *Vietnam Trauma*, 138.

14. Barrett, *Uncertain Warriors*, 156.

15. Ferguson, *Kissinger*, 816.

16. Edward Brooke to Henry Cabot Lodge Jr., April 2, 1968, Reel 2, Microfilm Edition, Henry Cabot Lodge, Jr. Papers II, Massachusetts Historical Society.

17. Memorandum from Dean Rusk to Lyndon Johnson, May 15, 1968, Box 147, Name File, Confidential File, White House Central File, Lyndon B. Johnson Presidential Library.

18. Heinz Barth, "A Member of the Pilgrim Fathers Aristocracy Henry Cabot Lodge, the New Ambassador in Bonn," *Die Welt*, April 4, 1968.

19. Angaben zur Persönlichkeit den neuen amerikanischen Botschafters, Henry Cabot Lodge, Jr., undated, Fiche 1, Bestell Nr. 273, B32, 1955–1969, North American File (11 A6), Foreign Office Archives (Politisches Archiv des Auswärtigen Amts), Berlin.

20. Telegram 13153 from Bonn to Washington, June 12, 1968, Box 16, Files of Walt W. Rostow, National Security File, Lyndon B. Johnson Presidential Library.

21. Lyndon Baines Johnson, *Vantage Point*, 505.

22. Dobbins, *Foreign Service*, 14.

23. Telegram 13837 from Bonn to Washington, June 26, 1968, Box 189, Europe and USSR, Germany, Country File, National Security File, Lyndon B. Johnson Presidential Library.

24. Telegram 13634 from Bonn to Washington, June 21, 1968, Box 189, Europe and USSR, Germany, Country File, National Security File, Lyndon B. Johnson Presidential Library.

25. Gespräch des Bundeskanzlers Kiesinger mit dem amerikanischen Botschafter Cabot Lodge, June 21, 1968, in *Akten zur Auswärtigen Politik, 1968, 1 Januar bis 30. Juni*, 199.

26. Cleveland, "NATO after the Invasion," 259.

27. Gespräch des Bundeskanzlers Kiesinger mit dem amerikanischen Botschafter Cabot Lodge, September 17, 1968, in *Akten zur Auswärtigen Politik, 1968, 1 Juli bis 31. Dezember*, 303.

28. Memorandum from Walt Rostow to Lyndon Johnson, September 4, 1968, Box 189, Europe and USSR, Germany, Country File, National Security File, Lyndon B. Johnson Presidential Library.

29. Telegram 16060 from Bonn to Washington, August 26, 1968, Box 189, Europe and USSR, Germany, Country File, National Security File, Lyndon B. Johnson Presidential Library.

30. Telegram 16454 from Bonn to Washington, September 5, 1968, Box 189, Europe and USSR, Germany, Country File, National Security File, Lyndon B. Johnson Presidential Library.

31. Memorandum of Conversation, June 14, 1968, Box 189, Europe and USSR, Germany, Country File, National Security File, Lyndon B. Johnson Presidential Library.

32. Clark Clifford to Henry Cabot Lodge Jr., October 15, 1968, Reel 3, Microfilm Edition, Henry Cabot Lodge, Jr. Papers II, Massachusetts Historical Society.

33. Memorandum of Conversation, October 11, 1968, Box 189, Europe and USSR, Germany, Country File, National Security File, Lyndon B. Johnson Presidential Library.

34. Telegram 17981 from Bonn to Washington, October 11, 1968, Box 189, Europe and USSR, Germany, Country File, National Security File, Lyndon B. Johnson Presidential Library.

35. Christian, *President Steps Down*, 24.

36. Walters, *Silent Missions*, 508.

37. "Behind the Bombing Halt," *New York Times*, November 11, 1968, pp. 1, 20.

38. Dobbins, *Foreign Service*, 20.

39. Norman Sherman, *From Nowhere to Somewhere*, 131–132.

40. Kattenberg, *Vietnam Trauma*, 140.

41. Kattenberg, *Vietnam Trauma*, 177.

42. Henry Cabot Lodge, "A Diplomat's Hail to His Chief," *New York Times*, February 3, 1973, p. 29.

43. Gespräch des Bundeskanzlers Kiesinger mit dem amerikanischen Botschafter Cabot Lodge, November 12, 1968, in *Akten zur Auswsärtigen Politik, 1968, 1 Juli bis 31. Dezember*, 371.

44. Memorandum of Conversation, October 15, 1968, Box 38, Henry Cabot Lodge, Jr. Papers I, Massachusetts Historical Society.

45. Christian, *President Steps Down*, 125.

46. Isaacson, *Kissinger*, 135.

47. Memorandum from Mr. Kolarek to Mr. Tarnoff, November 11, 1968, Box 65, Henry Cabot Lodge, Jr. Papers I, Massachusetts Historical Society.

48. Conversation with President-Elect Richard M. Nixon, November 9, 1968, 2:10–3:20 p.m., Key Biscayne, Florida, Reel 12, Microfilm Edition, Henry Cabot Lodge, Jr. Papers II, Massachusetts Historical Society.

49. Tien Hung Nguyen and Schecter, *Palace File*, 495.

50. Henry Kissinger to Henry Cabot Lodge Jr., December 10, 1968, Reel 9, Microfilm Edition, Henry Cabot Lodge, Jr. Papers II, Massachusetts Historical Society.

51. Coppolani, *Richard Nixon*, 396.

52. Suri, *Henry Kissinger,* 164.

53. Felzenberg, *A Man and His Presidents,* 207–208.

54. Ferguson, *Kissinger,* 860.

55. "Lodge for Harriman?," *Washington Post,* December 6, 1968, p. A24.

56. Gov's Comment on Lodge Nomination, undated, Box 484, Subject File, Kennedy-Johnson Administrations, 1958–1971, W. Averell Harriman Papers, Manuscript Division, Library of Congress.

57. Embassy of the United States of America, U.S. Information Service, Press Release No. 426, undated, Fiche 1, Bestell Nr. 273, B32, 1955–1969, North American File (11 A6), Foreign Office Archives (Politisches Archiv des Auswärtigen Amts), Berlin.

58. "Negotiator Lodge," *International Herald Tribune,* January 8, 1969.

59. Liebmann, *Last American Diplomat,* 34.

60. Barrett, *Uncertain Warriors,* 243.

61. Liebmann, *Last American Diplomat,* 34.

62. Nguyen Phu Duc, *Viet-Nam Peace Negotiations,* 178.

63. Sorley, *Vietnam War,* ix.

64. Lyndon Johnson to Henry Cabot Lodge Jr., January 18, 1969, Henry Cabot Lodge, Name File, White House Central File, Lyndon B. Johnson Presidential Library.

## 17. The Paris Peace Talks

1. Kalb and Kalb, *Kissinger,* 125.

2. Memorandum from Averell Harriman to Henry Cabot Lodge Jr., January 7, 1969, Reel 20, Microfilm Edition, Henry Cabot Lodge, Jr. Papers II, Massachusetts Historical Society.

3. Text Authorized by Bundy for Delivery by Lodge, Box 1071, Post-government, 1901–1988, Addition II: Special Files: Public Service, W. Averell Harriman Papers, Manuscript Division, Library of Congress.

4. Robert Hopkins Miller, *Vietnam and Beyond,* 119–120.

5. Robert Hopkins Miller, *Vietnam and Beyond,* 120.

6. Averell Harriman to Cyrus Vance, July 15, 1969, Box 41, Cyrus R. and Grace Sloane Vance Papers, Yale University.

7. Dobbins, *Foreign Service,* 21.

8. Edward Lansdale to Henry Cabot Lodge Jr., May 2, 1967, Reel 20, Microfilm Edition, Henry Cabot Lodge, Jr. Papers II, Massachusetts Historical Society.

9. "Negotiator Lodge," *International Herald Tribune,* January 8, 1969.

10. Ky, *Buddha's Child,* 302.

11. Notes from January 17, 1969, Box 5, Cyrus R. and Grace Sloane Vance Papers, Yale University.

12. Nguyen Phu Duc, *Viet-Nam Peace Negotiations,* 175.

13. Harvan File (Secret), Paris Peace Talks, January 16, 1969, Box 1, Additional Material, Cyrus R. and Grace Sloane Vance Papers, Yale University.

14. Kalb and Kalb, *Kissinger,* 130.

15. Robert Hopkins Miller, *Vietnam and Beyond,* 121.

16. Author interview with John Negroponte, October 18, 2017, Washington, DC, and email.

17. Henry Cabot Lodge Jr. to John Davis Lodge, September 25, 1969, Box 200, John Davis Lodge Papers, Hoover Institution.

18. Steven W. Bussard, "The Routine at the Hotel Majestic," *Harvard Crimson,* June 30, 1969.

19. Henry Cabot Lodge Jr. to Richard Nixon, March 5, 1969, Box 823, Name Files, National Security Council Files, Richard M. Nixon Presidential Library.

20. Sorley, *Vietnam War,* ix.

21. Kissinger, *White House Years,* 29.

22. Memorandum of Conversation, March 17, 1969, Box 180, Paris Talks/Meetings, National Security Council Files, Richard M. Nixon Presidential Library.

23. Kalb and Kalb, *Kissinger,* 131.

24. Kissinger, *White House Years,* 242.

25. Private Meetings, undated, Paris Peace, Reel 27, Microfilm Edition, Henry Cabot Lodge, Jr. Papers II, Massachusetts Historical Society.

26. Kissinger, *Ending the Vietnam War,* 66.

27. Kissinger, *White House Years,* 250.

28. Kissinger, *White House Years,* 263.

29. Henry Cabot Lodge Jr. to Richard Nixon, April 8, 1969, Box 823, Name Files, National Security Council Files, Richard M. Nixon Presidential Library.

30. Lien-Hang T. Nguyen, "Waging War on All Fronts," in Logevall and Preston, *Nixon in the World,* 187.

31. Johns, *Vietnam's Second Front,* 246.

32. Kissinger, *Ending the Vietnam War,* 74.

33. Nguyen Phu Duc, *Viet-Nam Peace Negotiations,* 178.

34. Kalb and Kalb, *Kissinger,* 131.

35. Stockdale and Stockdale, *In Love and War,* 305.

36. Henry Cabot Lodge Jr. to Henry Kissinger, September 19, 1969, Box 78, Vietnam Subject Files, National Security Council Files, Richard M. Nixon Presidential Library.

37. Van Atta, *With Honor,* 203.

38. Kissinger, *White House Years,* 282.

39. President's Daily Brief, July 22, 1969, CIA DOC_0005976891, Central Intelligence Agency.

40. Robert Hopkins Miller, *Vietnam and Beyond,* 124.

41. Memorandum from Henry Kissinger to Richard Nixon, June 24, 1969, Box 78, Vietnam Subject Files, National Security Council Files, Richard M. Nixon Presidential Library.

42. President's Daily Brief, July 24, 1969, CIA-RDP79T00936A007300210001-3, Central Intelligence Agency.

43. Dallek, *Nixon and Kissinger*, 149.

44. Kalb and Kalb, *Kissinger*, 138.

45. Henry Kissinger—Paris—Monday, August 4, 1969, Reel 9, Microfilm Edition, Henry Cabot Lodge, Jr. Papers II, Massachusetts Historical Society.

46. Hershberg, *Marigold*, 698.

47. Kissinger, *White House Years*, 282.

48. Walters, *Silent Missions*, 515.

49. Robert Hopkins Miller, *Vietnam and Beyond*, 124–125.

50. Lien-Hang T. Nguyen, *Hanoi's War*, 140.

51. Richard Nixon, *RN*, 397.

52. Henry Cabot Lodge Jr. to Henry Kissinger, August 9, 1969, Reel 9, Microfilm Edition, Henry Cabot Lodge, Jr. Papers II, Massachusetts Historical Society.

53. CAS Channel, for Kissinger from Ambassador Lodge, Box 839, Name Files, National Security Council Files, Richard M. Nixon Presidential Library.

54. Memorandum from Henry Kissinger to Richard Nixon, August 21, 1969, Box 839, Name Files, National Security Council Files, Richard M. Nixon Presidential Library.

55. Bill Safire later wrote with fascination about how myths like the "secret plan" get created, and how difficult they are to eradicate. See William Safire, "Secret Plan," in *Safire's Political Dictionary*, 647.

56. Haldeman, *Haldeman Diaries*, 98.

57. Haldeman, *Haldeman Diaries*, 107.

58. Memorandum of Telephone Conversation, September 2, 1969, Reel 9, Microfilm Edition, Henry Cabot Lodge, Jr. Papers II, Massachusetts Historical Society.

59. Kalb and Kalb, *Kissinger*, 141–142.

60. Telephone Conversation, October 31, 1969, 3:45 Paris Time, Reel 9, Microfilm Edition, Henry Cabot Lodge, Jr. Papers II, Massachusetts Historical Society.

61. John Paul Vann to Henry Kissinger, November 5, 1969, Box 28, Correspondence, circa 1950–1984, John Paul Vann, circa 1920–1984, Vann-Sheehan Vietnam War Collection, Neil Sheehan Papers, Manuscript Division, Library of Congress.

62. Kissinger, *White House Years*, 438.

63. Kalb and Kalb, *Kissinger*, 148.

64. Memorandum from Henry Kissinger to Richard Nixon, October 11, 1969, Box 78, Vietnam Subject Files, National Security Council Files, Richard M. Nixon Presidential Library.

65. Memorandum from Henry Kissinger to Richard Nixon, October 23, 1969, Box 78, Vietnam Subject Files, National Security Council Files, Richard M. Nixon Presidential Library.

66. Ambassador Lodge's Statement to the Media, October 16, 1969, Box 78, Vietnam Subject Files, National Security Council Files, Richard M. Nixon Presidential Library.

67. Conversation Pres. Nixon, Friday, December 11, 1969, 11:30 a.m., Reel 12, Microfilm Edition, Henry Cabot Lodge, Jr. Papers II, Massachusetts Historical Society.

68. John Paul Vann to Henry Kissinger, December 4, 1969, Box 28, Correspondence, circa 1950–1984, John Paul Vann, circa 1920–1984, Vann-Sheehan Vietnam War Collection, Neil Sheehan Papers, Manuscript Division, Library of Congress.

69. Interview with Phil Habib, May 24, 1984, Foreign Affairs Oral History Collection, Association for Diplomatic Studies and Training.

70. Kissinger, *Ending the Vietnam War*, 111.

71. Conversation Pres. Nixon, Friday, December 11, 1969, 11:30 a.m., Reel 12, Microfilm Edition, Henry Cabot Lodge, Jr. Papers II, Massachusetts Historical Society.

72. "Nixon Accepts Resignation of Paris Vietnam Negotiators," November 20, 1969, Box 200, John Davis Lodge Papers, Hoover Institution.

73. Kissinger, *Ending the Vietnam War*, 242.

74. Lien-Hang T. Nguyen, "Waging War on All Fronts," 192.

75. Memorandum of Conversation between Henry Kissinger and William Burchett, October 8, 1971, S-0871-0002-18-00001, Files of the Secretary-General, Archives and Records Management Section, United Nations.

76. Author interview with Winston Lord, February 10, 2017, Yorba Linda, California.

77. Kissinger, *White House Years*, 688.

78. Author interview with Henry A. Kissinger, June 27, 2018, New York, New York.

79. Undated Notes, Reel 3, Microfilm Edition, Henry Cabot Lodge, Jr. Papers II, Massachusetts Historical Society.

80. Henry Cabot Lodge Jr. to Marshall Green, December 1, 1969, Reel 3, Microfilm Edition, Henry Cabot Lodge, Jr. Papers II, Massachusetts Historical Society.

81. Memorandum from Henry Cabot Lodge Jr. to Henry Kissinger, February 3, 1970, Box 823, Name Files, National Security Council Files, Richard M. Nixon Presidential Library.

82. Memorandum from Henry Cabot Lodge Jr. to Henry Kissinger, January 23, 1970, Reel 9, Microfilm Edition, Henry Cabot Lodge, Jr. Papers II, Massachusetts Historical Society.

83. Undated Notes, Reel 3, Microfilm Edition, Henry Cabot Lodge, Jr. Papers II, Massachusetts Historical Society.

84. MacMillan, *Nixon and Mao*, 186.

85. Henry Cabot Lodge Jr. to Henry Kissinger, July 20, 1971, Box 361, Folder 22, Series II, Government Service, Henry A. Kissinger Papers, Part II.

86. Edward Brooke to Henry Cabot Lodge Jr., July 12, 1971, Reel 2, Microfilm Edition, Henry Cabot Lodge, Jr. Papers II, Massachusetts Historical Society.

87. Haldeman, *Haldeman Diaries*, 302.

88. Prados, *Family Jewels*, 286.

89. Prados, *Family Jewels*, 284.

90. Emery, *Watergate*, 72.

91. Lukas, *Nightmare*, 84.

92. Henry Cabot Lodge Jr. to Lyndon Johnson, May 4, 1972, LOD, Post-presidential Name File, Lyndon B. Johnson Presidential Library.

93. Henry Cabot Lodge, "A Diplomat's Hail to His Chief," *New York Times*, February 3, 1973, p. 29.

94. Asselin, *Hanoi's Road*, 211.

95. Suri, *Henry Kissinger*, 232.

## 18. Envoy to the Vatican

1. Califano, *Inside*, 178.

2. Robert S. Allen and Paul Scott, "Allen-Scott Report, Inside Washington," *Northern Virginia Sun*, May 1, 1965.

3. Memorandum from Henry A. Kissinger to Ron Ziegler, April 15, 1970, Box 823, Name Files, National Security Council Files, Richard M. Nixon Presidential Library.

4. Memorandum from Henry Cabot Lodge Jr. to Al Haig, undated, Reel 6, Microfilm Edition, Henry Cabot Lodge, Jr. Papers II, Massachusetts Historical Society.

5. Memorandum for the Files, undated, Reel 1, Microfilm Edition, Henry Cabot Lodge, Jr. Papers II, Massachusetts Historical Society.

6. Memorandum for the Files, undated, Reel 1, Microfilm Edition, Henry Cabot Lodge, Jr. Papers II, Massachusetts Historical Society.

7. Henry Cabot Lodge Jr. to John Paul Vann, January 5, 1970, Box 28, Correspondence, circa 1950–1984, John Paul Vann, circa 1920–1984, Vann-Sheehan Vietnam War Collection, Neil Sheehan Papers, Manuscript Division, Library of Congress.

8. Henry Cabot Lodge Jr. to Henry Kissinger, August 19, 1970, Box 823, Name Files, National Security Council Files, Richard M. Nixon Presidential Library.

9. Henry Cabot Lodge Jr. to Jimmy Carter, January 5, 1977, Reel 2, Microfilm Edition, Henry Cabot Lodge, Jr. Papers II, Massachusetts Historical Society.

10. Douglas Brinkley and Nichter, *Nixon Tapes: 1971–1972*, 103.

11. Henry Cabot Lodge Jr. to Richard Nixon, April 13, 1971, Reel 12, Microfilm Edition, Henry Cabot Lodge, Jr. Papers II, Massachusetts Historical Society.

12. Frank Sieverts to Henry Cabot Lodge Jr., August 27, 1970, Reel 2, Microfilm Edition, Henry Cabot Lodge, Jr. Papers II, Massachusetts Historical Society.

13. Henry Kissinger to Henry Cabot Lodge Jr., October 6, 1969, Box 68, Alphabetical Name Files, White House Central Files, Richard M. Nixon Presidential Library.

14. Telegram from White House Situation Room to Hanscom Air Force Base, December 19, 1970, Box 823, Name Files, National Security Council Files, Richard M. Nixon Presidential Library.

15. Aitken, *Charles W. Colson*, 133.

16. 3rd Draft—H. C. Lodge, undated, Working Paper, Box 823, Name Files, National Security Council Files, Richard M. Nixon Presidential Library.

17. Dean Acheson to Henry Cabot Lodge Jr., August 31, 1970, Reel 1, Microfilm Edition, Henry Cabot Lodge, Jr. Papers II, Massachusetts Historical Society.

18. Klein, *Making It Perfectly Clear*, 198.

19. Nichter, *Richard Nixon and Europe*, 29.

20. Kissinger, *White House Years*, 944.

21. Order, July 10, 1970, Box 67, Alphabetical Name Files, White House Central Files, Richard M. Nixon Presidential Library.

22. John Davis Lodge to Henry Cabot Lodge Jr., September 21, 1970, Box 200, John Davis Lodge Papers, Hoover Institution.

23. Henry Cabot Lodge Jr. to Alexander Haig, May 21, 1971, Box 823, Name Files, National Security Council Files, Richard M. Nixon Presidential Library.

24. Richard Nixon to Henry Cabot Lodge Jr., May 19, 1971, Box 68, Alphabetical Name Files, White House Central Files, Nixon Presidential Library.

25. Report of the President's Commission for the Observance of the Twenty-Fifth Anniversary of the United Nations, April 26, 1971, Box 823, Name Files, National Security Council Files, Richard M. Nixon Presidential Library.

26. Henry Cabot Lodge Jr. to Richard Nixon, August 17, 1971, Box 823, Name Files, National Security Council Files, Richard M. Nixon Presidential Library.

27. Henry Cabot Lodge Jr. to Richard Nixon, April 7, 1972, Box 823, Name Files, National Security Council Files, Richard M. Nixon Presidential Library.

28. Henry Cabot Lodge Jr. to Charles Colson, May 5, 1972, Reel 3, Microfilm Edition, Henry Cabot Lodge, Jr. Papers II, Massachusetts Historical Society.

29. Henry Cabot Lodge Jr. to Charles Colson, November 27, 1972, Box 72, Meeting Files, Charles W. Colson, Staff Member Office Files, White House Special Files, Richard M. Nixon Presidential Library.

30. Charles Colson to Henry Cabot Lodge Jr., October 10, 1972, Reel 3, Microfilm Edition, Henry Cabot Lodge, Jr. Papers II, Massachusetts Historical Society.

31. Statement—H. C. Lodge—Boston, August 1, Box 72, Meeting Files, Charles W. Colson, Staff Member Office Files, White House Special Files, Richard M. Nixon Presidential Library.

32. "Lodge, Pope Paul Swap What's New," *Boston Pilot*, October 21, 1972.

33. James O'Neil, untitled National Catholic News Service article, October 7, 1972, Box 72, Meeting Files, Charles W. Colson, Staff Member Office Files, White House Special Files, Richard M. Nixon Presidential Library.

34. Henry Cabot Lodge Jr., "The President Needs Item-Veto Power," *New York Times,* April 22, 1973.

35. Memorandum from Richard Smyser to Henry Kissinger, April 14, 1971, Box 823, Name Files, National Security Council Files, Richard M. Nixon Presidential Library.

36. Henry Cabot Lodge, "A Diplomat's Hail to His Chief," *New York Times,* February 3, 1973, p. 29.

37. Kissinger, *White House Years,* 1107.

38. Memorandum from A. Denis Clift to Brent Scowcroft, August 28, 1974, Box 41, NSC Europe, Canada, and Ocean Affairs Staff Files, National Security Adviser, Gerald R. Ford Presidential Library.

39. Henry Cabot Lodge Jr. to Gerald Ford, October 25, 1973, Reel 5, Microfilm Edition, Henry Cabot Lodge, Jr. Papers II, Massachusetts Historical Society.

40. Memorandum of Conversation with President Gerald Ford, April 21, 1975, Reel 5, Microfilm Edition, Henry Cabot Lodge, Jr. Papers II, Massachusetts Historical Society.

41. Call on the Vice President by Ambassador Henry Cabot Lodge, January 22, 1974, Box 65, Vice Presidential Meetings with Foreign and Diplomatic Officials, John O. Marsh, Office of Assistant for Defense and International Affairs, 1973–1974, Vice Presidential Papers, Gerald R. Ford Files, Gerald R. Ford Presidential Library.

42. Memorandum of Conversation between Gerald Ford, Brent Scowcroft, and Henry Cabot Lodge Jr., April 21, 1975, Box 11, National Security Adviser, Memoranda of Conversations, 1973–1977, Gerald R. Ford Presidential Library.

43. Meeting with Pope Paul VI, June 3, 1975, Box 9, National Security Adviser, Trip Briefing Books and Cables for President Ford, Gerald R. Ford Presidential Library.

44. Memorandum of Conversation between Gerald Ford, Jean Jadot, Raymond Powers, and Brent Scowcroft, December 22, 1975, Box 17, National Security Adviser, Memoranda of Conversations, 1973–1977, Gerald R. Ford Presidential Library.

45. Henry Cabot Lodge Jr. to Gerald Ford, July 14, 1974, Reel 5, Microfilm Edition, Henry Cabot Lodge, Jr. Papers II, Massachusetts Historical Society.

46. Memorandum from Terry O'Donnell to Richard Cheney, June 3, 1976, Box 1, Richard B. Cheney Files, Gerald R. Ford Presidential Library.

47. Memorandum of Conversation between Gerald Ford, Brent Scowcroft, and Henry Cabot Lodge Jr., April 21, 1975, Reel 4, Microfilm Edition, Henry Cabot Lodge, Jr. Papers II, Massachusetts Historical Society.

48. Memorandum from Robert Hartmann to Donald Rumsfeld, Henry Kissinger, and Douglas Bennett, August 18, 1975, Box 2, Robert T. Hartmann Files, Presidential Speeches and Statements, Gerald R. Ford Presidential Library. Regarding abortion, see

Memorandum from Bobbie Greene Kilberg to Gerald Ford, February 6, 1976, Box 1, David R. Gergen Files, Office of the Press Secretary, Gerald R. Ford Presidential Library.

49. Meeting with the U.S. Catholic Conference and the National Conference of Catholic Bishops, June 18, 1975, Box 16, William J. Baroody Files, Public Liaison Office, Gerald R. Ford Presidential Library.

50. George Dugan, "U.S. Bishops Urge Voter Involvement," *New York Times*, May 7, 1976.

51. The President's Special Envoy to the Vatican, undated, Box 41, NSC Europe, Canada, and Ocean Affairs Staff Files, National Security Adviser, Gerald R. Ford Presidential Library.

52. "Pope and Kissinger Discuss the Mideast," *New York Times*, July 9, 1976.

53. Eucharistic Congress, July 21, 1976, Box 9, Vernon C. Loen and Charles Leppert Files, Congressional Relations Office, Gerald R. Ford Presidential Library.

54. President's Remarks to the 41st International Eucharistic Congress, Philadelphia, August 8, 1976, Box 37, Reading Copies, Presidential Speeches, Gerald R. Ford Presidential Library.

55. Note, *New York Times*, December 3, 1975.

56. UPI Release, February 28, 1985, Research Office, Office of Speechwriting, Ronald Reagan Presidential Library.

57. Henry Cabot Lodge Jr. to Gerald Ford, August 9, 1976, Reel 5, Microfilm Edition, Henry Cabot Lodge, Jr. Papers II, Massachusetts Historical Society.

58. Conversation with Edward Brooke, Friday, May 2, 1975, at Lechner's Restaurant, Reel 2, Microfilm Edition, Henry Cabot Lodge, Jr. Papers II, Massachusetts Historical Society.

59. Memorandum of Conversation between President Ford, Henry Cabot Lodge Jr., and Brent Scowcroft, January 4, 1977, Box 21, Memoranda of Conversations, 1973–1977, National Security Adviser, Gerald R. Ford Presidential Library.

60. Henry Cabot Lodge Jr. to Jimmy Carter, January 5, 1977, Reel 2, Microfilm Edition, Henry Cabot Lodge, Jr. Papers II, Massachusetts Historical Society.

61. Henry Cabot Lodge Jr. to Gerald Ford, January 21, 1977, Box 1923, Name File, White House Central File, Gerald R. Ford Presidential Library.

## Retirement and Epilogue

1. Oral History Interview of Henry Cabot Lodge Jr. with Richard D. Challener, February 16, 1965, John Foster Dulles Oral History Collection, Seeley G. Mudd Manuscript Library, Princeton University.

2. Henry Cabot Lodge Jr. to Evan Thomas, July 4, 1964, Reel 27, Microfilm Edition, Henry Cabot Lodge, Jr. Papers II, Massachusetts Historical Society.

3. Notes, undated, Box 71, Individuals, 1957–1991, Vann-Sheehan Vietnam War Collection, Neil Sheehan Papers, Manuscript Division, Library of Congress.

4. Email from George Cabot Lodge to the author, May 8, 2018.

5. Henry Cabot Lodge Jr. to Dwight Eisenhower, January 7, 1957, Box 24, Administration Series, Ann Whitman File, Papers as President, Dwight D. Eisenhower Presidential Library.

6. Henry Cabot Lodge Jr., "Words I Live By," undated, Reel 3, Microfilm Edition, Henry Cabot Lodge, Jr. Papers II, Massachusetts Historical Society.

7. Henry Cabot Lodge Jr. to John Davis Lodge, March 17, 1978, Box 227, John Davis Lodge Papers, Hoover Institution.

8. Telegram from Henry Cabot Lodge Jr. to Jimmy Carter, December 4, 1978, Reel 1, Microfilm Edition, Henry Cabot Lodge, Jr. Papers II, Massachusetts Historical Society.

9. Henry Cabot Lodge, Doctor of Humane Letters, honoris causa, May 25, 1980, Reel 5, Microfilm Edition, Henry Cabot Lodge, Jr. Papers II, Massachusetts Historical Society.

10. Commencements, *Washington Post*, May 22, 1980.

11. Henry Cabot Lodge Jr. to John Davis Lodge, undated, Box 200, John Davis Lodge Papers, Hoover Institution.

12. George's Toast at H.C.L.'s Party, July 6, 1972, Box 200, John Davis Lodge Papers, Hoover Institution.

13. Beatty, *Rascal King*, 511.

14. Undated Notes, Reel 3, Microfilm Edition, Henry Cabot Lodge, Jr. Papers II, Massachusetts Historical Society.

15. Henry Cabot Lodge Jr. to David Halberstam, December 12, 1980, Box 10, Folder 12, Papers of David Halberstam, Howard Gotlieb Archival Research Center, Boston University.

16. Personal Assessment of the Roosevelt Years, United Nations, New York, Wednesday, June 16, 1982, Francis O. Wilcox Papers, University of Iowa.

17. Henry Cabot Lodge Jr. to John Davis Lodge, September 28, 1972, Box 200, John Davis Lodge Papers, Hoover Institution.

18. Henry Cabot Lodge Jr. to John Davis Lodge, February 23, 1973, Box 200, John Davis Lodge Papers, Hoover Institution.

19. John Davis Lodge to George Cabot Lodge, March 8, 1984, Box 271, John Davis Lodge Paper, Hoover Institution.

20. George Cabot Lodge to John Davis Lodge, March 15, 1984, Box 271, John Davis Lodge Paper, Hoover Institution.

21. George Cabot Lodge to John Davis Lodge, undated [early 1985], Box 271, John Davis Lodge Paper, Hoover Institution.

22. Emily Lodge, *Lodge Women*, 363.

23. Presidential Statement: Death of Henry Cabot Lodge, February 28, 1985, Box 33, Anthony Dolan Files, Ronald Reagan Presidential Library.

24. Memorandum from Henry Kissinger to Gerald Ford, September 27, 1976, Box 19, NSC Europe, Canada, and Ocean Affairs Staff Files, National Security Adviser, Gerald R. Ford Presidential Library.

25. UPI Release, February 28, 1985, Research Office, Office of Speechwriting, Ronald Reagan Presidential Library.

26. Telegram from John Davis Lodge to Emily Lodge, undated, Box 263, John Davis Lodge Papers, Hoover Institution.

27. Emily Lodge, *Lodge Women*, 360.

28. Forrester A. Clark to Henry Cabot Lodge Jr., March 14, 1961, Reel 3, Microfilm Edition, Henry Cabot Lodge, Jr. Papers II, Massachusetts Historical Society.

29. Richard Nixon to John Davis Lodge, February 28, 1985, Box Blue 30(D), Postpresidential Papers, Richard M. Nixon Presidential Library.

30. Frank, *Ike and Dick*, 202.

31. Halberstam, *Making of a Quagmire*, 136.

32. Hershberg, *Marigold*, 110.

# BIBLIOGRAPHY

## Archival Sources

### AUSTRALIA

National Archives of Australia—Canberra
  Cabinet Office
    Menzies and Holt Ministries (Series A4940)

### BELGIUM

North Atlantic Treaty Organization (NATO)—Brussels
  Archives Division
    North Atlantic Council (C-)
      Ministerial Meetings (C-M)
      Records of Meetings (C-R)

### GERMANY

Foreign Office Archives (Politisches Archiv des Auswärtigen Amts)—Berlin
  North American File (11 A6)
    B32, 1955–1969
      Bestell Nr. 273
      Fiche 1–4

### UNITED KINGDOM

National Archives—Kew, Surrey
  Foreign and Commonwealth Office (FCO)
    South East Asian Department (FCO 15)
  Foreign Office (FO)

Political Departments
General Correspondence from 1906–1966 (FO 371)
Security Service (KV)
Personal Files (KV 2)
United Nations Department (UN)
University of Cambridge—Cambridge
Churchill College
Winston Churchill Papers
Public and Political: General
Private and Personal: Correspondence
April 1952–May 1964

UNITED STATES

Archdiocese of Boston—Braintree, Massachusetts
Pastoral Center
Archives
Cushing Papers
Series I: Correspondence
Arizona State University Libraries—Tempe, Arizona
Arizona Collection
Personal and Political Papers of Senator Barry M. Goldwater
Series I: Personal
Sub-series A: Alpha Files
Sub-sub-series VI: Oversized
Sub-series I: Audio
Association for Diplomatic Studies and Training—Arlington, Virginia
Foreign Affairs Oral History Collection
Boston Public Library—Boston, Massachusetts
Print Department
Leslie Jones Collection
Boston University—Boston, Massachusetts
Howard Gotlieb Archival Research Center
Papers of David Halberstam
Central Intelligence Agency—Washington, DC
Electronic Reading Room
President's Daily Brief, 1961–1969
President's Daily Brief, 1969–1977
Columbia University—New York, New York
Columbia Center for Oral History
Eisenhower Administration Program: Oral History, 1962–1972

Dwight D. Eisenhower Presidential Library—Abilene, Kansas
  Audiovisual Collection
    National Park Service Photographs
  C. D. Jackson Records
    1931–1967 Series
    1953–1954 Series
  Christian A. Herter Papers
    1937–1967 Series
  Fred A. Seaton Papers
    Correspondence Series
      Routine Subseries
    Post-Eisenhower Administration Series
    Republican Party Series
    Subject Series
  Henry Cabot Lodge, Jr. Papers
    Selected Papers, 1942–1952
      Microfilm Edition
  John Foster Dulles Papers
    General Correspondence and Memoranda Series
    Memoranda of Conversations Subseries
    Telephone Conversations Subseries
  Maxwell M. Rabb Papers
    Cabinet Meeting Notes
    Correspondence
    General Office Files
    Photographs
  Oral Histories
  Papers of Dwight D. Eisenhower
    Papers as President, 1953–1961
      Ann Whitman File
        Administration Series
        DDE Diary Series
      Cabinet Series
      Dulles-Herter Series
    Post-presidential Papers, 1961–1969
      Principal Files (1962, 1963, 1964)
    Pre-presidential Papers, 1916–1952
      Principal Files
        Name Series
  Robert L. Schulz Papers
    Photographs

Franklin D. Roosevelt Presidential Library—Hyde Park, New York
    Coolidge T. Jefferson Papers
    Franklin D. Roosevelt, Jr. Papers
    Papers of Franklin D. Roosevelt
        President's Personal File
    Vertical File
Georgetown University—Washington, DC
    University Library
        Digital Georgetown
            Dean Peter Krogh Foreign Affairs Digital Archives
                George Cabot Lodge Interview
George Washington University—Washington, DC
    National Security Archive
        CNN.com/Cold War Interviews
            Episode 11: Vietnam
        Digital National Security Archive
        Electronic Briefing Books
            "Kennedy Considered Supporting Coup in South Vietnam, August 1963"
                (No. 302)
Gerald R. Ford Presidential Library—Ann Arbor, Michigan
    Agnes M. Waldron Files
    Betty Ford Papers
    Charles H. McCall Files
    David R. Gergen Files
    Gerald R. Ford Files
        Congressional Papers
            General Correspondence
            Press Secretary and Speech File, 1947–1973
        Vice Presidential Papers
            Office of Assistant for Defense and International Affairs Files,
                1973–1974
                John O. Marsh
                    Vice Presidential Meetings with Foreign and Diplomatic Officials
    Mildred V. Leonard Files
    National Security Adviser
        Memoranda of Conversations
        NSC Europe, Canada, and Ocean Affairs Staff Files
        Presidential Country Files for East Asia and the Pacific
        Saigon Embassy Files
        Trip Briefing Books and Cables
        Vietnam Information Group (VIG)

Oral History Project
Patricia Lindh and Jeanne Holm Files
Presidential Handwriting File
Presidential Speeches
    Reading Copies
Remote Archives Capture (RAC) Program
    Documents from National Security Adviser, Saigon Embassy File Kept by
        Ambassador Graham Martin
Richard B. Cheney Files
Robert T. Hartmann Files
    Presidential Speeches and Statements
Ron Nessen Files
Vernon C. Loen and Charles Leppert Files
White House Central Files
    Name File
White House Photographs
William J. Baroody Files
Harry S. Truman Presidential Library—Independence, Missouri
    Audiovisual Collection
    General File
    Oral History Interviews
        Francis O. Wilcox
    Paul G. Hoffman Papers
    President's Secretary's Files
    Stanley Andrews Papers
    White House Central Files
        President's Personal File
Harvard University—Cambridge, Massachusetts
    Harvard Business School
        Baker Library
            George C. Lodge Papers
                Series VI. Biographical, 1958–2009
                    Subseries B. Unpublished Memoir, 1997–2009
Herbert Hoover Presidential Library—West Branch, Iowa
    Bourke Hickenlooper Papers
        Personal Files
        Senate Files
    Hanford MacNider Papers
    Herbert Hoover Papers
        Individuals
        Post-presidential Papers

Hoover Commission I
Lewis Strauss Papers
    Atomic Energy Commission
    Name and Subject
Raymond Richmond Papers
Robert E. Wood Papers
William Castle Papers
Hoover Institution, Stanford University—Stanford, California
    Library & Archives
        John Davis Lodge Papers
            Biographical File, 1961–1969
            Biographical File, 1983–1985
            Correspondence, 1889–1932
            Correspondence, 1932–1942
            Correspondence, 1942–1945
            Correspondence, 1944–1961
            Correspondence, 1945–1950
            Correspondence, 1950–1955
            Correspondence, 1954–1969
            Correspondence, 1966–1975
            Correspondence, 1973–1983
            Correspondence, 1982–1987
            Speeches and Writings, 1933–1942
            Subject File, 1939–1945
            Subject File, 1943–1945
            Subject File, 1946–1949
            Subject File, 1949–1954
            Subject File, 1956–1960
            Subject File, 1962–1969, 1976
            Subject File, circa 1969–1974
            Subject File, 1974–1982
        Stanley Karnow Papers
            Series I: Subject Files, 1952–1982
            Series II: Philippines Research Materials, 1973–1987
John F. Kennedy Presidential Library—Boston, Massachusetts
    Personal Papers
        James C. Thompson
            Southeast Asia, 1961–1966
        Joseph P. Kennedy
            Senate Campaign, 1952
        Lawrence F. O'Brien

    John F. Kennedy Campaigns, 1954–1960
    Roger Hilsman
        Countries Files, 1961–1964
Oral Histories
Pre-presidential Papers
    Congressional Campaign Files, 1946–1958
        '52 Campaign
    House of Representatives Files
        Series 01.7 Scrapbooks
Presidential Papers
    National Security Files
        Country File
            Vietnam
        Meetings and Memoranda
    President's Office Files
        General Correspondence
        Special Correspondence
        Special Events through the Years
        Presidential Recordings
White House Central Subject Files
White House Photographs
Library of Congress—Washington, DC
    Manuscript Division
        Clare Booth Luce Papers
            Correspondence, 1914–1988
            Literary File, 1919–1987
            Subject File, 1903–1988
        Henry Robinson Luce Papers
            Business and Social Correspondence,
                1933–1967
            Special Correspondence
        James Schlesinger Papers
            Subject File, 1863–1979
        Joseph Alsop and Stewart Alsop Papers
            Part I
                Article, Book and Speech File, 1937–1963
                General Correspondence, 1934–1964
                Special Correspondence, 1946–1963
            Part II
                General Correspondence, 1964–1967
                Speeches and Writings, 1938–1966

Part III
General Correspondence, 1941–1975
Neil Sheehan Papers
Vann-Sheehan Vietnam War Collection
Individuals, 1957–1991
Interviews and Notes, 1972–1987
Tape Summaries, 1973–1975
John Paul Vann, circa 1920–1984
Correspondence, circa 1950–1984
Professional File
United Press International—Indochina, 1961–1964
Research File, circa 1920–1991
Robert A. Taft Papers
Legislative Papers, 1920–1953
Political File, 1924–1953
Subject File, 1946–1953
W. Averell Harriman Papers
Addition I: Special Files: Public Service
Post-government, 1942–1986
Addition II: Special Files: Public Service
Post-government, 1901–1988
Kennedy-Johnson Administrations, 1958–1971
Subject File
Lyndon B. Johnson Presidential Library—Austin, Texas
Audiovisual Archives
Lyndon Baines Johnson Archives
Famous Names File
Meeting Notes File
National Security File
Country File
Germany
Vietnam
Files of McGeorge Bundy
Files of Robert Komer
Files of Walt W. Rostow
Head of State Correspondence
Intelligence File
International Meetings
Memos to the President
National Security Council
Histories
Meetings

Situation Room File
Special Head of State Correspondence
Office Files of the White House Aides
    Busby, Horace
    Macy, John
    Panzer, Fred
Oral Histories
Personal Papers
    David Nes
    Democratic National Committee
    Drew Pearson
    Henry Cabot Lodge
    Tom Johnson
        Meeting Notes
    William Bundy
    William C. Westmoreland
Post-presidential Name File
President's Appointment File
Reference File
Remote Archives Capture (RAC) Program
Statements of Lyndon B. Johnson
White House Central File
    Confidential File
        Country File
            Vietnam
        Name File
    Name Files
White House Press Office Files
White House Social Files
White House Tapes
Vietnam Reference File
Massachusetts Historical Society—Boston, Massachusetts
Henry Cabot Lodge, Jr. Papers I
    Series I: Campaigns, 1932–1964
    Series II: Legislative Subject Files, 1947–1952
    Series III: General Subject Files, 1948–1975
    Series IV: Voting Record, 1933–1952
    Series V: Eisenhower Material, 1952–1957
    Series VI: United Nations, 1950–1976
    Series VII: Speeches, Writings, Etc.,
        1926–1967
    Series VIII: Vietnam 1963–1969

Series IX: Atlantic Institute, 1959–1963
Series X: Miscellaneous Material, 1922–1977
Series XI: Special Collections, 1920–1977
Series XII: Diaries, 1922–1969
Series XIII: Memorabilia—Passports, 1932–1964
Series XIV: Additions, 1948–1982
Series XV: Scrapbooks, 1923–1978
Series XVI: Photographs
Series XVII: Audio/Visual Material
Series XVIII: Oversize Material

Henry Cabot Lodge, Jr. Papers II
Series I: General Correspondence
Series II: Confidential Journal
Series III: Military Papers
Series IV: Senate Campaign of 1952
Series V: Vietnam Papers
Series VI: Emily Sears Lodge Saigon Papers
Series VII: Paris Peace Talks
Series VIII: Vietnam Memoir
Series IX: SALT II Papers
Series X: Books
Series XI: Lodge-Eisenhower Correspondence
Series XII: Newspapers Clippings
Series XIII: Miscellaneous Printed Material and Ephemera
Series XIV: Oversize Material

Henry Cabot Lodge, Jr. Photographs
Henry Cabot Lodge, Jr. Photographs II
Leverett Saltonstall Papers I
Series II: General Subject Files, 1923–1967
Leverett Saltonstall Papers II
Series I: Legislative Papers, 1945–1966
Series II: Appropriations Committee Papers, 1948–1966
Series IX: Campaign Materials, 1938–1967

Minnesota Historical Society—St. Paul, Minnesota
Manuscripts Collection
Harold E. Stassen Papers
Political Activity, 1952–1957
Hubert H. Humphrey Papers
1968 Presidential Campaign Files
Series 4: Correspondence
Series 6: Democratic National Committee Files

Series 7: Democratic National Convention, 1967–1968
Series 9: Personal Political Files, 1966–1969
Series 11: William Connell and Eiler Ravnholt, 1963–1969
Series 16: Miscellaneous Files, 1967–1968
Trip Files
Foreign Trips
Mount Auburn Cemetery—Cambridge, Massachusetts
Archives
Henry Cabot Lodge
Henry Cabot Lodge, Jr.
National Archives and Records Administration—College Park,
Maryland
CREST (CIA Records Search Tool)
Record Group 59: Department of State
Bureau of East Asia and Pacific Affairs
Office of the Assistant Secretary of State
Subject Files, 1954–1974
Central Foreign Policy Files, 1967–1969
Political and Defense
POL 7 US/Lodge
POL 7 US/Nixon
Files of the Ambassador At Large (Averell Harriman), 1967–1968
Office of the Executive Secretariat
Paris Peace Conference Telegrams and Special Caption Messages,
1966–1972
Paris Meeting Chronology
Delto Chrons
Todel Chrons
Subject Files of the Office of Vietnam Affairs (Vietnam Working Group),
1964–1974
Record Group 84: Records of the Foreign Service Posts
Top Secret Foreign Service Post Files, 1964
Embassy Saigon
Unclassified Central Subject Files, 1964–1971
Embassy Saigon
USIS Subject Files, 1965–1967
Embassy Saigon
Record Group 460: Records of the Watergate Special Prosecution Force
Plumbers Task Force
Investigation of Other Illegal Activities
Diem Cables Seized from E. Howard Hunt's Safe

New York Public Library—New York, New York
    William E. Weiner Oral History Library
        Maxwell Rabb
Pennsylvania State Archives—Harrisburg, Pennsylvania
    Manuscript Group 208
        William W. Scranton Papers (1962–1967)
            General Records
                General File, 1963–1966 (Series #208m1)
                Subject File, 1963–1967 (Series #208m2)
            James Reichley, Legislative Secretary
                Subject File (Series #208m11)
                    Clippings, 1963–1966
Pennsylvania State University—University Park, Pennsylvania
    Eberly Family Special Collections Library
        William Warren Scranton Papers, 1933–2005
            Series 2: Congressional Term, 1954–1971
            Series 3: Gubernatorial Papers, 1956–1978
                Subseries 2: Speeches and News Releases,
                1960–1978
Princeton University—Princeton, New Jersey
    Princeton University Library
        Seeley G. Mudd Manuscript Library
            Arthur Krock Papers
                Series 1: Works, 1909–1973
                    Subseries 1A: Memoranda, 1928–1963
                Series 2: Correspondence, 1916–1974
                    Subseries 2B: General, 1917–1974
            George Ball Papers
                Series 1, Subseries 1, Subject Files
                Series 2, Appointments
                Series 3, Writings
                Series 4, Public Statements
            John Foster Dulles Oral History Collection, 1964–1967
Richard M. Nixon Presidential Library—Yorba Linda, California
    Audiovisual Collection
    National Security Council Files
        HAK Administrative and Staff Files—Transition
        Name Files
        Paris Talks/Meetings
        Pentagon Papers
        Presidential/HAK MemCons
        Vietnam Subject Files

Post-presidential Papers
Pre-presidential Papers
    1960 Campaign
        Hamlin File
        Miscellaneous
    Series 134
        Series III
            1964 Campaign
                Clippings File
    Series 220
        Series I
            Correspondence
                Sub-series A
                    Alphabetical
    Series 238
        Wilderness Years
            Series I
                Correspondence
                    Sub-series A
                        Alphabetical
    Series 257
        Wilderness Years
            Series VIII
                Book Files
    Series 347
        Wilderness Years
            Series II
                Trip Files: 1963–1967
    Vice President
        General Correspondence
President's Personal File
Unpublished Memoirs
White House Central Files
    Alphabetical Name Files
White House Special Files
    Staff Member Office Files
        Charles W. Colson
White House Tapes
Rockefeller Archive Center—Sleepy Hollow, New York
    Nelson A. Rockefeller Papers
        Gubernatorial Records
            Campaigns

Series 5 (FA440)
    Subseries 6: Presidential Campaign 1960
Diane Van Wie
    Series 34 (FA373)
        Subseries 06: Meetings, Luncheons, and Dinners
Hugh Morrow
    Series 21 (FA 242)
        Subseries 2: Campaign Files, Presidential
New York Office
    Series 22 (FA 365)
        Subseries 1: Appointments Office
            Subseries 4: George Hinman and Ilene Slater Files
Personal Papers
    Ann C. Whitman—Politics
        Series P (FA351)
    Politics—George L. Hinman
        Series J.2 (FA346)
            Subseries 1: General Correspondence
    Projects
        Series L
    Photographs
        Gubernatorial
            Robert A. Wands
                Series 5: Nelson A. Rockefeller Photographs
        Gubernatorial Press Office
            Series 3
Ronald Reagan Presidential Library—Simi Valley, California
    Anthony Dolan Files
    Office of Speechwriting
        Research Office
        Speech Drafts
    White House Office of Records
        Management
            Presidential Handwriting File
Texas Tech University—Lubbock, Texas
    Vietnam Center and Archive
        Geoffrey Shaw Interview with General Nguyen Khanh
        Oral Histories
        Virtual Vietnam Archive
            David Lifton Collection
            Douglas Pike Collection

Rufus Phillips Collection
United Nations—New York, New York
  Archives and Records Management Section
    Executive Office of the Secretary-General (EOSG) (1946–)
      Martin W. Hill—numbered subject files
    Files of the General Assembly
      Official Records
    Files of the Secretary-General
      Dag Hammarskjöld (1953–1961)
        Operational Records
        Secretariat and Personnel Files (1948–1964)
      Kurt Waldheim (1972–1981)
        Correspondence—Outside Organizations and Individuals
      U Thant (1961–1971)
        Correspondence Files of the Secretary General: With Heads of State,
          Governments, Permanent Representatives and Observers to the
          United Nations
        Peacekeeping Operations
        Viet-Nam
    Files of the Security Council
      Official Records
    Office for Special Political Affairs (1955–1991)
      Office of the Executive Assistant and the Under-Secretary-General for
        Special Political Affairs (Cordier/Malania)
    Office of Public Information
      Press Services
        Notes
        Press Releases
    Peacekeeping—Middle East, 1945–1981
    United Nations Relief and Rehabilitation Administration
      (UNRRA)
      Bureau of Administration
United States Senate—Washington, DC
  Senate Historical Office
    Oral History Project
    Photographs
University of Iowa—Iowa City, Iowa
  Special Collections
    Francis O. Wilcox Papers
      General
        Correspondence

University of Massachusetts—Boston, Massachusetts
    Joseph P. Healey Library
        University Archives and Special Collections
            WGBH Educational Foundation Vietnam Project
            Interview Transcripts
            Restricted Interviews
University of Michigan—Ann Arbor, Michigan
    Bentley Historical Library
        Arthur H. Vandenberg Papers
            Correspondence, 1915–1951
University of Rochester—Rochester, New York
    River Campus Libraries
        Rare Books and Special Collections
            Thomas E. Dewey Papers
                First Term Governor
                    Personal Correspondence
                Personal
                    Dewey Correspondence
                Post Governor Correspondence
                    Early Personal
                Second Term Governor
                    Personal Correspondence
                Third Term Governor
                    General Correspondence
                    Personal Correspondence
University of South Carolina—Charleston, South Carolina
    South Caroliniana Library
        Special Collections
            General William Childs Westmoreland Papers
            Audio/Visual
            Military Papers
            Personal Papers
University of Southern California—Los Angeles, California
    University Archives
        Special Collections
            Papers of Herbert G. Klein
                Richard Nixon's Early Political Career, 1940–1962
                Working Files, 1957–1962
University of Virginia—Charlottesville, Virginia
    Miller Center of Public Affairs
        Scripps Library

Presidential Oral Histories
 Eisenhower Administration
 Ford Administration
 Hoover Administration
 Johnson Administration
 Kennedy Administration
 Nixon Administration
 Truman Administration
U.S. Military Academy—West Point, New York
 U.S. Military Academy Library
  Special Collections and Archives Division
  West Point Center for Oral History
WGBH Media Library and Archives—Boston, Massachusetts
 Vietnam Collection
  *Vietnam: A Television History,* "America's Mandarin (1954–1963)"
  Interviews
Yale University—New Haven, Connecticut
 Yale University Library
  Manuscripts and Archives
   Cyrus R. and Grace Sloane Vance Papers
    Series I. Government Service Papers (Kennedy and Johnson
     Presidential Administrations)
    Series III. Papers on Professional and Personal Activities, 1957–1992
    Series V. Personal and Routine Correspondence, 1960–1990
   Henry A. Kissinger Papers, Part II
    Series I. Early Career and Harvard University
     Professional Files
      Correspondence
      General
       Government Consulting for the Lyndon B. Johnson
        Administration
       Correspondence
     Nelson A. Rockefeller Work
      Gubernatorial Papers, 1965–1968
       Speeches
       Subject Files
    Series II. Government Service
     Correspondence
      White House Transition
     Subject Files
      Rodman (Peter W.) Files

Henry A. Kissinger Papers, Part III
    Series IV. Telephone Conversation Transcript Copies
    Series VII. Photographs
    William C. Bullitt Papers
    Series I. Correspondence
York County History Center—York, Pennsylvania
   General Jacob Devers Collection
   General Thomas E. Griess Research Collection

VIETNAM

National Archives Center II (Trung Tâm Lưu Trữ Quốc Gia II)—Ho Chi Minh City
   Ministry of Public Works and Communication, 1948–1966 (Bộ Công Chánh và
     Giao Thông)
   National Leadership Committee (Ủy Ban Lãnh Đạo Quốc Gia)
   Office of the President, 1954–1963 (Phông Phủ Tổng thống Đệ Nhất Cộng
     Hoà)
    Activities of the President
    Economics and Finance
    Foreign Affairs
    Organization
   Office of the Prime Minister, 1954–1975 (Phòng Phủ Thủ Tướng Việt Nam Cộng
     Hòa)
    Activities of the Prime Minister
    Awards and Commendations
    Internal Safety—Military Affairs—Security—Politics
   Photograph and Film Collections (Sưu Tập Tài Liệu Phim Ảnh)

## Author Interviews and Correspondence

### CABOT-LODGE-SEARS FAMILY

| | |
|---|---|
| Emily Sears Lodge | May 18, 2017—New York, NY, and email |
| | June 9, 2017—Paris, France, and email |
| George Cabot Lodge | January 24, 2017—Beverly, MA, and email |
| John Lodge | August 10, 2018—telephone and email |
| Henry Sears | June 21, 2018—Chestertown, MD, and email |

### SENATE YEARS (1937–1944, 1947–1953)

| | |
|---|---|
| George Cabot Lodge | January 24, 2017—Beverly, MA, and email |
| Ruth Rabb | July 11, 2017—New York, NY |

## WORLD WAR II SERVICE (1942, 1944–1945)

| | |
|---|---|
| George Cabot Lodge | January 24, 2017—Beverly, MA, and email |
| David Palmer | March 2, 2017—Belton, TX, and email |

## EISENHOWER ADMINISTRATION (1953–1961)

| | |
|---|---|
| Stephen Hess | August 4, 2017—Washington, DC, and email |
| Sergei Khrushchev | December 22, 2017—telephone |
| George Cabot Lodge | January 24, 2017—Beverly, MA, and email |
| Ruth Rabb | July 11, 2017—New York, NY |

## CAMPAIGN FOR VICE PRESIDENT (1960)

| | |
|---|---|
| Marjorie Acker | October 14, 2016—Newport Beach, CA |
| Tricia Nixon Cox | November 16, 2017—Washington, DC |
| David Eisenhower and Julie Nixon Eisenhower | July 22, 2017—telephone and email |
| Stephen Hess | August 4, 2017—Washington, DC, and email |
| Emily Lodge | May 18, 2017—New York, NY, and email |
| | June 9, 2017—Paris, France, and email |
| George Cabot Lodge | January 24, 2017—Beverly, MA, and email |
| Edward C. Nixon | June 12, 2018—telephone and email |

## U.S. EMBASSY, SAIGON (1963–1964)

| | |
|---|---|
| Peter Arnett | December 14, 2017—email |
| Leslie Gelb | October 16, 2018—New York, NY, and email |
| Thomas L. Hughes | August 5, 2017—Chevy Chase, MD, and email |
| Tran Thien Khiem | The ground rules for communication with Prime Minister Khiem were on background and through mutual intermediaries. Therefore, his reflections are included in this manuscript but are not cited. |
| William A. K. "Tony" Lake | May 25, 2017—telephone |
| Emily Lodge | May 18, 2017—New York, NY, and email |
| | June 9, 2017—Paris, France, and email |
| George Cabot Lodge | January 24, 2017—Beverly, MA, and email |
| Joseph C. Luman | July 10, 2017—Alexandria, VA, and email |
| Robert H. Miller | August 6, 2017—telephone |
| David Palmer | March 2, 2017—Belton, TX, and email |
| Rufus Phillips | March 18, 2017—Arlington, VA, and email |
| Charles Trueheart | June 9, 2017—Paris, France, and email |

Katherine "Kitsy" Westmoreland,   December 30, 2017—Charleston, SC, and email
    James R. Westmoreland, and
    Margaret Westmoreland

## LODGE FOR PRESIDENT (1964)

Lee Edwards                        August 29, 2017—telephone and email
David Franke                       August 21, 2016—email
David Goldberg                     June 29, 2017—Boston, MA, and email
George Cabot Lodge                 January 24, 2017—Beverly, MA, and email
David Palmer                       March 2, 2017—Belton, TX, and email
John Price                         May 11, 2017—Yorba Linda, CA, and email
Sally Saltonstall Willis and       May 29, 2017—email
    Caroline Williams Gay

## U.S. EMBASSY, SAIGON (1965–1967 AND LATER)

James Bullington                   December 19, 2017—Williamsburg, VA,
                                     and email
Joseph Califano                    June 27, 2018—New York, NY
Anna Chennault                     April 25, 2017—Washington, DC, and email
Charles Hill                       April 12, 2017—New Haven, CT, and email
Thomas L. Hughes                   August 5, 2017—Chevy Chase, MD, and email
Henry A. Kissinger                 June 27, 2018—New York, NY
Eva Kim McArthur                   June 19, 2018—telephone
Walter James McIntosh              December 11, 2017—email
Paul Miles                         February 24, 2017—telephone and email
Robert H. Miller                   August 6, 2017—telephone
John Negroponte                    October 18, 2017—Washington, DC, and email
William R. Polk                    May 5, 2017—email
Merle Pribbenow                    March 26, 2017—email
Katherine "Kitsy" Westmoreland,    December 30, 2017—Charleston, SC, and email
    James R. Westmoreland, and
    Margaret Westmoreland
Frank Wisner II                    June 4, 2018—telephone and email
Steve Young                        June 7, 2018—St. Paul, MN, and email

## U.S. EMBASSY, BONN, AND PARIS PEACE TALKS (1968–1969 AND LATER)

Anna Chennault                     April 25, 2017—Washington, DC, and email
Daniel I. Davidson                 October 16, 2017—Washington, DC, and email

| | |
|---|---|
| Bui Diem | August 7, 2017—Rockville, MD |
| David Engel | November 25, 2017—email |
| Henry A. Kissinger | June 27, 2018—New York, NY |
| John Negroponte | October 18, 2017—Washington, DC, and email |
| Hoang Duc Nha | May 22, 2017—Chicago, IL, and email |
| Henry Sears | June 21, 2018—Chestertown, MD, and email |

NIXON CAMPAIGN FOR PRESIDENT (1968)
AND NIXON/FORD ADMINISTRATIONS

| | |
|---|---|
| Richard V. Allen | February 10, 2017—Yorba Linda, CA, and email |
| James Bullington | December 19, 2017—Williamsburg, VA, and email |
| Charles W. Colson | December 13, 2007—telephone and email |
| Henry A. Kissinger | June 27, 2018—New York, NY |
| Sven Kraemer | March 17, 2017—Washington, DC, and email |
| Winston Lord | February 10, 2017—Yorba Linda, CA, and email |
| Henry Sears | June 21, 2018—Chestertown, MD, and email |

## Books, Articles, and Other Resources

Abramson, Rudy. *Spanning the Century: The Life of W. Averell Harriman, 1891–1986.* New York: William Morrow, 1992.

Absher, Kenneth Michael, Michael C. Desch, and Roman Popadiuk. *Privileged and Confidential: The Secret History of the President's Intelligence Advisory Board.* Lexington: University Press of Kansas, 2012.

Abshire, David M., and Richard V. Allen. *National Security: Political, Military, and Economic Strategies in the Decade Ahead.* New York: Frederick A. Praeger, 1963.

Adams, John A. *General Jacob Devers: World War II's Forgotten Four Star.* Bloomington: Indiana University Press, 2015.

Ahern, Thomas L., Jr. *CIA and Rural Pacification in South Vietnam.* Langley, VA: Center for the Study of Intelligence, 2001.

———. *CIA and the Generals: Covert Support to Military Government in South Vietnam.* Langley, VA: Center for the Study of Intelligence, 1998.

———. *CIA and the House of Ngo: Covert Action in South Vietnam, 1954–63.* Langley, VA: Center for the Study of Intelligence, 2000.

Aitken, Jonathan. *Charles W. Colson: A Life Redeemed.* Colorado Springs, CO: WaterBrook, 2005.

*Akten zur Auswärtigen Politik der Bundesrepublik Deutschland.* Munich: R. Oldenbourg Verlag.

   *1953*, vol. 1, *1 Januar bis 30. Juni.* Edited by Matthias Jaroch and Mechtild Lindemann. 2001.

*1968, vol. 1, 1 Januar bis 30. Juni.* Edited by Mechtild Lindemann and Matthias Peter. 2013.

*1968, vol. 2, 1 Juli bis 31. Dezember.* Edited by Mechtild Lindemann and Matthias Peter. 2013.

Allen, Michael J. *Until the Last Man Comes Home: POWs, MIAs, and the Unending Vietnam War.* Chapel Hill: University of North Carolina Press, 2009.

Ambrose, Stephen E. *Eisenhower.* Vol. 1, *Soldier, General of the Army, President-Elect, 1890–1952.* New York: Simon and Schuster, 1983.

———. *Eisenhower.* Vol. 2, *President and Elder-Statesman, 1952–1969.* New York: Simon and Schuster, 1984.

———. *Ike's Spies: Eisenhower and the Espionage Establishment.* Jackson: University Press of Mississippi, 1981.

Amory, Cleveland. *The Proper Bostonians.* Orleans, MA: Parnassus Imprints, 1984.

Anderson, Carol. *Eyes off the Prize: The United Nations and the African American Struggle for Human Rights, 1944–1955.* New York: Cambridge University Press, 2003.

Anderson, David L., ed. *Shadow on the White House: Presidents and the Vietnam War, 1945–1975.* Lawrence: University Press of Kansas, 1993.

Andrew, Christopher. *For the President's Eyes Only: Secret Intelligence and the American Presidency from Washington to Bush.* New York: HarperPerennial, 1995.

Arnett, Peter. *Live from the Battlefield: From Vietnam to Baghdad, 35 Years in the World's War Zones.* New York: Simon and Schuster, 1994.

Ashby, LeRoy, and Rod Gramer. *Fighting the Odds: The Life of Senator Frank Church.* Pullman: Washington State University Press, 1994.

Asselin, Pierre. *Hanoi's Road to the Vietnam War, 1954–1965.* Berkeley: University of California Press, 2013.

———. *Vietnam's American War: A History.* New York: Cambridge University Press, 2018.

Baker, Bobby. *Wheeling and Dealing: Confessions of a Capitol Hill Operator.* New York: W. W. Norton, 1978.

Baltzell, E. Digby. *The Protestant Establishment: Aristocracy and Caste in America.* New York: Random House, 1964.

———. *Puritan Boston and Quaker Philadelphia: Two Protestant Ethics and the Spirit of Class Authority and Leadership.* Boston: Beacon, 1979.

Barbrook, Alec. *God Save the Commonwealth: An Electoral History of Massachusetts.* Amherst: University of Massachusetts Press, 1973.

Barrett, David M. *The CIA and Congress: The Untold Story from Truman to Kennedy.* Lawrence: University Press of Kansas, 2005.

———. *Uncertain Warriors: Lyndon Johnson and His Vietnam Advisers.* Lawrence: University Press of Kansas, 1993.

Beatty, Jack. *The Rascal King: The Life and Times of James Michael Curley, 1874–1958.* Reading, MA: Addison-Wesley, 1992.

Beichman, Arnold. *The "Other" State Department: The United States Mission to the United Nations—Its Role in the Making of Foreign Policy.* New York: Basic Books, 1968.

Berkowitz, Edward D. *Something Happened: A Political and Cultural Overview of the Seventies.* New York: Columbia University Press, 2006.

Berle, Beatrice Bishop, and Travis Beal Jacobs, eds. *Navigating the Rapids, 1918–1971.* New York: Harcourt Brace Jovanovich, 1973.

Berman, Larry. *Planning a Tragedy: The Americanization of the War in Vietnam.* New York: W. W. Norton, 1982.

Beschloss, Michael, ed. *Jacqueline Kennedy, Historic Conversations on Life with John F. Kennedy: Interviews with Arthur M. Schlesinger, Jr., 1964.* New York: Hyperion, 2011.

———, ed. *Reaching for Glory: Lyndon Johnson's Secret White House Tapes, 1964–1965.* New York: Simon and Schuster, 2001.

———, ed. *Taking Charge: The Johnson White House Tapes, 1963–1964.* New York: Simon and Schuster, 1997.

Bird, Kai. *The Chairman: John J. McCloy and the Making of the American Establishment.* New York: Simon and Schuster, 1992.

———. *The Color of Truth: McGeorge Bundy and William Bundy, Brothers in Arms: A Biography.* New York: Simon and Schuster, 1998.

Blair, Anne E. "The Appointment of Henry Cabot Lodge as United States Ambassador to South Vietnam." Paper submitted to the History Department Seminar, Monash University, Melbourne, April 6, 1990.

———. *Lodge in Vietnam: A Portrait Abroad.* New Haven, CT: Yale University Press, 1995.

———. "No Time to Stop: Henry Cabot Lodge in Vietnam." PhD diss., Monash University, 1992.

———. "Special Consideration: The First Embassy of Henry Cabot Lodge in Vietnam." Working paper, Centre of Southeast Asian Studies, Monash University, Clayton, Victoria, Australia, 1992.

———. *Ted Serong: The Life of an Australian Counter-Insurgency Expert.* South Melbourne: Oxford University Press, 2002.

———. *There to the Bitter End: Ted Serong in Vietnam.* Crows Nest, Australia: Allen and Unwin, 2001.

Blake, David Haven. *Liking Ike: Eisenhower, Advertising, and the Rise of Celebrity Politics.* New York: Oxford University Press, 2016.

Blang, Eugenie M. *Allies at Odds: America, Europe, and Vietnam, 1961–1968.* Lanham, MD: Rowman and Littlefield, 2011.

Blight, James G., Janet M. Lang, and David A. Welch. *Vietnam If Kennedy Had Lived: Virtual JFK*. Lanham, MD: Rowman and Littlefield, 2009.

Boorstin, Daniel. *The National Experience*. New York: Vintage, 1965.

Boot, Max. *The Road Not Taken: Edward Lansdale and the American Tragedy in Vietnam*. New York: Liveright, 2018.

Bowden, Mark. *Hue 1968: A Turning Point of the American War in Vietnam*. New York: Atlantic Monthly Press, 2017.

Bowie, Robert R., and Richard H. Immerman. *Waging Peace: How Eisenhower Shaped an Enduring Cold War Strategy*. New York: Oxford University Press, 1998.

Bradlee, Ben. *A Good Life: Newspapering and Other Adventures*. New York: Simon and Schuster, 1995.

Braggiotti, Gloria. *Born in a Crowd*. New York: Thomas Y. Crowell, 1957.

Brands, H. W., Jr. *Cold Warriors: Eisenhower's Generation and American Foreign Policy*. New York: Columbia University Press, 1988.

Brennan, Sean. "Henry Cabot Lodge, Jr. and the Catholic Church." *U.S. Catholic Historian*, Vol. 37, No. 2 (Spring 2019): 47–72.

Briggs, L. Vernon. *History and Genealogy of the Cabot Family, 1475–1927*. Boston: Godspeed, 1927.

Brigham, Robert K. *Reckless: Henry Kissinger and the Tragedy of Vietnam*. New York: PublicAffairs, 2018.

Brinkley, Alan, and Davis Dyer, eds. *The American Presidency: The Authoritative Reference*. Boston: Houghton Mifflin, 2004.

Brinkley, Douglas. *Cronkite*. New York: Harper, 2012.

———. *Dean Acheson: The Cold War Years, 1953–1971*. New Haven, CT: Yale University Press, 1992.

Brinkley, Douglas, and Luke A. Nichter, eds. *The Nixon Tapes: 1971–1972*. Boston: Houghton Mifflin Harcourt, 2014.

———, eds. *The Nixon Tapes: 1973*. Boston: Houghton Mifflin Harcourt, 2015.

Brodie, Fawn M. *Richard Nixon: The Shaping of His Character*. New York: W. W. Norton, 1981.

Brown, John Mason. *Through These Men: Some Aspects of Our Passing History*. New York: Harper and Brothers, 1952.

Browne, Malcolm W. *The New Face of War*. Indianapolis: Bobbs-Merrill, 1965.

Brownell, Herbert. *Advising Ike: The Memoirs of Attorney General Herbert Brownell*. Lawrence: University Press of Kansas, 1993.

Bryant, Nick. *The Bystander: John F. Kennedy and the Struggle for Black Equality*. New York: Basic Books, 2007.

Buchanan, Patrick J. *The Greatest Comeback: How Richard Nixon Rose from Defeat to Create the New Majority*. New York: Crown Forum, 2014.

———. *Nixon's White House Wars: The Battles that Made and Broke a President and Divided America Forever*. New York: Crown, 2017.

———. *Right from the Beginning*. Boston: Little, Brown and Company, 1988.

Buckley, William F., Jr. *Flying High: Remembering Barry Goldwater*. New York: Basic Books, 2008.

———. *Miles Gone By: A Literary Autobiography*. Washington, DC: Regnery, 2004.

Bullington, James R. *Global Adventures on Less-Traveled Roads: A Foreign Service Memoir*. North Charleston, SC: CreateSpace, 2017.

Burke, Lee H. *Ambassador at Large: Diplomat Extra Ordinary*. The Hague: Martinus Nijoff, 1972.

Burns, James MacGregor. *Roosevelt: The Soldier of Freedom*. New York: Harcourt, Brace, Jovanovich, 1970.

Califano, Joseph A., Jr. *Inside: A Public and Private Life*. New York: PublicAffairs, 2004.

———. *The Triumph and Tragedy of Lyndon Johnson: The White House Years*. New York: Simon and Schuster, 2015.

Carlson, Peter. *K Blows Top: A Cold War Comic Interlude Starring Nikita Khrushchev, America's Most Unlikely Tourist*. New York: PublicAffairs, 2009.

Caro, Robert A. *Master of the Senate: The Years of Lyndon Johnson*. New York: Alfred A. Knopf, 2002.

———. *The Passage of Power: The Years of Lyndon Johnson*. New York: Alfred A. Knopf, 2012.

Catton, Philip E. *Diem's Final Failure: Prelude to America's War in Vietnam*. Lawrence: University Press of Kansas, 2002.

Chace, James. *Acheson: The Secretary of State Who Created the American World*. New York: Simon and Schuster, 1998.

Chernow, Ron. *The House of Morgan: An American Banking Dynasty and the Rise of Modern Finance*. New York: Atlantic Monthly Press, 1990.

Chomsky, Noam. *Rethinking Camelot: JFK, the Vietnam War, and U.S. Political Culture*. Boston: South End, 1993.

Christian, George. *The President Steps Down: A Personal Memoir of the Transfer of Power*. New York: Macmillan, 1971.

Cleveland, Harlan. "NATO after the Invasion." *Foreign Affairs*, January 1969.

Clifford, Clark. *Counsel to the President: A Memoir*. New York: Random House, 1991.

Cline, Ray S. *Secrets, Spies, and Scholars: Blueprint of the Essential CIA*. Washington, DC: Acropolis Books, 1976.

Colby, William. *Honorable Men: My Life in the CIA*. New York: Simon and Schuster, 1978.

———. *Lost Victory: A Firsthand Account of America's Sixteen-Year Involvement in Vietnam*. Chicago: Contemporary Books, 1989.

Cooper, Chester L. *In the Shadows of History: 50 Years behind the Scenes of Cold War Diplomacy*. Amherst, NY: Prometheus Books, 2005.

Coppolani, Antoine. *Richard Nixon*. Paris: Fayard, 2013.

Cosmas, Graham A. *MACV: The Joint Command in the Years of Escalation, 1962–1967*. Washington, DC: Center for Military History, 2006.

————. *MACV: The Joint Command in the Years of Withdrawal, 1968–1973.* Washington, DC: Center for Military History, 2006.

Costigliola, Frank. *The Kennan Diaries.* New York: W. W. Norton, 2014.

Critchlow, Donald T. *The Conservative Ascendancy: How the GOP Right Made Political History.* Cambridge, MA: Harvard University Press, 2007.

Crowley, John W. *George Cabot Lodge.* Boston: Twayne, 1976.

Crowley, Monica. *Nixon in Winter.* New York: Random House, 1998.

Curley, James Michael. *I'd Do It Again: A Record of All My Uproarious Years.* Englewood Cliffs, NJ: Prentice-Hall, 1957.

Cutler, Robert. *No Time for Rest.* Boston: Little, Brown, 1966.

Daalder, Ivo H., and I. M. Destler. *In the Shadow of the Oval Office: Profiles of the National Security Advisers and the Presidents They Served, from JFK to George W. Bush.* New York: Simon and Schuster, 2009.

Dallek, Robert. *Camelot's Court: Inside the Kennedy White House.* New York: Harper, 2013.

————. *Flawed Giant: Lyndon Johnson and His Times, 1961–1973.* New York: Oxford University Press, 1998.

————. *Lone Star Rising: Lyndon Johnson and His Times, 1908–1960.* New York: Oxford University Press, 1991.

————. *Nixon and Kissinger: Partners in Power.* New York: HarperCollins, 2007.

DeGroot, Gerard. *The Sixties Unplugged: A Kaleidoscopic History of a Disorderly Decade.* Cambridge, MA: Harvard University Press, 2008.

Demery, Monique Brinson. *Finding the Dragon Lady: The Mystery of Vietnam's Madame Nhu.* New York: PublicAffairs, 2013.

Department of Defense. *A Pocket Guide to Vietnam.* Oxford: Bodleian Library, 2011.

De Silva, Peer. *Sub Rosa: The CIA and the Uses of Intelligence.* New York: Times Books, 1978.

De Tassigny, Marshal de Lattre. *The History of the French First Army.* London: George Allen and Unwin, 1952.

Diem, Bui. *In the Jaws of History.* Boston: Houghton Mifflin, 1987.

DiLeo, David L. *George Ball, Vietnam, and the Rethinking of Containment.* Chapel Hill: University of North Carolina Press, 1991.

Dobbins, James F. *Foreign Service: Five Decades on the Frontlines of American Diplomacy.* Washington, DC: Brookings Institution Press, 2017.

Dobbs, Ricky F. *Yellow Dogs and Republicans: Allan Shivers and Texas Two-Party Politics.* College Station: Texas A&M University Press, 2005.

Dobrynin, Anatoly. *In Confidence: Moscow's Ambassador to America's Six Cold War Presidents, 1962–1986.* New York: Times Books, 1995.

Dommen, Arthur J. *The Indochinese Experience of the French and the Americans: Nationalism and Communism in Cambodia, Laos, and Vietnam.* Bloomington: Indiana University Press, 2001.

Don, Tran Van. *Our Endless War: Inside Vietnam.* Novato, CA: Presidio, 1978.

Donaldson, Gary A. *When America Liked Ike: How Moderates Won the 1952 Presidential Election and Reshaped American Politics.* Lanham, MD: Rowman and Littlefield, 2017.

Do Tho. *Nhat Ky Do Tho: Tuy Vien Mot Tong Thong Bi Giet* [The diary of Do Tho: Aide to a murdered president]. Saigon: Co So Xuat Ban Dai Nam, 1970.

Drea, Edward J. *McNamara, Clifford, and the Burdens of Vietnam, 1965–1969.* Washington, DC: Office of the Secretary of Defense, 2011.

Dulles, Allen. *The Craft of Intelligence.* New York: Harper and Row, 1963.

Eban, Abba. *The New Diplomacy: International Affairs in the Modern Age.* New York: Random House, 1983.

Eden, Anthony. *Full Circle: The Memoirs of Anthony Eden.* Boston: Houghton Mifflin Company, 1960.

Edwards, Lee. *Missionary for Freedom: The Life and Times of Walter Judd.* New York: Paragon House, 1990.

Eisenhower, David, and Julie Nixon Eisenhower. *Going Home to Glory: A Memoir of Life with Dwight D. Eisenhower, 1961–1969.* New York: Simon and Schuster, 2010.

Eisenhower, Dwight D. *The Eisenhower Diaries.* Edited by Robert H. Ferrell. New York: W. W. Norton, 1981.

———. *Mandate for Change: The White House Years, 1953–1956.* Garden City, NY: Doubleday, 1963.

———. *The Papers of Dwight David Eisenhower.* Edited by Alfred D. Chandler, Louis Galambos, and Daun Van Ee. Baltimore: Johns Hopkins Press.

Vols. 1–3, 5, *The War Years.* 1970.
Vols. 7, 9, *The Chief of Staff.* 1978.
Vols. 10, 11, *Columbia University.* 1984.
Vols. 12, 13, *NATO and the Campaign of 1952.* 1989.
Vols. 14–17, *The Presidency: The Middle Way.* 1996.
Vols. 18–21, *The Presidency: Keeping the Peace.* 2001.

———. *Waging Peace: The White House Years, 1956–1961.* Garden City, NY: Doubleday, 1965.

Eisenhower, John S. D. *Strictly Personal.* Garden City, NY: Doubleday, 1974.

Eisenhower, Milton S. *The President Is Calling.* Garden City, NY: Doubleday, 1974.

Elliott, David W. P. *The Vietnamese War: Revolution and Social Change in the Mekong Delta, 1930–1975.* Armonk, NY: M. E. Sharpe, 2007.

Ellsberg, Daniel. *Secrets: A Memoir of Vietnam and the Pentagon Papers.* New York: Viking, 2002.

Emery, Fred. *Watergate: The Corruption of American Politics and the Fall of Richard Nixon.* New York: Simon and Schuster, 1994.

Etkind, Alexander. *Roads Not Taken: An Intellectual Biography of William C. Bullitt.* Pittsburgh: University of Pittsburgh Press, 2017.

Farrell, Betty G. *Elite Families: Class and Power in Nineteenth Century Boston*. Albany: State University of New York Press, 1993.

Farrell, John A. *Richard Nixon: The Life*. New York: Doubleday, 2017.

Felzenberg, Alvin S. *A Man and His Presidents: The Political Odyssey of William F. Buckley, Jr*. New Haven, CT: Yale University Press, 2017.

Ferguson, Niall. *Kissinger*. Vol. 1, *1923–1968: The Idealist*. New York: Penguin, 2015.

Filipink, Richard M., Jr. *Dwight Eisenhower and American Foreign Policy during the 1960s: An American Lion in Winter*. Lanham, MD: Lexington Books, 2015.

Finger, Seymour Maxwell. *American Ambassadors at the UN: People, Politics, and Bureaucracy in Making Foreign Policy*. New York: Holmes and Meier, 1988.

Finley, Keith M. *Delaying the Dream: Southern Senators and the Fight against Civil Rights, 1938–1965*. Baton Rouge: Louisiana State University Press, 2008.

Frank, Jeffrey. *Ike and Dick: Portrait of a Strange Political Marriage*. New York: Simon and Schuster, 2013.

Frankel, Max. *The Times of My Life and My Life with The Times*. New York: Random House, 1999.

Frick, Daniel. *Reinventing Richard Nixon: A Cultural History of an American Obsession*. Lawrence: University Press of Kansas, 2008.

Gaddis, John Lewis. *Strategies of Containment: A Critical Appraisal of American National Security Policy during the Cold War*. Rev. and expanded ed. New York: Oxford University Press, 2005.

Gaiduk, Ilya V. *Confronting Vietnam: Soviet Policy toward the Indochina Conflict, 1954–1963*. Washington, DC: Woodrow Wilson Center Press, 2003.

———. *Divided Together: The United States and the Soviet Union in the United Nations, 1945–1965*. Washington, DC: Woodrow Wilson Center Press, 2012.

Galambos, Louis. *Eisenhower: Becoming the Leader of the Free World*. Baltimore: Johns Hopkins University Press, 2018.

Gallup, George H. *The Gallup Poll: Public Opinion, 1935–1971*. 3 vols. New York: Random House, 1972.

Garraty, John A. *Henry Cabot Lodge: A Biography*. New York: Alfred A. Knopf, 1953.

Gelb, Leslie H., and Richard K. Betts. *The Irony of Vietnam: The System Worked*. Washington, DC: Brookings Institution, 1979.

Gellman, Irwin F. *The President and the Apprentice: Eisenhower and Nixon, 1952–1961*. New Haven, CT: Yale University Press, 2015.

Gerard, E., and Bruce Kuklick. *Death in the Congo: Murdering Patrice Lumumba*. Cambridge, MA: Harvard University Press, 2015.

Germany, Kent, and Robert David Johnson, eds. *The Presidential Recordings, Lyndon B. Johnson: The Kennedy Administration and the Transfer of Power, November 1963–January 1964*. Vol. 3. New York: W. W. Norton, 2005.

Gibbs, Nancy, and Michael Duffy. *The President's Club: Inside the World's Most Exclusive Fraternity*. New York: Simon and Schuster, 2012.

Gifford, Laura Jane. *The Center Cannot Hold: The 1960 Presidential Election and the Rise of Modern Conservatism*. DeKalb: Northern Illinois Press, 2009.

Giglio, James N. *The Presidency of John F. Kennedy*. 2nd ed., rev. Lawrence: University Press of Kansas, 2006.

Goldberg, Robert Alan. *Barry Goldwater*. New Haven, CT: Yale University Press, 1995.

Goldwater, Barry M. *The Conscience of a Conservative*. Shepherdsville, KY: Victor, 1960.

———. *Goldwater*. New York: Doubleday, 1988.

———. *With No Apologies: The Personal and Political Memoirs of United States Senator Barry M. Goldwater*. New York: William Morrow, 1979.

Goodman, James, ed. *Letters to Kennedy*. Cambridge, MA: Harvard University Press, 1998.

Goscha, Christopher. *Vietnam: A New History*. New York: Basic Books, 2016.

Gottlieb, Robert. *Katherine Graham's Washington*. New York: Alfred A. Knopf, 2002.

Gould, Lewis L. *Grand Old Party: A History of the Republicans*. New York: Random House, 2003.

———. *1968: The Election That Changed America*. Chicago: Ivan R. Dee, 1993.

Graham, Billy. *Just As I Am: The Autobiography of Billy Graham*. New York: Harper-Collins, 1997.

Grant, Zalin. *Facing the Phoenix*. New York: W. W. Norton, 1991.

Gravel, Mike, ed. *The Pentagon Papers: Gravel Edition*. Vol. 2. Boston: Beacon, 1971.

Greene, Benjamin P. *Eisenhower, Science Advice, and the Nuclear Test-Ban Debate, 1945–1963*. Stanford, CA: Stanford University Press, 2007.

Greene, Graham. *The Quiet American*. New York: Viking, 1955.

Greene, John Robert. *I Like Ike: The Presidential Election of 1952*. Lawrence: University Press of Kansas, 2017.

Greenstein, Fred I. *The Hidden-Hand Presidency: Eisenhower as Leader*. New York: Basic Books, 1982.

Gromyko, Andrei. *Memoirs*. New York: Doubleday, 1990.

Grose, Peter. "Young U.S. Aides Score in Vietnam." *New York Times*, July 1, 1964.

Hagerty, James C. *The Diary of James C. Hagerty: Eisenhower in Mid-course, 1954–1955*. Edited by Robert H. Ferrell. Bloomington: Indiana University Press, 1983.

Hahn, Peter L. *Caught in the Middle East: U.S. Policy toward the Arab-Israeli Conflict, 1945–1961*. Chapel Hill: University of North Carolina Press, 2004.

———. *Crisis and Crossfire: The United States and the Middle East since 1945*. Washington, DC: Potomac Books, 2005.

———. *Missions Accomplished? The United States and Iraq since World War I*. New York: Oxford University Press, 2011.

Haig, Alexander M., Jr. *Inner Circles: How America Changed the World, a Memoir*. New York: Warner Books, 1992.

Halberstam, David. *The Best and the Brightest.* Twentieth anniversary ed. New York: Random House, 1992.

———. *The Coldest Winter: America and the Korean War.* New York: Hyperion, 2007.

———. *The Fifties.* New York: Villard Books, 1993.

———. *The Making of a Quagmire: America and Vietnam during the Kennedy Era.* New York: Alfred A. Knopf, 1964.

Haldeman, H. R. *The Haldeman Diaries: Inside the Nixon White House.* New York: G. P. Putnam's Sons, 1994.

Hammer, Ellen J. *A Death in November: America in Vietnam, 1963.* New York: E. P. Dutton, 1987.

Hanhimäki, Jussi. *The Flawed Architect: Henry Kissinger and American Foreign Policy.* New York: Oxford University Press, 2004.

Harper, Glyn. *The Battle for North Africa: El Alamein and the Turning Point for World War II.* Bloomington: Indiana University Press, 2017.

Hatch, Alden. *The Lodges of Massachusetts.* New York: Hawthorn Books, 1973.

Hatcher, Patrick Lloyd. *The Suicide of an Elite: American Internationalists and Vietnam.* Stanford, CA: Stanford University Press, 1990.

Herken, Gregg. *The Georgetown Set: Friends and Rivals in Cold War Washington.* New York: Alfred A. Knopf, 2014.

Hernon, Joseph Martin. *Profiles in Character: Hubris and Heroism in the U.S. Senate, 1789–1990.* Armonk, NY: M. E. Sharpe, 1997.

Herring, George C. *America's Longest War: The United States and Vietnam: 1950–1975.* 2nd ed. Philadelphia: Temple University Press, 1986.

Hersh, Seymour M. *The Dark Side of Camelot.* Boston: Little, Brown, 1997.

Hershberg, James G. *Marigold: The Lost Chance for Peace in Vietnam.* Washington, DC: Woodrow Wilson Center Press, 2012.

Hess, Gary R. *Vietnam and the United States: Origins and Legacy of War.* Boston: Twayne, 1990.

Hess, Stephen. *America's Political Dynasties: From Adams to Clinton.* Washington, DC: Brookings Institution Press, 2016.

Heymann, C. David. *The Georgetown Ladies' Social Club: Power, Passion, and Politics in the Nation's Capital.* New York: Atria Books, 2003.

Hill, Clint. *Five Presidents: My Extraordinary Journey with Eisenhower, Kennedy, Johnson, Nixon and Ford.* New York: Gallery Books, 2016.

Hillings, Pat. *The Irrepressible Irishman, a Republican Insider: The Story of a Political Life.* N.p.: Harold D. Dean, 1994.

Hilsman, Roger. "Commentary and Reply." *Parameters: U.S. Army War College Quarterly,* Vol. 22, No. 4 (Winter 1992–1993): 104–105.

———. *To Move a Nation: The Politics of Foreign Policy in the Administration of John F. Kennedy.* Garden City, NY: Doubleday, 1967.

Hitchcock, William I. *The Age of Eisenhower: America and the World in the 1950s.* New York: Simon and Schuster, 2018.

Hofstader, Richard. *Anti-intellectualism in American Life*. New York: Alfred A. Knopf, 1963.

Hogan, Michael J. *The Afterlife of John Fitzgerald Kennedy: A Biography*. New York: Cambridge University Press, 2017.

———. *A Cross of Iron: Harry S. Truman and the Origins of the National Security State, 1945–1954*. New York: Cambridge University Press, 1998.

Hoi-dang Quan-nhan Cach-mang. *Policy of the Military Revolutionary Council and the Provisional Government of the Republic of Vietnam*. Saigon: Ministry of Information, 1963.

Holbrooke, Richard. "Carpe Diem." *New Republic*, December 14, 1987.

Holland, Max, ed. *The Presidential Recordings, Lyndon B. Johnson: The Kennedy Administration and the Transfer of Power, November 1963–January 1964*. Vol. 1. New York: W. W. Norton, 2005.

Holmes, Oliver Wendell. *Elsie Venner: A Romance of Destiny*. Boston: Houghton Mifflin, 1861.

Hughes, Emmet John. *The Ordeal of Power: A Political Memoir of the Eisenhower Years*. New York: Atheneum, 1963.

Hughes, Thomas L. *Anecdotage: Some Authentic Retrievals*. Self-published, CreateSpace, 2013.

Humphrey, Hubert H. *The Education of a Public Man: My Life and Politics*. Garden City, NY: Doubleday, 1976.

Hunt, E. Howard. *Undercover: Memoirs of an American Secret Agent*. New York: Berkley, 1974.

Hunt, Michael H. *Lyndon Johnson's War: America's Cold War Crusade in Vietnam, 1945–1968*. New York: Hill and Wang, 1996.

Immerman, Richard H. *The CIA in Guatemala: The Foreign Policy of Intervention*. Austin: University of Texas Press, 1982.

———. *The Hidden Hand: A Brief History of the CIA*. Malden, MA: Wiley Blackwell, 2014.

———. *John Foster Dulles: Piety, Pragmatism, and Power in U.S. Foreign Policy*. Wilmington, DE: Scholarly Resources, 1999.

Isaacson, Walter. *Kissinger: A Biography*. New York: Simon and Schuster, 1992.

Isaacson, Walter, and Evan Thomas. *The Wise Men: Six Friends and the World They Made*. New York: Simon and Schuster, 1986.

Jacobs, Seth. *America's Miracle Man in Vietnam: Ngo Dinh Diem, Religion, Race, and U.S. Intervention in Southeast Asia*. Durham, NC: Duke University Press, 2004.

———. *Cold War Mandarin: Ngo Dinh Diem and the Origins of America's War in Vietnam, 1950–1963*. Lanham, MD: Rowman and Littlefield, 2006.

Jager, Sheila Miyoshi. *Brothers at War: The Unending Conflict in Korea*. New York: W. W. Norton, 2013.

Johns, Andrew L. *Vietnam's Second Front: Domestic Politics, the Republican Party, and the War*. Lexington: University Press of Kentucky, 2010.

Johnson, Lady Bird. *A White House Diary*. New York: Holt, Rinehart and Winston, 1970.

Johnson, Lyndon Baines. *The Vantage Point: Perspectives of the Presidency, 1963–1969*. New York: Holt, Rinehart and Winston, 1971.

Johnson, Robert David. *All the Way with LBJ: The 1964 Presidential Election*. New York: Cambridge University Press, 2009.

Johnson, Robert David, and David Shreve, eds. *The Presidential Recordings, Lyndon B. Johnson: The Kennedy Administration and the Transfer of Power, November 1963–January 1964*. Vol. 2. New York: W. W. Norton, 2005.

Jones, Howard. *Death of a Generation: How the Assassinations of Diem and JFK Prolonged the Vietnam War*. New York: Oxford University Press, 2003.

Judd, Walter H. *Walter H. Judd: Chronicles of a Statesman*. Edited by Edward J. Rozek. Denver: Grier, 1980.

Kabaservice, Geoffrey. *The Guardians: Kingman Brewster, His Circle, and the Rise of the Liberal Establishment*. New York: Henry Holt, 2004.

———. *Rule and Ruin: The Downfall of Moderation and the Destruction of the Republican Party, from Eisenhower to the Tea Party*. New York: Oxford University Press, 2012.

Kahin, George McT. *Intervention: How American Became Involved in Vietnam*. New York: Alfred A. Knopf, 1986.

Kaiser, David. *American Tragedy: Kennedy, Johnson, and the Origins of the Vietnam War*. Cambridge, MA: Belknap Press of Harvard University Press, 2002.

Kalb, Marvin. *The Road to War: Presidential Commitments Honored and Betrayed*. Washington, DC: Brookings Institution Press, 2013.

Kalb, Marvin, and Elie Abel. *Roots of Involvement: The U.S. in Asia, 1794–1971*. New York: W. W. Norton, 1971.

Kalb, Marvin, and Bernard Kalb. *Kissinger*. Boston: Little, Brown, 1974.

Kallina, Edmund F. *Kennedy v. Nixon: The Presidential Election of 1960*. Gainesville: University of Florida Press, 2010.

Kaplan, Lawrence S. *Harold Stassen: Eisenhower, the Cold War, and the Pursuit of Nuclear Disarmament*. Lexington: University Press of Kentucky, 2018.

———. *The Long Entanglement: NATO's First Fifty Years*. Westport, CT: Praeger, 1999.

Kaplan, Lawrence S., Ronald D. Landa, and Edward J. Drea. *The McNamara Ascendancy, 1961–1965*. Washington, DC: Office of the Secretary of Defense, 2006.

Karnow, Stanley. *Vietnam: A History*. New York: Viking, 1983.

Kattenberg, Paul M. "Vietnam and U.S. Diplomacy, 1940–1970." *Orbis*, Vol. 15, No. 3 (Fall 1971): 818–841.

———. *The Vietnam Trauma in American Foreign Policy, 1945–1975*. New Brunswick, NJ: Transaction Books, 1980.

Kaufman, Burton I. *The Post-presidency from Washington to Clinton*. Lawrence: University Press of Kansas, 2012.

Keever, Beverly Deepe. *Death Zones and Darling Spies: Seven Years of Vietnam War Reporting*. Lincoln: University of Nebraska Press, 2013.

Kennan, George F. *Memoirs: 1925–1950*. Boston: Little, Brown, 1967.

———. *Memoirs: 1950–1963*. Boston: Little, Brown, 1972.

Kenneally, James. "Prelude to the Last Hurrah: The Massachusetts Senatorial Election of 1936." *Mid-America*, Vol. 62 (January 1980): 3–20.

Kennedy, Edward M. *True Compass: A Memoir*. New York: Twelve, 2009.

Kennedy, Rose Fitzgerald. *Times to Remember*. Garden City, NY: Doubleday, 1974.

Kessel, John H. *The Goldwater Coalition: Republican Strategies in 1964*. New York: Bobbs-Merrill, 1968.

Kessler, Ronald. *The First Family Detail: Secret Service Agents Reveal the Hidden Lives of the Presidents*. New York: Crown Forum, 2014.

Khrushchev, Nikita Sergeyevich. *Khrushchev Remembers: The Glasnost Tapes*. Translated and edited by Jerrold L. Schecter and Vyacheslav V. Luchkov. Boston: Little, Brown, 1990.

———. *Memoirs of Nikita Khrushchev*. Vol. 3, *Statesman, 1953–1964*. Edited by Sergei Khrushchev. Translated by George Shriver. University Park: Pennsylvania State University Press, 2007.

Khrushchev, Sergei N. *Khrushchev on Khrushchev: An Inside Account of the Man and His Era*. Translated and edited by William Taubman. Boston: Little, Brown, 1990.

———. *Nikita Khrushchev and the Creation of a Superpower*. Translated by Shirley Benson. University Park: Pennsylvania State University Press, 2000.

Kiernan, Ben. *Viet Nam: A History from Earliest Times to the Present*. New York: Oxford University Press, 2017.

Kimball, Jeffrey. *The Vietnam War Files: Uncovering the Secret History of Nixon-Era Strategy*. Lawrence: University Press of Kansas, 2004.

Kirby, Alec, David G. Dalin, and John F. Rothmann. *Harold E. Stassen: The Life and Perennial Candidacy of the Progressive Republican*. Jefferson, NC: McFarland, 2013.

Kissinger, Henry A. *Ending the Vietnam War: A History of America's Involvement in and Extrication from the Vietnam War*. New York: Simon and Schuster, 2003.

———. *Nuclear Weapons and Foreign Policy*. New York: Harper and Brothers, 1957.

———. *The Troubled Partnership: A Re-appraisal of the Atlantic Alliance*. New York: McGraw-Hill, 1965.

———. *White House Years*. Boston: Little, Brown, 1979.

———. *Years of Renewal*. New York: Simon and Schuster, 1999.

Klein, Herbert G. *Making It Perfectly Clear: An Inside Account of Nixon's Love-Hate Relationship with the Media*. Garden City, NY: Doubleday, 1980.

Kleindienst, Richard G. *Justice: The Memoirs of Attorney General Richard Kleindienst*. Ottawa, IL: Jameson Books, 1985.

Kornitzer, Bela. *The Real Nixon: An Intimate Biography*. New York: Rand McNally, 1960.

Kotlowski, Dean J. *Nixon's Civil Rights: Politics, Principle, and Policy.* Cambridge, MA: Harvard University Press, 2001.

Kraemer, Sven F. *Inside the Cold War from Marx to Reagan: An Unprecedented Guide to the Roots, History, Strategies, and Key Documents of the Cold War.* Lanham, MD: University Press of America, 2015.

Krock, Arthur. *In the Nation: 1932–1966.* New York: McGraw-Hill, 1966.

———. *Memoirs: Sixty Years on the Firing Line.* New York: Funk and Wagnalls, 1968.

Kurlantzick, Joshua. *A Great Place to Have a War: America in Laos and the Birth of a Military CIA.* New York: Simon and Schuster, 2016.

Ky, Nguyen Cao. *Buddha's Child: My Fight to Save Vietnam.* New York: St. Martin's, 2002.

———. *How We Lost the Vietnam War.* New York: Cooper Square, 2002.

———. *Twenty Years and Twenty Days.* New York: Stein and Day, 1976.

Lankford, Nelson D. *The Last American Aristocrat: The Biography of David K.E. Bruce, 1898–1977.* Boston: Little, Brown, 1996.

Lansdale, Edward Geary. *In the Midst of Wars: An American's Mission to Southeast Asia.* New York: Harper and Row, 1972.

Large, David Clay. *Germans to the Front: West German Rearmament in the Adenauer Era.* Chapel Hill: University of North Carolina Press, 1996.

LaRosa, Michael, and Frank O'Mora. *Neighborly Adversaries: Readings in U.S.–Latin American Relations.* Lanham, MD: Rowman and Littlefield, 1999.

Lawrence, Mark Atwood. *The Vietnam War: A Concise International History.* New York: Oxford University Press, 2008.

Lee, Elsie. *Henry Cabot Lodge: Man and Statesman.* New York: Lancer Books, 1964.

Lee, Heath Hardage. *The League of Wives: The Untold Story of the Women Who Took on the U.S. Government to Bring Their Husbands Home.* New York: St. Martin's, 2019.

Leuchtenberg, William E. *The American President: From Teddy Roosevelt to Bill Clinton.* New York: Oxford University Press, 2015.

Lewis, David Levering. *The Improbable Wendell Willkie: The Businessman Who Saved the Republican Party and His Country, and Conceived a New World Order.* New York: Liveright, 2018.

Lie, Trygve. *In the Cause of Peace: Seven Years with the United Nations.* New York: Macmillan, 1954.

Liebmann, George W. *The Last American Diplomat: John D. Negroponte and the Changing Face of American Diplomacy.* New York: I. B. Tauris, 2012.

Locker, Ray. *Nixon's Gamble: How a President's Own Secret Government Destroyed his Administration.* Guilford, CT: Lyons, 2016.

Lodge, Emily. *The Lodge Women, Their Men, and Their Times.* Self-published, 2013.

Lodge, Henry Cabot. *The Life and Letters of George Cabot.* Boston: Little, Brown, 1878.

Lodge, Henry Cabot, Jr. *As It Was: An Inside View of Politics and Power in the '50s and '60s.* New York: W. W. Norton, 1976.

————. *The Cult of Weakness*. Boston: Houghton Mifflin, 1932.

————. "Eisenhower and the GOP." *Harper's*, May 1952, 34–39.

————. "Grandson Backs His Elder: U.S. Ambassador Tells How History Vindicates Lodge Stand on League." *Life*, September 14, 1963.

————. "Modernize the GOP." *Atlantic Monthly*, March 23, 1950, 23–28.

————. *The Storm Has Many Eyes: A Personal Narrative*. New York: W. W. Norton, 1973.

Logevall, Fredrik. *Choosing War: The Lost Chance for Peace and the Escalation of War in Vietnam*. Berkeley: University of California Press, 1999.

————. *Embers of War: The Fall of an Empire and the Making of America's Vietnam*. New York: Random House, 2012.

Logevall, Fredrik, and Andrew Preston, eds. *Nixon in the World: American Foreign Relations, 1969–1977*. New York: Oxford University Press, 2008.

Longley, Kyle. *LBJ's 1968: Power, Politics, and the Presidency in America's Year of Upheaval*. New York: Cambridge University Press, 2018.

Lukas, J. Anthony. *Nightmare: The Underside of the Nixon Years*. New York: Penguin Books, 1988.

Lytle, Mark H. *America's Uncivil Wars: The Sixties Era, from Elvis to the Fall of Richard Nixon*. New York: Oxford University Press, 2006.

MacKenzie, G. Calvin, and Robert Weisbrot. *The Liberal Hour: Washington and the Politics of Change in the 1960s*. New York: Penguin, 2008.

MacMillan, Margaret. *Nixon and Mao: The Week That Changed the World*. New York: Random House, 2007.

Magruder, Jeb Stuart. *An American Life: One Man's Road to Watergate*. New York: Atheneum, 1974.

Maneli, Mieczyslaw. *War of the Vanquished*. Translated by Maria de Görgey. New York: Harper and Row, 1971.

Mann, Robert. *Becoming Reagan: The Rise of a Conservative Icon*. Lincoln: Potomac Books, 2019.

Matthews, Chris. *Kennedy and Nixon: The Rivalry that Shaped Postwar America*. New York: Free Press, 2000.

Mayer, Jean-Paul. *RAND, Brookings, Harvard, et les autres: Les prophètes de la stratégie des États-Unis* [RAND, Brookings, Harvard, and the others: The prophets of American strategy]. Paris: ADDIM, 1997.

Mayer, Michael S. *The Eisenhower Years: Presidential Profiles*. New York: Facts on File, 2010.

Mazo, Earl. *Richard Nixon: A Political and Personal Portrait*. New York: Harper and Brothers, 1959.

McAllister, James. "A Fiasco of Noble Proportions." *Pacific Historical Review*, Vol. 73, No. 4 (November 2004): 619–652.

————. "The Lost Revolution: Edward Lansdale and the American Defeat in Vietnam, 1964–1968." *Small Wars and Insurgencies*, Vol. 14, No. 2 (2003): 1–26.

———. "'Only Religions Count in Vietnam': Thich Tri Quang and the Vietnam War." *Modern Asian Studies,* Vol. 42, No. 4 (July 2008): 751–782.

McAllister, James, and Ian Schulte. "The Limits of Influence in Vietnam: Britain, the United States and the Diem Regime, 1959–1963." *Small Wars and Insurgencies,* Vol. 17, No. 1 (2006): 22–43.

McCullough, David. *Truman.* New York: Simon and Schuster, 1992.

McLellan, David S. *Dean Acheson: The State Department Years.* New York: Dodd, Mead, 1976.

McMaster, H. R. *Dereliction of Duty: Lyndon Johnson, Robert McNamara, the Joint Chiefs of Staff, and the Lies That Led to Vietnam.* New York: HarperCollins, 1997.

McNamara, Robert S. *In Retrospect: The Tragedy and Lessons of Vietnam.* New York: Vintage Books, 1996.

McNamara, Robert S., James G. Blight, and Robert K. Brigham. *Argument without End: In Search of Answers to the Vietnam Tragedy.* New York: PublicAffairs, 1999.

Mecklin, John. *Mission in Torment: An Intimate Account of the U.S. Role in Vietnam.* Garden City, NY: Doubleday, 1965.

Meijer, Hendrik. *Arthur Vandenberg: The Man in the Middle of the American Century.* Chicago: University of Chicago Press, 2017.

Meir, Golda. *My Life.* New York: G. P. Putnam's Sons, 1975.

Mencken, H. L. *Thirty-Five Years of Newspaper Work.* Baltimore: Johns Hopkins University Press, 1994.

Merry, Robert. *Taking on the World: Joseph and Stewart Alsop—Guardians of the American Century.* New York: Viking, 1996.

Mickelson, Sig. *The Electric Mirror: Politics in an Age of Television.* New York: Dodd, Mead, 1972.

Miller, Edward. *Misalliance: Ngo Dinh Diem, the United States, and the Fate of South Vietnam.* Cambridge, MA: Harvard University Press, 2013.

———. *Nut Country: Right-Wing Dallas and the Birth of the Southern Strategy.* Chicago: University of Chicago Press, 2015.

———. "Religious Revival and the Politics of Nation Building: Reinterpreting the 1963 'Buddhist Crisis' in South Vietnam." *Modern Asia Studies,* Vol. 49, No. 6 (2015): 1903–1962.

Miller, Robert Hopkins. *Vietnam and Beyond: A Diplomat's Cold War Education.* Lubbock: Texas Tech University Press, 2002.

Miller, William J. *Henry Cabot Lodge: A Biography.* New York: James H. Heineman, 1967.

Milne, David. *America's Rasputin: Walt Rostow and the Vietnam War.* New York: Hill and Wang, 2008.

Miraldi, Robert. *Seymour Hersh: Scoop Artist.* Lincoln: Potomac Books, 2013.

Morrison, Samuel Eliot. *Maritime History of Massachusetts, 1783–1860.* Boston: Houghton Mifflin, 1921.

Morrow, E. Frederic. *Black Man in the White House: A Diary of the Eisenhower Years by the Administrative Officer for Special Projects, the White House, 1955–1961.* New York: Coward-McCann, 1963.

Moyar, Mark. *Triumph Forsaken: The Vietnam War, 1954–1965.* New York: Cambridge University Press, 2006.

Moynihan, Daniel Patrick. *Daniel Patrick Moynihan: A Portrait in Letters of an American Visionary.* Edited by Steven R. Weisman. New York: PublicAffairs, 2010.

———. *Miles to Go: A Personal History of Social Policy.* Cambridge, MA: Harvard University Press, 1996.

———. *Secrecy: The American Experience.* New Haven, CT: Yale University Press, 1998.

Murphy, Bruce Allen. *Wild Bill: The Legend and Life of William O. Douglas.* New York: Random House, 2003.

Murphy, George. *"Say . . . Didn't You Used to Be George Murphy?"* New York: Bartholomew House, 1970.

Murphy, Robert. *Diplomat among Warriors.* London: Collins, 1964.

Nasaw, David. *The Patriarch: The Remarkable Life and Turbulent Times of Joseph P. Kennedy.* New York: Penguin, 2012.

Neff, James. *Vendetta: Bobby Kennedy Versus Jimmy Hoffa.* New York: Little, Brown, 2015.

Nelson, Garrison. *John William McCormack: A Political Biography.* New York: Bloomsbury, 2017.

Nelson, Lawrence J., and Matthew G. Schoenbachler. *Nikita Khrushchev's Journey into America.* Lawrence: University Press of Kansas, 2019.

Newman, John M. *JFK and Vietnam: Deception, Intrigue, and the Struggle for Power.* New York: Warner Books, 1992.

Ngo-Dinh Quynh, Ngo-Dinh Le Quyen, and Jacqueline Willemetz. *La République du Vietnam et les Ngo-Dinh: 16 juin 1954–2 novembre 1963.* Paris: L'Harmattan, 2013.

Nguyen, Lien-Hang T. *Hanoi's War: An International History of the War for Peace in Vietnam.* Chapel Hill: University of North Carolina Press, 2012.

Nguyen Phu Duc. *The Viet-Nam Peace Negotiations: Saigon's Side of the Story.* Edited by Arthur J. Dommen. Christiansburg, VA: Dalley Book Service, 2005.

Nguyen, Tien Hung, and Jerrold L. Schecter. *The Palace File.* New York: Harper and Row, 1986.

Nichols, David A. *Ike and McCarthy: Dwight Eisenhower's Secret Campaign against Joseph McCarthy.* New York: Simon and Schuster, 2017.

Nichter, Luke A. *Lyndon B. Johnson: Pursuit of Populism, Paradox of Power.* New York: Nova History, 2013.

———. *Richard M. Nixon: In the Arena, from Valley to Mountaintop.* New York: Nova History, 2014.

———. *Richard Nixon and Europe: The Reshaping of the Postwar Atlantic World.* New York: Cambridge University Press, 2015.

Nitze, Paul H. *From Hiroshima to Glasnost: At the Center of Decision, a Memoir.* New York: Grove Weidenfeld, 1989.

Nixon, Ed, and Karen Olson. *The Nixons: A Family Portrait.* Bothell, WA: Book Publishing Network, 2009.

Nixon, Richard. *RN: The Memoirs of Richard Nixon.* New York: Grosset and Dunlap, 1978.

Nojeim, Michael J., and David P. Kilroy. *Days of Decision: Turning Points in U.S. Foreign Policy.* Washington, DC: Potomac Books, 2011.

Nolting, Frederick. *From Trust to Tragedy: The Political Memoirs of Frederick Nolting, Kennedy's Ambassador to Diem's Vietnam.* New York: Praeger, 1988.

O'Brien, Lawrence F. *No Final Victories: A Life in Politics—from John F. Kennedy to Watergate.* Garden City, NY: Doubleday, 1974.

O'Brien, Michael. *John F. Kennedy: A Biography.* New York: Thomas Dunne Books, 2005.

O'Connor, Thomas H. *The Boston Irish: A Political History.* Boston: Northeastern University Press, 1995.

O'Donnell, Kenneth P., and David F. Powers. *"Johnny, We Hardly Knew Ye": Memories of John Fitzgerald Kennedy.* Boston: Little, Brown, 1970.

Olmsted, Kathryn S. *Right Out of California: The 1930s and the Big Business Roots of Modern Conservatism.* New York: New Press, 2015.

O'Neill, Gerard. *Rogues and Redeemers: When Politics Was King in Irish Boston.* New York: Crown, 2012.

O'Neill, Tip. *Man of the House: The Life and Political Memoirs of Speaker Tip O'Neill.* New York: Random House, 1987.

O'Neill, William L. *Coming Apart: An Informal History of America in the 1960's.* Chicago: Quadrangle Books, 1971.

Packer, George. *Our Man: Richard Holbrooke and the End of the American Century.* New York: Alfred A. Knopf, 2019.

Palmer, Dave R. *Summons of the Trumpet: U.S.-Vietnam in Perspective.* Novato, CA: Presidio, 1978.

Parmet, Herbert S. *George Bush: The Life of a Lone Star Yankee.* New York: Scribner, 1997.

———. *JFK: The Presidency of John F. Kennedy.* New York: Dial, 1983.

———. *Richard Nixon and His America.* New York: Smithmark, 1990.

Patterson, James T. *Mr. Republican: A Biography of Robert A. Taft.* Boston: Houghton Mifflin, 1972.

Pearson, Drew. *Drew Pearson Diaries, 1949–1959.* Edited by Tyler Abell. New York: Holt, Rinehart and Winston, 1974.

———. *Washington Merry-Go-Round: The Drew Pearson Diaries, 1960–1969.* Edited by Peter Hannaford. Lincoln: Potomac Books, 2015.

Pedersen, Susan. *The Guardians: The League of Nations and the Crisis of Empire.* New York: Oxford University Press, 2015.

Perlstein, Rick. *Before the Storm: Barry Goldwater and the Unmaking of the American Consensus.* New York: Hill and Wang, 2001.

———. *Nixonland: The Rise of a President and the Fracturing of America.* New York: Scribner, 2008.

Pham Van Luu. "The Buddhist Crisis in Vietnam, 1963–1966." PhD diss., Monash University, 1991.

Phillips, Rufus. *Why Vietnam Matters: An Eyewitness Account of Lessons Not Learned.* Annapolis: Naval Institute Press, 2008.

Pietrusza, David. *1960: LBJ vs. JFK vs. Nixon: The Epic Campaign That Forged Three Presidencies.* New York: Union Square, 2008.

Polsky, Andrew J. *Elusive Victories: The American Presidency at War.* New York: Oxford University Press, 2012.

Prados, John, ed. "The Diem Coup after 50 Years: John F. Kennedy and South Vietnam, 1963." Electronic Briefing Book No. 444, National Security Archive, November 1, 2013. http://nsarchive.gwu.edu/NSAEBB/NSAEBB444/.

———. *The Family Jewels: The CIA, Secrecy, and Presidential Power.* Austin: University of Texas Press, 2013.

———. *Presidents' Secret Wars: CIA and Pentagon Covert Operations since World War II.* New York: William Morrow, 1986.

———. *Vietnam: The History of an Unwinnable War, 1945–1975.* Lawrence: University Press of Kansas, 2009.

Prados, John, and Margaret Pratt Porter, eds. *Inside the Pentagon Papers.* Lawrence: University Press of Kansas, 2004.

Price, Raymond. *With Nixon.* New York: Viking, 1977.

Prochnau, William. *Once upon a Distant War.* New York: Times Books, 1995.

Pruden, Caroline. *Conditional Partners: Eisenhower, the United Nations, and the Search for a Permanent Peace.* Baton Rouge: Louisiana State University Press, 1998.

Reagan, Ronald. *The Reagan Diaries.* Edited by Douglas Brinkley. New York: HarperCollins, 2007.

Reel, Monte. *A Brotherhood of Spies: The U-2 and the CIA's Secret War.* New York: Doubleday, 2018.

*Reporting Vietnam: Part One, American Journalism, 1959–1969.* New York: Library of America, 1998.

*Reporting Vietnam: Part Two, American Journalism, 1999–1975.* New York: Library of America, 1998.

Richardson, John H. *My Father the Spy: An Investigative Memoir.* New York: HarperCollins, 2005.

Riggs, Robert E. *Politics in the United Nations: A Study of United States Influence in the General Assembly.* Urbana: University of Illinois Press, 1958.

———. *US/UN: Foreign Policy and International Organization.* New York: Appleton-Century-Crofts, 1971.

•

Rivlin, Benjamin, and Leon Gordenker, eds. *The Challenging Role of the UN Secretary-General: Making "the Most Impossible Job in the World" Possible.* Westport, CT: Praeger, 1993.

Rudenstine, David. *The Day the Presses Stopped: A History of the Pentagon Papers Case.* Berkeley: University of California Press, 1996.

Rusk, Dean. *As I Saw It.* New York: W. W. Norton, 1990.

Rust, William J. *Eisenhower and Cambodia: Diplomacy, Covert Action, and the Origins of the Second Indochina War.* Lexington: University Press of Kansas, 2016.

———. *Kennedy in Vietnam.* New York: Charles Scribner's Sons, 1985.

Safire, William. *Before the Fall: An Inside View of the Pre-Watergate White House.* Garden City, NY: Doubleday, 1975.

———. *Safire's Political Dictionary.* New York: Oxford University Press, 2008.

Salisbury-Jones, Guy. *So Full a Glory: A Biography of Marshal de Lattre de Tassigny.* New York: Praeger, 1955.

Saltonstall, Leverett. *The Autobiography of Leverett Saltonstall: Massachusetts Governor, U.S. Senator, and Yankee Icon.* Lanham, MD: Rowman and Littlefield, 2015.

———. *Salty: Recollections of a Yankee in Politics.* Boston: Boston Globe, 1976.

Sander, Robert D. *Invasion of Laos, 1971: Lam Son 719.* Norman: University of Oklahoma Press, 2014.

Sankovitch, Nina. *The Lowells of Massachusetts: An American Family.* New York: St. Martin's, 2017.

Sarantakes, Nicholas Evan. "Lyndon Johnson, Foreign Policy, and the Election of 1960." *Southwestern Historical Quarterly*, Vol. 103, No. 2 (October 1999): 146–172.

Saunders, Elizabeth. *Leaders at War: How Presidents Shape Military Interventions.* Ithaca, NY: Cornell University Press, 2011.

Schandler, Herbert Y. *The Unmaking of a President: Lyndon Johnson and Vietnam.* Princeton, NJ: Princeton University Press, 1977.

Schlesinger, Arthur M., Jr., ed. *History of American Presidential Elections, 1789–1968.* New York: Chelsea House, 1971.

———. *Journals, 1952–2000.* New York: Penguin, 2007.

———. *The Letters of Arthur Schlesinger, Jr.* Edited by Andrew Schlesinger and Stephen Schlesinger. New York: Random House, 2013.

———. *Robert Kennedy, Jr. and His Times.* Boston: Houghton Mifflin, 1978.

———. *A Thousand Days: John F. Kennedy in the White House.* Boston: Houghton Mifflin Company, 1965.

———. *The Vital Center: The Politics of Freedom.* Boston: Houghton Mifflin, 1949.

Schmidt, Gustav, ed. *A History of NATO: The First Fifty Years.* Vol. 2. New York: Palgrave, 2001.

Schulman, Bruce J., and Julian E. Zelizer, eds. *Rightward Bound: Making America Conservative in the 1970s.* Cambridge, MA: Harvard University Press, 2008.

Schulzinger, Robert D., ed. *A Companion to American Foreign Relations*. Malden, MA: Blackwell, 2003.

———. *A Time for War: The United States and Vietnam, 1941–1975*. New York: Oxford University Press, 1997.

Scott, William A., and Stephen B. Withey. *The United States and the United Nations: The Public View, 1945–1955*. Westport, CT: Greenwood, 1974.

Selverstone, Marc J., ed. *A Companion to John F. Kennedy*. Malden, MA: Wiley Blackwell, 2014.

Shadegg, Stephen. *What Happened to Goldwater? The Inside Story of the 1964 Republican Campaign*. New York: Holt, Rinehart and Winston, 1965.

Shaplen, Robert. *The Lost Revolution: The Story of Twenty Years of Neglected Opportunities in Vietnam and of America's Failure to Foster Democracy There*. New York: Harper and Row, 1965.

———. *The Road from War: Vietnam, 1965–1970*. New York: Harper and Row, 1966.

Shaw, Geoffrey D. T. *The Lost Mandate of Heaven: The American Betrayal of Ngo Dinh Diem, President of Vietnam*. San Francisco: Ignatius, 2015.

Sheehan, Neil. *A Bright Shining Lie: John Paul Vann and America in Vietnam*. New York: Random House, 1988.

Shepard, Geoff. *The Secret Plot to Make Ted Kennedy President: Inside the Real Watergate Conspiracy*. New York: Sentinel, 2008.

Sherman, Casey, and Michael J. Tougias. *Above and Beyond: John F. Kennedy and America's Most Dangerous Cold War Spy Mission*. New York: PublicAffairs, 2018.

Sherman, Norman. *From Nowhere to Somewhere: My Political Journey, a Memoir of Sorts*. Minneapolis: First Avenue Editions, 2016.

Shinkle, Peter. *Ike's Mystery Man: The Secret Lives of Robert Cutler*. Hanover, NH: Steerforth, 2018.

Sieg, Kent G. "W. Averell Harriman, Henry Cabot Lodge, and the Quest for Peace in Vietnam." *Peace and Change*, Vol. 20 (April 1995): 237–249.

Slater, Ellis D. *The Ike I Knew*. N.p.: Ellis D. Slater Trust, 1980.

Small, Melvin, ed. *A Companion to Richard M. Nixon*. Malden, MA: Blackwell, 2011.

———. *The Presidency of Richard Nixon*. Lawrence: University Press of Kansas, 1999.

Smith, Gerard C. *Disarming Diplomat: The Memoirs of Gerard C. Smith, Arms Control Negotiator*. Lanham, MD: Madison Books, 1996.

———. *The Story of the First Strategic Arms Limitation Talks*. Garden City, NY: Doubleday, 1980.

Smith, Jean Edward. *Eisenhower: In War and Peace*. New York: Random House, 2012.

Smith, Richard Norton. *On His Own Terms: A Life of Nelson Rockefeller*. New York: Random House, 2014.

———. *Thomas E. Dewey and His Times*. New York: Simon and Schuster, 1982.

Sorley, Lewis. *A Better War: The Unexamined Victories and Final Tragedy of America's Last Years in Vietnam*. New York: Harcourt, 1999.

———, ed. *Vietnam Chronicles: The Abrams Tapes, 1968–1972*. Lubbock: Texas Tech University Press, 2004.

———, ed. *The Vietnam War: An Assessment by South Vietnam's Generals*. Lubbock: Texas Tech University Press, 2010.

———. *Westmoreland: The General Who Lost Vietnam*. Boston: Houghton Mifflin Harcourt, 2011.

Southwick, Leslie H., ed. *Presidential Also-Rans and Running Mates, 1788 through 1996*. 2nd ed. Jefferson, NC: McFarland, 1998.

Spaak, Paul-Henri. *The Continuing Battle: Memoirs of a European, 1936–1966*. Translated by Henry Fox. Boston: Little, Brown, 1971.

Stans, Maurice H. *The Terrors of Justice: The Untold Story of Watergate*. New York: Everest House, 1978.

Stassen, Harold, and Marshall Houts. *Eisenhower: Turning the World Toward Peace*. St. Paul, MN: Merrill/Magnus, 1990.

Steil, Benn. *The Battle of Bretton Woods: John Maynard Keyes, Harry Dexter White, and the Making of a New World Order*. Princeton, NJ: Princeton University Press, 2013.

———. *The Marshall Plan: Dawn of the Cold War*. New York: Simon and Schuster, 2018.

Stevens, George. *Speak for Yourself, John: The Life of John Mason Brown, with Some of His Letters and Many of His Opinions*. New York: Viking, 1974.

Stewart, Geoffrey C. *Vietnam's Lost Revolution: Ngo Dinh Diem's Failure to Build an Independent Nation, 1955–1963*. New York: Cambridge University Press, 2017.

Stimson, Henry L., and McGeorge Bundy. *On Active Service in Peace and War*. New York: Harper and Brothers, 1948.

Stockdale, Jim, and Sybil Stockdale. *In Love and War: The Story of a Family's Ordeal and Sacrifice during the Vietnam Years*. Rev. and updated ed. Annapolis: Naval Institute Press, 1990.

Stoessinger, John G. *The United Nations and the Superpowers: China, Russia, and America*. 4th ed. New York: Random House, 1977.

Strauss, Lewis L. *Men and Decisions*. Garden City, NY: Doubleday, 1962.

Strober, Deborah Hart, and Gerald S. Strober. *The Nixon Presidency: An Oral History of the Era*. Washington, DC: Brassey's, 2003.

Summers, Anthony. *The Arrogance of Power: The Secret World of Richard Nixon*. New York: Penguin Books, 2000.

Summers, Harry G., Jr. *On Strategy: A Critical Analysis of the Vietnam War*. Novato, CA: Presidio, 1982.

Suri, Jeremi. *Henry Kissinger and the American Century*. Cambridge, MA: Belknap Press of Harvard University Press, 2007.

Swift, Will. *Pat and Dick: The Nixons, an Intimate Portrait of a Marriage*. New York: Threshold Editions, 2014.

Taft, Robert A. *A Foreign Policy for Americans*. Garden City, NY: Doubleday, 1951.

———. *The Papers of Robert A. Taft*. Vol. 3, *1945–1948*. Edited by Clarence E. Wunderlin Jr. Kent, OH: Kent State University Press, 2003.

———. *The Papers of Robert A. Taft*. Vol. 4, *1949–1953*. Edited by Clarence E. Wunderlin Jr. Kent, OH: Kent State University Press, 2006.

Talbot, David. *Brothers: The Hidden History of the Kennedy Years*. New York: Free Press, 2007.

Tannenwald, Nina. *The Nuclear Taboo: The United States and the Non-use of Nuclear Weapons since 1945*. New York: Cambridge University Press, 2007.

Taraborrelli, J. Randy. *Jackie, Ethel, Joan: Women of Camelot*. New York: Warner Books, 2000.

Taylor, K. W. *A History of the Vietnamese*. New York: Cambridge University Press, 2013.

Taylor, Maxwell D. *Sword and Plowshares*. New York: W. W. Norton, 1972.

Theoharis, Athan, ed. *From the Secret Files of J. Edgar Hoover*. Chicago: Ivan R. Dee, 1993.

Thomas, Evan. *Being Nixon: A Man Divided*. New York: Random House, 2015.

———. *Ike's Bluff: President Eisenhower's Secret Battle to Save the World*. New York: Little, Brown, 2012.

———. *Robert Kennedy: A Life*. New York: Simon and Schuster, 2000.

———. *The Very Best Men: Four Who Dared: The Early Years of the CIA*. New York: Simon and Schuster, 1995.

———. *The War Lovers: Roosevelt, Lodge, Hearst, and the Rush to Empire, 1898*. Boston: Little, Brown, 2010.

Thomas, G. Scott. *Counting the Votes: A New Way to Analyze America's Presidential Elections*. Santa Barbara, CA: Praeger, 2015.

Thompson, James C., Jr. "How Could Vietnam Happen? An Autopsy." *Atlantic*, April 1968, 47–53.

Thurber, Timothy N. *Republicans and Race: The GOP's Frayed Relationship with African Americans, 1945–1974*. Lawrence: University Press of Kansas, 2013.

Tillett, Paul, ed. *Inside Politics: The National Conventions, 1960*. Dobby Ferry, NY: Oleana, 1962.

Torvar, B. Hugh. "Vietnam Revisited: The United States and Diem's Death." *International Journal of Intelligence and Counterintelligence*, Vol. 5, No. 3 (Fall 1991): 291–312.

Tran Ngoc Chau. *Vietnam Labyrinth: Allies, Enemies, and Why the U.S. Lost the War*. Lubbock: Texas Tech University Press, 2012.

Trento, Joseph J. *The Secret History of the CIA*. Roseville, CA: Prima, 2001.

Turner, Stansfield. *Burn before Reading: Presidents, CIA Directors, and Secret Intelligence*. New York: Hyperion, 2005.

United States Department of State. *History of the Bureau of Diplomatic Security of the United States Department of State*. Washington, DC: Global Publishing Solutions, 2011.

United States Senate, Committee on Foreign Relations. *U.S. Involvement in the Overthrow of Diem, 1963: A Staff Study Based on the Pentagon Papers.* Study No. 3. Washington, DC: U.S. Government Printing Office, 1972.

Uri, Pierre, ed. *Partnership for Progress: A Program for Transatlantic Action.* Westport, CT: Greenwood, 1963.

Urquhart, Brian. *Hammarskjold.* New York: W. W. Norton, 1994.

Valenti, Jack. *My Life: In War, the White House, and Hollywood.* New York: Harmony Books, 2007.

Van Atta, Dale. *With Honor: Melvin Laird in War, Peace, and Politics.* Madison: University of Wisconsin Press, 2008.

Vandenberg, Arthur H. *The Private Papers of Senator Vandenberg.* Edited by Arthur H. Vandenberg Jr. Boston: Houghton Mifflin, 1952.

Vasilew, Eugene. "The New Style in Political Campaigns: Lodge in New Hampshire, 1964." *Review of Politics,* Vol. 30, No. 2 (April 1968): 131–152.

Vazansky, Alexander. *An Army in Crisis: Social Conflict and the U.S. Army in Germany, 1968–1975.* Lincoln: University of Nebraska Press, 2019.

*Victory in Vietnam: The Official History of the People's Army of Vietnam, 1954–1975.* Translated by Merle L. Pribbenow. Lawrence: University Press of Kansas, 2002.

Wadsworth, James J. *The Glass House: The United Nations in Action.* New York: Frederick A. Praeger, 1966.

———. *The Price of Peace.* New York: Frederick A. Praeger, 1962.

———. *The Silver Spoon: An Autobiography.* Geneva, NY: W. F. Humphrey, 1980.

Walters, Vernon A. *Silent Missions.* Garden City, NY: Doubleday, 1978.

Warner, Denis. *The Last Confucian: Vietnam, South-East Asia, and the West.* Baltimore: Penguin Books, 1964.

Weiner, Tim. *Legacy of Ashes: The History of the CIA.* New York: Doubleday, 2007.

———. *One Man against the World: The Tragedy of Richard Nixon.* New York: Henry Holt, 2015.

Weisbrode, Kenneth. *The Atlantic Century: Four Generations of Extraordinary Diplomats Who Forged America's Vital Alliance with Europe.* Cambridge, MA: Da Capo, 2009.

Werle, Steve. *Stassen Again.* St. Paul: Minnesota Historical Press, 2015.

Westmoreland, William C. *A Soldier Reports.* Garden City, NY: Doubleday, 1976.

Whalen, Thomas J. *Kennedy versus Lodge: The 1952 Massachusetts Senate Race.* Boston: Northeastern University Press, 2000.

Wheeler, James Scott. *Jacob L. Devers: A General's Life.* Lexington: University Press of Kentucky, 2015.

White, Theodore H. *Breach of Faith: The Fall of Richard Nixon.* New York: Atheneum, 1975.

———. *In Search of History: A Personal Adventure.* New York: Harper and Row, 1978.

———. *The Making of the President, 1960.* New York: Atheneum, 1961.

———. *The Making of the President, 1964.* New York: Atheneum, 1965.

———. *The Making of the President, 1968.* New York: Atheneum, 1969.

Wicker, Tom. *One of Us: Richard Nixon and the American Dream.* New York: Random House, 1991.

Widenor, William C. *Henry Cabot Lodge and the Search for an American Foreign Policy.* Berkeley: University of California Press, 1980.

Widmer, Edward L. *Listening In: The Secret White House Recordings of John F. Kennedy.* New York: Hyperion, 2012.

Winters, Francis X. *The Year of the Hare: America in Vietnam, January 25, 1963–February 16, 1964.* Athens: University of Georgia Press, 1997.

Wise, David. *The American Police State: The Government against the People.* New York: Random House, 1976.

Witcover, Jules. *The Resurrection of Richard Nixon.* New York: G. P. Putnam's Sons, 1970.

———. *Very Strange Bedfellows: The Short and Unhappy Marriage of Richard Nixon and Spiro Agnew.* New York: PublicAffairs, 2007.

———. *The Year the Dream Died: Revisiting 1968 in America.* New York: Warner Books, 1997.

Worthen, James. *The Young Nixon and His Rivals: Four California Republicans Eye the White House, 1946–1958.* Jefferson, NC: McFarland, 2010.

Wright, Peter, and Paul Greengrass. *Spy Catcher: The Candid Autobiography of a Senior Intelligence Officer.* New York: Viking, 1987.

Young, Marilyn B., and Robert Buzzanco, eds. *A Companion to the Vietnam War.* Malden, MA: Blackwell, 2002.

Young, Nancy Beck. *Two Suns of the Southwest: Lyndon Johnson, Barry Goldwater, and the 1964 Battle between Liberalism and Conservatism.* Lawrence: University Press of Kansas, 2019.

Zacher, Mark W. *Dag Hammarskjold's United Nations.* New York: Columbia University Press, 1970.

Zasimczuk, Ivan A. "Maxwell M. Rabb: A Hidden Hand of the Eisenhower Administration in Civil Rights and Race Relations." MA thesis, Kansas State University, 2008.

Zeiger, Henry A. *The Remarkable Henry Cabot Lodge.* New York: Popular Library, 1964.

Zimmerman, Warren. *First Great Triumph: How Five Americans Made Their Country a World Power.* New York: Farrar, Straus and Giroux, 2002.

# Acknowledgments

The writing of history is a collaborative effort. An idea starts small and slowly builds momentum over time. Hypotheses are tested. Discussions, debates, and disagreements help to refine thinking. Without the input of many, I could not have written what you see here.

The National Endowment for the Humanities awarded me a Public Scholar Grant during 2017–2018. (The views expressed in this work do not necessarily represent those of the NEH.) The University of Oxford's Rothermere American Institute provided a Senior Visiting Research Fellowship during a semester-long sabbatical. I was supported by an Andrew W. Mellon Fellowship at the Massachusetts Historical Society, a visiting scholar position at the University of Michigan's Eisenberg Institute for Historical Studies, a visiting fellowship at the Norwegian Nobel Institute, and a visiting scholar position at the Department of History at Bowling Green State University—back where it all started fifteen years ago, and where I met my wife, Jennifer. Other institutions that supported this project include the London School of Economics, Duy Tan University, and the University of Social Sciences and Humanities at Vietnam National University.

A number of former officials and associates of Henry Cabot Lodge Jr. agreed—many eagerly—to share their memories and reflections. A total of fifty-three are acknowledged in the bibliography, too many to thank them all individually. Several went out of their way, including James Bullington; Thomas Hughes; Henry Kissinger; Sven Kraemer; William A. K. Lake; Joseph Luman; Robert Miller; John Negroponte; Rufus Phillips; Merle Pribbenow; the family of Maxwell Rabb, including his one-hundred-year-old widow, Ruth—Lodge was the best man at their 1937 nuptials—and children Bruce and Priscilla; and colleagues and family members of William Westmoreland, including Katherine Westmoreland, children Rip and Maggie, and former Westy aides David Palmer and Paul Miles. Most of all, I owe gratitude to members of the Lodge family, with whom I met at different times in Beverly, New York, and Paris, and corresponded throughout. George Cabot Lodge (and Susan), Emily Lodge, and Robert Pingeon offered every bit of assistance requested, and more. They did not ask for anyone to write a book. There will surely be parts they disagree with or do not like. They unselfishly shared their father/grandfather with this interloper.

There are too many archives and historic sites to thank all their staff individually. One institution I wish to single out is the Massachusetts Historical Society, specifically Conrad Wright, Kate Viens, Dan Hinchen, Peter Drummey, William Clendaniel, and Anna Clutterbuck-Cook. I placed more demands on them, the stewards of the Lodge papers, than on the staff of any other archive. I recognize them not only for their extensive help from a distance and onsite and their facilitation of a capacity crowd for a brown-bag talk but also for loaning boxes and boxes of the microfilmed portions of the Lodge papers. Various National Archives and Records Administration officials were also supportive. These include David Ferriero (a Beverly native), William "Jay" Bosanko, Maarja Krusten, Mary Burtzloff, Elizabeth Druga, Geir Gunderson, Mark Fischer, Tim Holtz, Matthew Schaefer, Allen Fisher, John Wilson, Chris Banks, Jenna De Graffenried, Abigail Malangone, Michael Desmond, Maura Porter, Michelle DeMartino, Cary McStay, Gregory Cumming, Michael Ellzey, Jason Schultz, Meghan Lee, Ryan Pettigrew, Michael Pinckney, Ray Wilson, Kendra Lightner, Patrick Fahy, Virginia Lewick, David Clark, Janice Davis, Laurie Austin, Samuel Rushay, and the entire Special Access/FOIA office in College Park—you are the best in the business. You can hide, but my FOIA requests will find you. A total of 270 FOIA requests were made to sixteen federal agencies in the course of preparing this manuscript, with many revealing fresh insights.

In Vietnam, Tram Pham helped me to navigate the National Archives Center II (Trung Tâm Lưu Trữ Quốc Gia II) in Ho Chi Minh City. On the ground in what many people continue to call Saigon, Tom Doling of Historic Vietnam and Paul Blizzard of Saigon-Cholon "Then and Now" answered queries and provided input on a study-abroad trip I am planning to coincide with the publication of this book. They provide a valuable public service by preserving Vietnamese history. They are in the right place at the right time as tourism explodes in Vietnam and many Americans are experiencing this fascinating place for the first time.

Many scholars offered advice and shared insights: Thomas Schwartz, Nigel Bowles, Irwin Gellman, Timothy Naftali, David Prentice, Edward Miller, Pierre Asselin, Lien-Hang Nguyen, Sean Fear, Jay Sexton, Douglas Forsyth, Gary Hess, Liette Gidlow, Niall Ferguson, Douglas Brinkley, Evan Thomas, Greg Daddis, Lewis "Bob" Sorley, Alvin S. Felzenberg, Mark Moyar, Sean Brennan, Peter Carlson, Max Holland, Monique Demery, Pierre Asselin, Richard Moss, Nicholas Sarantakes, Anand Toprani, Paul Stone, Kyle Longley, and George "Jay" Veith.

Two institutions provided a great deal of support and library resources. At Texas A&M University–Central Texas: Bridgit McCafferty, Bessie Miller, and Deniese Hart. At Bowling Green State University: Sara Ann Bushong, Mary Beth Zachary, Sherri

Long, Carol Ann Singer, and Amilcar Challu. Others who provided a sounding board or simply flexible teaching schedules semester after semester include Marc Nigliazzo, Peg Gray-Vickrey, Jerry Jones, and Allen Redmon. Over the course of this project I had a series of graduate assistants, including Bobbie Armstrong, Carmen Lewis, Amy Compton, and Julius Isaac. My longtime research assistant, Michael Cotten, keeps going no matter what I throw at him. I look forward to the next adventure.

At Yale University Press, William "Bill" Frucht, Karen Olson, and Mary Pasti were the best team one could have. Bill's vision for the book from the start was inspiring, and each challenged me to work harder than I thought I could. Karen, as well as Brian Ostrander and his team at Westchester Publishing Services, guided the manuscript through editing. Alex Hoyt was the ideal literary agent for the project. Without his support and enthusiasm, by which I mean prodding conversations over lunch in New York, it would never have come to fruition.

# INDEX

*HCL is used to indicate Henry Cabot Lodge Jr.; JFK to indicate John Fitzgerald Kennedy; and LBJ to indicate Lyndon Baines Johnson.*